The Philosophy of Mind

D0791641

The Philosophy of Mind: Classical Problems/Contemporary Issues

edited by Brian Beakley and Peter Ludlow

A Bradford Book
The MIT Press
Cambridge, Massachusetts
London, England

© 1992 Massachusetts Institute of Technology

All rights reserved. No part of this book may be reproduced in any form by any electronic or mechanical means (including photocopying, recording, or information storage and retrieval) without permission in writing from the publisher.

This book was set in Palatino by Asco Trade Typesetting Ltd., Hong Kong and was printed and bound in the United States of America.

Library of Congress Cataloging-in-Publication Data

The Philosophy of mind: classical problems/contemporary issues/edited by Brian Beakley and
  Peter Ludlow.
      p.   cm.
   Includes bibliographical references and index.
   "A Bradford book."
   ISBN 0-262-02340-7.—ISBN 0-262-52167-9 (pbk.)
   1. Philosophy of mind.   I. Beakley, Brian.   II. Ludlow, Peter Jay.
  BD418.3.P45   1992
  128'.2—dc20   91-31970
                                                                                 CIP

10 9 8 7 6 5

Contents

Preface

There is assuredly no more effectual method of clearing up one's own mind on any subject than by talking it over, so to speak, with [persons] of real power and grasp who have considered it from a totally different point of view. The parallax of time helps us to the true position of a conception, as the parallax of space helps us to that of a star.
T. H. Huxley

We assembled this volume with several goals in mind. First, we wanted to provide a pedagogical tool for those teaching the philosophy of mind to upper level undergraduates. We have each taught courses in the philosophy of mind, and we have each been frustrated by the lack of an introductory reader that contains historically relevant material. There are several excellent collections of recent writings in the philosophy of mind, but we thought it was important for students to see how certain problems have survived through the centuries. Our solution was to pull together the historical and contemporary work and organize the material by topics. Each section of the volume is dedicated to a single area and progresses from the relevant historical work (by, for example, Descartes) to more contemporary writings (by, for example, Fodor).

Our second goal was not pedagogical so much as ideological. Some philosophers have contended privately that the philosophy of mind is an irreducibly trendy branch of philosophy. We disagreed with this assessment and wanted this collection to show how many of the current concerns in the philosophy of mind have their roots in intellectual history.

Finally, we wanted to provide a helpful resource manual for those working in the philosophy of mind and the cognitive sciences. Few people will have all of these readings, and those who do will not have all of them at their fingertips. Of course we also hoped that by making some of the historical selections more accessible, they would become more widely read and appreciated. As the quote from Huxley suggests, there is much to be learned from dialogue with these thinkers.

It is customary to note that many excellent essays had to be left out due to space limitations. Sometimes this disclaimer is made merely to be polite, but not in this case. The writings in philosophy and psychology over the last 2500 years have been vast, and there is simply no way to include all of the worthy material. One can also envision additional sections that might be added to a collection of this nature. Candidate topics (which we have considered) include qualia, psychological content, and so forth. To some extent, all these topics are treated along the way, but we will be the first to admit that more extensive discussion of these topics is possible.

We have provided a brief introduction to each section. We prefer that the introductory material be viewed as articulating one interpretation of these works and their interrelationship, not as articulating some canonical view. The introductions should be read critically, as should all texts.

This collection was compiled with the help of a number of individuals. Ned Block, Stephen Neale, and Robert van Gulick read our initial proposal and made a number of very helpful suggestions for improvements. (Ned and Stephen also provided invaluable assistance with various aspects of preparation, ranging from help in securing permissions to advice on section introductions). We have also benefited from discussion with and suggestions from Marcos Bisticas-Cocoves, Nancy Franklin, Steve Fuller, Kathy Kemp, Peter Nagy, and Anderson Weekes. We also wish to thank Betty Stanton of Bradford Books for shepherding us through this process.

Finally, we welcome comments and criticisms from readers, especially students. Please write!

Brian Beakley
Dept of Philosophy
Eastern Illinois University
Charleston, IL 61920
email: cfbxb@ux1.eiu.edu

Peter Ludlow
Dept. of Philosophy
SUNY Stony Brook
Stony Brook, NY 11794
email: PLUDLOW@ccvm.sunysb.edu

Sources and Acknowledgments

Aristotle
From *Metaphysics*, book 7, and *On the Soul*, book 2
From W. D. Ross, ed., *The Oxford Aristotle*, vol. 8 (Oxford: Oxford University Press, 1928), by permission of the publisher.

Thomas Hobbes
Of Sense
From *Leviathan*, ed. Oakeshott (New York: Macmillan Publishing Company, 1962), by permission of the publisher.

René Descartes
From *Meditations* II and VI and from *Reply to Objections* II
From Haldane and Ross, eds., *The Philosophical Works of Descartes* (Cambridge: Cambridge University Press, 1911).

George Berkeley
From *The Principles of Human Knowledge*
From A. C. Fraser, ed., *The Works of George Berkeley* (London, 1871).

John Stuart Mill
Of the Laws of Mind
From *The System of Logic*, 8th edition (London, 1872).

Gilbert Ryle
Descartes' Myth
From *The Concept of Mind* (New York: Harper Collins Publishers, 1949), by permission of the publisher.

U. T. Place
Is Consciousness a Brain Process?
From the *British Journal of Psychology* (1956), by permission of the author and the British Psychological Society.

Saul Kripke
From "Identity and Necessity"
From Milton Munitz, ed., *Identity and Individuation* (New York: New York University Press, 1971), by permission of the author.

Noam Chomsky
From *Language and Problems of Knowledge* (Cambridge, MA: MIT Press, 1988), by permission of the author and publisher.

Hilary Putnam
The Nature of Mental States
Published as "Psychological Predicates" in W. H. Capitan and D. D. Merrill, eds., *Art, Mind and Religion* (Pittsburgh: University of Pittsburgh Press, 1967), by permission of the author and publisher.

Patricia Churchland
Reductionism and Antireductionism in Functionalist Theories of Mind
From *Neurophilosophy* (Cambridge, MA: MIT Press, 1986), by permission of the author and publisher.

Ned Block
Troubles with Functionalism
From C. W. Savage, ed., *Perception and Cognition: Issues in the Foundations of Psychology*, volume 9 of the

Minnesota Studies in the Philosophy of Science (Minneapolis: University of Minnesota Press, 1978), by permission of the author and publisher. This version has been significantly revised by the author.

Hilary Putnam
Philosophy and Our Mental Life
From *Mind, Language, and Reality*, volume 2 of Putnam's *Philosophical Papers* (Cambridge: Cambridge University Press, 1975), by permission of the author and publisher.

Plato
From *The Phaedo*
From *The Dialogues of Plato*, trans. B. Jowett (New York: Random House, 1892).

René Descartes
From *Passions of the Soul*
From *The Philosophical Works of Descartes*, trans. Haldane and Ross (Cambridge: Cambridge University Press, 1911).

Nicolas Malebranche
From "The Union of Soul and Body"
From *The Search after Truth*, trans. Thomas Lennon and Paul Olscamp (Columbus: Ohio State University Press, 1980), by permission of the publisher.

Gottfried Wilhelm Leibniz
The Nature and Communication of Substances ,
From Leroy Loemker, ed., *Philosophical Papers and Letters of Leibniz*, vol. 2 (Chicago: University of Chicago Press, 1956).

Immanuel Kant
The Third Antinomy
From *Critique of Pure Reason*, trans. F. Max Müller (London, 1881).

Thomas Henry Huxley
On the Hypothesis That Animals Are Automata
From *Collected Essays*, vol. 1 (London, 1893).

Donald Davidson
Mental Events
From Lawrence Foster and J. W. Swanson, eds., *Experience and Theory* (Amherst: University of Massachusetts Press, 1970), by permission of the author and publisher.

Jerry A. Fodor
Making Mind Matter More
From *Philosophical Topics*, vol. 17 (1989), by permission of the author and publisher.

Thomas Aquinas
That the Soul Never Thinks without an Image
From *Summa Theologica*, vol. 12 (New York: Blackfriars, McGraw-Hill, 1968), by permission of the publisher.

Thomas Hobbes
Of Imagination
From *Leviathan*, ed. Oakeshott (New York: Macmillan Publishing Company, 1962), by permission of the publisher.

René Descartes
From *Meditation* VI and from *Objection* IV and *Reply*
From Haldane and Ross, eds., *The Philosophical Works of Descartes* (Cambridge: Cambridge University Press, 1911).

David Hume
Of the Ideas of the Memory and Imagination
From *A Treatise of Human Nature*, ed. L. A. Selby-Bigge (Oxford University Press, 1888). (Original publication: London, 1739).

William James
Imagination
From *The Principles of Psychology*, vol. 2 (New York: Henry Holt, 1890).

Oswald Külpe
The Modern Psychology of Thinking
Originally given as a lecture in Berlin, 1912. Translation by G. Mandler and J. Mandler from *Thinking: From Association to Gestalt* (New York: Wiley, 1964), by permission of the translators and the publisher.

John Watson
Image and Affection in Behavior
From *The Journal of Philosophy, Psychology and Scientific Methods*, vol. 10, no. 16 (1913), pp. 421–424.

Gilbert Ryle
"The Theory of Special Status Pictures" and "Imagining"
From *The Concept of Mind* (New York: Harper Collins Publishers, 1949), by permission of the publisher.

Daniel Dennett
The Nature of Images and the Introspective Trap
From *Content and Consciousness* (London: Routledge and Kegan Paul, 1969), by permission of the author and publisher.

Roger Shepard and Jacqueline Metzler
Mental Rotation of Three-Dimensional Objects
From *Science*, vol. 171(1971), pp. 701–703, by permission of the authors and the American Association for the Advancement of Science.

Stephen Kosslyn
Scanning Visual Mental Images: The First Phase of the Debate
From Daniel Osherson, Stephen Kosslyn, and John Hollerbach, eds., *Visual Cognition and Action*, volume 2 of *An Invitation to Cognitive Science* (Cambridge, MA: MIT Press, 1990), by permission of the author and publisher.

Zenon W. Pylyshyn
Tacit Knowledge and "Mental Scanning"
From *Computation and Cognition* (Cambridge, MA: MIT Press, 1984), by permission of the publisher.

Stephen Kosslyn
Demand Characteristics?: The Second Phase of the Debate
From Daniel Osherson, Stephen Kosslyn, and John Hollerbach, eds., *Visual Cognition and Action*, volume 2 of *An Invitation to Cognitive Science* (Cambridge, MA: MIT Press, 1990), by permission of the author and publisher.

Thomas Hobbes
Of the Consequence or Train of Imaginations
From *Leviathan*, ed. Oakeshott (New York: Macmillan Publishing Company, 1962), by permission of the publisher.

John Locke
Of the Association of Ideas
From *An Essay Concerning Human Understanding*, fifth edition (London, 1706).

David Hume
Of the Connection or Association of Ideas
From *A Treatise of Human Nature*, ed. L. A. Selby-Bigge (Oxford University Press, 1888) (Original publication: London, 1739).

John Stuart Mill
The Principal Investigations of Psychology Characterised
From *A System of Logic*, vol. 2, book, 6 (London, 1843).

William James
The Elementary Law of Association
From *The Principles of Psychology*, vol. 2 (New York: Henry Holt, 1890).

James L. McClelland, David E. Rumelhart, and Geoffrey E. Hinton
The Appeal of Parallel Distributed Processing
From James L. Rumelhart, David E. McClelland, and the PDP Research Group, *Parallel Distributed Processing:*

Explorations in the Microstructure of Cognition, vol. 1 (Cambridge, MA: MIT Press, 1986), by permission of the authors and publisher.

Jerry A. Fodor and Zenon W. Pylyshyn
Connectionism and Cognitive Architecture: A Critical Analysis
From *Cognition*, vol. 20 (1988), by permission of the authors and Elsevier Science Publishers.

Paul Smolensky
The Constituent Structure of Connectionist Mental States: A Reply to Fodor and Pylyshyn
From *The Southern Journal of Philosophy*, vol. 26 supp. (1987), by permission of the journal and the author.

Seymour Papert
One AI or Many?
From *Daedalus, Journal of the American Academy of Arts and Sciences*, from the issue entitled, "Artificial Intelligence," vol. 117 (1988).

Plato
From *The Meno*
From *The Dialogues of Plato*, trans. B. Jowett (New York: Random House, 1892).

René Descartes
From "Comments on a Certain Broadsheet"
From *Philosophical Writings of Descartes*, trans. Cottingham, Stoothoff, and Murdoch (Cambridge: Cambridge University Press, 1985), by permission of the publisher.

John Locke
No Innate Principles in the Mind
From *An Essay Concerning Human Understanding*, fifth edition (London, 1706).

Jean Piaget
The Psychogenesis of Knowledge and Its Epistemological Significance
From Massimo Piatelli-Palmerini, ed., *Language and Learning: The Debate Between Jean Piaget and Noam Chomsky* (Cambridge, MA: Harvard University Press, 1980), by permission of the author and publisher. Copyright © 1980 by the President and Fellows of Harvard College.

Jerry A. Fodor
How There Could Be a Private Language and What It Must Be Like
From *The Language of Thought* (Cambridge, MA: Harvard University Press, 1975), by permission of the author and publisher. Copyright © 1975 by Thomas Y. Cromwell Company, Inc.

Noam Chomsky
On Cognitive Structures and Their Development: A Reply to Piaget
From Massimo Piatelli-Palmerini, ed., *Language and Learning: The Debate Between Jean Piaget and Noam Chomsky* (Cambridge, MA: Harvard University Press, 1980), by permission of the author and publisher. Copyright © 1980 by the President and Fellows of Harvard College.

Hilary Putnam
What Is Innate and Why: Comments on the Debate
From Massimo Piatelli-Palmerini, ed., *Language and Learning: The Debate Between Jean Piaget and Noam Chomsky* (Cambridge, MA: Harvard University Press, 1980), by permission of the author and publisher. Copyright © 1980 by the President and Fellows of Harvard College.

Noam Chomsky
Discussion of Putnam's Comments
From Massimo Piatelli-Palmerini, ed., *Language and Learning: The Debate Between Jean Piaget and Noam Chomsky* (Cambridge, MA: Harvard University Press, 1980), by permission of the author and publisher. Copyright © 1980 by the President and Fellows of Harvard College.

Jerry Fodor
Reply to Putnam
From Massimo Piatelli-Palmerini, ed., *Language and Learning: The Debate Between Jean Piaget and Noam Chomsky* (Cambridge, MA: Harvard University Press, 1980), by permission of the author and publisher. Copyright © 1980 by the President and Fellows of Harvard College.

Part I

The Mind/Body Problem

Introduction

Over the past 2500 years there have been many responses to the mind/body problem. The readings in this section represent a chronological sketch of the movement between four of the most influential general proposals: dualism, materialism, idealism, and functionalism. *Dualism* is the doctrine that there are two different types of substance: physical substance, which is the object of the natural sciences, and mental substance, which is the stuff of which our conscious states are comprised. *Materialism* is the position that there is only physical substance. For the materialist, mental states like pains, beliefs, desires, etc. are fundamentally physical states. *Idealism*, like materialism, holds that there is only one substance, but claims that the substance is mental. *Functionalism* steers a middle course between dualism and materialism. Against dualism, the functionalist holds that the mind is not something that exists apart from the physical. Against materialism, the functionalist denies that mental states are identical to physical states. Roughly, the idea is that it is not the physical substance itself that is important, but rather the way in which the physical substance is organized.

Although the claim is hotly debated among contemporary philosophers and classicists, Aristotle may be thought of as the first functionalist. In his discussion of definition—which he takes to express the formula, or essence, of a thing—Aristotle describes objects as combinations of *form* and *matter*. According to Aristotle, there are many cases where the form of the object is essential to the object, while the matter is not. For example, a word written in wax contains its letters as part of its formula but is only coincidentally made of wax (since it could equally well be engraved in stone, written on paper, etc.). Because the form of a word like "dog" can be realized in many different substances, we know that the form and the material substance are not identical. Contemporary philosophers call this a *multiple instantiation* argument, for it appeals to the fact that a single form can be instantiated (realized) in many different physical substances. Although, as it turns out, the formula of the soul is only realized in material like bones and muscle, Aristotle says that we should not make the mistake of thinking that the soul and body are identical. For if words were only written in wax, we would still be mistaken in supposing that words are identical to wax.

Thomas Hobbes provides an early and influential statement of identity theory in his account of perception: visual experiences are really only the action of external physical objects on our physical organs.

René Descartes provides the classical statement of dualism. Starting with the experience of his own mental existence, Descartes asks whether the idea of his mental existence is indistinguishable from the idea of his body. His answer is that it is not, concluding that the idea or essence of mind is different from the idea of body. Since two things that correspond to different ideas cannot be identical, the mind must be different from the body.

George Berkeley argues that a thorough empiricist will be led to adopt idealism. According to Berkeley, if all our knowledge comes to us through sense impressions, then we can never have knowledge of material substance itself. We may posit material substance as the cause of these impressions, but there is no direct evidence for such substance, and positing such substance may lead us into contradiction. His conclusion is that there are only minds and sense impressions.

John Stuart Mill introduces a new concern into the debate. Mill agrees that materialism is a plausible answer to the *ontological* question about the mind (the question of what the mind really is), but argues that we should not overlook the *methodological* question of how science should proceed to study the mind. Even if we hold that mental states are brain states, the brain is so complex and so poorly understood that we must study mental regularities independent of brain research. Thus, Mill concludes that the study of mind (psychology) should remain a separate science even if materialism should turn out to be true.

Gilbert Ryle, who is a *logical behaviorist*, provides an influential criticism of dualism. According to Ryle, dualists are guilty of a *category mistake*. For example, it is perfectly legitimate to talk about a football team winning a game, and it is also legitimate to talk about the individual members of a football team, but it would surely be a blunder to think that the team is something that exists in addition to the members of the team. For example, if someone were introduced to the members of the team and then exclaimed, "Now I'd like to meet the team," we would say that the person was fundamentally confused. Talk of the team is really just talk of the members of the team at a certain level of abstraction. Likewise, according to Ryle, we can talk about mental states (like pain) and we can talk of certain behaviors (like holding damaged body parts and moaning), but it would be a mistake to suppose that the mental state of pain exists *in addition to* some relevant class of behavior.

U. T. Place attempts to defuse certain arguments against the identity theory. Place argues that two things can turn out to be identical even if their definitions are different: "lightning", for example, doesn't mean the same thing as "electrical discharge", but we can discover that lightning and electrical discharge are identical. Likewise, though "mind" and "body" may have different definitions, we can nonetheless discover that mind and body are identical.

The selection from Saul Kripke presents a broadly Cartesian response in support of dualism. According to Kripke, science discovers essences. So, when we discover that lightning is electrical discharge, we discover that the essence of lightning is that of electrical discharge. Alternatively, if the essence of lightning and electrical discharge should turn out to be distinct, then lightning and electrical discharge would amount to distinct things. According to Kripke, the essence of mind may well be distinct from the essence of body. If this is so, then mind and body must be distinct as well.

Noam Chomsky sketches a radical approach to materialism. According to Chomsky, the notion of body is itself subject to revision by the sciences. For example, the concept of body employed by Descartes was soon superseded by the Newtonian notion of body, and research in particle physics during the last century has continually revised our understanding of the nature of physical bodies. This being the case, Chomsky argues that the very notion of the mind/body problem is ill defined. It is ill defined because we have no clear conception of what the body is. Moreover, he suggests that if our understanding of mental phenomena seems incompatible with our understanding of the physical body, then our understanding of the physical body will have to change to accommodate the mental. Our ultimate understanding of body will be shaped by (among other things) our theories of the mental.

Hilary Putnam initiates the contemporary discussion of functionalism. Like Aristotle, Putnam is concerned with the formula of the soul, though he suggests in "The Nature of

Our Mental States" that it can be thought of as a *Turing machine*, an abstract computing machine. Turing machines can be instantiated in many different kinds of hardware— silicon chips, Tinkertoy models, and, according to Putnam, the human body. Putnam argues against the identity theory by using a multiple instantiation argument: because a given psychological state (e.g., pain) can be realized in creatures with nervous systems quite different from our own, and indeed can presumably even be realized by the silicon-based creatures of science fiction, there is no single physical type that correlates with the psychological type pain. Consequently, no *reduction* of the psychological state pain to a single type of neurophysiological state is possible.

Patricia Churchland is unimpressed by this use of the multiple instantiation argument. She argues that Putnam's notion of reduction is far too restrictive—so restrictive that by Putnam's standards it is not clear that *any* science has been successfully reduced to a more fundamental science. Take, for example, the theory of thermodynamics, which is widely taken to have been reduced to statistical mechanics. As Churchland notes, a kind of multiple instantiation argument is possible here as well, for in gases, heat is reduced to mean kinetic energy, in solids something else, and in a vacuum something else again. But we don't conclude that there is no reduction.

Ned Block attacks functionalism from another direction, arguing that any functional definition of mental states will be either too liberal (ascribing mental states to creatures that don't really have them), or too chauvinistic (failing to ascribe mental states to creatures that do have them). In setting up his argument, he surveys a number of concerns that have been raised against functionalism, including the problem of accounting for the phenomenology of mental states. Block's article is also useful in providing an extensive classification of the various *types* of functionalism.

In "Philosophy and our Mental Life," Putnam criticizes his earlier formulation of functionalism, arguing that the multiple instantiation argument can also be extended to Turing machines—thus showing that mental states cannot be reduced to Turing machine states. But Putnam does not reject functionalism. Rather, he defines functional states more broadly as classes of structurally identical states, perhaps returning to something a bit more like Aristotle's notion of "form."

Further Reading

Several good collections are available on the mind/body problem, though they are primarily concerned with the debate between materialism and dualism. They include:

Borst, C. V., ed. 1970. *The Mind/Brain Identity Theory.* London: MacMillan.
Presley, C. F., ed. 1967. *The Identity Theory of Mind.* University of Queensland Press.
Rosenthal, David, ed. 1971. *Materialism and the Mind-Body Problem.* Englewood Cliffs, NJ: Prentice Hall.

The following collections are more general but also address the mind/body problem. The Block and Lycan collections have particularly good sections on functionalism.

Block, Ned, ed. 1980. *Readings in the Philosophy of Psychology vol. 1.* Cambridge, MA: Harvard University Press.
Hook, Sidney, ed. 1960. *Dimensions of Mind.* New York: Collier.
Lycan, William, ed. 1990. *Mind and Cognition: A Reader.* Oxford: Basil Blackwell.

Chapter 1

From *Metaphysics*, book 7, and *On the Soul*, book 2

Aristotle

Since a definition is a formula, and every formula has parts, and as the formula is to the thing, so is the part of the formula to the part of the thing, the question is already being asked whether the formula of the parts must be present in the formula of the whole or not. For in some cases the formulae of the parts are seen to be present, and in some not. The formula of the circle does not include that of the segments, but that of the syllable includes that of the letters; yet the circle is divided into segments as the syllable is into letters. And further if the parts are prior to the whole, and the acute angle is a part of the right angle and the finger a part of the animal, the acute angle will be prior to the right angle and the finger to the man. But the latter are thought to be prior; for in formula the parts are explained by reference to them, and in respect also of the power of existing apart from each other the wholes are prior to the parts.

... Let us inquire about the parts of which *substance* consists. If then matter is one thing, form another, the compound of these a third, and both the matter and the form and the compound are substance, even the matter is in a sense called part of a thing, while in a sense *it* is not, but only the elements of which the formula of the form consists. E.g., ... the bronze is a part of the concrete statue, but not of the statue when this is spoken of in the sense of the form. (For the form, or the thing as having form, should be said to be the thing, but the material element by itself must never be said to be so.) And so the formula of the circle does not include that of the segments, but the formula of the syllable includes that of the letters; for the letters are parts of the formula of the form, and not matter, but the segments are parts in the sense of matter on which the form supervenes; yet they are nearer the form than the bronze is when roundness is produced in bronze. But in a sense not even every kind of letter will be present in the formula of the syllable, e.g., particular waxen letters or the letters as movements in the air; for in these also we have already something that is part of the syllable only in the sense that it is its perceptible matter. For even if the line when divided passes away into its halves, or the man into bones and muscles and flesh, it does not follow that they are composed of these as parts of their essence, but rather as matter; and these are parts of the concrete thing, but not also of the form, i.e., of that to which the formula refers; wherefore also they are not present in the formulae. In one kind of formula, then, the formula of such parts will be present, but in another it must not be present, where the formula does not refer to the concrete object. For it is for this reason that some things have as their constituent principles parts into which they pass away, while some have not. Those things which are the form and the matter taken together, e.g., ... the bronze circle, pass away into these materials, and the matter is a part of them; but those things which do not involve matter but are without matter, and whose formulae are formulae of the form only, do not pass away.... Therefore these materials are principles and parts of the concrete things, while of the form they are neither parts nor principles. And therefore the clay statue is resolved into clay and the ball into bronze and Callias into flesh and bones, and again the circle into its segments; for there is a sense of 'circle' in which it involves matter. For 'circle' is used ambiguously, meaning both the circle, unqualified, and the individual circle, because there is no name peculiar to the individuals.

The truth has indeed now been stated, but still let us state it yet more clearly, taking up the question again. The parts of the formula, into which the formula is divided, are prior to it, either all or some of them. . . . The circle and the semicircle also are in such a relation; for the semicircle is defined by the circle; and so is the finger by the whole body, for a finger is 'such and such a part of a man.' Therefore the parts which are of the nature of matter, and into which as its matter a thing is divided, are posterior; but those which are of the nature of parts of the formula, and of the substance according to its formula, are prior, either all or some of them. And since the soul of animals (for this is the substance of a living being) is their substance according to the formula, i.e., the form and the essence of a body of a certain kind (at least we shall define each part, if we define it well, not without reference to its function, and this cannot belong to it without perception), so that the parts of soul are prior, either all or some of them, to the concrete 'animal,' and so too with each individual animal; and the body and its parts are posterior to this, the essential substance, and it is not the substance but the concrete thing that is divided into these parts as its matter: this being so, to the concrete thing these are in a sense prior, but in a sense they are not. For they cannot even exist if severed from the whole; for it is not a finger in any and every state that is the finger of a living thing, but a dead finger is a finger only in name. . . . 'A part' may be a part either of the form (i.e., of the essence), or of the compound of the form and the matter, or of the matter itself. But only the parts of the form are parts of the formula, and the formula is of the universal; for 'being a circle' is the same as the circle, and 'being a soul' the same as the soul. But when we come to the concrete thing, e.g., *this* circle, i.e., one of the individual circles, whether perceptible or intelligible (I mean by intelligible circles the mathematical, and by perceptible circles those of bronze and of wood)—of these there is no definition, but they are known by the aid of intuitive thinking or of perception . . . .

We have stated, then, how matters stand with regard to whole and part, and their priority and posteriority. But when any one asks whether the right angle and the circle and the animal are prior, or the things into which they are divided and of which they consist, i.e., the parts, we must meet the inquiry by saying that the question cannot be answered simply. For if even bare soul is the animal or the living thing, or the soul of each individual is the individual itself, and 'being a circle' is the circle, and 'being a right angle' and the essence of the right angle is the right angle, then the whole in one sense must be called posterior to the part in one sense, i.e., to the parts included in the formula and to the parts of the individual right angle (for both the material right angle which is made of bronze, and that which is formed by individual lines, are posterior to their parts); the immaterial right angle is posterior to the parts included in the formula, but prior to those included in the particular instance, and the question must not be answered simply. If the soul is something different and is not identical with the animal, even so some parts must, as we have maintained, be called prior and others must not.

. . . In the case of things which are found to occur in specifically different materials, as a circle may exist in bronze or stone or wood, it seems plain that these, the bronze or the stone, are no part of the essence of the circle, since it is found apart from them. Of things which are *not* seen to exist apart, [even here] there is no reason why the same may not be true, just as if all circles that had ever been seen were of bronze; for none the less the bronze would be no part of the form; but it is hard to eliminate it in thought.

E.g., the form of man is always found in flesh and bones and parts of this kind; are these then also parts of the form and the formula? No, they are matter; but because man is not found also in other matters we are unable to perform the abstraction.

We are in the habit of recognizing, as one determinate kind of [being], substance, and that in several senses, (a) in the sense of matter or that which in itself is not 'a [such-and-such],' and (b) in the sense of form or essence, which is that precisely in virtue of which a thing is called 'a [such-and-such],' and thirdly (c) in the sense of that which is compounded of both (a) and (b). Now matter is potentiality, form actuality; of the latter there are two grades related to one another as, e.g., knowledge to the exercise of knowledge.

Substances are, by general consent, [taken to include] bodies and especially natural bodies; for they are the principles of all other bodies. Of natural bodies some have life in them, others not; by life we mean self-nutrition and growth (with its correlative decay). It follows that every natural body which has life in it is a substance in the sense of a composite.

But since it is also a *body* of such and such a kind, viz. having life, the *body* cannot be soul; the body is the subject, or matter, not what is attributed to it. Hence the soul must be a substance in the sense of the form of a natural body having life potentially within it. But form is actuality, and thus soul is the actuality of a body as above characterized. Now the word actuality has two senses corresponding respectively to the possession of knowledge and the actual exercise of knowledge. It is obvious that the soul is actuality in the first sense, viz. that of knowledge as possessed, for both sleeping and waking presuppose the existence of soul, and of these waking corresponds to actual knowing, sleeping to knowledge possessed but not employed, and, in the history of the individual, knowledge comes before its employment or exercise.

That is why the soul is the first grade of actuality of a natural body having life potentially in it. The body so described is a body which is organized. The parts of plants in spite of their extreme simplicity are 'organs'; e.g., the leaf serves to shelter the pericarp, the pericarp to shelter the fruit, while the roots of plants are analogous to the mouth of animals, both serving for the absorption of food. If, then, we have to give a general formula applicable to all kinds of soul, we must describe it as the first grade of actuality of a natural organized body. That is why we can wholly dismiss as unnecessary the question whether the soul and the body are one: it is as meaningless as to ask whether the wax and the shape given to it by the stamp are one, or generally the matter of a thing and that of which it is the matter. ...

We have now given an answer to the question, What is soul?—an answer which applies to it in its full extent. It is substance in the sense which corresponds to the definitive formula of a thing's essence. That means that it is 'the essential whatness' of a body of the character just assigned. ... Suppose that the eye were an animal—sight would have been its soul, for sight is the substance, or *essence*, of the eye which corresponds to the formula, the eye being merely the matter of seeing; when seeing is removed the eye is no longer an eye, except in name—it is no more a real eye than the eye of a statue or of a painted figure. We must now extend our consideration from the 'parts' to the whole living body; for what the departmental sense is to the bodily part which is its organ, that the whole faculty of sense is to the whole sensitive body as such. ...

While waking is actuality in a sense corresponding to [actually] seeing, the soul is actuality in the sense corresponding to the power of sight ...; the body corresponds to what exists in potentiality; as the pupil *plus* the power of sight constitutes the eye, so the soul *plus* the body constitutes the animal.

From this it indubitably follows that the soul is inseparable from its body, or at any rate that certain parts of it are (if it has parts)—for the actuality of some of them is nothing but the actualities of their bodily parts.

Chapter 2

Of Sense

Thomas Hobbes

Sense

Concerning the thoughts of man, I will consider them first singly, and afterwards in train, or dependence upon one another. Singly, they are every one a *representation* or *appearance*, of some quality, or other accident of a body outside us, which is commonly called an *object*. Which object works on the eyes, ears, and other parts of a man's body; and by diversity of working, produceth diversity of appearances.

The original of them all, is that which we call sense, for there is no conception in a man's mind, which has not at first, totally, or by parts, been begotten [by] the organs of sense. The rest are derived from that original.

To know the natural cause of sense, is not very necessary to the business now in hand; and I have elsewhere written of the same at large. Nevertheless, to fill each part of my present method, I will briefly deliver the same in this place.

The cause of sense, is the external body, or object, which presseth the organ proper to each sense, either immediately, as in the taste and touch; or mediately, as in seeing, hearing, and smelling; which pressure, by the mediation of the nerves, and other strings and membranes of the body, continued inwards to the brain and heart, causeth there a resistance, or counter-pressure, or endeavour of the heart to deliver itself, which endeavour, because *outward*, seemeth to be some matter outside. And this *seeming*, or *fancy*, is that which men call *sense*; and consisteth, as to the eye, in a *light*, or *colour figured*; to the ear, in a *sound*; to the nostril, in an *odour*; to the tongue and palate, in a *savour*; and to the rest of the body, in *heat, cold, hardness, softness*, and such other qualities as we discern by *feeling*. All which qualities, called *sensible*, are, in the object that causeth them, [nothing] but so many several motions of the matter, by which it presseth our organs diversely. [Nor] in us that are pressed, are they any thing else, but divers motions; for motion produceth nothing but motion. But their appearance to us is fancy, the same waking, [as] dreaming. And as pressing, rubbing, or striking the eye, makes us fancy a light; and pressing the ear, produceth a din; so do the bodies we see, or hear, produce the same by their strong, though unobserved action. For if these colours and sounds were in the bodies, or objects that cause them, they could not be severed from them, as by glasses, and in echoes by reflection, we see they are; [so] we know the thing we see is in one place, the appearance in another. And though at some certain distance, the real and very object seems invested with the fancy it begets in us; yet the object is one thing, the image or fancy is another. So that sense, in all cases, is nothing else but original fancy, caused, as I have said, by the pressure, that is, by the motion of external things upon our eyes, ears, and other organs thereunto ordained.

Chapter 3

From *Meditations* II and VI and from *Reply to Objections* II

René Descartes

By the body I understand all that which can be defined by a certain figure: something which can be confined in a certain place, and which can fill a given space in such a way that every other body will be excluded from it; which can be perceived either by touch, or by sight, or by hearing, or by taste, or by smell: which can be moved in many ways not, in truth, by itself, but by something which is foreign to it, by which it is touched [and from which it receives impressions]: for to have the power of self-movement, as also of feeling or of thinking, I did not consider to appertain to the nature of body: on the contrary, I was rather astonished to find that faculties similar to them existed in some bodies.

But what am I, now that I suppose that there is a certain genius which is extremely powerful, and, if I may say so, malicious, who employs all his powers in deceiving me? Can I affirm that I possess the least of all those things which I have just said pertain to the nature of body? I pause to consider, I revolve all these things in my mind, and I find none of which I can say that it pertains to me. It would be tedious to stop to enumerate them. Let us pass to the attributes of soul and see if there is any one which is in me? What of nutrition or walking [the first mentioned]? But if it is so that I have no body it is also true that I can neither walk nor take nourishment. Another attribute is sensation. But one cannot feel without body, and besides I have thought I perceived many things during sleep that I recognised in my waking moments as not having been experienced at all. What of thinking? I find here that thought is an attribute that belongs to me; it alone cannot be separated from me. I am, I exist, that is certain. But how often? Just when I think; for it might possibly be the case if I ceased entirely to think, that I should likewise cease altogether to exist. I do not now admit anything which is not necessarily true: to speak accurately I am not more than a thing which thinks, that is to say a mind or a soul, or an understanding, or a reason, which are terms whose significance was formerly unknown to me. I am, however, a real thing and really exist; but what thing? I have answered: a thing which thinks.

And first of all, because I know that all things which I apprehend clearly and distinctly can be created by God as I apprehend them, it suffices that I am able to apprehend one thing apart from another clearly and distinctly in order to be certain that the one is different from the other, since they may be made to exist in separation at least by the omnipotence of God; and it does not signify by what power this separation is made in order to compel me to judge them to be different: and, therefore, just because I know certainly that I exist, and that meanwhile I do not remark that any other thing necessarily pertains to my nature or essence, excepting that I am a thinking thing, I

Bracketed text is translator's interpolation.

rightly conclude that my essence consists solely in the fact that I am a thinking thing [or a substance whose whole essence or nature is to think]. And although possibly (or rather certainly, as I shall say in a moment) I possess a body with which I am very intimately conjoined, yet because, on the one side, I have a clear and distinct idea of myself inasmuch as I am only a thinking and unextended thing, and as, on the other, I possess a distinct idea of body, inasmuch as it is only an extended and unthinking thing, it is certain that this I [that is to say, my soul by which I am what I am], is entirely and absolutely distinct from my body, and can exist without it.

Do you deny that in order to recognise a real distinctness between objects it is sufficient for us to conceive one of them clearly apart from the other? If so, offer us some surer token of real distinction. I believe that none such can be found. What will you say? That those things are really distinct each of which can exist apart from the other. But once more I ask how you will know that one thing can be apart from the other; this, in order to be a sign of the distinctness, should be known. Perhaps you will say that it is given to you by the senses, since you can see, touch, etc., the one thing while the other is absent. But the trustworthiness of the senses is inferior to that of the intellect, and it is in many ways possible for one and the same thing to appear under various guises or in several places or in different manners, and so to be taken to be two things. And finally if you bear in mind what was said at the end of the Second Meditation about wax, you will see that properly speaking not even are bodies themselves perceived by sense, but that they are perceived by the intellect alone, so that there is no difference between perceiving by sense one thing apart from another, and having an idea of one thing and understanding that that idea is not the same as an idea of something else. Moreover, this knowledge can be drawn from no other source than the fact that the one thing is perceived apart from the other; nor can this be known with certainty unless the ideas in each case are clear and distinct. Hence that sign you offer of real distinctness must be reduced to my criterion in order to be infallible.

But if any people deny that they have distinct ideas of mind and body, I can do nothing further than ask them to give sufficient attention to what is said in the Second Meditation. I beg them to note that the opinion they perchance hold, namely, that the parts of the brain join their forces with the soul to form thoughts, has not arisen from any positive ground, but only from the fact that they have never had experience of separation from the body, and have not seldom been hindered by it in their operations, and that similarly if anyone had from infancy continually worn irons on his legs, he would think that those irons were part of his own body and that he needed them in order to walk.

Chapter 4

From *The Principles of Human Knowledge*

George Berkeley

It is evident to any one who takes a survey of the *objects* of human knowledge, that they are either ideas actually imprinted on the senses; or else such as are perceived by attending to the passions and operations of the mind; or lastly, ideas formed by help of memory and imagination—either compounding, dividing, or barely representing those originally perceived in the aforesaid ways. By sight I have the ideas of light and colours, with their several degrees and variations. By touch I perceive hard and soft, heat and cold, motion and resistance, and of all these more and less either as to quantity or degree. Smelling furnishes me with odours; the palate with tastes; and hearing conveys sounds to the mind in all their variety of tone and composition. And as several of these are observed to accompany each other, they come to be marked by one name, and so to be reputed as one thing. Thus, for example, a certain colour, taste, smell, figure and consistence having been observed to go together, are accounted one distinct thing, signified by the name *apple*; other collections of ideas constitute a stone, a tree, a book, and the like sensible things—which as they are pleasing or disagreeable excite the passions of love, hatred, joy, grief, and so forth.

But, besides all that endless variety of ideas or objects of knowledge, there is likewise something which knows or perceives them, and exercises divers operations, as willing, imagining, remembering, about them. This perceiving, active being is what I call *mind, spirit, soul,* or *myself.* By which words I do not denote any one of my ideas, but a thing entirely distinct from them, wherein they exist, or, which is the same thing, whereby they are perceived—for the existence of an idea consists in being perceived.

That neither our thoughts, nor passions, nor ideas formed by the imagination, exist without the mind, is what everybody will allow. And to me it is no less evident that the various sensations or ideas imprinted on the sense, however blended or combined together (that is, whatever objects they compose), cannot exist otherwise than in a mind perceiving them. I think an intuitive knowledge may be obtained of this by any one that shall attend to what is meant by the term *exist* when applied to sensible things. The table I write on I say exists, that is, I see and feel it; and if I were out of my study I should say it existed—meaning thereby that if I was in my study I might perceive it, or that some other spirit actually does perceive it. There was an odour, that is, it was smelt; there was a sound, that is, it was heard; a colour or figure, and it was perceived by sight or touch. This is all that I can understand by these and the like expressions. For as to what is said of the absolute existence of unthinking things without any relation to their being perceived, that is to me perfectly unintelligible. Their *esse* is *percipi*, nor is it possible they should have any existence out of the minds or thinking things which perceive them.

It is indeed an opinion strangely prevailing amongst men, that houses, mountains, rivers, and in a word all sensible objects, have an existence, natural or real, distinct from their being perceived by the understanding. But, with how great an assurance and acquiescence soever this principle may be entertained in the world, yet whoever shall find in his heart to call it in question may, if I mistake not, perceive it to involve a manifest contradiction. For, what are the forementioned objects but the things we perceive by sense? and what do we perceive besides our own ideas or sensations? and is it not plainly repugnant that any one of these, or any combination of them, should exist unperceived?

If we throughly examine this tenet it will, perhaps, be found at bottom to depend on the doctrine of *abstract ideas*. For can there be a nicer strain of abstraction than to distinguish the existence of sensible objects from their being perceived, so as to conceive them existing unperceived? Light and colours, heat and cold, extension and figures—in a word the things we see and feel—what are they but so many sensations, notions, ideas, or impressions on the sense? and is it possible to separate, even in thought, any of these from perception? For my part, I might as easily divide a thing from itself. I may, indeed, divide in my thoughts, or conceive apart from each other, those things which, perhaps, I never perceived by sense so divided. Thus, I imagine the trunk of a human body without the limbs, or conceive the smell of a rose without thinking on the rose itself. So far, I will not deny, I can abstract—if that may properly be called *abstraction* which extends only to the conceiving separately such objects as it is possible may really exist or be actually perceived asunder. But my conceiving or imagining power does not extend beyond the possibility of real existence or perception. Hence, as it is impossible for me to see or feel anything without an actual sensation of that thing, so is it impossible for me to conceive in my thoughts any sensible thing or object distinct from the sensation or perception of it. [In truth, the object and the sensation are the same thing, and cannot therefore be abstracted from each other.]

Some truths there are so near and obvious to the mind that a man need only open his eyes to see them. Such I take this important one to be, viz. that all the choir of heaven and furniture of the earth, in a word all those bodies which compose the mighty frame of the world, have not any subsistence without a mind, that their *being* is to be perceived or known; that consequently so long as they are not actually perceived by me, or do not exist in my mind or that of any other created spirit, they must either have no existence at all, or else subsist in the mind of some Eternal Spirit—it being perfectly unintelligible, and involving all the absurdity of abstraction, to attribute to any single part of them an existence independent of a spirit. [To be convinced of which, the reader need only reflect, and try to separate in his own thoughts the *being* of a sensible thing from its *being perceived*.]

From what has been said it is evident there is not any other Substance than *Spirit*, or that which perceives. But, for the fuller demonstration of this point, let it be considered the sensible qualities are colour, figure, motion, smell, taste, etc., i.e., the ideas perceived by sense. Now, for an idea to exist in an unperceiving thing is a manifest contradiction, for to have an idea is all one as to perceive; that therefore wherein colour, figure, etc. exist must perceive them; hence it is clear there can be no unthinking substance or *substratum* of those ideas.

But, say you, though the ideas themselves do not exist without the mind, yet there may be things like them, whereof they are copies or resemblances, which things exist without the mind in an unthinking substance. I answer, an idea can be like nothing but an idea; a colour or figure can be like nothing but another colour or figure. If we look but never so little into our thought, we shall find it impossible for us to conceive a likeness except only between our ideas. Again, I ask whether those supposed originals or external things, of which our ideas are the pictures or representations, be themselves perceivable or no? If they are, then they are ideas and we have gained our point; but if you say they are not, I appeal to any one whether it be sense to assert a colour is like something which is invisible; hard or soft, like something which is intangible; and so of the rest.

Some there are who make a distinction betwixt *primary* and *secondary* qualities. By the former they mean extension, figure, motion, rest, solidity or impenetrability, and number; by the latter they denote all other sensible qualities, as colours, sounds, tastes, and so forth. The ideas we have of these they acknowledge not to be the resemblances of anything existing without the mind, or unperceived, but they will have our ideas of the primary qualities to be patterns or images of things which exist without the mind, in an unthinking substance which they call Matter. By Matter, therefore, we are to understand an inert, senseless substance, in which extension, figure, and motion do actually subsist. But it is evident, from what we have already shewn, that extension, figure, and motion are only ideas existing in the mind, and that an idea can be like nothing but another idea, and that consequently neither they nor their archetypes can exist in an unperceiving substance. Hence, it is plain that the very notion of what is called *Matter* or *corporeal substance*, involves a contradiction in it. [Insomuch that I should not think it necessary to spend more time in exposing its absurdity. But, because the tenet of the existence of Matter seems to have taken so deep a root in the minds of philosophers, and draws after it so many ill consequences, I choose rather to be thought prolix and tedious than omit anything that might conduce to the full discovery and extirpation of that prejudice.]

Chapter 5
Of the Laws of Mind
John Stuart Mill

What Is Meant by Laws of Mind

What the Mind is, as well as what Matter is, or any other question respecting Things in themselves, as distinguished from their sensible manifestations, it would be foreign to the purposes of this treatise to consider. Here, as throughout our inquiry, we shall keep clear of all speculations respecting the mind's own nature, and shall understand by the laws of mind those of mental phenomena—of the various feelings or states of consciousness of sentient beings. These, according to the classification we have uniformly followed, consist of Thoughts, Emotions, Volitions, and Sensations; the last being as truly states of Mind as the three former. It is usual, indeed, to speak of sensations as states of body, not of mind. But this is the common confusion of giving one and the same name to a phenomenon and to the proximate cause or conditions of the phenomenon. The immediate antecedent of a sensation is a state of body, but the sensation itself is a state of mind. If the word mind means anything, it means that which feels. Whatever opinion we hold respecting the fundamental identity or diversity of matter and mind, in any case the distinction between mental and physical facts, between the internal and the external world, will always remain as a matter of classification; and in that classification, sensations, like all other feelings, must be ranked as mental phenomena. The mechanism of their production, both in the body itself and in what is called outward nature, is all that can with any propriety be classed as physical.

The phenomena of mind, then, are the various feelings of our nature, both those improperly called physical and those peculiarly designated as mental; and by the laws of mind I mean the laws according to which those feelings generate one another.

Is There a Science of Psychology?

All states of mind are immediately caused either by other states of mind or by states of body. When a state of mind is produced by a state of mind, I call the law concerned in the case a law of Mind. When a state of mind is produced directly by a state of body, the law is a law of Body, and belongs to physical science.

With regard to those states of mind which are called sensations, all are agreed that these have for their immediate antecedents states of body. Every sensation has for its proximate cause some affection of the portion of our frame called the nervous system, whether this affection originate in the action of some external object, or in some pathological condition of the nervous organisation itself. The laws of this portion of our nature—the varieties of our sensations and the physical conditions on which they proximately depend—manifestly belong to the province of Physiology.

Whether the remainder of our mental states are similarly dependent on physical conditions, is one of the *vexatae questiones* in the science of human nature. It is still disputed whether our thoughts, emotions, and volitions are generated through the intervention of material mechanism; whether we have organs of thought and of emotion in the same sense in which we have organs of sensation. Many eminent physiologists hold the affirmative. These contend that a thought (for example) is as much the result of nervous agency as a sensation; that some particular state of our nervous system, in particular of that central portion of it called the brain, invariably precedes, and is presupposed by, every state of our consciousness. According to this theory, one state of mind is never really produced by another; all are produced by states of body. When one thought seems to call up another by association, it is not really a thought which recalls a thought; the association did not exist between the two thoughts, but between the two states of the brain or nerves which preceded the thoughts: one of those states recalls the other, each being attended, in its passage, by the particular state of consciousness which is consequent on it. On this theory the uniformities of succession among states of mind would be mere derivative uniformities, resulting from the laws of succession of the bodily states which cause them. There would be no original mental laws, no Laws of Mind in the sense in which I use the term, at all; and mental science would be a mere branch, though the highest and most recondite branch, of the science of Physiology. M. Comte, accordingly, claims the scientific cognisance of moral and intellectual phenomena exclusively for physiologists; and not only denies to Psychology, or Mental Philosophy properly so called, the character of a science, but places it, in the chimerical nature of its objects and pretensions, almost on a par with astrology.

But, after all has been said which can be said, it remains incontestable that there exist uniformities of succession among states of mind, and that these can be ascertained by observation and experiment. Further, that every mental state has a nervous state for its immediate antecedent and proximate cause, though extremely probable, cannot hitherto be said to be proved, in the conclusive manner in which this can be proved of sensations; and even were it certain, yet every one must admit that we are wholly ignorant of the characteristics of these nervous states; we know not, and at present have no means of knowing, in what respect one of them differs from another; and our only mode of studying their successions or co-existences must be by observing the successions and co-existences of the mental states of which they are supposed to be the generators or causes. The successions, therefore, which obtain among mental phenomena do not admit of being deduced from the physiological laws of our nervous organisation; and all real knowledge of them must continue, for a long time at least, if not always, to be sought in the direct study, by observation and experiment, of the mental successions themselves. Since, therefore, the order of our mental phenomena must be studied in those phenomena, and not inferred from the laws of any phenomena more general, there is a distinct and separate Science of Mind.

The relations, indeed, of that science to the science of physiology must never be overlooked or undervalued. It must by no means be forgotten that the laws of mind may be derivative laws resulting from laws of animal life, and that their truth therefore may ultimately depend on physical conditions; and the influence of physiological states or physiological changes in altering or counteracting the mental successions is one of the most important departments of psychological study. But, on the other hand, to reject the resource of psychological analysis, and construct the theory of the mind solely on such data as physiology at present affords, seems to me as great an error in principle, and an even more serious one in practice. Imperfect as is the science of mind, I do not scruple to affirm that it is in a considerably more advanced state than the portion of physiology which corresponds to it; and to discard the former for the latter appears to me an infringement of the true canons of inductive philosophy, which must produce, and which does produce, erroneous conclusions in some very important departments of the science of human nature.

Chapter 6
Descartes' Myth
Gilbert Ryle

The Official Doctrine

There is a doctrine about the nature and place of minds which is so prevalent among theorists and even among laymen that it deserves to be described as the official theory. Most philosophers, psychologists and religious teachers subscribe, with minor reservations, to its main articles and, although they admit certain theoretical difficulties in it, they tend to assume that these can be overcome without serious modifications being made to the architecture of the theory. It will be argued here that the central principles of the doctrine are unsound and conflict with the whole body of what we know about minds when we are not speculating about them.

The official doctrine, which hails chiefly from Descartes, is something like this. With the doubtful exceptions of idiots and infants in arms every human being has both a body and a mind. Some would prefer to say that every human being is both a body and a mind. His body and his mind are ordinarily harnessed together, but after the death of the body his mind may continue to exist and function.

Human bodies are in space and are subject to the mechanical laws which govern all other bodies in space. Bodily processes and states can be inspected by external observers. So a man's bodily life is as much a public affair as are the lives of animals and reptiles and even as the careers of trees, crystals and planets.

But minds are not in space, nor are their operations subject to mechanical laws. The workings of one mind are not witnessable by other observers; its career is private. Only I can take direct cognisance of the states and processes of my own mind. A person therefore lives through two collateral histories, one consisting of what happens in and to his body, the other consisting of what happens in and to his mind. The first is public, the second private. The events in the first history are events in the physical world, those in the second are events in the mental world.

It has been disputed whether a person does or can directly monitor all or only some of the episodes of his own private history; but, according to the official doctrine, of at least some of these episodes he has direct and unchallengeable cognisance. In consciousness, self-consciousness and introspection he is directly and authentically apprised of the present states and operations of his mind. He may have great or small uncertainties about concurrent and adjacent episodes in the physical world, but he can have none about at least part of what is momentarily occupying his mind.

It is customary to express this bifurcation of his two lives and of his two worlds by saying that the things and events which belong to the physical world, including his own body, are external, while the workings of his own mind are internal. This antithesis of outer and inner is of course meant to be construed as a metaphor, since minds, not being in space, could not be described as being spatially inside anything else, or as having things going on spatially inside themselves. But relapses from this good intention are common and theorists are found speculating how stimuli, the physical sources of which are yards or miles outside a person's skin, can generate mental responses inside his skull, or how decisions framed inside his cranium can set going movements of his extremities.

Even when 'inner' and 'outer' are construed as metaphors, the problem how a person's mind and body influence one another is notoriously charged with theoretical difficulties. What the mind wills, the legs, arms and the tongue execute; what affects the ear and the eye has something to do with what the mind perceives; grimaces and smiles betray the mind's moods and bodily castigations lead, it is hoped, to moral improvement. But the actual transactions between the episodes of the private history and those of the public history remain mysterious, since by definition they can belong to neither series. They could not be reported among the happenings described in a person's autobiography of his inner life, but nor could they be reported among those described in some one else's biography of that person's overt career. They can be inspected neither by introspection nor by laboratory experiment. They are theoretical shuttlecocks which are forever being bandied from the physiologist back to the psychologist and from the psychologist back to the physiologist.

Underlying this partly metaphorical representation of the bifurcation of a person's two lives there is a seemingly more profound and philosophical assumption. It is assumed that there are two different kinds of existence or status. What exists or happens may have the status of physical existence, or it may have the status of mental existence. Somewhat as the faces of coins are either heads or tails, or somewhat as living creatures are either male or female, so, it is supposed, some existing is physical existing, other existing is mental existing. It is a necessary feature of what has physical existence that it is in space and time, it is a necessary feature of what has mental existence that it is in time but not in space. What has physical existence is composed of matter, or else is a function of matter; what has mental existence consists of consciousness, or else is a function of consciousness.

There is thus a polar opposition between mind and matter, an opposition which is often brought out as follows. Material objects are situated in a common field, known as 'space', and what happens to one body in one part of space is mechanically connected with what happens to other bodies in other parts of space. But mental happenings occur in insulated fields, known as 'minds', and there is, apart maybe from telepathy, no direct causal connection between what happens in one mind and what happens in another. Only through the medium of the public physical world can the mind of one person make a difference to the mind of another. The mind is its own place and in his inner life each of us lives the life of a ghostly Robinson Crusoe. People can see, hear and jolt one another's bodies, but they are irremediably blind and deaf to the workings of one another's minds and inoperative upon them.

What sort of knowledge can be secured of the workings of a mind? On the one side, according to the official theory, a person has direct knowledge of the best imaginable kind of the workings of his own mind. Mental states and processes are (or are normally) conscious states and processes, and the consciousness which irradiates them can engender no illusions and leaves the door open for no doubts. A person's present thinkings, feelings and willings, his perceivings, rememberings and imaginings are intrinsically 'phosphorescent'; their existence and their nature are inevitably betrayed to their owner. The inner life is a stream of consciousness of such a sort that it would be absurd to suggest that the mind whose life is that stream might be unaware of what is passing down it.

True, the evidence adduced recently by Freud seems to show that there exist channels tributary to this stream, which run hidden from their owner. People are actuated by impulses the existence of which they vigorously disavow; some of their thoughts differ from the thoughts which they acknowledge; and some of the actions which they think they will to perform they do not really will. They are thoroughly gulled by some of their own hypocrisies and they successfully ignore facts about their mental lives which on the official theory ought to be patent to them. Holders of the official theory tend, however, to maintain that anyhow in normal circumstances a person must be directly and authentically seized of the present state and workings of his own mind.

Besides being currently supplied with these alleged immediate data of consciousness, a person is also generally supposed to be able to exercise from time to time a special kind of perception, namely inner perception, or introspection. He can take a (non-optical) 'look' at what is passing in his mind. Not only can he view and scrutinize a flower through his sense of sight and listen to and discriminate the notes of a bell through his sense of hearing; he can also reflectively or introspectively watch, without any bodily organ of sense, the current episodes of his inner life. This self-observation is also commonly supposed to be immune from illusion, confusion or doubt. A mind's reports of its own affairs have a certainty superior to the best that is possessed by its reports of matters in the physical world. Sense-perceptions can, but consciousness and introspection cannot, be mistaken or confused.

On the other side, one person has no direct access of any sort to the events of the inner life of another. He cannot do better than make problematic inferences from the observed behaviour of the other person's body to the states of mind which, by analogy from his own conduct, he supposes to be signalised by that behaviour. Direct access to the workings of a mind is the privilege of that mind itself; in default of such privileged access, the workings of one mind are inevitably occult to everyone else. For the supposed arguments from bodily movements similar to their own to mental workings similar to their own would lack any possibility of observational corroboration. Not unnaturally, therefore, an adherent of the official theory finds it difficult to resist this consequence of his premises, that he has no good reason to believe that there do exist minds other than his own. Even if he prefers to believe that to other human bodies there are harnessed minds not unlike his own, he cannot claim to be able to discover their individual characteristics, or the particular things that they undergo and do. Absolute solitude is on this showing the ineluctable destiny of the soul. Only our bodies can meet.

As a necessary corollary of this general scheme there is implicitly prescribed a special way of construing our ordinary concepts of mental powers and operations. The verbs, nouns and adjectives, with which in ordinary life we describe the wits, characters and higher-grade performances of the people with whom we have do, are required to be construed as signifying special episodes in their secret histories, or else as signifying tendencies for such episodes to occur. When someone is described as knowing, believing or guessing something, as hoping, dreading, intending or shirking something, as designing this or being amused at that, these verbs are supposed to denote the occurrence of specific modifications in his (to us) occult stream of consciousness. Only his own privileged access to this stream in direct awareness and introspection could provide authentic testimony that these mental-conduct verbs were correctly or incorrectly applied. The onlooker, be he teacher, critic, biographer or friend, call never assure himself that his comments have any vestige of truth. Yet it was just because we do in fact all know how to make such comments, make them with general correctness and correct them when they turn out to be confused or mistaken, that philosophers found it necessary to construct their theories of the nature and place of minds. Finding mental-conduct concepts being regularly and effectively used, they properly sought to fix their logical geography. But the logical geography officially recommended would entail that there could be no regular or effective use of these mental-conduct concepts in our descriptions of, and prescriptions for, other people's minds.

The Absurdity of the Official Doctrine

Such in outline is the official theory. I shall often speak of it, with deliberate abusiveness, as 'the dogma of the Ghost in the Machine'. I hope to prove that it is entirely false, and false not in detail but in principle. It is not merely an assemblage of particular mistakes. It is one big mistake and a mistake of a special kind. It is, namely, a category-mistake. It represents the facts of mental life as if they belonged to one logical type or category (or range of types or categories), when they actually belong to another. The dogma is therefore a philosopher's myth. In attempting to explode the myth I shall probably be taken to be denying well-known facts about the mental life of human beings, and my plea that I aim at doing nothing more than rectify the logic of mental-conduct concepts will probably be disallowed as mere subterfuge.

I must first indicate what is meant by the phrase 'Category-mistake'. This I do in a series of illustrations.

A foreigner visiting Oxford or Cambridge for the first time is shown a number of colleges, libraries, playing fields, museums, scientific departments and administrative offices. He then asks 'But where is the University? I have seen where the members of the Colleges live, where the Registrar works, where the scientists experiment and the rest. But I have not yet seen the University in which reside and work the members of your University.' It has then to be explained to him that the University is not another collateral institution, some ulterior counterpart to the colleges, laboratories and offices which he has seen. The University is just the way in which all that he has already seen is organized. When they are seen and when their co-ordination is understood, the University has been seen. His mistake lay in his innocent assumption that it was correct to speak of Christ Church, the Bodleian Library, the Ashmolean Museum *and* the University, to speak, that is, as if 'the University' stood for an extra member of the class of which these other units are members. He was mistakenly allocating the University to the same category as that to which the other institutions belong.

The same mistake would be made by a child witnessing the march-past of a division, who, having had pointed out to him such and such battalions, batteries, squadrons, etc., asked when the division was going to appear. He would be supposing that a division was a counterpart to the units already seen, partly similar to them and partly unlike them. He would be shown his mistake by being told that in watching the battalions, batteries and squadrons marching past he had been watching the division marching past. The march-past was not a parade of battalions, batteries, squadrons *and* a division; it was a parade of the battalions, batteries and squadrons *of* a division.

One more illustration. A foreigner watching his first game of cricket learns what are the functions of the bowlers, the batsmen, the fielders, the umpires and the scorers. He then says 'But there is no one left on the field to contribute the famous element of team-spirit. I see who does the bowling, the batting and the wicket-keeping; but I do not see whose role it is to exercise *esprit de corps.*' Once more, it would have to be explained that he was looking for the wrong type of thing. Team-spirit is not another cricketing-operation supplementary to all of the other special tasks. It is, roughly, the keenness with which each of the special tasks is performed, and performing a task keenly is not performing two tasks. Certainly exhibiting team-spirit is not the same thing as bowling or catching, but nor is it a third thing such that we can say that the bowler first bowls *and* then exhibits team-spirit or that a fielder is at a given moment *either* catching *or* displaying *esprit de corps*.

These illustrations of category-mistakes have a common feature which must be noticed. The mistakes were made by people who did not know how to wield the concepts *University*, *division* and *team-spirit*. Their puzzles arose from inability to use certain items in the English vocabulary.

The theoretically interesting category-mistakes are those made by people who are perfectly competent to apply concepts, at least in the situations with which they are familiar, but are still liable in their abstract thinking to allocate those concepts to logical types to which they do not belong. An instance of a mistake of this sort would be the following story. A student of politics has learned the main differences between the British, the French and the American Constitutions, and has learned also the differences and connections between the Cabinet, Parliament, the various Ministries, the Judicature and the Church of England. But he still becomes embarrassed when asked questions about the connections between the Church of England, the Home Office and the British Constitution. For while the Church and the Home Office are institutions, the British Constitution is not another institution in the same sense of that noun. So inter-institutional relations which can be asserted or denied to hold between the Church and the Home Office cannot be asserted or denied to hold between either of them and the British Constitution. 'The British Constitution is not a term of the same logical type as 'the Home Office' and 'the Church of England'. In a partially similar way, John Doe may be a relative, a friend, an enemy or a stranger to Richard Roe; but he cannot be any of these things to the Average Taxpayer. He knows how to talk sense in certain sorts of discussions about the Average Taxpayer, but he is baffled to say why he could not come across him in the street as he can come across Richard Roe.

It is pertinent to our main subject to notice that, so long as the student of politics continues to think of the British Constitution as a counterpart to the other institutions, he will tend to describe it as a mysteriously occult institution; and so long as John Doe continues to think of the Average Taxpayer as a fellow-citizen, he will tend to think of him as an elusive insubstantial man, a ghost who is everywhere yet nowhere.

My destructive purpose is to show that a family of radical category-mistakes is the source of the double-life theory. The representation of a person as a ghost mysteriously ensconced in a machine derives from this argument. Because, as is true, a person's thinking, feeling and purposive doing cannot be described solely in the idioms of physics, chemistry and physiology, therefore they must be described in counterpart idioms. As the human body is a complex organised unit, so the human mind must be another complex organised unit, though one made of a different sort of stuff and with a different sort of structure. Or, again, as the human body, like any other parcel of matter, is a field of causes and effects, so the mind must be another field of causes and effects, though not (Heaven be praised) mechanical causes and effects.

The Origin of the Category-Mistake

One of the chief intellectual origins of what I have yet to prove to be the Cartesian category-mistake seems to be this. When Galileo showed that his methods of scientific discovery were competent to provide a mechanical theory which should cover every occupant of space, Descartes found in himself two conflicting motives. As a man of scientific genius he could not but endorse the claims of mechanics, yet as a religious and moral man he could not accept, as Hobbes accepted, the discouraging rider to those claims, namely that human nature differs only in degree of complexity from clockwork. The mental could not be just a variety of the mechanical.

He and subsequent philosophers naturally but erroneously availed themselves of the following escape-route. Since mental-conduct words are not to be construed as signifying the occurrence of mechanical processes, they must be construed as signifying the occurrence of non-mechanical processes; since mechanical laws explain movements in space as the effects of other movements in space, other laws must explain some of the non-spatial workings of minds as the effects of other non-spatial workings of minds. The difference between the human behaviours which we describe as intelligent and those which we describe as unintelligent must be a difference in their causation; so, while some movements of human tongues and limbs are the effects of mechanical causes, others must be the effects of non-mechanical causes, i.e. some issue from movements of particles of matter, others from workings of the mind.

The differences between the physical and the mental were thus represented as differences inside the common framework of the categories of 'thing', 'stuff', 'attribute', 'state', 'process', 'change', 'cause' and 'effect'. Minds are things, but different sorts of things from bodies; mental processes are causes and effects, but different sorts of causes and effects from bodily movements. And so on. Somewhat as the foreigner expected the University to be an extra edifice, rather like a college but also considerably different, so the repudiators of mechanism represented minds as extra centres of causal processes, rather like machines but also considerably different from them. Their theory was a para-mechanical hypothesis.

That this assumption was at the heart of the doctrine is shown by the fact that there was from the beginning felt to be a major theoretical difficulty in explaining how minds can influence and be influenced by bodies. How can a mental process, such as willing, cause spatial movements like the movements of the tongue? How can a physical change in the optic nerve have among its effects a mind's perception of a flash of light? This notorious crux by itself shows the logical mould into which Descartes pressed his theory of the mind. It was the self-same mould into which he and Galileo set their mechanics. Still unwittingly adhering to the grammar of mechanics, he tried to avert disaster by describing minds in what was merely an obverse vocabulary. The workings of minds had to be described by the mere negatives of the specific descriptions given to bodies; they are not in space, they are not motions, they are not modifications of matter, they are not accessible to public observation. Minds are not bits of clockwork, they are just bits of not-clockwork.

As thus represented, minds are not merely ghosts harnessed to machines, they are themselves just spectral machines. Though the human body is an engine, it is not quite an ordinary engine, since some of its workings are governed by another engine inside it—this interior governor-engine being one of a very special sort. It is invisible, inaudible and it has no size or weight. It cannot be taken to bits and the laws it obeys are not those known to ordinary engineers. Nothing is known of how it governs the bodily engine.

A second major crux points the same moral. Since, according to the doctrine, minds belong to the same category as bodies and since bodies are rigidly governed by mechanical laws, it seemed to many theorists to follow that minds must be similarly governed by rigid non-mechanical laws. The physical world is a deterministic system, so the mental world must be a deterministic system. Bodies cannot help the modifications that they undergo, so minds cannot help pursuing the careers fixed for them. *Responsibility, choice, merit* and *demerit* are therefore inapplicable concepts—unless the compromise solution is adopted of saying that the laws governing mental processes, unlike those governing physical processes, have the congenial attribute of being only rather rigid. The problem of the Freedom of the Will was the problem how to reconcile the hypothesis that minds are to be described in terms drawn from the categories of mechanics with the knowledge that higher-grade human conduct is not of a piece with the behaviour of machines.

It is an historical curiosity that it was not noticed that the entire argument was broken-backed. Theorists correctly assumed that any sane man could already recognise the differences between, say, rational and non-rational utterances or between purposive and automatic behaviour. Else there would have been nothing requiring to be salved from mechanism. Yet the explanation given presupposed that one person could in principle never recognise the difference between the rational and the irrational utterances issuing from other human bodies, since he could never get access to the postulated immaterial causes of some of their utterances. Save for the doubtful exception of himself, he could never tell the difference between a man and a Robot. It would have to be conceded, for example, that, for all that we can tell, the inner lives of persons who are classed as idiots or lunatics are as rational as those of anyone else. Perhaps only their overt behaviour is disappointing; that is to say, perhaps 'idiots' are not really idiotic, or 'lunatics' lunatic. Perhaps, too, some of those who are classed as sane are really idiots. According to the theory, external observers could never know how the overt behaviour of others is correlated with their mental powers and processes and so they could never know or even plausibly conjecture whether their applications of mental-conduct concepts to these other people were correct or incorrect. It would then be hazardous or impossible for a man to claim sanity or logical consistency even for himself, since he would be debarred from comparing his own performances with those of others. In short, our characterisations of persons and their performances as intelligent, prudent and virtuous or as stupid, hypocritical and cowardly could never have been made, so the problem of providing a special causal hypothesis to serve as the basis of such diagnoses would never have arisen. The question, 'How do persons differ from machines?' arose just because everyone already knew how to apply mental-conduct concepts before the new causal hypothesis was introduced. This causal hypothesis could not therefore be the source of the criteria used in those applications. Nor, of course, has the causal hypothesis in any degree improved our handling of those criteria. We still distinguish good from bad arithmetic, politic from impolitic conduct and fertile from infertile imaginations in the ways in which Descartes himself distinguished them before and after he speculated how the applicability of these criteria was compatible with the principle of mechanical causation.

He had mistaken the logic of his problem. Instead of asking by what criteria intelligent behaviour is actually distinguished from non-intelligent behaviour, he asked 'Given that the principle of mechanical causation does not tell us the difference, what other causal principle will tell us?' He realised that the problem was not one of mechanics and assumed that it must therefore be one of some counterpart to mechanics. Not unnaturally psychology is often cast for just this role.

When two terms belong to the same category, it is proper to construct conjunctive propositions embodying them. Thus a purchaser may say that he bought a left-hand glove and a right-hand glove, but not that he bought a left-hand glove, a right-hand glove and a pair of gloves. 'She came home in a flood of tears and a sedan-chair' is a well-known joke based on the absurdity of conjoining terms of different types. It would have been equally ridiculous to construct the disjunction 'She came home either in a flood of tears or else in a sedan-chair'. Now the dogma of the Ghost in the Machine does just this. It maintains that there exist both bodies and minds; that there occur physical processes and mental processes; that there are mechanical causes of corporeal movements and mental causes of corporeal movements. I shall argue that these and other analogous conjunctions are absurd; but, it must be noticed, the argument will not show that either of the illegitimately conjoined propositions is absurd in itself. I am not, for example, denying that there occur mental processes. Doing long division is a mental process and so is making a joke. But I am saying that the phrase 'there occur mental processes' does not mean the same sort of thing as 'there occur physical processes', and, therefore, that it makes no sense to conjoin or disjoin the two.

If my argument is successful, there will follow some interesting consequences. First, the hallowed contrast between Mind and Matter will be dissipated, but dissipated not by either of the equally hallowed absorptions of Mind by Matter or of Matter by Mind, but in quite a different way. For the seeming contrast of the two will be shown to be as illegitimate as would be the contrast of 'she came home in a flood of tears' and 'she came home in a sedan-chair'. The belief that there is a polar opposition between Mind and Matter is the belief that they are terms of the same logical type.

It will also follow that both Idealism and Materialism are answers to an improper question. The 'reduction' of the material world to mental states and processes, as well as the 'reduction' of mental states and processes to physical states and processes, presuppose the legitimacy of the disjunction 'Either there exist minds or there exist bodies (but not both)'. It would be like saying, 'Either she bought a left-hand and a right-hand glove or she bought a pair of gloves (but not both)'.

It is perfectly proper to say, in one logical tone of voice, that there exist minds and to say, in another logical tone of voice, that there exist bodies. But these expressions do not indicate two different species of existence, for 'existence' is not a generic word like 'coloured' or 'sexed'. They indicate two different senses of 'exist', somewhat as 'rising' has different senses in 'the tide is rising', 'hopes are rising', and 'the average age of death is rising'. A man would be thought to be making a poor joke who said that three things are now rising, namely the tide, hopes and the average age of death. It would be just as good or bad a joke to say that there exist prime numbers and Wednesdays and public opinions and navies; or that there exist both minds and bodies. . . . I try to prove that the official theory does rest on a batch of category-mistakes by showing that logically absurd corollaries follow from it. The exhibition of these absurdities will have the constructive effect of bringing out part of the correct logic of mental-conduct concepts.

Historical Note

It would not be true to say that the official theory derives solely from Descartes' theories, or even from a more widespread anxiety about the implications of seventeenth century mechanics. Scholastic and Reformation theology had schooled the intellects of the scientists as well as of the laymen, philosophers and clerics of that age. Stoic-Augustinian theories of the will were embedded in the Calvinist doctrines of sin and grace; Platonic and Aristotelian theories of the intellect shaped the orthodox doctrines of the immortality of the soul. Descartes was reformulating already prevalent theological doctrines of the soul in the new syntax of Galileo. The theologian's privacy of conscience became the philosopher's privacy of consciousness, and what had been the bogy of Predestination reappeared as the bogy of Determinism.

It would also not be true to say that the two-worlds myth did no theoretical good. Myths often do a lot of theoretical good, while they are still new. One benefit bestowed by the para-mechanical myth was that it partly superannuated the then prevalent para-political myth. Minds and their Faculties had previously been described by analogies with political superiors and political subordinates. The idioms used were those of ruling, obeying, collaborating and rebelling. They survived and still survive in many ethical and some epistemological discussions. As, in physics, the new myth of occult Forces was a scientific improvement on the old myth of Final Causes, so, in anthropological and psychological theory, the new myth of hidden operations, impulses and agencies was an improvement on the old myth of dictations, deferences and disobediences.

Chapter 7

Is Consciousness a Brain Process?

U. T. Place

Introduction

The view that there exists a separate class of events, mental events, which cannot be described in terms of the concepts employed by the physical sciences no longer commands the universal and unquestioning acceptance amongst philosophers and psychologists which it once did. Modern physicalism, however, unlike the materialism of the seventeenth and eighteenth centuries, is behaviouristic. Consciousness on this view is either a special type of behaviour, 'sampling' or 'running-back-and-forth' behaviour as Tolman (1932, p. 206) has it, or a disposition to behave in a certain way, an itch for example being a temporary propensity to scratch. In the case of cognitive concepts like 'knowing', 'believing', 'understanding', 'remembering' and volitional concepts like 'wanting' and 'intending', there can be little doubt, I think, that an analysis in terms of dispositions to behave (Wittgenstein 1953, Ryle 1949) is fundamentally sound. On the other hand, there would seem to be an intractable residue of concepts clustering around the notions of consciousness, experience, sensation and mental imagery, where some sort of inner process story is unavoidable (Place 1954). It is possible, of course, that a satisfactory behaviouristic account of this conceptual residuum will ultimately be found. For our present purposes, however, I shall assume that this cannot be done and that statements about pains and twinges, about how things look, sound and feel, about things dreamed of or pictured in the mind's eye, are statements referring to events and processes which are in some sense private or internal to the individual of whom they are predicated. The question I wish to raise is whether in making this assumption we are inevitably committed to a dualist position in which sensations and mental images form a separate category of processes over and above the physical and physiological processes with which they are known to be correlated. I shall argue that an acceptance of inner processes does not entail dualism and that the thesis that consciousness is a process in the brain cannot be dismissed on logical grounds.

The 'Is' of Definition and the 'Is' of Composition

I want to stress from the outset that in defending the thesis that consciousness is a process in the brain, I am not trying to argue that when we describe our dreams, fantasies and sensations we are talking about processes in our brains. That is, I am not claiming that statements about sensations and mental images are reducible to or analysable into statements about brain processes, in the way in which 'cognition statements' are analysable into statements about behaviour. To say that statements about consciousness are statements about brain processes is manifestly false. This is shown (a) by the fact that you can describe your sensations and mental imagery without knowing anything about your brain processes or even that such things exist, (b) by the fact that statements about one's consciousness and statements about one's brain processes are verified in entirely different ways and (c) by the fact that there is nothing self-contradictory about the statement 'X has a pain but there is nothing going on in his brain'. What I do want to assert, however, is that the statement 'consciousness is a process in the brain', although not necessarily true, is not necessarily false. 'Consciousness is a process in the brain', on my view is neither self-contradictory nor self-evident; it is a reasonable scientific hypothesis, in the way that the statement 'lightning is a motion of electric charges' is a reasonable scientific hypothesis.

The all but universally accepted view that an assertion of identity between consciousness and brain processes can be ruled out on logical grounds alone, derives, I suspect, from a failure to distinguish between what we may call the 'is' of definition and the 'is' of composition. The distinction I have in mind here is the difference between the function of the word 'is' in statements like 'a square is an equilateral rectangle', 'red is a colour', 'to understand an instruction is to be able to act appropriately under the appropriate circumstances', and its function in statements like 'his table is an old packing case ', 'her hat is a bundle of straw tied together with string', 'a cloud is a mass of water droplets or other particles in suspension'. These two types of 'is' statements have one thing in common. In both cases it makes sense to add the qualification 'and nothing else'. In this they differ from those statements in which the 'is' is an 'is' of predication; the statements 'Toby is 80 years old and nothing else', 'her hat is red and nothing else' or 'giraffes are tall and nothing else', for example, are nonsense. This logical feature may be described by saying that in both cases both the grammatical subject and the grammatical predicate are expressions which provide an adequate characterization of the state of affairs to which they both refer.

In another respect, however, the two groups of statements are strikingly different. Statements like 'a square is an equilateral rectangle' are necessary statements which are true by definition. Statements like 'his table is an old packing case', on the other hand, are contingent statements which have to be verified by observation. In the case of statements like 'a square is an equilateral rectangle' or 'red is a colour', there is a relationship between the meaning of the expression forming the grammatical predicate and the meaning of the expression forming the grammatical subject, such that whenever the subject expression is applicable the predicate must also be applicable. If you can describe something as red then you must also be able to describe it as coloured. In the case of statements like 'his table is an old packing case', on the other hand, there is no such relationship between the meanings of the expressions 'his table' and 'old packing case'; it merely so happens that in this case both expressions are applicable to and at the same time provide an adequate characterization of the same object. Those who contend that the statement 'consciousness is a brain process' is logically untenable base their claim, I suspect, on the mistaken assumption that if the meanings of two statements or expressions are quite unconnected, they cannot both provide an adequate characterization of the same object or state of affairs: if something is a state of consciousness, it cannot be a brain process, since there is nothing self-contradictory in supposing that someone feels a pain when there is nothing happening inside his skull. By the same token we might be led to conclude that a table cannot be an old packing case, since there is nothing self-contradictory in supposing that someone has a table, but is not in possession of an old packing case.

The Logical Independence of Expressions and the Ontological Independence of Entities

There is, of course, an important difference between the table/packing case case and the consciousness/brain process case in that the statement 'his table is an old packing case' is a particular proposition which refers only to one particular case, whereas the state-ment 'consciousness is a process in the brain' is a general or universal proposition applying to all states of consciousness whatever. It is fairly clear, I think, that if we lived in a world in which all tables without exception were packing cases, the concepts of 'table' and 'packing case' in our language would not have their present logically inde-pendent status. In such a world a table would be a species of packing case in much the same way that red is a species of colour. It seems to be a rule of language that whenever a given variety of object or state of affairs has two characteristics or sets of characteris-tics, one of which is unique to the variety of object or state of affairs in question, the expression used to refer to the characteristic or set of characteristics which defines the variety of object or state of affairs in question will always entail the expression used to refer to the other characteristic or set of characteristics. If this rule admitted of no exception it would follow that any expression which is logically independent of another expression which uniquely characterizes a given variety of object or state of affairs, must refer to a characteristic or set of characteristics which is not normally or necessarily associated with the object or state of affairs in question. It is because this rule applies almost universally, I suggest, that we are normally justified in arguing from the logical independence of two expressions to the ontological independence of the states of affairs to which they refer. This would explain both the undoubted force of the argument that consciousness and brain processes must be independent entities because the expressions used to refer to them are logically independent and, in general, the curious phenomenon whereby questions about the furniture of the universe are often fought and not infrequently decided merely on a point of logic.

The argument from the logical independence of two expressions to the ontological independence of the entities to which they refer breaks down in the case of brain processes and consciousness, I believe, because this is one of a relatively small number of cases where the rule stated above does not apply. These exceptions are to be found, I suggest, in those cases where the operations which have to be performed in order to verify the presence of the two sets of characteristics inhering in the object or state of affairs in question can seldom if ever be performed simultaneously. A good example here is the case of the cloud and the mass of droplets or other particles in suspension. A cloud is a large semi-transparent mass with a fleecy texture suspended in the atmo-sphere whose shape is subject to continual and kaleidoscopic change. When observed at close quarters, however, it is found to consist of a mass of tiny particles, usually water droplets, in continuous motion. On the basis of this second observation we conclude that a cloud is a mass of tiny particles and nothing else. But there is no logical connexion in our language between a cloud and a mass of tiny particles; there is nothing self-contradictory in talking about a cloud which is not composed of tiny particles in suspension. There is no contradiction involved in supposing that clouds consist of a dense mass of fibrous tissue; indeed, such a consistency seems to be implied by many of the functions performed by clouds in fairy stories and mythology. It is clear from this that the terms 'cloud' and 'mass of tiny particles in suspension' mean quite different things. Yet we do not conclude from this that there must be two things, the mass of particles in suspension and the cloud. The reason for this, I suggest, is that although the characteristics of being a cloud and being a mass of tiny particles in suspension are invariably associated, we never make the observations necessary to verify the statement 'that is a cloud' and those necessary to verify the statement 'this is a mass of tiny particles in suspension' at one and the same time. We can observe the micro-structure of a cloud only when we are enveloped by it, a condition which effectively prevents us from observing those characteristics which from a distance lead us to describe it as a cloud. Indeed, so disparate are these two experiences that we use different words to describe them. That which is a cloud when we observe it from a distance becomes a fog or mist when we are enveloped by it.

When Are Two Sets of Observations Observations of the Same Event?

The example of the cloud and the mass of tiny particles in suspension was chosen because it is one of the few cases of a general proposition involving what I have called the 'is' of composition which does not involve us in scientific technicalities. It is useful because it brings out the connexion between the ordinary everyday cases of the 'is' of composition like the table/packing case example and the more technical cases like 'lightning is a motion of electric charges' where the analogy with the consciousness/ brain process case is most marked. The limitation of the cloud/tiny particles in suspension case is that it does not bring out sufficiently clearly the crucial problem of how the identity of the states of affairs referred to by the two expressions is established. In the cloud case the fact that something is a cloud and the fact that something is a mass of tiny particles in suspension are both verified by the normal processes of visual observation. It is arguable, moreover, that the identity of the entities referred to by the two expressions is established by the continuity between the two sets of observations as the observer moves towards or away from the cloud. In the case of brain processes and consciousness there is no such continuity between the two sets of observations involved. A closer introspective scrutiny will never reveal the passage of nerve impulses over a thousand synapses in the way that a closer scrutiny of a cloud will reveal a mass of tiny particles in suspension. The operations required to verify statements about consciousness and statements about brain processes are fundamentally different.

To find a parallel for this feature we must examine other cases where an identity is asserted between something whose occurrence is verified by the ordinary processes of observation and something whose occurrence is established by special scientific procedures. For this purpose I have chosen the case where we say that lightning is a motion of electric charges. As in the case of consciousness, however closely we scrutinize the lightning we shall never be able to observe the electric charges, and just as the operations for determining the nature of one's state of consciousness are radically different from those involved in determining the nature of one's brain processes, so the operations for determining the occurrence of lightning are radically different from those involved in determining the occurrence of a motion of electric charges. What is it, therefore, that leads us to say that the two sets of observations are observations of the same event? It cannot be merely the fact that the two sets of observations are systematically correlated such that whenever there is lightning there is always a motion of electric charges. There are innumerable cases of such correlations where we have no temptation to say that the two sets of observations are observations of the same event. There is a systematic correlation, for example, between the movement of the tides and the stages of the moon, but this does not lead us to say that records of tidal levels are records of the moon's stages or vice versa. We speak rather of a causal connexion between two independent events or processes.

The answer here seems to be that we treat the two sets of observations as observations of the same event, in those cases where the technical scientific observations set in the context of the appropriate body of scientific theory provide an immediate explanation of the observations made by the man in the street. Thus we conclude that lightning is nothing more than a motion of electric charges, because we know that a motion of electric charges through the atmosphere, such as occurs when lightning is reported, gives rise to the type of visual stimulation which would lead an observer to report a flash of lightning. In the moon/tide case, on the other hand, there is no such direct causal connexion between the stages of the moon and the observations made by the man who measures the height of the tide. The causal connexion is between the moon and the tides, not between the moon and the measurement of the tides.

The Physiological Explanation of Introspection and the Phenomenological Fallacy

If this account is correct, it should follow that in order to establish the identity of consciousness and certain processes in the brain, it would be necessary to show that the introspective observations reported by the subject can be accounted for in terms of processes which are known to have occurred in his brain. In the light of this suggestion it is extremely interesting to find that when a physiologist as distinct from a philosopher finds it difficult to see how consciousness could be a process in the brain, what worries him is not any supposed self-contradiction involved in such an assumption, but the apparent impossibility of accounting for the reports given by the subject of his conscious processes in terms of the known properties of the central nervous system. Sir Charles Sherrington has posed the problem as follows: 'The chain of events stretching from the sun's radiation entering the eye to, on the one hand, the contraction of the pupillary muscles, and on the other, to the electrical disturbances in the brain-cortex are all straightforward steps in a sequence of physical "causation", such as, thanks to science, are intelligible. But in the second serial chain there follows on, or attends, the stage of brain-cortex reaction an event or set of events quite inexplicable to us, which both as to themselves and as to the causal tie between them and what preceded them science does not help us; a set of events seemingly incommensurable with any of the events leading up to it. The self "sees" the sun; it senses a two-dimensional disc of brightness, located in the "sky", this last a field of lesser brightness, and overhead shaped as a rather flattened dome, coping the self and a hundred other visual things as well. Of hint that this is within the head there is none. Vision is saturated with this strange property called "projection", the unargued inference that what it sees is at a "distance" from the seeing "self". Enough has been said to stress that in the sequence of events a step is reached where a physical situation in the brain leads to a psychical, which however contains no hint of the brain or any other bodily part. ... The supposition has to be, it would seem, two continuous series of events, one physico-chemical, the other psychical, and at times interaction between them' (Sherrington, 1947, pp. xx–xxi).

Just as the physiologist is not likely to be impressed by the philosopher's contention that there is some self-contradiction involved in supposing consciousness to be a brain process, so the philosopher is unlikely to be impressed by the considerations which lead Sherrington to conclude that there are two sets of events, one physico-chemical, the other psychical. Sherrington's argument for all its emotional appeal depends on a fairly simple logical mistake, which is unfortunately all too frequently made by psychologists and physiologists and not infrequently in the past by the philosophers themselves. This logical mistake, which I shall refer to as the 'phenomenological fallacy', is the mistake of supposing that when the subject describes his experience, when he describes how things look, sound, smell, taste or feel to him, he is describing the literal properties of objects and events on a peculiar sort of internal cinema or television screen, usually referred to in the modern psychological literature as the 'phenomenal field'. If we assume, for example, that when a subject reports a green after-image he is asserting the occurrence inside himself of an object which is literally green, it is clear that we have on our hands an entity for which there is no place in the world of physics. In the case of the green after-image there is no green object in the subject's environment corresponding to the description that he gives. Nor is there anything green in his brain; certainly there is nothing which could have emerged when he reported the appearance of the green after-image. Brain processes are not the sort of things to which colour concepts can be properly applied.

The phenomenological fallacy on which this argument is based depends on the mistaken assumption that because our ability to describe things in our environment depends on our consciousness of them, our descriptions of things are primarily descriptions of our conscious experience and only secondarily, indirectly and inferentially descriptions of the objects and events in our environments. It is assumed that because we recognize things in our environment by their look, sound, smell, taste and feel, we begin by describing their phenomenal properties, i.e., the properties of the looks, sounds, smells, tastes and feels which they produce in us, and infer their real properties from their phenomenal properties. In fact, the reverse is the case. We begin by learning to recognize the real properties of things in our environment. We learn to recognize them, of course, by their look, sound, smell, taste and feel; but this does not mean that we have to learn to describe the look, sound, smell, taste and feel of things before we can describe the things themselves. Indeed, it is only after we have learnt to describe the things in our environment that we can learn to describe our consciousness of them. We describe our conscious experience not in terms of the mythological 'phenomenal properties' which are supposed to inhere in the mythological 'objects' in the mythological 'phenomenal field', but by reference to the actual physical properties of the concrete physical objects, events and processes which normally, though not perhaps in the present instance, give rise to the sort of conscious experience which we are trying to describe. In other words when we describe the after-image as green, we are not saying that there is something, the after-image, which is green, we are saying that we are having the sort of experience which we normally have when, and which we have learnt to describe as, looking at a green patch of light.

Once we rid ourselves of the phenomenological fallacy we realize that the problem of explaining introspective observations in terms of brain processes is far from insuperable. We realize that there is nothing that the introspecting subject says about his conscious experiences which is inconsistent with anything the physiologist might want to say about the brain processes which cause him to describe the environment and his consciousness of that environment in the way he does. When the subject describes his experience by saying that a light which is in fact stationary, appears to move, all the physiologist or physiological psychologist has to do in order to explain the subject's introspective observations, is to show that the brain process which is causing the subject to describe his experience in this way, is the sort of process which normally occurs when he is observing an actual moving object and which therefore normally causes him to report the movement of an object in his environment. Once the mechanism whereby the individual describes what is going on in his environment has been worked out, all that is required to explain the individual's capacity to make introspective observations is an explanation of his ability to discriminate between those cases where his normal habits of verbal description are appropriate to the stimulus situation and those cases where they are not and an explanation of how and why, in those cases where the appropriateness of his normal descriptive habits is in doubt, he learns to issue his ordinary descriptive protocols preceded by a qualificatory phrase like 'it appears', 'seems', 'looks', 'feels', etc.

Acknowledgments

I am greatly indebted to my fellow-participants in a series of informal discussions on this topic which took place in the Department of Philosophy, University of Adelaide, in particular to Mr C. B. Martin for his persistent and searching criticism of my earlier attempts to defend the thesis that consciousness is a brain process, to Prof. D. A. T. Gasking, of the University of Melbourne, for clarifying many of the logical issues involved and to Prof J. J. C. Smart for moral support and encouragement in what often seemed a lost cause.

References

Place, U. T. (1954). The concept of heed. *Brit. J. Psychol.* 45, 243—55.

Ryle, G. (1949). *The Concept of Mind.* London: Hutchinson.

Sherrington, Sir Charles (1947). Foreword to the 1947 edition of *The Integrative Action of the Nervous System.* Cambridge University Press.

Tolman, E. C. (1932). *Purposive Behaviour in Animals and Men.* Berkeley and Los Angeles: University of California Press.

Wittgenstein, L. (1953). *Philosophical Investigations.* Oxford: Blackwell.

Chapter 8

From "Identity and Necessity"

Saul Kripke

Let me turn to the case of heat and the motion of molecules. Here surely is a case that is contingent identity! Recent philosophy has emphasized this again and again. So, if it is a case of contingent identity, then let us imagine under what circumstances it would be false. Now, concerning this statement I hold that the circumstances philosophers apparently have in mind as circumstances under which it would have been false are not in fact such circumstances. First, of course, it is argued that "Heat is the motion of molecules" is an a posteriori judgment; scientific investigation might have turned out otherwise. As I said before, this shows nothing against the view that it is necessary—at least if I am right. But here, surely, people had very specific circumstances in mind under which, so they thought, the judgment that heat is the motion of molecules would have been false. What were these circumstances? One can distill them out of the fact that we found out empirically that heat is the motion of molecules. How was this? What did we find out first when we found out that heat is the motion of molecules? There is a certain external phenomenon which we can sense by the sense of touch, and it produces a sensation which we call "the sensation of heat." We then discover that the external phenomenon which produces this sensation, which we sense, by means of our sense of touch, is in fact that of molecular agitation in the thing that we touch, a very high degree of molecular agitation. So, it might be thought, to imagine a situation in which heat would not have been the motion of molecules, we need only imagine a situation in which we would have had the very same sensation and it would have been produced by something other than the motion of molecules. Similarly, if we wanted to imagine a situation in which light was not a stream of photons, we could imagine a situation in which we were sensitive to something else in exactly the same way, producing what we call visual experiences, though not through a stream of photons. To make the case stronger, or to look at another side of the coin, we could also consider a situation in which we *are* concerned with the motion of molecules but in which such motion does not give us the sensation of heat. And it might also have happened that we, or, at least, the creatures inhabiting this planet, might have been so constituted that, let us say, an increase in the motion of molecules did not give us this sensation but that, on the contrary, a slowing down of the molecules did give us the very same sensation. This would be a situation, so it might be thought, in which heat would not be the motion of molecules, or, more precisely, in which temperature would not be mean molecular kinetic energy.

But I think it would not be so. Let us think about the situation again. First, let us think about it in the actual world. Imagine right now the world invaded by a number of Martians, who do indeed get the very sensation that we call "the sensation of heat" when they feel some ice which has slow molecular motion, and who do not get a sensation of heat—in fact, maybe just the reverse—when they put their hand near a fire which causes a lot of molecular agitation. Would we say, "Ah, this casts some doubt on heat being the motion of molecules, because there are these other people who don't get the same sensation"? Obviously not, and no one would think so. We would say instead that the Martians somehow feel the very sensation we get when we feel heat when they feel cold and that they do not get a sensation of heat when they feel heat. But now let us think of a counterfactual situation.[1] Suppose the earth had from the very beginning been inhabited by such creatures. First, imagine it inhabited by no creatures at all: then there is no one to feel any sensations of heat. But we would not say that under such circumstances it would necessarily be the case that heat did not exist; we would say that heat might have existed, for example, if there were fires that heated up the air.

Let us suppose the laws of physics were not very different: Fires do heat up the air. Then there would have been heat even though there were no creatures around to feel it. Now let us suppose evolution takes place, and life is created, and there are some creatures around. But they are not like us, they are more like the Martians. Now would we say that heat has suddenly turned to cold, because of the way the creatures of this planet sense it? No, I think we should describe this situation as a situation in which, though the creatures on this planet got our sensation of heat, they did not get it when they were exposed to heat. They got it when they were exposed to cold. And that is something we can surely well imagine. We can imagine it just as we can imagine our planet being invaded by creatures of this sort. Think of it in two steps. First there is a stage where there are no creatures at all, and one can certainly imagine the planet still having both heat and cold, though no one is around to sense it. Then the planet comes through an evolutionary process to be peopled with beings of different neural structure from ourselves. Then these creatures could be such that they were insensitive to heat; they did not feel it in the way we do; but on the other hand, they felt cold in much the same way that we feel heat. But still, heat would be heat, and cold would be cold. And particularly, then, this goes in no way against saying that in this counterfactual situation heat would still *be* the molecular motion, *be* that which is produced by fires, and so on, just as it would have been if there had been no creatures on the planet at all. Similarly, we could imagine that the planet was inhabited by creatures who got visual sensations when there were sound waves in the air. We should not therefore say, "Under such circumstances, sound would have been light." Instead we should say, "The planet was inhabited by creatures who were in some sense visually sensitive to sound, and maybe even visually sensitive to light." If this is correct, it can still be and will still be a necessary truth that heat is the motion of molecules and that light is a stream of photons.

To state the view succinctly: we use both the terms 'heat' and 'the motion of molecules' as rigid designators for a certain external phenomenon. Since heat is in fact the motion of molecules, and the designators are rigid, by the argument I have given here, it is going to be *necessary* that heat is the motion of molecules. What gives us the illusion of contingency is the fact we have identified the heat by the contingent fact that there happen to be creatures on this planet—(namely, ourselves) who are sensitive to it in a certain way, that is, who are sensitive to the motion of molecules or to heat—these are one and the same thing. And this is contingent. So we use the description, 'that which causes such and such sensations, or that which we sense in such and such a way', to identify heat. But in using this fact we use a contingent property of heat, just as we use the contingent property of Cicero as having written such and such works to identify him. We then use the terms 'heat' in the one case and 'Cicero' in the other *rigidly* to designate the objects for which they stand. And of course the term 'the motion of molecules' is rigid; it always stands for the motion of molecules, never for any other phenomenon. So, as Bishop Butler said, "everything is what it is and not another thing." Therefore, "Heat is the motion of molecules" will be necessary, not contingent, and one only has the *illusion* of contingency in the way one could have the illusion of contingency in thinking that this table might have been made of ice. We might think one could imagine it, but if we try, we can see on reflection that what we are really imagining is just there being another lectern in this very position here which was in fact made of ice. The fact that we may identify this lectern by being the object we see and touch in such and such a position is something else.

Now how does this relate to the problem of mind and body? It is usually held that this is a contingent identity statement just like "Heat is the motion of molecules." That cannot be. It cannot be a contingent identity statement just like "Heat is the motion of molecules" because, if I am right, "Heat is the motion of molecules" is not a contingent identity statement. Let us look at this statement. For example, "My being in pain at such and such a time is my being in such and such a brain state at such and such a time," or, "Pain in general is such and such a neural (brain) state."

This is held to be contingent on the following grounds. First, we can imagine the brain state existing though there is no pain at all. It is only a scientific fact that whenever we are in a certain brain state we have a pain. Second, one might imagine a creature being in pain, but not being in any specified brain state at all, maybe not having a brain at all. People even think, at least prima facie, though they may be wrong, that they can imagine totally disembodied creatures, at any rate certainly not creatures with bodies anything like our own. So it seems that we can imagine definite circumstances under which this relationship would have been false. Now, if these circumstances are circumstances, notice that we cannot deal with them simply by saying that this is just an illusion, something we can apparently imagine, but in fact cannot in the way we thought erroneously that we could imagine a situation in which heat was not the motion of molecules. Because although we can say that we pick out heat contingently by the contingent property that it affects us in such and such a way, we cannot similarly say that we pick out pain contingently by the fact that it affects us in such and such a way. On such a picture there would be the brain state, and we pick it out by the contingent fact that it affects us as pain. Now that might be true of the brain state, but it cannot be true of the pain. The experience itself has to be *this experience*, and I cannot say that it is a contingent property of the pain I now have that it is a pain.[2] In fact, it would seem that both the terms, 'my pain' and 'my being in such and such a brain state' are, first of all, both rigid designators. That is, whenever anything is such and such a pain, it is essentially that very object, namely, such and such a pain, and wherever anything is such and such a brain state, it is essentially that very object, namely, such and such a brain state. So both of these are rigid designators. One cannot say this pain might have been something else, some other state. These are both rigid designators.

Second, the way we would think of picking them out—namely, the pain by its being an experience of a certain sort, and the brain state by its being the state of a certain material object, being of such and such molecular configuration—both of these pick out their objects essentially and not accidentally, that is, they pick them out by essential properties. Whenever the molecules *are* in this configuration, we *do* have such and such a brain state. Whenever you feel *this*, you do have a pain. So it seems that the identity theorist is in some trouble, for, since we have two rigid designators, the identity statement in question is necessary. Because they pick out their objects essentially, we cannot say the case where you seem to imagine the identity statement false is really an illusion like the illusion one gets in the case of heat and molecular motion, because that illusion depended on the fact that we pick out heat by a certain contingent property. So there is very little room to maneuver; perhaps none.[3] The identity theorist, who holds that pain is the brain state, also has to hold that it necessarily is the brain state. He therefore cannot concede, but has to deny, that there would have been situations under which one would have had pain but not the corresponding brain state. Now usually in arguments on the identity theory, this is very far from being denied. In fact, it is conceded from the outset by the materialist as well as by his opponent. He says, "Of course, it *could* have been the case that we had pains without the brain states. It is a contingent identity." But that cannot be. He has to hold that we are under some illusion in thinking that we can imagine that there could have been pains without brain states. And the only model I can think of for what the illusion might be, or at least the model given by the analogy the materialists themselves suggest, namely, heat and molecular motion, simply does not work in this case. So the materialist is up against a very stiff challenge. He has to show that these things we think we can see to be possible are in fact not possible. He has to show that these things which we can imagine are not in fact things we can imagine. And that requires some very different philosophical argument from the sort which has been given in the case of heat and molecular motion. And it would have to be a deeper and subtler argument than I can fathom and subtler than has ever appeared in any materialist literature that I have read. So the conclusion of this investigation would be that the analytical tools we are using go against the identity thesis and so go against the general thesis that mental states are just physical states.[4]

The next topic would be my own solution to the mind-body problem, but that I do not have.

Notes

1. Isn't the situation I just described also counterfactual? At least it may well be, if such Martians never in fact invade. Strictly speaking, the distinction I wish to draw compares how we *would* speak *in* a (possibly counterfactual) situation, *if* it obtained, and how we *do* speak *of* a counterfactual situation, knowing that it does not obtain—i.e., the distinction between the language we would have used in a situation and the language we *do* use to describe it. (Consider the description: "Suppose we all spoke German." This description is in English.) The former case can be made vivid by imagining the counterfactual situation to be actual.

2. The most popular identity theories advocated today explicitly fail to satisfy this simple requirement. For these theories usually hold that a mental state is a brain state, and that what makes the brain state into a mental state is its 'causal role', the fact that it tends to produce certain behavior (as intentions produce actions, or pain, pain behavior) and to be produced by certain stimuli (e.g., pain, by pinpricks). If the relations between the brain state and its causes and effects are regarded as contingent, then *being such-and-such-a-mental state* is a contingent property of the brain state. Let X be a pain. The causal-role identity theorist holds (1) that X is a brain state, (2) that the fact that X is a pain is to be analyzed (roughly) as the fact that X is produced by certain stimuli and produces certain behavior. The fact mentioned in (2) is, of course, regarded as contingent: the brain state X might well exist and not tend to produce the appropriate behavior in the absence of other conditions. Thus (1) and (2) assert that a certain pain X might have existed, yet not have been a pain. This seems to me self-evidently absurd. Imagine any pain: is it possible that *it itself* could have existed, yet not have been a pain?

   If $X = Y$, then X and Y share all properties, including modal properties. If X is a pain and Y the corresponding brain state, then *being a pain* is an essential property of X, and *being a brain state* is an essential property of Y. If the correspondence relation is, in fact, identity, then it must be *necessary* of Y that it corresponds to a pain, and *necessary* of X that it correspond to a brain state, indeed to this particular brain state, Y. Both assertions seem false; it *seems* clearly possible that X should have existed without the corresponding brain state; or that the brain state should have existed without being felt as pain. Identity theorists cannot, contrary to their almost universal present practice, accept these intuitions; they must deny them, and explain them away. This is none too easy a thing to do.

3. A brief restatement of the argument may be helpful here. If "pain" and "C-fiber stimulation" are rigid designators of phenomena, one who identifies them must regard the identity as necessary. How can this necessity be reconciled with the apparent fact that C-fiber stimulation might have turned out not to be correlated with pain at all? We might try to reply by analogy to the case of heat and molecular motion; the latter identity, too, is necessary, yet someone may believe that, before scientific

investigation showed otherwise, molecular motion might have turned out not to be heat. The reply is, of course, that what really is possible is that people (or some rational sentient beings) could have been in the *same epistemic situation* as we actually are, and identify *a phenomenon* in the same way we identify heat, namely, by feeling it by the sensation we call "the sensation of heat," without the phenomenon being molecular motion. Further, the beings might not have been sensitive to molecular motion (i.e., to heat) by any neural mechanism whatsoever. It is impossible to explain the apparent possibility of C-fiber stimulations not having been pain in the same way. Here, too, we would have to suppose that we could have been in the same epistemological situation, and identify something in the same way we identify pain, without its corresponding to C-fiber stimulation. But the way we identify pain is by feeling it, and if a C-fiber stimulation could have occurred without our feeling any pain, then the C-fiber stimulation would have occurred without there *being* any pain, contrary to the necessity of the identity. The trouble is that although 'heat' is a rigid designator, heat is picked out by the contingent property of its being felt in a certain way; pain, on the other hand, is picked out by an essential (indeed necessary and sufficient) property. For a sensation to be *felt* as pain is for it to *be* pain.

4. All arguments against the identity theory which rely on the necessity of identity, or on the notion of essential property, are, of course, inspired by Descartes' argument for his dualism. The earlier arguments which superficially were rebutted by the analogies of heat and molecular motion, and the bifocals inventor who was also Postmaster General, had such an inspiration; and so does my argument here. R. Albritton and M. Slote have informed me that they independently have attempted to give essentialist arguments against the identity theory, and probably others have done so as well.

The simplest Cartesian argument can perhaps be restated as follows: Let 'A' be a *name* (rigid designator) of Descartes' body. Then Descartes argues that since he could exist even if A did not, ◇ (Descartes $\neq A$), hence Descartes $\neq A$. Those who have accused him of a modal fallacy have forgotten that 'A' is rigid. His argument is valid, and his conclusion is correct, provided its (perhaps dubitable) premise is accepted. On the other hand, provided that Descartes is regarded as having ceased to exist upon his death. "Descartes $\neq A$" can be established without the use of a modal argument; for if so, no doubt A survived Descartes when A was a corpse. Thus A had a property (existing at a certain time) which Descartes did not. The same argument can establish that a statue is not the hunk of stone, or the congery of molecules, of which it is composed. Mere non-identity, then, may be a weak conclusion. (See D. Wiggins, *Philosophical Review*, Vol. 77 (1968), pp. 90 ff.) The Cartesian modal argument, however, surely can be deployed to maintain relevant stronger conclusions as well.

Chapter 9

From *Language and Problems of Knowledge*

Noam Chomsky

It is interesting to observe the fate of the Cartesian version of the mind-body problem and the problem of the existence of other minds. The mind-body problem can be posed sensibly only insofar as we have a definite conception of body. If we have no such definite and fixed conception, we cannot ask whether some phenomena fall beyond its range. The Cartesians offered a fairly definite conception of body in terms of their contact mechanics, which in many respects reflects commonsense understanding. Therefore they could sensibly formulate the mind-body problem and the problem of other minds. There was important work attempting to develop the concept of mind further, including studies by British Neoplatonists of the seventeenth century that explored the categories and principles of perception and cognition along lines that were later extended by Kant and that were rediscovered, independently, in twentieth-century Gestalt psychology.

Another line of development was the "general and philosophical grammar" (in our terms, scientific grammar) of the seventeenth, eighteenth, and early nineteenth centuries, which was much influenced by Cartesian conceptions, particularly in the early period. These inquiries into universal grammar sought to lay bare the general principles of language. These were regarded as not essentially different from the general principles of thought, so that language is "a mirror of mind," in the conventional phrase. For various reasons—some good, some not—these inquiries were disparaged and abandoned for a century, to be resurrected, again independently, a generation ago, though in quite different terms and without recourse to any dualist assumptions.

It is also interesting to see how the Cartesian conception of body and mind entered social thought, most strikingly in the libertarian ideas of Jean-Jacques Rousseau, which were based on strictly Cartesian conceptions of body and mind. Because humans, possessing minds, are crucially distinct from machines (including animals), so Rousseau argued, and because the properties of mind crucially surpass mechanical determinacy, therefore any infringement on human freedom is illegitimate and must be confronted and overcome. Although the later development of such thinking abandoned the Cartesian framework, its origins lie in significant measure in these classical ideas.

The Cartesian conception of a second substance was generally abandoned in later years, but it is important to recognize that it was not the theory of mind that was refuted (one might argue that it was hardly clear enough to be confirmed or refuted). Rather, the Cartesian concept of *body* was refuted by seventeenth-century physics, particularly in the work of Isaac Newton, which laid the foundations for modern science. Newton demonstrated that the motions of the heavenly bodies could not be explained by the principles of Descartes's contact mechanics, so that the Cartesian concept of body must be abandoned. In the Newtonian framework there is a "force" that one body exerts on another, without contact between them, a kind of "action at a distance." Whatever this force may be, it does not fall within the Cartesian framework of contact mechanics. Newton himself found this conclusion unsatisfying. He sometimes referred to gravitational force as "occult" and suggested that his theory gave only a mathematical description of events in the physical world, not a true "philosophical" (in more modern terminology, "scientific") explanation of these events. Until the late nineteenth century it was still widely held that a true explanation must be framed somehow in mechanical or quasi-mechanical terms. Others, notably the chemist and philosopher Joseph Priestley, argued that bodies themselves possess capacities that go beyond the limits of contact mechanics, specifically the property of attracting other bodies, but perhaps far more. Without pursuing subsequent developments further, the general conclusion is that the Cartesian concept of body was found to be untenable.

What is the concept of body that finally emerged? The answer is that there is no clear and definite concept of body. If the best theory of the material world that we can construct includes a variety of forces, particles that have no mass, and other entities that would have been offensive to the "scientific common sense" of the Cartesians, then so be it: We conclude that these are properties of the physical world, the world of body. The conclusions are tentative, as befits empirical hypotheses, but are not subject to criticism because they transcend some a priori conception of body. There is no longer any definite conception of body. Rather, the material world is whatever we discover it to be, with whatever properties it must be assumed to have for the purposes of explanatory theory. Any intelligible theory that offers genuine explanations and that can be assimilated to the core notions of physics becomes part of the theory of the material world, part of our account of body. If we have such a theory in some domain, we seek to assimilate it to the core notions of physics, perhaps modifying these notions as we carry out this enterprise. In the study of human psychology, if we develop a theory of some cognitive faculty (the language faculty, for example) and find that this faculty has certain properties, we seek to discover the mechanisms of the brain that exhibit these properties and to account for them in the terms of the physical sciences—keeping open the possibility that the concepts of the physical sciences might have to be modified, just as the concepts of Cartesian contact mechanics had to be modified to account for the motion of the heavenly bodies, and as has happened repeatedly in the evolution of the natural sciences since Newton's day.

In short, there is no definite concept of body. Rather, there is a material world, the properties of which are to be discovered, with no a priori demarcation of what will count as "body." The mind-body problem can therefore not even be formulated. The problem cannot be solved, because there is no clear way to state it. Unless someone proposes a definite concept of body, we cannot ask whether some phenomena exceed its bounds. Similarly, we cannot pose the problem of other minds. We can, and I think should, continue to use mentalistic terminology, as I have done throughout in discussing mental representations and operations that form and modify them in mental computation. But we do not see ourselves as investigating the properties of some "second substance," something crucially distinct from body that interacts with body in some mysterious way, perhaps through divine intervention. Rather, we are studying the properties of the material world at a level of abstraction at which we believe, rightly or wrongly, that a genuine explanatory theory can be constructed, a theory that provides genuine insight into the nature of the phenomena that concern us. These phenomena, in fact, are of real intellectual interest not so much in themselves but in the avenue that they provide for us to penetrate into the deeper workings of the mind. Ultimately, we hope to assimilate this study to the mainstream of the natural sciences, much as the study of genes or of valence and the properties of the chemical elements was assimilated to more fundamental sciences. We recognize, however, that, as in the past, it may turn out that these fundamental sciences must be modified or extended to provide foundations for the abstract theories of complex systems, such as the human mind.

Our task, then, is to discover genuine explanatory theories and to use these discoveries to facilitate inquiry into physical mechanisms with the properties outlined in these theories. Wherever this inquiry leads, it will be within the domain of "body." Or more accurately, we simply abandon the whole conception of body as possibly distinct from something else and use the methods of rational inquiry to learn as much as we can about the world—what we call the material world, whatever exotic properties it turns out to have.

The mind-body problem remains the subject of much controversy, debate, and speculation, and in this regard the problem is still very much alive. But the discussion seems to me incoherent in fundamental respects. Unlike the Cartesians, we have no definite concept of body. It is therefore quite unclear how we can even ask whether some phenomena lie beyond the range of the study of body, falling within the separate study of mind.

Recall the logic of Descartes's argument for the existence of a second substance, *res cogitans*. Having defined "body" in terms of contact mechanics, he argued that certain phenomena lie beyond its domain, so that some new principle was required; given his metaphysics, a second substance must be postulated. The logic is essentially sound; it is, in fact, much like Newton's, when he demonstrated the inadequacy of Cartesian contact mechanics for the explanation of the motion of the heavenly bodies so that a new principle, the principle of gravitational attraction, had to be postulated. The crucial difference between the Cartesian and the Newtonian enterprises was that the latter offered a genuine explanatory theory of the behavior of bodies, whereas the Cartesian theory offered no satisfactory account of properties such as the creative aspect of language use that lie beyond mechanical explanation in Descartes's view. Therefore Newton's conceptions came to be the "scientific common sense" of later generations of scientists, while Descartes's fell by the wayside.

Chapter 10

The Nature of Mental States

Hilary Putnam

The typical concerns of the Philosopher of Mind might be represented by three questions: (1) How do we know that other people have pains? (2) Are pains brain states? (3) What is the analysis of the concept *pain*? I do not wish to discuss questions (1) and (3) in this chapter. I shall say something about question (2).

Identity Questions

'Is pain a brain state?' (Or, 'Is the property of having a pain at time *t* a brain state?')[1] It is impossible to discuss this question sensibly without saying something about the peculiar rules which have grown up in the course of the development of 'analytical philosophy'—rules which, far from leading to an end to all conceptual confusions, themselves represent considerable conceptual confusion. These rules—which are, of course, implicit rather than explicit in the practice of most analytical philosophers—are (1) that a statement of the form 'being *A* is being *B*' (e.g., 'being in pain is being in a certain brain state') can be *correct* only if it follows, in some sense, from the meaning of the terms *A* and *B*; and (2) that a statement of the form 'being *A* is being *B*' can be philosophically *informative* only if it is in some sense reductive (e.g., 'being in pain is having a certain unpleasant sensation' is not philosophically informative; 'being in pain is having a certain behavior disposition' is, if true, philosophically informative). These rules are excellent rules if we still believe that the program of reductive analysis (in the style of the 1930s) can be carried out; if we don't, then they turn analytical philosophy into a mug's game, at least so far as 'is' questions are concerned.

In this paper I shall use the term 'property' as a blanket term for such things as being in pain, being in a particular brain state, having a particular behavior disposition, and also for magnitudes such as temperature, etc.—i.e., for things which can naturally be represented by one-or-more-place predicates or functors. I shall use the term 'concept' for things which can be identified with synonymy-classes of expressions. Thus the concept *temperature* can be identified (I maintain) with the synonymy-class of the word 'temperature'.[2] (This is like saying that the number 2 can be identified with the class of all pairs. This is quite a different statement from the peculiar statement that 2 *is* the class of all pairs. I do not maintain that concepts *are* synonymy-classes, whatever that might mean, but that they can be identified with synonymy-classes, for the purpose of formalization of the relevant discourse.)

The question 'What is the concept *temperature*?' is a very 'funny' one. One might take it to mean 'What is temperature? Please take my question as a conceptual one.' In that case an answer might be (pretend for a moment 'heat' and 'temperature' are synonyms) 'temperature is heat', or even 'the concept of temperature is the same concept as the concept of heat'. Or one might take it to mean 'What are *concepts*, really? For example, what is "the concept of temperature"?' In that case heaven knows what an 'answer' would be. (Perhaps it would be the statement that concepts *can be identified with synonymy-classes*.)

Of course, the question 'What is the property temperature?' is also 'funny'. And one way of interpreting it is to take it as a question about the concept of temperature. But this is not the way a physicist would take it.

The effect of saying that the property P_1 can be identical with the property P_2 only if the terms P_1, P_2 are in some suitable sense 'synonyms' is, to all intents and purposes, to collapse the two notions of 'property' and 'concept' into a single notion. The view that concepts (intensions) *are* the same as properties has been explicitly advocated by Carnap (e.g., in *Meaning and Necessity*). This seems an unfortunate view, since 'temperature is mean molecular kinetic energy' appears to be a perfectly good example of a true statement of identity of properties, whereas 'the concept of temperature is the same concept as a concept of mean molecular kinetic energy' is simply false.

Many philosophers believe that the statement 'pain is a brain state' violates some rules or norms of English. But the arguments offered are hardly convincing. For example, if the fact that I can know that I am in pain without knowing that I am in brain state S shows that pain cannot be brain state S, then, by exactly the same argument, the fact that I can know that the stove is hot without knowing that the mean molecular kinetic energy is high (or even that molecules exist) shows that it is *false* that temperature is mean molecular kinetic energy, physics to the contrary. In fact, all that immediately follows from the fact that I can know that I am in pain without knowing that I am in brain state S is that the concept of pain is not the same concept as the concept of being in brain state S. But either pain, or the state of being in pain, or some pain, or some pain state, might still be brain state S. After all, the concept of temperature is not the same concept as the concept of mean molecular kinetic energy. But temperature is mean molecular kinetic energy.

Some philosophers maintain that both 'pain is a brain state' and 'pain states are brain states' are unintelligible. The answer is to explain to these philosophers, as well as we can, given the vagueness of all scientific methodology, what sorts of considerations lead one to make an empirical reduction (i.e., to say such things as 'water is H_2O', 'light is electromagnetic radiation', 'temperature is mean molecular kinetic energy'). If, without giving reasons, he still maintains in the face of such examples that one cannot imagine parallel circumstances for the use of 'pains are brain states' (or, perhaps, 'pain states are brain states'), one has grounds to regard him as perverse.

Some philosophers maintain that 'P_1 is P_2' is something that can be true, when the 'is' involved is the 'is' of empirical reduction, only when the properties P_1 and P_2 are (a) associated with a spatio-temporal region; and (b) the region is one and the same in both cases. Thus 'temperature is mean molecular kinetic energy' is an admissible empirical reduction, since the temperature and the molecular energy are associated with the same space-time region, but 'having a pain in my arm is being in a brain state' is not, since the spatial regions involved are different.

This argument does not appear very strong. Surely no one is going to be deterred from saying that mirror images are light reflected from an object and then from the surface of a mirror by the fact that an image can be 'located' three feet *behind* the mirror! (Moreover, one can always find *some* common property of the reductions one is willing to allow—e.g., temperature is mean molecular kinetic energy—which is not a property of some one identification one wishes to disallow. This is not very impressive unless one has an argument to show that the very purposes of such identification depend upon the common property in question.)

Again, other philosophers have contended that all the predictions that can be derived from the conjunction of neurophysiological laws with such statements as 'pain states are such-and-such brain states' can equally well be derived from the conjunction of the same neurophysiological laws with 'being in pain is correlated with such-and-such brain states', and hence (sic!) there can be no methodological grounds for saying that pains (or pain states) *are* brain states, as opposed to saying that they are *correlated* (invariantly) with brain states. This argument, too, would show that light is only correlated with electromagnetic radiation. The mistake is in ignoring the fact that, although the theories in question may indeed lead to the same predictions, they open and exclude different *questions*. 'Light is invariantly correlated with electromagnetic radiation' would leave open the questions 'What is the light then, if it isn't the same as the electromagnetic radiation?' and 'What makes the light accompany the electromagnetic radiation?'—questions which are excluded by saying that the light *is* the electromagnetic radiation. Similarly, the purpose of saying that pains are brain states is precisely to exclude from empirical meaningfulness the questions 'What is the pain, then, if it isn't the same as the brain state?' and 'What makes the pain accompany the brain state?' If there are grounds to suggest that these questions represent, so to speak, the wrong way to look at the matter, then those grounds are grounds for a theoretical identification of pains with brain states.

If all arguments to the contrary are unconvincing, shall we then conclude that it is meaningful (and perhaps true) to say either that pains are brain states or that pain states are brain states?

> 1. It is perfectly meaningful (violates no 'rule of English', involves no 'extension of usage') to say 'pains are brain states'.
> 2. It is not meaningful (involves a 'changing of meaning' or 'an extension of usage', etc.) to say 'pains are brain states'.

My own position is not expressed by either 1 or 2. It seems to me that the notions 'change of meaning' and 'extension of usage' are simply so ill defined that one cannot in fact say *either* 1 or 2. I see no reason to believe that either the linguist, or the man-on-the-street, or the philosopher possesses today a notion of 'change of meaning' applicable to such cases as the one we have been discussing. The *job* for which the notion of change of meaning was developed in the history of the language was just a *much* cruder job than this one.

But, if we don't assert either 1 or 2—in other words, if we regard the 'change of meaning' issue as a pseudo-issue in this case—then how are we to discuss the question with which we started? 'Is pain a brain state?'

The answer is to allow statements of the form 'pain is A', where 'pain' and 'A' are in no sense synonyms, and to see whether any such statement can be found which might be acceptable on empirical and methodological grounds. This is what we shall now proceed to do.

Is Pain a Brain State?

We shall discuss 'Is pain a brain state?' then. And we have agreed to waive the 'change of meaning' issue.

Since I am discussing not what the concept of pain comes to, but what pain is, in a sense of 'is' which requires empirical theory-construction (or, at least, empirical speculation), I shall not apologize for advancing an empirical hypothesis. Indeed, my strategy will be to argue that pain is *not* a brain state, not on *a priori* grounds, but on the grounds that another hypothesis is more plausible. The detailed development and verification of my hypothesis would be just as Utopian a task as the detailed development and verification of the brain-state hypothesis. But the putting-forward, not of detailed and scientifically 'finished' hypotheses, but of schemata for hypotheses, has long been a function of philosophy. I shall, in short, argue that pain is not a brain state, in the sense of a physical-chemical state of the brain (or even the whole nervous system), but another *kind* of state entirely. I propose the hypothesis that pain, or the state of being in pain, is a functional state of a whole organism.

To explain this it is necessary to introduce some technical notions. In previous papers I have explained the notion of a Turing Machine and discussed the use of this notion as a model for an organism. The notion of a Probabilistic Automaton is defined similarly to a Turing Machine, except that the transitions between 'states' are allowed to be with various probabilities rather than being 'deterministic'. (Of course, a Turing Machine is simply a special kind of Probabilistic Automaton, one with transition probabilities 0, 1). I shall assume the notion of a Probabilistic Automaton has been generalized to allow for 'sensory inputs' and 'motor outputs'—that is, the Machine Table specifies, for every possible combination of a 'state' and a complete set of 'sensory inputs', an 'instruction' which determines the probability of the next 'state', and also the probabilities of the 'motor outputs'. (This replaces the idea of the Machine as printing on a tape.) I shall also assume that the physical realization of the sense organs responsible for the various inputs, and of the motor organs, is specified, but that the 'states' and the 'inputs' themselves are, as usual, specified only 'implicitly'—i.e., by the set of transition probabilities given by the Machine Table.

Since an empirically given system can simultaneously be a 'physical realization' of many different Probabilistic Automata, I introduce the notion of a *Description* of a system. A Description of S where S is a system, is any true statement to the effect that S possesses distinct states $S_1, S_2 \ldots S_n$ which are related to one another and to the motor outputs and sensory inputs by the transition probabilities given in such-and-such a Machine Table. The Machine Table mentioned in the Description will then be called the Functional Organization of S relative to that Description, and the S_i such that S is in state S_i at a given time will be called the Total State of S (at the time) relative to that Description. It should be noted that knowing the Total State of a system relative to a Description involves knowing a good deal about how the system is likely to 'behave', given various combinations of sensory inputs, but does *not* involve knowing the physical realization of the S_i as, e.g., physical-chemical states of the brain. The S_i, to repeat, are specified only *implicitly* by the Description—i.e., specified *only* by the set of transition probabilities given in the Machine Table.

The hypothesis that 'being in pain is a functional state of the organism' may now be spelled out more exactly as follows:

1. All organisms capable of feeling pain are Probabilistic Automata.
2. Every organism capable of feeling pain possesses at least one Description of a certain kind (i.e., being capable of feeling pain *is* possessing an appropriate kind of Functional Organization).
3. No organism capable of feeling pain possesses a decomposition into parts which separately possess Descriptions of the kind referred to in 2.
4. For every Description of the kind referred to in 2, there exists a subset of the sensory inputs such that an organism with that Description is in pain when and only when some of its sensory inputs are in that subset.

This hypothesis is admittedly vague, though surely no vaguer than the brain-state hypothesis in its present form. For example, one would like to know more about the kind of Functional Organization that an organism must have to be capable of feeling pain, and more about the marks that distinguish the subset of the sensory inputs referred to in 4. With respect to the first question, one can probably say that the Functional Organization must include something that resembles a 'preference function', or at least a preference partial ordering and something that resembles an 'inductive logic' (i.e., the Machine must be able to 'learn from experience'). In addition, it seems natural to require that the Machine possess 'pain sensors', i.e., sensory organs which normally signal damage to the Machine's body, or dangerous temperatures, pressures, etc., which transmit a special subset of the inputs, the subset referred to in 4. Finally, and with respect to the second question, we would want to require at least that the inputs in the distinguished subset have a high disvalue on the Machine's preference function or ordering (further conditions are discussed in the previous chapter). The purpose of condition 3 is to rule out such 'organisms' (if they can count as such) as swarms of bees as single pain-feelers. The condition 1 is, obviously, redundant, and is only introduced for expository reasons. (It is, in fact, empty, since everything is a Probabilistic Automaton under *some* Description.)

I contend, in passing, that this hypothesis, in spite of its admitted vagueness, is far *less* vague than the 'physical-chemical state' hypothesis is today, and far more susceptible to investigation of both a mathematical and an empirical kind. Indeed, to investigate this hypothesis is just to attempt to produce 'mechanical' models of organisms—and isn't this, in a sense, just what psychology is about? The difficult step, of course, will be to pass from models of *specific* organisms to a *normal form* for the psychological description of organisms—for this is what is required to make 2 and 4 precise. But this too seems to be an inevitable part of the program of psychology.

I shall now compare the hypothesis just advanced with (a) the hypothesis that pain is a brain state, and (b) the hypothesis that pain is a behavior disposition.

Functional State versus Brain State

It may, perhaps, be asked if I am not somewhat unfair in taking the brain-state theorist to be talking about *physical-chemical* states of the brain. But (a) these are the only sorts of states ever mentioned by brain-state theorists. (b) The brain-state theorist usually mentions (with a certain pride, slightly reminiscent of the Village Atheist) the incompatibility of his hypothesis with all forms of dualism and mentalism. This is natural if physical-chemical states of the brain are what is at issue. However, functional states of whole systems are something quite different. In particular, the functional-state hypothesis is *not* incompatible with dualism! Although it goes without saying that the hypothesis is 'mechanistic' in its inspiration, it is a slightly remarkable fact that a system consisting of a body and a 'soul', if such things there be, can perfectly well be a Probabilistic Automaton. (c) One argument advanced by Smart is that the brain-state theory assumes only 'physical' properties, and Smart finds 'non-physical' properties unintelligible. The Total States and the 'inputs' defined above are, of course, neither mental nor physical *per se*, and I cannot imagine a functionalist advancing this argument. (d) If the brain-state theorist does mean (or at least allow) states other than physical-chemical states, then his hypothesis is completely empty, at least until he specifies *what* sort of 'states' he *does* mean.

Taking the brain-state hypothesis in this way, then, what reasons are there to prefer the functional-state hypothesis over the brain-state hypothesis? Consider what the brain-state theorist has to do to make good his claims. He has to specify a physical-chemical state such that *any* organism (not just a mammal) is in pain if and only if (a) it possesses a brain of a suitable physical-chemical structure; and (b) its brain is in that physical-chemical state. This means that the physical-chemical state in question must be a possible state of a mammalian brain, a reptilian brain, a mollusc's brain (octopuses are mollusca, and certainly feel pain), etc. At the same time, it must *not* be a possible (physically possible) state of the brain of any physically possible creature that cannot feel pain. Even if such a state can be found, it must be nomologically certain that it will also be a state of the brain of any extraterrestrial life that may be found that will be capable of feeling pain before we can even entertain the supposition that it may *be* pain.

It is not altogether impossible that such a state will be found. Even though octopus and mammal are examples of parallel (rather than sequential) evolution, for example, virtually identical structures (physically speaking) have evolved in the eye of the octopus and in the eye of the mammal, notwithstanding the fact that this organ has evolved from different kinds of cells in the two cases. Thus it is at least possible that parallel evolution, all over the universe, might *always* lead to *one and the same* physical 'correlate' of pain. But this is certainly an ambitious hypothesis.

Finally, the hypothesis becomes still more ambitious when we realize that the brain-state theorist is not just saying that *pain* is a brain state; he is, of course, concerned to maintain that *every* psychological state is a brain state. Thus if we can find even one psychological predicate which can clearly be applied to both a mammal and an octopus (say 'hungry'), but whose physical-chemical 'correlate' is different in the two cases, the brain-state theory has collapsed. It seems to me overwhelmingly probable that we can do this. Granted, in such a case the brain-state theorist can save himself by *ad hoc* assumptions (e.g., defining the disjunction of two states to be a single 'physical-chemical state'), but this does not have to be taken seriously.

Turning now to the considerations *for* the functional-state theory, let us begin with the fact that we identify organisms as in pain, or hungry, or angry, or in heat, etc., on the basis of their *behavior*. But it is a truism that similarities in the behavior of two systems are at least a reason to suspect similarities in the functional organization of the two systems, and a much *weaker* reason to suspect similarities in the actual physical details. Moreover, we expect the various psychological states—at least the basic ones, such as hunger, thirst, aggression, etc.—to have more or less similar 'transition probabilities' (within wide and ill-defined limits, to be sure) with each other and with behavior in the case of different species, because this is an artifact of the way in which we identify these states. Thus, we would not count an animal as *thirsty* if its 'unsatiated' behavior did not seem to be directed toward drinking and was not followed by 'satiation for liquid'. Thus any animal that we count as capable of these various states will at least *seem* to have a certain rough kind of functional organization. And, as already remarked, if the program of finding psychological laws that are not species-specific—i.e., of finding a normal form for psychological theories of different species—ever succeeds, then it will bring in its wake a delineation of the kind of functional organization that is necessary and sufficient for a given psychological state, as well as a precise definition of the notion 'psychological state'. In contrast, the brain-state theorist has to hope for the eventual development of neurophysiological laws that are species-independent, which seems much less reasonable than the hope that psychological laws (of a sufficiently general kind) may be species-independent, or, still weaker, that a species-independent *form* can be found in which psychological laws can be written.

Functional State versus Behavior-Disposition

The theory that being in pain is neither a brain state nor a functional state but a behavior disposition has one apparent advantage: it appears to agree with the way in which we verify that organisms are in pain. We do not in practice know anything about the brain state of an animal when we say that it is in pain; and we possess little if any knowledge of its functional organization, except in a crude intuitive way. In fact, however, this 'advantage' is no advantage at all: for, although statements about how we verify that *x* is *A* may have a good deal to do with what the concept of being *A* comes to, they have precious little to do with what the property *A is*. To argue on the ground just mentioned that pain is neither a brain state nor a functional state is like arguing that heat is not mean molecular kinetic energy from the fact that ordinary people do not (they think) ascertain the mean molecular kinetic energy of something when they verify that it is hot or cold. It is not necessary that they should; what is necessary is that the marks that they take as indications of heat should in fact be explained by the mean molecular kinetic energy. And, similarly, it is necessary to our hypothesis that the marks that are taken as behavioral indications of pain should be explained by the fact that the organism is a functional state of the appropriate kind, but not that speakers should *know* that this is so.

The difficulties with 'behavior disposition' accounts are so well known that I shall do little more than recall them here. The difficulty—it appears to be more than a 'difficulty,' in fact—of specifying the required behavior disposition except as 'the disposition of X to behave as if X were in *pain*', is the chief one, of course. In contrast, we *can* specify the functional state with which we propose to identify pain, at least roughly, without using the notion of pain. Namely, the functional state we have in mind is the state of receiving sensory inputs which play a certain role in the Functional Organization of the organism. This role is characterized, at least partially, by the fact that the sense organs responsible for the inputs in question are organs whose function is to detect damage to the body, or dangerous extremes of temperature, pressure, etc., and by the fact that the 'inputs' themselves, whatever their physical realization, represent a condition that the organism assigns a high disvalue to. As I stressed in 'The mental life of some machines', this does *not* mean that the Machine will always *avoid* being in the condition in question ('pain'); it only means that the condition will be avoided unless not avoiding it is necessary to the attainment of some more highly valued goal. Since the behavior of the Machine (in this case, an organism) will depend not merely on the sensory inputs, but also on the Total State (i.e., on other values, beliefs, etc.), it seems hopeless to make any general statement about how an organism in such a condition *must* behave; but this does not mean that we must abandon hope of characterizing the condition. Indeed, we have just characterized it.

Not only does the behavior-disposition theory seem hopelessly vague; if the 'behavior' referred to is peripheral behavior, and the relevant stimuli are peripheral stimuli (e.g., we do not say anything about what the organism will do if its brain is operated upon), then the theory seems clearly false. For example, two animals with all motor nerves cut will have the same actual and potential 'behavior' (namely, none to speak of); but if one has cut pain fibers and the other has uncut pain fibers, then one will feel pain and the other won't. Again, if one person has cut pain fibers, and another suppresses all pain responses deliberately due to some strong compulsion, then the actual and potential peripheral behavior may be the same, but one will feel pain and the other won't. (Some philosophers maintain that this last case is conceptually impossible, but the only evidence for this appears to be that *they* can't, or don't want to, conceive of it.) If, instead of pain, we take some sensation the 'bodily expression' of which is easier to suppress—say, a slight coolness in one's left little finger—the case becomes even clearer.

Finally, even if there *were* some behavior disposition invariantly correlated with pain (species-independently!), and specifiable without using the term 'pain', it would still be more plausible to identify being in pain with some state whose presence *explains* this behavior disposition—the brain state or functional state—than with the behavior disposition itself. Such considerations of plausibility may be somewhat subjective; but if other things *were* equal (of course, they aren't) why shouldn't we allow considerations of plausibility to play the deciding role?

Methodological Considerations

So far we have considered only what might be called the 'empirical' reasons for saying that being in pain is a functional state, rather than a brain state or a behavior disposition; namely, that it seems more likely that the functional state we described is invariantly 'correlated' with pain, species-independently, than that there is either a physical-chemical state of the brain (must an organism have a *brain* to feel pain? perhaps some ganglia will do) or a behavior disposition so correlated. If this is correct, then it follows that the identification we proposed is at least a candidate for consideration. What of methodological considerations?

The methodological considerations are roughly similar in all cases of reduction, so no surprises need be expected here. First, identification of psychological states with functional states means that the laws of psychology can be derived from statements of the form 'such-and-such organisms have such-and-such Descriptions' together with the identification statements ('being in pain is such-and-such a functional state', etc.). Secondly, the presence of the functional state (i.e., of inputs which play the role we have described in the Functional Organization of the organism) is not merely 'correlated with' but actually explains the pain behavior on the part of the organism. Thirdly, the identification serves to exclude questions which (if a naturalistic view is correct) represent an altogether wrong way of looking at the matter, e.g., 'What *is* pain if it isn't either the brain state or the functional state?' and 'What causes the pain to be always accompanied by this sort of functional state?' In short, the identification is to be tentatively accepted as a theory which leads to both fruitful predictions and to fruitful *questions*, and which serves to discourage fruitless and empirically senseless questions, where by 'empirically senseless' I mean 'senseless' not merely from the standpoint of verification, but from the standpoint of what there in fact *is*.

Notes

1. In this paper I wish to avoid the vexed question of the relation between *pains* and *pain states*. I only remark in passing that one common argument *against* identification of these two—namely, that a pain can be in one's arm but a state (of the organism) cannot be in one's arm—is easily seen to be fallacious.

2. There are some well-known remarks by Alonzo Church on this topic. Those remarks do not bear (as might at first be supposed) on the identification of concepts with synonymy-classes as such, but rather support the view that (in formal semantics) it is necessary to retain Frege's distinction between the normal and the 'oblique' use of expressions. That is, even if we say that the concept of temperature *is* the synonymy-class of the word 'temperature', we must not thereby be led into the error of supposing that 'the concept of temperature' is synonymous with 'the synonymy-class of the word "temperature"'—for then 'the concept of temperature' and '*der Begriff der Temperatur*' would not be synonymous, which they are. Rather, we must say that the concept of 'temperature' *refers to* the synonymy-class of the word 'temperature' (on this particular reconstruction); but that class is *identified* not as 'the synonymy-class to which such-and-such a word belongs', but in another way (e.g., as the synonymy-class whose members have such-and-such a characteristic use).

Chapter 11

Reductionism and Antireductionism in Functionalist Theories of Mind

Patricia Churchland

Antireductionism in Functionalist Theories of the Mind

Functional Types and Structural Implementations

The core idea of functionalism is the thesis that mental states are defined in terms of their abstract causal roles within the wider information-processing system. A given mental state is characterized in terms of its abstract causal relations to environmental input, to other internal states, and to output. Being in pain, on this account, is a state characterized by its causal relations to behavior such as wincing and crying out, by its causal relations to external input such as the skin being burned, by its causal relations to other internal states such as the desire to make the pain go away, beliefs about the source of the pain and about what will bring relief, and so forth. The characterization of having the goal of, say, finding a mate will follow a similar pattern: the goal state will be connected to a complex range of beliefs and desires, will prompt a diverse range of plans and actions, and will be connected in rich and complicated ways to perceptual states (Putnam 1967, Fodor 1975, Lycan 1981b).

In general, functional kinds are specified by reference to their roles or relational profiles, not by reference to the material structure in which they are instantiated. What makes a certain part of an engine a valve lifter is that, given a specified input, it has a certain output, namely the lifting of the valves, and it might be instantiated in various physical devices, such as a rotating camshaft or a hydraulic device. More humbly, "mousetrap" is a functional kind, being implementable in all manner of physically different devices: spring traps, assorted cage traps, a sack of grain falling when a trip line is wriggled, or perhaps even a cat or a specially bred killer rat. There is nothing in the specification "mousetrap" that says it must have a tin spring or a wooden housing. Being a mousetrap or a valve lifter is therefore a functional kind, not a physical kind, though mousetraps and valve lifters are implemented in physical stuff and every implementation or "token" is a physical device.

According to functionalism, then, mental states and processes are functional kinds. Functionalists have typically sided with physicalism by claiming that our mental states are implemented in neural stuff, not, as the dualist would have it, in spiritual stuff. At one level of description we can talk about the causal and logical relations among perceptions, beliefs, desires, and behavior, and at the structural level we can talk about spiking frequencies of neurons, patterns of excitations, and so forth. It is because neurons are orchestrated as they are that the system has the functional organization it does, and thus the physical substratum subserves the functional superstratum. In our case the functional organization that is our psychology is realized in our neural "gubbins." In similar fashion, it is because on-off switches in a computer are orchestrated as they are that it adds, finds square roots, and so forth. The computer's program is realized in its electronic "gubbins." The functionalist theory is thus as roundly physicalist as it can be, yet despite their adherence to physicalist principles, functionalists have typically rejected reductionism and ignored neuroscience. Why?

Plainly, it is not because functionalists suppose that mental states have no material realization. Rather, it is because they envision that types of mental states could have *too many* distinct material realizations for a reductive mold to fit. As functionalists see it, for a reductive strategy to succeed, a type of mental state must be identical to a type of physical state, but, they argue, the identities are not forthcoming. The reason is that one and the same cognitive organization might be realized or embodied in various ways in various stuffs, which entails that there cannot be one-to-one relations between functional types and structural types. A cognitive organization is like the computational organization of a computer executing a program: computational processes are logical, or at least semantically coherent, and they operate on symbols as a function of the symbol's meaning, not as a function of its physical etiology in the machine, and the same program can be run on different machines (Putnam 1967, Pylyshyn 1984). There is nothing in the specification of a cognitive organization, the functionalist will remind us, that says that pain must be subserved by substance P in a given set of neurons or that a goal-to-find-a-mate state must be linked to testosterone. This oversimplifies, of course, but the main point is clear enough.

In a general way one can imagine that on another planet there might have evolved creatures who, though very different from us in physical structure, might have a cognitive organization much like our own. Suppose, for example, they were silicon-based instead of carbon-based as we are. For these animals, having a goal will be functionally like our having a goal, but such a state will not be identical to having neurons $n-m$ responding thus and so, though to be sure the goal state will be embodied in their physical structure. Or suppose that in time we figure out how to manufacture a robot that has the same functional organization as a human: it has goals, beliefs, and pains, and it solves problems, sees, and moves about. Its information-processing innards are not neurons but microchips, and its cognitive organization cannot therefore be identical to a particular neuronal organization, since *neural* stuff it has not got. Instead, its cognitive economy will be instantiated in electronic stuff. As we shall see, the plausibility of these thought-experiments depends on a crucial and highly suspect assumption—namely, that we know at what level the biology does not matter.

Fictional examples are not really needed to make the point anyhow, since there are certain to be neural (structural) differences between functionally identical states in distinct species. An echidna and a yak may both be in pain or have the goal of finding a mate and hence be in the same functional state, though the neural events and processes subserving their states may differ considerably. The same is probably true of more closely related species such as chimpanzees and gorillas. Moreover, it is continued, there may be nontrivial differences in structural detail between two *humans* in a functionally identical state: the neural events that subserve my adding 29 and 45 may not be the same as those in the brain of a calculating prodigy or a mathematician or a child or a street vendor. Indeed, on different occasions different neuronal events may realize *my* adding 29 and 45, depending on what else my brain is doing and heaven knows what other matters. We know quite well that two computers can be in the same type of functional state and yet have very different structural states. For example, two computers can be executing the same program written in BASIC, though their hardware and even their assembly language may be quite different (Fodor 1975).

Identity of functional-state types with structural-state types, argues the functionalist, is therefore hopelessly unrealistic, and since reduction requires such identities, *tant pis* for reduction. Physicalist principles are in no way sundered, however, for all that physicalism requires is that any given *instance* of a functional-state type (a token of that type) be realized in physical stuff, and this the functionalist heartily agrees to and insists upon. He therefore describes himself as espousing *token-token* identity of mental states with physical states, but denying *type-type* identity and therewith reductionism (Putnam 1967, Dennett 1978b).

This foray against the reductionist program is known as the argument from *multiple instantiability* or *multiple realizability*. Functional states are multiply instantiable, and the range of physical implementations will be so diverse that we cannot expect it to form a natural kind. Apart from its implications for the theory that mental states are identical with brain states, the argument has been deployed to methodological purpose in the following way.

If mental states and processes are functional kinds, then to understand how cognitively adept organisms solve problems, think, reason, and comport themselves intelligently, what we need to understand is their functional organization. Research on neurons is not going to reveal the nature of the functional organization, but only something about the embodiment of the functional organization—and just one sort of instantiation at that. Neuroscience, it has been argued, is focused on the engineering details rather than on the functional scheme, and to this extent it is removed from the level of description that is appropriate to answering questions concerning learning, intelligence, problem solving, memory, and so forth. Knowledge of the structural minutiae is important for repairs, of course, and to this extent neuroscience has obvious medical significance, but structural theory will not enlighten functional hypotheses and functional models. To put it crudely, it will not tell us how the mind works. Cognitive psychology, in contrast, is focused at the appropriate level of description, and in cooperation with research in artificial intelligence it constitutes the best strategy for devising a theory of our functional cognitive economy. Thus the crux of the argument.

As Pylyshyn (1980) sees it, the research labor can be divided along these lines: the cognitive scientists will figure out the functional/cognitive theory, and the neuroscientists can untangle the underlying physical devices that instantiate the cognitive "program." On an extreme version of this view, nothing much of the details of neuronal business need be known by the cognitive scientist—or the philosopher, either—since the way the functional organization is instantiated in the brain is a quite separate and *independent* matter from the way our cognitive economy is organized. Pylyshyn comes close to this in his claim that computational questions can be addressed exclusively at a privileged (functional) level of algorithms and symbolic manipulation (1980:111). He says, "... in studying computation it is possible, and in certain respects essential, to factor apart the nature of the symbolic process from the properties of the physical device in which it is realized" (p. 115).

Neuroscience, on this picture, is irrelevant to the computational questions of cognitive science. What it is relevant to are implementation issues, such as whether a particular computational model of cognitive business is in fact implemented in the neural structure. Computational (functional) psychology is thus conceived as an *autonomous* science, with its proprietary vocabulary and its own domain of questions, the answers to which, as Pylyshyn remarks, "... can be given without regard to the material or hardware properties of the device on which these processes are executed" (p. 115). It may even be suggested that the less known about the actual pumps and pulleys of the embodiment of mental life, the better, for the less there is to clutter up one's functionally oriented research.

Whether anyone really holds the extreme version of the research ideology is doubtful, but certainly milder versions have won considerable sympathy, and sometimes cognitive science programs permit or encourage neglect of neuroscience, where the autonomy of psychology is the rationale. How influential the view is I cannot estimate, but some philosophers are still wont to excuse those colleagues who take neuroscience seriously as having not quite managed to master the distinction between functional and structural descriptions. The methodological point should be taken seriously because functionalism is now the dominant theory of the mind espoused by philosophers as well as by many cognitive scientists. Even so, there are significant differences among functionalists on a number of issues, including the relevance of theories of brain function to theories of psychological function. Dissent from the methodological point is not without voice in cognitive psychology (for example, McClelland and Rumelhart 1981, Posner, Pea, and Volpe 1982), philosophy (for example, Enç 1983, Hooker 1981, Paul M. Churchland 1981), and computer science (for example, Anderson and Hinton 1981). My lot is thrown in with the dissenters, because I think both the antireductionist argument and the research ideology it funds are theoretically unjustified and pragmatically unwise to boot. In what follows I shall try to show why.

In Defense of Reductionism

There are two principal sources of error in the antireductionist views I have outlined. The first concerns the background assumptions about the nature of intertheoretic reduction; the second concerns the conception of levels—how many there are, their nature, their discovery, and their interconnections. These sources of error will be considered in sequence.

Intertheoretic Reduction and Functionalism

Functionalists appear to assume that intertheoretic reduction cannot come off unless the properties in the reduced theory have a *unique* realization in physical stuff. This assumption is crucial in the case against reduction, and it is what floats the methodological claim for the autonomy of cognitive psychology. Is the assumption justified?

One way to test the claim is to see whether it conflicts with or comports with the paradigm cases of reduction in the history of science. "Temperature" is a predicate of thermodynamics, and as thermodynamics and molecular theory co-evolved, the temperature of gases was found to reduce to the mean kinetic energy of the constituent molecules. That is, a corrected version of the classical ideal gas law was derived from statistical mechanics together with certain assumptions. Several features of this case are immediately relevant to the issue at hand. Notice that what was reduced was not temperature tout court, but temperature of a gas. The temperature of a gas *is* mean kinetic energy of the constituent molecules, but the temperature of a solid is something else again; the temperature of a plasma cannot be a matter of kinetic energy of the molecules, because plasmas are high-energy states consisting not of molecules but of dissociated atoms; the temperature of empty space as embodied in its transient electromagnetic radiation is different yet again. (Paul M. Churchland 1984 and Enç 1983 also make this point.) And perhaps there are states as yet undiscovered for which temperature is specified in none of these ways. The initial reduction in thermodynamics was relative to a certain domain of phenomena, to wit, gases, but it was a bona fide reduction for all that. Nor is this domain-relativity used as grounds for saying that thermodynamics is an autonomous science, independent and separate from physics. Quite the contrary, the co-evolution of corpuscular physics and thermodynamics was of the first importance to both physics and thermodynamics.

Yet if we heed the functionalist assumption at issue, we ought to withhold the stamp of reduction on grounds that temperature must be a functional property that is multiply realized in distinct physical structures. Now, however, this looks like a merely verbal recommendation about what to call reductions in cases where the predicates in the reducing theory are relativized to certain domains (cf. Cummins 1983). As such, it implies nothing about the derivation of one theory from another or about the autonomy of the sciences. No grand methodological strictures about what is and is not relevant to the "functional" theory will be in order. As a merely verbal recommendation it is not especially objectionable, but it has no obvious utility either.

Dialectically, it does the functionalist no good to deny reduction in thermodynamics, for then he loses the basis for saying that psychology is on an entirely different footing from the rest of science (Enç 1983). After all, if psychology is no worse off than thermodynamics, then reductionists can be cheerful indeed. At any rate, the requirements for the reduction of psychology should not be made stiffer than those for intertheoretic reduction elsewhere in science. (See also Richardson 1979, Paul M. Churchland 1984.)

The main point of the example drawn from thermodynamics is that reductions may be reductions *relative to a domain of phenomena*. Though this is called "multiple instantiability" and is draped in black by the functionalist, it is seen as part of normal business in the rest of science. By analogy with the thermodynamics example, if human brains and electronic brains both enjoy a certain type of cognitive organization, we may get two distinct, domain-relative reductions. Or we may, in the fullness of time and after much co-evolution in theories, have one reductive account of, say, goals or pain in vertebrates, a different account for invertebrates, and so forth. In and of itself, the mere fact that there are differences in hardware has no implications whatever for whether the psychology of humans will eventually be explained in neuroscientific terms, whether the construction of psychological theories can benefit from neuroscientific information, and whether psychology is an autonomous and independent science. That reductions are domain-relative does not mean they are phony reductions or reductions manqué, and it certainly does not mean that psychology can justify methodological isolation from neuroscience.

Enç (1983) draws a further point out of the thermodynamics case. Two volumes of a gas might have the same temperature, but the distributions of velocities of their constituent molecules will be quite different even while their mean value is the same. To be consistent, functionalists should again deny reductive success to statistical mechanics since, as they would put it, *temperature of a gas* is differently realized in the two cases. If, on the other hand, they want to concede reduction here but withhold its possibility from psychology, they need to do more than merely predict hardware differences between species or between individuals.

If it turns out that we are lucky enough to get a reduction (domain-relative) of *human* psychology to neuroscience, what does this do to the thesis that mental kinds are functional kinds? Nothing, for that thesis is independent of the antireductionist argument, and it stands on its own feet after the argument from multiple instantiability falls. The thesis that mental states are identified in terms of their abstract causal roles in the wider information-processing system is the core conception that makes functionalism functionalism, and it is entirely neutral on the question of reducibility. Functionalists can be true blue functionalists without naysaying reduction. Functionalism as it lives and breathes, however, is another matter, and frequently functionalists have wished to argue for a package: the functional characterization of mental states, the nonreducibility of psychology, and the autonomy (in some degree) of psychology from the more basic sciences. As a result, the term "functionalism" is typically if inappropriately associated with the whole package.

The point of this section has been a very general one: intertheoretic reductions are not conditional on a one-to-one mapping of predicates of the higher-level theory onto predicates of the reducing theory. Antireductionists may wish to concede the general point but to continue by arguing that the details of the case at hand rule out reduction. In so arguing, they will point to radical differences between the neuronal level of explanation and the functional-computational level, and they will point out that the multiplicity of instantiations of psychological predicates can be so profuse, diverse, and arbitrary that the case cannot be likened to the thermodynamics-statistical mechanics example. In a word, they claim that the case of psychology is special.

Levels of Organization in the Mind-Brain

There is a good deal that is uncontroversial in the antireductionist's appreciation that there must *be* a set of levels of organization. A theory of cellular and synaptic changes occurring during learning will be more fine-grained than a theory of how an interactive network learns, which will be more fine-grained than a theory of what anatomical structures subserve learning, which will be more fine-grained than a theory that postulates a coding mechanism, retrieval mechanisms, and so forth. What is controversial is the assumption that the trilevel model suitable to Von Neumann computers is also suitable to organic brains. That there should be some division of labor is also beyond dispute; no one since Bacon could take all knowledge as his province. Indeed, no one since Helmholtz could take even all of neuroscience as his province. What is regrettable, however, is the divisive research ideology based on the trilevel model.

As we have seen, the hypothesis based on the computer analogy is that the mind-brain has three levels of organization: the semantic, the syntactic, and the mechanistic—the level of *content*, the level of the *algorithm*, and the level of *structural implementation*. The principal problem with the computer metaphor is that on the basis of the complexity we already know to be found in the brain, it is evident that there are *many* levels of organization between the topmost level and the level of intracellular dynamics. (See also Lycan 1981a.) And even if there were just three, neurobiological theory challenges that way of specifying their organizational description. How many levels there are, and how they should be described, is not something to be decided in advance of empirical theory. Pretheoretically, we have only rough and ready—and eminently revisable—hunches about what constitutes a level of organization.

As a first approximation, we can distinguish the following levels of organization: the membrane, the cell, the synapse, the cell assembly, the circuit, the behavior. And within each level further substrata can be distinguished. If, however, neurons are organized into modules, each perhaps playing a role in several distinct information-processing modules, and if modules themselves are members of higher-order "metamodules," again with membership being a diverse and distributed affair, or if some cell assemblies or modules have a transient membership or a transient existence, we may then find a description of levels that is orthogonal to the first.

Another preliminary and related way to demarcate a level is to characterize it in terms of the research methods used. Certainly this is a very rough way of defining levels of organization, but it may be useful until the research reveals enough for us to see what the levels really are. For example, in research on learning and memory one can discern many different methods that, compared to one another, are more or less fine-grained. The cellular approach taken by Kandel and his colleagues (Hawkins and Kandel 1984) showing modification in presynaptic neurotransmitter release in habituation is in some sense at a lower level than studies by Lynch and his colleagues (Lee et al. 1980) showing modification of synapse numbers and synaptic morphology correlated with plasticity in behavior, which in turn is at a (slightly) lower level than the studies by Greenough and his colleagues (Greenough, Juraska, and Volkmar 1979) on the effect of maze training on dendritic branching. We then ascend to the multicellular studies in the hippocampus done by Berger, Latham, and Thompson (1980), and from there up (a bit) to the cell assembly studies in the olfactory bulb by Freeman (1979), which uses an 8 × 8 electrode array and evoked response potential averaging techniques. Upward again to the studies of Nottebohm (1981) on the seasonal changes in the "songster" nuclei of the canary brain or to the animal models of human amnesia studied by Zola-Morgan and Squire (1984). At yet a different level are the studies by Jernigan (1984) and Volpe et al. (1983) of correlations between neural tissue atrophy and memory performance using neural imaging techniques (CBF, PET). Finally there are neurological studies of human amnesia (Weiskrantz 1978, Squire and Cohen 1984), ethological studies of such things as how bees remember flowers (Gould 1985), and psychological studies of memory capacities and skills of college undergraduates (Norman 1973, Tulving 1983). This is obviously a very fast Cook's ascent at just one point through the research strata, but a more leisurely tour will reinforce the impressions.

It is simply not rewarding to sort out this research in terms of the trilevel computer analogy, nor is there any useful purpose to be served by trying to force a fit. Moreover, at each of the research levels one can distinguish among questions concerning the nature of the capacity, questions concerning the processes subserving the capacity, and the matter of the physical implementation. The point is, even at the level of *cellular* research, one can view the cell as being the functional unit with a certain input-output profile, as having a specifiable dynamics, and as having a structural implementation in certain proteins and other subcellular structures.

What this means is that one cannot foist on the brain a monolithic distinction between function and structure, and then appoint psychologists to attend to function and neuroscientists to attend to structure. Relative to a lower research level a neuroscientist's research can be considered functional, and relative to a higher level it can be considered structural. Thus, Thompson's work on multicellular response profiles in the hippocampus is perhaps structural relative to Squire's work on the recognition capacities of amnesic humans but functional relative to Lynch's work on plasticity of synaptic morphology. The structure-function distinction, though not without utility, is a *relative*, not an absolute, distinction, and even then it is insufficiently precise to support any sweeping research ideology.

In addition, we simply do not know at what level of organization one can assume that the physical implementation can vary but the capacities will remain the same. In brief, it may be that if we had a complete cognitive neurobiology we would find that to build a computer with the same capacities as the human brain, we had to use as structural elements things that behaved very like neurons. That is, the artificial units would have to have both action potentials and graded potentials, and a full repertoire of synaptic modifiability, dendritic growth, and so forth, though unlike neurons they might not need to have, say, mitochondria or ribosomes. But, for all we know now, to mimic nervous plasticity efficiently, we might have to mimic very closely even certain subcellular structures.

There is a further assumption, usually unstated, that lends credence to the ideology of autonomy and should be debunked. This assumption is that neuroscience, because it tries to understand the physical device—the brain itself—will not produce *theories* of functional organization. Now we have already seen that the functional-structural distinction will not support the simplistic idea that psychology does functional analysis and neuroscience does structural analysis, and that there are bound to be many levels of organization between the level of the single cell and the level at which most cognitive psychologists work. It is important as well to emphasize that when neuroscientists do address such questions as how neurons manage to store information, or how cell assemblies do pattern recognition, or how they manage to effect sensorimotor control, they are addressing questions concerning neurodynamics—concerning information and how the brain processes it. In doing so, they are up to their ears in theorizing, and even more shocking, in theorizing about representations and computations. If the representations postulated are not sentencelike, and if the transformations postulated do not resemble reasoning, this does not mean the theory is not functional theory, or not real theory, or not relevant to theories at a higher level.... The existence of bona fide *neurofunctional* theorizing is perhaps the most resounding refutation of the second assumption.

My general conclusion, therefore, is that it is supremely naive to assume that we know what level is functional and what is structural, and that neurons can be ignored as we get on with the functional specification of the mind-brain. This explains my earlier warning about the multiple instantiation thought-experiments that are endlessly invoked by antireductionists. Nevertheless, antireductionists will argue for the autonomy of cognitive psychology not merely on the basis of the trilevel hypothesis but also on the grounds that the categories and generalizations appropriate to the cognitive levels are special. For reasons to be examined, these categories are believed to have an invulnerable theoretical integrity and to be irreducible to physical categories.

Bibliography

Anderson, James A. and Geoffrey Hinton, 1981. "Models of Information Processing in the Brain." In Hinton and Anderson, eds., *Parallel Models of Associative Memory*. Hillsdale NJ: Erlbaum.

Berger, T. W., R. I. Latham, and R. F. Thomson, 1980. "Hippocampal Unit Behavior Correlations During Classical Conditioning," *Brain Research* 193: 483–85.

Churchland, Paul M., 1981. "Eliminative Materialism and the Propositional Attitudes." *Journal of Philosophy* 78, no. 2, 67–90.

Churchland, Paul M., 1984. *Matter and Consciousness: A Contemporary Introduction to the Philosophy of Mind.* Cambridge MA: MIT Press.

Cummins, Robert, 1983. *The Nature of Psychological Explanation.* Cambridge MA: MIT Press.

Dennett, Daniel C., 1978b. *Brainstorms: Philosophical Essays on Mind and Psychology.* Cambridge MA: MIT Press.

Enç, Berent, 1983. "In Defense of the Identity Theory," *Journal of Philosophy* 80: 279–98.

Fodor, Jerry A., 1975. *The Language of Thought.* New York: Crowell.

Freeman, Walter, 1979. "Nonlinear dynamics of paleocortex manifested in the olfactory EEG," *Biological Cybernetics* 3: 21–37.

Gould, James L., 1985. "How Bees Remember Flower Shapes," *Science* 227: 1492–94.

Greenough, W. T., J. M. Juraska, and F. R. Volkmar, 1979. "Maze Training Effects on Dendritic Branching in Occipital Cortex of Adult Rats," *Behavioral and Neural Biology* 26: 287–97.

Hawkins, Robert D., and Eric R. Kandel, 1984. "Steps Toward a Cell-Biological Alphabet for Elementary Forms of Learning." In G. Lynch, J. L. McGaugh, and N. M. Weinberger, eds., *Neurobiology of Learning and Memory.* New York: Guilford.

Hooker, Clifford A., 1981. "Toward a General Theory of Reduction," *Dialogue* 20: 38–59, 201–236, 496–529.

Jernigan, Terry L., 1984. "The Study of Human Memory with Neuro-Imaging Techniques." In L. R. Squire and N. Butters, eds., *Neuropsychology of Memory*. New York: Guilford.

Lee, K. S., F. Schottler, M. Oliver, and G. Lynch, 1980. "Brief Bursts of High-Frequency Produce Two Types of Structural Change in Rat Hippocampus," *Journal of Neurophysiology* 44: 247–58.

Lycan, William G., 1981a. "Form, Function, and Feel," *Journal of Philosophy* 78: 24–50.

Lycan, William G., 1981b. "Toward a Homuncular Theory of Believing," *Cognition and Brain Theory* 4: 139–59.

McClelland, James L., and David E. Rumelhart, 1981. "An Interactive Activation Model of the Effect of Context in Letter Perception. Part I: An Account of Basic Findings," *Psychological Review* 88: 375–407.

Norman, D. A., 1973. "Memory, Knowledge, and the Answering of Questions." In R. Solso, ed., *The Loyola Symposium on Cognitive Psychology*. Washington D.C.: Winston.

Nottebohm, F., 1981. "Laterality, Seasons, and Space Governing the Learning of a Motor Skill," *Trends in Neuroscience* 4, no. 5: 104–6.

Posner, Michael I., Roy Pea, and Bruce Volpe, 1982. "Cognitive Neuroscience: Developments Toward a Science of Synthesis." In J. Mehler, E. Walker, and M. Garrett, eds., *Perspectives on Mental Representation*. Hillsdale NJ: Erlbaum.

Putnam, Hilary, 1967. "The Nature of Mental States." In W. H. Capitan and D. D. Merrill, eds., *Art, Mind, and Religion*. Pittsburgh: Univ. Pittsburgh Press.

Pylyshyn, Zenon, 1980. "Computation and Cognition: Issues in the Foundation of Cognitive Science," *Behavioral and Brain Sciences* 3, no. 1: 111–34.

Pylyshyn, Zenon, 1984. *Computation and Cognition*. Cambridge MA: MIT Press.

Richardson, Robert, 1979. "Functionalism and Reduction," *Philosophy of Science* 46: 533–58.

Squire, Larry R., and Neal J. Cohen, 1984. "Human Memory and Amnesia." In G. Lynch, J. L. McGaugh, and N. M. Weinberger, eds., *Neurobiology of Learning and Memory*. New York: Guilford.

Tulving, Endel, 1983. *Elements of Episodic Memory*. Oxford: Clarendon Press.

Volpe, B. T., P. Herscovitch, M. E. Raichle, M. S. Gazzaniga, and W. Hirst, 1983. "Cerebral Blood Flow and Metabolism in Human Amnesia," *Journal of Cerebral Blood Flow and Metabolism* 3: 5.

Weiskrantz, L., 1978. "A Comparison of Hippocampal Pathology in Man and Other Animals." In *Functions of the Septo-Hippocampal System*. Amsterdam: Elsevier.

Zola-Morgan, S., and L. R. Squire, 1984. "Preserved Learning in Monkeys with Medial Temporal Lesions: Sparing of Motor and Cognitive Skills," *Journal of Neuroscience* 4: 1072–85.

Chapter 12
Troubles with Functionalism
Ned Block

Functionalism, Behaviorism, and Physicalism

The functionalist view of the nature of the mind is now widely accepted.[1] Like behaviorism and physicalism, functionalism seeks to answer the question "What are mental states?" I shall be concerned with identity thesis formulations of functionalism. They say, for example, that pain is a functional state, just as identity thesis formulations of physicalism say that pain is a physical state.

I shall begin by describing functionalism, and sketching the functionalist critique of behaviorism and physicalism. Then I shall argue that the troubles ascribed by functionalism to behaviorism and physicalism infect functionalism as well.

One characterization of functionalism that is probably vague enough to be acceptable to most functionalists is: each type of mental state is a state consisting of a disposition to act in certain ways *and to have certain mental states*, given certain sensory inputs and certain mental states. So put, functionalism can be seen as a new incarnation of behaviorism. Behaviorism identifies mental states with dispositions to act in certain ways in certain input situations. But as critics have pointed out (Chisholm 1957, Geach 1957, Putnam 1963), desire for goal G cannot be identified with, say, the disposition to do A in input circumstances in which A leads to G, since, after all, the agent might not *know* that A leads to G and thus might not be disposed to do A. Functionalism replaces behaviorism's "sensory inputs" with "sensory inputs and mental states"; and functionalism replaces behaviorism's "dispositions to act" with "dispositions to act and have certain mental states." Functionalists want to individuate mental states causally, and since mental states have mental causes and effects as well as sensory causes and behavioral effects, functionalists individuate mental states partly in terms of causal relations to other mental states. One consequence of this difference between functionalism and behaviorism is that there are possible organisms that according to behaviorism, have mental states but, according to functionalism, do not have mental states.

So, necessary conditions for mentality that are postulated by functionalism are in one respect stronger than those postulated by behaviorism. According to behaviorism, it is necessary and sufficient for desiring that G that a system be characterized by a certain set (perhaps infinite) of input-output relations; that is, according to behaviorism, a system desires that G just in case a certain set of conditionals of the form "It will emit O given I" are true of it. According to functionalism, however, a system might have these input-output relations, yet not desire that G; for according to functionalism, whether a system desires that G depends on whether it has internal states which have certain causal relations to other internal states (and to inputs and outputs). Since behaviorism makes no such "internal state" requirement, there are possible systems of which behaviorism affirms and functionalism denies that they have mental states.[2] One way of stating this is that, according to functionalism, behaviorism is guilty of *liberalism*—ascribing mental properties to things that do not in fact have them.

Despite the difference just sketched between functionalism and behaviorism, functionalists and behaviorists need not be far apart in spirit.[3] Shoemaker (1975), for example, says, "On one construal of it, functionalism in the philosophy of mind is the doctrine that mental, or psychological, terms are, in principle, eliminable in a certain way" (pp. 306–307). Functionalists have tended to treat the mental-state terms in a functional characterization of a mental state quite differently from the input and output terms. Thus in the simplest Turing-machine version of the theory (Putnam 1967, Block and Fodor 1972), mental states are identified with the total Turing-machine states, which are themselves *implicitly* defined by a machine table that *explicitly* mentions inputs and outputs, described nonmentalistically.

In Lewis's version of functionalism, mental-state terms are defined by means of a modification of Ramsey's method, in a way that eliminates essential use of mental terminology from the definitions but does not eliminate input and output terminology. That is, 'pain' is defined as synonymous with a definite description containing input and output terms but no mental terminology (see Lewis 1972).

Furthermore, functionalism in both its machine and nonmachine versions has typically insisted that characterizations of mental states should contain descriptions of inputs and outputs in *physical* language. Armstrong (1968), for example, says,

> We may distinguish between 'physical behaviour', which refers to any merely physical action or passion of the body, and 'behaviour proper' which implies relationship to mind. ... Now, if in our formula ["state of the person apt for bringing about a certain sort of behaviour"] 'behaviour' were to mean 'behaviour proper', then we would be giving an account of mental concepts in terms of a concept that already presupposes mentality, which would be circular. So it is clear that in our formula, 'behaviour' must mean 'physical behaviour'. (p. 84)

Therefore, functionalism can be said to "tack down" mental states only at the periphery—that is, through physical, or at least nonmental, specification of inputs and outputs. One major thesis of this article is that, because of this feature, functionalism fails to avoid the sort of problem for which it rightly condemns behaviorism. Functionalism, too, is guilty of liberalism, for much the same reasons as behaviorism. Unlike behaviorism, however, functionalism can naturally be altered to avoid liberalism—but only at the cost of falling into an equally ignominious failing.

The failing I speak of is the one that functionalism shows *physicalism* to be guilty of. By 'physicalism', I mean the doctrine that pain, for example, is identical to a physical (or physiological) state.[4] As many philosophers have argued (notably Fodor 1965, Putnam 1966, see also Block and Fodor 1972), if functionalism is true, physicalism is probably false. The point is at its clearest with regard to Turing-machine versions of functionalism. Any given abstract Turing machine can be realized by a wide variety of physical devices; indeed, it is plausible that, given any putative correspondence between a Turing-machine state and a configurational physical (or physiological) state, there will be a possible realization of the Turing machine that will provide a counterexample to that correspondence. (See Kalke 1969, Gendron 1971, and Mucciolo 1974, for unconvincing arguments to the contrary; see also Kim 1972.) Therefore, if pain is a functional state, it cannot, for example, be a brain state, because creatures without brains can realize the same Turing machine as creatures with brains.

I must emphasize that the functionalist argument against physicalism does not appeal merely to the fact that one abstract Turing machine can be realized by systems of different *material composition* (wood, metal, glass, etc.). To argue this way would be like arguing that temperature cannot be a microphysical magnitude because the same temperature can be had by objects with *different* microphysical structures (Kim 1972). Objects with different microphysical structures, such as objects made of wood, metal, glass, etc., can have many interesting microphysical properties in common, such as molecular kinetic energy of the same average value. Rather, the functionalist argument against physicalism is that it is difficult to see how there *could be* a nontrivial first-order (see note 4) physical property in common to all and only the possible physical realizations of a given Turing-machine state. Try to think of a remotely plausible candidate! At the very least, the onus is on those who think such physical properties are conceivable to show us how to conceive of one.

One way of expressing this point is that, according to functionalism, physicalism is a *chauvinist* theory: it withholds mental properties from systems that in fact have them. In saying mental states are brain states, for example, physicalists unfairly exclude those poor brainless creatures who nonetheless have minds.

A second major point of this paper is that the very argument which functionalism uses to condemn physicalism can be applied equally well against functionalism; indeed, any version of functionalism that avoids liberalism falls, like physicalism, into chauvinism.

This article has three parts. The first argues that functionalism is guilty of liberalism, the second that one way of modifying functionalism to avoid liberalism is to tie it more closely to empirical psychology, and the third that no version of functionalism can avoid both liberalism and chauvinism.

More about What Functionalism Is

One way of providing some order to the bewildering variety of functionalist theories is to distinguish between those that are couched in terms of a Turing machine and those that are not.

A Turing-machine table lists a finite set of machine-table states, $S_1 \ldots S_n$; inputs, $I_1 \ldots I_m$; and outputs, $O_1 \ldots O_p$. The table specifies a set of conditionals of the form: if the machine is in state S_i and receives input I_j, it emits output O_k and goes into state S_1. That is, given any state and input, the table specifies an output and a next state. Any system with a set of inputs, outputs, and states related in the way specified by the table is described by the table and is a realization of the abstract automaton specified by the table.

To have the power for computing any recursive function, a Turing machine must be able to control its input in certain ways. In standard formulations, the output of a Turing machine is regarded as having two components. It prints a symbol on a tape, then moves the tape, thus bringing a new symbol into the view of the input reader. For the Turing machine to have full power, the tape must be infinite in at least one direction and movable in both directions. If the machine has no control over the tape, it is a "finite transducer," a rather limited Turing machine. Finite transducers need not be regarded as having tape at all. Those who believe that machine functionalism is true must suppose that just what power automaton we are is a substantive empirical question. If we are "full power" Turing machines, the environment must constitute part of the tape. . . .

One very simple version of machine functionalism (Block and Fodor 1972) states that each system having mental states is described by at least one Turing-machine table of a specifiable sort and that each type of mental state of the system is identical to one of the machine-table states. Consider, for example, the Turing machine described in table 12.1 (cf. Nelson 1975). One can get a crude picture of the simple version of machine functionalism by considering the claim that S_1 = dime-desire, and S_2 = nickel-desire. Of course, no functionalist would claim that a Coke machine desires anything. Rather, the

Table 12.1

	S_1	S_2
nickel	Emit no output	Emit a Coke
input	Go to S_2	Go to S_1
dime	Emit a Coke	Emit a Coke and a nickel
input	Stay in S_1	Go to S_1

simple version of machine functionalism described above makes an analogous claim with respect to a much more complex hypothetical machine table. Notice that machine functionalism specifies inputs and outputs explicitly, internal states implicitly (Putnam 1967, p. 434 says: "The S_i, to repeat, are specified only *implicitly* by the description, i.e., specified *only* by the set of transition probabilities given in the machine table"). To be described by this machine table, a device must accept nickels and dimes as inputs and dispense nickels and Cokes as outputs. But the states S_1 and S_2 can have virtually any natures (even nonphysical natures), so long as those natures connect the states to each other and to the inputs and outputs specified in the machine table. All we are told about S_1 and S_2 are these relations; thus machine functionalism can be said to reduce mentality to input-output structures. This example should suggest the force of the functionalist argument against physicalism. Try to think of a first-order (see note 4) physical property that can be shared by all (and only) realizations of this machine table!

One can also categorize functionalists in terms of whether they regard functional identities as part of a priori psychology or empirical psychology. ... The a priori functionalists (such as Smart, Armstrong, Lewis, Shoemaker) are the heirs of the logical behaviorists. They tend to regard functional analyses as analyses of the meanings of mental terms, whereas the empirical functionalists (such as Fodor, Putnam, Harman) regard functional analyses as substantive scientific hypotheses. In what follows, I shall refer to the former view as 'Functionalism' and the latter as 'Psychofunctionalism'. (I shall use 'functionalism' with a lowercase 'f' as neutral between Functionalism and Psychofunctionalism. When distinguishing between Functionalism and Psychofunctionalism, I shall always use capitals.)

Functionalism and Psychofunctionalism and the difference between them can be made clearer in terms of the notion of the Ramsey sentence of a psychological theory. Mental-state terms that appear in a psychological theory can be defined in various ways by means of the Ramsey sentence of the theory ... All functional state identity theories ... can be understood as defining a set of functional states ... by means of the Ramsey sentence of a psychological theory—with one functional state corresponding to each mental state. The functional state corresponding to pain will be called the 'Ramsey functional correlate' of pain, with respect to the psychological theory. In terms of the notion of a Ramsey functional correlate with respect to a theory, the distinction between Functionalism and Psychofunctionalism can be defined as follows: Functionalism identifies mental state S with S's Ramsey functional correlate with respect to a *common-sense* psychological theory; Psychofunctionalism identifies S with S's Ramsey functional correlate with respect to a *scientific* psychological theory.

This difference between Functionalism and Psychofunctionalism gives rise to a difference in specifying inputs and outputs. Functionalists are restricted to specification of inputs and outputs that are plausibly part of commonsense knowledge; Psychofunctionalists are under no such restriction. Although both groups insist on physical—or at least nonmental—specification on inputs and outputs, Functionalists require externally observable classifications (such as inputs characterized in terms of objects present in the vicinity of the organism, outputs in terms of movements of body parts). Psychofunctionalists, on the other hand, have the option to specify inputs and outputs in terms of internal parameters, such as signals in input and output neurons. ...

Let T be a psychological theory of either commonsense or scientific psychology. T may contain generalizations of the form: anyone who is in state w and receives input x emits output y, and goes into state z. Let us write T as

$$T(S_1 \ldots S_n, I_1 \ldots I_k, O_1 \ldots O_m)$$

where the Ss are mental states, the Is are inputs, and the Os are outputs. The 'S's are to be understood as mental state *constants* such as 'pain', not variables, and likewise for the 'I's and 'O's. Thus, one could also write T as

T(pain ..., light of 400 nanometers entering left eye ..., left big toe moves 1 centimeter left ...)

To get the Ramsey sentence of T, replace the mental state terms—*but not the input and output terms*—by variables, and prefix an existential quantifier for each variable:

$$\exists F_1 \ldots \exists F_n T(F_1 \ldots F_n,$$
$$I_1 \ldots I_k, O_1 \ldots O_m)$$

If 'F_{17}' is the variable that replaced the word 'pain' when the Ramsey sentence was formed, then we can define pain as follows in terms of the Ramsey sentence:

x is in pain $\Leftrightarrow \exists F_1 \ldots \exists F_n$
$T[(F_1 \ldots F_n, I_1 \ldots I_k, O_1 \ldots O_m)$ and x has $F_{17}]$

The Ramsey functional correlate of pain is the property expressed by the predicate on the right hand side of this biconditional. Notice that this predicate contains input and output constants, but no mental constants since the mental constants were replaced by variables. The Ramsey functional correlate for pain is defined in terms of inputs and outputs, but not in mental terms.

For example, let T be the theory that pain is caused by skin damage and causes worry and the emission of "ouch", and worry, in turn, causes brow wrinkling. Then the Ramsey definition would be:

x is in pain $\Leftrightarrow$ There are 2 states (properties), the first of which is caused by skin damage and causes both the emission of "ouch" and the second state, and the second state causes brow wrinkling, and x is in the first state.

The Ramsey functional correlate of pain with respect to this "theory" is the property of being in a state that is caused by skin damage and causes the emission of "ouch" and another state that in turn causes brow wrinkling. (Note that the words 'pain' and 'worry' have been replaced by variables, but the input and output terms remain.)

The Ramsey functional correlate of a state S is a state that has much in common with S. Specifically, S and its Ramsey functional correlate share the structural properties specified by the theory T. But, there are two reasons why it is natural to suppose that S and its Ramsey functional correlate will be distinct. First, the Ramsey functional correlate of S with respect to T can "include" at most those aspects of S that are captured by T; any aspects not captured by T will be left out. Second, the Ramsey functional correlate may even leave out some of what T does capture, for the Ramsey definition does not contain the "theoretical" vocabulary of T. The example theory of the last paragraph is true only of pain-feeling organisms—but trivially, in virtue of its use of the word 'pain'. However, the predicate that expresses the Ramsey functional correlate does not contain this word (since it was replaced by a variable), and so can be true of things that don't feel pain. It would be easy to make a simple machine that has some artificial skin, a brow, a tape-recorded "ouch", and two states that satisfy the mentioned causal relations, but no pain.

The bold hypothesis of functionalism is that for *some* psychological theory, this natural supposition that a state and its Ramsey functional correlate are distinct is false. Functionalism says that there is a theory such that pain, for example, *is* its Ramsey functional correlate with respect to that theory.

One final preliminary point: I have given the misleading impression that functionalism identifies *all* mental states with functional states. Such a version of functionalism is obviously far too strong. Let X be a newly created cell-for-cell duplicate of you (which, of course, is functionally equivalent to you). Perhaps you remember being bar mitzvahed. But X does not remember being bar mitzvahed, since X never was bar mitzvahed. Indeed, something can be functionally equivalent to you but fail to know what you know, or [verb], what you [verb], for a wide variety of "success" verbs. Worse still, if Putnam (1975b) is right in saying that "meanings are not in the head," systems functionally equivalent to you may, for similar reasons, fail to have many of your other propositional attitudes. Suppose you believe water is wet. According to plausible arguments advanced by Putnam and Kripke, a condition for the possibility of your believing water is wet is a certain kind of causal connection between you and water. Your "twin" on Twin Earth, who is connected in a similar way to XYZ rather than H_2O, would not believe water is wet.

If functionalism is to be defended, it must be construed as applying only to a subclass of mental states, those "narrow" mental states such that truth conditions for their application are in some sense "within the person." But even assuming that a notion of narrowness of psychological state can be satisfactorily formulated, the interest of functionalism may be diminished by this restriction. I mention this problem only to set it aside.

I shall take functionalism to be a doctrine about all "narrow" mental states.

Homunculi-Headed Robots

In this section I shall describe a class of devices that are prima facie embarrassments for all versions of functionalism in that they indicate functionalism is guilty of liberalism—classifying systems that lack mentality as having mentality.

Consider the simple version of machine functionalism already described. It says that each system having mental states is described by at least one Turing-machine table of a certain kind, and each mental state of the system is identical to one of the machine-table states specified by the machine table. I shall consider inputs and outputs to be specified by descriptions of neural impulses in sense organs and motor-output neurons. This assumption should not be regarded as restricting what will be said to Psychofunctionalism rather than Functionalism. As already mentioned, every version of functionalism assumes *some* specification of inputs and outputs. A Functionalist specification would do as well for the purposes of what follows.

Imagine a body externally like a human body, say yours, but internally quite different. The neurons from sensory organs are connected to a bank of lights in a hollow cavity in the head. A set of buttons connects to the motor-output neurons. Inside the cavity resides a group of little men. Each has a very simple task: to implement a "square" of an adequate machine table that describes you. On one wall is a bulletin board on which is posted a state card; that is, a card that bears a smybol designating one of the states specified in the machine table. Here is what the little men do: Suppose the posted card has a 'G' on it. This alerts the little men who implement G squares—'G-men' they call themselves. Suppose the light representing input I_{17} goes on. One of the G-men has the following as his sole task: when the card reads 'G' and the I_{17} light goes on, he presses output button O_{191} and changes the state card to 'M'. This G-man is called upon to exercise his task only rarely. In spite of the low level of intelligence required of each little man, the system as a whole manages to simulate you because the functional organization they have been trained to realize is yours. A Turing machine can be represented as a finite set of quadruples (or quintuples, if the output is divided into two parts): current state, current input; next state, next output. Each little man has the task corresponding to a single quadruple. Through the efforts of the little men, the system realizes the same (reasonably adequate) machine table as you do and is thus functionally equivalent to you.[5]

I shall describe a version of the homunculi-headed simulation, which has more chance of being nomologically possible. How many homunculi are required? Perhaps a billion are enough.

Suppose we convert the government of China to functionalism, and we convince its officials ... to realize a human mind for an hour. We provide each of the billion people in China (I chose China because it has a billion inhabitants) with a specially designed two-way radio that connects them in the appropriate way to other persons and to the artificial body mentioned in the previous example. We replace each of the little men with a citizen of China plus his or her radio. Instead of a bulletin board, we arrange to have letters displayed on a series of satellites placed so that they can be seen from anywhere in China.

The system of a billion people communicating with one another plus satellites plays the role of an external "brain" connected to the artifical body by radio. There is nothing absurd about a person being connected to his brain by radio. Perhaps the day will come when our brains will be periodically removed for cleaning and repairs. Imagine that this is done initially by treating neurons attaching the brain to the body with a chemical that allows them to stretch like rubber bands, thereby assuring that no brain-body connections are disrupted. Soon clever businessmen discover that they can attract more customers by replacing the stretched neurons with radio links so that brains can be cleaned without inconveniencing the customer by immobilizing his body.

It is not at all obvious that the China-body system is physically impossible. It could be functionally equivalent to you for a short time, say an hour.

"But," you may object, "how could something be functionally equivalent to me for *an hour*? Doesn't my functional organization determine, say, how I would react to doing nothing for a week but reading the *Reader's Digest*?" Remember that a machine table specifies a set of conditionals of the form: if the machine is in S_i and receives input I_j, it emits output O_k and goes into S_1. These conditionals are to be understood *subjunctively*. What gives a system a functional organization at a time is not just what it *does* at that time, but also the counterfactuals true of it at that time: what it *would* have done (and what its state transitions would have been) had it had a different input or been in a different state. If it is true of a system at time t that it *would* obey a given machine table no matter which of the states it is in and no matter which of the inputs it receives, then the system is described at t by the machine table (and realizes at t the abstract automaton specified by the table), even if it exists for only an instant. For the hour the Chinese system is "on," it *does* have a set of inputs, outputs, and states of which such subjunctive conditionals are true. This is what makes any computer realize the abstract automaton that it realizes.

Of course, there are signals the system would respond to that you would not respond to—for example, massive radio interference or a flood of the Yangtze River. Such events might cause a malfunction, scotching the simulation, just as a bomb in a computer can make it fail to realize the machine table it was built to realize. But just as the computer *without* the bomb *can* realize the machine table, the system consisting of the people and artificial body can realize the machine table so long as there are no catastrophic interferences, such as floods, etc.

"But," someone may object, "there is a difference between a bomb in a computer and a bomb in the Chinese system, for in the case of the latter (unlike the former), inputs as specified in the machine table can be the cause of the malfunction. Unusual neural activity in the sense organs of residents of Chungking Province caused by a bomb or by a flood of the Yangtze can cause the system to go haywire."

Reply: The person who says what system he or she is talking about gets to say what signals count as inputs and outputs. I count as inputs and outputs only neural activity in the artificial body connected by radio to the people of China. Neural signals in the people of Chungking count no more as inputs to this system than input tape jammed by a saboteur between the relay contacts in the innards of a computer counts as an input to the computer.

Of course, the object consisting of the people of China + the artificial body has *other* Turing-machine descriptions under which neural signals in the inhabitants of Chungking *would* count as inputs. Such a new system (that is, the object under such a new Turing-machine description) would not be functionally equivalent to you. Likewise, any commercial computer can be redescribed in a way that allows tape jammed into its innards to count as inputs. In describing an object as a Turing machine, one draws a line between the inside and the outside. (If we count only neural impulses as inputs and outputs, we draw that line inside the body; if we count only peripheral stimulations as inputs, ... we draw that line at the skin.) In describing the Chinese system as a Turing machine, I have drawn the line in such a way that it satisfies a certain type of functional description—one that you *also* satisfy, and one that, according to functionalism, justifies attributions of mentality. Functionalism does not claim that every mental system has a machine table of a sort that justifies attributions of mentality with respect to *every* specification of inputs and outputs, but rather, only with respect to *some* specification.

Objection: The Chinese system would work too slowly. The kind of events and processes with which we normally have contact would pass by far too quickly for the system to detect them. Thus, we would be unable to converse with it, play bridge with it, etc.

Reply: It is hard to see why the system's time scale should matter. ... Is it really contradictory or nonsensical to suppose we could meet a race of intelligent beings with whom we could communicate only by devices such as time-lapse photography? When we observe these creatures, they seem almost inanimate. But when we view the time-lapse movies, we see them conversing with one another. Indeed, we find they are saying that the only way they can make any sense of us is by viewing movies greatly slowed down. To take time scale as all important seems crudely behavioristic. ...

What makes the homunculi-headed system (count the two systems as variants of a single system) just described a prima facie counterexample to (machine) functionalism is that there is prima facie doubt whether it has any mental states at all—especially whether it has what philosophers have variously called "qualitative states," "raw feels," or "immediate phenomenological qualities." (You ask: What is it that philosophers have called qualitative states? I answer, only half in jest: As Louis Armstrong said when asked what jazz is, "If you got to ask, you ain't never gonna get to know.") In Nagel's terms (1974), there is a prima facie doubt whether there is anything which it is like to be the homunculi-headed system.[6] ...

Putnam's Proposal

One way functionalists can try to deal with the problem posed by the homunculi-headed counterexamples is by the ad hoc device of stipulating them away. For example, a functionalist might stipulate that two systems cannot be functionally equivalent if one contains parts with functional organizations characteristic of sentient beings and the other does not. In his article hypothesizing that pain is a functional state, Putnam stipulated that "no organism capable of feeling pain possesses a decomposition into parts which separately possess Descriptions" (as the sort of Turing machine which can be in the functional state Putnam identifies with pain). The purpose of this condition is "to rule out such 'organisms' (if they count as such) as swarms of bees as single pain feelers" (Putnam 1967, pp. 434–435).

One way of filling out Putnam's requirement would be: a pain-feeling organism cannot possess a decomposition into parts *all* of which have a functional organization characteristic of sentient beings. But this would not rule out my homunculi-headed example, since it has nonsentient parts, such as the mechanical body and sense organs. It will not do to go to the opposite extreme and require that *no* proper parts be sentient. Otherwise pregnant women and people with sentient parasites will fail to count as pain-feeling organisms. What seems to be important to examples like the homunculi-headed simulation I have described is that the sentient beings *play a crucial role* in giving the thing its functional organization. This suggests a version of Putnam's proposal which requires that a pain-feeling organism has a certain functional organization and that it has no parts which (1) themselves possess that sort of functional organization and also (2) play a crucial role in giving the whole system its functional organization.

Although this proposal involves the vague notion "crucial role," it is precise enough for us to see it will not do. Suppose there is a part of the universe that contains matter quite different from ours, matter that is infinitely divisible. In this part of the universe, there are intelligent creatures of many sizes, even humanlike creatures much smaller than our elementary particles. In an intergalactic expedition, these people discover the existence of our type of matter. For reasons known only to them, they decide to devote the next few hundred years to creating out of *their* matter substances with the chemical and physical characteristics (except at the subelementary particle level) of *our* elements. They build hordes of space ships of different varieties about the sizes of our electrons, protons, and other elementary particles, and fly the ships in such a way as to mimic the behavior of these elementary particles. The ships also contain generators to produce the type of radiation elementary particles give off. Each ship has a staff of experts on the nature of our elementary particles. They do this so as to produce huge (by our standards) masses of substances with the chemical and physical characteristics of oxygen, carbon, etc. Shortly after they accomplish this, you go off on an expedition to that part of the universe, and discover the "oxygen," "carbon," etc. Unaware of its real nature, you set up a colony, using these "elements" to grow plants for food, provide "air" to breathe, etc. Since one's molecules are constantly being exchanged with the environment, you and other colonizers come (in a period of a few years) to be composed mainly of the "matter" made of the tiny people in space ships. Would you be any less capable of feeling pain, thinking, etc. just because the matter of which you are composed contains (and depends on for its characteristics) beings who themselves have a functional organization characteristic of sentient creatures? I think not. The basic electrochemical mechanisms by which the synpase operates are now fairly well understood. As far as is known, changes that do not affect these electrochemical mechanisms do not affect the operation of the brain, and do not affect mentality. The electrochemical mechanisms in your synapses would be unaffected by the change in your matter.[7]

It is interesting to compare the elementary-particle-people example with the homunculi-headed examples the chapter started with. A natural first guess about the source of our intuition that the initially described homunculi-headed simulations lack mentality is that they have *too much* internal mental structure. The little men may be sometimes bored, sometimes excited. We may even imagine that they deliberate about the best way to realize the given functional organization and make changes intended to give them more leisure time. But the example of the elementary-particle people just described suggests this first guess is wrong. What seems important is *how* the mentality of the parts contributes to the functioning of the whole.

There is one very noticeable difference between the elementary-particle-people example and the earlier homunculus examples. In the former, the change in you as you become homunculus-infested is not one that makes any difference to your psychological processing (that is, information processing) or neurological processing but only to your microphysics. No techniques proper to human psychology or neurophysiology would reveal any difference in you. However, the homunculi-headed simulations described in the beginning of the chapter are not things to which neurophysiological theories true of us apply, and *if they are construed as Functional* (rather than Psychofunctional) simulations, they need not be things to which psychological (information-processing) theories true of us apply. This difference suggest that our intuitions are in part controlled by the not unreasonable view that our mental states depend on our having the psychology and/or neurophysiology we have. So something that differs markedly from us in both regards (recall that it is a Functional rather than Psychofunctional simulation) should not be assumed to have mentality just on the ground that it has been designed to be Functionally equivalent to us.

Is the Prima Facie Doubt Merely Prima Facie?
The Absent Qualia Argument rested on an appeal to the intuition that the homunculi-headed simulations lacked mentality or at least qualia. I said that this intuition gave rise to prima facie doubt that functionalism is true. But intuitions unsupported by principled argument are hardly to be considered bedrock. Indeed, intuitions incompatible with well-supported theory (such as the pre-Copernican intuition that the earth does not move) thankfully soon disappear. Even fields like linguistics whose data consist mainly in intuitions often reject such intuitions as that the following sentences are ungrammatical (on theoretical grounds):

> The horse raced past the barn fell.
> The boy the girl the cat bit scratched died.

These sentences are in fact grammatical though hard to process.[8]

Appeal to intuitions when judging possession of mentality, however, is *especially* suspicious. *No* physical mechanism seems very intuitively plausible as a seat of qualia, least of all a *brain*. Is a hunk of quivering gray stuff more intuitively appropriate as a seat of qualia than a covey of little men? If not, perhaps there is a prima facie doubt about the qualia of brain-headed systems too?

However, there is a very important difference between brain-headed and homunculi-headed systems. Since we know that *we are brain-headed systems*, and that *we* have qualia, we know that brain-headed systems can have qualia. So even though we have no theory of qualia which explains how this is *possible*, we have overwhelming reason to disregard whatever prima facie doubt there is about the qualia of l rain-headed systems. Of course, this makes my argument partly *empirical*—it depends on knowledge of what makes us tick. But since this is knowledge we in fact possess, dependence on this knowledge should not be regarded as a defect.[9]

There is another difference between us meat-heads and the homunculi-heads: they are systems designed to mimic us, but we are not designed to mimic anything (here I rely on another empirical fact). This fact forestalls any attempt to argue on the basis of an inference to the best explanation for the qualia of homunculi-heads. The best explanation of the homunculi-heads' screams and winces is not their pains, but that they were designed to mimic our screams and winces.

Some people seem to feel that the complex and subtle behavior of the homunculi-heads (behavior just as complex and subtle—even as "sensitive" to features of the environment, human and nonhuman, as your behavior) is itself sufficient reason to disregard the prima facie doubt that homunculi-heads have qualia. But this is just crude behaviorism. . . .

My case against Functionalism depends on the following principle: if a doctrine has an absurd conclusion which there is no independent reason to believe, and if there is no way of explaining away the absurdity or showing it to be misleading or irrelevant, and if there is no good reason to believe the doctrine that leads to the absurdity in the first place, then don't accept the doctrine. I claim that there is no independent reason to believe in the mentality of the homunculi-head, and I know of no way of explaining away the absurdity of the conclusion that it has mentality (though of course, my argument is vulnerable to the introduction of such an explanation). The issue, then, is whether there is any good reason to believe Functionalism. One argument for Functionalism is that it is the best solution available to the mind-body problem. I think this is a bad form of argument, but since I also think that Psychofunctionalism is preferable to Functionalism (for reasons to be mentioned below), I'll postpone consideration of this form of argument to the discussion of Psychofunctionalism.

The only other argument for Functionalism that I know of is that Functional identities can be shown to be true on the basis of analyses of the meanings of mental terminology. According to this argument, Functional identities are to be justified in the way one might try to justify the claim that the state of being a bachelor is identical to the state of being an unmarried man. A similar argument appeals to commonsense platitudes about mental states instead of truths of meaning. Lewis says that functional characterizations of mental states are in the province of "commonsense psychology— folk science, rather than professional science" (Lewis 1972, p. 250). (See also Shoemaker 1975, and Armstrong 1968. Armstrong equivocates on the analyticity issue. See Armstrong 1968, pp. 84–5, and p. 90.) And he goes on to insist that Functional characterizations should "include only platitudes which are common knowledge among us—everyone knows them, everyone knows that everyone else knows them, and so on" (Lewis 1972, p. 256). I shall talk mainly about the "platitude" version of the argument. The analyticity version is vulnerable to essentially the same considerations, as well as Quinean doubts about analyticity. . . .

I am willing to concede, for the sake of argument, that it is possible to define any given mental state term in terms of platitudes concerning other mental state terms, input terms, and output terms. But this does not commit me to the type of definition of mental terms in which all mental terminology has been eliminated via Ramsification or some other device. It is simply a fallacy to suppose that if each mental term is definable in terms of the others (plus inputs and outputs), then each mental term is definable nonmentalistically. To see this, consider the example given earlier. Indeed, let's simplify matters by ignoring the inputs and outputs. Let's define pain as the cause of worry, and worry as the effect of pain. Even a person so benighted as to accept this needn't accept a definition of pain as *the cause of something*, or a definition of worry as *the effect of something*. Lewis claims that it is analytic that pain is the occupant of a certain causal role. Even if he is right about a causal role, specified in part mentalistically, one cannot conclude that it is analytic that pain is the occupant of any causal role, nonmentalistically specified.

I don't see any decent argument for Functionalism based on platitudes or analyticity. Further, the conception of Functionalism as based on platitudes leads to trouble with cases that platitudes have nothing to say about. Recall the example of brains being removed for cleaning and rejuvenation, the connections between one's brain and one's body being maintained by radio while one goes about one's business. The process takes a few days and when it is completed, the brain is reinserted in the body. Occasionally it may happen that a person's body is destroyed by an accident while the brain is being cleaned and rejuvenated. If hooked up to input sense organs (but not output organs) such a brain would exhibit *none* of the usual platitudinous connections between behavior and clusters of inputs and mental states. If, as seems plausible, such a brain could have almost all the same (narrow) mental states as we have (and since such a state of affairs could become typical), Functionalism is wrong.

It is instructive to compare the way Psychofunctionalism attempts to handle brains in bottles. According to Psychofunctionalism, what is to count as a system's inputs and outputs is an empirical question. Counting neural impulses as inputs and outputs would avoid the problems just sketched, since the brains in bottles and paralytics could have the right neural impulses even without bodily movements. Objection: There could be paralysis that affects the nervous system, and thus affects the neural impulses, so the problem which arises for Functionalism arises for Psychofunctionalism as well. Reply: Nervous system diseases can actually *change mentality*: for example they can render victims incapable of having pain. So it might actually be true that a widespread nervous system disease that caused intermittent paralysis rendered people incapable of certain mental states.

According to plausible versions of Psychofunctionalism, the job of deciding what neural processes should count as inputs and outputs is in part a matter of deciding *what malfunctions count as changes in mentality and what malfunctions count as changes in peripheral input and output connections*. Psychofunctionalism has a resource that Functionalism does not have, since Psychofunctionalism allows us to *adjust the line we draw between the inside and the outside of the organism so as to avoid problems of the sort discussed*. All versions of Functionalism go wrong in attempting to draw this line on the basis of only commonsense knowledge; "analyticity" versions of Functionalism go especially wrong in attempting to draw the line a priori.

Psychofunctionalism

In criticizing Functionalism, I appealed to the following principle: if a doctrine has an absurd conclusion which there is no independent reason to believe, and if there is no way of explaining away the absurdity or showing it it to be misleading or irrelevant, and if there is no good reason to believe the doctrine that leads to the absurdity in the first place, then don't accept the doctrine. I said that there was no independent reason to believe that the homunculi-headed Functional simulation has any mental states. However, there *is* an independent reason to believe that the homunculi-headed *Psycho*functional simulation has mental states, namely that a Psychofunctional simulation of you would be Psychofunctionally equivalent to you, so any psychological theory true of you would be true of it too. What better reason could there be to attribute to it whatever mental states are in the domain of psychology?

This point shows that any Psychofunctional simulation of you shares your *non*-qualitative mental states. However, in the next section I shall argue that there is nonetheless some doubt that it shares your qualitative mental states.

Are Qualia Psychofunctional States?
I began this chapter by describing a homunculi-headed device and claiming there is prima facie doubt about whether it has any mental states at all, especially whether it has qualitative mental states like pains, itches, and sensations of red. The special doubt about qualia can perhaps be explicated by thinking about *inverted* qualia rather than *absent* qualia. It makes sense, or seems to make sense, to suppose that objects we both call green look to me the way objects we both call red look to you. It seems that we could be functionally equivalent even though the sensation fire hydrants evoke in you is qualitatively the same as the sensation grass evokes in me. Imagine an inverting lens which when placed in the eye of a subject results in exclamations like "Red things now look the way green things used to look, and vice versa." Imagine further, a pair of identical twins one of whom has the lenses inserted at birth. The twins grow up normally, and at age 21 are functionally equivalent. This situation offers at least some evidence that each's spectrum is inverted relative to the other's. (See Shoemaker 1975, note 17, for a convincing description of intrapersonal spectrum inversion.) However, it is very hard to see how to make sense of the analog of spectrum inversion with respect to nonqualitative states. Imagine a pair of persons one of whom believes that p is true and that q is false while the other believes that q is true and that p is false. Could these persons be functionally equivalent? It is hard to see how they could.[10] Indeed, it is hard to see how two persons could have only this difference in beliefs and yet there be no possible circumstance in which this belief difference would reveal itself in different behavior. Qualia seem to be supervenient on functional organization in a way that beliefs are not . . .

There is another reason to firmly distinguish between qualitative and nonqualitative mental states in talking about functionalist theories: Psychofunctionalism avoids Functionalism's problems with nonqualitative states—for example propositional attitudes like beliefs and desires. But Psychofunctionalism may be no more able to handle qualitative states than is Functionalism. The reason is that qualia may well not be in the domain of psychology.

To see this let us try to imagine what a homunculi-headed realization of human psychology would be like. Current psychological theorizing seems directed toward the description of information-flow relations among psychological mechanisms. The aim seems to be to decompose such mechanisms into psychologically primitive mechanisms, "black boxes" whose internal structure is in the domain of physiology rather than in the domain of psychology. (See Fodor 1968, Dennett 1975, and Cummins 1975; interesting objections are raised in Nagel 1969.) For example, a near-primitive mechanism might be one that matches two items in a representational system and determines if they are tokens of the same type. Or the primitive mechanisms might be like those in a digital computer—for example, they might be (a) *add 1 to a given register*, and (b) *subtract 1 from a given register, or if the register contains 0, go to the nth (indicated) instruction*. (These operations can be combined to accomplish any digital computer operation; see

Minsky 1967, p. 206.) Consider a computer whose machine-language code contains only two instructions corresponding to (a) and (b). If you ask how it multiplies or solves differential equations or makes up payrolls, you can be answered by being shown a program couched in terms of the two machine-language instructions. But if you ask how it adds 1 to a given register, the appropriate answer is given by a wiring diagram, not a program. The machine is hard-wired to add 1. When the instruction corresponding to (a) appears in a certain register, the contents of another register "automatically" change in a certain way. The computational structure of a computer is determined by a set of primitive operations and the ways nonprimitive operations are built up from them. Thus it does not matter to the computational structure of the computer whether the primitive mechanisms are realized by tube circuits, transistor circuits, or relays. Likewise, it does not matter to the psychology of a mental system whether its primitive mechanisms are realized by one or another neurological mechanism. Call a system a "realization of human psychology" if every psychological theory true of us is true of it. Consider a realization of human psychology whose primitive psychological operations are accomplished by little men, in the manner of the homunculi-headed simulations discussed. So, perhaps one little man produces items from a list, one by one, another compares these items with other representations to determine whether they match, etc.

Now there is good reason for supposing this system has some mental states. Propositional attitudes are an example. Perhaps psychological theory will identify remembering that P with having "stored" a sentencelike object which expresses the proposition that P (Fodor 1975). Then if one of the little men has put a certain sentencelike object in "storage," we may have reason for regarding the system as remembering that P. But unless having qualia is just a matter of having certain information processing (at best a controversial proposal), there is no such theoretical reason for regarding the system as having qualia. In short, there is perhaps as much doubt about the qualia of this homunculi-headed system as there was about the qualia of the homunculi-headed Functional simulation discussed early in the chapter.

But the system we are discussing is *ex hypothesi* something of which any true psychological theory is true. *So any doubt that it has qualia is a doubt that qualia are in the domain of psychology.*

It may be objected: "The kind of psychology you have in mind is *cognitive* psychology, that is, psychology of thought processes; and it is no wonder that qualia are not in the domain of *cognitive* psychology!" But I *do not* have cognitive psychology in mind, and if it sounds that way, this is easily explained: nothing we know about the psychological processes underlying our conscious mental life has anything to do with qualia. What passes for the "psychology" of sensation or pain, for example, is (a) physiology, (b) psychophysics (that is, the study of the mathematical functions relating stimulus variables and sensation variables; for example, the intensity of sound as a function of the amplitude of the sound waves), or (c) a grab bag of descriptive studies (see Melzack 1973, ch. 2). Of these, only psychophysics could be construed as being about qualia *per se*. And it is obvious that psychophysics touches only the *functional* aspect of sensation, not its qualitative character. Psychophysical experiments done on you would have the same results if done on any system Psychofunctionally equivalent to you, even if it had inverted or absent qualia. If experimental results would be unchanged whether or not the experimental subjects have inverted or absent qualia, they can hardly be expected to cast light on the nature of qualia.

Indeed, on the basis of the kind of conceptual apparatus now available in psychology, I do not see how psychology in anything like its present incarnation *could* explain qualia. We cannot now conceive how psychology could explain qualia, though we *can* conceive how psychology could explain believing, desiring, hoping, etc. (see Fodor 1975). That something is currently inconceivable is not a good reason to think it is impossible. Concepts could be developed tomorrow that would make what is now inconceivable conceivable. But all we have to go on is what we know, and on the basis of what we have to go on, it looks as if qualia are not in the domain of psychology. . . .

It is no objection to the suggestion that qualia are not psychological entities that qualia are the very paradigm of something in the domain of psychology. As has often been pointed out, it is in part an empirical question what is in the domain of any particular branch of science. The liquidity of water turns out not to be explainable by chemistry, but rather by subatomic physics. Branches of science have at any given time a set of phenomena they seek to explain. But it can be discovered that some phenomenon which seemed central to a branch of science is actually in the purview of a different branch. . . .

The Absent Qualia Argument exploits the possibility that the Functional or Psychofunctional state Functionalists or Psychofunctionalists would want to identify with pain can occur without any quale occurring. It also seems to be conceivable that the latter occur without the former. Indeed, there are facts that lend plausibility to this view. After frontal lobotomies, patients typically report that they still have pains, though the pains no longer bother them (Melzack 1973, p. 95). These patients show all the "sensory" signs of pain (such as recognizing pin pricks as sharp), but they often have little or no desire to avoid "painful" stimuli.

One view suggested by these observations is that each pain is actually a *composite* state whose components are a quale and a Functional or Psychofunctional state.[11] Or what amounts to much the same idea, each pain is a quale playing a certain Functional or Psychofunctional role. If this view is right, it helps to explain how people can have believed such different theories of the nature of pain and other sensations; they have emphasized one component at the expense of the other. Proponents of behaviorism and functionalism have had one component in mind; proponents of private ostensive definition have had the other in mind. Both approaches err in trying to give one account of something that has two components of quite different natures.

Chauvinism vs. Liberalism

It is natural to understand the psychological theories Psychofunctionalism adverts to as theories of *human* psychology. On Psychofunctionalism, so understood, it is impossible for a system to have beliefs, desires, etc., except in so far as psychological theories true of us are true of it. Psychofunctionalism (so understood) stipulates that Psychofunctional equivalence to us is necessary for mentality.

But even if Psychofunctional equivalence to us is a condition on our *recognition of mentality*, what reason is there to think it is a condition on mentality itself? Could there not be a wide variety of possible psychological processes that can underlie mentality, of which we instantiate only one type? Suppose we meet Martians and find that they are roughly Functionally (but not Psychofunctionally) equivalent to us. When we get to know Martians, we find them about as different from us as humans we know. We develop extensive cultural and commercial intercourse with them. We study each other's science and philosophy journals, go to each other's movies, read each other's novels, etc. Then Martian and Earthian psychologists compare notes, only to find that in underlying psychology, Martians and Earthians are very different. They soon agree that the difference can be described as follows. Think of humans and Martians as if they were products of conscious design. In any such design project, there will be various options. Some capacities can be built in (innate), others learned. The brain can be designed to accomplish tasks using as much memory capacity as necessary in order to minimize use of computation capacity; or, on the other hand, the designer could choose to conserve memory space and rely mainly on computation capacity. Inferences can be accomplished by systems which use a few axioms and many rules of inference, or, on the other hand, few rules and many axioms. Now imagine that what Martian and Earthian psychologists find when they compare notes is that Martians and Earthians differ as if they were the end products of maximally different design choices (compatible with rough Functional equivalence in adults). Should we reject our assumption that Martains can enjoy our films, believe their own apparent scientific results, etc.? Should they "reject" their "assumption" that we "enjoy" their novels, "learn" from their textbooks, etc.? Perhaps I have not provided enough information to answer this question. After all, there may be many ways of filling in the description of the Martian-human differences in which it would be reasonable to suppose there simply is no fact of the matter, or even to suppose that the Martians do not deserve mental ascriptions. But surely there are many ways of filling in the description of the Martian-Earthian difference I sketched on which it would be perfectly clear that even if Martains behave differently from us on subtle psychological experiments, they none the less think, desire, enjoy, etc. To suppose otherwise would be crude human chauvinism. (Remember theories are chauvinist in so far as they falsely *deny* that systems have mental properties and liberal in so far as they falsely *attribute* mental properties.) . . .

An obvious suggestion of a way out of this difficulty is to identify mental states with Psychofunctional states, taking the domain of psychology to include *all creatures with mentality*, including Martians. The suggestion is that we define "Psychofunctionalism" in terms of "universal" or "cross-system" psychology, rather than the human psychology I assumed earlier. Universal psychology however, is a suspect enterprise. For how are we to decide what systems should be included in the *domain* of universal psychology? One possible way of deciding what systems have mentality, and are thus in the domain of universal psychology, would be to use some *other* developed theory of mentality such as behaviorism or Functionalism. But such a procedure would be at least as ill-justified as the other theory used. Further, if Psychofunctionalism must presuppose some other theory of mind, we might just as well accept the other theory of mind instead.

Perhaps universal psychology will avoid this "domain" problem in the same way other branches of science avoid it or seek to avoid it. Other branches of science start with tentative domains based on intuitive and prescientific versions of the concepts the sciences are supposed to explicate. They then attempt to develop natural kinds in a way which allows the formulations of lawlike generalizations which apply to all or most of the entities in the prescientific domains. In the case of many branches of science—including biological and social sciences such as genetics and linguistics—the prescientific domain turned out to be suitable for the articulation of lawlike generalizations.

Now it may be that we shall be able to develop universal psychology in much the same way we develop Earthian psychology. We decide on an intuitive and prescientific basis what creatures to include in its domain, and work to develop natural kinds of psychological theory which apply to all or at least most of them. Perhaps the study of a wide range of organisms found on different worlds will one day lead to theories that determine truth conditions for the attribution of mental states like belief, desire, etc., applicable to systems which are pretheoretically quite different from us. Indeed, such cross-world psychology will no doubt require a whole new range of mentalistic concepts. Perhaps there will be families of concepts corresponding to belief, desire, etc.; that is, a family of belief-like concepts, desire-like concepts, etc. If so, the universal psychology we develop shall, no doubt, be somewhat dependent on which new organisms we discover first. Even if universal psychology is in fact possible, however, there will certainly be many possible organisms whose mental status is indeterminate.

On the other hand, it may be that universal psychology is *not* possible. Perhaps life in the universe is such that we shall simply have no basis for reasonable decisions about what systems are in the domain of psychology and what systems are not.

If universal psychology *is* possible, the problem I have been raising vanishes. Universal-Psychofunctionalism avoids the liberalism of Functionalism and the chauvinism of human-Psychofunctionalism. But the question of whether universal psychology is possible is surely one which we have no way of answering now.

Here is a summary of the argument so far:

1. Functionalism has the bizarre consequence that a homunculi-headed simulation of you has qualia. This puts the burden of proof on the Functionalist to give us some reason for believing his doctrine. However, the one argument for Functionalism in the literature is no good, and so Functionalism shows no sign of meeting the burden of proof.

2. Psychofunctional simulations of us share whatever states are in the domain of psychology, so the Psychofunctional homunculi-head does not cast doubt on Psychofunctional theories of cognitive states, but only on Psychofunctionalist theories of qualia, there being a doubt as to whether qualia are in the domain of psychology.

3. Psychofunctionalist theories of mental states that are in the domain of psychology, however, are hopelessly chauvinist.

So one version of functionalism has problems with liberalism, the other has problems with chauvinism. As to qualia, if they are in the domain of psychology, then Psychofunctionalism with respect to qualia is just as chauvinist as Psychofunctionalism with respect to belief. On the other hand, if qualia are not in the domain of psychology, the Psychofunctionalist homunculi-head can be used against Psychofunctionalism with respect to qualia. For the only thing that shields Psychofunctionalism with respect to mental state S from the homunculi-head argument is that if you have S, then any Psychofunctional simulation of you must have S, because the correct theory of S applies to it just as well as to you.

The Problem of the Inputs and the Outputs

I have been supposing all along (as Psychofunctionalists often do—see Putnam 1967) that inputs and outputs can be specified by neural impulse descriptions. But this is a chauvinist claim, since it precludes organisms without neurons (such as machines) from having functional descriptions. How can one avoid chauvinism with respect to specification of inputs and outputs? One way would be to characterize the inputs and outputs *only as* inputs and outputs. So the functional description of a person might list outputs by number: $output_1$, $output_2$, ... Then a system could be functionally equivalent to you if it had a set of states, inputs, and outputs causally related to one another in the way yours are, no matter what the states, inputs, and outputs were like. Indeed, though this approach violates the demand of some functionalists that inputs and outputs be physically specified, other functionalists—those who insist only that input and output descriptions be *nonmental*—may have had something like this in mind. This version of functionalism does not "tack down" functional descriptions at the periphery with relatively specific decriptions of inputs and outputs; rather, this version of functionalism treats inputs and outputs just as all versions of functionalism treat internal states. That is, this version specifies states, inputs, and outputs only by requiring that they *be* states, inputs, and outputs.

The trouble with this version of functionalism is that it is wildly liberal. Economic systems have inputs and outputs, such as influx and outflux of credits and debits. And economic systems also have a rich variety of internal states, such as having a rate of increase of GNP equal to double the Prime Rate. It does not seem impossible that a wealthy sheik could gain control of the economy of a small country, for example Bolivia, and manipulate its financial system to make it functionally equivalent to a person, for example himself. If this seems implausible, remember that the economic states, inputs, and outputs designated by the sheik to correspond to his mental states, inputs, and outputs need not be "natural" economic magnitudes. Our hypothetical sheik could pick *any* economic magnitudes at all—for example, the fifth time derivative of the balance of payments. His only constraint is that the magnitudes he picks be economic, that their having such-and-such values be inputs, outputs, and states, and that he be able to set up a financial structure which can be made to fit the intended formal mold. The mapping from psychological magnitudes to economic magnitudes could be as bizarre as the sheik requires.

This version of functionalism is far too liberal and must therefore be rejected. If there are any fixed points when discussing the mind-body problem, one of them is that the economy of Bolivia could not have mental states, no matter how it is distorted by powerful hobbyists. Obviously, we must be more specific in our descriptions of inputs and outputs. The question is: is there a description of inputs and outputs specific enough to avoid liberalism, yet general enough to avoid chauvinism? I doubt that there is.

Every proposal for a description of inputs and outputs I have seen or thought of is guilty of either liberalism or chauvinism. Though this paper has concentrated on liberalism, chauvinism is the more pervasive problem. Consider standard Functional and Psychofunctional descriptions. Functionalists tend to specify inputs and outputs in the manner of behaviorists: outputs in terms of movements of arms and legs, sound emitted and the like; inputs in terms of light and sound falling on the eyes and ears. ... Such descriptions are blatantly *species-specific*. Humans have arms and legs, but snakes do not—and whether or not snakes have mentality, one can easily imagine snake-like creatures that do. Indeed, one can imagine creatures with all manner of input-output devices, for example creatures that communicate and manipulate by emitting strong magnetic fields. Of course, one could formulate Functional descriptions for each such species, and somewhere in disjunctive heaven there is a disjunctive description which will handle all species that ever actually exist in the universe (the description may be infinitely long). But even an appeal to such suspicious entities as infinite disjunctions will not bail out Functionalism, since even the amended view will not tell us what there is in common to pain-feeling organisms in virtue of which they all have pain. And it will not allow the ascription of pain to some hypothetical (but nonexistent) pain-feeling creatures. Further, these are just the grounds on which functionalists typically acerbically reject the disjunctive theories sometimes advanced by desperate physicalists. If functionalists suddenly smile on wildly disjunctive states to save themselves from chauvinism, they will have no way of defending themselves from physicalism.

Standard Psychofunctional descriptions of inputs and outputs are also species-specific (for example in terms of neural activity) and hence chauvinist as well.

The chauvinism of standard input-output descriptions is not hard to explain. The variety of possible intelligent life is enormous. Given any fairly specific descriptions of inputs and outputs, any high-school-age science-fiction buff will be able to describe a sapient sentient being whose inputs and outputs fail to satisfy that description.

I shall argue that *any physical description* of inputs and outputs (recall that many functionalists have insisted on physical descriptions) yields a version of functionalism that is inevitably chauvinist or liberal. Imagine yourself so badly burned in a fire that your optimal way of communicating with the outside world is via modulations of your EEG pattern in Morse Code. You find that thinking an exciting thought produces a pattern that your audience agrees to interpret as a dot, and a dull thought produces a "dash". Indeed, this fantasy is not so far from reality. According to a recent newspaper article (*Boston Globe*, 21 March 1976), "at UCLA scientists are working on the use of EEG to control machines. . . . A subject puts electrodes on his scalp, and thinks an object through a maze." The "reverse" process is also presumably possible: others communicating with you in Morse Code by producing bursts of electrical activity that affect your brain (for example causing a long or short afterimage). Alternatively, if the cerebroscopes that philosophers often fancy become a reality, your thoughts will be readable directly from your brain. Again, the reverse process also seems possible. In these cases, *the brain itself becomes an essential part of one's input and output devices.* This possibility has embarrassing consequences for functionalists. You will recall that functionalists pointed out that physicalism is false because a single mental state can be realized by an indefinitely large variety of physical states that have no necessary and sufficient physical characterization. But if this functionalist point against physicalism is right, *the same point applies to inputs and outputs,* since the physical realization of mental states can serve as an essential part of the input and output devices. That is, on any sense of 'physical' in which the functionalist criticism of physicalism is correct, *there will be no physical characterization that applies to all and only mental systems' inputs and outputs.* Hence, any attempt to formulate a functional description with physical characterizations of inputs and outputs will inevitably either exclude some systems with mentality or include some systems without mentality. Hence, . . . *functionalists cannot avoid both chauvinism and liberalism.*

So physical specifications of inputs and outputs will not do. Moreover, mental or "action" terminology (such as "punching the offending person") cannot be used either, since to use such specifications of inputs or outputs would be to give up the functionalist program of characterizing mentality in nonmental terms. On the other hand, as you will recall, characterizing inputs and ouputs simply *as* inputs and outputs is inevitably liberal. I, for one, do not see how there can be a vocabulary for describing inputs and outputs that avoids both liberalism and chauvinism. I do not claim that this is a conclusive argument against functionalism. Rather, like the functionalist argument against physicalism, it is best construed as a burden-of-proof argument. The functionalist says to the physicalist: "It is very hard to see how there could be a single physical characterization of the internal states of all and only creatures with mentality." I say to the functionalist: "It is very hard to see how there could be a single physical characterization of the inputs and outputs of all and only creatures with mentality." In both cases, enough has been said to make it the responsibility of those who think there could be such characterizations to sketch how they could be possible.[12]

Notes

1. See Fodor 1965; Lewis 1972; Putnam 1966, 1967, 1970, 1975a; Armstrong 1968; Locke 1968; perhaps Sellars 1968; perhaps Dennett 1969, 1978b; Nelson 1969, 1975 (but see also Nelson 1976); Pitcher 1971; Smart 1971; Block and Fodor 1972; Harman 1973; Grice 1975; Shoemaker 1975; Wiggins 1975.

2. The converse is also true.

3. Indeed, if one defines 'behaviorism' as the view that mental terms can be defined in nonmental terms, then functionalism *is* a version of behaviorism....

4. State type, not state token. Throughout the chapter, I shall mean by 'physicalism' the doctrine that says each distinct type of mental state is identical to a distinct type of physical state; for example, pain (the universal) is a physical state. Token physicalism, on the other hand, is the (weaker) doctrine that each particular datable pain is a state of some physical type or other. Functionalism shows that type physicalism is false, but it does not show that token physicalism is false.

   By 'physicalism', I mean *first-order* physicalism, the doctrine that, e.g., the property of being in pain is a first-order (in the Russell-Whitehead sense) physical property. (A first-order property is one whose definition does not require quantification over properties; a second-order property is one whose definition requires quantification over first-order properties—and not other properties.) The claim that being in pain is a second-order physical property is actually a (physicalist) form of functionalism. See Putnam 1970.

5. The basic idea for this example derives from Putnam (1967). I am indebted to many conversations with Hartry Field on the topic. Putnam's attempt to defend functionalism from the problem posed by such examples is discussed in the section entitled Putnam's Proposal of this chapter.

6. Shoemaker (1975) argues (in reply to Block and Fodor 1972) that absent qualia are logically impossible; that is, that it is logically impossible that two systems be in the same functional state yet one's state have and the other's state lack qualitative content....

7. Since there is a difference between the role of the little people in producing your functional organization in the situation just described and the role of the homunculi in the homunculi-headed simulations this chapter began with, presumably Putnam's condition could be reformulated to rule out the latter without ruling out the former. But this would be a most *ad hoc* maneuver.

8. Compare the first sentence with 'The fish eaten in Boston stank.' The reason it is hard to process is that 'raced' is naturally read as active rather than passive. See Fodor et al., 1974, p. 360. For a discussion of why the second sentence is grammatical, see Fodor and Garrett 1967, Bever 1970, and Fodor et al., 1974.

9. We often fail to be able to conceive of how something is possible because we lack the relevant theoretical concepts. For example, before the discovery of the mechanism of genetic duplication, Haldane argued persuasively that no conceivable physical mechanism could do the job. He was right. But instead of urging that scientists should develop ideas that would allow us to conceive of such a physical mechanism, he concluded that a *non*physical mechanism was involved. (I owe the example to Richard Boyd.)

10. Suppose a man who has good color vision mistakenly uses 'red' to denote green and 'green' to denote red. That is, he simply confuses the two words. Since his confusion is purely linguistic, though he says of a green thing that it is red, he does not *believe* that it is red, any more than a foreigner who has confused 'ashcan' with 'sandwich' believes people eat ashcans for lunch. Let us say that the person who has confused 'red' and 'green' in this way is a victim of Word Switching.

    Now consider a different ailment: having red/green inverting lenses placed in your eyes without your knowledge. Let us say a victim of this ailment is a victim of Stimulus Switching. Like the victim of Word Switching, the victim of Stimulus Switching applies 'red' to green things and vice versa. But the victim of Stimulus Switching *does* have false color beliefs. If you show him a green patch he says *and believes* that it is red.

    Now suppose that a victim of Stimulus Switching suddenly becomes a victim of Word Switching as well. (Suppose as well that he is a lifelong resident of a remote Arctic village, and has no standing beliefs to the effect that grass is green, fire hydrants are red, and so forth.) He speaks normally, applying 'green' to green patches and 'red' to red patches. Indeed, he is functionally normal. But his *beliefs* are just as abnormal as they were before he became a victim of Word Switching. Before he confused the words 'red' and 'green', he applied 'red' to a green patch, and mistakenly believed the patch to be red. Now he (correctly) says 'red', but his belief is still wrong.

    So two people can be functionally the same, yet have incompatible beliefs. Hence, the inverted qualia problem infects belief as well as qualia (though presumably only qualitative belief). This fact should be of concern not only to those who hold functional state identity theories of belief, but also to those who are attracted by Harman-style accounts of meaning as functional role. Our double victim—

of Word and Stimulus Switching—is a counterexample to such accounts. For his word 'green' plays the normal role in his reasoning and inference, yet since in saying of something that it "is green," he expresses his belief that it is *red*, he uses 'green' with an abnormal meaning. I am indebted to Sylvain Bromberger for discussion of this issue.

11. The quale might be identified with a physico-chemical state. This view would comport with a suggestion Hilary Putnam made in the late 1960s in his philosophy of mind seminar. See also ch. 5 of Gunderson 1971.

12. I am indebted to Sylvain Bromberger, Hartry Field, Jerry Fodor, David Hills, Paul Horwich, Bill Lycan, Georges Rey, and David Rosenthal for their detailed comments on one or another earlier draft of this paper. Beginning in the fall of 1975, parts of earlier versions were read at Tufts University, Princeton University, the University of North Carolina at Greensboro, and the State University of New York at Binghamton.

References

Armstrong, D. (1968) *A materialist theory of mind*. London: Routledge & Kegan Paul.

Bever, T. (1970) "The cognitive basis for linguistic structures," in J. R. Hayes (ed.), *Cognition and the Development of Language*. New York: Wiley.

Block, N. (1980) "Are absent qualia impossible?" *Philosophical Review*, 89(2).

Block, N. and Fodor, J. (1972) "What psychological states are not," *Philosophical Review*, 81, 159–81.

Chisholm, Roderick (1957) *Perceiving*. Ithaca: Cornell University Press.

Cummins, R. (1975) "Functional analysis," *Journal of Philosophy*, 72, 741–64.

Davidson, D. (1970) "Mental events," in L. Swanson and J. W. Foster (eds), *Experience and Theory*. Amherst: University of Massachusetts Press.

Dennett, D. (1969) *Content and Consciousness*. London: Routledge & Kegan Paul.

Dennett, D. (1975) "Why the law of effect won't go away," *Journal for the Theory of Social Behavior*, 5, 169–87.

Dennett, D. (1978a) "Why a computer can't feel pain," *Synthese*, 38, 3.

Dennett, D. (1978b) *Brainstorms*, Montgomery, Vt.: Bradford.

Feldman, F. (1973) "Kripke's argument against materialism," *Philosophical Studies*, 416–19.

Fodor, J. (1965) "Explanations in psychology," in M. Black (ed.), *Philosophy in America*. London: Routledge & Kegan Paul.

Fodor, J. (1968) "The appeal to tacit knowledge in psychological explanation," *Journal of Philosophy*, 65, 627–40.

Fodor, J. (1974) "Special sciences," *Synthese*, 28, 97–115.

Fodor, J. (1975) *The Language of Thought*. New York: Crowell.

Fodor, J., Bever, T. and Garrett, M. (1974) *The Psychology of Language*. New York: McGraw-Hill.

Fodor, J. and Garrett, M. (1967) "Some syntactic determinants of sentential complexity," *Perception and Psychophysics*, 2, 289–96.

Geach, P. (1957) *Mental Acts*. London: Routledge & Kegan Paul.

Gendron, B. (1971) "On the relation of neurological and psychological theories: A critique of the hardware thesis," in R. C. Buck and R. S. Cohen (eds), *Boston Studies in the Philosophy of Science VIII*. Dordrecht: Reidel.

Grice, H. P. (1975) "Method in philosophical psychology (from the banal to the bizarre)," *Proceedings and Addresses of the American Philosophical Association*.

Gunderson, K. (1971) *Mentality and Machines*. Garden City: Doubleday Anchor.

Harman, G. (1973) *Thought*. Princeton: Princeton University Press.

Hempel, C. (1970) "Reduction: Ontological and linguistic facets," in S. Morgenbesser, P. Suppes and M. White (eds), *Essays in Honor of Ernest Nagel*. New York: St. Martins Press.

Kalke, W. (1969) "What is wrong with Fodor and Putnam's functionalism?" *Noûs*, 3, 83–93.

Kim, J. (1972) "Phenomenal properties, psychophysical laws, and the identity theory," *The Monist*, 56(2), 177–92.

Lewis, D. (1972) "Psychophysical and theoretical identifications," *Australasian Journal of Philosophy*, 50(3), 249–58.

Locke, D. (1968) *Myself and Others*. Oxford: Oxford University Press.

Melzack, R. (1973) *The Puzzle of Pain*. New York: Basic Books.

Minsky, M. (1967) *Computation*. Englewood Cliffs NJ: Prentice-Hall.

Mucciolo, L. F. (1974) "The identity thesis and neuropsychology," *Noûs*, 8, 327–42.

Nagel, T. (1969) "The boundaries of inner space," *Journal of Philosophy*, 66, 452–8.

Nagel, T. (1970) "Armstrong on the mind," *Philosophical Review*, 79, 394–403.

Nagel, T. (1972) "Review of Dennett's *Content and Consciousness*," *Journal of Philosophy*, 50, 220–34.

Nagel, T. (1974) "What is it like to be a bat?" *Philosophical Review*, 83, 435–50.

Nelson, R. J. (1969) "Behaviorism is false," *Journal of Philosophy*, 66, 417–52.

Nelson, R. J. (1975) "Behaviorism, finite automata and stimulus response theory," *Theory and Decision*, 6, 249–67.

Nelson, R. J. (1976) "Mechanism, functionalism, and the identity theory," *Journal of Philosophy*, 73, 365–86.

Oppenheim, P. and Putnam, H. (1958) "Unity of science as a working hypothesis," in H. Feigl, M. Scriven and G. Maxwell (eds), *Minnesota Studies in the Philosophy of Science II*. Minneapolis: University of Minnesota Press.

Pitcher, G. (1971) *A Theory of Perception*. Princeton: Princeton University Press.

Putnam, H. (1963) "Brains and behavior"; reprinted as are all Putnam's articles referred to here (except "On properties") in *Mind, Language and Reality: Philosophical Papers*, vol. 2. London: Cambridge University Press, 1975.

Putnam, H. (1966) "The mental life of some machines".

Putnam, H. (1967) "The nature of mental states" (originally published under the title "Psychological Predicates").

Putnam, H. (1970) "On properties," in *Mathematics, Matter and Method: Philosophical Papers*, vol. 1. London: Cambridge University Press.

Putnam, H. (1975a) "Philosophy and our mental life".

Putnam, H. (1975b) "The meaning of 'meaning'."

Rorty, R. (1972) "Functionalism, machines and incorrigibility," *Journal of Philosophy*, 69, 203–20.

Scriven, M. (1966) *Primary Philosophy*. New York: McGraw-Hill.

Sellars, W. (1956) "Empiricism and the philosophy of mind," in H. Feigl and M. Scriven (eds), *Minnesota Studies in Philosophy of Science I*. Minneapolis: University of Minnesota Press.

Sellars, W. (1968) *Science and Metaphysics* (ch. 6). London: Routledge & Kegan Paul.

Shoemaker, S. (1975) "Functionalism and qualia," *Philosophical Studies*," 27, 271–315.

Shoemaker, S. (1976) "Embodiment and behavior," in A. Rorty (ed.), *The Identities of Persons*. Berkeley: University of California Press.

Shallice, T. (1972) "Dual functions of consciousness," *Psychological Review*, 79, 383–93.

Smart, J. J. C. (1971) "Reports of immediate experience," *Synthese*, 22, 346–59.

Wiggins, D. (1975) "Identity, designation, essentialism, and physicalism," *Philosophia*, 5, 1–30.

Chapter 13

Philosophy and Our Mental Life

Hilary Putnam

The question which troubles laymen, and which has long troubled philosophers, even if it is somewhat disguised by today's analytic style of writing philosophy, is this: are we made of matter or soul-stuff? To put it as bluntly as possible, are we just material beings, or are we 'something more'? In this chapter, I will argue as strongly as possible that this whole question rests on false assumptions. My purpose is not to dismiss the question, however, so much as to speak to the real concern which is behind the question. The real concern is, I believe, with the autonomy of our mental life.

People are worried that we may be debunked, that our behavior may be exposed as really explained by something mechanical. Not, to be sure, mechanical in the old sense of cogs and pulleys, but in the newer sense of electricity and magnetism and quantum chemistry and so forth. In this paper, part of what I want to do is to argue that this can't happen. Mentality is a real and autonomous feature of our world.

But even more important, at least in my feeling, is the fact that this whole question has nothing to do with our substance. Strange as it may seem to common sense and to sophisticated intuition alike, the question of the autonomy of our mental life does not hinge on and has nothing to do with that all too popular, all too old question about matter or soul-stuff. We could be made of Swiss cheese and it wouldn't matter.

Failure to see this, stubborn insistence on formulating the question as *matter or soul*, utterly prevents progress on these questions. Conversely, once we see that our substance is not the issue, I do not see how we can help but make progress.

The concept which is key to unravelling the mysteries in the philosophy of mind, I think, is the concept of *functional isomorphism*. Two systems are functionally isomorphic if *there is a correspondence between the states of one and the states of the other that preserves functional relations*. To start with computing machine examples, if the functional relations are just sequence relations, e.g., *state A is always followed by state* B, then, for F to be a functional isomorphism, it must be the case that state A is followed by state B in system 1 if and only if state $F(A)$ is followed by state $F(B)$ in system 2. If the functional relations are, say, data or print-out relations, e.g., *when print π is printed on the tape, system 1 goes into state A*, these must be preserved. *When print π is printed on the tape, system 2 goes into state $F(A)$*, if F is a functional isomorphism between system 1 and system 2. More generally, if T is a correct theory of the functioning of system 1, at the functional or psychological level, then an isomorphism between system 1 and system 2 must map each property and relation defined in system 2 in such a way that T comes out true when all references to system 1 are replaced by references to system 2, and all property and relation symbols in T are reinterpreted according to the mapping.

The difficulty with the notion of functional isomorphism is that it *presupposes the notion of a thing's being a functional or psychological description*. It is for this reason that, in various papers on this subject, I introduced and explained the notion in terms of Turing machines. And I felt constrained, therefore, to defend the thesis that *we* are Turing machines. Turing machines come, so to speak, with a normal form for their functional description, the so-called machine table—a standard style of program. But it does not seem fatally sloppy to me, although it is sloppy, if we apply the notion of functional isomorphism to systems for which we have no detailed idea at present what the normal form description would look like—systems like ourselves. The point is that even if we don't have any idea what a comprehensive psychological theory would look like, I claim that we know enough (and here analogies from computing machines, economic systems, games and so forth are helpful) to point out illuminating differences between any possible psychological theory of a human being, or even a functional description of a computing machine or an economic system, and a physical or chemical description. Indeed, Dennett and Fodor have done a great deal along these lines in recent books.

This brings me back to the question of *copper, cheese, or soul*. One point we can make immediately as soon as we have the basic concept of functional isomorphism is this: two systems can have quite different constitutions and be functionally isomorphic. For example, a computer made of electrical components can be isomorphic to one made of cogs and wheels. In other words, for each state in the first computer there is a corresponding state in the other, and, as we said before, the sequential relations are the same—if state S is followed by state B in the case of the electronic computer, state A would be followed by state B in the case of the computer made of cogs and wheels, and it doesn't matter at all that the *physical realizations* of those states are totally different. So a computer made of electrical components can be isomorphic to one made of cogs and wheels or to human clerks using paper and pencil. A computer made of one sort of wire, say copper wire, or one sort of relay, etc. will be in a different physical and chemical state when it computes than a computer made of a different sort of wire and relay. But the functional description may be the same.

We can extend this point still further. Assume that one thesis of materialism (I shall call it the 'first thesis') is correct, and we are, as wholes, just material systems obeying physical laws. Then the second thesis of classical materialism cannot be correct—namely, our mental states, e.g., *thinking about next summer's vacation*, cannot be *identical* with any physical or chemical states. For it is clear from what we already know about computers etc., that whatever the program of the brain may be, it must be physically possible, though not necessarily feasible, to produce something with that same program but quite a different physical and chemical constitution. Then to identify the state in question with its physical or chemical realization would be quite absurd, given that that realization is in a sense quite accidental, from the point of view of psychology, anyway (which is the relevant science).[1] It is as if we met Martians and discovered that they were in all functional respects isomorphic to us, but we refused to admit that they could feel pain because their C fibers were different.

Now, imagine two possible universes, perhaps 'parallel worlds', in the science fiction sense, in one of which people have good old fashioned souls, operating through pineal glands, perhaps, and in the other of which they have complicated brains. And suppose that the souls in the soul world are functionally isomorphic to the brains in the brain world. Is there any more sense to attaching importance to this difference than to the difference between copper wires and some other wires in the computer? Does it matter that the soul people have, so to speak, immaterial brains, and that the brain people have material souls? What matters is the common structure, the theory T of which we are, alas, in deep ignorance, and not the hardware, be it ever so ethereal.

One may raise various objections to what I have said. I shall try to reply to some of them.

One might, for example, say that if the souls of the soul people are isomorphic to the brains of the brain people, then their souls must be automata-like, and that's not the sort of soul we are interested in. 'All your argument really shows is that there is no need to distinguish between a brain and an automaton-like soul.' But what precisely does that objection come to?

I think there are two ways of understanding it. It might come to the claim that the notion of functional organization or functional isomorphism only makes sense for automata. But that is totally false. Sloppy as our notions are at present, we at least know this much, as Jerry Fodor has emphasized: we know that the notion of functional organization applies to anything to which the notion of a psychological theory applies. I explained the most general notion of functional isomorphism by saying that two systems are functionally isomorphic if there is an isomorphism that makes both of them models for the same psychological theory. (That is stronger than just saying that they are both models for the same psychological theory—they are isomorphic realizations of the same abstract structure.) To say that real old fashioned souls would not be in the domain of definition of the concept of functional organization or of the concept of functional isomorphisms would be to take the position that whatever we mean by the soul, it is something for which there can be no theory. That seems pure obscurantism. I will assume, henceforth, that it is not built into the notion of mind or soul or whatever that it is unintelligible or that there couldn't be a theory of it.

Secondly, someone might say more seriously that even if there is a theory of the soul or mind, the soul, at least in the full, rich old fashioned sense, is supposed to have powers that no mechanical system could have. In the latter part of this chapter I shall consider this claim.

If it is built into one's notions of the soul that the soul can do things that violate the laws of physics, then I admit I am stumped. There cannot be a soul which is isomorphic to a brain, if the soul can read the future clairvoyantly, in a way that is not in any way explainable by physical law. On the other hand, if one is interested in more modest forms of magic like telepathy, it seems to me that there is no reason in principle why we couldn't construct a device which would project subvocalized thoughts from one brain to another. As to reincarnation, if we are, as I am urging, a certain kind of functional structure (my identity is, as it were, my functional structure), there seems to be in principle no reason why that could not be reproduced after a thousand years or a million years or a billion years. Resurrection: as you know, Christians believe in resurrection in the flesh, which completely bypasses the need for an immaterial vehicle. So even if one is interested in those questions (and they are not my concern in this paper, although I am concerned to speak to people who have those concerns), even then one doesn't need an immaterial brain or soul-stuff.

So if I am right, and the question of matter or soul-stuff is really irrelevant to any question of philosophical or religious significance, why so much attention to it, why so much heat? The crux of the matter seems to be that both the Diderots of this world and the Descartes of this world have agreed that if we are matter, then there is a physical explanation for how we behave, disappointing or exciting. I think the traditional dualist says *'wouldn't it be terrible if we turned out to be just matter, for then there is a physical explanation for everything we do'*. And the traditional materialist says *'if we are just matter, then there is a physical explanation for everything we do. Isn't that exciting!'* (It is like the distinction between the optimist and the pessimist: an optimist is a person who says 'this is the best of all possible worlds'; and a pessimist is a person who says 'you're right'.)[2]

I think they are both wrong. I think Diderot and Descartes were both wrong in assuming that if we are matter, or our souls are material, then there is a physical explanation for our behavior.

Let me try to illustrate what I mean by a very simple analogy. Suppose we have a very simple physical system—a board in which there are two holes, a circle one inch in diameter and a square one inch high, and a cubical peg one-sixteenth of an inch less than one inch high. We have the following very simple fact to explain: *the peg passes through the square hole, and it does not pass through the round hole.*

In explanation of this, one might attempt the following. One might say that the peg is, after all, a cloud or, better, a rigid lattice of atoms. One might even attempt to give a description of that lattice, compute its electrical potential energy, worry about why it does not collapse, produce some quantum mechanics to explain why it is stable, etc. The board is also a lattice of atoms. I will call the peg 'system A', and the holes 'region 1' and 'region 2'. One could compute all possible trajectories of system A (there are, by the way, very serious questions about these computations, their effectiveness, feasibility, and so on, but let us assume this), and perhaps one could deduce from just the laws of particle mechanics or quantum electrodynamics that system A never passes through region 1, but that there is at least one trajectory which enables it to pass through region 2. Is this an explanation of the fact that the peg passes through the square hole and not the round hole?

Very often we are told that if something is made of matter, its behavior must have a physical explanation. And the argument is that if it is made of matter (and we make a lot of assumptions), then there should be a deduction of its behavior from its material structure. *What makes you call this deduction an explanation?*

On the other hand, if you are not 'hipped' on the idea that *the* explanation must be at the level of the ultimate constituents, and that in fact the explanation might have the property that *the ultimate constituents don't matter*, that *only the higher level structure matters*, then there is a very simple explanation here. The explanation is that the board is rigid, the peg is rigid, and as a matter of geometrical fact, the round hole is smaller than the peg, the square hole is bigger than the cross-section of the peg. The peg passes through the hole that is large enough to take its cross-section, and does not pass through the hole that is too small to take its cross-section. That is a correct explanation whether the peg consists of molecules, or continuous rigid substance, or whatever. (If one wanted to amplify the explanation, one might point out the geometrical fact that a square one inch high is bigger than a circle one inch across.)

Now, one can say that in this explanation certain *relevant structural features of the situation* are brought out. The geometrical features are brought out. It is *relevant* that a square one inch high is bigger than a circle one inch around. And the relationship between the size and shape of the peg and the size and shape of the holes is *relevant*. It is *relevant* that both the board and the peg are *rigid* under transportation. And nothing else is relevant. The same explanation will go in any world (whatever the microstructure) in which those *higher level structural features* are present. In that sense *this explanation is autonomous.*

People have argued that I am wrong to say that the microstructural deduction is not an explanation. I think that in terms of the *purposes for which we use the notion of explanation*, it is not an explanation. If you want to, let us say that the deduction *is* an explanation, it is just a terrible explanation, and why look for terrible explanations when good ones are available?

Goodness is not a subjective matter. Even if one agrees with the positivists who saddled us with the notion of explanation as deduction from laws, one of the things we do in science is to look for laws. Explanation is superior not just subjectively, but *methodologically*, in terms of facilitating the aims of scientific inquiry, if it brings out relevant laws. An explanation is superior if it is more general.

Just taking those two features, and there are many many more one could think of, compare the explanation at the higher level of this phenomenon with the atomic explanation. The explanation at the higher level brings out the relevant geometrical relationships. The lower level explanation conceals those laws. Also notice that the higher level explanation applies to a much more interesting class of systems (of course that has to do with what we are interested in).

The fact is that we are much more interested in generalizing to other structures which are rigid and have various geometrical relations, than we are in generalizing to *the next peg that has exactly this molecular structure*, for the very good reason that there is not going to *be* a next peg that has exactly this molecular structure. So in terms of real life disciplines, real life ways of slicing up scientific problems, the higher level explanation is far more general, which is why it is *explanatory*.

We were only able to deduce a statement which is lawful at the *higher* level, that the peg goes through the hole which is larger than the cross-section of the peg. When we try to deduce the possible trajectories of 'system *A*' from statements about the individual atoms, we use premises which are totally accidental—this atom is here, this carbon atom is there, and so forth. And that is one reason that it is very misleading to talk about a reduction of a science like economics to the level of the elementary particles making up the players of the economic game. In fact, their motions—buying this, selling that, arriving at an equilibrium price—these motions cannot be deduced from just the equations of motion. Otherwise they would be *physically necessitated*, not *economically necessitated*, to arrive at an equilibrium price. They play that game because they are particular systems with particular boundary conditions which are totally accidental from the point of view of physics. This means that the derivation of the laws of economics from *just* the laws of physics is *in principle* impossible. The derivation of the laws of economics from the laws of physics and *accidental statements about which particles were where when* by a Laplacian supermind might be in principle possible, but why want it? A few chapters of, e.g., von Neumann, will tell one far more about regularities at the level of economic structure than such a deduction ever could.

The conclusion I want to draw from this is that we do have the kind of autonomy that we are looking for in the mental realm. Whatever our mental functioning may be, there seems to be no serious reason to believe that it is *explainable* by our physics and chemistry. And what we are interested in is not: given that we consist of such and such particles, could someone have predicted that we would have this mental functioning? because such a prediction is not *explanatory*, however great a feat it may be. What we are interested in is: can we say at this autonomous level that since we have this sort of structure, this sort of program, it follows that we will be able to learn this, we will tend to like that, and so on? These are the problems of mental life—the description of this autonomous level of mental functioning—and that is what is to be discovered.

In previous papers, I have argued for the hypothesis that (1) a whole human being is a Turing machine, and (2) that psychological states of a human being are Turing machine states or disjunctions of Turing machine states. In this section I want to argue that this point of view was essentially wrong, and that I was too much in the grip of the reductionist outlook.

Let me begin with a technical difficulty. A *state* of a Turing machine is described in such a way that a Turing machine can be in exactly one state at a time. Moreover, memory and learning are not represented in the Turing machine model as acquisition of new states, but as acquisition of new information printed on the machine's tape. Thus, if human beings have any states at all which resemble Turing machine states, those states must (1) be states the human can be in at any time, independently of learning and memory; and (2) be *total* instantaneous states of the human being—states which determine, together with learning and memory, what the next state will be, as well as totally specifying the present condition of the human being ('totally' from the standpoint of psychological theory, that means).

These characteristics establish that *no* psychological state in any customary sense can be a Turing machine state. Take a particular kind of pain to be a 'psychological state'. If I *am* a Turing machine, then my present 'state' must determine not only whether or not I am having that particular kind of pain, but also whether or not I am about to say 'three', whether or not I am hearing a shrill whine, etc. So the psychological state in question (the pain) is not the same as my 'state' in the sense of *machine state*, although it is possible (so far) that my machine state *determines* my psychological state. Moreover, *no* psychological theory would pretend that having a pain of a particular kind, being about to say 'three', or hearing a shrill whine, etc., all belong to *one* psychological state, although there could well be a machine state characterized by the fact that I was in it only when simultaneously having that pain, being about to say 'three', hearing a shrill whine, etc. So, even if I am a Turing machine, my machine states are *not* the same as my psychological states. My description *qua* Turing machine (machine table) and my description *qua* human being (*via* a psychological theory) are descriptions at two totally different levels of organization.

So far it is still possible that a psychological state is a large disjunction (practically speaking, an almost infinite disjunction) of machine states, although no *single* machine state is a psychological state. But this is very unlikely when we move away from states like 'pain' (which are almost *biological*) to states like 'jealousy' or 'love' or 'competitiveness'. Being jealous is certainly not an *instantaneous* state, and it depends on a great deal of information and on many learned facts and habits. But Turing machine states are instantaneous and are independent of learning and memory. That is, learning and memory may cause a Turing machine to go into a state, but the identity of the state does not depend on learning and memory, whereas, no matter what state I am in, identifying that state as 'being jealous of X's regard for Y' involves specifying that I have learned that X and Y are persons and a good deal about social relations among persons. Thus jealousy can neither be a machine state nor a disjunction of machine states.

One might attempt to modify the theory by saying that being jealous = either being in State A and having tape c_1 *or* being in State A and having tape c_2 *or*... being in State B and having tape d_1 *or* being in State B and having tape d_2...being in State Z and having tape y_1... or being in State Z and having tape y_n—i.e., define a psychological state as disjunction, the individual disjuncts being not Turing machine states, as before, but conjunctions of a machine state and a tape (i.e., a total description of the content of the memory bank). Besides the fact that such a description would be literally infinite, the theory is now without content, for the original purpose was to use the machine table as a model of a psychological theory, whereas it is now clear that the machine table description, although different from the description at the elementary particle level, is as removed from the description *via* a psychological theory as the physico-chemical description is.

What is the importance of machines in the philosophy of mind? I think that machines have both a positive and a negative importance. The positive importance of machines was that it was in connection with machines, computing machines in particular, that the notion of functional organization first appeared. Machines forced us to distinguish between an abstract structure and its concrete realization. Not that that distinction came into the world for the first time with machines. But in the case of computing machines, we could not avoid rubbing our noses against the fact that what we had to count as to all intents and purposes the same structure could be realized in a bewildering variety of different ways; that the important properties were not physical-chemical. That the machines made us catch on to the idea of functional organization is extremely important. The negative importance of machines, however, is that they tempt us to oversimplification. The notion of functional organization became clear to us through systems with a very restricted, very specific functional organization. So the temptation is present to assume that we must have that restricted and specific kind of functional organization.

Now I want to consider an example—an example which may seem remote from what we have been talking about, but which may help. This is not an example from the philosophy of mind at all. Consider the following fact. The earth does not go around the sun in a circle, as was once believed, it goes around the sun in an ellipse, with the sun at one of the foci, not in the center of the ellipse. Yet one statement which would hold true if the orbit was a circle and the sun was at the centre still holds true, surprisingly. That is the following statement: the radius vector from the sun to the earth sweeps out equal areas in equal times. If the orbit were a circle, and the earth were moving with a constant velocity, that would be trivial. But the orbit is not a circle. Also the velocity is not constant—when the earth is farthest away from the sun, it is going most slowly, when it is closest to the sun, it is going fastest. The earth is speeding up and slowing down. But the earth's radius vector sweeps out equal areas in equal times.[3] Newton deduced that law in his *Principia*, and his deduction shows that the only thing on which that law depends is that the force acting on the earth is in the direction of the sun. That is absolutely the only fact one needs to deduce that law. Mathematically it is equivalent to that law.[4] That is all well and good when the gravitational law is that every body attracts every other body according to an inverse square law, because then there is always a force on the earth in the direction of the sun. If we assume that we can neglect all the other bodies, that their influence is slight, then that is all we need, and we can use Newton's proof, or a more modern, simpler proof.

But today we have very complicated laws of gravitation. First of all, we say what is really going is that the world lines of freely falling bodies in space-time are geodesics. And the geometry is determined by the mass-energy tensor, and the ankle bone is connected to the leg bone, etc. So, one might ask, how would a modern relativity theorist explain Kepler's law? He would explain it very simply. *Kepler's laws are true because Newton's laws are approximately true.* And, in fact, an attempt to replace that argument by a deduction of Kepler's laws from the field equations would be regarded as almost as ridiculous (but not quite) as trying to deduce that the peg will go through one hole and not the other from the positions and velocities of the individual atoms.

I want to draw the philosophical conclusion that Newton's laws *have a kind of reality in our world* even though they are not *true*. The point is that it will be necessary to appeal to Newton's laws in order to explain Kepler's laws. Methodologically, I can make that claim at least plausible. One remark—due to Alan Garfinkel—is that *a good explanation is invariant under small perturbations of the assumptions*. One problem with deducing Kepler's laws from the gravitational field equations is that if we do it, tomorrow the gravitational field equations are likely to be different. Whereas the explanation which consists in showing that whichever equation we have implies Newton's equation to a first approximation is invariant under even moderate perturbations, quite big perturbations, of the assumptions. One might say that every explanation of Kepler's laws 'passes through' Newton's laws.

Let me come back to the philosophy of mind, now. If we assume a thorough atomic structure of matter, quantization and so forth, then, at first blush, it looks as if *continuities* cannot be relevant to our brain functioning. Mustn't it all be discrete? Physics says that the deepest level is discrete.

There are two problems with this argument. One is that there are continuities even in quantum mechanics, as well as discontinuities. But ignore that, suppose quantum mechanics were a thoroughly discrete theory.

The other problem is that if that were a good argument, it would be an argument against the utilizability of the model of air as a continuous liquid, which is the model on which aeroplane wings are constructed, at least if they are to fly at anything less than supersonic speeds. There are two points: one is that a discontinuous structure, a discrete structure, can approximate a continuous structure. The discontinuities may be irrelevant, just as in the case of the peg and the board. The fact that the peg and the board are not continuous solids is irrelevant. One can say that the peg and the board only approximate perfectly rigid continuous solids. But if the error in the approximation is irrelevant to the level of description, so what? It is not just that discrete systems can approximate continuous systems; the fact is that the system may behave in the way it does *because* a continuous system would behave in such and such a way, and the system approximates a continuous system.

This is not a Newtonian world. Tough. Kepler's law comes out true because the sun-earth system approximates a Newtonian system. And the error in the approximation is quite irrelevant at that level.

This analogy is not perfect because physicists are interested in laws to which the error in the approximation is relevant. It seems to me that in the psychological case the analogy is even better, that continuous models (for example, Hull's model for rote learning which used a continuous potential) could perfectly well be correct, whatever the ultimate structure of the brain is. We cannot deduce that a digital model has to be the correct model from the fact that ultimately there are neurons. The brain may work the way it does because it approximates some system whose laws are best conceptualized in terms of continuous mathematics. What is more, the errors in that approximation may be irrelevant at the level of psychology.

What I have said about *continuity* goes as well for many other things. Let us come back to the question of the soul people and the brain people, and the isomorphism between the souls in one world and the brains in the other. One objection was, if there is a functional isomorphism between souls and brains, wouldn't the souls have to be rather simple? The answer is no. Because brains can be essentially infinitely complex. A system with as many degrees of freedom as the brain can imitate to within the accuracy relevant to psychological theory any structure one can hope to describe. It might be, so to speak, that the ultimate physics of the soul will be quite different from the ultimate physics of the brain, but that at the level we are interested in, the level of functional organization, the same description might go for both. And also that that description might be formally incompatible with the actual physics of the brain, in the way that the description of the air flowing around an aeroplane wing as a continuous incompressible liquid is *formally incompatible with the actual structure of the air.*

Let me close by saying that these examples support the idea that our substance, what we are made of, places almost no first order restrictions on our form. And that what we are really interested in, as Aristotle saw,[5] is form and not matter. *What is our intellectual form?* is the question, not what the matter is. And whatever our substance may be, soul-stuff, or matter or Swiss cheese, it is not going to place any interesting first order restrictions on the answer to this question. It may, of course, place interesting higher order restrictions. Small effects may have to be explained in terms of the actual physics of the brain. But when we are not even at the level of an *idealized* description of the functional organization of the brain, to talk about the importance of small perturbations seems decidedly premature. My conclusion is that we have what we always wanted— an autonomous mental life. And we need no mysteries, no ghostly agents, no *élan vital* to have it.

Notes

This paper was presented as a part of a Foerster symposium on "Computers and the Mind" at the University of California (Berkeley) in October, 1973. I am indebted to Alan Garfinkel for comments on earlier versions of this paper.

1. Even if it were not physically possible to realize human psychology in a creature made of anything but the usual protoplasm, DNA, etc., it would still not be correct to say that psychological states are identical with their physical realizations. For, as will be argued below, such an identification has no *explanatory* value *in psychology.* On this point, compare Fodor, 1968.
2. Joke credit: Joseph Weizenbaum.
3. This is one of Kepler's Laws.
4. Provided that the two bodies—the sun and the earth—are the whole universe. If there are other forces, then, of course, Kepler's law cannot be *exactly* correct.
5. E.g., Aristotle says: "...we can wholly dismiss as unnecessary the question whether the soul and the body are one: it is as meaningless to ask whether the wax and the shape given to it by the stamp are one, or generally the matter of a thing and that of which it is the matter." (See *De Anima*, 412 a6–b9.)

Part II
Mental Causation

Introduction

While the first section of this book was concerned with what mental states are, this section considers the question of how mental states can have causal powers.

In the seventeenth century most philosophers were dualists, but this agreement did not by itself answer the question of how mind influences the body and vice versa. Likewise, in the twentieth century many philosophers of mind are materialists, yet the problem of what role, if any, mental states play in causing our behavior remains open. So while the mind/body problem is concerned with the *nature* of mental states, the question of mental causation turns on the *causal powers* of mental states (whatever their nature). One's position on the first question certainly constrains the possible answers one can give to the second, but it falls far short of determining a specific answer.

Plato provides an interesting view on what counts as a proper psychological explanation. Here Plato dismisses the idea that human behavior could be explained physically (in terms of muscles, motions, etc.) not because we couldn't give such an account, but because it wouldn't pick out the true causes of behavior. To cite the cause of something is, according to Plato, to explain it purposively, to show the ultimate end or good it is aimed at. A purely physical account of what causes our actions would be unable to show the relationship between human action and its end.

Adopting the modern conception of causality, René Descartes insists that mind and body interact causally—the soul interacting with the body most particularly in a small gland in the center of the brain—the *pineal gland*.

Nicolas Malebranche and Gottfried Wilhelm Leibniz retain Descartes' dualism but reject his straightforward interactionism. Malebranche argues for *occasionalism*: mind and body are incapable of directly influencing one another, but God intervenes to bring about the effect, giving the appearance that one has directly affected the other. For example, if I will my arm to move, this willing is itself powerless, but on each such occasion God raises my arm for me.

Leibniz, while agreeing that mind and body cannot causally interact directly, suggests that the system of occasional causes is not a plausible strategy for an intelligent God. Instead, at the beginning of time God instituted a "preestablished harmony" such that each object would react in the appropriate way at the appropriate time. While we might, for example, believe that one billiard ball caused another to move, in fact God "programmed" the second ball to move at exactly the same moment the first ball contacted it. Likewise, while I may believe that my mind caused my arm to move, Leibniz holds that in fact God designed my arm so that it would move spontaneously exactly when I will it to move—once again creating the illusion of direct causation.

Since Immanuel Kant's position forms part of his general system of philosophy, a bit of background is called for in explaining it. Kant argues that space and time are not objects in themselves, but subjective conditions of our "sensible intuition"—that is, part of the very structure of our sense perception. Since ordinary spatiotemporal objects are the objects of our knowledge, it follows that we know things only through these conditions. Hence Kant calls objects as known by us "appearances" or "phenomena." At the same time he holds that appearances must be appearances *of* something, so he postulates a "thing in itself" or "noumenon" behind these appearances; but since the thing in itself falls outside the conditions of knowledge (space and time), Kant concludes that we can know nothing about it in itself. The intractability of problems in classical metaphysics stems, according to Kant, from pure reason's attempts to go beyond the appearances and have knowledge of things in themselves. Arguments concerning the existence of God or the immortality of the soul, for example, are forever inconclusive because they ignore the fact that we can only know phenomena, and try to talk about noumena. In the passage included here, Kant demonstrates the dead-end nature of such arguments by showing how both sides of a metaphysical debate look equally reasonable; he sets the argument that only physical causation exists, against the opposing view that free will constitutes a second kind of causation. We can never resolve this debate, since it concerns things in themselves, but Kant argues that in any case the two views are compatible. Within the realm of space and time—that is, on the level of appearances—my action may be entirely caused by past conditioning, brain states, and so forth. But at the same time my behavior, if rational, can be interpreted as reflecting free will on the level of things in themselves.

Most recent philosophers, while adopting Kant's deterministic view of the universe, steer clear of his two-world metaphysics. Thomas Huxley argues that mental states have no causal powers—but that they do, nonetheless, exist. Huxley is led to the conclusion that consciousness is a mere *epiphenomenon* of brain states: just as my shadow accompanies my movements without affecting them, so my conscious states accompany my brain states but are powerless to causally influence them in any way.

The positions of Huxley and Kant have faint echoes in the writings of Davidson and Fodor. According to Davidson, there are two ways in which we can describe mental events: in either physical or mental language. But, while a physical description permits the application of causal laws, a mentalistic description of the same event cannot be accommodated within those laws. That is, true causality holds only at the level of physics. If we use mentalistic language to say that one mental event caused another, we can do so because the mentalistic descriptions *supervene* on the physical descriptions. Many philosophers have suggested that Davidson's position amounts to a new form of epiphenomenalism, but the charge is a matter of some controversy.

Fodor agrees with Davidson that there are two ways of describing mental events, and he also agrees that to be causally efficacious, an event must fall under causal laws; but he argues that sciences other than physics have such laws. These higher level "special sciences" differ from physics in requiring certain lower level conditions for their instantiation (whereas physics, being on the lowest level, requires no such conditions). Thus special science laws hold only *ceteris paribus* (all other things being equal). But, Fodor insists, this does not block them from being genuine causal laws. Put another way, physics does not own causality, and causal connections can be appropriately described in mentalistic language.

Further Reading

Block, N., 1990. "Can the Mind Change the World?" in *Meaning and Method: Essays in Honor of Hilary Putnam.* ed. George Boolos. Cambridge: Cambridge University Press.

Dretske, F., 1988. *Explaining Behavior: Reasons in a World of Causes.* Cambridge, MA: MIT Press. (There is a symposium on Dretske's book in *Philosophy and Phenomenological Research* Vol L, 783–840.)

Enc, B., 1986. "Essentialism with Individual Essences: Causation, Kinds, Supervenience and Restricted Identities." In *Midwest Studies in Philosophy XI*, Minneapolis: University of Minnesota Press.

Jackson, F., and Pettit, P., 1988. "Functionalism and Broad Content," *Mind* 97, 381–400.

Kim, J., 1984. "Epiphenomenal and Supervenient Causation." In P. A. French et al., *Midwest Studies in Philosophy IX*, Minneapolis: University of Minnesota Press.

Segal, G., and Sober, E., 1991. "The Causal Efficacy of Content" *Philosophical Studies* 63, 1–30.

Sosa, E., 1984. "Mind-Body Interaction and Supervenient Causation." In *Midwest Studies in Philosophy IX*. Minneapolis: University of Minnesota Press.

Chapter 14

From *The Phaedo*

Plato

Then I heard some one reading, as he said, from a book of Anaxagoras, that mind was the disposer and cause of all, and I was delighted at this notion, which appeared quite admirable, and I said to myself: If mind is the disposer, mind will dispose all for the best, and put each particular in the best place; and I argued that if any one desired to find out the cause of the generation or destruction or existence of anything, he must find out what state of being or doing or suffering was best for that thing, and therefore a man had only to consider the best for himself and others, and then he would also know the worse, since the same science comprehended both. And I rejoiced to think that I had found in Anaxagoras a teacher of the causes of existence such as I desired, and I imagined that he would tell me first whether the earth is flat or round; and whichever was true, he would proceed to explain the cause and the necessity of this being so, and then he would teach me the nature of the best and show that this was best; and if he said that the earth was in the centre, he would further explain that this position was the best, and I should be satisfied with the explanation given, and not want any other sort of cause. And I thought that I would then go on and ask him about the sun and moon and stars, and that he would explain to me their comparative swiftness, and their returnings and various states, active and passive, and how all of them were for the best. For I could not imagine that when he spoke of mind as the disposer of them, he would give any other account of their being as they are, except that this was best; and I thought that when he had explained to me in detail the cause of each and the cause of all, he would go on to explain to me what was best for each and what was good for all. These hopes I would not have sold for a large sum of money, and I seized the books and read them as fast as I could in my eagerness to know the better and the worse.

What expectations I had formed, and how grievously was I disappointed! As I proceeded, I found my philosopher altogether forsaking mind or any other principle of order, but having recourse to air, and ether, and water, and other eccentricities. I might compare him to a person who began by maintaining generally that mind is the cause of the actions of Socrates, but who, when he endeavoured to explain the causes of my several actions in detail, went on to show that I sit here because my body is made up of bones and muscles; and the bones, as he would say, are hard and have joints which divide them, and the muscles are elastic, and they cover the bones, which have also a covering or environment of flesh and skin which contains them; and as the bones are lifted at their joints by the contraction or relaxation of the muscles, I am able to bend my limbs, and this is why I am sitting here in a curved posture—that is what he would say; and he would have a similar explanation of my talking to you, which he would attribute to sound, and air, and hearing, and he would assign ten thousand other causes of the same sort, forgetting to mention the true cause, which is, that the Athenians have thought fit to condemn me, and accordingly I have thought it better and more right to remain here and undergo my sentence; for I am inclined to think that these muscles and bones of mine would have gone off long ago to Megara or Boeotia—by the dog, they would, if they had been moved only by their own idea of what was best, and if I had not chosen the better and nobler part, instead of playing truant and running away, of enduring any punishment which the state inflicts. There is surely a strange confusion of causes and conditions in all this. It may be said, indeed, that without bones and muscles and the other parts of the body I cannot execute my purposes. But to say that I do as I do because of them, and that this is the way in which mind acts, and not from the choice of the best, is a very careless and idle mode of speaking. I wonder that they cannot distinguish the cause from the condition, which the many, feeling about in the dark, are always mistaking and misnaming.

Chapter 15

From *Passions of the Soul*

René Descartes

Article V

That it is an error to believe that the soul supplies the movement and heat to body.

By this means we shall avoid a very considerable error into which many have fallen; so much so that I am of opinion that this is the primary cause which has prevented our being able hitherto satisfactorily to explain the passions and the other properties of the soul. It arises from the fact that from observing that all dead bodies are devoid of heat and consequently of movement, it has been thought that it was the absence of soul which caused these movements and this heat to cease; and thus, without any reason, it was thought that our natural heat and all the movements of our body depend on the soul: while in fact we ought on the contrary to believe that the soul quits us on death only because this heat ceases, and the organs which serve to move the body disintegrate.

Article VI

The difference that exists between a living body and a dead body.

In order, then, that we may avoid this error, let us consider that death never comes to pass by reason of the soul, but only because some one of the principal parts of the body decays; and we may judge that the body of a living man differs from that of a dead man just as does a watch or other automaton (i.e., a machine that moves of itself), when it is wound up and contains in itself the corporeal principle of those movements for which it is designed along with all that is requisite for its action, from the same watch or other machine when it is broken and when the principle of its movement ceases to act.

Article XIII

That this action of outside objects may lead the spirits into the muscles in diverse ways.

And I have explained in the Dioptric how all the objects of sight communicate themselves to us only through the fact that they move locally by the intermission of transparent bodies which are between them and us, the little filaments of the optic nerves which are at the back of our eyes, and then the parts of the brain from which these nerves proceed; I explained, I repeat, how they move them in as many diverse ways as the diversities which they cause us to see in things, and that it is not immediately the movements which occur in the eye, but those that occur in the brain which represent these objects to the soul. To follow this example, it is easy to conceive how sounds, scents, tastes, heat, pain, hunger, thirst and generally speaking all objects of our other external senses as well as of our internal appetites, also excite some movement in our nerves which by their means pass to the brain; and in addition to the fact that these diverse movements of the brain cause diverse perceptions to become evident to our soul, they can also without it cause the spirits to take their course towards certain muscles rather than towards others, and thus to move our limbs, which I shall prove here by one example only. If someone quickly thrusts his hand against our eyes as if to strike us, even though we know him to be our friend, that he only does it in fun, and that he will take great care not to hurt us, we have all the same trouble in preventing ourselves from closing them; and this shows that it is not by the intervention of our soul that they close, seeing that it is against our will, which is its only, or at least its principal activity; but it is because the machine of our body is so formed that the movement of this hand towards our eyes excites another movement in our brain, which conducts the animal spirits into the muscles which cause the eyelids to close.

Article XVI

How all the members may be moved by the objects of the senses and by the animal spirits without the aid of the soul.

We must finally remark that the machine of our body is so formed that all the changes undergone by the movement of the spirits may cause them to open certain pores in the brain more than others, and reciprocally that when some one of the pores is opened more or less than usual (to however small a degree it may be) by the action of the nerves which are employed by the senses, that changes something in the movement of the spirits and causes them to be conducted into the muscles which serve to move the body in the way in which it is usually moved when such an action takes place. In this way all the movements which we make without our will contributing thereto (as frequently happens when we breathe, walk, eat, and in fact perform all those actions which are common to us and to the brutes), only depend on the conformation of our members, and on the course which the spirits, excited by the heat of the heart, follow naturally in the brain, nerves, and muscles, just as the movements of a watch are produced simply by the strength of the springs and the form of the wheels.

Article XVII

What the functions of the soul are.

After having thus considered all the functions which pertain to the body alone, it is easy to recognise that there is nothing in us which we ought to attribute to our soul excepting our thoughts, which are mainly of two sorts, the one being the actions of the soul, and the other its passions. Those which I call its actions are all our desires, because we find by experience that they proceed directly from our soul, and appear to depend on it alone: while, on the other hand, we may usually term one's passions all those kinds of perception or forms of knowledge which are found in us, because it is often not our soul which makes them what they are, and because it always receives them from the things which are represented by them.

Article XVIII

Of the Will.

Our desires, again, are of two sorts, of which the one consists of the actions of the soul which terminate in the soul itself, as when we desire to love God, or generally speaking, apply our thoughts to some object which is not material; and the other of the actions which terminate in our body, as when from the simple fact that we have the desire to take a walk, it follows that our legs move and that we walk.

Article XXX

That the soul is united to all the portions of the body conjointly.

But in order to understand all these things more perfectly, we must know that the soul is really joined to the whole body, and that we cannot, properly speaking, say that it exists in any one of its parts to the exclusion of the others, because it is one and in some manner indivisible, owing to the disposition of its organs, which are so related to one another that when any one of them is removed, that renders the whole body defective; and because it is of a nature which has no relation to extension, nor dimensions, nor other properties of the matter of which the body is composed, but only to the whole conglomerate of its organs, as appears from the fact that we could not in any way conceive of the half or the third of a soul, nor of the space it occupies, and because it does not become smaller owing to the cutting off of some portion of the body, but separates itself from it entirely when the union of its assembled organs is dissolved.

Article XXXI

That there is a small gland in the brain in which the soul exercises its functions more particularly than in the other parts.

It is likewise necessary to know that although the soul is joined to the whole body, there is yet in that a certain part in which it exercises its functions more particularly than in all the others; and it is usually believed that this part is the brain, or possibly the heart: the brain, because it is with it that the organs of sense are connected, and the heart because it is apparently in it that we experience the passions. But, in examining the matter with care, it seems as though I had clearly ascertained that the part of the body in which the soul exercises its functions immediately is in nowise the heart, nor the whole of the brain, but merely the most inward of all its parts, to wit, a certain very small gland which is situated in the middle of its substance and so suspended above the duct whereby the animal spirits in its anterior cavities have communication with those in the posterior, that the slightest movements which take place in it may alter very greatly the course of these spirits; and reciprocally that the smallest changes which occur in the course of the spirits may do much to change the movements of this gland.

Article XXXII

How we know that this gland is the main seat of the soul.

The reason which persuades me that the soul cannot have any other seat in all the body than this gland wherein to exercise its functions immediately, is that I reflect that the other parts of our brain are all of them double, just as we have two eyes, two hands, two ears, and finally all the organs of our outside senses are double; and inasmuch as we have but one solitary and simple thought of one particular thing at one and the same moment, it must necessarily be the case that there must somewhere be a place where the two images which come to us by the two eyes, where the two other impressions which proceed from a single object by means of the double organs of the other senses, can unite before arriving at the soul, in order that they may not represent to it two objects instead of one. And it is easy to apprehend how these images or other impressions might unite in this gland by the intermission of the spirits which fill the cavities of the brain; but there is no other place in the body where they can be thus united unless they are so in this gland.

Article XXXIV

How the soul and the body act on one another.

Let us then conceive here that the soul has its principal seat in the little gland which exists in the middle of the brain, from whence it radiates forth through all the remainder of the body by means of the animal spirits, nerves, and even the blood, which, participating in the impressions of the spirits, can carry them by the arteries into all the members. And recollecting what has been said above about the machine of our body, i.e., that the little filaments of our nerves are so distributed in all its parts, that on the occasion of the diverse movements which are there excited by sensible objects, they open in diverse ways the pores of the brain, which causes the animal spirits contained in these cavities to enter in diverse ways into the muscles, by which means they can move the members in all the different ways in which they are capable of being moved; and also that all the other causes which are capable of moving the spirits in diverse ways suffice to conduct them into diverse muscles; let us here add that the small gland which is the main seat of the soul is so suspended between the cavities which contain the spirits that it can be moved by them in as many different ways as there are sensible diversities in the object, but that it may also be moved in diverse ways by the soul, whose nature is such that it receives in itself as many diverse impressions, that is to say, that it possesses as many diverse perceptions as there are diverse movements in this gland. Reciprocally, likewise, the machine of the body is so formed that from the simple fact that this gland is diversely moved by the soul, or by such other cause, whatever it is, it thrusts the spirits which surround it towards the pores of the brain, which conduct them by the nerves into the muscles, by which means it causes them to move the limbs.

Article XXXV

Example of the mode in which the impressions of the objects unite in the gland which is in the middle of the brain.

Thus, for example, if we see some animal approach us, the light reflected from its body depicts two images of it, one in each of our eyes, and these two images form two others, by means of the optic nerves, in the interior surface of the brain which faces its cavities; then from there, by means of the animal spirits with which its cavities are filled, these images so radiate towards the little gland which is surrounded by these spirits, that the movement which forms each point of one of the images tends towards the same point of the gland towards which tends the movement which forms the point of the other image, which represents the same part of this animal. By this means the two images which are in the brain form but one upon the gland, which, acting immediately upon the soul, causes it to see the form of this animal.

Article XLI

The power of the soul in regard to the body.

But the will is so free in its nature, that it can never be constrained; and of the two sorts of thoughts which I have distinguished in the soul (of which the first are its actions, i.e., its desires, the others its passions, taking this word in its most general significance, which comprises all kinds of perceptions), the former are absolutely in its power, and can only be indirectly changed by the body, while on the other hand the latter depend absolutely on the actions which govern and direct them, and they can only indirectly be altered by the soul, excepting when it is itself their cause. And the whole action of the soul consists in this, that solely because it desires something, it causes the little gland to which it is closely united to move in the way requisite to produce the effect which relates to this desire.

Article XLII

How we find in the memory the things which we desire to remember.

Thus when the soul desires to recollect something, this desire causes the gland, by inclining successively to different sides, to thrust the spirits towards different parts of the brain until they come across that part where the traces left there by the object which we wish to recollect are found; for these traces are none other than the fact that the pores of the brain, by which the spirits have formerly followed their course because of the presence of this object, have by that means acquired a greater facility than the others in being once more opened by the animal spirits which come towards them in the same way. Thus these spirits in coming in contact with these pores, enter into them more easily than into the others, by which means they excite a special movement in the gland which represents the same object to the soul, and causes it to know that it is this which it desired to remember.

Article XLVII

In what the strife consists which we imagine to exist between the lower and higher part of the soul.

And it is only in the repugnance which exists between the movements which the body by its animal spirits, and the soul by its will, tend to excite in the gland at the same time, that all the strife which we are in the habit of conceiving to exist between the inferior part of the soul, which we call the sensuous, and the superior which is rational, or as we may say, between the natural appetites and the will, consists. For there is within us but one soul, and this soul has not in itself any diversity of parts; the same part that is subject to sense impressions is rational, and all the soul's appetites are acts of will. The error which has been committed in making it play the part of various personages, usually in opposition one to another, only proceeds from the fact that we have not properly distinguished its functions from those of the body, to which alone we must attribute every thing which can be observed in us that is opposed to our reason; so that there is here no strife, excepting that the small gland which exists in the middle of the brain, being capable of being thrust to one side by the soul, and to the other by the animal spirits, which are mere bodies, as I have said above, it often happens that these two impulses are contrary, and that the stronger prevents the other from taking effect. We may, however, distinguish two sorts of movement excited by the animal spirits in the gland—the one sort represents to the soul the objects which move the senses, or the impressions which are met with in the brain, and makes no attempt to affect its will; the others do make an effort to do so—i.e., those which cause the passions or the movements of the body which accompany the passions. And as to the first, although they often hinder the actions of the soul, or else are hindered by them, yet, because they are not directly contrary to them, we do not notice any strife between them. We only notice the strife between the latter and the acts of·will which conflict with them: e.g., between the effort with which the spirits impel the gland in order to cause a desire for something in the soul, and that with which the soul repels it again by the desire which it has to avoid the very same thing. And what causes this strife to come into evidence for the most part is that the will, not having the power to excite the passions directly, as has just been said, is constrained to use its best endeavours, and to apply itself to consider successively several things as to which, though it happens that one has the power to change for a moment the course taken by the spirits, it may come to pass that that which succeeds does not have it, and that they immediately afterwards revert to that same course because the disposition which has before held its place in the nerves, heart, and blood has not changed, and thus it comes about that the soul feels itself almost at the same time impelled to desire and not to desire the same thing. It is from this that occasion has been taken to imagine in the soul two powers which strive one with the other. At the same time we may still conceive a sort of strife to exist, inasmuch as often the same cause which excites some passion in the soul, also excites certain movements in the body to which the soul does not contribute, and which it stops, or tries to stop, directly it perceives them; as we see when what excites fear also causes the spirits to enter into the muscles which serve to move the legs with the object of flight, and when the wish which we have to be brave stops them from doing so.

Chapter 16

From "The Union of Soul and Body"

Nicolas Malebranche

One need not imagine, as do most philosophers, that the mind becomes material when united with the body, and that the body becomes mind when it unites with the mind. The soul is not spread through all parts of the body, in order to give life and movement to it, as the imagination might have it; and the body does not become capable of sensation through its union with the mind, as our false and misleading senses seem to convince us. Each substance remains what it is, and as the soul is incapable of extension and movement, so the body is incapable of sensation and inclinations. The only alliance of mind and body known to us consists in a natural and mutual correspondence of the soul's thoughts with the brain traces, and of the soul's emotions with the movements of the animal spirits.

As soon as the soul receives some new ideas, new traces are imprinted in the brain: and as soon as objects produce new traces, the soul receives new ideas. It is not that it considers these traces, since it has no knowledge of them; nor that these traces include these ideas, for they have no relation to them; nor, finally, that the soul receives its ideas from these traces: for, as we shall explain in the third book, it is inconceivable that the mind receive anything from the body and become more enlightened by turning toward it, as these philosophers claim who would have it that it is by *transformation* to fantasms, or brain traces, *per conversionem ad phantasmata*, that the mind perceives all things. But that all takes place according to the general laws of the union of soul and body, which I shall also explain in the third book.

Likewise as soon as the soul wills that the arm be moved, it is moved, even though the soul does not know what it must do in order to move it; and as soon as the animal spirits are agitated, the soul is affected, even though it might not even know whether there are animal spirits in its body.

When I come to speak of the passions, I shall talk about the connection between the brain traces and the movements of the spirits, and that between the ideas and the emotions of the soul, for all the passions depend on them. Right now, I need only mention the connection between the ideas and the traces, and the connection of the traces with each other.

There are three very important causes of the connection of ideas with traces. The first, and the one the others presuppose, is nature, or the constant and immutable will of the Creator. There is, for example, a natural connection, independent of our will, between the traces producing a tree or a mountain we see and the ideas of tree or mountain, between the traces that produce in our brain the cry of a suffering man or animal and our understanding him to complain, between the expression of a man who threatens or fears us and the ideas of pain, strength, weakness, and even among the feelings of compassion, fear, and courage arising in us.

These natural connections are the strongest of all. They are generally similar in all men, and they are absolutely necessary for the preservation of life. This is why they do not depend at all upon our wills. For, if the connection of ideas with sounds and certain characters is weak, and quite different in different countries, it is because it depends upon the weak and changeable will of men. And the reason why this connection depends upon it is that this connection is not absolutely necessary for living, but only for living as men, who should form a rational society among themselves.

The *passions* of the soul are impressions from the Author of nature that incline us toward loving our body and all that might be of use in its preservation. . . . It is through this continuous action by God that our volitions are followed by all those movements in the body designed to carry them out, and that the movements of our body that are mechanically excited in us at the sight of some object are accompanied by a passion of our soul that inclines us to will what seems to be useful to the body.

It is this continuous and efficacious impression of the will of God on us that binds us so closely to one part of matter, and if this impression of His will should cease for but a moment, we would immediately be freed from our dependence upon the body and all the changes it undergoes. For I cannot understand how certain people imagine that there is an absolutely necessary relation between the movements of the spirits and blood and the emotions of the soul. A few tiny particles of bile are rather violently stirred up in the brain—therefore, the soul must be excited by some passion, and the passion must be anger rather than love. What relation can be conceived between the idea of an enemy's faults, or a passion of contempt or hatred, on the one hand, and the corporeal movement of the blood's parts striking against certain parts of the brain on the other? How can they convince themselves that the one depends on the other, and that the union or connection of two things so remote and incompatible as mind and matter could be caused and maintained in any way other than by the continuous and all-powerful will of the Author of nature?

. . . Now it appears to me quite certain that the will of minds is incapable of moving the smallest body in the world; for it is clear that there is no necessary connection between our will to move our arms, for example, and the movement of our arms. It is true that they are moved when we will it, and that thus we are the natural cause of the movement of our arms. But *natural* causes are not true causes; they are only *occasional* causes that act only through the force and efficacy of the will of God, as I have just explained.

For how could we move our arms? To move them, it is necessary to have animal spirits, to send them through certain nerves toward certain muscles in order to inflate and contract them, for it is thus that the arm attached to them is moved; or according to the opinion of some others, it is still not known how that happens. And we see that men who do not know that they have spirits, nerves, and muscles move their arms, and even move them with more skill and ease than those who know anatomy best. Therefore, men will to move their arms, and only God is able and knows how to move them. If a man cannot turn a tower upside down, at least he knows what must be done to do so; but there is no man who knows what must be done to move one of his fingers by means of animal spirits. How, then, could men move their arms? These things seem obvious to me and, it seems to me, to all those willing to think, although they are perhaps incomprehensible to all those willing only to sense.

But not only are men not the true causes of the movements they produce in their bodies, there even seems to be some contradiction (in saying) that they could be. A true cause as I understand it is one such that the mind perceives a necessary connection between it and its effect. Now the mind perceives a necessary connection only between the will of an infinitely perfect being and its effects. Therefore, it is only God who is the true cause and who truly has the power to move bodies. I say further (a) that it is inconceivable that God could communicate His power to move bodies to men or angels, and (b) that those who claim that our power to move our arms is a true power should admit that God can also give to minds the power to create, annihilate, and to do all possible things; in short, that He can render them omnipotent, as I shall show.

God needs no instruments to act; it suffices that He wills[1] in order that a thing be, because it is a contradiction that He should will and that what He wills should not happen. Therefore, His power is His will, and to communicate His power is to communicate the efficacy of His will. But to communicate this efficacy to a man or an angel signifies nothing other than to will that when a man or an angel shall will this or that body to be moved it will actually be moved. Now in this case, I see two wills concurring when an angel moves a body; that of God and that of the angel; and in order to know which of the two is the true cause of the movement of this body, it is necessary to know which one is efficacious. There is a necessary connection between the will of God and the thing He wills. God wills in this case that, when an angel wills this or that body be moved, it will be moved. Therefore, there is a necessary connection between the will of God and the movement of the body; and consequently it is God who is the true cause of its movement, whereas the will of the angel is only the occasional cause.

But to show this still more clearly, let us suppose that God wills to produce the opposite of what some minds will, as might be thought in the case of demons or some other minds that deserve this punishment. One could not say in this case that God would communicate His power to them, since they could do nothing they willed to do. Nevertheless, the wills of these minds would be the natural causes of the effects produced. Such bodies would be moved to the right only because these minds willed them moved to the left; and the volitions of these minds would determine the will of God to act, as our willing to move the parts of our bodies determines the first cause to move them. Thus, all the volitions of minds are only occasional causes.

There is therefore only one single true God and one single cause that is truly a cause, and one should not imagine that what precedes an effect is its true cause. God cannot even communicate His power to creatures, if we follow the lights of reason; He cannot make true causes of them, He cannot make them gods. But even if He could, we cannot conceive why He would. Bodies, minds, pure intelligences, all these can do nothing. It is He who made minds, who enlightens and activates them. It is He who created the sky and the earth, and who regulates their motions. In short, it is the Author of our being who executes our wills: *semel jussit, semper paret.* He moves our arms even when we use them against His orders; for He complains through His prophet that we make Him serve our unjust and criminal desires.

If religion teaches us that there is only one true God, this philosophy shows us that there is only one true cause. If religion teaches us that all the divinities of paganism are merely stones and metals without life or motion, this philosophy also reveals to us that all secondary causes, or all the divinities of philosophy, are merely matter and inefficacious wills. Finally, if religion teaches us that we must not genuflect before false gods, this philosophy also teaches us that our imaginations and minds must not bow before the imaginary greatness and power of causes that are not causes at all; that we must neither love nor fear them; that we must not be concerned with them; that we must think only of God alone, see God in all things, fear and love God in all things.

Note

1. It is clear that I am speaking here about practical volitions, or those God has when He wills to act.

Chapter 17

The Nature and Communication of Substances

Gottfried Wilhelm Leibniz

When I began to think about the union of the soul with the body, it was like casting me back into the open sea, for I found no way to explain how the body causes anything to take place in the soul, or vice versa, or how one substance can communicate with another created substance. So far as we can know from his writings, Descartes gave up the struggle over this problem. But seeing that the common opinion is inconceivable, his disciples concluded that we sense the qualities of bodies because God causes thoughts to arise in our soul on the occasion of material movements and that, when our soul in its turn wishes to move the body, God moves the body for it. And since the communication of motion also seemed inconceivable to them, they believed that God imparts motion to a body on the occasion of the motion of another body. This they call the *System of Occasional Causes*; it has had great vogue as a result of the beautiful reflections of the author of the *Recherche de la vérite*.

It must be admitted that this has definitely penetrated the difficulty in showing us what cannot take place. But it does not seem to have removed the difficulty by showing us what actually does happen. It is quite true that, speaking with metaphysical rigor, there is no real influence of one created substance upon another and that all things, with all their reality, are continually produced by the power of God. But problems are not solved merely by making use of a general cause and calling in what is called the *deus ex machina*. To do this without offering any other explanation drawn from the order of secondary causes is, properly speaking, to have recourse to miracle. In philosophy we must try to give a reason which will show how things are brought about by the Divine Wisdom in conformity with the particular concept of the subject in question.

Being constrained, then, to admit that it is impossible for the soul or any other true substance to receive something from without, except by the divine omnipotence, I was led insensibly to an opinion which surprised me, but which seems inevitable, and which has in fact very great advantages and very significant beauties. This is that we must say that God has originally created the soul, and every other real unity, in such a way that everything in it must arise from its own nature by a perfect *spontaneity* with regard to itself, yet by a perfect *conformity* to things without. And thus, since our internal sensations, that is, those which are in the soul itself and not in the brain or in the subtle parts of the body, are merely phenomena which follow upon external events or, better, are really appearances or like well-ordered dreams, it follows that these perceptions internal to the soul itself come to it through its own original constitution, that is to say, through its representative nature, which is capable of expressing entities outside of itself in agreement with its organs—this nature having been given it from its creation and constituting its individual character. It is this that makes each substance represent the entire universe accurately in its own way and according to a definite point of view. And the perceptions or expressions of external things reach the soul at the proper time by virtue of its own laws, as in a world apart, and as if there existed nothing but God and itself (to make use of the expression of a person of exalted mind and renowned piety). So there will be a perfect accord between all these substances which produces the same effect that would be noticed if they all communicated with each other by a transmission of species or of qualities, as the common run of philosophers imagine. Furthermore, the organized mass in which the point of view of the soul is found is itself expressed more immediately by the soul and is in turn ready to act by itself following the laws of the corporeal mechanism, at the moment at which the soul wills but without either disturbing the laws of the other, the animal spirits and the blood taking on, at exactly the right moment, the motions required to correspond to the passions and the perceptions of the soul. It is this mutual agreement, regulated in advance in every substance of the universe, which produces what we call their communication and which alone constitutes the union of soul and body. This makes it clear how the soul has its seat in the body by an immediate presence which could not be closer, since the soul is in it as a unity is in the resultant of unities which is a multitude.

This hypothesis is entirely possible. For why should God be unable to give to substance in the beginning a nature or internal force which enables it to produce in regular order—as in an *automaton that is spiritual or formal but free* in the case of that substance which has a share of reason—everything which is to happen to it, that is, all the appearances or expressions which it is to have, and this without the help of any created being? Especially since the nature of substance necessarily demands and essentially involves progress or change and would have no force of action without it. And since it is the nature of the soul to represent the universe in a very exact way, though with relative degrees of distinctness, the sequence of representations which the soul produces will correspond naturally to the sequence of changes in the universe itself. So the body, in turn, has also been adapted to the soul to fit those situations in which the soul is thought of as acting externally. This is all the more reasonable inasmuch as bodies are made solely for the spirits themselves, who are capable of entering into a society with God and of extolling his glory. Thus as soon as one sees the possibility of this *hypothesis of agreement*, one sees also that it is the most reasonable one and that it gives a wonderful idea of the harmony of the universe and of the perfection of the works of God.

There is also in it the great advantage that, instead of saying that we are free only in appearance and in a manner adequate for practical purposes, as several intelligent persons have thought, we must rather say that we are determined only in appearance and that in metaphysical strictness we are in a state of perfect independence as concerns the influence of all the other created beings. This throws a wonderful light on the immortality of our soul as well and on the always uniform conservation of our individual being, which is perfectly regulated by its own nature and fully sheltered from all accidents from without, whatever appearance there may be to the contrary. Never has a system so clearly exhibited our elevation. Since each mind is as a world apart and sufficient unto itself, independent of every other created being, enveloping the infinite and expressing the universe, it is as durable, as subsistent, as absolute as the universe of creatures itself. We must therefore conclude that it must always play such a part as is most fitting to contribute to the perfection of the society of all minds, which is their moral union in the City of God. A new proof of the existence of God can also be found here, one of surprising clarity. For the perfect agreement of so many substances which have no communication whatever with each other can come only from a common source.

Imagine two clocks or watches which are in perfect agreement. Now this can happen in *three ways*. The *first* is that of a natural influence. This is the way with which Mr. Huygens experimented, with results that greatly surprised him. He suspended two pendulums from the same piece of wood. The continued strokes of the pendulums transmitted similar vibrations to the particles of wood, but these vibrations could not continue in their own frequency without interfering with each other, at least when the two pendulums did not beat together. The result, by a kind of miracle, was that even when their strokes had been intentionally disturbed, they came to beat together again, somewhat like two strings tuned to each other. The *second* way of making two clocks, even poor ones, agree always is to assign a skilled craftsman to them who adjusts them and constantly sets them in agreement. The *third* way is to construct these two time-pieces at the beginning with such skill and accuracy that one can be assured of their subsequent agreement.

Now put the soul and the body in the place of these two timepieces. Then their agreement or sympathy will also come about in one of these three ways. The *way of influence* is that of the common philosophy. But since it is impossible to conceive of material particles or of species or immaterial qualities which can pass from one of these substances into the other, this view must be rejected. The *way of assistance* is that of the system of occasional causes. But I hold that this makes a *deus ex machina* intervene in a natural and ordinary matter where reason requires that God should help only in the way in which he concurs in all other natural things. Thus there remains only my hypothesis, that is, the *way of preestablished harmony*, according to which God has made each of the two substances from the beginning in such a way that, though each follows only its own laws which it has received with its being, each agrees throughout with the other, entirely as if they were mutually influenced or as if God were always putting forth his hand, beyond his general concurrence. I do not think that there is anything more than this that I need to prove—unless someone should demand that I prove that God is skilful enough to make use of this foresighted artifice, of which we see samples even among men, to the extent that they are able men. And, assuming that God can do it, it is clear that this way is the most beautiful and the most worthy of him. You had suspected that my explanation would be opposed to the different idea we have of the mind and of the body. But now you clearly see that no one could establish their independence more effectively. For as long as one was obliged to explain their communication by means of a miracle, one always gave opportunity for some people to fear that the distinction between body and soul is not as real as is thought, since we were forced to go to such lengths to maintain it. Now all these scruples will cease.

Chapter 18

The Third Antinomy

Immanuel Kant

THE ANTINOMY OF PURE REASON

THIRD CONFLICT OF THE TRANSCENDENTAL IDEAS

Thesis

Causality, according to the laws of nature, is not the only causality from which all the phenomena of the world can be deduced. In order to account for these phenomena it is necessary also to admit another causality, that of freedom.

Proof

Let us assume that there is no other causality but that according to the laws of nature. In that case everything that *takes place*, presupposes an anterior state, on which it follows inevitably according to a rule. But that anterior state must itself be something which has taken place (which has come to be in time, and did not exist before), because, if it had always existed, its effect too would not have only just arisen, but have existed always. The causality, therefore, of a cause, through which something takes place, is itself an *event*, which again, according to the law of nature, presupposes an anterior state and its causality, and this again an anterior state, and so on. If, therefore, everything takes place according to mere laws of nature, there will always be a secondary only, but never a primary beginning, and therefore no completeness of the series, on the side of successive causes. But the law of nature consists in this, that nothing

Antithesis

There is no freedom, but everything in the world takes place entirely according to the laws of nature.

Proof

If we admit that there is *freedom*, in the transcendental sense, as a particular kind of causality, according to which the events in the world could take place, that is a faculty of absolutely originating a state, and with it a series of consequences, it would follow that not only a series would have its absolute beginning through this spontaneity, but the determination of that spontaneity itself to produce the series, that is, the causality, would have an absolute beginning, nothing preceding it by which this act is determined according to permanent laws. Every beginning of an act, however, presupposes a state in which the cause is not yet active, and a dynamically primary beginning of an act presupposes a state which has no causal connection with the preceding state of that cause, that is, in no wise follows from it. Transcendental freedom is therefore opposed to the law of causality, and represents such a connection of suc-

takes place without a cause sufficiently determined *a priori*. Therefore the proposition, that all causality is possible according to the laws of nature only, contradicts itself, if taken in unlimited generality, and it is impossible, therefore, to admit that causality as the only one.

We must therefore admit another causality, through which something takes place, without its cause being further determined according to necessary laws by a preceding cause, that is, an *absolute spontaneity* of causes, by which a series of phenomena, proceeding according to natural laws, begins by itself; we must consequently admit transcendental freedom, without which, even in the course of nature, the series of phenomena on the side of causes, can never be perfect.

cessive states of effective causes, that no unity of experience is possible with it. It is therefore an empty fiction of the mind, and not to be met with in any experience.

We have, therefore, nothing but *nature*, in which we must try to find the connection and order of events. Freedom (independence) from the laws of nature is no doubt a *deliverance* from restraint, but also from the *guidance* of all rules. For we cannot say that, instead of the laws of nature, laws of freedom may enter into the causality of the course of the world, because, if determined by laws, it would not be freedom, but nothing else but nature. Nature, therefore, and transcendental freedom differ from each other like legality and lawlessness. The former, no doubt, imposes upon the understanding the difficult task of looking higher and higher for the origin of events in the series of causes, because their causality is always conditioned. In return for this, however, it promises a complete and well-ordered unity of experience; while, on the other side, the fiction of freedom promises, no doubt, to the enquiring mind, rest in the chain of causes, leading him up to an unconditioned causality, which begins to act by itself, but which, as it is blind itself, tears the thread of rules by which alone a complete and coherent experience is possible.

OBSERVATION ON THE THIRD ANTINOMY

I On the Thesis

The transcendental idea of freedom is ... the real stone of offence in the eyes of philosophy, which finds its unsurmountable difficulties in admitting this kind of unconditioned causality. That element in the question of the freedom of the will, which has always so much embarrassed speculative reason, is

II On the Antithesis

He who stands up for the omnipotence of nature (transcendental *physiocracy*), in opposition to the doctrine of freedom, would defend his position against the sophistical conclusions of that doctrine in the following manner. *If you do not admit something mathematically the first in the world with reference to time, there is*

therefore in reality *transcendental* only, and refers merely to the question whether we must admit a faculty of *spontaneously* originating a series of successive things or states. How such a faculty is possible need not be answered, because, with regard to the causality, according to the laws of nature also, we must be satisfied to know *a priori* that such a causality has to be admitted, though we can in no wise understand the possibility how, through one existence, the existence of another is given, but must for that purpose appeal to experience alone. The necessity of a first beginning of a series of phenomena from freedom has been proved so far only as it is necessary in order to comprehend an origin of the world, while all successive states may be regarded as a result in succession according to mere laws of nature. But as the faculty of originating a series in time by itself has been proved, though by no means understood, it is now permitted also to admit, within the course of the world, different series, beginning by themselves, with regard to their causality, and to attribute to their substances a faculty of acting with freedom. But we must not allow ourselves to be troubled by a misapprehension, namely that, as every successive series in the world can have only a relatively primary beginning, some other state of things always preceding in the world, therefore no absolutely primary beginning of different series is possible in the course of the world. For we are speaking here of the absolutely first beginning, *not according to time*, but *according to causality*. If, for instance, at this moment I rise from my chair with perfect freedom, without the necessary determining influence of natural causes, a new series has its absolute beginning in this event, with all its natural consequences *ad infinitum*, although, *with regard to time*, this event is only the continuation of a preceding series. For this determination and this act do not belong to the succession of merely natu-

no necessity why you should look for something dynamically the first with reference to causality. Who has told you to invent an absolutely first state of the world, and with it an absolute beginning of the gradually progressing series of phenomena, and to set limits to unlimited nature in order to give to your imagination something to rest on? As substances have always existed in the world, or as the unity of experience renders at least such a supposition necessary, there is no difficulty in assuming that a change of their states, that is, a series of their changes, has always existed also, so that there is no necessity for looking for a first beginning either mathematically or dynamically. It is true we cannot render the possibility of such an infinite descent comprehensible without the first member to which everything else is subsequent. But, if for this reason you reject this riddle of nature, you will feel yourselves constrained to reject many fundamental properties (natural forces), which you cannot comprehend any more....

And, even if the transcendental faculty of freedom might somehow be conceded to start the changes of the world, such faculty would at all events have to be outside the world (though it would always remain a bold assumption to admit, outside the sum total of all possible intuitions, an object that cannot be given in any possible experience). But to attribute in the world itself a faculty to substances can never be allowed, because in that case the connection of phenomena determining each other by necessity and according to general laws, which we call nature, and with it the test of empirical truth, which distinguishes experience from dreams, would almost entirely disappear. For by the side of such a lawless faculty of freedom, nature could hardly be conceived any longer, because the laws of the latter would be constantly changed through the influence of the former, and the play of phenomena

ral effects, nor are they a mere continuation of them, but the determining natural causes completely stop before it, so far as this event is concerned, which no doubt follows them, and does not *result* from them, and may therefore be called an absolutely first beginning in a series of phenomena, not with reference to time, but with reference to causality.

This requirement of reason to appeal in the series of natural causes to a first and free beginning is fully confirmed if we see that, with the exception of the Epicurean school, all philosophers of antiquity have felt themselves obliged to admit, for the sake of explaining all cosmical movements, a *prime mover*, that is, a freely acting cause which, first and by itself, started this series of states. They did not attempt to make a first beginning comprehensible by an appeal to nature only.

which, according to nature, is regular and uniform, would become confused and incoherent.

III

Solution of the Cosmological Ideas with Regard to the Totality of the Derivation of Cosmical Events from their Causes   We can conceive two kinds of causality only with reference to events, causality either of *nature* or of *freedom*. The former is the connection of one state in the world of sense with a preceding state, on which it follows according to a rule. As the *causality* of phenomena depends on conditions of time, and as the preceding state, if it had always existed, could not have produced an effect, which first takes place in time, it follows that the causality of the cause of that which happens or arises must, according to the principle of the understanding, have itself *arisen* and require a cause.

By freedom, on the contrary, in its cosmological meaning, I understand the faculty of beginning a state *spontaneously*. Its causality, therefore, does not depend, according to the law of nature, on another cause, by which it is determined in time. In this sense freedom is a purely transcendental idea, which, first, contains nothing derived from *experience*, and, secondly, the object of which cannot be determined in any *experience*; because it is a general rule, even of the possibility of all *experience*, that everything which happens has a cause, and that therefore the causality also of the cause, which *itself* has happened or arisen, must again have a cause. In this manner the whole field of experience, however far it may extend, has been changed into one great whole of nature. As, however, it is impossible in this way to arrive at an absolute totality of the conditions in causal relations, reason creates for itself the idea of spontaneity, or the power of beginning by itself, without an antecedent cause determining it to action, according to the law of causal connection.

It is extremely remarkable, that the practical concept of freedom is founded on the *transcendental idea of freedom*, which constitutes indeed the real difficulty which at all times has surrounded the question of the possibility of freedom. *Freedom*, in its *practical sense*, is the independence of our (arbitrary) will from the *coercion* through sensuous impulses....

It can easily be seen that, if all causality in the world of sense belonged to nature, every event would be determined in time through another, according to necessary laws. As therefore the phenomena, in determining the will, would render every act necessary as their natural effect, the annihilation of transcendental freedom would at the same time destroy all practical freedom. Practical freedom presupposes that, although something has not happened, it *ought* to have happened, and that its cause therefore had not that determining force among phenomena, which could prevent the causality of our will from producing, independently of those natural causes, and even contrary to their force and influence, something determined in the order of time, according to empirical laws, and from originating *entirely by itself* a series of events.

What happens here is what happens generally in the conflict of reason venturing beyond the limits of possible experience, namely, that the problem is not *physiological*, but *transcendental*. Hence the question of the possibility of freedom concerns no doubt psychology; but its solution, as it depends on dialectical arguments of pure reason, belongs entirely to transcendental philosophy. In order to enable that philosophy to give a satisfactory answer, which it cannot decline to do, I must first try to determine more accurately its proper procedure in this task.

If phenomena were things in themselves, and therefore space and time forms of the existence of things in themselves, the conditions together with the conditioned would always belong, as members, to one and the same series.... All depends here only on the dynamical relation of conditions to the conditioned, so that in the question on nature and freedom we at once meet with the difficulty, whether freedom is indeed possible, and whether, if it is possible, it can exist together with the universality of the natural law of causality. The question in fact arises, whether it is a proper disjunctive proposition to say, that every effect in the world must arise, *either* from nature, *or* from freedom, or whether *both* cannot coexist in the same event in different relations. The correctness of the principle of the unbroken connection of all events in the world of sense, according to unchangeable natural laws, is firmly established ... and admits of no limitation. The question, therefore, can only be whether, in spite of it, freedom also can be found in the same effect which is determined by nature; or whether freedom is entirely excluded by that inviolable rule? Here the common but fallacious supposition of the *absolute reality* of phenomena shows at once its pernicious influence in embarrassing reason. For if phenomena are things in themselves, freedom cannot be saved. Nature in that case is the complete and sufficient cause determining every event, and its condition is always contained in that series of phenomena only which, together with their effect, are necessary under the law of nature. If, on the contrary, phenomena are taken for nothing except what they are in reality, namely, not things in themselves, but representations only, which are connected with each other according to empirical laws, they must themselves have causes, which are not phenomenal. Such an intelligible cause, however, is not determined with reference to its causality by phenomena, although its effects become phenomenal, and can thus be determined by other phenomena. That intelligible cause, therefore, with its causality, is outside the series, though its *effects* are to be found *in* the series of empirical conditions. The effect therefore can, with reference to its *intelligible* cause, be considered as free, and yet at the same time, with reference to *phenomena*, as resulting from them according to the necessity of nature; a distinction which, if thus represented, in a general and entirely abstract form, may seem extremely subtle and obscure, but will become clear in its practical application. Here I only wished to remark that, as the unbroken *connection* of all phenomena in the context of nature, is an unalterable law, it would necessarily destroy all freedom, if we were to defend obstinately the reality of phenomena. Those, therefore, who follow the common opinion on this subject, have never been able to reconcile nature and freedom.

Possibility of a Causality through Freedom, in Harmony with the Universal Law of Natural Necessity   Whatever in an object of the senses is not itself phenomenal, I call *intelligible*. If, therefore, what in the world of sense must be considered as phenomenal, possesses in itself a faculty which is not the object of sensuous intuition, but through which it can become the cause of phenomena, the *causality* of that being may be considered from *two sides*, as *intelligible* in its *action*, as the causality of a thing in itself, and as *sensible* in the *effects* of the action, as the causality of a phenomenon in the world of sense. Of the faculty of such a being we should have to form both an *empirical* and an *intellectual concept* of its causality, both of which consist together in one and the same effect. This twofold way of conceiving the faculty of an object of the senses does not contradict any of the concepts which we have to form of phenomena and of a possible experience. For since all phenomena, not being things in themselves, must have for their foundation a transcendental object, determining them as mere representations, there is nothing to prevent us from attributing to that transcendental object, besides the quality through which it becomes phenomenal, a *causality* also which is not phenomenal, although its *effect* appears in the phenomenon. Every efficient cause, however, must have a *character*, that is, a rule according to which it manifests its causality, and without which it would not be a cause. According to this we should have in every subject of the world of sense, first, an *empirical character*, through which its acts, as phenomena, stand with other phenomena in an unbroken connection, according to permanent laws of nature, and could be derived from them as their conditions, and in connection with them form the links of one and the same series in the order of nature. Secondly, we should have to allow to it an *intelligible character* also, by which, it is true, it becomes the cause of the same acts as phenomena, but which itself is not subject to any conditions of sensibility, and never phenomenal. We might call the former the character of such a thing as a phenomenon, in the latter the character of the thing in itself.

According to its intelligible character, this active subject would not depend on conditions of time, for time is only the condition of phenomena, and not of things in themselves. In it no *act* would *arise* or *perish*, neither would it be subject therefore to the law of determination in time and of all that is changeable, namely, that everything *which happens* must have its cause in *the phenomena* (of the previous state). In one word its causality, so far as it is intelligible, would not have a place in the series of empirical conditions by which the event is rendered necessary in the world of sense. It is true that that intelligible character could never be known immediately, because we cannot perceive anything, except so far as it appears, but it would nevertheless have to be conceived, according to the empirical character, as we must always admit in thought a transcendental object, as the foundation of phenomena, though we know nothing of what it is in itself.

In its empirical character, therefore, that subject, as a phenomenon, would submit, according to all determining laws, to a causal nexus, and in that respect it would be nothing but a part of the world of sense, the effects of which, like every other phenomenon, would arise from nature without fail. As soon as external phenomena began to influence it, and as soon as its empirical character, that is the law of its causality, had been known through experience, all its actions ought to admit of explanation, according to the laws of nature, and all that is requisite for its complete and necessary determination would be found in a possible experience.

In its intelligible character, however (though we could only have a general concept of it), the same subject would have to be considered free from all influence of sensibility, and from all determination through phenomena: and as in it, so far as it is a *noumenon*, nothing *happens*, and no change which requires dynamical determination of time, and therefore no connection with phenomena as causes, can exist, that active being would so far be quite independent and free in its acts from all natural necessity, which can exist in the world of sense only. One might say of it with perfect truth that it originates its effects in the world of sense *by itself*, though the act does not begin *in itself*. And this would be perfectly true, though the effects in the world of sense need not therefore originate by themselves, because in it they are always determined previously through empirical conditions in the previous time, though only by means of the empirical character (which is the phenomenal appearance of the intelligible character), and therefore impossible, except as a continuation of the series of natural causes. In this way freedom and nature, each in its complete signification, might exist together and without any conflict in the same action, according as we refer it to its intelligible or to its sensible cause.

Explanation of the Cosmological Idea of Freedom in Connection with the General Necessity of Nature   I thought it best to give first this sketch of the solution of our transcendental problem, so that the course which reason has to adopt in its solution might be more clearly surveyed. We shall now proceed to explain more fully the points on which the decision properly rests, and examine each by itself.

That our reason possesses causality, or that we at least represent to ourselves such a causality in it, is clear from the *imperatives* which, in all practical matters, we impose as rules on our executive powers. The *ought* expresses a kind of necessity and connection with causes, which we do not find elsewhere in the whole of nature. The understanding can know in nature only what is present, past, or future. It is impossible that anything in it *ought to be* different from what it is in reality, in all these relations of time. Nay, if we only look at the course of nature, the ought has no meaning whatever. We cannot ask, what ought to be in nature, as little as we can ask, what qualities a circle ought to possess. We can only ask what happens in it, and what qualities that which happens has.

This ought expresses a possible action, the ground of which cannot be anything but a mere concept; while in every merely natural action the ground must always be a phenomenon. Now it is quite true that the action to which the ought applies must be possible under natural conditions, but these natural conditions do not affect the determination of the will itself, but only its effects and results among phenomena. There may be ever so many natural grounds which impel me to *will* and ever so many sensuous temptations, but they can never produce the *ought*, but only a willing which is always conditioned, but by no means necessary, and to which the ought, pronounced by reason, opposes measure, ay, prohibition and authority. Whether it be an object of the senses merely (pleasure), or of pure reason (the good), reason does not yield to the impulse that is given empirically, and does not follow the order of things, as they present themselves as phenomena, but frames for itself, with perfect spontaneity, a new order according to ideas to which it adapts the empirical conditions, and according to which it declares actions to be necessary, even though they *have not taken place*, and, maybe, never will take place. Yet it is presupposed that reason may have causality with respect to them, for otherwise no effects in experience could be expected to result from these ideas.

Now let us take our stand here and admit it at least as possible, that reason really possesses causality with reference to phenomena. In that case, reason though it be, it must show nevertheless an empirical character, because every cause presupposes a rule according to which certain phenomena follow as effects, and every rule requires in the effects a homogeneousness, on which the concept of cause (as a faculty) is founded. This, so far as it is derived from mere phenomena, may be called the empirical character, which is *permanent*, while the effects, according to a diversity of concomitant, and in part, restraining conditions, appear in *changeable* forms.

Every man therefore has an empirical character of his (arbitrary) will, which is nothing but a certain causality of his reason, exhibiting in its phenomenal actions and effects a rule, according to which one may infer the motives of reason and its actions, both in kind and in degree, and judge of the subjective principles of his will. As that empirical character itself must be derived from phenomena, as an effect, and from their rule which is supplied by experience, all the acts of a man, so far as they are phenomena, are determined from his empirical character and from the other concomitant causes, according to the order of nature; and if we could investigate all the manifestations of his will to the very bottom, there would be not a single human action which we could not predict with certainty and recognise from its preceding conditions as necessary. There is no freedom therefore with reference to this empirical character, and yet it is only with reference to it that we can consider man, when we are merely *observing*, and, as is the case in anthropology, trying to investigate the motive causes of his actions physiologically.

If, however, we consider the same actions with reference to reason ... solely so far as reason is the cause which *produces* them; in one word, if we compare actions with reason, with reference to *practical* purposes, we find a rule and order, totally different from the order of nature. For, from this point of view, everything, it may be, *ought not to have happened*, which according to the course of nature *has happened*, and according to its empirical grounds, was inevitable. And sometimes we find, or believe at least that we find, that the ideas of reason have really proved their causality with reference to human actions as phenomena, and that these actions have taken place, not because they were determined by empirical causes, but by the causes of reason.

Now supposing one could say that reason possesses causality in reference to phenomena, could the action of reason be called free in that case, as it is accurately determined by the empirical character (the disposition) and rendered necessary by it? That character again is determined in the intelligible character (way of thinking). The latter, however, we do not know, but signify only through phenomena, which in reality give us immediately a knowledge of the disposition (empirical character) only.[1] ... Pure reason, as a simple intelligible faculty, is not subject to the form of time, or to the conditions of the succession of time. The causality of reason in its intelligible character does *not arise* or begin at a certain time in order to produce an effect; for in that case it would be subject to the natural law of phenomena, which determines all causal series in time, and its causality would then be nature and not freedom. What, therefore, we can say is, that if reason can possess causality with reference to phenomena, it is a faculty *through which* the sensuous condition of an empirical series of effects first begins. For the condition that lies in reason is not sensuous, and therefore does itself not begin. Thus we get what we missed in all empirical series, namely, that the *condition* of a successive series of events should itself be empirically unconditioned. For here the condition is really *outside* the series of phenomena (in the intelligible), and therefore not subject to any sensuous condition, nor to any temporal determination through preceding causes.

Nevertheless the same cause belongs also, in another respect, to the series of phenomena. Man himself is a phenomenon. His will has an empirical character, which is the (empirical) cause of all his actions. There is no condition, determining man according to this character, that is not contained in the series of natural effects and subject to their law, according to which there can be no empirically unconditioned causality of anything that happens in time. No given action therefore (as it can be perceived as a phenomenon only) can begin absolutely by itself. Of pure reason, however, we cannot say that the state in which it determines the will is preceded by another in which that state itself is determined. For as reason itself is not a phenomenon, and not subject to any of the conditions of sensibility, there exists in it, even in reference to its causality, no succession of time, and the dynamical law of nature, which determines the succession of time according to rules, cannot be applied to it.

Reason is therefore the constant condition of all free actions by which man takes his place in the phenomenal world. Every one of them is determined beforehand in his empirical character, before it becomes actual. With regard to the intelligible character, however, of which the empirical is only the sensuous schema, there is neither *before* nor *after*; and every action, without regard to the temporal relation which connects it with other phenomena, is the immediate effect of the intelligible character of pure reason. That reason therefore acts freely, without being determined dynamically, in the chain of natural causes, by external or internal conditions, anterior in time. That freedom must then not only be regarded negatively, as independence of empirical conditions (for in that case the faculty of reason would cease to be a cause of phenomena), but should be determined positively also, as the faculty of beginning spontaneously a series of events. Hence nothing begins in reason itself, and being itself the unconditioned condition of every free action, reason admits of no condition antecedent in time above itself, while nevertheless its effect takes its beginning in the series of phenomena, though it can never constitute in that series an *absolutely* first beginning.

In order to illustrate the regulative principle of reason by an example of its empirical application, not in order to confirm it (for such arguments are useless for transcendental propositions), let us take a voluntary action, for example, a malicious lie, by which a man has produced a certain confusion in society, and of which we first try to find out the motives, and afterwards try to determine how far it and its consequences may be imputed to the offender. With regard to the first point, one has first to follow up his empirical character to its very sources, which are to be found in wrong education, bad society, in part also in the viciousness of a natural disposition, and a nature insensible to shame, or ascribed to frivolity and heedlessness, not omitting the occasioning causes at the time. In all this the procedure is exactly the same as in the investigation of a series of determining causes of a given natural effect. But although one believes that the act was thus determined, one nevertheless blames the offender, and not on account of his unhappy natural disposition, not on account of influencing circumstances, not even on account of his former course of life, because one supposes one might leave entirely out of account what that course of life may have been, and consider the past series of conditions as having never existed, and the act itself as totally unconditioned by previous states, as if the offender had begun with it a new series of effects, quite by himself. This blame is founded on a law of reason, reason being considered as a cause which, independent of all the before-mentioned empirical conditions, would and should have determined the behaviour of the man otherwise. Nay, we do not regard the causality of reason as a concurrent agency only, but as complete in itself, even though the sensuous motives did not favour, but even oppose it. The action is imputed to a man's intelligible character. At the moment when he tells the lie, the guilt is entirely his; that is, we regard reason, in spite of all empirical conditions of the act, as completely free, and the act has to be imputed entirely to a fault of reason.

Such an imputation clearly shows that we imagine that reason is not affected at all by the influences of the senses, and that it does not change (although its manifestations, that is the mode in which it shows itself by its effects, do change): that in it no state precedes as determining a following state, in fact, that reason does not belong to the series of sensuous conditions which render phenomena necessary, according to laws of nature. Reason, it is supposed, is present in all the actions of man, in all circumstances of time, and always the same; but it is itself never in time, never in a new state in which it was not before; it is *determining*, never *determined*. . . .

We thus see that, in judging of voluntary actions, we can, so far as their causality is concerned, get only so far as the intelligible cause, but not beyond. We can see that that cause is free, that it determines as independent of sensibility, and therefore is capable of being the sensuously unconditioned condition of phenomena. To explain why that intelligible character should, under present circumstances, give these phenomena and this empirical character, and no other, transcends all the powers of our reason, nay, all its rights of questioning, as if we were to ask why the transcendental object of our external sensuous intuition gives us intuition in *space* only and no other. But the problem which we have to solve does not require us to ask or to answer such questions. Our problem was, whether freedom is contradictory to natural necessity in one and the same action: and this we have sufficiently answered by showing that freedom may have relation to a very different kind of conditions from those of nature, so that the law of the latter does not affect the former, and both may exist independent of, and undisturbed by, each other.

It should be clearly understood that, in what we have said, we had no intention of establishing the *reality* of freedom, as one of the faculties which contain the cause of the phenomenal appearances in our world of sense. For not only would this have been no transcendental consideration at all, which is concerned with concepts only, but it could never have succeeded, because from experience we can never infer anything but what must be represented in thought according to the laws of experience. It was not even our intention to prove the *possibility* of freedom, for in this also we should not have succeeded, because from mere concepts *a priori* we can never know the possibility of any real ground or any causality. We have here treated freedom as a transcendental idea only, which makes reason imagine that it can absolutely begin the series of phenomenal conditions through what is sensuously unconditioned, but by which reason becomes involved in an antinomy with its own laws, which it had prescribed to the empirical use of the understanding. That this antinomy rests on a mere illusion, and that nature does *not contradict* the causality of freedom, that was the only thing which we could prove, and cared to prove.

Note

1. The true morality of actions (merit or guilt), even that of our own conduct, remains therefore entirely hidden. Our imputations can refer to the empirical character only. How much of that may be the pure effect of freedom, how much should be ascribed to nature only, and to the faults of temperament, for which man is not responsible, or its happy constitution (*merito fortunae*), no one can discover, and no one can judge with perfect justice.

Chapter 19

On the Hypothesis That Animals Are Automata

Thomas Henry Huxley

Descartes' line of argument is perfectly clear. He starts from reflex action in man, from the unquestionable fact that, in ourselves, co-ordinate, purposive actions may take places, without the intervention of consciousness or volition, or even contrary to the latter. As actions of a certain degree of complexity are brought about by mere mechanism, why may not actions of still greater complexity be the result of a more refined mechanism? What proof is there that brutes are other than a superior race of marionettes, which eat without pleasure, cry without pain, desire nothing, know nothing, and only simulate intelligence as a bee simulates a mathematician?

The Port Royalists adopted the hypothesis that brutes are machines, and are said to have carried its practical applications so far as to treat domestic animals with neglect, if not with actual cruelty. As late as the middle of the eighteenth century, the problem was discussed very fully and ably by Bouillier, in his *"Essai philosophique sur l'Âme des Bêtes,"* while Condillac deals with it in his *"Traité des Animaux;"* but since then it has received little attention. Nevertheless, modern research has brought to light a great multitude of facts, which not only show that Descartes' view is defensible, but render it far more defensible than it was in his day.

And would Descartes not have been justified in asking why we need deny that animals are machines, when men, in a state of unconsciousness, perform, mechanically, actions as complicated and as seemingly rational as those of any animals?

But though I do not think that Descartes' hypothesis can be positively refuted, I am not disposed to accept it. The doctrine of continuity is too well established for it to be permissible to me to suppose that any complex natural phenomenon comes into existence suddenly, and without being preceded by simpler modifications; and very strong arguments would be needed to prove that such complex phenomena as those of consciousness, first make their appearance in man. We know, that, in the individual man, consciousness grows from a dim glimmer to its full light, whether we consider the infant advancing in years, or the adult emerging from slumber and swoon. We know, further, that the lower animals possess, though less developed, that part of the brain which we have every reason to believe to be the organ of consciousness in man; and as, in other cases, function and organ are proportional, so we have a right to conclude it is with the brain; and that the brutes, though they may not possess our intensity of consciousness, and though, from the absence of language, they can have no trains of thoughts, but only trains of feelings, yet have a consciousness which, more or less distinctly, foreshadows our own.

I confess that, in view of the struggle for existence which goes on in the animal world, and of the frightful quantity of pain with which it must be accompanied, I should be glad if the probabilities were in favour of Descartes' hypothesis; but, on the other hand, considering the terrible practical consequences to domestic animals which might ensue from any error on our part, it is as well to err on the right side, if we err at all, and deal with them as weaker brethren, who are bound, like the rest of us, to pay their toll for living, and suffer what is needful for the general good. As Hartley finely says, "We seem to be in the place of God to them;" and we may justly follow the precedents He sets in nature in our dealings with them.

But though we may see reason to disagree with Descartes' hypothesis that brutes are unconscious machines, it does not follow that he was wrong in regarding them as automata. They may be more or less conscious, sensitive, automata; and the view that they are such conscious machines is that which is implicitly, or explictly, adopted by most persons. When we speak of the actions of the lower animals being guided by instinct and not by reason, what we really mean is that, though they feel as we do, yet their actions are the results of their physical organisation. We believe, in short, that they are machines, one part of which (the nervous system) not only sets the rest in motion, and co-ordinates its movements in relation with changes in surrounding bodies, but is provided with special apparatus, the function of which is the calling into existence of those states of consciousness which are termed sensations, emotions, and ideas. I believe that this generally accepted view is the best expression of the facts at present known.

It is experimentally demonstrable—any one who cares to run a pin into himself may perform a sufficient demonstration of the fact—that a mode of motion of the nervous system is the immediate antecedent of a state of consciousness. All but the adherents of "Occasionalism," or of the doctrine of "Pre-established Harmony" (if any such now exist), must admit that we have as much reason for regarding the mode of motion of the nervous system as the cause of the state of consciousness, as we have for regarding any event as the cause of another. How the one phenomenon causes the other we know, as much or as little, as in any other case of causation; but we have as much right to believe that the sensation is an effect of the molecular change, as we have to believe that motion is an effect of impact; and there is as much propriety in saying that the brain evolves sensation, as there is in saying that an iron rod, when hammered, evolves heat.

As I have endeavoured to show, we are justified in supposing that something analogous to what happens in ourselves takes place in the brutes, and that the affections of their sensory nerves give rise to molecular changes in the brain, which again give rise to, or evolve, the corresponding states of consciousness. Nor can there be any reasonable doubt that the emotions of brutes, and such ideas as they possess, are similarly dependent upon molecular brain changes. Each sensory impression leaves behind a record in the structure of the brain—an "ideagenous" molecule, so to speak, which is competent, under certain conditions, to reproduce, in a fainter condition, the state of consciousness which corresponds with that sensory impression; and it is these "ideagenous molecules" which are the physical basis of memory.

It may be assumed, then, that molecular changes in the brain are the causes of all the states of consciousness of brutes. Is there any evidence that these states of consciousness may, conversely, cause those molecular changes which give rise to muscular motion? I see no such evidence. The frog walks, hops, swims, and goes through his gymnastic performances quite as well without consciousness, and consequently without volition, as with it; and, if a frog, in his natural state, possesses anything corresponding with what we call volition, there is no reason to think that it is anything but a concomitant of the molecular changes in the brain which form part of the series involved in the production of motion.

The consciousness of brutes would appear to be related to the mechanism of their body simply as a collateral product of its working, and to be as completely without any power of modifying that working as the steam-whistle which accompanies the work of a locomotive engine is without influence upon it machinery. Their volition, if they have any, is an emotion indicative of physical changes, not a cause of such changes.

This conception of the relations of states of consciousness with molecular changes in the brain—of *psychoses* with *neuroses*—does not prevent us from ascribing free will to brutes. For an agent is free when there is nothing to prevent him from doing that which he desires to do. If a greyhound chases a hare, he is a free agent, because his action is in entire accordance with his strong desire to catch the hare; while so long as he is held back by the leash he is not free, being prevented by external force from following his inclination. And the ascription of freedom to the greyhound under the former circumstances is by no means inconsistent with the other aspect of the facts of the case—that he is a machine impelled to the chase, and caused, at the same time, to have the desire to catch the game by the impression which the rays of light proceeding from the hare make upon his eyes, and through them upon his brain.

Much ingenious argument has at various times been bestowed upon the question: How is it possible to imagine that volition, which is a state of consciousness, and, as such, has not the slightest community of nature with matter in motion, can act upon the moving matter of which the body is composed, as it is assumed to do in voluntary acts? But if, as is here suggested, the voluntary acts of brutes—or, in other words, the acts which they desire to perform—are as purely mechanical as the rest of their actions, and are simply accompanied by the state of consciousness called volition, the inquiry, so far as they are concerned, becomes superfluous. Their volitions do not enter into the chain of causation of their actions at all.

The hypothesis that brutes are conscious automata is perfectly consistent with any view that may be held respecting the often discussed and curious question whether they have souls or not; and, if they have souls, whether those souls are immortal or not. It is obviously harmonious with the most literal adherence to the text of Scripture concerning "the beast that perisheth"; but it is not inconsistent with the amiable conviction ascribed by Pope to his "untutored savage," that when he passes to the happy hunting-grounds in the sky, "his faithful dog shall bear him company." If the brutes have consciousness and no souls, then it is clear that, in them, consciousness is a direct function of material changes; while, if they possess immaterial subjects of consciousness, or souls, then, as consciousness is brought into existence only as the consequence of molecular motion of the brain, it follows that it is an indirect product of material changes. The soul stands related to the body as the bell of a clock to the works, and consciousness answers to the sound which the bell gives out when it is struck.

Thus far I have strictly confined myself to the problem with which I proposed to deal at starting—the automatism of brutes. The question is, I believe, a perfectly open one, and I feel happy in running no risk of either Papal or Presbyterian condemnation for the views which I have ventured to put forward. And there are so very few interesting questions which one is, at present, allowed to think out scientifically—to go as far as reason leads, and stop where evidence comes to an end—without speedily being deafened by the tattoo of "the drum ecclesiastic"—that I have luxuriated in my rare freedom, and would now willingly bring the disquisition to an end if I could hope that other people would go no farther. Unfortunately, past experience debars me from entertaining any such hope, even if

that drum's discordant sound
Parading round and round and round,

were not, at present, as audible to me as it was to the mild poet who ventured to express his hatred of drums in general, in that well-known couplet.

It will be said, that I mean that the conclusions deduced from the study of the brutes are applicable to man, and that the logical consequences of such application are fatalism, materialism, and atheism—whereupon the drums will beat the *pas de charge*.

One does not do battle with drummers; but I venture to offer a few remarks for the calm consideration of thoughtful persons, untrammelled by foregone conclusions, unpledged to shore-up tottering dogmas, and anxious only to know the true bearings of the case.

It is quite true that, to the best of my judgment, the argumentation which applies to brutes holds equally good of men; and, therefore, that all states of consciousness in us, as in them, are immediately caused by molecular changes of the brain-substances. It seems to me that in men, as in brutes, there is no proof that any state of consciousness is the cause of change in the motion of the matter of the organism. If these positions are well based, it follows that our mental conditions are simply the symbols in consciousness of the changes which take place automatically in the organism; and that, to take an extreme illustration, the feeling we call volition is not the cause of a voluntary act, but the symbol of that state of the brain which is the immediate cause of that act. We are conscious automata, endowed with free will in the only intelligible sense of that much-abused term—inasmuch as in many respects we are able to do as we like—but nonetheless parts of the great series of causes and effects which, in unbroken continuity, composes that which is, and has been, and shall be—the sum of existence.

Chapter 20
Mental Events
Donald Davidson

Mental events such as perceivings, rememberings, decisions, and actions resist capture in the nomological net of physical theory.[1] How can this fact be reconciled with the causal role of mental events in the physical world? Reconciling freedom with causal determinism is a special case of the problem if we suppose that causal determinism entails capture in, and freedom requires escape from, the nomological net. But the broader issue can remain alive even for someone who believes a correct analysis of free action reveals no conflict with determinism. *Autonomy* (freedom, self-rule) may or may not clash with determinism; *anomaly* (failure to fall under a law) is, it would seem, another matter.

I start from the assumption that both the causal dependence, and the anomalousness, of mental events are undeniable facts. My aim is therefore to explain, in the face of apparent difficulties, how this can be. I am in sympathy with Kant when he says,

> it is as impossible for the subtlest philosophy as for the commonest reasoning to argue freedom away. Philosophy must therefore assume that no true contradiction will be found between freedom and natural necessity in the same human actions, for it cannot give up the idea of nature any more than that of freedom. Hence even if we should never be able to conceive how freedom is possible, at least this apparent contradiction must be convincingly eradicated. For if the thought of freedom contradicts itself or nature . . . it would have to be surrendered in competition with natural necessity.[2]

Generalize human actions to mental events, substitute anomaly for freedom, and this is a description of my problem. And of course the connection is closer, since Kant believed freedom entails anomaly.

Now let me try to formulate a little more carefully the "apparent contradiction" about mental events that I want to discuss and finally dissipate. It may be seen as stemming from three principles.

The first principle asserts that at least some mental events interact causally with physical events. (We could call this the Principle of Causal Interaction.) Thus for example if someone sank the *Bismarck*, then various mental events such as perceivings, notings, calculations, judgments, decisions, intentional actions and changes of belief played a causal role in the sinking of the *Bismarck*. In particular, I would urge that the fact that someone sank the *Bismarck* entails that he moved his body in a way that was caused by mental events of certain sorts, and that this bodily movement in turn caused the *Bismarck* to sink.[3] Perception illustrates how causality may run from the physical to the mental: if a man perceives that a ship is approaching, then a ship approaching must have caused him to come to believe that a ship is approaching. (Nothing depends on accepting these as examples of causal interaction.)

Though perception and action provide the most obvious cases where mental and physical events interact causally, I think reasons could be given for the view that all mental events ultimately, perhaps through causal relations with other mental events, have causal intercourse with physical events. But if there are mental events that have no physical events as causes or effects, the argument will not touch them.

The second principle is that where there is causality, there must be a law: events related as cause and effect fall under strict deterministic laws. (We may term this the Principle of the Nomological Character of Causality.) This principle, like the first, will be treated here as an assumption, though I shall say something by way of interpretation.[4]

The third principle is that there are no strict deterministic laws on the basis of which mental events can be predicted and explained (the Anomalism of the Mental).

The paradox I wish to discuss arises for someone who is inclined to accept these three assumptions or principles, and who thinks they are inconsistent with one another. The inconsistency is not, of course, formal unless more premises are added. Nevertheless it is natural to reason that the first two principles, that of causal interaction, and that of the nomological character of causality, together imply that at least some mental events can be predicted and explained on the basis of laws, while the principle of the anomalism of the mental denies this. Many philosophers have accepted, with or without argument, the view that the three principles do lead to a contradiction. It seems to me, however, that all three principles are true, so that what must be done is to explain away the appearance of contradiction; essentially the Kantian line.

The rest of this paper falls into three parts. The first part describes a version of the identity theory of the mental and the physical that shows how the three principles may be reconciled. The second part argues that there cannot be strict psychophysical laws; this is not quite the principle of the anomalism of the mental, but on reasonable assumptions entails it. The last part tries to show that from the fact that there can be no strict psychophysical laws, and our other two principles, we can infer the truth of a version of the identity theory, that is, a theory that identifies at least some mental events with physical events. It is clear that this "proof" of the identity theory will be at best conditional, since two of its premises are unsupported, and the argument for the third may be found less than conclusive. But even someone unpersuaded of the truth of the premises may be interested to learn how they may be reconciled and that they serve to establish a version of the identity theory of the mental. Finally, if the argument is a good one, it should lay to rest the view, common to many friends and some foes of identity theories, that support for such theories can come only from the discovery of psychophysical laws.

I

The three principles will be shown consistent with one another by describing a view of the mental and the physical that contains no inner contradiction and that entails the three principles. According to this view, mental events are identical with physical events. Events are taken to be unrepeatable, dated individuals such as the particular eruption of a volcano, the (first) birth or death of a person, the playing of the 1968 World Series, or the historic utterance of the words, "You may fire when ready, Gridley." We can easily frame identity statements about individual events; examples (true or false) might be:

> The death of Scott = the death of the author of *Waverley*;
> The assassination of the Archduke Ferdinand = the event that started the First World War;
> The eruption of Vesuvius in A.D. 79 = the cause of the destruction of Pompeii.

The theory under discussion is silent about processes, states, and attributes if these differ from individual events.

What does it mean to say that an event is mental or physical? One natural answer is that an event is physical if it is describable in a purely physical vocabulary, mental if describable in mental terms. But if this is taken to suggest that an event is physical, say, if some physical predicate is true of it, then there is the following difficulty. Assume that the predicate 'x took place at Noosa Heads' belongs to the physical vocabulary; then so also must the predicate 'x did not take place at Noosa Heads' belong to the physical vocabulary. But the predicate 'x did or did not take place at Noosa Heads' is true of every event, whether mental or physical.[5] We might rule out predicates that are tautologically true of every event, but this will not help since every event is truly describable either by 'x took place at Noosa Heads' or by 'x did not take place at Noosa Heads.' A different approach is needed.[6]

We may call those verbs mental that express propositional attitudes like believing, intending, desiring, hoping, knowing, perceiving, noticing, remembering, and so on. Such verbs are characterized by the fact that they sometimes feature in sentences with subjects that refer to persons, and are completed by embedded sentences in which the usual rules of substitution appear to break down. This criterion is not precise, since I do not want to include these verbs when they occur in contexts that are fully extensional ('He knows Paris,' 'He perceives the moon' may be cases), nor exclude them whenever they are not followed by embedded sentences. An alternative characterization of the desired class of mental verbs might be that they are psychological verbs as used when they create apparently nonextensional contexts.

Let us call a description of the form 'the event that is M' or an open sentence of the form 'event x is M' a *mental description* or a *mental open sentence* if and only if the expression that replaces 'M' contains at least one mental verb essentially. (Essentially, so as to rule out cases where the description or open sentence is logically equivalent to one not containing mental vocabulary.) Now we may say that an event is mental if and only if it has a mental description, or (the description operator not being primitive) if there is a mental open sentence true of that event alone. Physical events are those picked out by descriptions or open sentences that contain only the physical vocabulary essentially. It is less important to characterize a physical vocabulary because relative to the mental it is, so to speak, recessive in determining whether a description is mental or physical. (There will be some comments presently on the nature of a physical vocabulary, but these comments will fall far short of providing a criterion.)

On the proposed test of the mental, the distinguishing feature of the mental is not that it is private, subjective, or immaterial, but that it exhibits what Brentano called intentionality. Thus intentional actions are clearly included in the realm of the mental along with thoughts, hopes, and regrets (or the events tied to these). What may seem doubtful is whether the criterion will include events that have often been considered paradigmatic of the mental. Is it obvious, for example, that feeling a pain or seeing an afterimage will count as mental? Sentences that report such events seem free from taint of nonextensionality, and the same should be true of reports of raw feels, sense data, and other uninterpreted sensations, if there are any.

However, the criterion actually covers not only the havings of pains and afterimages, but much more besides. Take some event one would intuitively accept as physical, let's say the collision of two stars in distant space. There must be a purely physical predicate 'Px' true of this collision, and of others, but true of only this one at the time it occurred. This particular time, though, may be pinpointed as the same time that Jones notices that a pencil starts to roll across his desk. The distant stellar collision is thus *the* event x such that Px and x is simultaneous with Jones' noticing that a pencil starts to roll across his desk. The collision has now been picked out by a mental description and must be counted as a mental event.

This strategy will probably work to show every event to be mental; we have obviously failed to capture the intuitive concept of the mental. It would be instructive to try to mend this trouble, but it is not necessary for present purposes. We can afford Spinozistic extravagance with the mental since accidental inclusions can only strengthen the hypothesis that all mental events are identical with physical events. What would matter would be failure to include bona fide mental events, but of this there seems to be no danger.

I want to describe, and presently to argue for, a version of the identity theory that denies that there can be strict laws connecting the mental and the physical. The very possibility of such a theory is easily obscured by the way in which identity theories are commonly defended and attacked. Charles Taylor, for example, agrees with protagonists of identity theories that the sole "ground" for accepting such theories is the supposition that correlations or laws can be established linking events described as mental with events described as physical. He says, "It is easy to see why this is so: unless a given mental event is invariably accompanied by a given, say, brain process, there is no ground for even mooting a general identity between the two."[7] Taylor goes on (correctly, I think) to allow that there may be identity without correlating laws, but my present interest is in noticing the invitation to confusion in the statement just quoted. What can "a given mental event" mean here? Not a particular, dated, event, for it would not make sense to speak of an individual event being "invariably accompanied" by another. Taylor is evidently thinking of events of a given *kind*. But if the only identities are of kinds of events, the identity theory presupposes correlating laws.

One finds the same tendency to build laws into the statement of the identity theory in these typical remarks:

> When I say that a sensation is a brain process or that lightning is an electrical discharge, I am using 'is' in the sense of strict identity . . . there are not two things: a flash of lightning and an electrical discharge. There is one thing, a flash of lightning, which is described scientifically as an electrical discharge to the earth from a cloud of ionized water molecules.[8]

The last sentence of this quotation is perhaps to be understood as saying that for every lightning flash there exists an electrical discharge to the earth from a cloud of ionized water molecules with which it is identical. Here we have a honest ontology of individual events and can make literal sense of identity. We can also see how there could be identities without correlating laws. It is possible, however, to have an ontology of events with the conditions of individuation specified in such a way that any identity implies a correlating law. Kim, for example, suggests that Fa and Gb "describe or refer to the same event" if and only if $a = b$ and the property of being F = the property of being G. The identity of the properties in turn entails that $(x)(\text{F}x \leftrightarrow \text{G}x)$.[9] No wonder Kim says:

> If pain is identical with brain state B, there must be a concomitance between occurrences of pain and occurrences of brain state B. . . . Thus, a necessary condition of the pain-brain state B identity is that the two expressions 'being in pain' and 'being in brain state B' have the same extension. . . . There is no conceivable observation that would confirm or refute the identity but not the associated correlation.[10]

It may make the situation clearer to give a fourfold classification of theories of the relation between mental and physical events that emphasizes the independence of claims about laws and claims of identity. On the one hand there are those who assert, and those who deny, the existence of psychophysical laws; on the other hand there are those who say mental events are identical with physical and those who deny this. Theories are thus divided into four sorts: *Nomological monism*, which affirms that there are correlating laws and that the events correlated are one (materialists belong in this category); *nomological dualism*, which comprises various forms of parallelism, interactionism, and epiphenomenalism; *anomalous dualism*, which combines ontological dualism with the general failure of laws correlating the mental and the physical (Cartesianism). And finally there is *anomalous monism*, which classifies the position I wish to occupy.[11]

Anomalous monism resembles materialism in its claim that all events are physical, but rejects the thesis, usually considered essential to materialism, that mental phenomena can be given purely physical explanations. Anomalous monism shows an ontological bias only in that it allows the possibility that not all events are mental, while insisting that all events are physical. Such a bland monism, unbuttressed by correlating laws or conceptual economies, does not seem to merit the term "reductionism"; in any case it is not apt to inspire the nothing-but reflex ("Conceiving the *Art of the Fugue* was nothing but a complex neural event," and so forth).

Although the position I describe denies there are psychophysical laws, it is consistent with the view that mental characteristics are in some sense dependent, or supervenient, on physical characteristics. Such supervenience might be taken to mean that there cannot be two events alike in all physical respects but differing in some mental respect, or that an object cannot alter in some mental respect without altering in some physical respect. Dependence or supervenience of this kind does not entail reducibility through law or definition: if it did, we could reduce moral properties to descriptive, and this there is good reason to *believe* cannot be done; and we might be able to reduce truth in a formal system to syntactical properties, and this we *know* cannot in general be done.

This last example is in useful analogy with the sort of lawless monism under consideration. Think of the physical vocabulary as the entire vocabulary of some language L with resources adequate to express a certain amount of mathematics, and its own syntax. L' is L augmented with the truth predicate 'true-in-L,' which is "mental." In L (and hence L') it is possible to pick out, with a definite description or open sentence, each sentence in the extension of the truth predicate, but if L is consistent there exists no predicate of syntax (of the "physical" vocabulary), no matter how complex, that applies to all and only the true sentences of L. There can be no "psychophysical law" in the form of a biconditional, '(x) (x is true-in-L if and only if x is ϕ)' where, 'ϕ' is replaced by a "physical" predicate (a predicate of L). Similarly, we can pick out each mental event using the physical vocabulary alone, but no purely physical predicate, no matter how complex, has, as a matter of law, the same extension as a mental predicate.

It should now be evident how anomalous monism reconciles the three original principles. Causality and identity are relations between individual events no matter how described. But laws are linguistic; and so events can instantiate laws, and hence be explained or predicted in the light of laws, only as those events are described in one or another way. The principle of causal interaction deals with events in extension and is therefore blind to the mental-physical dichotomy. The principle of the anomalism of the mental concerns events described as mental, for events are mental only as described. The principle of the nomological character of causality must be read carefully: it says that when events are related as cause and effect, they have descriptions that instantiate a law. It does not say that every true singular statement of causality instantiates a law.[12]

II

The analogy just bruited, between the place of the mental amid the physical, and the place of the semantical in a world of syntax, should not be strained. Tarski proved that a consistent language cannot (under some natural assumptions) contain an open sentence 'Fx' true of all and only the true sentences of that language. If our analogy were pressed, then we would expect a proof that there can be no physical open sentence 'Px' true of all and only the events having some mental property. In fact, however, nothing I can say about the irreducibility of the mental deserves to be called a proof; and the kind of irreducibility is different. For if anomalous monism is correct, not only can every mental event be uniquely singled out using only physical concepts, but since the number of events that falls under each mental predicate may, for all we know, be finite, there may well exist a physical open sentence coextensive with each mental predicate, though to construct it might involve the tedium of a lengthy and uninstructive alternation. Indeed, even if finitude is not assumed, there seems no compelling reason to deny that there could be coextensive predicates, one mental and one physical.

The thesis is rather that the mental is nomologically irreducible: there may be *true* general statements relating the mental and the physical, statements that have the logical form of a law; but they are not *lawlike* (in a strong sense to be described). If by absurdly remote chance we were to stumble on a nonstochastic true psychophysical generalization, we would have no reason to believe it more than roughly true.

Do we, by declaring that there are no (strict) psychophysical laws, poach on the empirical preserves of science—a form of *hubris* against which philosophers are often warned? Of course, to judge a statement lawlike or illegal is not to decide its truth outright; relative to the acceptance of a general statement on the basis of instances, ruling it lawlike must be a priori. But such relative apriorism does not in itself justify philosophy, for in general the grounds for deciding to trust a statement on the basis of its instances will in turn be governed by theoretical and empirical concerns not to be distinguished from those of science. If the case of supposed laws linking the mental and the physical is different, it can only be because to allow the possibility of such laws would amount to changing the subject. By changing the subject I mean here: deciding not to accept the criterion of the mental in terms of the vocabulary of the propositional attitudes. This short answer cannot prevent further ramifications of the problem, however, for there is no clear line between changing the subject and changing what one says on an old subject, which is to admit, in the present context at least, that there is no clear line between philosophy and science. Where there are no fixed boundaries only the timid never risk trespass.

It will sharpen our appreciation of the anomological character of mental-physical generalizations to consider a related matter, the failure of definitional behaviorism. Why are we willing (as I assume we are) to abandon the attempt to give explicit definitions of mental concepts in terms of behavioral ones? Not, surely, just because all actual tries are conspicuously inadequate. Rather it is because we are persuaded, as we are in the case of so many other forms of definitional reductionism (naturalism in ethics, instrumentalism and operationalism in the sciences, the causal theory of meaning, phenomenalism, and so on—the catalogue of philosophy's defeats), that there is system in the failures. Suppose we try to say, not using any mental concepts, what it is for a man to believe there is life on Mars. One line we could take is this: when a certain sound is produced in the man's presence ("Is there life on Mars?") he produces another ("Yes"). But of course this shows he believes there is life on Mars only if he understands English, his production of the sound was intentional, and was a response to the sounds as meaning something in English; and so on. For each discovered deficiency, we add a new proviso. Yet no matter how we patch and fit the nonmental conditions, we always find the need for an additional condition (provided he *notices*, *understands*, etc.) that is mental in character.[13]

A striking feature of attempts at definitional reduction is how little seems to hinge on the question of synonymy between definiens and definiendum. Of course, by imagining counterexamples we do discredit claims of synonymy. But the pattern of failure prompts a stronger conclusion: if we were to find an open sentence couched in behavioral terms and exactly coextensive with some mental predicate, nothing could reasonably persuade us that we had found it. We know too much about thought and behavior to trust exact and universal statements linking them. Beliefs and desires issue in behavior only as modified and mediated by further beliefs and desires, attitudes and attendings, without limit. Clearly this holism of the mental realm is a clue both to the autonomy and to the anomalous character of the mental.

These remarks apropos definitional behaviorism provide at best hints of why we should not expect nomological connections between the mental and the physical. The central case invites further consideration.

Lawlike statements are general statements that support counterfactual and subjunctive claims, and are supported by their instances. There is (in my view) no nonquestion-begging criterion of the lawlike, which is not to say there are no reasons in particular cases for a judgment. Lawlikeness is a matter of degree, which is not to deny that there may be cases beyond debate. And within limits set by the conditions of communication, there is room for much variation between individuals in the pattern of statements to which various degrees of nomologicality are assigned. In all these respects, nomologicality is much like analyticity, as one might expect since both are linked to meaning.

'All emeralds are green' is lawlike in that its instances confirm it, but 'all emeralds are grue' is not, for 'grue' means 'observed before time t and green, otherwise blue,' and if our observations were all made before t and uniformly revealed green emeralds, this would not be a reason to expect other emeralds to be blue. Nelson Goodman has suggested that this shows that some predicates, 'grue' for example, are unsuited to laws (and thus a criterion of suitable predicates could lead to a criterion of the lawlike). But it seems to me the anomalous character of 'All emeralds are grue' shows only that the predicates 'is an emerald' and 'is grue' are not suited to one another: grueness is not an inductive property of emeralds. Grueness *is* however an inductive property of entities of other sorts, for instance of emerires. (Something is an emerire if it is examined before t and is an emerald, and otherwise is a sapphire.) Not only is 'All emerires are grue' entailed by the conjunction of the lawlike statements 'All emeralds are green' and 'All sapphires are blue,' but there is no reason, as far as I can see, to reject the deliverance of intuition, that it is itself lawlike.[14] Nomological statements bring together predicates that we know a priori are made for each other—know, that is, independently of knowing whether the evidence supports a connection between them. 'Blue,' 'red,' and 'green' are made for emeralds, sapphires, and roses; 'grue,' 'bleen,' and 'gred' are made for sapphalds, emerires, and emeroses.

The direction in which the discussion seems headed is this: mental and physical predicates are not made for one another. In point of lawlikeness, psychophysical statements are more like 'All emeralds are grue' than like 'All emeralds are green.'

Before this claim is plausible, it must be seriously modified. The fact that emeralds examined before *t* are grue not only is no reason to believe all emeralds are grue; it is not even a reason (if we know the time) to believe *any* unobserved emeralds are grue. But if an event of a certain mental sort has usually been accompanied by an event of a certain physical sort, this often is a good reason to expect other cases to follow suit roughly in proportion. The generalizations that embody such practical wisdom are assumed to be only roughly true, or they are explicitly stated in probabilistic terms, or they are insulated from counterexample by generous escape clauses. Their importance lies mainly in the support they lend singular causal claims and related explanations of particular events. The support derives from the fact that such a generalization, however crude and vague, may provide good reason to believe that underlying the particular case there is a regularity that could be formulated sharply and without caveat.

In our daily traffic with events and actions that must be foreseen or understood, we perforce make use of the sketchy summary generalization, for we do not know a more accurate law, or if we do, we lack a description of the particular events in which we are interested that would show the relevance of the law. But there is an important distinction to be made within the category of the rude rule of thumb. On the one hand, there are generalizations whose positive instances give us reason to believe the generalization itself could be improved by adding further provisos and conditions stated in the same general vocabulary as the original generalization. Such a generalization points to the form and vocabulary of the finished law: we may say that it is a *homonomic* generalization. On the other hand there are generalizations which when instantiated may give us reason to believe there is a precise law at work, but one that can be stated only by shifting to a different vocabulary. We may call such generalizations *heteronomic*.

I suppose most of our practical lore (and science) is heteronomic. This is because a law can hope to be precise, explicit, and as exceptionless as possible only if it draws its concepts from a comprehensive closed theory. This ideal theory may or may not be deterministic, but it is if any true theory is. Within the physical sciences we do find homonomic generalizations, generalizations such that if the evidence supports them, we then have reason to believe they may be sharpened indefinitely by drawing upon further physical concepts: there is a theoretical asymptote of perfect coherence with all the evidence, perfect predictability (under the terms of the system), total explanation (again under the terms of the system). Or perhaps the ultimate theory is probabilistic, and the asymptote is less than perfection; but in that case there will be no better to be had.

Confidence that a statement is homonomic, correctible within its own conceptual domain, demands that it draw its concepts from a theory with strong constitutive elements. Here is the simplest possible illustration; if the lesson carries, it will be obvious that the simplification could be mended.

The measurement of length, weight, temperature, or time depends (among many other things, of course) on the existence in each case of a two-place relation that is transitive and asymmetric: warmer than, later than, heavier than, and so forth. Let us take the relation *longer than* as our example. The law or postulate of transitivity is this:

(L) $L(x, y)$ and $L(y, z) \rightarrow L(x, z)$

Unless this law (or some sophisticated variant) holds, we cannot easily make sense of the concept of length. There will be no way of assigning numbers to register even so much as ranking in length, let alone the more powerful demands of measurement on a ratio scale. And this remark goes not only for any three items directly involved in an intransitivity: it is easy to show (given a few more assumptions essential to measurement of length) that there is no consistent assignment of a ranking to any item unless (L) holds in full generality.

Clearly (L) alone cannot exhaust the import of 'longer than'—otherwise it would not differ from 'warmer than' or 'later than.' We must suppose there is some empirical content, however difficult to formulate in the available vocabulary, that distinguishes 'longer than' from the other two-place transitive predicates of measurement and on the basis of which we may assert that one thing is longer than another. Imagine this empirical content to be partly given by the predicate 'O(x, y)'. So we have this "meaning postulate":

$$(M) \quad O(x, y) \rightarrow O(x, y)$$

that partly interprets (L). But now (L) and (M) together yield an empirical theory of great strength, for together they entail that there do not exist three objects a, b, and c such that $O(a, b)$, $O(b, c)$, and $O(c, a)$. Yet what is to prevent this happening if 'O(x, y) is a predicate we can ever, with confidence, apply? Suppose we *think* we observe an intransitive triad; what do we say? We could count (L) false, but then we would have no application for the concept of length. We could say (M) gives a wrong test for length; but then it is unclear what we thought was the *content* of the idea of one thing being longer than another. Or we could say that the objects under observation are not, as the theory requires, *rigid* objects. It is a mistake to think we are forced to accept some one of these answers. Concepts such as that of length are sustained in equilibrium by a number of conceptual pressures, and theories of fundamental measurement are distorted if we force the decision, among such principles as (L) and (M): analytic or synthetic. It is better to say the whole set of axioms, laws, or postulates for the measurement of length is partly constitutive of the idea of a system of macroscopic, rigid, physical objects. I suggest that the existence of lawlike statements in physical science depends upon the existence of constitutive (or synthetic a priori) laws like those of the measurement of length within the same conceptual domain.

Just as we cannot intelligibly assign a length to any object unless a comprehensive theory holds of objects of that sort, we cannot intelligibly attribute any propositional attitude to an agent except within the framework of a viable theory of his beliefs, desires, intentions, and decisions.

There is no assigning beliefs to a person one by one on the basis of his verbal behavior, his choices, or other local signs no matter how plain and evident, for we make sense of particular beliefs only as they cohere with other beliefs, with preferences, with intentions, hopes, fears, expectations, and the rest. It is not merely, as with the measurement of length, that each case tests a theory and depends upon it, but that the content of a propositional attitude derives from its place in the pattern.

Crediting people with a large degree of consistency cannot be counted mere charity: it is unavoidable if we are to be in a position to accuse them meaningfully of error and some degree of irrationality. Global confusion, like universal mistake, is unthinkable, not because imagination boggles, but because too much confusion leaves nothing to be confused about and massive error erodes the background of true belief against which alone failure can be construed. To appreciate the limits to the kind and amount of blunder and bad thinking we can intelligibly pin on others is to see once more the inseparability of the question what concepts a person commands and the question what he does with those concepts in the way of belief, desire, and intention. To the extent that we fail to discover a coherent and plausible pattern in the attitudes and actions of others we simply forego the chance of treating them as persons.

The problem is not bypassed but given center stage by appeal to explicit speech behavior. For we could not begin to decode a man's sayings if we could not make out his attitudes towards his sentences, such as holding, wishing, or wanting them to be true. Beginning from these attitudes, we must work out a theory of what he means, thus simultaneously giving content to his attitudes and to his words. In our need to make him make sense, we will try for a theory that finds him consistent, a believer of truths, and a lover of the good (all by our own lights, it goes without saying). Life being what it is, there will be no simple theory that fully meets these demands. Many theories will effect a more or less acceptable compromise, and between these theories there may be no objective grounds for choice.

The heteronomic character of general statements linking the mental and the physical traces back to this central role of translation in the description of all propositional attitudes, and to the indeterminacy of translation.[15] There are no strict psychophysical laws because of the disparate commitments of the mental and physical schemes. It is a feature of physical reality that physical change can be explained by laws that connect it with other changes and conditions physically described. It is a feature of the mental that the attribution of mental phenomena must be responsible to the background of reasons, beliefs, and intentions of the individual. There cannot be tight connections between the realms if each is to retain allegiance to its proper source of evidence. The nomological irreducibility of the mental does not derive merely from the seamless nature of the world of thought, preference and intention, for such interdependence is common to physical theory, and is compatible with there being a single right way of interpreting a man's attitudes without relativization to a scheme of translation. Nor is the irreducibility due simply to the possibility of many equally eligible schemes, for this is compatible with an arbitrary choice of one scheme relative to which assignments of mental traits are made. The point is rather that when we use the concepts of belief, desire and the rest, we must stand prepared, as the evidence accumulates, to adjust our theory in the light of considerations of overall cogency: the constitutive ideal of rationality partly controls each phase in the evolution of what must be an evolving theory. An arbitrary choice of translation scheme would preclude such opportunistic tempering of theory; put differently, a right arbitrary choice of a translation manual would be of a manual acceptable in the light of all possible evidence, and this is a choice we cannot make. We must conclude, I think, that nomological slack between the mental and the physical is essential as long as we conceive of man as a rational animal.

III

The gist of the foregoing discussion, as well as its conclusion, will be familiar. That there is a categorial difference between the mental and the physical is a commonplace. It may seem odd that I say nothing of the supposed privacy of the mental, or the special authority an agent has with respect to his own propositional attitudes, but this appearance of novelty would fade if we were to investigate in more detail the grounds for accepting a scheme of translation. The step from the categorial difference between the mental and the physical to the impossibility of strict laws relating them is less common, but certainly not new. If there is a surprise, then, it will be to find the lawlessness of the mental serving to help establish the identity of the mental with that paradigm of the lawlike, the physical.

The reasoning is this. We are assuming, under the Principle of the Causal Dependence of the Mental, that some mental events at least are causes or effects of physical events; the argument applies only to these. A second Principle (of the Nomological

Character of Causality) says that each true singular causal statement is backed by a strict law connecting events of kinds to which the events mentioned as cause and effect belong. Where there are rough, but homonomic, laws, there are laws drawing on concepts from the same conceptual domain and upon which there is no improving in point of precision and comprehensiveness. We urged in the last section that such laws occur in the physical sciences. Physical theory promises to provide a comprehensive closed system guaranteed to yield a standardized, unique description of every physical event couched in a vocabulary amenable to law.

It is not plausible that mental concepts alone can provide such a framework, simply because the mental does not, by our first principle, constitute a closed system. Too much happens to affect the mental that is not itself a systematic part of the mental. But if we combine this observation with the conclusion that no psychophysical statement is, or can be built into, a strict law, we have the Principle of the Anomalism of the Mental: there are no strict laws at all on the basis of which we can predict and explain mental phenomena.

The demonstration of identity follows easily. Suppose m, a mental event, caused p, a physical event; then under some description m and p instantiate a strict law. This law can only be physical, according to the previous paragraph. But if m falls under a physical law, it has a physical description; which is to say it is a physical event. An analogous argument works when a physical event causes a mental event. So every mental event that is causally related to a physical event is a physical event. In order to establish anomalous monism in full generality it would be sufficient to show that every mental event is cause or effect of some physical event; I shall not attempt this.

If one event causes another, there is a strict law which those events instantiate when properly described. But it is possible (and typical) to know of the singular causal relation without knowing the law or the relevant descriptions. Knowledge requires reasons, but these are available in the form of rough heteronomic generalizations, which are lawlike in that instances make it reasonable to expect other instances to follow suit without being lawlike in the sense of being indefinitely refinable. Applying these facts to knowledge of identities, we see that it is possible to know that a mental event is identical with some physical event without knowing which one (in the sense of being able to give it a unique physical description that brings it under a relevant law). Even if someone knew the entire physical history of the world, and every mental event were identical with a physical, it would not follow that he could predict or explain a single mental event (so described, of course).

Two features of mental events in their relation to the physical—causal dependence and nomological independence—combine, then, to dissolve what has often seemed a paradox, the efficacy of thought and purpose in the material world, and their freedom from law. When we portray events as perceivings, rememberings, decisions and actions, we necessarily locate them amid physical happenings through the relation of cause and effect; but that same mode of portrayal insulates mental events, as long as we do not change the idiom, from the strict laws that can in principle be called upon to explain and predict physical phenomena.

Mental events as a class cannot be explained by physical science; particular mental events can when we know particular identities. But the explanations of mental events in which we are typically interested relate them to other mental events and conditions. We explain a man's free actions, for example, by appeal to his desires, habits, knowledge and perceptions. Such accounts of intentional behavior operate in a conceptual framework removed from the direct reach of physical law by describing both cause and effect, reason and action, as aspects of a portrait of a human agent. The anomalism of the mental is thus a necessary condition for viewing action as autonomous. I conclude with a second passage from Kant:

> It is an indispensable problem of speculative philosophy to show that its illusion respecting the contradiction rests on this, that we think of man in a different sense and relation when we call him free, and when we regard him as subject to the laws of nature.... It must therefore show that not only can both of these very well co-exist, but that both must be thought *as necessarily united* in the same subject....[16]

Notes

1. I was helped and influenced by Daniel Bennett, Sue Larson, and Richard Rorty, who are not responsible for the result. My research was supported by the National Science Foundation and the Center for Advanced Study in the Behavioral Sciences.
2. *Fundamental Principles of the Metaphysics of Morals*, trans. T. K. Abbott (London, 1909), pp. 75–76.
3. These claims are defended in my "Actions, Reasons and Causes," *The Journal of Philosophy*, LX (1963), pp. 685–700 and in "Agency," a paper forthcoming in the proceedings of the November, 1968, colloquium on Agent, Action, and Reason at the University of Western Ontario, London, Canada.
4. In "Causal Relations," *The Journal of Philosophy*, LXIV (1967), pp. 691–703, I elaborate on the view of causality assumed here. The stipulation that the laws be deterministic is stronger than required by the reasoning, and will be relaxed.
5. The point depends on assuming that mental events may intelligibly be said to have a location; but it is an assumption that must be true if an identity theory is, and here I am not trying to prove the theory but to formulate it.
6. I am indebted to Lee Bowie for emphasizing this difficulty.
7. Charles Taylor, "Mind-Body Identity, a Side Issue?" *The Philosophical Review*, LXXVI (1967), p. 202.
8. J. J. C. Smart, "Sensations and Brain Processes," *The Philosophical Review*, LXVIII (1959), pp. 141–56. The quoted passages are on pp. 163–165 of the reprinted version in *The Philosophy of Mind*, ed. V. C. Chappell (Englewood Cliffs, N. J., 1962). For another example, see David K. Lewis, "An Argument for the Identity Theory," *The Journal of Philosophy*, LXIII (1966), pp. 17–25. Here the assumption is made explicit when Lewis takes events as universals (p. 17, footnotes 1 and 2). I do not suggest that Smart and Lewis are confused, only that their way of stating the identity theory tends to obscure the distinction between particular events and kinds of events on which the formulation of my theory depends.
9. Jaegwon Kim, "On the Psycho-Physical Identity Theory," *American Philosophical Quarterly*, III (1966), p. 231.
10. Ibid., pp. 227–228. Richard Brandt and Jaegwon Kim propose roughly the same criterion in "The Logic of the Identity Theory," *The Journal of Philosophy* LIV (1967), pp. 515–537. They remark that on their conception of event identity, the identity theory "makes a stronger claim than merely that there is a pervasive phenomenal-physical correlation" (p. 518). I do not discuss the stronger claim.
11. Anomalous monism is more or less explicitly recognized as a possible position by Herbert Feigl, "The 'Mental' and the 'Physical,'" in *Concepts, Theories and the Mind-Body Problem*, vol. II, Minnesota Studies in the Philosophy of Science (Minneapolis, 1958); Sydney Shoemaker, "Ziff's Other Minds," *The Journal of Philosophy*, LXII (1965), p. 589; David Randall Luce, "Mind-Body Identity and Psycho-Physical Correlation," *Philosophical Studies*, XVII (1966), pp. 1–7; Charles Taylor, op. cit., p. 207. Something like my position is tentatively accepted by Thomas Nagel, "Physicalism," *The Philosophical Review*, LXXIV (1965), pp. 339–356, and briefly endorsed by P. F. Strawson in *Freedom and the Will*, ed. D. F. Pears (London, 1963), pp. 63–67.
12. The point that substitutivity of identity fails in the context of explanation is made in connection with the present subject by Norman Malcolm, "Scientific Materialism and the Identity Theory," *Dialogue*, III (1964–65), pp. 123–124. See also my "Actions, Reasons and Causes," *The Journal of Philosophy*, LX (1963), pp. 696–699 and "The Individuation of Events" in *Essays in Honor of Carl G. Hempel*, ed. N. Rescher, et al. (Dordrecht, 1969).
13. The theme is developed in Roderick Chisholm, *Perceiving* (Ithaca, New York, 1957), chap. 11.
14. This view is accepted by Richard C. Jeffrey, "Goodman's Query," *The Journal of Philosophy*, LXII (1966), p. 286 ff., John R. Wallace, "Goodman, Logic, Induction," same journal and issue, p. 318, and John M. Vickers, "Characteristics of Projectible Predicates," *The Journal of Philosophy*, LXIV (1967), p. 285. On pp. 328–329 and 286–287 of these journal issues respectively Goodman disputes the lawlikeness of

statements like "All emerires are grue." I cannot see, however, that he meets the point of my "Emeroses by Other Names," *The Journal of Philosophy*, LXIII (1966), pp. 778–780.

15. The influence of W. V. Quine's doctrine of the indeterminacy of translation, as in chap. 2 of *Word and Object* (MIT Press: Cambridge, Mass., 1960), is, I hope, obvious. In § 45 Quine develops the connection between translation and the propositional attitudes, and remarks that "Brentano's thesis of the irreducibility of intentional idioms is of a piece with the thesis of indeterminacy of translation" (p. 221).

16. Op. cit., p. 76.

Chapter 21

Making Mind Matter More

Jerry A. Fodor

An outbreak of epiphobia (epiphobia is the fear that one is turning into an epiphenomenalist) appears to have much of the philosophy of mind community in its grip. Though it is generally agreed to be compatible with physicalism that intentional states should be causally responsible for behavioral outcomes, epiphobics worry that it is *not* compatible with physicalism that intentional states should be causally responsible for behavioral outcomes *qua intentional*. So they fear that the very successes of a physicalistic (and/or a computational) psychology will entail the causal inertness of the mental. Fearing this makes them unhappy.

In this paper, I want to argue that epiphobia is a neurotic worry; if there is a problem, it is engendered not by the actual-or-possible successes of physicalistic psychology, but by two philosophical mistakes: (a) a wrong idea about what it is for a property to be causally responsible; and (b) a complex of wrong ideas about the relations between special-science laws and the events that they subsume.[1] Here's how I propose to proceed: First, we'll have a little psychodrama; I want to give you a feel for how an otherwise healthy mind might succumb to epiphobia. Second, I'll provide a brief, sketchy, but I hope good-enough-for-present-purposes account of what it is for a property to be causally responsible. It will follow from this account that intentional properties are causally responsible if there are intentional causal laws. I'll then argue that (contrary to the doctrine called "anomalous monism") there is no good reason to doubt that there are intentional causal laws. I'll also argue that, so far as the matter affects the cluster of issues centering around epiphenomenalism, the sorts of relations that intentional causal laws can bear to the individuals they subsume are much the same as the sorts of relations that *non*intentional causal laws can bear to the individuals that they subsume. So then everything will be all right.

I Causal Responsibility

There are many routes to epiphobia. One of them runs via two premises and a stipulation.

> 1. Premise (Supervenience of Causal Powers): The causal powers of an event are entirely determined by its physical properties. Suppose two events are identical in their physical properties; then all causal hypotheticals true of one event are true of the other. If, for example, e1 and e2 are events identical in their physical properties, then all hypotheticals of the form "if e1 occurred in situation S, it would cause...." remain true if "e2" is substituted for "e1" and vice versa.
> 2. Premise (Property Dualism): Intentional properties supervene on physical properties, but no intentional property is identical to any physical property. (A physical property is a property expressible in the vocabulary of physics. Never mind,

for now, what the vocabulary of physics is; just assume that it contains no intentional terms.)

3. Stipulation: A property is "causally responsible" iff it affects the causal powers of things that have it. And (also by stipulation) all properties that aren't causally responsible are epiphenomenal.

But then, consider the mental event m (let's say, an event which consists of you desiring to lift your arm) which is the cause of the behavioral event b (let's say, an event which consists of you lifting your arm). m does, of course, have certain intentional properties. But, according to 2, none of its intentional properties is identical to any of its physical properties. And, according to 1, m's physical properties fully determine its causal powers (including, of course, its power to cause b). So, it appears that m's being the cause of your lifting your arm doesn't depend on its being a desire to lift your arm; m would have caused your lifting of your arm even if it hadn't had its intentional properties, so long as its physical properties were preserved.[2] So it appears that m's intentional properties don't affect its causal powers. So it appears that m's intentional properties are causally inert. Clearly, this argument iterates to *any* intentional property of the cause of any behavioral effect. So the intentional properties of mental events are epiphenomenal. Epiphobia!

Now, the first thing to notice about this line of argument is that it has *nothing to do with intentionality as such*. On the contrary, it applies equally happily to prove the epiphenomenality of *any* non-physical property, so long as property dualism is assumed. Consider, for example, the property of being a mountain; and suppose (what is surely plausible) that being a mountain isn't a physical property. (Remember, this just means that "mountain" and its synonyms aren't items in the lexicon of physics.) Now, untutored intuition might suggest that many of the effects of mountains are attributable *to their being* mountains. Thus, untutored intuition suggests, it is because Mt. Everest is a mountain that Mt. Everest has glaciers on its top; and it is because Mt. Everest is a mountain that it casts such a long shadow; and it is because Mt. Everest is a mountain that so many people try to climb Mt. Everest . . . and so on. But not so according to the present line of argument. For surely the causal powers of Mt. Everest are fully determined by its physical properties, and we've agreed that *being a mountain* isn't one of the physical properties of mountains. So then Mt. Everest's being a mountain doesn't affect its causal powers. So then—contrary to what one reads in geology books—the property of being a mountain is causally inert. Geoepiphobia!

No doubt there will be those who are prepared to bite this bullet. Such folk may either (i) deny that property dualism applies to mountainhood (because, on reflection, *being a mountain* is a physical property after all) or (ii) assert that it *is* intuitively plausible that *being a mountain* is causally inert (because, on reflection, it is intuitively plausible that it's not *being a mountain* but some other of Mt. Everest's properties—specifically, some of its physical properties—that are causally responsible for its effects). So be it; I do not want this to turn into a squabble about cases. Instead, let me emphasize that there are lots and lots and *lots* of examples where, on the one hand, considerations like multiple realizability make it implausible that a certain property is expressible in physical vocabulary; and, on the other hand, claims for the causal inertness of the property appear to be wildly implausible, at least prima facie.

Consider the property of being a sail. I won't bore you with the fine points (terribly tempted, though I am, to exercise my hobbyhorse[3]). Suffice it that sails are *airfoils* and there is quite a nice little theory about the causal properties of airfoils. Typically, airfoils generate lift in a direction, and in amounts, that are determined by their geometry, their rigidity, and many, many details of their relations to the (liquid or gaseous) medium through which they move. The basic idea is that lift is propagated at right angles to the surface of the airfoil along which the medium flows fastest, and is proportional to the relative velocity of the flow. Hold a flat piece of paper by one edge and blow across the top. The free side of the paper will move *up* (i.e., towards the air flow), and the harder you blow, the more it will do so. (*Ceteris paribus.*)

Now, the relative velocity of the airfoil may be increased by forcing the medium to flow through a "slot" (a constriction, one side of which is formed by the surface of the airfoil). The controlling law is that the narrower the slot, the faster the flow. (On sailboats of conventional Bermuda rig, the slot is the opening between the jib and the main. But perhaps you didn't want to know that.) Anyhow, airfoils and slots can be made out of all sorts of things; sails are airfoils, but so are keel-wings, and airplane wings and bird's wings. Slots are multiply realizable too: You can have a slot both sides of which are made of sailcloth, as in the jib/mainsail arrangement, but you can also have a slot one side of which is made of sailcloth and the other side of which is made of *air*. (That's part of the explanation of why you can sail towards the wind even if you haven't got a jib.) So then, if one of your reasons for doubting that *believing that P* is a physical property is that believing is multiply realizable, then you have the same reason for doubting that *being an airfoil* or *being a slot* counts as a physical property.

And yet, of course, it would seem to be quite mad to say that *being an airfoil* is causally inert. Airplanes fall down when you take their wings off; and sailboats come to a stop when you take down their sails. Everybody who isn't a philosopher agrees that these and other such facts are explained by the story about lift being generated by causal interactions between the airfoil and the medium. If that *isn't* the right explanation, what keeps the plane up? If that *is* the right explanation, how could it be that *being an airfoil* is causally inert?

Epiphobics primarily concerned with issues in the philosophy of mind might well stop here. The geological and aerodynamic analogies make it plausible that if there's a case for epiphenomenalism in respect of psychological properties, then there is the same case for epiphenomenalism in respect of *all* the non-physical properties mentioned in theories in the special sciences. I pause, for a moment, to moralize about this.

Many philosophers have the bad habit of thinking about only two sciences when they think about sciences at all; these being psychology and physics. When in the grip of this habit, they are likely to infer that if psychological theories have some property that physical theories don't, that must be because psychological states (qua psychological) are intentional and physical states (qua physical) are not. In the present case, if there's an argument that psychological properties are epiphenomenal, and no corresponding argument that physical properties are epiphenomenal, that must show that there is something funny about intentionality.

But we now see that it shows no such thing since, if the causal inertness of psychological properties is maintained along anything like the lines of 1–3, there are likely to be parallel arguments that *all properties are causally inert except those expressed by the vocabulary of physics*. In which case, *why should anybody care* whether psychological properties are epiphenomenal? All that anybody could reasonably want for psychology is that its constructs should enjoy whatever sort of explanatory/causal role is proper to the constructs of the special sciences. If beliefs and desires are as well off ontologically as mountains, wings, spiral nebulas, trees, gears, levers and the like, then surely they're as well off as anyone could need them to be.

But, in fact, we shouldn't stop here. Because, though it's true that claims for the epiphenomenality of mountainhood and airfoilhood and, in general, of any non-physical-property-you-like-hood will follow from the same sorts of arguments that imply claims for the epiphenomenality of beliefhood and desirehood. It's also true that such claims are prima facie absurd. Whatever you may think about beliefs and desires and the other paraphernalia of intentional psychology, it's a fact you have to live with that there are all these *non*intentional special sciences around; and that many, many—maybe even all—of the properties that figure in their laws are nonphysical too. Surely something *must* have gone wrong with arguments that show that all these properties are epiphenomenal. How could there be laws about airfoils (notice, laws about *the causal consequences of something's being an airfoil*) if airfoilhood is epiphenomenal? How could there be a science of geology if geological properties are causally inert?

It seems to me, in light of the foregoing, that it ought to be a minimal condition upon a theory of what it is for something to be a causally responsible property that it does not entail the epiphenomenality of winghood, mountainhood, gearhood, leverhood, beliefhood, desirehood and the like. I'm about to propose a theory which meets this condition, and thereby commends itself as a tonic for epiphobics. It isn't, as you will see, very shocking, or surprising or anything; actually it's pretty dull. Still, I need a little stage setting before I can tell you about it. In particular, I need some caveats and some assumptions.

Caveats   First, curing epiphobia requires making it plausible that intentional properties can meet sufficient conditions for causal responsibility; but one is not also required to show that they can meet *necessary and sufficient* conditions for causal responsibility. This is just as well, since necessary and sufficient conditions for causal responsibility might be sort of hard to come by (necessary and sufficient conditions for *anything* tend to be sort of hard to come by) and I, for one, don't claim to have any.

Second, the question "What makes a property causally responsible?" needs to be distinguished from the probably much harder question. "What determines which property is responsible in a given case when one event causes another?" Suppose that e1 causes e2; then, trivially, it must do so in virtue of some or other of its causally responsible properties; i.e., in virtue of some or other property in virtue of which it is able to be a cause. But it may be that e1 has many—perhaps many, many—such properties; so it must not be assumed that if e1 is capable of being a cause in virtue of having a certain property P, then P is ipso facto the property in virtue of which e1 is the cause of e2. Indeed, it must not even be assumed that if e1 is capable of being a cause of e2 in virtue of its having P, then P is ipso facto the property in virtue of which e1 causes e2. For again it may be that e1 has many—even many, many—properties in virtue of which it is capable of being the cause of e2, and it need not be obvious which one of these properties is the one in virtue of which it actually *is* the cause of e2. At least, I can assure you, it need not be obvious to me.

It is, to put all this a little less pedantically, one sort of success to show that it was in virtue of its intentional content that your desire to raise your hand made something happen. It is another, and lesser, sort of success to show that *being a desire to raise your hand* is the kind of property in virtue of which things *can* be made to happen. Curing epiphobia requires only a success of the latter, lesser sort.

Assumptions   I assume that singular causal statements need to be covered by causal laws. That means something like:

> 4. Covering Principle: If an event e1 causes an event e2, then there are properties F, G such that;

4.1. e1 instantiates F;

4.2. e2 instantiates G;

and

4.3. "F instantiations are sufficient for G instantiations" is a causal law.[4]

When a pair of events bears this relation to a law, I'll say that the individuals are each *covered* or *subsumed* by that law and I'll say that the law *projects* the properties in virtue of which the individuals are subsumed by it. Notice that when an individual is covered by a law, it will always have some property in virtue of which the law subsumes it. If, for example, the covering law is that Fs cause Gs, then individuals that get covered by this law do so either in virtue of being Fs (in case they are subsumed by its antecedent) or in virtue of being Gs (in case they are subsumed by its consequent). This could all be made more precise, but I see no reason to bother.

OK, I can now tell you my sufficient condition for a property to be causally responsible:

5. P is a causally responsible property if it's a property in virtue of which individuals are subsumed by causal laws; or, equivalently,

5.1. P is a causally responsible property if it's a property projected by a causal law; or, equivalently (since the satisfaction of the antecedent of a law is ipso facto nomologically sufficient for the satisfaction of its consequent),

5.2. P is a causally responsible property if it's a property in virtue of the instantiation of which the occurrence of one event is nomologically sufficient for the occurrence of another.[5]

If this is right, then intentional properties are causally responsible in case there are intentional causal laws; aerodynamic properties are causally responsible in case there are aerodynamic causal laws; geological properties are causally responsible in case there are geological causal laws . . . and so forth. To all intents and purposes, on this view the question whether the property P is causally responsible *reduces to* the question whether there are causal laws about P. To settle the second question *is* to settle the first.

I don't mind if you find this proposal dull, but I would be distressed if you found it circular. How, you might ask, can one possibly make progress by defining "*causally responsible property*" in terms of "covering *causal* law"? And yet it's unclear that we can just drop the requirement that the covering law *be* causal because there are *non-causal* laws (e.g., the gas law about pressure and volume varying inversely) and perhaps an event's being covered by those sorts of laws *isn't* sufficient for its having a causally responsible property.

I can think of two fairly plausible ways out of this. First, it may be that any property in virtue of which some law covers an individual will be a property in virtue of which some causal law covers an individual;[6] i.e., that no property figures *only* in noncausal laws. This is, I think, an interesting metaphysical possibility; if it is true, then we can just identify the causally responsible properties with the properties in virtue of which individuals are covered by laws.

And, even if it's not true, it may be that what makes a law causal can itself be specified in noncausal terms. Perhaps it involves such properties as covering temporal successions, being asymmetric, and the like. In that case it would be okay to construe "causally responsible" in terms of "causal law" since the latter could be independently defined. Barring arguments to the contrary, I'm prepared to suppose that this will work.

We're now in a position to do a little diagnosis. According to the present view, the properties projected in the laws of basic science are causally responsible, and so too are the properties projected in the laws of the special sciences. This is truistic since the present view just is that being projected is sufficient for being causally responsible. Notice, in particular, that even if the properties that the special sciences talk about are supervenient upon the properties that the basic sciences talk about, that does *not* argue that the properties that the special sciences talk about are epiphenomenal. Not, at least, if there are causal laws of the special sciences. The causal laws of the special sciences and causal laws of basic sciences have in common that they *both* license ascriptions of causal responsibility. Or so, at least, the present view would have it.

This is not, however, to deny that there are metaphysically interesting differences between special-science laws and basic science laws. Let me introduce here a point that I propose to make a fuss of later.

Roughly, the satisfaction of the antecedent of a law is nomologically sufficient for the satisfaction of its consequent.[7] (I'll sometimes say that the truth of the antecedent of a law *nomologically necessitates* the truth of its consequent.) But a metaphysically interesting difference between basic and nonbasic laws is that, in the case of the latter but not the former, there always has to be a *mechanism in virtue of which* the satisfaction of its antecedent brings about the satisfaction of its consequent. If 'Fs cause Gs' is basic, then there is no answer to the question *how* do Fs cause Gs; they just do, and that they do is among the not-to-be-further-explained facts about the way the world is put together. Whereas, if 'Fs cause Gs' is *non*basic, then there is always a story about what goes on when—and in virtue of which—Fs cause Gs.

Sometimes it's a microstructure story: Meandering rivers erode their outside banks; facts about the abrasive effects of particles suspended in moving water explain why there is erosion; and the Bernouli effect explains why it's the *outside* banks that get eroded most. Sometimes there's a story about chains of macrolevel events that intervene between F-instantiations and G-instantiations. Changes in CO_2 levels in the atmosphere cause changes in fauna. There's a story about how CO_2 blocks radiation from the earth's surface; and there's a story about how the blocked radiation changes the air temperature; and there's a story about how changes in the air temperature cause climactic changes; and there's a (Darwinian) story about how climactic changes have zoological impacts. (I try to be as topical as I can.)

Or, to get closer home, consider the case in computational psychology: There are—so I fondly suppose—intentional laws that connect, for example, states of believing that P & (P → Q) to states of believing that Q. (*Ceteris paribus*, of course. More of that later.) Because there are events covered by such laws, it follows (trivially) that intentional properties (like *believing that P & (P → Q)* are causally responsible. And because nobody (except, maybe, panpsychists; who I am prepared not to take seriously for present purposes) thinks that intentional laws are basic, it follows that there must be a mechanism in virtue of which believing that P & (P → Q) *brings it about* that one believes Q.

There are, as it happens, some reasonably persuasive theories about the nature of such mechanisms currently on offer. The one I like best says that the mechanisms that implement intentional laws are computational. Roughly, the story goes: believing (etc.) is a relation between an organism and a mental representation. Mental representations have (*inter alia*) syntactic properties; and the mechanisms of belief-change are defined over the syntactic properties of mental representations. Let's not worry, for the moment, about whether this story is right; let's just worry about whether it's epiphobic.

Various philosophers have supposed that it is. Steven Stich, for example, has done some public handwringing about how anybody (a fortiori, how *I*) could hold *both* that intentional properties are causally responsible *and* the ("methodologically solipsistic") view that mental processes are entirely computational (/syntactic). And Norbert Hornstein[8] has recently ascribed to me the view that "the generalizations of psychology, the laws and the theories, are stated over syntactic objects, i.e., it is over syntactic representations that computations proceed." (p. 18). But: THE CLAIM THAT MENTAL PROCESSES ARE SYNTACTIC DOES NOT ENTAIL THE CLAIM THAT THE LAWS OF PSYCHOLOGY ARE SYNTACTIC. On the contrary THE LAWS OF PSYCHOLOGY ARE INTENTIONAL THROUGH AND THROUGH. This is a point to the reiteration of which my declining years seems somehow to have become devoted. What's syntactic is not the laws of psychology but the mechanisms by which the laws of psychology are implemented. Cf: The mechanisms of geological processes are—as it might be—chemical and molecular; it does not follow that chemical or molecular properties are projected by geological laws (on the contrary, it's geological properties that are projected by geological laws); and it does not follow that geological properties are causally inert (on the contrary, it's because Mt. Everest is such a very damned big mountain that it's so very damned cold on top).

It is, I should add, not in the least unusual to find that the vocabulary that's appropriate to articulate a special-science law is systematically different from the vocabulary that's appropriate to articulate its implementing mechanism(s). Rather, shift of vocabulary as one goes from the law to the mechanism is the *general* case. If you want to talk laws of inheritance, you talk recessive traits and dominant traits and homozygotes and heterozygotes; if you want to talk mechanisms of inheritance, you talk chromosomes and genes and how the DNA folds. If you want to talk psychological law, you talk intentional vocabulary; if you want to talk psychological mechanism, you talk syntactic (or maybe neurological) vocabulary. If you want to talk geological law, you talk mountains and glaciers; if you want to talk geological mechanism, you talk abrasion coefficients and cleavage planes. If you want to talk aerodynamic law, you talk airfoils and lift forces; if you want to talk aerodynamic mechanism, you talk gas pressure and laminar flows. It doesn't follow that the property of being a belief or an airfoil or a recessive trait is causally inert; all that follows is that *specifying the causally responsible macroproperty isn't the same as specifying the implementing micromechanism.*

It's a confusion to suppose that, if there's a law, then there needn't be an implementing mechanism; and it's a confusion to suppose that, if there's a mechanism that implements a law, then the properties that the law projects must be causally inert. If you take great care to avoid both these confusions, you will be delighted to see how rapidly your epiphobia disappears. You really will. Trust me.

II   Intentional Laws

According to the position just developed, the question whether a property is causally responsible reduces to the question whether it is a property in virtue of which individuals are subsumed by covering causal laws. So, in particular, if there are intentional laws, then it follows that intentional properties aren't epiphenomenal. But maybe there aren't intentional laws; or, if there are, maybe they can't cover individual causes in the way that causal laws are supposed to cover the events that they subsume. The view that this is so is widespread in recent philosophy of mind. Clearly, if intentional covering doesn't actually happen, the question whether it would be sufficient for the causal responsibility of the mental is academic even by academic standards. And the treatment for epiphobia that I prescribed in part I won't work. The rest of the paper will be devoted to this issue, with special attention to a very interesting recent discussion by Barry Loewer and Ernie LePore.

There seems to be some tension between the following three principles, each of which I take to be prima facie sort of plausible:

6. Strict covering: Just like 4 except with the following in place of 4.3: "P1 instantiations are causally sufficient for P2 instantiations" is a *strict* causal law.

7. Anomia of the mental: The only strict laws are laws of physics. Specifically, there are no strict 'psychophysical' laws relating types of brain states to types of intentional states; and there are no strict 'psychological' laws relating types of mental events to one another or to types of behavioral outcomes.

8. Causal responsibility of the mental: Intentional properties aren't epiphenomenal.

6 means something like: Causal transactions must be covered by exceptionless laws; the satisfaction of the antecedent of a covering law has to provide literally nomologically sufficient conditions for the satisfaction of its consequent so that its consequent is satisfied in every nomologically possible situation in which its antecedent is satisfied.

7 means something like this: The laws of physics differ in a characteristic way from the laws of the special sciences (notably including psychology). Special science laws are typically hedged with 'ceteris paribus' clauses, so that whereas physical laws say what has to happen come what may, special-science laws only say what has to happen all else being equal.[9]

How we should construe 8 has, of course, been a main concern throughout; but, according to the account of causal responsibility that I've been trying to sell you, it effectively reduces to the requirement that mental causes be covered by intentional laws. So now we can see where the tension between the three principles (6–8) arises. The responsibility of the mental requires covering by intentional laws. But given the revised notion of covering, according to which causes have to be covered by *strict* laws, it must be *physical* laws, and not intentional ones, that cover mental causes. So it turns out that the intentional properties are causally inert even according to the count of causal responsibility commended in part I.[10]

Something has to be done, and I assume it has to be done to 6 or 8 (or both) since 7 would seem to be okay. It is quite generally true about special-science laws that they hold only 'barring breakdowns', or 'under appropriately idealized conditions', or 'when the effects of interacting variables are ignored'. If even geological laws have to be hedged—as indeed they do—then it's more than plausible that the 'all else equal' proviso in psychological laws will prove not to be eliminable. On balance, we had best assume that 7 stays.

What about 8 then? Surely we want 8 to come out true on *some* reasonable construal. I've opted for a robust reading: mental properties are causally responsible because they are the properties in virtue of which mental causes are subsumed by covering laws; which is to say that mental properties are causally responsible because there are intentional generalizations which specify nomologically sufficient conditions for behavioral outcomes. But this reading of 8 looks to be incompatible with 7. 7 suggests that there *aren't* intentionally specifiable sufficient conditions for behavioral outcomes since, at best, intentional laws hold only ceteris paribus. So, maybe the notion of causal responsibility I've been selling is too strong. Maybe we could learn to make do with less.[11]

This is, more or less explicitly, the course that LePore and Loewer recommend in "Mind Matters": If the causal *responsibility* of the intentional can somehow be detached from its causal *sufficiency* for behavioral outcomes, we could then maybe reconcile causal responsibility with anomicness. In effect, L&L's idea is to hold on to 6 and 7 at the cost of not adopting a nomological subsumption reading of 8. Prima facie, this strategy is plausible in light of a point that L&L emphasize in their discussion of Sosa: The very fact that psychological laws are hedged would seem to rule out any construal of causal responsibility that requires mental causes qua mental to be nomologically sufficient for behavior. If it's only true ceteris paribus that someone who wants a drink reaches for the locally salient glass of water, then it's epiphobic to hold that desiring is causally responsible for reaching only if literally everyone who desires would thereupon reach. After all, quite aside from what you think of 6, it's simply not coherent to require the antecedents of hedged laws to provide literally nomologically sufficient conditions for the satisfaction of their consequents.

That's the stick; but Loewer and LePore also have a carrot on offer. They concede that, if the only strict laws are physical, then instantiations of intentional properties are not strictly sufficient for determining behavioral outcomes. But they observe that granting 6 and 7 *doesn't* concede that the *physical* properties of mental events are *necessary* for their behavioral effects. To see this, assume an event m which instantiates the mental property M and the physical property P. Assume that m has the behavioral outcome b, an event with the behavioral property B, and that it does so in virtue of a physical law which strictly connects the instantiation of P with the instantiation of B. LePore and Loewer point out that all this is fully compatible with the truth of the counterfactual:— $Pm \& Mm \rightarrow Bb$ (i.e., with it being the case that m would have caused Bb even if it hadn't been P.) Think of the case where M events are "multiply realized," e.g., not just by P instantiations but also by P* instantiations. And suppose that there's a strict law connecting P* events with B events. Then $Mm \rightarrow Bb$ will be true not only when m is a P instantiation, but also when m is a P* instantiation. The point is that *one* way that—$Pm \& Mm \rightarrow Bb$ can be true is if there are strict psychological laws; i.e., if being an M instantiation is strictly sufficient for being a B instantiation. But the counterfactual could also be true on the assumption that B instantiations have *disjoint physically sufficient conditions*. And that assumption can be allowed by someone who claims that only physical laws can ground mental causes (e.g., because he claims that only physical laws articulate strictly sufficient conditions for behavioral outcomes).

In short, LePore and Loewer show us that we can get quite a lot of what we want from the causal responsibility of the mental without assuming that intentional events are nomologically sufficient for behavioral outcomes; i.e., without assuming that intentional laws nomologically necessitate their consequents; i.e., without denying that the mental is anomic. Specifically, we can get that the particular constellation of physical properties that a mental cause exhibits needn't be necessary for its behavioral outcomes. I take LePore and Loewer's advice to be that we should settle for this; that we should construe the causal responsibility of the mental in some way that doesn't require mental events to be nomologically sufficient for their behavioral consequences. In effect, given a conflict between 6 and a covering law construal of 8, LePore and Loewer opt for 6; keep the idea that causes have to be strictly covered, and give up on the idea that the causal responsibility of the mental is the nomological necessitation of the behavioral by the intentional.

Now, this may be good advice, but I seem to detect a not-very-hidden agenda. Suppose, just for the sake of argument, that there *is* some way of providing intentionally sufficient conditions for behavioral outcomes. Then this would not only allow for an intuitively satisfying construal of the causal responsibility of the mental (viz., mental properties are causally responsible if mental causes are covered by intentional laws, as per part I), it would also undermine the idea that mental causes have to be covered by *physical* laws. If the laws of psychology have in common with the laws of physics that both strictly necessitate their consequents, then presumably either would do equally well to satisfy the constraints that 6 imposes on the laws that cover mental causes. But the idea that mental causes have to be covered by physical laws is the key step in the famous Davidsonian argument from the anomia of the mental to physicalism. It may be that LePore and Loewer would like to hang onto the Davidsonian argument; it's pretty clear that Davidson would.

I take Davidson's argument to go something like this:

> 9.1. Mental causes have to be covered by some strict law (strict covering);
> 9.2. but not by intentional laws because intentional laws aren't strict; the satisfaction of their antecedents isn't nomologically sufficient for the satisfaction of their consequents (anomia of the mental);
> 9.3. so mental causes must be covered by physical laws;
> 9.4. so they must have physical properties. Q.E.D.

But if there are intentionally sufficient conditions for behavioral outcomes you lose step 9.2; and if you lose step 9.2, you lose the argument. It appears that the cost of an intuitively adequate construal of mental responsibility is that there's no argument from mental causation to physicalism.

Well, so much for laying out the geography. Here's what happens next: First, I'll try to convince you that your intuitions really do cry out for some sort of causal sufficiency account of causal responsibility; something like that if it's m's being M that's causally responsible for b's being B, then b is B in all nearby worlds where m is M. (This is, to repeat, a consequence of defining causal responsibility in terms of strict covering laws, since it is a defining property of such laws that the satisfaction of their antecedents necessitates the satisfaction of their consequents.) I'll then suggest that, appearances to the contrary, it really isn't very hard to square such an account with the admission that even the best psychological laws are very likely to be hedged. In effect, I'm claiming that, given a conflict between 6 and 8, there's a natural replacement for 8. At this point the question about physicalism becomes moot since it will no longer be clear why hedged psychological laws can't ground mental causes; and, presumably, if hedged psychological laws can, then strict physical laws needn't. It still might turn out, however, that you can get a physicalist conclusion from considerations about mental causation, though by a slightly different route from the one that Davidson follows—a route that doesn't require the subsumption of causes by strict laws as a lemma.

My first point, then, is that, Loewer and LePore to the contrary notwithstanding, the notion of the causal responsibility of the mental that your intuitions demand is that Ms should be a nomologically sufficient condition for Bs. Accept no substitutes, is what I say. I'm not, however, exactly sure how to convince you that this is indeed what your intuitions cry out for; perhaps the following considerations will seem persuasive.

There aren't, of course, any reliable procedures for scientific discovery. But one might think of the procedures that have sometimes been proposed as, in effect, codifying our intuitions about causal responsibility. For example, it's right to say that Pasteur used the 'method of differences' to discover that contact with stuff in the air—and not spontaneous generation in the nutrient—is responsible for the breeding of maggots. This is not, however, a comment on how Pasteur went about thinking up his hypotheses or his experiments. The method of differences doesn't tell you *how* to find out what is causally responsible. Rather, it tells you *what* to find out to find out what's causally responsible. It says: thrash about in the nearby nomologically possible worlds and find a property such that you get the maggots just when you get that property instantiated. *That* will be the property whose instantiation is causally responsible for the maggots.

I'm claiming that Pasteur had in mind to assign causal responsibility for the maggots, and that, in doing so, it was preeminantly reasonable of him to have argued according to the method of differences: viz., that if the infestation is airborne, then fitting a gauze top to the bottle should get rid of the maggots, and taking the gauze top off the bottle should bring the maggots back again. Assigning causal responsibility to contact with stuff in the air involved showing that such contact is necessary *and sufficient* for getting the maggots; that was what the method of differences required, and that was what Pasteur figured out how to do. If those intuitions about causal responsibility were good enough for Pasteur, I guess they ought to be good enough for you and me.

So then, I assume that the method of differences codifies our intuitions about causal responsibility. But this implies that assigning causal responsibility to the mental requires the truth of more counterfactuals than L&L are prepared to allow. Intuitively, what we need is that m's being M is what *makes the difference* in determining whether b is B, hence that 'Bb whenever Mm' is true in all nearby worlds. If the method of differences tells us what causal responsibility is, then what it tells us is that causal responsibility requires nomological sufficiency.[12] So the causal responsibility of the mental must be the nomological sufficiency of intentional states for producing behavioral outcomes.

The first—and crucial—step in getting what a robust construal of the causal responsibility of the mental requires is to square the idea that Ms are nomologically sufficient for Bs with the fact that psychological laws are hedged. How can you have it *both* that special laws only necessitate their consequents ceteris paribus *and* that we must get Bs *whenever* we get Ms. Answer: you can't. But what you can have is just as good: viz., that if it's a law that M $\rightarrow$ B ceteris paribus, then it follows that you get Bs whenever you get Ms *and* the ceteris paribus conditions are satisfied.[13] This shows us how ceteris paribus laws can do serious scientific business, since it captures the difference between the (substantive) claim that Fs cause Gs ceteris paribus, and the (empty) claim that Fs cause Gs except when they don't.

So, it's sufficient for M to be a causally responsible property if it's a property in virtue of which Ms cause Bs. And here's what it is for M to be a property in virtue of which Ms cause Bs:

10.1. Ms cause Bs;
10.2. 'M $\rightarrow$ B ceteris paribus' is a law;[14] and
10.3. the ceteris paribus conditions are satisfied in respect of some Ms.

I must say, the idea that hedged (including intentional) laws necessitate their consequents when their ceteris paribus clauses are discharged seems to me to be so obviously the pertinent proposal that I'm hard put to see how anybody could seriously object to it. But no doubt somebody will.

One might, I suppose, take the line that there's no fact of the matter about whether, in a given case, the ceteris paribus conditions on a special science law are satisfied. Or that, even if there is a fact of the matter, still one can't ever know what the fact of the matter is. But, surely that would be mad. After all, Pasteur did demonstrate, to the satisfaction of all reasonable men, that ceteris paribus you get maggots when and only when the nutrients are in contact with stuff in the air. And presumably he did it *by* investigating experimental environments in which the ceteris paribus condition was satisfied and known to be so. Whatever is actual is possible; what Pasteur could do in fact, even you and I can do in principle.

I remark, in passing, that determining that ceteris paribus stuff in the air causes maggots did not require that Pasteur be able to *enumerate* the ceteris paribus conditions, only that he be able to recognize some cases in which they were in fact satisfied. *Sufficient* conditions for the satisfaction of ceteris paribus clauses may be determinate and epistemically accessible even when *necessary and sufficient* conditions for their satisfaction aren't. A fortiori, hedged laws whose ceteris paribus conditions cannot be enumerated may nevertheless be satisfied in particular cases. Perhaps we should say that M is causally responsible only if Ms cause Bs in *any* world in which the ceteris paribus clause of 'M → B all else equal' is discharged. This would leave it open, and not very important, whether '*all and only* the worlds in which the ceteris paribus conditions are discharged' is actually well-defined. It's not very important because what determines whether a given law can cover a given event is whether the law is determinately satisfied by the event. It is not also required that it be determinate whether the law would be satisfied by arbitrary other events (or by that same event in arbitrary other worlds). It seems to me that the plausibility of Davidson's assumption that hedged laws can't ground causes may depend on overlooking this point.

Finally, it might be argued that, although the ceteris paribus conditions on other special-science laws are sometimes known to be satisfied, there is nevertheless something peculiar about *intentional* laws, so that their ceteris paribus conditions can't be. I take it that Davidson thinks that something of this sort is true; but I have never been able to follow the arguments that are supposed to show that it is. And I notice (with approval) that LePore and Loewer are apparently not committed to any such claim.

Where does all this leave us with respect to the classical Davidsonian argument that infers physicalism from the anomalousness of the mental? It seems to me that we are now lacking any convincing argument for accepting principle 6. Suppose it's true that causes need to be covered by laws that necessitate their consequents; it doesn't follow that they need to be covered by *strict* laws. Hedged laws necessitate their consequents in worlds where their ceteris paribus conditions are satisfied. Why, then, should mental causes that are covered by hedged intentional laws with satisfied antecedents and satisfied ceteris paribus conditions require *further* covering by a strict law of physics?

The point till now has been that if strict laws will do to cover causes, so too will hedged laws in worlds where the hedges are discharged. I digress to remark that hedged laws can play the same role as strict ones in covering law explanations, so long as it's part of the explanation that the ceteris paribus conditions are satisfied.

When the antecedent of a strict law is satisfied, you are *guaranteed* the satisfaction of its consequent, and the operation of strict laws in covering law explanations depends on this. What's typically in want of a covering law explanation is some such fact as that an event *m* caused an event *b* (and not, nb, that an event *m* caused an event *b* ceteris paribus).[15] Indeed, it's not clear to me that there are facts of this latter sort. Hedged generalizations are one thing; hedged singularly causal statements would be quite another. Well, the point is that strict laws can explain *m*'s causing *b* precisely because if it's strict that Ms cause Bs and it's true that there is an M, then it *follows* that there is an M-caused *b*. "You got a B because you had an M, and it's a law that you get a B *whenever* you get an M." But if that sort of explanation is satisfying, then so too ought to be: "You got a B in world *w* because you had an M in world *w*, and it's a law that ceteris paribus you get a B whenever you have an M, and the ceteris paribus conditions were satisfied in world *w*." The long and short is: One reason you might think that causes have to be covered by strict laws is that covering law explanations depend on this being so. But they don't. Strict laws and hedged laws with satisfied ceteris paribus conditions operate alike in respect of their roles in covering causal relations and in respect of their roles in covering law explanations. Surely this is as it should be: Strict laws are just the special case of hedged laws where the ceteris paribus clauses are discharged *vacuously*; they're the hedged laws for which 'all else' is *always* equal.

Still, I think that there is *something* to be said for the intuition that strict physical laws play a special role in respect of the metaphysical under-pinnings of causal relations, and I think there may after all be a route from considerations about mental causation to physicalism. I'll close by saying a little about this.

In my view, the metaphysically interesting fact about special-science laws isn't that they're hedged; it's that they're *not basic*. Correspondingly, the metaphysically interesting contrast isn't between physical laws and special science laws; it's between basic laws and the rest. For present purposes, I need to remind you of a difference between special laws and basic laws that I remarked on in part I: If it's nonbasically lawful that Ms cause Bs, there's always a story to tell about how (typically, by what transformations of microstructures) instantiating M brings about the instantiation of B. Nonbasic laws want implementing mechanisms; basic laws don't. (That, I imagine, is what makes them basic.)

It is therefore surely no accident that *hedged* laws are typically—maybe always—*not* basic. On the one hand, it's intrinsic to a law being hedged that it is nomologically possible for its ceteris paribus conditions not to be satisfied. And, on the other hand, a standard way to account for the failure of a ceteris paribus condition is to point to the breakdown of an intervening mechanism. Thus, meandering rivers erode their outside banks ceteris paribus, but not when the speed of the river is artificially controlled (no Bernoulli effect); and not when the river is chemically pure (no suspended particles); and not when somebody has built a wall on the outside bank (not enough abrasion to overcome adhesion). In such cases, the ceteris paribus clause fails to be satisfied *because* an intervening mechanism fails to operate. By contrast, this strategy is unavailable in the case of *non*basic laws; basic laws don't rely on mechanisms of implementation, so if they have exceptions that must be because they're nondeterministic.

We see here one way in which ceteris paribus clauses do their work. Nonbasic laws *rely on* mediating mechanisms which they do not, however, *articulate* (sometimes because the mechanisms aren't known; sometimes because As can cause Bs in many different ways, so that the same law has a variety of implementations). Ceteris paribus clauses can have the effect of existentially quantifying over these mechanisms, so that 'As cause Bs ceteris paribus' can mean something like 'There exists an intervening mechanism such that As cause Bs when it's intact.' I expect that the ceteris paribus clauses in special science laws can do other useful things as well. It is a scandal of the philosophy of science that we haven't got a good taxonomy of their functions.

However, I digress. The present point is that:

11. non-basic laws require mediation by intervening mechanisms; and
12. there are surely no basic laws of psychology.

Let us now make the following bold assumption: all the mechanisms that mediate the operation of nonbasic laws are eventually physical.[16] I don't, I confess, know exactly what this bold assumption means (because I don't know exactly what it *is* for a mechanism to be physical as opposed, say, to spiritual); and I confess that I don't know exactly why it seems to me to be a reasonable bold assumption to make. But I do suspect that if it could be stated clearly, it would be seen to be a sort of bold assumption for which the past successes of our physicalistic world view render substantial inductive support.

Well, if all the mechanisms that nonbasic laws rely on are eventually physical, then the mechanisms of mental causation must be eventually physical, too. For, on the current assumptions, mental causes have their effects in virtue of being subsumed by psychological laws and, since psychological laws aren't basic, they require mediation by intervening mechanisms. However, it seems to me that to admit that mental causes must be related to their effects (including, notice, their *mental* effects) by physical mechanisms *just is* to admit that mental causes are physical. Or, if it's not, then it's to admit something so close that I can't see why the difference matters.

So, then, perhaps there's a route to physicalism from stuff about mental causation that *doesn't* require the claim that ceteris paribus laws can't ground mental causes. If so, then my story gives us both physicalism and a reasonable account of the causal responsibility of the mental; whereas Davidson's story gives us at most the former.[17] But if we *can't* get both the causal responsibility of the mental and an argument for physicalism, then it seems to me that we ought to give up the argument for physicalism. I'm not really convinced that it matters very much whether the mental is physical; still less that it matters very much whether we can prove that it is. Whereas, if it isn't literally true that my wanting is causally responsible for my reaching, and my itching is causally responsible for my scratching, and my believing is causally responsible for my saying.... if none of that is literally true, then practically everything I believe about anything is false and it's the end of the world.

Notes

This paper is a revised and extended version of some remarks presented at an APA symposium on December 30, 1987, in reply to Ernest LePore and Barry Loewer's "Mind Matters," *Journal of Philosophy* 84.11 (Nov. 1987): 630–642. I am grateful to them and to Brian McLaughlin, for much stimulating conversation on these and related issues.

1. I shall more or less assume, in what follows, that events are the individuals that causal laws subsume and to which causal powers are ascribed. Nothing will turn on this; it's just a bore to always be having to say "events, or situations, or things or whatever...."

2. It facilitates the discussion not to worry about which of their properties events have essentially. In particular, I shall assume that we can make sense of counterfactuals in which a certain mental event is supposed to have *no* intentional content, or an intentional content or a physical constituency different from its actual content or constituency. Nothing germane to the present issues hangs on this since, as far as I can tell, the same sorts of points I'll be making about counterfactual properties of events could just as well be made about relations between events and their counterparts.

3. What follows is a very crude approximation of the aerodynamic facts. Enthusiasts will find a serious exposition in W. Ross, *Sail Power* (New York: Alfred A. Knopf, 1975).

4. The Covering Principle is generally in the spirit of the proposals of Donald Davidson, except that, unlike Davidson, I'm prepared to be shameless about properties.

5. 5.2 is in the text to emphasize that the nomological subsumption account of the causal responsibility of the mental is closely connected to the idea that mental events are nomologically sufficient for behavioral outcomes. We will thus have to consider how to square the nomological subsumption story with the fact that the antecedents of psychological laws generally do *not* specify nomologically sufficient conditions for the satisfaction of their consequents (because, like the laws of the other special sciences, the laws of psychology typically have essential ceteris paribus causes). See part II.

6. I'm leaving statistical laws out of consideration. If some laws are irremediably statistical, then the proposal in the text should be changed to read: "any property in virtue of which some deterministic law covers an individual will be a property in virtue of which some causal law covers an individual."

7. But this will have to be hedged to deal with ceteris paribus laws. Part II is about what's the right way to hedge it.

8. N. Hornstein, "The Heartbreak of Semantics," *Mind and Language* 3 (1988): 18.

9. Special science laws are unstrict not just de facto, but in principle. Specifically, they are characteristically "*heteronomic*": You can't convert them into strict laws by elaborating their antecedents. One reason why this is so is that special science laws typically fail in limiting conditions, or in conditions where the idealizations presupposed by the science aren't approximated; and, generally speaking, you have to go outside the vocabulary of the science to say what these conditions are. Old rivers meander, but not

when somebody builds a levee. Notice that "levee" is not a *geological* term. (Neither, for that matter, is "somebody.")

I emphasize this point because it's sometimes supposed that heteronomicity is a proprietary feature of *intentional* laws qua intentional. Poppycock.

10. It could, no doubt, be said that accepting 6 doesn't really make the mental properties drop out of the picture because, even if mental causes have to be covered by physical laws, it can still be true that they are *also* covered by intentional laws (*viz.*, in the old 4.3 sense of "covering" which didn't require covering laws to be strict). As Brian McLaughlin (ms) has rightly pointed out, it's perfectly consistent to hold that covering by strict laws is necessary and sufficient for causal relations and *also to hold that covering by loose laws is necessary, or even sufficient, for causal relations*, so long as you are prepared to assume that every cause that is loosely covered is strictly covered, too.

However, it is not clear that this observation buys much relief from epiphobia. After all, if mental properties really are causally active, why isn't intentional covering *all by itself* sufficient to ground the causal relations of mental events? I've been urging that intentional properties are causally responsible if mental causes are covered by intentional laws. But that seems plausible only if mental events are causes *in virtue of* their being covered by intentional laws. But how could mental causes be causes qua intentionally covered if, in order to *be* causes, they are further required to be subsumed by nonintentional laws? Taken together, 6 and 7 make it look as though, even if mental events are covered qua intentional, they're causes only qua physical. So again it looks like the intentional properties of mental events aren't doing any of the work.

11. I'm doing a little pussyfooting here, so perhaps I'd better put the point exactly: On the view that I will presently commend, there *are* circumstances in which instantiations of mental properties nomologically necessitate behavioral outcomes. What isn't, however, quite the case is that these circumstances are fully specified by the antecedents of intentional laws. On my view, only *basic* laws have the property that their antecedents fully specify the circumstances that nomologically necessitate the satisfaction of their consequents (and then only if they're deterministic).

12. It will be noticed that I'm stressing the importance of causal sufficiency for causal responsibility, whereas it was causal necessity that Pasteur cared about most. Pasteur was out to show that contact with stuff in the air and *only* contact with stuff in the air is causally responsible for maggots; specifically that contact with stuff in the air accounts for *all* of the maggots, hence that spontaneous generation accounts for none. I take it that it is *not* among our intuitions that a certain mental property is causally responsible for a certain behavior only if that sort of behavior can have no other sort of cause.

13. So, what I said above—that a law is a hypothetical the satisfaction of whose antecedent nomologically necessitates the satisfaction of its consequent—wasn't quite true since it doesn't quite apply to hedged laws. What *is* true is that a law is a hypothetical the satisfaction of whose antecedent nomologically necessitates the satisfaction of its consequent *when its ceteris paribus conditions are satisfied*.

14. If it's a strict law, then the ceteris paribus clause is vacuously satisfied.

15. To put it another way: Suppose you're feeling Hempelian about the role of covering laws in scientific explanations. Then you might worry that (i) ceteris paribus As cause Bs together with (ii) Aa yields something like (iii) ceteris paribus Bb which isn't strong enough to explain the datum (Bb). 'Ceteris paribus Bb' doesn't look to have the form of a possible data statement. I wonder in the text whether it even has the form of a possible truth.

16. "Eventually" means: either the law is implemented by a physical mechanism, or its implementation depends on a lower level law which is itself either implemented by a physical mechanism or is dependent on a still lower level law which is itself either implemented by a physical mechanism or ..., etc. Since only finite chains of implementation are allowed, you have to get to a physical mechanism "eventually."

We need to put it this way because, as we've been using it, a "physical" mechanism is one whose means of operation is covered by a physical law (i.e., by a law articulated in the language of physics). And though, presumably, physical mechanisms implement every high-level law, they usually do so via lots of levels of intermediate laws and implementations. So, for example, intentional laws are implemented by syntactic mechanisms that are governed by syntactic laws that are implemented by neurological mechanisms that are governed by neurological laws that are implemented by biochemical mechanisms that ... and so on down to physics.

None of this really matters for present purposes, of course. A demonstration that mental events have neural properties would do to solve the mind/body problem since nobody doubts that neural events have physical properties.

17. On the other hand, I don't pretend to do what Davidson seems to think he can: viz., to get physicalism *just* from considerations about the constraints that causation places on covering laws together with the

truism that psychological laws aren't strict. That project was breathtakingly ambitious but maybe not breathtakingly well advised. My guess is: If you want to get a lot of physicalism out, you're going to have to put a lot of physicalism in; what I put in was the independent assumption that the mechanism of intentional causation is physical.

Part III
Mental Imagery

Introduction

The selections from Thomas Aquinas, Thomas Hobbes, and René Descartes raise the question of whether thought is imagistic. For Aquinas the answer is yes (for people) and no (for noncorporeal beings). For Hobbes the answer is yes. For Descartes the answer is no. According to this trio of writers, imagery is something that only embodied creatures can have. This may seem surprising in the case of Descartes, for imagery seems to be a canonical mental phenomenon. But Descartes believes that if we were disembodied, we could no longer have images. Descartes makes a distinction between images and ideas, pointing out that you can have an idea of a chiliagon (a thousand-sided figure) but not an image of one.

Hobbes also articulates two important themes that recur in later philosophy: that mental imagery is decaying sense, and that the faculty of imagination is identical to the faculty of memory.

David Hume addresses the relation between perception, memory, and imagination. Like Hobbes, he argues that memories and mental images are merely sense perceptions that are less vivid. The crucial difference between memories and images, he argues, is that memories (though less vivid than perceptions) are still more vivid than images.

William James takes up the themes introduced by Hobbes and Hume. He argues for the physiological basis of mental images, maintaining that the processes underlying imagery are identical to the processes underlying perception. He cites turn-of-the-century neurophysiological data, including a study that suggests that if the vision center of a sighted person is severely damaged, the person not only loses vision but will not even be aware of a deficit. The reason, according to James, is that the person can no longer have mental images and thus can have no idea of what is now unseen.

Following Hume, James argues that images are simply less vivid sense impressions. James suggests that there are common experiences that support this idea. For example, if a baby cries in a distant room, one may be unsure whether one is actually perceiving a baby or imagining it. That is because the perception is so faint that it is no more vivid than an auditory image.

James also addresses the question of whether thoughts (ideas) are identical to images. He denies both that general thoughts correspond to vague images and that thoughts about particular objects correspond to sharp images. So, for example, he approves of Berkeley's observation that the idea of a triangle does not correspond to a vague or confused image. There may rather be a sharp image of some prototypical triangle. The converse also holds. One may have a vague image of a particular individual.

Oswald Külpe (a continental psychologist at the turn of the century) also takes exception to the claim that all thought is imagistic. Külpe notes that introspective experiments show that certain mental activities cannot be reduced to images. For example, the acts of attending, willing, and so forth, do not appear to be imagistic.

John Watson argues that mental images merely stand in the way of a proper scientific psychology (specifically, behaviorism) and suggests that they must be dispensed with altogether. According to Watson, mental images have no place in behavioral psychology for they are not publicly observable.

Gilbert Ryle challenges the idea of mental pictures as well, but on conceptual grounds rather than scientific grounds. He notes that if a child imagines a smile on a doll's face, the child does not actually see a smile floating in front of the doll. Rather the child is playing (behaving) as though the doll is smiling. Ryle goes on to note that the case for mental images is not so appealing when we consider the other sensory modalities. While we are quick to talk of the "mind's eye" seeing a mental picture, Ryle suggests that no one would speak of the "mind's nose" smelling a mental aroma.

Ryle also takes issue with the idea (from Hobbes, Hume, and James) that images can be thought of as less vivid sense impressions. Ryle notes that while dolls may be lifelike, we would never say that a real baby is lifelike. Likewise we may call an image vivid, but we would never consider an actual sense impression vivid. Moreover, an image of a loud noise is not loud and will not even drown out someone whispering. Ryle concludes that it is a simple confusion to try and compare the vividness of an image with that of a sense impression.

Daniel Dennett suggests several additional reasons for doubting that there can be anything like pictures in the head. First, he notes that most images share some physical property with the object they represent. So, for example, an image of an orange must be either round, or orange, or both. The question is, what physical properties could mental images possibly share with the things they are images of?

Second, Dennett notes that images, unlike pictures are incomplete. Close your eyes and imagine a tiger for a second or two. Now, how many stripes were visible in the image? Probably there is no answer to the question because the image was vague. On the other hand, there is a determinate answer to how many stripes are visible in a picture of a tiger.

In response to such doubts there is a great deal of work in cognitive psychology that attempts to establish the existence of visual mental images. Shepard and Metzler report an experiment in which subjects are given two pictures of geometrical figures and are asked to indicate whether the figures are identical. In some cases the second figure is identical to the first but rotated; in such cases the amount of time it takes the subject to indicate that the figures are identical is directly correlated with the degree to which the second figure has been rotated. The further the image has been rotated, the longer it takes the subject to respond. Shepard and Metzler conclude that the subject forms a mental image of the figure and rotates the mental image at a certain limiting rate.

Stephen Kosslyn reports the results of scanning experiments in which subjects must scan (with their "mind's eye") between points on an image. For example, a subject might be instructed to attend to a particular location on a mental image of a map and indicate whether there is a lake in another location on the mental map. The greater the relative distance between the two points, the longer it takes the subject to respond. Kosslyn concludes that this time difference can be accounted for if we suppose that the subject is scanning a mental picture at a certain limiting rate.

Zenon Pylyshyn remains unconvinced by these experiments. He argues that the experimental conditions are such that the subjects understand their task as imagining that they are actually scanning a map. Utilizing their real-world knowledge about scanning maps, they delay their reaction times to correspond to the time that they realize it would take to scan an actual map.

Kosslyn replies to Pylyshyn on this point, citing a number of recent experiments designed to show that the subject has no expectation that it should take longer to scan greater distances.

Further Reading

Block, N., ed. 1981. *Imagery*. Cambridge, MA: MIT Press.
Finke, R. 1989. *Principles of Mental Imagery*, Cambridge, MA: MIT Press.
Kosslyn S. 1980. *Image and Mind*. Cambridge, MA: Harvard University Press.
Pinker, S., ed. 1984. *Visual Cognition*. Cambridge, MA: MIT Press.
Shepard R., and L. Cooper. 1982. *Mental Images and their Transformations*. Cambridge, MA: MIT Press.
Tye, M., 1991. *The Imagery Debate*, Cambridge, MA: MIT Press.

Chapter 22

That the Soul Never Thinks without an Image

Thomas Aquinas

It is impossible for our intellect, in its present state of being joined to a body capable of receiving impressions, actually to understand anything without turning to sense images. This is evident on two counts. First, because, since it is a faculty which does not use a corporeal organ, the intellect would be in no sense impeded by an injury to a corporeal organ if for its act another act of a faculty that does use a corporeal organ were not required. But the senses, the imagination, and the other faculties of the sense part of man do use corporeal organs. Hence it is obvious that, for the intellect actually to understand (not only in acquiring new knowledge but also in using knowledge already acquired), acts of the imagination and the other faculties are necessary.

We see, in fact, that if acts of the imagination are impeded by an injury to its organ—for instance, in a seizure—or, similarly, if acts of sense memory are impeded—for instance, in coma—a man is impeded from actually understanding even things which he had known before.

The second count is this. As anyone can experience for himself, if he attempts to understand anything, he will form images for himself which serve as examples in which he can, as it were, look at what he is attempting to understand. This is the reason, indeed, why, when we want to help someone understand something, we propose examples to him so that he can form images for himself in order to understand.

The reason for all this is that cognitive faculties are proportioned to their objects. For instance, an angel's intellect, which is totally separate from corporeal reality, has as its proper object intelligible substances separate from corporeal reality, and it is by means of these intelligible objects that it knows material realities. The proper object of the human intellect, on the other hand, since it is joined to a body, is a nature or 'whatness' found in corporeal matter—the intellect, in fact, rises to the limited knowledge it has of invisible things by way of the nature of visible things. But by definition a nature of this kind exists in an individual which has corporeal matter, for instance, it is of the nature of stone that it should exist in this or that particular stone, or of the nature of horse that it should exist in this or that particular horse, etc. Thus the nature of stone or any other material reality cannot be known truly and completely except in so far as it exists in a particular thing. Now we apprehend the particular through the senses and imagination. Therefore if it is actually to understand its proper object, then the intellect must needs turn to sense images in order to look at universal natures existing in particular things.

Whereas if the proper object of our intellect were an immaterial form, or if the natures of sensible things subsisted apart from particulars, as the Platonists think, it would not be necessary for our intellect when understanding always to be turning to sense images. Hence:

    1. Species stored up in the possible intellect remain there in a habitual way when the intellect is not actually understanding, as was said above. Thus, in order for us actually to understand, a mere storing of species is not sufficient; we must also use

them, and indeed in accord with the things of which they are images, which are natures existing in particulars.

2. Since the sense image is itself a likeness of a particular thing, the imagination does not need a further likeness of a particular, as does the intellect.

3. We know incorporeal realities, which have no sense images, by analogy with sensible bodies, which do have images, just as we understand truth in the abstract by a consideration of things in which we see truth. God we know, according to Dionysius, as cause about which we ascribe the utmost perfection and negate any limit. Furthermore, we cannot, in our present state, know other incorporeal substances except negatively and by analogy with corporeal realities. Thus when we understand anything of these beings, we necessarily have to turn to images of sensible bodies even though they do not themselves have such images.

Chapter 23

Of Imagination

Thomas Hobbes

Imagination

That when a thing lies still, unless somewhat else stir it, it will lie still for ever, is a truth that no man doubts of. But that when a thing is in motion, it will eternally be in motion, unless somewhat else stay it, though the reason be the same, namely, that nothing can change itself, is not so easily assented to. For men measure, not only other men, but all other things, by themselves; and because they find themselves subject after motion to pain, and lassitude, think every thing else grows weary of motion, and seeks repose of its own accord; little considering, whether it be not some other motion, wherein that desire of rest they find in themselves, consisteth. . . .

When a body is once in motion, it moveth, unless something else hinder it, eternally; and whatsoever hindreth it, cannot in an instant, but in time, and by degrees, quite extinguish it; and as we see in the water, though the wind cease, the waves give not over rolling for a long time after: so also it happeneth in that motion, which is made in the internal parts of a man, then, when he sees, dreams, etc. For after the object is removed, or the eye shut, we still retain an image of the thing seen, though more obscure than when we see it. And this is it, the Latins call *imagination*, from the image made in seeing; and apply the same, though improperly, to all the other senses. But the Greeks call it *fancy*; which signifies *appearance*, and is as proper to one sense, as to another. Imagination therefore is nothing but *decaying sense*; and is found in men, and many other living creatures, as well sleeping, as waking.

The decay of sense in men waking, is not the decay of the motion made in sense; but an obscuring of it, in such manner as the light of the sun obscureth the light of the stars; which stars do no less exercise their virtue, by which they are visible, in the day than in the night. But because amongst many strokes, which our eyes, ears, and other organs receive from external bodies, the predominant only is sensible; therefore, the light of the sun being predominant, we are not affected with the action of the stars. And any object being removed from our eyes, though the impression it made in us remain, yet other objects more present succeeding, and working on us, the imagination of the past is obscured, and made weak, as the voice of a man is in the noise of the day. From whence it followeth, that the longer the time is, after the sight or sense of any object, the weaker is the imagination. For the continual change of man's body destroys in time the parts which in sense were moved: so that distance of time, and of place, hath one and the same effect in us. For as at a great distance of place, that which we look at appears dim, and without distinction of the smaller parts; and as voices grow weak, and inarticulate; so also, after great distance of time, our imagination of the past is weak; and we lose, for example, of cities we have seen, many particular streets, and of actions, many particular circumstances. This *decaying sense*, when we would express the thing itself, I mean *fancy* itself, we call *imagination*, as I said before: but when we would express the decay, and signify that the sense is fading, old, and past, it is called *memory*.

So that imagination and memory are but one thing, which for divers considerations hath divers names.

Memory

Much memory, or memory of many things, is called *experience*. Again, imagination being only of those things which have been formerly perceived by sense, either all at once, or by parts at several times; the former, which is the imagining the whole object as it was presented to the sense, is *simple* imagination, as when one imagineth a man, or horse, which he hath seen before. The other is *compounded*; as when, from the sight of a man at one time, and of a horse at another, we conceive in our mind a Centaur. So when a man compoundeth the image of his own person with the image of the actions of another man, as when a man imagines himself a Hercules or an Alexander, which happeneth often to them that are much taken with reading of romances, it is a compound imagination, and properly but a fiction of the mind. There be also other imaginations that rise in men, though waking, from the great impression made in sense: as from gazing upon the sun, the impression leaves an image of the sun before our eyes a long time after; and from being long and vehemently attent upon geometrical figures, a man shall in the dark, though awake, have the images of lines and angles before his eyes; which kind of fancy hath no particular name, as being a thing that doth not commonly fall into men's discourse.

Dreams

The imaginations of them that sleep are those we call *dreams*. And these also, as all other imaginations, have been before, either totally or by parcels, in the sense. And because in sense, the brain and nerves, which are the necessary organs of sense, are so benumbed in sleep, as not easily to be moved by the action of external objects, there can happen in sleep on imagination, and therefore no dream, but what proceeds from the agitation of the inward parts of man's body; which inward parts, for the connexion they have with the brain, and other organs, when they be distempered, do keep the same in motion; whereby the imagination there formerly made, appear as if a man were waking; saving that the organs of sense being now benumbed, so as there is no new object, which can master and obscure them with a more vigorous impression, a dream must needs be more clear, in this silence of sense, than our waking thoughts. And hence it cometh to pass, that it is a hard matter, and by many thought impossible, to distinguish exactly between sense and dreaming. For my part, when I consider that in dreams I do not often nor constantly think of the same persons, places, objects, and actions, that I do waking; nor remember so long a train of coherent thoughts, dreaming, as at other times; and because waking I often observe the absurdity of dreams, but never dream of the absurdities of my waking thoughts; I am well satisfied, that being awake, I know I dream not, though when I dream I think myself awake.

And seeing dreams are caused by the distemper of some of the inward parts of the body, divers distempers must needs cause different dreams. And hence it is that lying cold breedeth dreams of fear, and raiseth the thought and image of some fearful object, the motion from the brain to the inner parts and from the inner parts to the brain being reciprocal; and that as anger causeth heat in some parts of the body when we are awake, so when we sleep the overheating of the same parts causeth anger, and raises up in the brain the imagination of an enemy. In the same manner, as natural kindness, when we are awake, causeth desire, and desire makes heat in certain other parts of the body; so also too much heat in those parts, while we sleep, raiseth in the brain an imagination of some kindness shown. In sum, our dreams are the reverse of our waking imaginations; the motion when we are awake beginning at one end, and when we dream at another.

Understanding

The imagination that is raised in man, or any other creature endued with the faculty of imagining, by words, or other voluntary signs, is that we generally call *understanding*; and is common to man and beast. For a dog by custom will understand the call, or the rating of his master; and so will many other beasts. That understanding which is peculiar to man, is the understanding not only his will, but his conceptions and thoughts, by the sequel and contexture of the names of things into affirmations, negations, and other forms of speech; and of this kind of understanding I shall speak hereafter.

Chapter 24

From *Meditation* VI and from *Objection* IV and *Reply*

René Descartes

Nothing further now remains but to inquire whether material things exist. And certainly I at least know that these may exist insofar as they are considered as the objects of pure mathematics, since in this aspect I perceive them clearly and distinctly. For there is no doubt that God possesses the power to produce everything that I am capable of perceiving with distinctness, and I have never deemed that anything was impossible for Him, unless I found a contradiction in attempting to conceive it clearly. Further, the faculty of imagination which I possess, and of which, experience tells me, I make use when I apply myself to the consideration of material things, is capable of persuading me of their existence; for when I attentively consider what imagination is, I find that it is nothing but a certain application of the faculty of knowledge to the body which is immediately present to it, and which therefore exists.

And to render this quite clear, I remark in the first place the difference that exists between the imagination and pure intellection [or conception]. For example, when I imagine a triangle, I do not conceive it only as a figure comprehended by three lines, but I also apprehend these three lines as present by the power and inward vision of my mind, and this is what I call imagining. But if I desire to think of a chiliagon, I certainly conceive truly that it is a figure composed of a thousand sides, just as easily as I conceive of a triangle that it is a figure of three sides only; but I cannot in any way imagine the thousand sides of a chiliagon [as I do the three sides of a triangle], nor do I, so to speak, regard them as present [with the eyes of my mind]. And although in accordance with the habit I have formed of always employing the aid of my imagination when I think of corporeal things, it may happen that in imagining a chiliagon I confusedly represent to myself some figure, yet it is very evident that this figure is not a chiliagon, since it in no way differs from that which I represent to myself when I think of a myriagon or any other many-sided figure; nor does it serve my purpose in discovering the properties which go to form the distinction between a chiliagon and other polygons. But if the question turns upon a pentagon, it is quite true that I can conceive its figure as well as that of a chiliagon without the help of my imagination; but I can also imagine it by applying the attention of my mind to each of its five sides, and at the same time to the space which they enclose. And thus I clearly recognise that I have need of a particular effort of mind in order to effect the act of imagination, such as I do not require in order to understand, and this particular effort of mind clearly manifests the difference which exists between imagination and pure intellection.

I remark besides that this power of imagination which is in one, inasmuch as it differs from the power of understanding, is in no wise a necessary element in my nature, or in [my essence, that is to say, in] the essence of my mind; for although I did not possess it I should doubtless ever remain the same as I now am, from which it appears that we might conclude that it depends on something which differs from me. And I easily conceive that if some body exists with which my mind is conjoined and united in such a way that it can apply itself to consider it when it pleases, it may be that by this means it can imagine corporeal objects; so that this mode of thinking differs from pure intellection only inasmuch as mind in its intellectual activity in some manner turns on itself, and considers some of the ideas which it possesses in itself; while in imagining it turns towards the body, and there beholds in it something conformable to the idea which it has either conceived of itself or perceived by the senses. I easily understand, I say, that the imagination could be thus constituted if it is true that body exists; and because I can discover no other convenient mode of explaining it, I conjecture with probability that body does exist; but this is only with probability, and although I examine all things with care, I nevertheless do not find that from this distinct idea of corporeal nature, which I have in my imagination, I can derive any argument from which there will necessarily be deduced the existence of body.

Objection IV [By Thomas Hobbes]

Hence it is left for me to concede that I do not even understand by the imagination what this wax is, but conceive it by the mind alone.

There is a great difference between imagining, i.e., having some idea, and conceiving with the mind, i.e., inferring, as the result of a train of reasoning, that something is, or exists. But M. Descartes has not explained to us the sense in which they differ. The ancient peripatetics also have taught clearly enough that substance is not perceived by the senses, but is known as a result of reasoning.

But what shall we now say, if reasoning chance to be nothing more than the uniting and stringing together of names or designations by the word is? It will be a consequence of this that reason gives us no conclusion about the nature of things, but only about the terms that designate them, whether, indeed, or not there is a convention (arbitrarily made about their meanings) according to which we join these names together. If this be so, as is possible, reasoning will depend on names, names on the imagination, and imagination, perchance, as I think, on the motion of the corporeal organs. Thus mind will be nothing but the motions in certain parts of an organic body.

Reply

I have here explained the difference between imagination and a pure mental concept, as when in my illustration I enumerated the features in wax that were given by the imagination and those solely due to a conception of the mind. But elsewhere also I have explained how it is that one and the same thing, e.g., a pentagon, is in one way an object of the understanding, in another way of the imagination [for example how in order to imagine a pentagon a particular mental act is required which gives us this figure (i.e., its five sides and the space they enclose) which we dispense with wholly in our conception]. Moreover, in reasoning we unite not names but the things signified by the names; and I marvel that the opposite can occur to anyone. For who doubts whether a Frenchman and a German are able to reason in exactly the same way about the same things, though they yet conceive the words in an entirely diverse way? And has not my opponent condemned himself in talking of conventions arbitrarily made about the meanings of words? For, if he admits that words signify anything, why will he not allow our reasonings to refer to this something that is signified, rather than to the words alone? But, really, it will be as correct to infer that earth is heaven or anything else that is desired, as to conclude that mind is motion [for there are no other two things in the world between which there is not as much agreement as there is between motion and spirit, which are of two entirely different natures].

Chapter 25

Of the Ideas of the Memory and Imagination

David Hume

We find by experience, that when any impression has been present with the mind, it again makes its appearance there as an idea; and this it may do after two different ways: either when in its new appearance it retains a considerable degree of its first vivacity, and is somewhat intermediate betwixt an impression and an idea; or when it intirely loses that vivacity, and is a perfect idea. The faculty, by which we repeat our impressions in the first manner, is called the Memory, and the other the Imagination. 'Tis evident at first sight, that the ideas of the memory are much more lively and strong than those of the imagination, and that the former faculty paints its objects in more distinct colours, than any which are employ'd by the latter. When we remember any past event, the idea of it flows in upon the mind in a forcible manner; whereas in the imagination the perception is faint and languid, and cannot without difficulty be preserv'd by the mind steddy and uniform for any considerable time. Here then is a sensible difference betwixt one species of ideas and another. But of this more fully hereafter.

There is another difference betwixt these two kinds of ideas, which is no less evident, namely that tho' neither the ideas of the memory nor imagination, neither the lively nor faint ideas can make their appearance in the mind, unless their correspondent impressions have gone before to prepare the way for them, yet the imagination is not restrain'd to the same order and form with the original impressions; while the memory is in a manner ty'd down in that respect, without any power of variation.

'Tis evident, that the memory preserves the original form, in which its objects were presented, and that where-ever we depart from it in recollecting any thing, it proceeds from some defect or imperfection in that faculty. An historian may, perhaps, for the more convenient carrying on of his narration, relate an event before another, to which it was in fact posterior; but then he takes notice of this disorder, if he be exact; and by that means replaces the idea in its due position. 'Tis the same case in our recollection of those places and persons, with which we were formerly acquainted. The chief exercise of the memory is not to preserve the simple ideas, but their order and position. In short, this principle is supported by such a number of common and vulgar phænomena, that we may spare ourselves the trouble of insisting on it any farther.

The same evidence follows us in our second principle, *of the liberty of the imagination to transpose and change its ideas*. The fables we meet with in poems and romances put this entirely out of question. Nature there is totally confounded, and nothing mentioned but winged horses, fiery dragons, and monstrous giants. Nor will this liberty of the fancy appear strange, when we consider, that all our ideas are copy'd from our impressions, and that there are not any two impressions which are perfectly inseparable. Not to mention, that this is an evident consequence of the division of ideas into simple and complex. Whereever the imagination perceives a difference among ideas, it can easily produce a separation.

Chapter 26

Imagination

William James

Sensations, once experienced, modify the nervous organism, so that copies of them arise again in the mind after the original outward stimulus is gone. No mental copy, however, can arise in the mind, of any kind of sensation which has never been directly excited from without.

The blind may dream of sights, the deaf of sounds, for years after they have lost their vision or hearing;[1] but the man *born* deaf can never be made to imagine what sound is like, nor can the man *born* blind ever have a mental vision. In Locke's words, already quoted, "the mind can frame unto itself no one new simple idea." The originals of them all must have been given from without. Fantasy, or Imagination, are the names given to the faculty of reproducing copies of originals once felt. The imagination is called 'reproductive' when the copies are literal; 'productive' when elements from different originals are recombined so as to make new wholes.

After-images belong to sensation rather than to imagination; so that the most immediate phenomena of imagination would seem to be those tardier images (due to what the Germans all *Sinnesgedächtniss*)—coercive hauntings of the mind by echoes of unusual experiences for hours after the latter have taken place. The phenomena ordinarily ascribed to imagination, however, are those mental pictures of possible sensible experiences, to which the ordinary processes of associative thought give rise.

When represented with surroundings concrete enough to constitute a *date*, these pictures, when they revive, form *recollections*. When the mental pictures are of data freely combined, and reproducing no past combination exactly, we have acts of imagination properly so called.

Our Images Are Usually Vague

For the ordinary 'analytic' psychology, each sensibly discernible element of the object imagined is represented by its own separate idea, and the total object is imagined by a 'cluster' or 'gang' of ideas. We have seen abundant reason to reject this view. An imagined object, however complex, is at any one moment thought in one idea, which is aware of all its qualities together. If I slip into the ordinary way of talking, and speak of various ideas 'combining,' the reader will understand that this is only for popularity and convenience, and he will not construe it into a concession to the atomistic theory in psychology.

Hume was the hero of the atomistic theory. Not only were ideas copies of original impressions made on the sense-organs, but they were, according to him, completely adequate copies, and were all so separate from each other as to possess no manner of connection. Hume proves ideas in the imagination to be completely adequate copies, not by appeal to observation, but by *a priori* reasoning, as follows:

The mind cannot form any notion of quantity or quality, without forming a precise notion of the degrees of each, [for] 'tis confessed that no object can appear to the senses; or in other words, that no impression[2] can become present to the mind, without being determined in its degrees both of quantity and quality. The confusion in which impressions are sometimes involved proceeds only from their faintness and unsteadiness, not from any capacity in the mind to receive any impression, which in its real existence has no particular degree nor proportion. That is a contradiction in terms; and even implies the flattest of all contradictions, *viz.*, that 'tis possible for the same thing both to be and not to be. Now since all ideas are derived from impressions, and are nothing but copies and representations of them, whatever is true of the one must be acknowledged concerning the other. Impressions and ideas differ only in their strength and vivacity. The foregoing conclusion is not founded on any particular degree of vivacity. It cannot therefore be affected by any variation in that particular. An idea is a weaker impression; and as a strong impression must necessarily have a determinate quantity and quality, the case must be the same with its copy or representative.[3]

The slightest introspective glance will show to anyone the falsity of this opinion. Hume surely had images of his own works without seeing distinctly every word and letter upon the pages which floated before his mind's eye. His dictum is therefore an exquisite example of the way in which a man will be blinded by *a priori* theories to the most flagrant facts. It is a rather remarkable thing, too, that the psychologists of Hume's own empiricist school have, as a rule, been more guilty of this blindness than their opponents. The fundamental *facts* of consciousness have been, on the whole, more accurately reported by the spiritualistic writers. None of Hume's pupils, so far as I know, until Taine and Huxley, ever took the pains to contradict the opinion of their master. Prof. Huxley in his brilliant little work on Hume set the matter straight in the following words:

When complex impressions or complex ideas are reproduced as memories, it is probable that the copies never give all the details of the originals with perfect accuracy, and it is certain that they rarely do so. No one possesses a memory so good, that if he has only once observed a natural object, a second inspection does not show him something that he has forgotten. Almost all, if not all, our memories are therefore sketches, rather than portraits, of the originals—the salient features are obvious, while the subordinate characters are obscure or unrepresented.

Now, when several complex impressions which are more or less different from one another—let us say that out of ten impressions in each, six are the same in all, and four are different from all the rest—are successively presented to the mind, it is easy to see what must be the nature of the result. The repetition of the six similar impressions will strengthen the six corresponding elements of the complex idea, which will therefore acquire greater vividness; while the four differing impressions of each will not only acquire no greater strength than they had at first, but, in accordance with the law of association, they will all tend to appear at once, and will thus neutralize one another.

This mental operation may be rendered comprehensible by considering what takes place in the formation of compound photographs—when the images of the faces of six sitters, for example, are each received on the same photographic plate, for a sixth of the time requisite to take one portrait. The final result is that all those points in which the six faces agree are brought out strongly, while all those in which they differ are left vague; and thus what may be termed a *generic* portrait of the six, in contradistinction to a *specific* portrait of any one, is produced.

Thus our ideas of single complex impressions are incomplete in one way, and those of numerous, more or less similar, complex impressions are incomplete in another way; that is to say, they are *generic*, not *specific*. And hence it follows that our ideas of the impressions in question are not, in the strict sense of the word, copies of those impressions; while, at the same time, they may exist in the mind independently of language.

The generic ideas which are formed from several similar, but not identical complex experiences are what are called *abstract* or *general* ideas; and Berkeley endeavored to prove that all general ideas are nothing but particular ideas annexed to a certain term, which gives them a more extensive signification, and makes them recall, upon occasion, other individuals which are similar to them. Hume says that he regards this as 'one of the greatest and the most valuable discoveries that has been made of late years in the republic of letters,' and endeavors to confirm it in such a manner that it shall be 'put beyond all doubt and controversy.'

I may venture to express a doubt whether he has succeeded in his object; but the subject is an abstruse one; and I must content myself with the remark, that though Berkeley's view appears to be largely applicable to such general ideas as are formed after language has been acquired, and to all the more abstract sort of conceptions, yet that general ideas of sensible objects may nevertheless be produced in the way indicated, and may exist independently of language. In dreams, one sees houses, trees, and other objects, which are perfectly recognizable as such, but which remind one of the actual objects as seen 'out of the corner of the eye,' or of the pictures thrown by a badly-focussed magic lantern. A man addresses us who is like a figure seen in twilight; or we travel through countries where every feature of the scenery is vague; the outlines of the hills are ill-marked, and the rivers have no defined banks. They are, in short, generic ideas of many past impressions of men, hills, and rivers. An anatomist who occupies itself intently with the examination of several specimens of some new kind of animal, in course of time acquires so vivid a conception of its form and structure that the idea may take visible shape and become a sort of waking dream. But the figure which thus presents itself is generic, not specific. It is no copy of any one specimen, but, more or less, a mean of the series; and there seems no reason to doubt that the minds of children before they learn to speak, and of deaf-mutes, are peopled with similarly generated generic ideas of sensible objects.[4]

Are Vague Images 'Abstract Ideas'?

The only point which I am tempted to criticise in this account is Prof. Huxley's *identification of these generic images with 'abstract or general ideas' in the sense of universal conceptions.* Taine gives the truer view. He writes:

Some years ago I saw in England, in Kew Gardens, for the first time, araucarias, and I walked along the beds looking at these strange plants, with their rigid bark and compact, short, scaly leaves, of a sombre green, whose abrupt, rough, bristling form cut in upon the fine softly-lighted turf of the fresh grass-plat. If I now inquire what this experience has left in me, I find, first, the sensible representation of an araucaria; in fact, I have been able to describe almost exactly the form and color of the plant. But there is a difference between this representation and the former sensations, of which it is the present echo. The internal semblance, from which I have just made my description, is vague, and my past sensations were precise. For, assuredly, each of the araucarias I saw then excited in me a distinct visual sensation; there are no two absolutely similar plants in nature; I observed perhaps twenty or thirty araucarias; without a doubt each one of them differed from the others in size, in girth, by the more or less obtuse angles of its branches, by the more or less abrupt jutting out of its scales, by the style of its texture; consequently, my twenty or thirty visual sensations were different. But no one of these sensations has completely survived in its echo; the twenty or thirty revivals have blunted one another; thus upset and agglutinated by their resemblance they are confounded together, and my present representation is their residue only. This is the product, or rather the fragment, which is deposited in us, when we have gone through a series of similar facts or individuals. Of our numerous experiences there remain on the following day four or five more or less distinct recollections, which, obliterated themselves, leave behind in us a simple colorless, vague representation, into which enter as components various reviving sensations, in an utterly feeble, incomplete, and abortive state.—*But this representation is not the general and abstract idea. It is but its accompaniment*, and, if I may say so, the ore from which it is extracted. For the representation, though badly sketched, is a sketch, the sensible sketch of a distinct individual.... But my abstract idea corresponds to the whole class; it differs, then, from the representation of an individual.—Moreover, my abstract idea is perfectly clear and determinate; now that I possess it, I never fail to recognize an araucaria among the various plants which may be shown me; it differs then from the confused and floating representation I have of some particular araucaria.[5]

In other words, a blurred picture is just as much a single mental fact as a sharp picture is; and *the use of either picture by the mind to symbolize a whole class of individuals is a new mental function*, requiring some other modification of consciousness than the mere perception that the picture is distinct or not. I may bewail the indistinctness of my mental image of my absent friend. That does not prevent my thought from meaning *him* alone, however. And I may mean all mankind, with perhaps a very sharp image of one man in my mind's eye. The meaning is a function of the more 'transitive' parts of consciousness, the 'fringe' of relations which we feel surrounding the image, be the latter sharp or dim.

Our ideas or images of past sensible experience may then be either distinct and adequate or dim, blurred, and incomplete. It is likely that the different degrees in which different men are able to make them sharp and complete has had something to do with keeping up such philosophic disputes as that of Berkeley with Locke over abstract ideas. Locke had spoken of our possessing 'the general idea of a triangle' which "must be neither oblique nor rectangle, neither equilateral, equicrural, nor scalenon, but all and none of these at once." Berkeley says:

> If any man has the faculty of framing in his mind such an idea of a triangle as is here described, it is in vain to pretend to dispute him out of it, nor would I go about it. All I desire is that the reader would fully and certainly inform himself whether *he* has such an idea or no.[6]

Until very recent years it was supposed by all philosophers that there was a typical human mind which all individual minds were like, and that propositions of universal validity could be laid down about such faculties as 'the Imagination.' Lately, however, a mass of revelations have poured in, which make us see how false a view this is. There are imaginations, not 'the Imagination,' and they must be studied in detail.

The Neural Process which Underlies Imagination?

The commonly-received idea is that it is only a milder degree of the same process which took place when the thing now imagined was sensibly perceived. Professor Bain writes:

> Since a sensation in the first instance diffuses nerve-currents through the interior of the brain outwards to the organs of expression and movement,—the persistence of that sensation, after the outward exciting cause is withdrawn, can be but a continuance of the same diffusive currents, perhaps less intense, but not otherwise different. The shock remaining in the ear and brain, after the sound of thunder, must pass through the same circles, and operate in the same way as during the actual sound. We can have no reason for believing that, in this self-sustaining condition, the impression changes its seat, or passes into some new circles that have the special property of retaining it. Every part actuated *after* the shock must have been actuated *by* the shock, only more powerfully. With this single difference of intensity, the mode of existence of a sensation existing after the fact is essentially the same as its mode of existence during the fact.... Now if this be the case with impressions *persisting* when the cause has ceased, what view are we to adopt concerning impressions *reproduced* by mental causes alone, or without the aid of the original, as in ordinary recollection? What is the manner of occupation of the brain with a resuscitated feeling of resistance, a smell or a sound? There is only one answer that seems admissable. *The renewed feeling occupies the very same parts, and in the same manner, as the original feeling, and no other parts, nor in any other assignable manner.* I imagine that if our present knowledge of the brain had been present to the earliest speculators, this is the only hypothesis that would have occurred to them. For where should a past feeling be embodied, if not in the same organs as the feeling when present? It is only in this way that its identity can be preserved; a feeling differently embodied would be a different feeling.[7]

It is not plain from Professor Bain's text whether by the 'same parts' he means only the same parts *inside the brain*, or the same *peripheral* parts also, as those occupied by the original feeling. The examples which he himself proceeds to give are almost all cases of imagination of *movement*, in which the peripheral organs are indeed affected, for actual movements of a weak sort are found to accompany the idea. This is what we should expect. All currents tend to run forward in the brain and discharge into the muscular system; and the idea of a movement tends to do this with peculiar facility. But the question remains: Do currents run *backward*, so that if the optical centres (for example) are excited by 'association' and a visual object is imagined, a current runs *down to the retina* also, and excites that sympathetically with the higher tracts? In other words, *can peripheral sense-organs be excited from above, or only from without? Are they excited in imagination?* Professor Bain's instances are almost silent as to this point. All he says is this:

> We might think of a blow on the hand until the skin were actually irritated and inflamed. The attention very much directed to any part of the body, as the great toe, for instance, is apt to produce a distinct feeling in the part, which we account for only by supposing a revived nerve-current to flow there, making a sort of false sensation, an influence from within mimicking the influences from without in

sensation proper.—(See the writings of Mr. Braid, of Manchester, on Hypnotism, etc.)

If I may judge from my own experience, all feelings of this sort are consecutive upon motor currents invading the skin and producing contraction of the muscles there, the muscles whose contraction gives 'goose-flesh' when it takes place on an extensive scale. I never get a *feeling* in the skin, however strongly I *imagine* it, until some actual change in the condition of the skin itself has occurred. The truth seems to be that the cases where peripheral sense-organs are directly excited in consequence of imagination are exceptional rarities, if they exist at all. *In common cases of imagination it would seem more natural to suppose that the seat of the process is purely cerebral, and that the sense-organ is left out.* Reasons for such a conclusion would be briefly these:

1. In imagination the *starting-point* of the process must be in the brain. Now we know that currents usually flow one way in the nervous system; and for the peripheral sense-organs to be excited in these cases, the current would have to flow backward.

2. There is between imagined objects and felt objects a difference of conscious quality which may be called almost absolute. It is hardly possible to confound the liveliest image of fancy with the weakest real sensation. The felt object has a plastic reality and outwardness which the imagined object wholly lacks. Moreover, as Fechner says, in imagination the attention feels as if drawn backwards to the brain; in sensation (even of after-images) it is directed forward towards the sense-organ. The difference between the two processes feels like one of kind, and not like a mere 'more' or 'less' of the same.[8] If a sensation of sound were only a strong imagination, and an imagination a weak sensation, there ought to be a border-line of experience where we never could tell whether we were hearing a weak sound or imagining a strong one. In comparing a present sensation felt with a past one imagined, it will be remembered that we often judge the imagined one to *have been the stronger*. This is inexplicable if the imagination be simply a weaker excitement of the sensational process.

To these reasons the following objections may be made:

To 1: The current demonstrably *does* flow backward down the optic nerve in Meyer's and Féré's negative afterimage. Therefore it *can* flow backward; therefore it *may* flow backward in some, however slight, degree, in all imagination.[9]

To 2: The difference alleged is not absolute, and sensation and imagination *are* hard to discriminate where the sensation is so weak as to be just perceptible. At night hearing a very faint striking of the hour by a far-off clock, our imagination reproduces both rhythm and sound, and it is often difficult to tell which was the last real stroke. So of a baby crying in a distant part of the house, we are uncertain whether we still hear it, or only imagine the sound. Certain violin-players take advantage of this in diminuendo terminations. After the pianissimo has been reached they continue to bow as if still playing, but are careful not to touch the strings. The listener hears in imagination a degree of sound fainter still than the preceding pianissimo. This phenomenon is not confined to hearing:

If we slowly approach our finger to a surface of water, we often deceive ourselves about the moment in which the wetting occurs. The apprehensive patient believes himself to feel the knife of the surgeon whilst it is still at some distance.[10]

Visual perception supplies numberless instances in which the same sensation of vision is perceived as one object or another according to the interpretation of the mind.

Taken together, all these facts would force us to admit that *the subjective difference between imagined and felt objects is less absolute than has been claimed, and that the cortical processes which underlie imagination and sensation are not quite as discrete as one at first is tempted to suppose. That peripheral sensory processes are ordinarily involved in imagination seems improbable; that they may sometimes be aroused from the cortex downwards cannot, however, be dogmatically denied.*

The imagination-process can *then pass over into the sensation-process.* In other words, genuine sensations *can* be centrally originated. When we come to study hallucinations in the chapter on Outer Perception, we shall see that this is by no means a thing of rare occurrence. At present, however, we must admit that *normally the two processes do* NOT *pass over into each other*; and we must inquire why. One of two things must be the reason. Either

1. Sensation-processes occupy a different *locality* from imagination-processes; or
2. Occupying the same locality, they have an *intensity* which under normal circumstances currents from other cortical regions are incapable of arousing, and to produce which currents from the periphery are required.

It seems almost certain that the imagination-process differs from the sensation-process by its intensity rather than by its locality. However it may be with lower animals, the assumption that ideational and sensorial centres are locally distinct appears to be supported by no facts drawn from the observation of human beings. After occipital destruction, the hemianopsia which results in man is sensorial blindness, not mere loss of optical ideas. Were there centres for crude optical sensation below the cortex, the patients in these cases would still feel light and darkness. Since they do not preserve even this impression on the lost half of the field, we must suppose that there are no centres for vision of any sort whatever below the cortex, and that the corpora quadrigemina and other lower optical ganglia are organs for reflex movement of eye-muscles and not for conscious sight. Moreover there are no facts which oblige us to think that, within the occipital cortex, one part is connected with sensation and another with mere ideation or imagination. The pathological cases assumed to prove this are all better explained by disturbances of conduction between the optical and other centres. In bad cases of hemianopsia the patient's images depart from him together with his sensibility to light. They depart so completely that he does not even know what is the matter with him. To perceive that one is blind to the right half of the field of view one must have an idea of that part of the field's possible existence. But the defect in these patients has to be revealed to them by the doctor, they themselves only knowing that there is 'something wrong' with their eyes. What you have no idea of you cannot miss; and their not definitely missing this great region out of their sight seems due to the fact that their very idea and memory of it is lost along with the sensation. A man blind of his eyes merely, sees *darkness*. A man blind of his visual brain-centers can no more see darkness out of the parts of his retina which are connected with the brain-lesion than he can see it out of the skin of his back. He cannot see at all in that part of the field; and he cannot think of the light which he ought to be feeling *there*, for the very notion of the existence of that particular 'there' is cut out of his mind.[11]

Now if we admit that sensation and imagination are due to the activity of the same centres in the cortex, we can see a very good teleological reason why they should correspond to discrete kinds of process in these centres, and why the process which gives the sense that the object is really there ought normally to be arousable only by currents entering from the periphery and not by currents from the neighboring cortical parts. We can see, in short, why *the sensational process* OUGHT TO *be discontinuous with all normal ideational processes, however intense.* For, as Dr. Münsterberg justly observes:

> Were there not this peculiar arrangement we should not distinguish reality and fantasy, our conduct would not be accommodated to the facts about us, but would be inappropriate and senseless, and we could not keep ourselves alive. . . . That our thoughts and memories should be copies of sensations with their intensity greatly reduced is thus a consequence deducible logically from the natural adaptation of the cerebral mechanism to its environment.[12]

Mechanically the discontinuity between the ideational and the sensational kinds of process must mean that when the greatest ideational intensity has been reached, an order of *resistance* presents itself which only a new order of force can break through. The current from the periphery is the new order of force required; and what happens after the resistance is overcome is the sensational process. We may suppose that the latter consists in some new and more violent sort of disintegration of the neural matter, which now explodes at a deeper level than at other times.

Now how shall we conceive of the 'resistance' which prevents this sort of disintegration from taking place, this sort of intensity in the process from being attained, so much of the time? It must be either an intrinsic resistance, some force of cohesion in the neural molecules themselves; or an extrinsic influence, due to other cortical cells. When we come to study the process of hallucination we shall see that both factors must be taken into account. There is a degree of inward molecular cohesion in our brain-cells which it probably takes a sudden inrush of destructive energy to spring apart. Incoming peripheral currents possess this energy from the outset. Currents from neighboring cortical regions might attain to it if they could *accumulate* within the centre which we are supposed to be considering. But since during waking hours every centre communicates with others by association-paths, no such accumulation can take place. The cortical currents which run in run right out again, awakening the next ideas; the level of tension in the cells does not rise to the higher explosion-point; and the latter must be gained by a sudden current from the periphery or not at all.

Notes

1. Prof. Jastrow has ascertained by statistical inquiry among the blind that if their blindness have occurred before a period embraced between the fifth and seventh years the visual centres seem to decay, and visual dreams and images are gradually outgrown. If sight is lost after the seventh year, visual imagination seems to survive through life. See Prof. J.'s interesting article on the Dreams of the Blind, in the New Princeton Review for January 1888.
2. Impression means sensation for Hume.
3. Treatise on Human Nature, part I. § VII.
4. Huxley's Hume, pp. 92–94.
5. On Intelligence (N.Y.), vol. II. p. 139.
6. Principles, Introd. § 18.
7. Senses and Intellect, p. 338.
8. V. Kandinsky (*Kritische u. klinische Betrachtungen in Gebiete der Sinnestäuschungen* (Berlin, 1885), p. 135ff.) insists that in even the liveliest pseudo-hallucinations, which may be regarded as the intensest possible results of the imaginative process, there is no outward objectivity perceived in the thing represented, and that a *ganzer Abgrund* separates these 'ideas' from true hallucination and objective perception.
9. It seems to also flow backwards in certain hypnotic hallucinations. Suggest to a 'Subject' in the hypnotic trance that a sheet of paper has a red cross upon it, then pretend to remove the imaginary cross, whilst you tell the Subject to look fixedly at a dot upon the paper, and he will presently tell you that he sees a 'bluish-green' cross. The genuineness of the result has been doubted, but there seems no good reason for rejecting M. Binet's account (*Le Magnétisme Animal*, 1887, p. 188). M. Binet, following M. Parinaud, and on the faith of a certain experiment, at one time believed, the optical brain-centres and not the retina to be the seat of ordinary negative after-images. The experiment is this: Look

fixedly, with one eye open, at a colored spot on a white background. Then close that eye and look fixedly with the *other* eye at a plain surface. A negative after-image of the colored spot will presently appear. (*Psychologie du Raisonnement*, 1886, p. 45.) But Mr. Delabarre has proved (American Journal of Psychology, II. 326) that this after-image is due, not to a higher cerebral process, but to the fact that the retinal process in the *closed* eye affects consciousness at certain moments, and that its object is then projected into the field seen by the eye which is open. M. Binet informs me that he is converted by the proofs given by Mr. Delabarre.

The fact remains, however, that the negative after- images of Herr Meyer, M. Féré, and the hypnotic subjects, form an exception to all that we know of nerve-currents, if they are due to a refluent centrifugal current to the retina. It may be that they will hereafter be explained in some other way. Meanwhile we can only write them down as a paradox. Sig. Sergi's theory that there is *always* a refluent wave in perception hardly merits serious consideration (Psychologie Physiologique, pp. 99, 189). Sergi's theory has recently been reaffirmed with almost incredible crudity by Lombroso and Ottolenghi in the *Revue Philosophique*, XXIX. 70 (Jan. 1890).

10. Lotze, *Med. Psych.* p. 509.
11. See an important article by Binet in the *Revue Philosophique*, XXVI. 481 (1888); also Dufour, in *Revue Méd. de la Suisse Romande*, 1889, No. 8, cited in the *Neurologisches Centralblatt*, 1890, p. 48.
12. *Die Willenshandlung* (1888), pp. 129- 40.

References

Bain, Alexander. *The Senses and the Intellect*. London: J. W. Parker & Son, 1855.

Fechner, G. T. *Elemente der Psychophysik*. Leipzig: Breitkopf und Härtel, 1860.

Féré, Charles. *Sensation et Mouvement*. Paris: F. Alcon, 1887.

Galton, Sir Francis. *Inquiries into Human Faculty*. London: MacMillan & Co., 1880.

Huxley, Thomas Henry, *Hume*. London: MacMillan & Co., 1879.

Meyer, G. H. *Untersuchungen üb. d. Physiol. d. Nervenfaser*. Tübingen: H. Laupp., 1843.

Taine, H. *On Intelligence*. Vol. II London: L. Reeve & Co., 1871.

Chapter 27
The Modern Psychology of Thinking
Oswald Külpe

The study of thinking, which in Germany has been nurtured primarily at the Würz-burger Psychological Institute, belongs to [the] developmental phase of experimental psychology.

While earlier psychology in general did not pay adequate attention to thinking, the new experimental direction was so busy bringing order into the more solid institutions of sensations, images, and feelings, that it was quite late before it could devote itself to the airy thoughts. The first mental contents to be noted in consciousness were those of pressures and punctures, tastes and smells, sounds and colors. They were the easiest to perceive, followed by their images and the pleasures and pains. That there was any-thing else without the palpable* constitution of these formations escaped the eye of the scientist who had not been trained to perceive it. The experience of natural science directed the researcher's attention toward sensory stimuli and sensations, after-images, contrast phenomena and fantastic variations of reality. Whatever did not have such characteristics simply did not seem to exist. And thus when the first experimental psychologists undertook experiments about the meaning of words they were able to report anything at all only if self-evident representations or their accompanying phenomena made an appearance. In many other cases, particularly when the words signified something abstract or general, they found "nothing." The fact that a word could be understood without eliciting images, that a sentence could be understood and judged even though only its sounds appeared to be present in consciousness, never gave these psychologists cause to postulate or to determine imageless as well as imageable contents.

The prejudice upon which we have touched here has a long history. Aristotle de-clared that there were no thoughts without an image and during the scholastic period this position was held fast. The division between perception and thinking, between objects of the senses and objects of thought, made repeatedly by Plato, had never been psychologically pursued. In modern times one found words, and nothing but words when the perceptions were missing that were supposed to give them meaning and understanding. In the pedagogy of Pestalozzi and Herbart, perception was honored as the ABC of all mental development. Kant considered concepts without images as empty, and Schopenhauer wanted to base all of mathematics upon imagery; he even wanted to ban proof from geometry. Similar conceptions were added in poetry. Poetic art could only function through images; the more it tried to follow Horace and emulate painting—to create with the brush of perception—the more completely did it seem to fulfill its mission. . . .

What finally led us in psychology to another theory was the *systematic application of self-observation*. Previously it was the rule not to obtain reports about all experiences that occurred during an experiment as soon as it was concluded, but only to obtain occasional reports from subjects about exceptional or abnormal occurrences. Only at the conclusion of a whole series was a general report requested about the main facts that were still remembered. In this fashion only the grossest aspects came to light. Furthermore, the commitment to the traditional concepts of sensations, feelings, and images prevented the observation or labelling of that which was neither sensation nor feeling nor image. However, as soon as persons trained in self-observation were allowed to make complete and unprejudiced reports about their experiences of an experiment immediately after its completion, the necessity for an extension of the previous concepts and definitions became obvious. We found in ourselves processes, states, directions, and acts which did not fit the schema of the older psychology. Subjects started to speak in the language of everyday life and to give images only a subordinate importance in their private world. They knew and thought, judged and understood, apprehended meaning and interpreted connections, without receiving any real support from occasionally appearing sensory events [*Versinnlichungen*]. Consider the following examples. [There follow two examples, only one of which will be presented here.] The subject is asked: "Do you understand the sentence: Thinking is so extraordinarily difficult that many prefer to judge?" The protocol reads: "I knew immediately after the conclusion of the sentence what the point was. But the thought was still quite unclear. In order to gain clarity, I slowly repeated the sentence and when I was finished with that the thought was clear so that I can now repeat it: To judge here implies thoughtless speech and a dismissal of the subject matter in contrast to the searching activity of thinking. Apart from the words of the sentence that I heard and which I then reproduced, there was nothing in the way of images in my consciousness." This is not just a simple process of imageless thought. What is notable is that [subjects] stated that understanding proceeded generally in this fashion with difficult sentences. It is thus not an artificial product of the laboratory, but the blossoming life of reality that has been opened up by these experiments. [There follows a string of aphorisms and sayings to demonstrate examples from daily experience that produce just such thinking, e.g., Man is noble, charitable and good: that alone differentiates him from all other known beings.] Who would experience images here and for whom would such images be the basis, the inescapable condition of comprehension? And who wants to maintain that words alone suffice to represent the meaning? No, these cases provide proof for the existence of imageless conscious contents, especially thoughts.

But if thoughts differ from the images of colors and sounds, of forests and gardens, of men and animals, then this difference will also be found in their behavior, in their forms, and in their course. We know what lawfulness governs images. Everybody speaks of association and reproduction, of the appearance of an image, of its elicitation by others, of its connection with other images. We learn a poem or a new vocabulary. Here knowledge of content, knowledge of meaning is not sufficient; we must learn one word after another so that we can later faithfully reproduce the whole. We develop strong associations between the succeeding or coordinated members of a poem or a list of words, and for this we need a long period of time and a large number of repetitions. If thoughts are nothing but images, then the same tediousness should govern their memorization. Any reflection about the manner in which we assimilate the meaning of a poem shows immediately that the state of affairs is different here. One attentive reading is frequently sufficient to reproduce the thought content. And thus we progress through sheer mental exposure to such comprehensive feats as the reproduction of the thoughts contained in a sermon, a lecture, a dramatic production, a novel, a scientific work, or a long conversation. We not infrequently find to our sorrow how independent we are of the actual words. Sometimes we would like very much to be able to reproduce faithfully a striking expression, the pregnant form of a sentence, or an attractive picture.

But even though the sense of what has been said is quite available to us, we cannot reproduce its form.

[There follows a discussion of some of Bühler's experiments.] It is notable that one of the first results of our psychology of thought was negative: The old conceptual notions that experimental psychology had provided for descriptions of sensation, feeling, and imagination, and their relations, did not permit comprehension or definition of intellectual processes. But similarly the new concept of dispositions of consciousness [Bewusstseinslage] which was pressed upon us by factual observation, was not sufficient and only made possible circumscription rather than description. Even the study of primitive processes of thinking soon showed that the imageless can be known. Self-observation, in contrast to observations of nature, can perceive the presence and definite characteristics of what is neither color nor sound, of what may be given without image or feeling. The meaning of abstract and general expressions can be shown to exist in consciousness when nothing perceptual may be discovered apart from the words, and these meanings may be experienced and realized even without words or other signs. The new concept of conscious knowing [Bewusstheit] gave expression to these facts. And thus the inflexible schema of the previously accepted elements of mental life was extended in an important direction.

Experimental psychology is thus confronted with new problems which disclose many and varied perspectives. Not only do imageless states include known, meant, and thought objects with all their characteristics and relations, and states of affairs that can be expressed in judgments, but also the many actions whereby we take a position toward a given conscious content, whereby we order, classify, recognize or reject it. Although one once could use sensations and images to construct a mosaic of mental life and an automatic lawfulness of the coming and going of conscious elements, such a simplification and dependence upon chemical analogies has now lost its footing. Perceptual [anschaulich] contents could only persist as artificial abstractions, as arbitrarily isolated and separated components. Within a complete consciousness, however, they have become partial phenomena, dependent upon a variety of different conceptions, and it was only when they were placed in a complex of mental processes that they gained meaning and value for the experiencing subject. Just as perception could not be characterized as a mere having of sensation, no less could thinking be conceived as the associative course of images. Association psychology, as it had been founded by Hume, lost its hegemony.

The fact that thoughts are independent of the signs in which they are expressed, and that they have peculiar and fluid interrelations, uninfluenced by the laws of the association of images, demonstrated their autonomy as a special class of conscious contents. As a result, the area of self-observation has been extended to a considerable degree. Not only images and sensations and their characteristics and colorations belong to our mental life, but we can also include thought and knowledge, in which we can perceive neither color nor form, neither pleasure nor unpleasure. We know from daily experience that we have at our disposal a great spontaneity in our search for objects, their registration and comprehension, in our activity with and our actions upon them. Psychology has taken little notice of this activity of the mind. F. A. Lange coined the phrase about the scientific psychology without a soul, a psychology in which sensations and images and their feeling tones are the sole contents of consciousness. Such a psychology had to be watchful that no mystical force such as the ego should insinuate itself into this psychological world. More exactly, one had to say: "Thinking occurs," but not: "I think," and the process of such thinking consisted in nothing but the coming and going of images regulated by the laws of association. Even today there are psychologists who have not risen above this point of view. Their psychology can rightly be accused of unreality, of moving in an abstract region where it neither seeks nor finds entry to full experience. These are the psychologists who offer stones instead of bread to those representatives of the humanities [*Geisteswissenschaften*] who are asking for psychological justification; nor can these psychologists advise or help a biology that is seeking a connection with psychology....

[The psychology of] thinking unlocked the door to the true internal world, and it was no mysticism that led us there, but the abandoning of a prejudice. Bacon already knew that the road to truth is paved with prejudices. In the present instance they happen to derive from the exact natural sciences, for whom in the last decades sensory observation meant everything and for whom concepts were only an expedient used to represent, in the simplest possible fashion, facts based on sensory experience. But now thoughts became not only signs for sensations but independent structures and values that could be ascertained with certainty just as any sensory impression. They were even more faithful, lasting, and freer than the pictures with which our memory and fantasy otherwise operate. But they did not, of course, admit to the same immediate observation as perceptual objects. The discovery was made that the ego could not be divided. To think with a certain devotion and depth and to observe the thoughts at the same time—that could not be done. First one and then the other, that was the watchword of the young psychology of thought. And it succeeded surprisingly well. Once a mental task was solved, the process that had been experienced became in all its phases an object of intensive determination by the retrospective observer. Comparison of several subjects and of several results from the same subject demonstrated that the procedure was unobjectionable. The pronounced agreement of our studies in the psychology of thought, whereby one could be built upon another, was a beautiful confirmation of our results. Once again it became clear why the previously used methods of observation could not find any thinking or other expressions of our conscious activity. Observation itself is a particular act, a committed activity of the ego. No other activity can be executed next to it at the same time. Our mental efficiency is limited, our personality is a unitary whole. But observation can take place after the completion of a function and can make it the object of self-perception. And now many acts were recognized which previously had not existed for psychology: attending and recognizing, willing and rejecting, comparing and differentiating, and many more. All of them were lacking the perceptual [*anschaulich*] character of sensations, images, and feelings, even though these phenomena could accompany the newly found actions. It is characteristic of the helplessness of the previous psychology that it thought it could define these acts through their symptoms. Attention was considered as a group of tension and muscle sensations, because so-called strained attention gives rise to such sensations. Similarly, willing was dissolved into images of motions because they usually precede an external act of the will. These constructions, whose artificiality immediately becomes apparent, were left without a leg to stand on as soon as the existence of special psychic acts was recognized, thus robbing sensations and images of their sole dominion in consciousness.

With the recognition of these acts another important innovation came to the fore. The center of gravity of mental life had to be moved. Previously one could say: We are attentive because our eyes are fixed on a particular point in the visual field and the muscles that keep the eyes in that position are tensed. It now became clear that this conception inverted the real state of affairs and that what it should rather say is: We direct our eyes toward a certain point and strain our muscles because we want to observe it. *Activity became the central focus*, receptivity and the mechanism of images secondary....

The actions of the ego are always subject to points of view and tasks [*Aufgaben*] and through them are moved to activity. One could also say that they serve a purpose, either self-generated or set by others. The thinking of the theoretician is no more nor less aimless than that of the practitioner. Psychologists are used to taking this into consideration. The subject receives a task, a direction or instruction as to the point of view which he must adopt toward the presented stimulus. He may have to compare two light intensities one with another, to execute a movement upon a pressure or a sound, to reply quickly to a called-out word with the first word that he can think of, to understand a sentence, to draw a conclusion, and so forth. All such tasks, if they are willingly undertaken and remembered, exercise a great determining force upon the behavior of the subject. This force is called the determining tendency. In a sense the ego contains an unlimited variety of response possibilities. If one of these is to come to the fore to the exclusion of all others, then a determination, a selection, is needed.

The independence of the task and the determining tendency that was derived from it was also fateful for association psychology. Such a task is not some ordinary type of reproductive motive. It must be accepted, the subject must support it, and it gives his activity a certain direction. Sensations, feelings, and images are not given tasks; a task is set for a subject, whose mental character does not dissolve into these contents, but whose spontaneity alone can adopt the instructions and execute them. Since in all thinking such determining viewpoints play a role, since abstraction and combination, judgment and conclusion, comparison and differentiation, the finding and construction of relations, all become carriers of determining tendencies, the psychology of the task became an essential part of the modern investigation of thinking. And even the psychology of the task proved to have an importance that significantly transcended the narrower area in which it was developed. No psychological experiments are imaginable without tasks! The tasks must, therefore, be considered just as important an experimental condition as the apparatus and the stimuli that it presents. A variation in the task is at least as important an experimental procedure as a change in external experimental conditions.

This importance of the task and its effects on the structure and course of mental events could not be explained with the tools of association psychology. Rather, Ach was able to show that even associations of considerable strength could be overcome with a counteracting task. The force with which a determining tendency acts is not only greater than the familiar reproductive tendencies, it also derives from a different source and its effectiveness is not tied to associative relations.

Notes

* Translators' note: In facing the troublesome problem of translating "*anschaulich*" and "*unanschaulich*," we have generally translated the latter as "imageless" in keeping with traditional usage. However, the word "*anschaulich*" seemed more amenable to a variety of translations such as "palpable," "self-evident," "perceptual," and "specifiable." We have used these words in keeping with the context and have also, at times, substituted such choices as "non-perceptual" or "impalpable" for "*unanschaulich*" in order to point up the generality of the notion which relieves it from the suggestion of the visual that "imageless" implies.

Chapter 28

Image in Behavior

John Watson

In the thesis which I recently advanced[1] I had scant time to discuss two topics, which may seem to many to be stumbling blocks in the way of a free passage from structuralism to *behaviorism*.

The first of these, and by all odds the more serious of the obstacles, is the "centrally aroused sensation" or "image." If thought goes on in terms of centrally aroused sensations, as is maintained by the majority of both structural and functional psychologists, we should have to admit that there is a serious limitation on the side of method in behaviorism. Imagery from Galton on has been the inner stronghold of a psychology based on introspection. All of the outer defenses might be given over to the enemy, but the cause could never be wholly lost as long as the pass (introspection) to this stronghold (image) could be maintained.

So well guarded is the image that it would seem almost foolhardy for us to make an attack upon it. If I did not perceive certain signs of weakening on the part of the garrison, I think I should agree with Professor Cattell that I am becoming too radical, and that I should better admit the claims of imagery and try to work out a scheme for behaviorism which will embrace the image. Suppose we consider this aspect of the question first: Does the inclusion of the image weaken the claims of the behaviorist? I am ready to admit that it does. Take a case like that ordinarily urged. Some one suggests in words that I borrow one thousand dollars and go abroad for a year. I think over the situation—the present condition of my research problems, my debts, whether I can leave my family, etc. I am in a brown study for days, trying to make up my mind. Now the train of thoughts going on in my mind, according to the upholders of the image, has no adequate behavior counterpart while it is in transit. The behaviorist, observing me, might note that my appetite had departed, that I was smoking and drinking more than usual, and that I was distrait. Finally, experimental tests might show that my ability to make fine coordination had been seriously interfered with, that my dynamometric threshold was lowered, and so *ad infinitum*. The introspectionists would say that all of these tests failed to give anything like a complete record of my "mental content" or of the "totality of conscious processes." Indeed, they would urge that such tests have only an analogical reference. Only direct observation of the mental states themselves by the method of introspection will ever tell whether I am grieving over past sins or whether I am really trying to reach a decision about going abroad! If we grant this, and such an impulse is very strong, the behaviorist must content himself with this reflection: "I care not what goes on in his so-called mind; the important thing is that, given the stimulation (in this case a series of spoken words) it must produce response, or else modify responses which have been already initiated. This is the all-important thing and I will be content with it." In other words, he contents himself with observing the initial object (stimulation) and the end object (the reaction). Possibly the old saying "a half loaf is better than no bread at all" expresses the attitude the behaviorist ought to take; and yet I for one dislike to admit anything which may be construed as an admission of even partial defeat.

Feeling so, I prefer to attack rather than to remain upon the defensive. I spoke above of certain signs of disaffection and mutiny among the ranks of the faithful. These signs manifest themselves in three different ways: (1) The attempt on the part of Woodworth, Thorndike, and others to question the dogma of the image and to show that thought processes may go on independently of imagery—or, indeed, as I understand it, even independently of peripherally initiated processes. To this last contention I do not accede, as I shall undertake later to show. It is needless for me to discuss this phase of the problem at any length before this laboratory. (2) The failure on the part of the most earnest upholders of the doctrine of the centrally aroused sensation to obtain any objective experimental evidence of the presence of different image-types. I refer here to the researches of Angell and of Fernald. I think this admission paves the way for the complete dismissal of the image from psychology. Furthermore, I believe that most psychologists are willing to admit that introspection furnishes no guide for the determination of one's own image-type. In this field, above all others, introspection, if it is a legitimate method at all, ought to yield its best results. It is just here that it has failed, except in the case of a few fortunate men who seem to have become adept in the use of it. We who are less happy in its use must forever do without this wonderful Aladdin's lamp which, upon demand, illumines the dark places of the human mind. (3) The attempts even of the structuralists to reduce the so-called higher thought processes to groups of obscure organic processes. I have in mind the recent work on recognition, abstraction, etc.

All of these tendencies, initiated by the psychologists themselves, lead directly over to my principal contention, viz., that there are no centrally initiated processes.[2]

The environment in the widest sense forces the formation of habits. These are exhibited first in the organs which are most mobile: the arms, hands, fingers, legs, etc. By this I do not mean to imply that there is any fixed order in their formation. After such general bodily habits are well under way, speech habits begin. All of the recent work shows that these reach enormous complexity in a comparatively short time. Furthermore, as language habits become more and more complex there arise associations (neural) between words and acts. Behavior then takes on refinement: short cuts are formed, and finally words come to be, on occasion, substituted for acts. That is, a stimulus which, in early stages, would produce an act (and which will always do so under appropriate conditions) now produces merely a spoken word or a mere movement of the larynx (or of some other expressive organ).

When the stimulus produces either an *immediate overt response* (as, for example, when I tell John to go to the sideboard and get an apple, taking it for granted that he goes), or a *delayed overt response* (as, for example, when I ask an engineer to think out and make an apparatus for the conversion of salt water into sweet, which may consume years before overt action begins), we have examples of what one may call *explicit behavior*. In contrast to behavior of this type, which involves the larger musculature in a way plainly apparent to direct observation, we have behavior involving only the speech mechanisms (or the larger musculature in a minimal way; for example, bodily attitudes or sets). This form of behavior, for lack of a better name, I will call *implicit behavior*.[3] Where explicit behavior is delayed (i.e., where deliberation ensues), the intervening time between stimulus and response is given over to implicit behavior (to "thought processes").

Now it is this type of implicit behavior that the introspectionist claims as his own and denies to us because its neural seat is cortical and because it goes on without adequate bodily portrayal. Why in psychology the stage for the neural drama was ever transferred from periphery to cortex must remain somewhat of a mystery. The old idea of strict localization of brain function is in part responsible. I feel, however, that religious convictions are even more largely responsible for it. I do not mean that the men originally responsible for the transfer were aware of this religious tendency at all. When the psychologist threw away the soul he compromised with his conscience by setting up a "mind" which was to remain always hidden and difficult of access.[4] The transfer from periphery to cortex has been the incentive for driving psychology into vain and fruitless searches of the unknown and unknowable. I am quite sure that if the idea of the image had never taken such firm hold upon us we would never have originated the notion that we are seeking to explain consciousness. We would have been content to study the very tangible phenomena of the growth and control of explicit and implicit habits.

It is implied in my words that there exists or ought to exist a method of observing implicit behavior. There is none at present. The larynx, I believe, is the seat of most of the phenomena. If its movements could be adequately portrayed we should obtain a record similar in character to that of the phonogram.[5] Certainly nothing so definite as this could be obtained, but we should get a record, at least, which would largely reveal the subject's word-habits, which, if I am not mistaken, make up the bulk of the implicit forms of behavior.

Now it is admitted by all of us that words spoken or faintly articulated belong really in the realm of behavior as much as do movements of the arms and legs. If implicit behavior can be shown to consist of nothing but word movements (or expressive movements of the word-type) the behavior of the human being as a whole is as open to objective observation and control as is the behavior of the lowest organism.

Notes

1. "Psychology as the Behaviorist Views It," *Psychological Review*, March, 1913.
2. I may have to grant a few sporadic cases of imagery to him who will not be otherwise convinced, but I insist that the images of such a one are sporadic, and as unnecessary to his well-being and *well-thinking* as a few hairs more or less on his head.
3. It may be said in passing that the explicit and implicit forms of behavior referred to throughout the paper are acquired and not congenital.
4. The tendency to make the brain itself something more than a mechanism for coordinating incoming and outgoing impulses has been very strong among psychologists, and even among psychologically inclined neurologists.
5. I have been trying to find out whether any of the spoken phonographic records can be read by experts in that work. I have not been able to ascertain this information, but I am sure there is nothing inherently difficult about the problem. Records of laryngeal movements could likewise be read directly.

Chapter 29
"The Theory of Special Status Pictures" and "Imagining"
Gilbert Ryle

Let us first consider some implications of the other doctrine, that in visualising I am, in a nearly ordinary sense of the verb, seeing a picture with a special status. It is part of this doctrine that the picture that I see is not, as snapshots are, in front of my face; on the contrary, it has to be not in physical space, but in a space of another kind. The child, then, who imagines her wax-doll smiling is seeing a picture of a smile. But the picture of the smile is not where the doll's lips are, since they are in front of the child's face. So the imagined smile is not on the doll's lips at all. Yet this is absurd. No one can imagine an unattached smile, and no doll-owner would be satisfied with an unsmiling doll plus a separate and impossible simulacrum of a smile suspended somewhere else. In fact she does not really see a Cheshire smile elsewhere than on the doll's lips; she fancies she sees a smile on the doll's lips in front of her face, though she does not see one there and would be greatly frightened if she did. Similarly the conjuror makes us 'see' (not see) rabbits coming out of the hat in his hand on the stage in front of our noses; he does not induce us to see (not 'see') shadow-rabbits coming out of a second spectral hat, which is not in his hand, but in a space of another kind.

The pictured smile is not, then, a physical phenomenon, i.e. a real contortion of the doll's face; nor yet is it a non-physical phenomenon observed by the child taking place in a field quite detached from her perambulator and her nursery. There is not a smile at all, and there is not an effigy of a smile either. There is only a child fancying that she sees her doll smiling. So, though she is really picturing her doll smiling, she is not looking at a picture of a smile; and though I am fancying that I see rabbits coming out of the hat, I am not seeing real phantasms of rabbits coming out of real phantasms of hats. There is not a real life outside, shadowily mimicked by some bloodless likenesses inside; there are just things and events, people witnessing some of these things and events, and people fancying themselves witnessing things and events that they are not witnessing.

Take another case. I start to write down a long and unfamiliar word and after a syllable or two, I find that I am not sure how the word should go on. I then, perhaps, imagine myself consulting a dictionary and in some cases I can then 'see' how the last three syllables are printed. In this sort of case it is tempting to say that I am really seeing a picture of a printed word, only the picture is 'in my head', or 'in my mind', since reading off the letters of the word that I 'see' feels rather like reading off the letters from a dictionary-item, or a photograph of such an item, which I really do see. But in another case, I start writing the word and I 'see' the next syllable or two on the page on which I am writing and in the place where I am to write them. I feel rather as if I were merely inking in a word-shadow lying across the page. Yet here it is impossible to say that I am having a peep at a picture or ghost of a word in a queer space other than physical space, for what I 'see' is on my page just to the right of my nib. Again we must say that though I picture the word in a certain place, printed in a certain type, or written in a certain handwriting, and though I can read off the spelling of the word from the way I picture it as printed or written, yet there exists no picture, shadow or ghost of the word and I see no picture, shadow or ghost of it. I seem to see the word on the page itself, and the more vividly and sustainedly I seem to see it, the more easily can I transcribe what I seem to see on to my paper with my pen.

Hume notoriously thought that there exist both 'impressions' and 'ideas', that is, both sensations and images; and he looked in vain for a clear boundary between the two sorts of 'perceptions'. Ideas, he thought, tend to be fainter than impressions, and in their genesis they are later than impressions, since they are traces, copies or reproductions of impressions. Yet he recognised that impressions can be of any degree of faintness, and that though every idea is a copy, it does not arrive marked 'copy' or 'likeness', any more than impressions arrive marked 'original' or 'sitter'. So, on Hume's showing, simple inspection cannot decide whether a perception is an impression or an idea. Yet the crucial difference remains between what is heard in conversation and what is 'heard' in day-dreams, between the snakes in the Zoo and the snakes 'seen' by the dipsomaniac, between the study that I am in and the nursery in which 'I might be now'. His mistake was to suppose that 'seeing' is a species of seeing, or that 'perception' is the name of a genus of which there are two species, namely impressions and ghosts or echoes of impressions. There are no such ghosts, and if there were, they would merely be extra impressions; and they would belong to seeing, not to 'seeing'.

Hume's attempt to distinguish between ideas and impressions by saying that the latter tend to be more lively than the former was one of two bad mistakes. Suppose, first, that 'lively' means 'vivid'. A person may picture vividly, but he cannot see vividly. One 'idea' may be more vivid than another 'idea', but impressions cannot be described as vivid at all, just as one doll can be more lifelike than another, but a baby cannot be lifelike or unlifelike. To say that the difference between babies and dolls is that babies are more lifelike than dolls is an obvious absurdity. One actor may be more convincing than another actor; but a person who is not acting is neither convincing nor unconvincing, and cannot therefore be described as more convincing than an actor. Alternatively, if Hume was using 'vivid' to mean not 'lifelike' but 'intense', 'acute' or 'strong', then he was mistaken in the other direction; since, while sensations can be compared with other sensations as relatively intense, acute or strong, they cannot be so compared with images. When I fancy I am hearing a very loud noise, I am not really hearing either a loud or a faint noise; I am not having a mild auditory sensation, as I am not having an auditory sensation at all, though I am fancying that I am having an intense one. An imagined shriek is not ear-splitting, nor yet is it a soothing murmur, and an imagined shriek is neither louder nor fainter than a heard murmur. It neither drowns it nor is drowned by it.

Similarly, there are not two species of murderers, those who murder people, and those who act the parts of murderers on the stage; for these last are not murderers at all. They do not commit murders which have the elusive attribute of being shams; they pretend to commit ordinary murders, and pretending to murder entails, not murdering, but seeming to murder. As mock-murders are not murders, so imagined sights and sounds are not sights or sounds. They are not, therefore, dim sights, or faint sounds. And they are not private sights or sounds either. There is no answer to the spurious question, 'Where have you deposited the victim of your mock-murder?' since there was no victim. There is no answer to the spurious question, 'Where do the objects reside that we fancy we see?' since there are no such objects.

It will be asked, 'How can a person seem to hear a tune running in his head, unless there is a tune to hear?' Part of the answer is easy, namely that he would not be seeming to hear, or fancying that he heard, a tune, if he were really hearing one, any more than the actor would be simulating murder, if he were really murdering someone. But there is more to be said than this. The question, 'How can a person seem to hear a tune, when there is no tune to be heard?' has the form of a 'wires and pulleys' question. It suggests that there exists a mechanical or para-mechanical problem, (like those that are properly asked about conjuring-tricks and automatic telephones), and that we need to have described to us the hidden workings that constitute what a person does, when he fancies himself listening to a tune. But to understand what is meant by saying that someone is fancying that he hears a tune does not require information about any ulterior processes which may be going on when he does so. We already know, and have known since childhood, in what situations to describe people as imagining that they see or hear or do things. The problem, so far as it is one, is to construe these descriptions without falling back into the idioms in which we talk of seeing horse-races, hearing concerts and committing murders. It is into these idioms that we fall back the moment we say that to fancy one sees a dragon is to see a real dragon-phantasm, or that to pretend to commit a murder is to commit a real mock-murder, or that to seem to hear a tune is to hear a real mental tune. To adopt such linguistic practices is to try to convert into species-concepts concepts which are designed, anyhow partly, to act as factual disclaimers. To say that an action is a mock-murder is to say, not that a certain sort of mild or faint murder has been committed, but that no sort of murder has been committed; and to say that someone pictures a dragon is to say, not that he dimly sees a dragon of a peculiar kind, or something else very like a dragon, but that he does not see a dragon, or anything dragon-like at all. Similarly a person who 'sees Helvellyn in his mind's eye' is not seeing either the mountain, or a likeness of the mountain; there is neither a mountain in front of the eyes in his face, nor a mock-mountain in front of any other non-facial eyes. But it is still true that he 'might be seeing Helvellyn now' and even that he may fail to realise that he is not doing so.

Let us consider another sort of imaging. Sometimes, when someone mentions a blacksmith's forge, I find myself instantaneously back in my childhood, visiting a local smithy. I can vividly 'see' the glowing red horseshoe on the anvil, fairly vividly 'hear' the hammer ringing on the shoe and less vividly 'smell' the singed hoof. How should we describe this 'smelling in the mind's nose'? Ordinary language provides us with no means of saying that I am smelling a 'likeness' of a singed hoof. As has been said already, in the ordinary daylit world there are visible faces and mountains, as well as other visible objects, which are pictures of faces and mountains; there are visible people and visible effigies of people. Both trees and reflections of trees can be photographed or reflected in mirrors. The visual comparison of seen things with the seen likenesses of those things is familiar and easy. With sounds we are not quite so well placed, but there are heard noises and heard echoes of noises, songs sung and recordings of songs played, voices and mimicries of them. So it is easy and tempting to describe visual imaging as if it were a case of looking at a likeness instead of looking at its original, and it may pass muster to describe auditory imaging as if it were a case of hearing a sort of echo or recording, instead of hearing the voice itself. But we have no such analogies for smelling, tasting or feeling. So when I say that I 'smell' the singed hoof, I have no way of paraphrasing my statement into a form of words which says instead 'I smell a copy of a singed hoof'. The language of originals and copies does not apply to smells.

None the less, I may certainly say that I vividly 'smell' the singed hoof, or that its smell comes back to me vividly, and the use of this adverb shows by itself that I know that I am not smelling, but only 'smelling'. Smells are not vivid, faithful or lifelike; they are only more or less strong. Only 'smells' can be vivid, and correspondingly they cannot be more or less strong, though I can seem to be getting a more or less strong smell. However vividly I may be 'smelling' the smithy, the smell of lavender in my room, however faint, is in no degree drowned. There is no competition between a smell and a 'smell', as there can be a competition between the smell of onions and the smell of lavender.

If a person who has recently been in a burning house reports that he can still 'smell' the smoke, he does not think that the house in which he reports it is itself on fire. However vividly he 'smells' the smoke, he knows that he smells none; at least, he realises this, if he is in his right mind, and if he does not realise it, he will say not that the 'smell' is vivid, but, erroneously, that the smell is strong. But if the theory were true that to 'smell' smoke were really to smell a likeness of smoke, he could have no way of distinguishing between 'smelling' and smelling, corresponding to the familiar ways in which we distinguish between looking at faces and looking at likenesses of them, or between hearing voices and hearing recordings of voices.

There are usually ocular ways of distinguishing between things and snapshots or effigies of them; a picture is flat, has edges and perhaps a frame; it can be turned round and turned upside down, crumpled and torn. Even an echo, or a recording, of a voice can be distinguished, if not audibly, at least by certain mechanical criteria from the voice itself. But no such discriminations can be made between a smell and a copy of a smell, a taste and a likeness of a taste, a tickle and a dummy-tickle; indeed, it makes no sense to apply words like 'copy', 'likeness' and 'dummy' to smells, tastes and feelings. Consequently we have no temptation to say that a person who 'smells' the smithy is really smelling a facsimile or likeness of anything. He seems to smell, or he fancies he smells, something, but there is no way of talking as if there existed an internal smell replica, or smell facsimile, or smell echo. In this case, therefore, it is clear that to 'smell' entails not smelling and therefore that imaging is not perceiving a likeness, since it is not perceiving at all.

Why, then, is it tempting and natural to misdescribe 'seeing things' as the seeing of pictures of things? It is not because 'pictures' denotes a genus of which snapshots are one species and mental pictures are another, since 'mental pictures' no more denotes pictures than 'mock-murders' denotes murders. On the contrary, we speak of 'seeing' as if it were a seeing of pictures, because the familiar experience of seeing snapshots of things and persons so often induces the 'seeing' of those things and persons. This is what snapshots are for. When a visible likeness of a person is in front of my nose, I often seem to be seeing the person himself in front of my nose, though he is not there and may be long since dead. I should not keep the portrait if it did not perform this function. Or when I hear a recording of a friend's voice, I fancy I hear him singing or speaking in the room, though he is miles away. The genus is seeming to perceive, and of this genus one very familiar species is that of seeming to see something, when looking at an ordinary snapshot of it. Seeming to see, when no physical likeness is before the nose, is another species. Imaging is not having shadowy pictures before some shadow-organ called 'the mind's eye'; but having paper pictures before the eyes in one's face is a familiar stimulus to imaging.

An oil painting of a friend is described as lifelike, if it makes me seem to see the friend in great clarity and detail, when I am not actually seeing him. A mere cartoon may be lifelike without being at all similar to a lifelike oil painting of the same person. For a picture to be lifelike it is not necessary or sufficient that it should be an accurate replica of the contours or colouring of the subject's face. So when I vividly 'see' a face, this does not entail my seeing an accurate replica, since I might see an accurate replica without being helped to 'see' the face vividly and *vice versa*. But finding a picture of a person lifelike or 'speaking' entails being helped to seem to see the person, since that is what 'lifelike' and 'speaking' mean.

People have tended to describe 'seeing' as a seeing of genuine but ghostly likenesses, because they wanted to explain vividness or lifelikeness in terms of similarity, as if, for me vividly to 'see' Helvellyn, I must be actually seeing something else very similar to Helvellyn. But this is erroneous. Seeing replicas, however accurate, need not result in 'seeing' vividly, and the speakingness of a physical likeness has to be described, not in terms of similarity, but in terms of the vividness of the 'seeing' which it induces.

In short, there are no such objects as mental pictures, and if there were such objects, seeing them would still not be the same thing as seeming to see faces or mountains. We do picture or visualise faces and mountains, just as we do, more rarely, 'smell' singed hoofs, but picturing a face or a mountain is not having before us a picture of the face or mountain, it is something that having a physical likeness in front of one's nose commonly helps us to do, though we can and often do do it without any such promptings. Dreaming, again, is not being present at a private cinematograph show; on the contrary, witnessing a public cinematograph show is one way of inducing a certain sort of dreaming. The spectator there is seeing a variously illuminated sheet of linen, but he is 'seeing' rolling prairies. So it would invert the true state of affairs to say that the dreamer is regarding a variously illuminated sheet of 'mental' linen; for there is no mental linen, and if there were, seeing it variously illuminated would not be dreaming that one was galloping over the prairies.

The tendency to describe visualising as seeing genuine, but internal, likenesses, reinforces and is reinforced by the Sense Datum Theory. Many holders of this theory, supposing, erroneously, that in 'seeing' I am seeing a peculiar paper-less snapshot, though one which, oddly, cannot be turned upside down, think that *a fortiori* in seeing proper I am seeing a peculiar non-physical colour expanse. And supposing, erroneously, that having a visual sensation is descrying a flat patchwork of colours spread out in 'a private space', they find it all the easier to say that in imaging we are scanning a more ghostly patchwork of colours hung up in the same gallery with that original patchwork of colours. As in my study there may be both a person and a shadow or a portrait of that person, so in my private sight-gallery there might be both sense data and reproductions of sense data. My objections to the interpretation of picturing as picture-seeing do not in themselves demolish the Sense Datum Theory of sensations; but they do demolish, I hope, the ancillary theory that picturing is looking at reproductions of sense data. And if I am right in saying that having a visual sensation is wrongly described as some sort of observing of a patchwork of colours, since the concept of sensation is different from the concept of observing, it will follow, as can be established on other grounds, that imaging is not only not any sort of observing of anything; it is also not having a sensation of a special sort. Seeming to hear a very loud noise is not being in any degree deafened, nor is seeming to see a very bright light being in any degree dazzled. So far are ideas from being impressions of a special sort, that to describe something as an idea, in this sense, is to deny that an impression is being had.

It will probably be asked, 'What then is it for a person to fancy that he sees or smells something? How can he seem to hear a tune that he does not really hear? And, in particular, how can a person fail to be aware that he is only seeming to hear or see, as the dipsomaniac certainly fails? In what precise respects is 'seeing' so like seeing that the victim often cannot, with the best will and the best wits, tell which he is doing?' Now if we divest these questions of associations with any 'wires and pulleys' questions, we can see that they are simply questions about the concept of imagining or make-believe, a concept of which I have so far said nothing positive. I have said nothing about it so far, because it seemed necessary to begin by vaccinating ourselves against the theory, often tacitly assumed, that imagining is to be described as the seeing of pictures with a special status.

But I hope I have now shown that what people commonly describe as 'having a mental picture of Helvellyn' or 'having Helvellyn before the mind's eye' is actually a special case of imagining, namely imagining that we see Helvellyn in front of our noses, and that having a tune running in one's head is imagining that one has the tune being played in one's hearing, maybe in a concert-hall. If successful, then I have also shown that the notion that a mind is a 'place', where mental pictures are seen and reproductions of voices and tunes are heard, is also wrong.

There are hosts of widely divergent sorts of behaviour in the conduct of which we should ordinarily and correctly be described as imaginative. The mendacious witness in the witness-box, the inventor thinking out a new machine, the constructor of a romance, the child playing bears, and Henry Irving are all exercising the imaginations; but so, too, are the judge listening to the lies of the witness, the colleague giving his opinion on the new invention, the novel reader, the nurse who refrains from admonishing the 'bears' for their subhuman noises, the dramatic critic and the theatre-goers. Nor do we say that they are all exercising their imaginations because we think that, embedded in a variety of often widely different operations, there is one common nuclear operation which all alike are performing, any more than we think that what makes two men both farmers is some nuclear operation which both do in exactly the same way. Just as ploughing is one farming job and tree-spraying is another farming job, so inventing a new machine is one way of being imaginative and playing bears is another. No one thinks that there exists a nuclear farming operation by the execution of which alone a man is entitled to be called 'a farmer'; but the concepts wielded in theories of knowledge are apt to be less generously treated. It is often assumed that there does exist one nuclear operation in which imagination proper consists; it is assumed, that is, that the judge following the witness's mendacities, and the child playing bears, are both exercising their imaginations only if they are both executing some specifically identical ingredient operation. This supposed nuclear operation is often supposed to be that of seeing things in the mind's eye, hearing things in one's head and so on, i.e. some piece of fancied perceiving. Of course, it is not denied that the child is doing lots of other things as well; he roars, he pads around the floor, he gnashes his teeth and he pretends to sleep in what he pretends is a cave. But, according to this view, only if he sees pictures in his mind's eye of his furry paws, his snowbound den and so on, is he imagining anything. His noises and antics may be a help to his picturing, or they may be special effects of it, but it is not in making these noises, or performing these antics, that he is exercising his imagination, but only in his 'seeing', 'hearing', 'smelling', 'tasting' and 'feeling' things which are not there to be perceived. And the corresponding things will be true of the attentive, if sceptical, judge.

Put as bluntly as this, the doctrine is patently absurd. Most of the things for which we ordinarily describe children as imaginative are ruled out in favour of a limited number of operations the occurrence and qualities of which it is difficult to ascertain, especially from relatively inarticulate children. We see and hear them play, but we do not see or hear them 'seeing' or 'hearing' things. We read what Conan Doyle wrote, but we do not get a view of what he saw in his mind's eye. So, on this theory, we cannot easily tell whether children, actors or novelists are imaginative or not, though the word 'imagination' came to be wielded in theories of knowledge just because we all know how to wield it in our everyday descriptions of children, actors and novelists.

There is no special Faculty of Imagination, occupying itself single-mindedly in fancied viewings and hearings. On the contrary, 'seeing' things is one exercise of imagination, growling somewhat like a bear is another; smelling things in the mind's nose is an uncommon act of fancy, malingering is a very common one, and so forth. Perhaps the chief motive from which many theorists have limited the exercises of imagination to the special class of fancied perceptions is that they have supposed that, since the mind is officially tri-partitioned into the Three Estates of Cognition, Volition and Emotion, and since imagination was born into the first, it must therefore be excluded from the others. Cognitive malpractices are notoriously due to the pranks of undisciplined Imagination, and some cognitive successes are in debt to its primmer activities. So, being an (erratic) Squire of Reason, it cannot serve the other masters. But we need not pause to discuss this feudal allegory. Indeed, if we are asked whether imagining is a cognitive or a noncognitive activity , our proper policy is to ignore the question. 'Cognitive' belongs to the vocabulary of examination papers.

Chapter 30

The Nature of Images and the Introspective Trap

Daniel Dennett

Although few philosophers these days will express outright allegiance to the doctrine of mental imagery, these ghostly snapshots have not yet been completely exorcized from current thinking. Introspection is often held to tell us that consciousness is filled with a variety of peculiar objects and qualities that cannot be accounted for by a purely physical theory of mind, and this chapter is devoted to demolishing this view. The imagistic view of consciousness has been in the past a prolific source of confusions, such as the perennial problems of hallucinations, 'perceptual spaces' and colour qualities, to name a few. Once the distinction between the personal and sub-personal level is made clear and mental images are abandoned these problems vanish.

Although the myth of mental imagery is beginning to lose its grip on thinkers in the field, it is still worth a direct examination and critique.[1] I shall restrict the examination to visual perception and mental imagery, since the results obtained there can be applied directly to the other sense modalities. We are less inclined to strike up the little band in the brain for auditory perception than we are to set up the movie screen, so if images can be eliminated, mental noises, smells, feels and tastes will go quietly.

The difficulty with mental images has always been that they are not very much like physical images—paintings and photographs, for example. The concept of a mental image must always be hedged in a variety of ways: mental images are in a different space, do not have dimensions, are subjective, are Intentional, or even, in the end, just quasi-images. Once mental images have been so qualified, in what respects are they *like* physical images at all? Paintings and photographs are our exemplary images, and if mental images are not like them, our use of the word 'image' is systematically misleading, regardless of how well entrenched it is in our ordinary way of speaking.

Let me propose an acid test for images. An image is a *representation* of something, but what sets it aside from other representations is that an image represents something else always in virtue of having at least one quality or characteristic of shape, form or colour in common with what it represents. Images can be in two or three dimensions, can be manufactured or natural, permanent or fleeting, but they must *resemble* what they represent and not merely represent it by playing a role—symbolic, conventional or functional—in some system. Thus an image of an orange need not be orange (e.g., it could be a black-and-white photograph), but something hard, square and black just cannot be an image of something soft, round and white. It might be intended as a *symbol* of something soft, round and white, and—given the temper of contemporary art—might even be labelled a *portrait* of something soft, round and white, but it would not be an image. Now I take the important question about mental images to be: are there elements in perception that represent in virtue of resembling what they represent and hence deserve to be called images?

First let us attack this question from the point of view of a sub-personal account of perception. Consider how images *work*. It is one thing just to be an image—e.g., a reflection in a pool in the wilderness—and another to function as an image, to be taken as an image, to be used as an image. For an image to work as an image there must be a person (or an analogue of a person) to see or observe it, to recognize or ascertain the qualities in virtue of which it is an image of something. Imagine a fool putting a television camera on his car and connecting it to a small receiver under the bonnet so the engine could 'see where it is going'. The madness in this is that although an image has been provided, no provision has been made for anyone or anything analogous to a perceiver to watch the image. This makes it clear that if an image is to function as an element in *perception*, it will have to function as the raw material and not the end product, for if we suppose that the product of the perceptual process is an image, we shall have to design a perceiver-analogue to sit in front of the image and yet another to sit in front of the image which is the end product of perception in the perceiver-analogue and so forth *ad infinitum*. Just as the brain-writing view discussed earlier required brain-writing readers, so the image view requires image-watchers; both views merely postpone true analysis by positing unanalysed man-analogues as functional parts of men.

In fact the last image in the physical process of perception is the image of stimulation on the retina. The process of afferent analysis begins on the surface of the retina and continues up the optic nerve, so that the exact pattern of stimulation on the retina is 'lost' and replaced with information about characteristics of this pattern and eventually about characteristics of the environment.[2] The particular physiological facts about this neural analysis are not directly relevant to the philosophical problem of images. The nervous system *might* have transmitted the mosaic of stimulation on the retina deep into the brain and then reconstituted the image there, in the manner of television, but in that case the analysis that must occur as the first step in perception would simply be carried out at a deeper anatomical level. Once perceptual analysis has begun there will indeed be elements of the process that can be said to be representations, but only in virtue of being interrelated parts of an essentially arbitrary system. The difference between a neural representation of a square and that of a circle will no more be a difference in the shape of the neural things, than the difference between the *words* 'ox' and 'butterfly' is that one is heavier and uglier than the other. The upshot of this is that there is no room in the sub-personal explanation of the perceptual process, whatever its details, for images. Let us turn then to the personal level account of mental imagery to see if it is as compelling, after all, as we often think.

Shorter, in 'Imagination',[3] describes imagining as more like depicting—in words—than like painting a picture. We can, and usually do, imagine things without going into great detail. If I imagine a tall man with a wooden leg I need not also have imagined him as having hair of a certain colour, dressed in any particular clothes, having or not having a hat. If, on the other hand, I were to draw a picture of this man, I would have to go into details. I can make the picture fuzzy, or in silhouette, but unless something positive is drawn in where the hat should be, obscuring that area, the man in the picture must either have a hat on or not. As Shorter points out, my not going into details about hair colour in my imagining does not mean that his hair is coloured 'vague' in my imagining; his hair is simply not 'mentioned' in my imagining at all. This is quite unlike drawing a picture that is deliberately ambiguous, as one can readily see by first imagining a tall man with a wooden leg and then imagining a tall man with a wooden leg who maybe does and maybe does not have blond hair, and comparing the results.

If I write down a description of a person it would be absurd for anyone to say that my description cannot fail to mention whether or not the man is wearing a hat. My description can be as brief and undetailed as I like. Similarly it would be absurd to insist that one's imagining someone must go into the question of his wearing a hat. It is one thing to imagine a man wearing a hat, another to imagine him not wearing a hat, a third to imagine his head so obscured you can't tell, and a fourth to imagine him without going into the matter of headgear at all. Imagining is depictional or descriptional, not pictorial, and is bound only by this one rule borrowed from the rules governing sight: it must be from a point of view—I cannot imagine the inside and outside of a barn at once.[4]

A moment's reflection should convince us that it is not just imagining, however, that is like description in this way; all 'mental imagery', including seeing and hallucinating, is descriptional. Consider the film version of *War and Peace* and Tolstoy's book; the film version goes into immense detail and in one way cannot possibly be *faithful* to Tolstoy's words, since the 'picture painted' by Tolstoy does not go into the detail the film cannot help but go into (such as the colours of the eyes of each filmed soldier). Yet Tolstoy's descriptions are remarkably vivid. The point of this is that the end product of perception, what we are aware of when we perceive something, is more like the written Tolstoy than the film. The writing analogy has its own pitfalls, but is still a good antidote to the picture analogy. When we perceive something in the environment we are not aware of every fleck of colour all at once, but rather of the highlights of the scene, an edited commentary on the things of interest.

As soon as images are abandoned even from the personal level account of perception in favour of a descriptional view of awareness, a number of perennial philosophical puzzles dissolve. Consider the Tiger and his Stripes. I can dream, imagine or see a striped tiger, but must the tiger I experience have a particular number of stripes? If seeing or imagining is having a mental image, then the image of the tiger *must*—obeying the rules of images in general—reveal a definite number of stripes showing, and one should be able to pin this down with such questions as 'more than ten?', 'less than twenty?'. If, however, seeing or imagining has a descriptional character, the questions need have no definite answer. Unlike a snapshot of a tiger, a description of a tiger need not go into the number of stripes at all; 'numerous stripes' may be all the description says. Of course in the case of actually seeing a tiger, it will often be possible to corner the tiger and count his stripes, but then one is counting real tiger stripes, not stripes on a mental image.[5]

Another familiar puzzle is Wittgenstein's duck-rabbit, the drawing that looks now like a duck, now like a rabbit. What can possibly be the difference between seeing it first one way and then the other? The image (on the paper or the retina) does not change, but there can be more than one description of that image. To be aware of it first as a rabbit and then as a duck can be just a matter of the content of the signals crossing the awareness line, and this in turn could depend on some weighting effect occurring in the course of afferent analysis. One says at the personal level 'First I was aware of it *as* a rabbit, and then *as* a duck', but if the question is asked 'What is the difference between the two experiences?', one can only answer at this level by repeating one's original remark. To get to other more enlightening answers to the question one must resort to the sub-personal level, and here the answer will invoke no images beyond the unchanging image on the retina.

Of all the problems that have led philosophers to posit mental imagery, the most tenacious has been the problem of hallucinations, and yet it need hardly be mentioned that there is no problem of hallucinations *unless* one is thinking of awareness imagistically. On the sub-personal level, there can be little doubt that hallucinations are caused by abnormal neuronal discharges. Stimulation by electrode of micro-areas on the visual cortex produces specific and repeatable hallucinations.[6] Having a visual hallucination is then just being aware of the content of a non-veridical visual 'report' caused by such a freak discharge. And where is this report, and what space does it exist in? It is in the brain and exists in the space taken up by whatever event it is that has this non-veridical content, just as my description of hallucinations takes up a certain amount of space on paper. Since spatiality is irrelevant to descriptions, freak descriptions do not require ghostly spaces to exist in.[7]

The one familiar philosophical example that may seem at first to resist the descriptional view of perception and awareness in favour of the imagistic is the distinction, drawn by Descartes, between imagining and conceiving. We can imagine a pentagon or a hexagon, and imagining one of these is introspectively distinguishable from imagining the other, but we cannot imagine a chiliagon (a thousand-sided figure) in a way that is introspectively distinct from imagining a 999-sided figure. We can, however, *conceive* of a chiliagon (without trying to imagine one) and this experience is perfectly distinct from conceiving of a 999-sided figure. From this it might be tempting to argue that whereas conceiving might well be descriptional and not imagistic, imagining must be imagistic, for our inability to imagine a chiliagon is just like our inability to tell a *picture* of a chiliagon from the *picture* of a 999-sided figure. All this shows, however, is that imagining is like *seeing*, not that imagining is like making pictures. In fact, it shows that imagining is *not* like making pictures, for I certainly *can* make a picture of a chiliagon if I have a great deal of patience and very sharp pencils, and when it is done I can tell it from a picture of a 999-sided figure, but this deliberate, constructive activity is unparalleled by anything I can do when I 'frame mental images'. Although I can *put together* elements to make a mental 'image' the result is always bound by a limitation of seeing: I can only imagine what I could see in a glance; differences below the threshold of discrimination of casual observation cannot be represented in imagination. The distinction between imagining and conceiving is real enough; it is like the distinction between seeing and listening to someone. Conceiving depends on the ability to understand words, such as the formula 'regular thousand-sided figure', and what we can describe in words far outstrips what we can see in one gaze.

If seeing is rather like reading a novel at breakneck speed, it is also the case that the novel is written to order at breakneck speed. This allows introspection to lay a trap for us and lead us naturally to the picture theory of seeing. Whenever we examine our own experience of seeing, whenever we set out to discover what we can say about what we are seeing, we find all the details we think of looking for. When we read a novel, questions can come to mind that are not answered in the book, but when we are looking at something, as soon as questions come up they are answered immediately by new information as a result of the inevitable shift in the focus and fixation point of our eyes. The reports of perception are written to order; whatever detail interests us is immediately brought into focus and reported on. When this occurs one is not scanning some stable mental image or sense-datum. One is scanning the outside world—quite literally. One can no more become interested in a part of one's visual experience without bringing the relevant information to the fore than one can run away from one's shadow. For this reason it is tempting to suppose that everything one *can* know about via the eyes is *always* 'present to consciousness' in some stable picture.

To sit and introspect one's visual experience for a while is not to examine normal sight. When one does this one is tempted to say that it is all very true that there is only a small, central part of the visual field of which one is aware at any moment, and that to describe the whole scene our eyes, our fixation point, and our 'focus of interest' must scan the sensory presentation, but that the parts we are not scanning at any moment persist or remain, as a sort of vague, coloured background. Of this background we are only 'semi-aware'. Here, however, introspection runs into trouble, for as soon as one becomes interested in what is going on outside the beam of the fixation point one immediately becomes aware of the contents of peripheral signals, and this phenomenon is quite different from the ordinary one. While it is true that one can focus on a spot on the wall and yet direct one's attention to the periphery of one's visual field and come up with reports like 'There is something blue and book-sized on the table to my right; it is vague and blurred and I am not sure it is a book', it cannot be inferred from this that when one is *not* doing this one is still aware of the blue, booklike shape. We are led to such conclusions by the natural operation of our eyes, which is to make a cursory scanning of the environment whenever it changes and as soon as it changes, and by the operation of short-term memory, which holds the results of this scanning for a short period of time. In familiar surroundings we do not have to see or pay attention to the objects in their usual places. If anything had been moved or removed we *would* have noticed, but that does not mean we notice their presence, or even that we had the experience (in any sense) of their presence. We enter a room and we know what objects are in it, because if it is a familiar room we do not notice that anything is missing and thus it is filled with all the objects we have noticed or put there in the past. If it is an unfamiliar room we automatically scan it, picking out the objects that fill it and catch our attention. I may spend an afternoon in a strange room without ever being aware (in any sense) of the colour of the walls, and while it is no doubt true that had the walls been bright red I would have been aware of this, it does not follow that I must have been aware that they were beige, or aware that they were colourless or vaguely coloured—whatever that might mean.[8]

It is true, of course, that when we see we do not simply see *that* there is a table in front of us, but a table of a particular colour and shape in a particular position and so forth. All this need mean is that the information we receive is vivid and rich in detail. This is not true of the vision of many lower animals. The frog, for example, can see that there is a small moving object before him, but he cannot see that it is a fly or a bit of paper on a string. If the small object is not moving, *he cannot see it at all*, because motion signals are required for the production of the higher-level signals that will initiate a behavioural response. A frog left in a cage with freshly killed (unmoving) flies will starve to death, because it has no equipment for sending the signal: there is a fly (moving or still). Dangle a dead fly on a string and the frog will eat it.[9] The difference in degree of complexity and vividness between frog and human perception does not warrant the assumption that there is a difference in kind—however much we may feel that a picture is worth a thousand words.[10]

Notes

1. Optimists who doubt that mental images are still taken seriously in philosophy and even in science are invited to peruse two recent anthologies, R. J. Hirst, ed., *Perception and the External World*, New York, 1965, and J. R. Smythies, ed., *Brain and Mind, Modern Concepts of the Nature of Mind*, London, 1965. The wealth of cross-disciplinary confusions over mental images is displayed in both volumes, which both include papers by philosophers, psychologists and neurophysiologists. Neither editor seems to think that much of what he presents is a dead horse, which strengthens my occasionally flagging conviction that I am not beating one. On the other hand there are scientists who have expressed clear and explicit rejections of imagistic confusions. See, e.g., G. W. Zopf, 'Sensory Homeostasis' in Wiener and Schadé, *Nerve, Brain and Memory Models*, New York, 1963, p. 71, esp. p. 118, and D. M. MacKay, 'Internal Representation of the External World', unpublished, read at the Avionics Panel Symposium on Nature and Artificial Logic Processors, Athens, July 15–19, 1963.
2. H. B. Barlow, 'Possible Principles Underlying the Transformations of Sensory Messages' in W. A. Rosenblith, (ed.) *Sensory Communication*, New York, 1961, offers a particularly insightful account of the

'editorial' function of afferent neural activity and the depletion of information that is the necessary concomitant of such analysis.

3. J. M. Shorter, 'Imagination', *Mind*, LXI, 1952, pp. 528–42.

4. Counter-examples spring to mind, but are they really counter-examples? All the ones that have so far occurred to me turn out on reflection to be cases of imagining myself seeing—with the aid of large mirrors—the inside and outside of the barn, imagining a (partially) transparent barn, imagining looking in the windows and so forth. These are all from a point of view in the sense I mean. A written description, however, is not bound by these limitations; from what point of view is the description: 'the barn is dark red with black rafters and a pine floor'?

5. In the unusual phenomenon of 'eidetic imagery', the subject *can* read off or count off the details of his 'memory image', and this may seem to provide the fatal counter-example to this view. (See G. Allport, 'Eidetic Imagery', *British Journal of Psychology*, XV, 1924, pp. 99–120.) Yet the fact that such 'eidetic memory images' actually appear to be projected or superimposed on the subject's normal visual field (so that if the subject shifts his gaze the position of the memory image in his visual field remains fixed, and 'moves with the eye') strongly suggests that in these cases the actual image of retinal stimulation is somehow retained at or very near the retina and superimposed on incoming stimulation. In these rare cases, then, the memory mechanism must operate *prior to* afferent analysis, at a time when there still is a physical image.

6. Penfield, *The Excitable Cortex in Conscious Man*, Liverpool, 1958. Some of Penfield's interpretations of his results have been widely criticized, but the results themselves are remarkable. It would be expected that hallucinations would have to be the exception rather than the rule in the brain for event—types to *acquire* content in the first place, and this is in fact supported by evidence. Amputees usually experience 'phantom limb' sensations that seem to come from the missing limb; an amputee may feel that he not only still has the leg, but that it is itching or hot or bent at the knee. These phenomena, which occur off and on for years following amputation, are nearly universal in amputees, with one interesting exception. In cases where the amputation occurred in infancy, before the child developed the use and coordination of the limb, phantom limb is rarely experienced, and in cases where amputation occurred just after birth, no phantom limb is ever experienced (see M. Simmel, 'Phantom Experiences following Amputation in Childhood', *Journ. of Neurology, Neurosurgery and Psychiatry* XXV, 1962, pp. 69–78).

7. Other phenomena less well known to philosophers also favour a descriptional explanation. See, e.g., W. R. Brain's account of the reports of patients who have their sight surgically restored, in 'Some Reflections on Mind and Brain,' *Brain*, LXXXVI, 1963, p. 381; the controversial accounts of newly sighted adults' efforts to learn to see, in M. von Senden, *Raum- und Gestaltauffassung bei operierten Blindgeborenen vor und nach der Operation*, Leipzig, 1932, translated with appendices by P. Heath as *Space and Sight, the Perception of Space and Shape in the congenitally blind before and after operation*, London, 1960; I. Kohler's experiments with inverting spectacles (a good account of these and similar experiments is found in J. G. Taylor, *The Behavioral Basis of Perception*, New Haven, 1962); and the disorder called simultanagnosia, M. Kinsbourne and E. K. Warrington, 'A Disorder of Simultaneous Form Perception', *Brain*, LXXXV, 1962, pp. 461–86 and A. R. Luria, *et al.*, 'Disorders of Ocular Movement in a Case of Simultanagnosia', *Brain*, LXXXVI, 1963, pp. 219–28.

8. Cf. Wittgenstein, 'But the existence of this feeling of strangeness does not give us a reason for saying that every object we know well and which does not seem strange to us gives us a feeling of familiarity', *Philosophical Investigations*, Oxford, 1953, i. 596. See also i. 597, i. 605.

9. Muntz, 'Vision in Frogs', *Scientific American*, 210, 1964, pp. 757–76, and Wooldridge, *The Machinery of the Brain*, New York, 1963, pp. 46–50.

10. Having found no room for images in the sub-personal account of perception, we can say that 'mental image' and its kin are poor candidates for referring expressions in science; having found further that nothing with the traits of genuine images is to be found at the personal level either allows us to conclude that 'mental image' is valueless as a referring expression under *any* circumstances.

Chapter 31

Mental Rotation of Three-Dimensional Objects

Roger Shepard and Jacqueline Metzler

Human subjects are often able to determine that two two-dimensional pictures portray objects of the same three-dimensional shape even though the objects are depicted in very different orientations. The experiment reported here was designed to measure the time that subjects require to determine such identity of shape as a function of the angular difference in the portrayed orientations of the two three-dimensional objects.

This angular difference was produced either by a rigid rotation of one of two identical pictures in its own picture plane or by a much more complex, nonrigid transformation, of one of the pictures, that corresponds to a (rigid) rotation of the three-dimensional object in depth.

This reaction time is found (i) to increase linearly with the angular difference in portrayed orientation and (ii) to be no longer for a rotation in depth than for a rotation merely in the picture plane. These findings appear to place rather severe constraints on possible explanations of how subjects go about determining identity of shape of differently oriented objects. They are, however, consistent with an explanation suggested by the subjects themselves. Although introspective reports must be interpreted with caution, all subjects claimed (i) that to make the required comparison they first had to imagine one object as rotated into the same orientation as the other and that they could carry out this "mental rotation" at no greater than a certain limiting rate; and (ii) that, since they perceived the two-dimensional pictures as objects in three-dimensional space, they could imagine the rotation around whichever axis was required with equal ease.

In the experiment each of eight adult subjects was presented with 1600 pairs of perspective line drawings. For each pair the subject was asked to pull a right-hand lever as soon as he determined that the two drawings portrayed objects that were congruent with respect to three-dimensional shape and to pull a left-hand lever as soon as he determined that the two drawings depicted objects of different three-dimensional shapes. According to a random sequence, in half of the pairs (the "same" pairs) the two objects could be rotated into congruence with each other (as in figure 31.1, a and b), and in the other half (the "different" pairs) the two objects differed by a reflection as well as a rotation and could not be rotated into congruence (as in figure 31.1c).

The choice of objects that were mirror images or "isomers" of each other for the "different" pairs was intended to prevent subjects from discovering some distinctive feature possessed by only one of the two objects and thereby reaching a decision of noncongruence without actually having to carry out any mental rotation. As a further precaution, the ten different three-dimensional objects depicted in the various perspective drawings were chosen to be relatively unfamiliar and meaningless in overall three-dimensional shape.

Each object consisted of ten solid cubes attached face-to-face to form a rigid armlike structure with exactly three right-angled "elbows" (see figure 31.1). The set of all ten

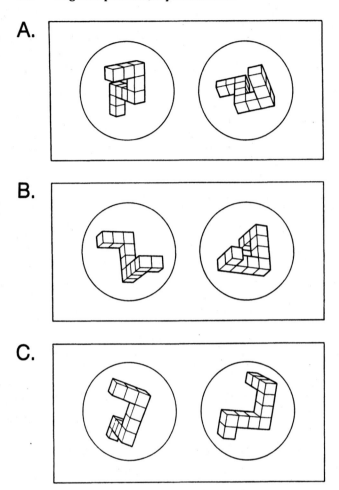

Figure 31.1
Examples of pairs of perspective line drawings presented to the subjects. (a) A "same" pair, which differs by an 80° rotation in the picture plane; (b) a "same" pair, which differs by an 80° rotation in depth; and (c) a "different" pair, which cannot be brought into congruence by *any* rotation.

shapes included two subsets of five: within either subset, no shape could be transformed into itself or any other by any reflection or rotation (short of 360°). However, each shape in either subset was the mirror image of one shape in the other subset, as required for the construction of the "different" pairs.

For each of the ten objects, 18 different perspective projections—corresponding to one complete turn around the vertical axis by 20° steps—were generated by digital computer and associated graphical output (1). Seven of the 18 perspective views of each object were then selected so as (i) to avoid any views in which some part of the object was wholly occluded by another part and yet (ii) to permit the construction of two pairs that differed in orientation by each possible angle, in 20° steps, from 0° to 180°. These 70 line drawings were then reproduced by photo-offset process and were attached to cards in pairs for presentation to the subjects.

Half of the "same" pairs (the "depth" pairs) represented two objects that differed by some multiple of a 20° rotation about a vertical axis (figure 31.1b). For each of these pairs, copies of two appropriately different perspective views were simply attached to the cards in the orientation in which they were originally generated. The other half of the "same" pairs (the "picture-plane" pairs) represented two objects that differed by some multiple of a 20° rotation in the plane of the drawings themselves (figure 31.1a). For each of these, one of the seven perspective views was selected for each object and two copies of this picture were attached to the card in appropriately different orientations. Altogether, the 1600 pairs presented to each subject included 800 "same" pairs, which consisted of 400 unique pairs (20 "depth" and 20 "picture-plane" pairs at each of the ten angular differences from 0° to 180°), each of which was presented twice. The remaining 800 pairs, randomly intermixed with these, consisted of 400 unique "different" pairs, each of which (again) was presented twice. Each of these 'different" pairs corresponded to one "same" pair (of either the "depth" or "picture-plane" variety) in which, however, one of the three-dimensional objects had been reflected about some plane in three-dimensional space. Thus the two objects in each "different" pair differed, in general, by both a reflection and a rotation.

The 1600 pairs were group into blocks of not more than 200 and presented over eight to ten 1-hour sessions (depending upon the subject). Also, although it is only of incidental interest here, each such block of presentations was either "pure," in that all pairs involved rotations of the same type ("depth" or "picture-plane"), or "mixed," in that the two types of rotation were randomly intermixed within the same block.

Each trial began with a warning tone, which was followed half a second later by the presentation of a stimulus pair and the simultaneous onset of a timer. The lever-pulling response stopped the timer, recorded the subject's reaction time and terminated the visual display. The line drawings, which averaged between 4 and 5 cm in maximum linear extent, appeared at a viewing distance of about 60 cm. They were positioned, with a center-to-center spacing that subtended a visual angle of 9°, in two circular apertures in a vertical black surface (see figure 31.1, a to c).

The subjects were instructed to respond as quickly as possible while keeping errors to a minimum. On the average only 3.2 percent of the responses were incorrect (ranging from 0.6 to 5.7 percent for individual subjects). The reaction-time data presented blow include only the 96.8 percent correct responses. However, the data for the incorrect responses exhibit a similar pattern.

In figure 31.2, the overall means of the reaction times as a function of angular difference in orientation for all correct (right-hand) responses to "same" pairs are plotted separately for the pairs differing by a rotation in the picture plane (figure 31.2a) and for the pairs differing by a rotation in depth (figure 31.2b). In both cases, reaction time is

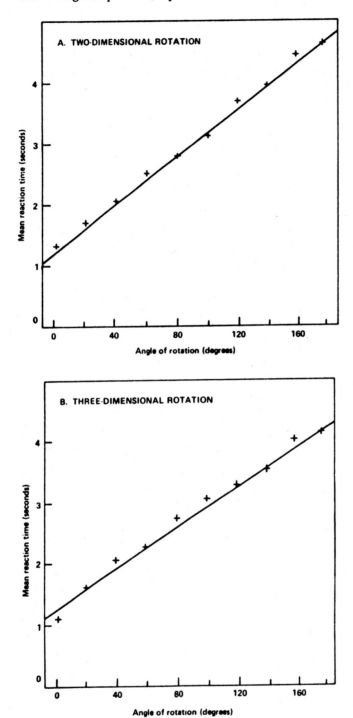

Figure 31.2
Mean reaction times to two perspective line drawings portraying objects of the same three-dimensional shape. Times are plotted as a function of angular difference in portrayed orientation: (a) for pairs differing by a rotation in the picture plane only; and (b) for pairs differing by a rotation in depth.

a strikingly linear function of the angular difference between the two three-dimensional objects portrayed. The mean reaction times for individual subjects increased from a value of about 1 second at 0° of rotation for all subjects to values ranging from 4 to 6 seconds at 180° of rotation, depending upon the particular individual. Moreover, despite such variations in slope, the *linearity* of the function is clearly evident when the data are plotted separately for individual three-dimensional objects or for individual subjects. Polynomial regression lines were computed separately for each subject under each type of rotation. In all 16 cases the functions were found to have a highly significant linear component ($P < .001$) when tested against deviations from linearity. No significant quadratic or higher-order effects were found ($P > .05$, in all cases).

The angle through which different three-dimensional shapes must be rotated to achieve congruence is not, of course, defined. Therefore, a function like those plotted in figure 31.2 cannot be constructed in any straightforward manner for the "different" pairs. The *overall* mean reaction time for these pairs was found, however, to be 3.8 seconds—nearly a second longer than the corresponding overall means for the "same" pairs. (In the postexperimental interview, the subjects typically reported that they attempted to rotate one end of one object into congruence with the corresponding end of the other object; they discovered that the two objects were *different* when, after this "rotation," the two free ends still remained noncongruent.)

Not only are the two functions shown in figure 31.2 both linear but they are very similar to each other with respect to intercept and slope. Indeed, for the larger angular differences the reaction times were, if anything, somewhat shorter for rotation in depth than for rotation in the picture plane. However, since this small difference is either absent or reversed in four of the eight subjects, it is of doubtful significance. The determination of identity of shape may therefore be based, in both cases, upon a process of the same general kind. If we can describe this process as some sort of "mental rotation in three-dimensional space," then the slope of the obtained functions indicates that the average rate at which these particular objects can be thus "rotated" is roughly 60° per second.

Of course the plotted reaction times necessarily include any times taken by the subjects to decide how to process the pictures in each presented pair as well as the time taken actually to carry out the process, once it was chosen. However, even for these highly practiced subjects, the reaction times were still linear and were no more than 20 percent lower in the "pure" blocks of presentations (in which the subjects knew both the axis and the direction of the required rotation in advance of each presentation) than in the "mixed" blocks (in which the axis of rotation was unpredictable). Tentatively, this suggests that 80 percent of a typical one of these reaction times may represent some such process as "mental rotation" itself, rather than a preliminary process of preparation or search. Nevertheless, in further research now underway, we are seeking clarification of this point and others.

References and Notes

1. Mrs. Jih-Jie Chang of the Bell Telephone Laboratories generated the 180 perspective projections for us by means of the Bell Laboratories' Stromberg-Carlson 4020 microfilm recorder and the computer program for constructing such projections developed there by A. M. Noll. See, for example, A. M. Noll, *Computers Automation* 14, 20 (1965).

2. We thank Mrs. Chang [see (1)]; and we also thank Dr. J. D. Elashoff for her suggestions concerning the statistical analyses. Assistance in the computer graphics was provided by the Bell Telephone Laboratories. Supported by NSF grant GS-2283 to R.N.S.

Chapter 32

Scanning Visual Mental Images: The First Phase of the Debate

Stephen Kosslyn

The modern debate about mental imagery has gone through two distinct phases. The first began in 1973, with the publication of Pylyshyn's paper "What the Mind's Eye Tells the Mind's Brain: A Critique of Mental Imagery" and Anderson and Bower's book *Human Associative Memory*. Pylyshyn's critique of mental imagery focused on arguments that the very idea of imagery was paradoxical (Who looks at the images?) or muddled (In what ways are images like pictures? Why can't you see the number of stripes on an imaged tiger?). The thrust of the critique of imagery was that a depictive representation does not occur in the brain when we experience mental images; instead, propositional representations are used for all forms of cognition—including imagery. The depictive features of images that are evident to introspection were thus taken to be "epiphenomenal": these features have nothing to do with the representation used to perform the task, just as the lights flashing on the outside of a mainframe computer have nothing to do with carrying out the internal processing (the lights could be removed and it would keep working just as well).

By their very nature, depictions embody space (recall that "distance" is an intrinsic part of the representation). Thus, if depictive representations underlie the experience of "having an image," then the spatial nature of the representation should affect how images are processed. On the other hand, if the underlying representation is propositional, we have no reason to expect distance to affect processing times (given that the description of an object's appearance would be stored in a list or network of some kind, just as in language).

Different Mechanisms? The First Phase of the Debate

In this section we will consider a series of experiments that were carried out largely by my colleagues and me; these experiments represent a kind of "case study," illustrating how one can make abstract ideas concrete and how one can grasp a conceptual issue by the horns, so to speak.

We reasoned that one way to discover whether image representations embody space is to see whether it takes more time to shift attention greater distances across an imaged object. If subjects take more time to scan a long distance across an imaged object than to scan a short distance, we would have evidence that distance was indeed embodied in the representation of the object.

The first experiment began by asking subjects to memorize a set of drawings (Kosslyn 1973). Half of these drawings were vertical and half were horizontal, as illustrated in figure 32.1. After the subjects had memorized the drawings, they closed their eyes, heard the name of one (say, "speedboat"), and visualized it. Once it was

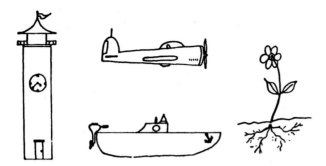

Figure 32.1
Examples of the drawings used by Kosslyn (1973) to study image scanning

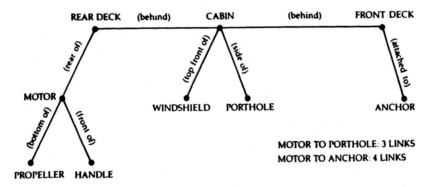

Figure 32.2
A propositional representation of the drawing of a speedboat illustrated in figure 32.1. The greater the distance between two parts on the drawing, the larger the number of links between them in the network.

imaged, the subjects were asked to mentally focus ("stare" with the "mind's eye") at one end of the object in the image. Then the name of a possible component of the object (say, "motor") was presented on tape. On half the trials the name labeled part of the drawing, and on the other half it did not. The subjects were asked to "look for" the named component on the image object.

An important aspect of this experiment was that the probed parts were either at one end or the other of a drawing or in the middle. The subjects were told that we were interested in how long it took to "see" a feature on an imaged object (the word *scan* was never mentioned in the instructions), and they pressed the "true" button only after "seeing" the named component and the "false" button only after "looking" but failing to find it. We reasoned that if image representations depict information, then it ought to take more time to locate the representations of parts located farther from the point of focus. And in fact this is exactly what occurred.

At first glance, the results from this experiment seemed to show that depictive representations are used in imagery. But it soon became clear that a propositional explanation could easily be formulated. Bobrow (personal communication) suggested that the visual appearance of an object is stored in a propositional structure like that illustrated in figure 32.2. This representation is a series of linked hierarchies of propositions, with each hierarchy describing a part of the object. Note that we could rewrite the propositions illustrated here as BOTTOM-OF (PROPELLER, MOTOR), REAR-OF

(MOTOR, REAR DECK), and so on. That is, each link is a relation that combines the symbols at the connected nodes into a proposition.

According to Bobrow's theory, people automatically (and unconsciously) construct these sorts of propositional descriptions when asked to memorize the appearance of drawings. When the subjects were asked to focus on one end of the drawing, they would then activate one part of the representation (for instance, for speedboat, the node for motor). When subsequently asked about a part, they then searched the network for its name. The more links they had to traverse through the network before locating the name, the more time it took to respond. For example, for speedboat it took more time to find "anchor" than "porthole" after having been focused on the motor because four links had to be traversed from motor to anchor but only three from motor to porthole. Thus, the effect of "distance" on scanning time may have nothing to do with distance being embodied in an underlying depictive representation but may instead simply reflect the organization of a propositional network (see also Lea 1975). The conscious experience of scanning a pictorial mental image may somehow be produced by processing this network, and the depictive aspects of images open to introspection may simply be epiphenomenal.

It should now be clear why it was necessary to go into so much detail in characterizing the differences between the types of representations: we need a reasonably precise characterization of the two representations if we are to perform experiments to discriminate between them. According to our characterization, although propositional structures can be formulated to capture the spatial arrangement of the drawings, they are not depictions. Recall that in depictions, in contrast to this sort of propositional representation, the shape of empty space is represented as clearly as the shape of filled space and there is no explicit representation of relations (such as REAR-OF).

The next experiment was designed to eliminate the problem with the first one. In this experiment we independently varied the distance scanned across and the number of items scanned over. The results of this experiment were straightforward: both distance and amount of material scanned over affected the reaction times. Time increased linearly with increasing distance scanned over, even when the amount of material scanned over was kept constant (for details, see Kosslyn, Ball, and Reiser 1978), as expected if images depict.

The notion of depiction leads us to expect that image representations embody distance in at least two dimensions. To test this idea, we asked subjects to memorize the map illustrated in figure 32.3. On this map were seven objects, which could be related by twos to form 21 pairs. The subjects learned to draw the locations of each of the seven objects on the map. These objects were positioned in such a way that the members of each of the 21 pairs were a different distance apart.

As is evident in figure 32.4, time to scan the image increased linearly with increasing distance scanned across. This result is exactly as predicted by the idea that image representations depict information. But it is possible to create a propositional counterexplanation even here. Now the network contains "dummy nodes" that mark off distance. That is, these nodes convey no information other than the fact that an increment of distance (say, 5 centimeters) exists between one object and another; hence, there would be more nodes between nodes representing parts separated by greater distances on the map. By putting enough dummy nodes into a network, the propositional theory developed for the original results can be extended to these results as well.

To attempt to rule out this propositional counterexplanation, we conducted a control experiment, which involved a variation on the map-scanning task. In this experiment subjects again imaged the map and focused their attention on a particular point, but

Figure 32.3
A map that was memorized and later imaged and scanned. The seven objects were placed in such a way that the members of each of the 21 pairs were a different distance apart.

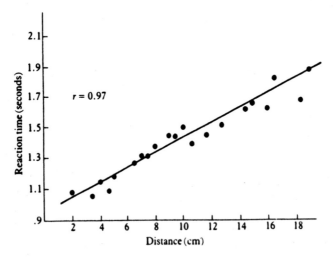

Figure 32.4
The time to scan between pairs of objects on an image of the map illustrated in figure 32.3

now they were told simply to decide as quickly as possible whether the probe named an object on the map. If the propositional theory is correct, we reasoned, then we should find effects of distance here too; after all, we asked the subjects to form the image (which corresponds to accessing the appropriate network). However, there were absolutely no effects of the distance from the focus to target objects on response times.

In other experiments we varied the size of the imaged objects being scanned, asking subjects to adjust the size of an object in the image after they memorized it. Not only did time increase with the distance scanned, but more time was required to scan across larger images. The finding of effects of size on scanning time allows us to eliminate yet another nondepictive explanation for the effects of distance on response times. One could argue that the closer two parts are on an object or drawing, the more likely it is that they will be grouped into a single perceptual "chunk" and stored as a single unit, and hence the easier it will later be to look up two parts in succession. Because the size of the image was not manipulated until after the actual drawing was removed, this explanation cannot account for the effects of size on scanning time.

Chapter 33

Tacit Knowledge and "Mental Scanning"
Zenon W. Pylyshyn

The Empirical Phenomena: Mental Scanning

In the following I examine some specific claims made about the phenomenon of reasoning with the aid of images. Since the study of mental imagery came back into fashion in the 1960s, hundreds of studies have been published, purporting to show that theories of imagery must make allowances for some fairly special properties, properties not shared by other modes of reasoning. Beginning in the 1970s, these studies have concentrated on the role of imagery in reasoning and problem solving rather than on imagery as a form of memory or imagery as an intervening variable in experiments on learning.

Among the best-known research on imaginal reasoning is that of Roger Shepard and his students (Shepard 1978, Shepard and Cooper 1982) and Steve Kosslyn and his associates. Kosslyn's work has been extensively reported—in numerous papers, in a summary in a review paper by Kosslyn et al. (1979), and in a book (Kosslyn 1980). Because Kosslyn, having developed a detailed computer model of imagery, takes a more theoretical approach than most writers, and because his work is among the most influential of the "pictorialists"—to use Block's (1981) term—most of what follows is directed specifically at claims made by Kosslyn. My intention, however, is not to single out this one piece of research; everything I say applies equally to those "pictorialists" who feel that a special form of representation (often called an analogue medium) is needed to account for various experimental results in imaginal reasoning. It is just that Kosslyn's productivity and the explicitness of his claims make him an excellent spokesman for that approach.

The finding that became the basis for much of Kosslyn's theorizing is the "mental scanning result," used not only to argue that "images preserve distances"[1] and that they "depict information in a spatial medium" but also as a way to calibrate "imaginal distance" for such purposes as measuring the visual angle of the "mind's eye" (Kosslyn 1978). Kosslyn's work has also been cited by Attneave (1974) as one of two results that most clearly demonstrate the analogue nature of the representational medium (the other is the "mental rotation" result that will be mentioned here only in passing). Hence, it seems a good place to start.

The scanning experiment (for example, Kosslyn, Ball, and Reiser 1978) has been done many times, so there are quite a few variants. Here is a typical one. Subjects are asked to memorize a simple map of a fictitious island containing about seven visually distinct places (a beach, church, lighthouse, bridge, and so on), until they can reproduce the map to within a specified tolerance. The subjects are then asked to image the map "in their mind's eye" and focus their attention on one of the places, for example, the church. Then they are told the name of a second place, which might or might not be on the map. They are asked to imagine a spot moving from the first to the second place named (or, in some variants, to "move their attention" to the second place). When the subjects can clearly see the second place on their image, they are to press a "yes" button, or, if the named place is not on the map, the "no" button. The latter condition is usually there only as a foil. The result, which is quite robust when the experiment is conducted over hundreds of trials, shows that the time it takes to make the decision is a linear function of the distance traversed on the map. Because, to go from one point on an imagined map to a second point the mind's eye apparently scans through intermediate points, theorists conclude that all the intermediate points are on the mental map; hence, the representation is said to be a form of analogue.

This description, though accurate, does justice neither to the range of experiments carried out nor to the extremely intricate, detailed, highly interconnected model used to explain these and other results. I do not take the reader through the details of the model (they are summarized in the review papers and the book already cited), principally because I do not believe the details matter, neither for the main point of my criticism nor for what makes the model attractive to "pictorialists." The important point is that the explanation of the "scanning result" is to be found in the *intrinsic properties of the representational medium* rather than the tacit knowledge subjects have of the situation they are imagining. Therefore, it is an instance of explicitly positing a property of the functional architecture to account for a generalization.

Some Preliminary Considerations

In examining what occurs in studies such as the scanning experiment and those discussed in Kosslyn (1980), it is crucial that we note the difference between the following two tasks:

> 1a. Solve a problem by using a certain prescribed form of representation or a certain medium or mechanism; and
>
> 1b. Attempt to re-create as accurately as possible the sequence of perceptual events that would occur if you actually observed a certain real event happening.

The reason this difference is crucial is that substantially different criteria of success apply in the two cases. For example, solving a problem by using a certain representational format does not necessarily entail that various incidental properties of a known situation be considered, let alone simulated. On the other hand, this is precisely what is required of someone solving task 1b. Here, failure to duplicate such conditions as the speed at which an event occurs constitutes failure to perform the task correctly. Take the case of imagining. The task of imagining something is the case, or considering an imagined situation in order to answer questions about it, does not entail (as part of the specification of the task itself) that it take a particular length of time. On the other hand, the task of imagining that an event actually happens before your eyes does entail, for a successful realization of this task, consideration of as many characteristics of the event as possible, even if they are irrelevant to the discrimination task itself, as well as entailing that you attempt to place them in the correct time relationships.

In discussing how he imaged his music, Mozart claimed: "Nor do I hear in my imagination, the parts successively, but I hear them, as it were, all at once...." (See Mozart's letter, reproduced in Ghiselin 1952, p. 45.) Mozart felt that he could "hear a whole symphony" in his imagination "all at once" and apprehend its structure and beauty. He must have had in mind a task best described in terms of task 1a. Even the word *hear*, taken in the sense of having an auditorylike imaginal experience, need entail nothing about the duration of the experience. We can be reasonably certain Mozart did not intend the sense of imagining implied in task 1b, simply because, if what he claimed to be doing was that he imagined witnessing the real event of, say, sitting in the Odeon Conservatoire in Munich and hearing his Symphony Number 40 in G Minor being played with impeccable precision by the resident orchestra under the veteran Kapellmeister, and if he imagined that it was actually happening before him in real time and in complete detail—including the most minute flourishes of the horns and the trills of the flute and oboe, all in the correct temporal relations and durations—he would have taken nearly 22 minutes for the task. If he had taken less time, it would signify only that Mozart had not been doing exactly what he said he was doing; that is, he would not have been imagining that he witnessed the actual event in which every note was being played at its proper duration—or we might conclude that what he had, in fact, been imagining was not a good performance of his symphony. In other words, if it takes *n* seconds to witness a certain event, then an accurate mental simulation of the act of witnessing the same event should also take *n* seconds, simply because, how well the latter task is performed, by definition, depends on the accuracy with which it mimics various properties of the former task. On the other hand, the same need not apply merely to the act of imagining that the event has a certain set of properties, that is, imagining a situation to be the case but without the additional requirements specified in the 1b version of the task. These are not empirical assertions about how people imagine and think; they are merely claims about the existence of two distinct, natural interpretations of the specification of a certain task.

In applying this to the case of mental scanning, we must be careful to distinguish between the following two tasks, which subjects might set themselves:

2a. Using a mental image, and focusing your attention on a certain object in the image, decide as quickly as possible whether a second named object is present elsewhere in that image; or

2b. Imagine yourself in a certain real situation in which you are viewing a certain scene and are focusing directly on a particular object in that scene. Now imagine that you are looking for (scanning toward, glancing up at, seeing a speck moving across the scene toward) a second named object in the scene. When you succeed in imagining yourself finding (and seeing) the object (or when you see the speck arrive at the object), press the button.

The relevant differences between 2a and 2b should be obvious. As in the preceding examples, the criteria of successful completion of the task are different in the two cases. In particular, task 2b includes, as part of its specification, such requirements as, subjects should attempt to imagine various intermediate states (corresponding to those they believe would be passed through in actually carrying out the corresponding real task), and that they spend more time visualizing those episodes they believe (or infer) would take more time in the corresponding, real task (perhaps because they recall how long it once took, or because they have some basis for predicting how long it would take). Clearly, the latter conditions are not part of the specification of task 2a, as there is nothing about task 2a which requires that such incidental features of the visual task be considered in answering the question. In the words of Newell and Simon (1972), the two tasks have quite different "task demands."

To demonstrate that subjects actually carry out task 2b in the various studies reported by Kosslyn (and, therefore, that the proper explanation of the findings should appeal to subjects' tacit knowledge of the depicted situation rather than to properties of their imaginal medium), I shall attempt to establish several independent points. First, it is independently plausible that the methods used in experiments reported in the literature should be inviting subjects to carry out task 2b rather than task 2a, and that, in fact, this explanation has considerable generality and can account for a variety of imaginal phenomena. Second, independent experimental evidence exists showing that subjects can, indeed, be led to carry out task 2a rather than 2b, and that when they do, the increase in reaction time with increase in imagined distance disappears. Finally, I consider several objections raised to the "tacit-knowledge" explanation, principally, cases in which subjects appear to have no knowledge of how the results would have turned out in the visual case. I then consider a number of interesting, important cases, possibly not explained by the tacit-knowledge view, in which subjects combine visual and imaginal information by, for example, superimposing images on the scene they are examining visually. I argue that these do not bear on the question under debate—namely, the necessity of postulating a special, noninferential (and noncomputational) mechanism in order to deal with the imagistic mode of reasoning.

Task Demands of Imagery Experiments

With respect to the first point, all published studies of which I am aware, in which larger image distances led to longer reaction times, used instructions that explicitly required subjects to imagine witnessing the occurrence of a real physical event. In most scanning experiments subjects are asked to imagine a spot moving from one point to another, although, in a few experiments (for example, Kosslyn 1973; Kosslyn, Ball, and Reiser 1978, experiment 4), they are asked to imagine "shifting their attention" or their "glance" from one imagined object to another in the same imagined scene. In each case, what subjects were required to imagine was a real, physical event (because such terms as *move* and *shift* refer to physical processes) about whose duration they would clearly have some reasonable, though sometimes only tacit, knowledge. For example, the subjects would know implicitly that, for instance, it takes a moving object longer to move through a greater distance, that it takes longer to shift one's attention through greater distances (both transversely and in depth).

It is important to see that what is at issue is not a contamination of results by the sort of experimental artifact psychologists refer to as "experimenter demand characteristics" (see, for example, Rosenthal and Rosnow 1969) but simply a case of subjects solving a task as they interpret it (or as they choose to interpret it, for one reason or another) by bringing to bear everything they know about a class of physical events, events they take to be those they are to imagine witnessing. If the subjects take the task to be that characterized as 2b, they will naturally attempt to reproduce a temporal sequence of representations corresponding to the sequence they believe will arise from actually viewing the event of scanning across a scene or seeing a spot move across it. Thus, beginning with the representation corresponding to "imagining seeing the initial point of focus," the process continues until a representation is reached that corresponds to "imagining seeing the named point." According to this view there is no need to assume that what is happening is that the imaging process continues until the occurrence of a certain imagined state is independently detected (by the mind's eye), say, because a certain "visual" property is noticed. The process could just as plausibly proceed according to a rhythm established by some independent psychophysical mechanism that paces the time between each viewpoint imagined, according to the speed the subject sets for the mental scanning. (We know such mechanisms exist, since subjects can generate time intervals corresponding to known magnitudes with even greater reliability than they can estimate them; see Fraisse 1963.) Neither is it required that the process consist of a discrete sequence—all that is required is that there be psychophysical mechanisms for estimating and creating both speeds and time intervals. My point here is simply that the skill involved does not necessarily have anything to do with properties specific to a medium of visual imagery.

For the purpose of this account of the scanning results, we need assume little or nothing about intrinsic constraints on the process or about the form of the sequence of representations generated. It could be that the situation here is like that where a sequence of numbers is computed in conventional digital manner and displayed in analogue form. In that example, I claim that positing an analogue representation is theoretically irrelevant. A similar point applies here. We might, for instance, simply have a sequence consisting of a series of representations of the scene, each with a different location singled out in some manner. In that case, the representation's form is immaterial as far as the data at hand are concerned. For example, we could view the representations as a sequence of beliefs whose contents are something like that the spot is now *here*, and now it is *there*—where the locative demonstratives are pointers to parts of the symbolic representations being constructed and updated.

Although the sequence almost certainly is more complex than I have described it, we need not assume that it is constrained by a special property of the representational medium—as opposed simply to being governed by what subjects believe or infer about likely intermediate stages of the event being imagined and about the relative times at which they will occur. Now, such beliefs and inferences obviously can depend on anything the subject might tacitly know or believe concerning what usually happens in corresponding perceptual situations. Thus the sequence could, in one case, depend on tacit knowledge of the dynamics of physical objects, and, in another, on tacit knowledge of some aspects of eye movements or what happens when one must "glance up" or refocus on an object more distant, or even on tacit knowledge of the time required to notice or recognize certain kinds of visual patterns. For example, I would not be surprised, for this reason, to find that it took subjects longer to imagine trying to see something in dim light or against a camouflage background.

The Generality of the "Tacit Knowledge" View

The sort of "tacit knowledge" view I have been discussing has considerable generality in explaining various imagery research findings, especially when we take into account the plausibility that subjects are actually attempting to solve a problem of type 1b. For instance, the list of illustrative examples presented at the beginning of this chapter clearly show that, to imagine the episode of "seeing" certain physical events, one must have access to tacit knowledge of physical regularities. In some cases, it even seems reasonable that one needs an implicit theory, since a variety of related generalizations must be brought to bear to correctly predict what some imagined process will do (for example, the sugar solution or the color filter case). In other cases, the mere knowledge or recollection that certain things typically happen in certain ways, and that they take certain relative lengths of time suffices.

Several other findings, allegedly revealing properties of the mind's eye, might also be explainable on this basis, including the finding (Kosslyn 1975) that it takes longer to report properties of objects when the objects are imagined as being small. Consider that the usual way to inspect an object is to take up a viewing position at some convenient distance from the object that depends on the object's size and, in certain cases, other things as well (for example, consider imagining a deadly snake or a raging fire). So long as we have a reasonably good idea of the object's true size, we can imagine viewing it at the appropriate distance. Now, if someone told me to imagine an object as especially small, I might perhaps think of myself as being farther away or as seeing it through, say, the wrong end of a telescope. If I were then asked to do something, such as report some properties of the object, and if the instructions were to imagine that I could *see* the property I was reporting (which was the case in the experiments reported), or even if, for some obscure reason, I simply chose to make that my task, I would naturally try to imagine the occurrence of some real sequence of events in which I went from seeing the object as small to seeing it as large enough for me to easily discern details (that is, I probably would take the instructions as indicating I should carry out task 1b). In that case, I probably would imagine something that, in fact, is a plausible visual event, such as a zooming-in sequence (indeed, that is what many of Kosslyn's subjects reported). If such were the case, we would expect the time relations to be as they are actually observed.

Although this account may sound similar to the one given by some analogue theorists (for example, Kosslyn 1975), from a theoretical standpoint, there is one critical difference. In my account, no appeals need be made to knowledge-independent properties of the functional architecture, especially not to geometrical properties. No doubt, the architecture—what I have been calling the representational medium—has some relevant, intrinsic properties that restrict how things can be represented. These properties, however, appear to play no role in accounting for any phenomena we are considering. These phenomena can be viewed as arising from (a) subjects' tacit knowledge of how, in reality, things typically happen, and (b) subjects' ability to carry out such psychophysical tasks as generating time intervals that correspond to inferred durations of certain possible, physical events. This is not to deny the importance of different forms of representation, of certain inferential capacities, or of the nature of the underlying mechanisms; I am merely suggesting that these findings do not necessarily tell us anything about such matters.

Everyone intuitively feels that the visual image modality (format, or medium) severely constrains both the form and the content of potential representations; at the same time, it is no easy matter to state exactly what these constraints are (the informal examples already given should at least cast suspicion on the validity of such intuitions in general). For instance, it seems clear that we cannot image every object whose properties we can describe; this lends credence to the view that images are more constrained than descriptions. While it is doubtless true that imagery, in some sense, is not as flexible as such discursive symbol systems as language, it is crucial that we know the nature of this constraint if we are to determine whether it is a constraint imposed by the medium or is merely a habitual way of doing things or is related to our understanding of what it *means* to image something. It might even be a limitation attributable to the absence of certain knowledge or a failure to draw certain inferences. Once again, I would argue that we cannot tell a priori whether certain patterns which arise when we use imagery ought to be attributed to the character of the biological medium of representation (the analogue view), or whether they should be attributed to the subject's possession and use, either voluntary or habitual, of certain tacit knowledge.

Consider the following proposals made by Kosslyn et al. (1979) concerning the nature of the constraints on imagery. The authors take such constraints to be given by the intrinsic nature of the representational medium, suggesting that what they call the "surface display" (a reference to their cathode ray tube proto-model) gives imagery certain fixed characteristics. For example, they state,

> We predict that this component will not allow cognitive penetration: that a person's knowledge, beliefs, intentions, and so on will not alter the spatial structure that we believe the display has. Thus we predict that a person cannot at will make

his surface display four-dimensional, or non-Euclidean.... (Kosslyn et al. 1979 p. 549)

It does seem true that one cannot image a four-dimensional or non-Euclidean space; yet the very oddness of the supposition that we could do so should make us suspicious as to the reason. To understand why little can be concluded from this, let us suppose a subject insists that he or she could image a non-Euclidean space. Suppose further that mental scanning experiments are consistent with the subject's claim (for example, the scan time conforms to, say, a city block metric). Do we believe this subject, or do we conclude that what the subject really does is "simulate such properties in imagery by filling in the surface display with patterns of a certain sort, in the same way that projections of non-Euclidean surfaces can be depicted on two-dimensional Euclidean paper" (Kosslyn et al. 1979, p. 547)?

We, of course, conclude the latter. The reason we do so is exactly the same as that given for discounting a possible interpretation of what Mozart meant in claiming to be able to imagine a whole symphony "at once." That reason has to do solely with the implications of a particular sense of the phrase "imagine a symphony"—namely, that the task-1b sense demands that certain conditions be fulfilled. If we transpose this to the case of the spatial property of visual imagery, we can see that it is also the reason why the notion of imagining four-dimensional space in the sense of task 1b is incoherent. The point is sufficiently central that it merits a brief elaboration.

Let us first distinguish, as I have been insisting we should, between two senses of "imaging." The first sense of imagining (call it "$imagine_{think}$ X") means to think of X or to consider the hypothetical situation that X is the case or to mentally construct a symbolic model or a "description" of a "possible world" in which X is the case. The second sense of imagining (call this "$imagine_{see}$ X") means to imagine that you are seeing X or that you observe the actual event X as it occurs. Then the reason for the inadmissibility of four-dimensional or non-Euclidean imaginal space becomes clear, as does its irrelevance to the question of what properties an imaginal medium has. The reason we cannot $imagine_{see}$ such spaces is, they are not the sort of thing that can be seen. Our inability to $imagine_{see}$ such things has nothing to do with intrinsic properties of a "surface display" but, instead, with lack of a certain kind of knowledge: We do not know what it is like to see such a thing. For example, we have no idea what configuration of light and dark contours would be necessary, what visual features would need to appear, and so on. Presumably for similar reasons, congenitally color-blind people cannot $imagine_{see}$ a colored scene, in which case, it would hardly seem appropriate to attribute this failure to a defect in their "surface display." On the other hand, we do know, in nonvisual (that is, nonoptical) terms, what a non-Euclidean space is like, hence we might still be able to $imagine_{think}$ there being such a space in reality (certainly, Einstein did) and thus solve problems about it. Perhaps, given sufficient familiarity with the facts of such spaces, we could even produce mental scanning results in conformity with non-Euclidean geometries. There have been frequent reports of people who claim to have an intuitive grasp of four-dimensional space in the sense that they can, for instance, mentally rotate a four-dimensional tesseract and $imagine_{see}$ its three-dimensional projection from a new four-dimensional orientation (Hinton, 1906, provides an interesting discussion of what is involved). If this were true, these people might be able to do a four-dimensional version of the Shepard mental rotation task.

If one drops all talk about the *geometry* (that is, the "spatial character") of the display and considers the general point regarding the common conceptual constraints imposed on vision and imagery, there can be no argument: *something* is responsible for the way in which we cognize the world. Whatever that something is probably also explains both the way we see the world and how we image it. But that's as far as we can go. From this, we can no more draw conclusions about the geometry, topology, or other structural property of a representational medium than we can about the structure of a language by considering the structure of things that can be described in that language. There is no reason for believing that the relation is anything but conventional—which is precisely what the doctrine of functionalism claims (and what most of us implicitly believe).

The distinction between the two senses of *imagine* we discussed also serves to clarify why various empirical findings involving imagery tend to occur together. For example, Kosslyn et al. (1979), in their response section, provide a brief report on a study by Kosslyn, Jolicoeur, and Fliegel which shows that when stimuli are sorted according to whether subjects tend to visualize them in reporting certain of their properties, that is, whether subjects typically *imagine*$_{see}$ them in such tasks; then it is only those stimulus-property pairs that are classified as mental image evokers that yield the characteristic reaction time functions in mental scanning experiments. This is hardly surprising, since anything that leads certain stimuli habitually to be processed in the *imagine*$_{see}$ mode will naturally tend to exhibit numerous other characteristics associated with *imagine*$_{see}$ processing, including scanning time results and such phenomena as the "visual angle of the mind's eye" or the relation between latency and imagined size of objects (see the summary in Kosslyn et al. 1979). Of course, nobody knows why certain features of a stimulus or a task tend to elicit the *imagine*$_{see}$ habit, nor why some stimuli should do so more than others; but that is not a problem that distinguishes the analogue from the tacit knowledge view.

Some Empirical Evidence

Finally, it may be useful to consider some provisional evidence suggesting that subjects can be induced to use their visual image to perform a task such as 2a in a way that does not entail imagining oneself observing an actual sequence of events. Recall that the question is whether mental scanning effects (that is, the linear relation between time and distance) should be viewed as evidence for an intrinsic property of a representational medium or as evidence for, say, people's tacit knowledge of geometry and dynamics, as well as their understanding of the task. If the former interpretation is the correct one, then it must not merely be the case that people usually take longer to retrieve information about more distant objects in an imagined scene. That could arise, as already noted, merely from some habitual or preferred way of imagining or from a preferred interpretation of task demands. If the phenomenon is due to an intrinsic property of the imaginal medium, it must be a *necessary* consequence of using this medium; that is, the linear (or, at least, the monotonic) relation between time and distance represented must hold whenever information is accessed through the medium of imagery.

As it happens, there exists a strong preference for interpreting tasks involving doing something imaginally as tasks of type 1b—that is, as requiring one to *imagine*$_{see}$ an actual, physically realizable event happening over time. In most mental scanning cases it is the event of moving one's attention from place to place, or of witnessing something moving between two points. It could also involve imagining such episodes as drawing or extrapolating a line, and watching its progression. The question remains, however: *Must* a subject imagine such a physically realizable event in order to access information from an image or, more precisely, to produce an answer which the subject claims is based on an examination of the image?

A number of studies have been carried out in my laboratory suggesting that conditions can be set up which enable a subject to use an image to access information, yet which is done without the subject having to imagine the occurrence of a particular, real life, temporal event. That is, the subject can be induced to imagine$_{think}$ rather than imagine$_{see}$. For purposes of illustration, I mention two of these studies. The design of the experiments follows closely that of experiments reported in Kosslyn, Ball, and Reiser (1978). (See Pylyshyn 1981, for additional details, and Bannon 1981, for all the details of the design and analysis.) The subjects were required to memorize a map containing approximately seven visually distinct places (a church, castle, beach, and so on). Then they were asked to image the map in front of them and focus their attention on a particular named place, while keeping the rest of the map in view in their mind's eye. We then investigated various conditions under which the subjects were given different instructions concerning what to do next, all of which (a) emphasized that the task was to be carried out exclusively by consulting their image, and (b) required them to notice, on cue, a second named place on the map and to make some discriminatory response with respect to that place as quickly and as accurately as possible.

So far this description of the method is identical to that of the experiments by Kosslyn, Ball, and Reiser (1978). Indeed, when we instructed subjects to imagine a speck moving from the place of initial focus to another, named place, we obtained the same strongly linear relation between distance and reaction time as did Kosslyn, Ball, and Reiser. When, however, the instructions specified merely that subjects give the compass bearing of the second place—that is, to state whether the second place was north, northeast, east, southeast, and so on of the first, there was no relation between distance and reaction time. Similar results have also been obtained since by Finke and Pinker (1982).

These results suggest that it is possible to arrange a situation in which subjects use their image to retrieve information, yet where they do not feel compelled to imagine the event of scanning their attention between the two points—that is, to imagine$_{see}$. While this result is suggestive, it is by no means compelling, since it lacks controls for a number of alternative explanations. In particular, because a subject must, in any case, know the bearing of the second place on the map before scanning to it (even in Kosslyn's experiments), we might, for independent reasons, wish to claim that in this experiment the relative bearing of pairs of points on the map was retrieved from a symbolic, as opposed to an imaginal, representation, despite subjects' insistence that they did use their images in making judgments. Whereas this tends to weaken the imagery story somewhat (because it allows a crucial spatial property to be represented off the display and thus raises the question, Why not represent other spatial properties this way?, and because it discounts subjects' reports of how they were carrying out the task in this case while accepting such reports in other comparable situations), nonetheless, it is a possible avenue of retreat.

Consequently, another instructional condition was investigated, one aimed at making it more plausible to believe that subjects had to consult their image in order to make the response, while at the same time making it more compelling that they be focused on the second place and mentally "see" both the original and the second place at the time of the response. The only change in instructions made for this purpose was explicitly to require subjects to focus on the second place after they heard its name (for example, church) and, using it as the new origin, give the orientation of the first place (the place initially focused on) relative to the second. Thus the instructions strongly emphasized the necessity of focusing on the second place and the need actually to see both places before making an orientation judgment. Subjects were not told how to get to the second place from the first, only to keep the image before their mind's eye and use the image to read off the correct answer. In addition, for reasons to be mentioned, the same experiment was run (using a different group of subjects) entirely in the visual modality; thus, instead of having to image the map, subjects could actually examine the map in front of them.

What we found was that in the visual condition there is a significant correlation between response time (measured from the presentation of the name of the second place) and the distance between places, whereas in the imaginal condition no such relation holds. These results indicate clearly that even though the linear relation between distance and time (the "scanning phenomenon") is a frequent concomitant of imaging a transition between "seeing" two places on an image, it is not a necessary consequence of using the visual imagery modality, as it is in the case of actual visual perception; consequently, the linear-reaction time function is not due to an intrinsic (hence, knowledge- and goal-independent) property of the representational medium for visual images.

Such experiments demonstrate that image examination is unencumbered by at least one putative constraint of the "surface display" postulated by Kosslyn and others. Further, it is reasonable to expect other systematic relations between reaction time and image properties to disappear when appropriate instructions are given that are designed to encourage subjects to interpret the task as in 1a instead of 1b. For example, if subjects could be induced to generate what they consider small but highly detailed, clear images, the effect of image size on time to report the presence of features (Kosslyn, 1975) might disappear as well. There is evidence from one of Kosslyn's own studies that this might be the case. In a study reported in Kosslyn, Reiser, Farah, and Fliegel (1983), the time to retrieve information from images was found to be independent of image size. From the description of this experiment, it seems that a critical difference between it and earlier experiments (Kosslyn, 1975), in which an effect of image size was found, is that, here, subjects had time to study the actual objects, with instructions to practice generating equally clear images of each object. The subjects were also tested with the same instructions—which, I assume, encouraged them to entertain equally detailed images at all sizes.

Thus it seems possible, when subjects are encouraged to make available detailed information, they can put as fine a grain of detail as desired into their imaginal constructions, though, presumably, the total amount of information in the image remains limited along some dimension, if not the dimension of resolution. Unlike the case of real vision, such imaginal vision need not be limited by problems of grain or resolution or any other difficulty associated with making visual discriminations. As I have remarked, subjects can exhibit some of the behavioral characteristics associated with such limitations (for example taking longer to recall fine details); but that may be because the subjects know what real vision is like and are simulating it as best they can rather than because of the intrinsic nature of the imaginal medium.

Note

1. This claim is worded differently at different times, and depending on how careful Kosslyn is. Thus, in Kosslyn et al. (1979), it is put two different ways in two consecutive sentences. In the first, the authors claim that "these results seem to indicate that images do represent metrical distance"; in the second, they take the more radical approach, claiming that "images have spatial extent." (Kosslyn et al., p. 537) I contend that this vacillation between *representing* and *having* is no accident. Indeed, the attraction of the theory—what appears to give it a principled explanation—is the strong version (that images "have spatial extent"); but the only one that can be defended is the weaker version, a version, in fact,

indistinguishable from the tacit knowledge view I have been advocating. Computerization of the theory does not remove the equivocation: There are still two options on how to interpret the simulation—as a simulation of an analogue or a surface with "spatial extent," or as a simulation of the knowledge the subject possesses about space.

References

Attneave, F. 1974. "How Do You Know?", *American Psychologist* 29: 493–499.

Bannon, L. J. 1981. "An Investigation of Image Scanning: Theoretical Claims and Empirical Evidence," Ph.D. diss., University of Western Ontario. Ann Arbor, Mich.: University Microfilms, no. 81–50, 599.

Block, N. J., ed. 1981 *Imagery*. Cambridge, Mass.: MIT Press, a Bradford Book.

Finke, R. A., and S. Pinker. 1982. "Spontaneous Imagery Scanning in Mental Extrapolation," *Journal of Experimental Psychology: Learning, Memory, and Cognition* 8:2: 142–147.

Fraisse, P. 1963. *The Psychology of Time*. New York: Harper & Row.

Ghiselin, B. 1952. *The Creative Process*. New York: New American Library.

Kosslyn, S. M. 1973. "Scanning Visual Images: Some Structural Implications," *Perception and Psychophysics* 14: 90–94.

Kosslyn, S. M. 1975. "The Information Represented in Visual Images," *Cognitive Psychology* 7: 341–370.

Kosslyn, S. M. 1978. "Measuring the Visual Angle of the Mind's Eye," *Cognitive Psychology* 10: 356–389.

Kosslyn, S. M. 1980. *Image and Mind*. Cambridge, Mass.: Harvard Univ. Press.

Kosslyn, S. M., B. J. Reiser, M. J. Farah, and L. Fliegel. 1983. "Generating Visual Images: Units and Relations," *Journal of Experimental Psychology: General*, 112:2: 278–303.

Kosslyn, S. M., T. M. Ball, and B. J. Reiser. 1978. "Visual Images Preserve Metric Spatial Information: Evidence from Studies of Image Scanning," *Journal of Experimental Psychology: Human Perception and Performance* 4: 46–60.

Kosslyn, S. M., S. Pinker, G. Smith, and S. P. Shwartz. 1979. "On The Demystification of Mental Imagery," *Behavioral and Brain Sciences* 2:4: 535–548.

Newell, A., and H. A. Simon. 1972. *Human Problem Solving*. Englewood Cliffs, N. J.: Prentice-Hall.

Pylyshyn, Z. W. 1981. "The Imagery Debate: Analogue Media versus Tacit Knowledge," *Psychological Review* 88: 16–45.

Rosenthal, R., and R. L. Rosnow, eds. 1969. *Artifact in Behavioral Research*. New York: Academic Press.

Shepard, R. N., and L. A. Cooper. 1982. *Mental Images and Their Transformations*. Cambridge, Mass.: MIT Press, a Bradford Book.

Chapter 34

Demand Characteristics?: The Second Phase of the Debate

Stephen Kosslyn

The second phase of the debate began about eight years after the first, when Pylyshyn elaborated his views (Pylyshyn 1981). This phase of the debate focused on the data collected earlier. Whereas the proponents of depictive representation claimed that the data reflected the processing of depictive representations, the propositionalists now focused on possible methodological problems with the experiments. Two such problems were raised: "experimenter expectancy effects" and "task demands."

Intons-Peterson (1983) performed an experiment in which she compared scanning images to scanning physically present displays. Half of the experimenters were told that the image scanning should be faster and half were told that the perceptual scanning should be faster. She found that the experimenters' expectations influenced the results: when experimenters expected faster perceptual scanning, the subjects produced this result; when they expected faster image scanning, there was no difference in overall times. Thus, the experimenters were somehow leading the subjects to respond as the experimenters expected.

Jolicoeur and Kosslyn (1985) decided to test the idea that the increases in times with increasing distance scanned reflect the subjects' responding to experimenter expectancy effects. We performed a series of experiments using Intons-Peterson's methodology. For example, we told one experimenter that we expected a U-shaped function, with the most time being required to scan the shortest and longest distances. The reason for this prediction, we explained, was that the four closest objects "group" into a single chunk—because of the Gestalt laws of similarity and proximity—and so they are "cluttered" together, making it difficult to scan among them. And the longest distances require more time than the medium ones because more scanning is involved.

The results from this experiment were identical to those found previously: times increased linearly with increasing distance. In additional experiments Jolicoeur and Kosslyn varied experimenter expectancy in different ways, none of which affected scan times. Indeed, these experimenters failed to replicate Intons-Peterson's original finding. What could be going on here? Many details of such experiments can differ from laboratory to laboratory (for instance, making sure subjects always keep their fingers on the response buttons), and these details could be critical for obtaining experimenter expectancy effects. The important point is that, whatever caused the experimenter expectancy effect in Intons-Peterson's study, it was not present in the procedures used in the initial studies of image scanning. Thus, these results cannot be explained away as simply reflecting how well subjects can satisfy the expectations of the experimenter.

Taking an alternative tack, Pylyshyn (1981) claimed that the very instruction to scan an image induces subjects to pretend to scan an actual object—which leads them to take more time to respond when they think they would have taken more time to scan across a visible object. The way the subjects estimate how long to wait (unconsciously) would involve propositional processing of some sort.

This potential concern was ruled out by image-scanning experiments that eliminated all references to imagery in the instructions. Finke and Pinker (1982, 1983; see also Pinker, Choate, and Finke 1984) showed subjects a set of random dots on a card, removed the card, and presented an arrow. The question was, if the arrow were superimposed over the card containing the dots, would it point directly at a dot? Subjects reported using imagery to perform this task, and Finke and Pinker found that the response times increased linearly with increasing distance from the arrow to a dot. Furthermore, the rate of increase in time with distance was almost identical to what we had found in our earlier experiments. Because no imagery instructions were used, let alone mention of scanning an image, a task-demands explanation seems highly implausible.

Goldston, Hinrichs, and Richman (1985) actually went so far as to tell the subjects the predictions, which is never done in typical psychological experiments. Even when subjects were told that the experimenter expected longer times with shorter distances, they still displayed increased times with distance scanned. Telling subjects different predictions did affect the degree of the increase with distance, but this result is not surprising: given the purposes of imagery, one had better be able to control imaged events! What is impressive is that even when subjects were, if anything, trying for the opposite result, they still took longer to scan across longer distances.

Finally, Denis and Carfantan (1985) described the basic scanning experiment to naive subjects and asked them to predict the outcome. Although these subjects were good at predicting many of the effects of imagery (for example, that it will help one to memorize information), they were very poor at predicting the results of scanning experiments and the like. If subjects are using knowledge about perception and physics to "fake" the data in the experiments, it is puzzling that they evince no such knowledge in this situation.

Bibliography

Anderson, J., and Bower, G. 1973. *Human Associative Memory.* New York: V. H. Winston and Sons.

Denis, M. and M. Carfantan. 1985. People's knowledge about images. *Cognition* 20: 49–60.

Finke, R. A., and S. Pinker. 1982. Spontaneous imagery scanning in mental extrapolation. *Journal of Experimental Psychology: Human Learning and Memory* 8: 142–147.

Finke, R. A., and S. Pinker. 1983. Directional scanning of remembered visual patterns. *Journal of Experimental Psychology: Learning, Memory, and Cognition* 9: 398–410.

Goldston, D. B., J. V. Hinrichs, and C. L. Richman. 1985. Subject's expectations, individual variability, and the scanning of mental images. *Memory and Cognition* 13: 365–370.

Intons-Peterson, M. J. 1983. Imagery paradigms: How vulnerable are they to experimenters' expectations? *Journal of Experimental Psychology: Human Perception and Performance* 9: 394–412.

Jolicoeur, P., and S. M. Kosslyn. 1985. Is time to scan images due to demand characterisitics? *Memory and Cognition* 13: 320–332.

Kosslyn, S. M. 1973. Scanning visual images: Some structural implications. *Perception and Psychophysics* 14: 90–94.

Kosslyn, S. M., Ball, T. M., and B. J. Reiser. 1978. Visual images preserve metric spatial information: Evidence from studies of image scanning. *Journal of Experimental Psychology: Human Perception and Performance* 4: 47–60.

Lea, G. 1975. Chronometric analysis of the method of loci. *Journal of Experimental Psychology: Human Perception and Performance* 2: 95–104.

Pinker, S. 1980. Mental imagery and the third dimension. *Journal of Experimental Psychology: General* 109: 354–371.

Pinker, S., P. A. Choate, and R. A. Finke. 1984. Mental extrapolation in patterns constructed from memory. *Memory and Cognition* 12: 207–218.

Pylyshyn, Z. 1973. What the mind's eye tells the mind's brain: A critique of mental imagery. *Psychological Bulletin* 80: 1–24.

Pylyshyn, Z. 1981. The imagery debate: Analogue media versus tacit knowledge. *Psychological Review* 87: 16–45.

Part IV

Associationism/Connectionism

Introduction

Connectionism is a loosely organized research program involving researchers in computer science, psychology, and in some cases neurobiology. The research program has received considerable attention both in academia and the popular press, and is sometimes touted as a radical breakthrough in our understanding of the human mind. On the other hand, there are those who argue that connectionism is nothing more than "high tech" Lockean associationism. In fact, the truth probably lies somewhere between these positions. Careful study of associationist and connectionist writings reveals not only marked differences, but a number of fundamental similarities as well.

The basic idea underlying associationism certainly is not new (it can be found in Aristotle, according to some). We begin with Thomas Hobbes, who is interested in giving an account of our train of thinking. The section contains a famous passage in which Hobbes shows how the discussion of a civil war could be causally related to someone asking the price of a Roman penny. The idea of the war triggers a sequence of related or connected ideas, resulting in the seemingly anomalous question.

John Locke develops the associationist doctrine somewhat, arguing that some ideas come to be associated by natural connections holding between them while other ideas come to be associated through custom (education, interests, etc.). Locke also argues that association can account for certain kinds of pathological thinking. For example, if one has a bad experience in a particular room, one might be unable to enter the room again without thinking of the experience. This is because the ideas of the room and the experience will have become inextricably associated. David Hume proposes certain additional principles that govern the association of ideas: resemblance, contiguity, and cause and effect.

Willam James gives a helpful survey of work in associationist psychology and addresses two very important issues: the question of whether any general associative principle might underlie the proposed associationist laws, and the question of whether neural mechanisms underlie associationist psychology. James thus anticipates those contemporary philosophers who take connectionism to be grounded in neural mechanisms.

We begin the contemporary debate with an introduction (by James McClelland, David Rumelhart, and Geoffrey Hinton) to a version of connectionism known as parallel distributed processing (PDP). While these writers do not make explicit reference to the early associationist psychologists, it is clear that they share certain fundamental views. In PDP models of memory, for example, properties might be associated with mutually excitatory units (processors). So, if a unit representing René Descartes were activated, there might be a corresponding excitation of a unit representing the property of being a philosopher, or the property of being French. The connection strengths between units within the network are set by training the network with a general learning algorithm that may be considered a descendent of the principles first enunciated by Locke, Hume, and subsequent associationists.

The PDP perspective stands in marked contrast to what is sometimes called the classical theory of computation, in which computation consists of formal operations on complex syntactic objects. For example, on the classical view the inference from the sentence P&Q to the sentence P is executed by a formal mechanism sensitive only to the syntactic form of P&Q. Jerry Fodor and Zenon Pylyshyn take strong exception to the PDP paradigm, suggesting that there are several reasons for preferring the classical theory. They argue that PDP models, by eschewing structure-sensitive processes, give up the ability to account for a number of phenomena including (i) the productivity of human linguistic processes (i.e., the ability to create and comprehend sentences of unbounded length like "This is the cat that ate the rat that lived in the house that...."), (ii) systematicity (understanding "Jack likes Jill" entails understanding "Jill likes Jack"), (iii) compositionality (the meaning of a sentence is a function of the meaning of its parts), and (iv) inferential coherence (inferences from, e.g., P&Q to P).

Paul Smolensky is unconvinced that these arguments pose a problem for connectionism. Smolensky notes that the kinds of problems raised by Fodor and Pylyshyn do not argue against connectionist treatments of "soft" mental processes but merely its ability to handle "hard" processes such as logical inference as well. Smolensky concedes that there are structure-sensitive processes, speculating that they need not be handled in a classical model but could be accounted for by supposing that "the mind is a statistics-sensitive engine operating on structure-sensitive numerical representations."

Claims and counterclaims regarding PDP systems abound today, but Seymour Papert offers some deflationary remarks. He notes that the mathematical properties of PDP networks have yet to be explored and suggests that even for very simple ancestors of these networks, the actual properties are difficult to determine, and once determined, often unexpected. The abilities of full-blown connectionist systems (as opposed to toy implementations) are simply unknown.

Further Reading

Some classical works in associationist psychology:

Hartley, D. 1749. *Observations on Man, His Frame, His Duty, and His Expectations*. London.
Hebb, C. O. 1949. *The Organization of Behavior*. New York: John Wiley.
Mandler, G., and Mandler, J., eds. 1964. *Thinking: From Association to Gestalt*. New York: John Wiley.
Mill, J. 1829. *Analysis of the Phenomena of the Human Mind*. London.

Some further reading on connectionism:

Bechtel, W., and A. Abrahamson. 1990. *Connectionism and the Mind: An Introduction to Parallel Processing Networks*. Oxford: Basil Blackwell.
Fodor, J., and B. McLaughlin. 1990. "Connectionism and the Problem of Systematicity: Why Smolensky's Solution Doesn't Work." *Cognition* 35, 183–204.
Minsky, M., and S. Papert. 1986. *Perceptrons*. Expanded edition. Cambridge, MA: MIT Press.
Rumelhart, D., J. McClelland, and the PDP Research Group. 1986. *Parallel Distributed Processing*, vol. 1. Cambridge, MA: MIT Press.
McClelland, J., D. Rumelhart, and the PDP Research Group. 1986. *Parallel Distributed Processing*, vol. 2. Cambridge, MA: MIT Press.

Chapter 35

Of the Consequence or Train of Imaginations

Thomas Hobbes

By *consequence*, or *train of thoughts*, I understand that succession of one thought to another, which is called, to distinguish it from discourse in words, *mental discourse*.

When a man thinks on any thing whatsoever, his next thought after, is not altogether so casual as it seems to be. Not every thought to every thought succeeds indifferently. But as we have no imagination, whereof we have not formerly had sense, in whole, or in parts; so we have no transition from one imagination to another, whereof we never had the like before in our senses. The reason whereof is this. All fancies are motions within us, relics of those made in the sense: and those motions that immediately succeeded one another in the sense, continue also together after sense: insomuch as the former coming again to take place, and be predominant, the latter follows, by coherence of the matter moved, in such manner, as water upon a plane table is drawn which way any one part of it is guided by the finger. But because in sense, to one and the same thing perceived, sometimes one thing, sometimes another succeeds, it comes to pass in time, that in the imagining of any thing, there is no certainty what we shall imagine next; only this is certain, it shall be something that succeeded the same before, at one time or another.

Train of Thoughts Unguided

This train of thoughts, or mental discourse, is of two sorts. The first is *unguided, without design*, and inconstant; wherein there is no passionate thought, to govern and direct those that follow, to itself, as the end and scope of some desire, or other passion: in which case the thoughts are said to wander, and seem impertinent one to another, as in a dream. Such are commonly the thoughts of men, that are not only without company, but also without care of any thing; though even then their thoughts are as busy as at other times, but without harmony; as the sound which a lute out of tune would yield to any man; or in tune, to one that could not play. And yet in this wild ranging of the mind, a man may oft-times perceive the way of it, and the dependence of one thought upon another. For in a discourse of our present civil war, what could seem more impertinent, than to ask, as one did, what was the value of a Roman penny? Yet the coherence to me was manifest enough. For the thought of the war, introduced the thought of the delivering up the king to his enemies; the thought of that, brought in the thought of the delivering up of Christ; and that again the thought of the thirty pence, which was the price of that treason; and thence easily followed that malicious question, and all this in a moment of time; for thought is quick.

Train of Thoughts Regulated

The second is more constant; as being *regulated* by some desire, and design. For the impression made by such things as we desire, or fear, is strong, and permanent, or, if it cease for a time, of quick return: so strong it is sometimes, as to hinder and break our sleep. From desire, arises the thought of some means we have seen produce the like of that which we aim at; and from the thought of that, the thought of means to that mean; and so continually, till we come to some beginning within our own power. And because the end, by the greatness of the impression, comes often to mind, in case our thoughts begin to wander, they are quickly again reduced into the way: which observed by one of the seven wise men, made him give men this precept, which is now worn out, *Respice finem*; that is to say, in all your actions, look often upon what you would have, as the thing that directs all your thoughts in the way to attain it.

Remembrance

The train of regulated thoughts is of two kinds; one, when of an effect imagined we seek the causes, or means that produce it: and this is common to man and beast. The other is, when imagining any thing whatsoever, we seek all the possible effects, that can by it be produced; that is to say, we imagine what we can do with it, when we have it. Of which I have not at any time seen any sign, but in man only; for this is a curiosity hardly incident to the nature of any living creature that has no other passion but sensual, such as are hunger, thirst, lust, and anger. In sum, the discourse of the mind, when it is governed by design, is nothing but *seeking*, or the faculty of invention, which the Latins called *sagacitas*, and *solertia*; a hunting out of the causes, of some effect, present or past; or of the effects, of some present or past cause. Sometimes a man seeks what he has lost; and from that place, and time, wherein he misses it, his mind runs back, from place to place, and time to time, to find where, and when he had it; that is to say, to find some certain, and limited time and place, in which to begin a method of seeking. Again, from thence, his thoughts run over the same places and times, to find what action, or other occasion might make him lose it. This we call *remembrance*, or calling to mind: the Latins call it *reminiscentia*, as it were a *re-conning* of our former actions.

Sometimes a man knows a place determinate, within the compass whereof he is to seek; and then his thoughts run over all the parts thereof, in the same manner as one would sweep a room, to find a jewel; or as a spaniel ranges the field, till he find a scent; or as a man should run over the alphabet, to start a rhyme.

Prudence

Sometimes a man desires to know the event of an action; and then he thinks of some like action past, and the events thereof one after another; supposing like events will follow like actions. As he that foresees what will become of a criminal, re-cons what he has seen follow on the like crime before; having this order of thoughts, the crime, the officer, the prison, the judge, and the gallows. Which kind of thoughts, is called *foresight*, and *prudence*, or *providence*; and sometimes *wisdom*; though such conjecture, through the difficulty of observing all circumstances, be very fallacious. But this is certain; by how much one man has more experience of things past, than another, by so much also he is more prudent, and his expectations the seldomer fail him. The *present* only has a being in nature; things *past* have a being in the memory only, but things *to come* have no being at all; the *future* being but a fiction of the mind, applying the sequels of actions past, to the actions that are present; which with most certainty is done by him that has most experience, but not with certainty enough. And though it be called prudence, when the event answers our expectation; yet in its own nature, it is but presumption. For the foresight of things to come, which is providence, belongs only to him by whose will they are to come. From him only, and supernaturally, proceeds prophecy. The best prophet naturally is the best guesser; and the best guesser, he that is most versed and studied in the matters he guesses at: for he has most *signs* to guess by.

Signs

A *sign* is the evident antecedent of the consequent; and contrarily, the consequent of the antecedent, when the like consequences have been observed, before: and the oftener they have been observed, the less uncertain is the sign. And therefore he that has most experience in any kind of business, has most signs, whereby to guess at the future time; and consequently is the most prudent: and so much more prudent than he that is new in that kind of business, as not to be equalled by any advantage of natural and extemporary wit: though perhaps many young men think the contrary.

Nevertheless it is not prudence that distinguisheth man from beast. There be beasts, that at a year old observe more, and pursue that which is for their good, more prudently, than a child can do at ten.

Conjecture of the Time Past

As prudence is a *presumption* of the *future*, contracted from the *experience* of time *past*: so there is a presumption of things past taken from other things, not future, but past also. For he that hath seen by what courses and degrees a flourishing state hath first come into civil war, and then to ruin; upon the sight of the ruins of any other state, will guess, the like war, and the like courses have been there also. But this conjecture, has the same uncertainty almost with the conjecture of the future; both being grounded only upon experience.

There is no other act of man's mind, that I can remember, naturally planted in him, so as to need no other thing, to the exercise of it, but to be born a man, and live with the use of his five senses. Those other faculties, of which I shall speak by and by, and which seem proper to man only, are acquired and increased by study and industry; and of most men learned by instruction, and discipline; and proceed all from the invention of words, and speech. For besides sense, and thoughts, and the train of thoughts, the mind of man has no other motion; though by the help of speech, and method, the same faculties may be improved to such a height, as to distinguish men from all other living creatures.

Infinite

Whatsoever we imagine is *finite*. Therefore there is no idea, or conception of any thing we call *infinite*. No man can have in his mind an image of infinite magnitude; nor conceive infinite swiftness, infinite time, or infinite force, or infinite power. When we say any thing is infinite, we signify only, that we are not able to conceive the ends, and bounds of the things named; having no conception of the thing, but of our own inability. And therefore the name of God is used, not to make us conceive him, for he is incomprehensible; and his greatness, and power are unconceivable; but that we may honour him. Also because, whatsoever, as I said before, we conceive, has been perceived first by sense, either all at once, or by parts; a man can have no thought, representing any thing, not subject to sense. No man therefore can conceive any thing, but he must conceive it in some place; and endued with some determinate magnitude; and which may be divided into parts; nor that any thing is all in this place, and all in another place at the same time; nor that two, or more things can be in one, and the same place at once: for none of these things ever have, nor can be incident to sense; but are absurd speeches, taken upon credit, without any signification at all, from deceived philosophers, and deceived, or deceiving Schoolmen.

Chapter 36

Of the Association of Ideas

John Locke

There is scarce any one that does not observe something that seems odd to him, and is in it self really Extravagant in the Opinions, Reasonings, and Actions of other Men. The least flaw of this kind, if at all different from his own, every one is quick-sighted enough to espie in another, and will by the Authority of Reason forwardly condemn, though he be guilty of much greater Unreasonableness in his own Tenets and Conduct, which he never perceives, and will very hardly, if at all, be convinced of.

This proceeds not wholly from Self-love, though that has often a great hand in it. Men of fair Minds, and not given up to the over weening of Self-flattery, are frequently guilty of it; and in many Cases one with amazement hears the Arguings, and is astonish'd at the Obstinacy of a worthy Man, who yields not to the Evidence of Reason, though laid before him as clear as Day-light.

This sort of Unreasonableness is usually imputed to Education and Prejudice, and for the most part truly enough, though that reaches not the bottom of the Disease, nor shews distinctly enough whence it rises, or wherein it lies. Education is often rightly assigned for the Cause, and Prejudice is a good general Name for the thing it self: But yet, I think, he ought to look a little farther who would trace this sort of Madness to the root it springs from, and so explain it, as to shew whence this flaw has its Original in very sober and rational Minds, and wherein it consists.

I shall be pardon'd for calling it by so harsh a name as *Madness*, when it is considered, that opposition to Reason deserves that Name, and is really Madness; and there is scarce a Man so free from it, but that if he should always on all occasions argue or do as in some cases he constantly does, would not be thought fitter for *Bedlam*, than Civil Conversation. I do not here mean when he is under the power of an unruly Passion, but in the steady calm course of his Life. That which will yet more apologize for this harsh Name, and ungrateful Imputation on the greatest part of Mankind is, that enquiring a little by the bye into the Nature of Madness, I found it to spring from the very same Root, and to depend on the very same Cause we are here speaking of. This consideration of the thing it self, at a time when I thought not the least on the Subject which I am now treating of, suggested it to me. And if this be a Weakness to which all Men are so liable; if this be a Taint which so universally infects Mankind, the greater care should be taken to lay it open under its due Name, thereby to excite the greater care in its Prevention and Cure.

Some of our *Ideal* have a natural Correspondence and Connexion one with another: It is the Office and Excellency of our Reason to trace these, and hold them together in that Union and Correspondence which is founded in their peculiar Beings. Besides this there is another Connexion of *Ideas* wholly owing to Chance or Custom; *Ideas* that in themselves are not at all of kin, come to be so united in some Mens Minds, that 'tis very hard to separate them, they always keep in company, and the one no sooner at any time comes into the Understanding but its Associate appears with it; and if they are more than two which are thus united, the whole gang always inseparable shew themselves together.

This strong Combination of *Ideas*, not ally'd by Nature, the Mind makes in it self either voluntarily, or by chance, and hence it comes in different Men to be very different, according to their different Inclinations, Educations, Interests, *etc.* Custom settles habits of Thinking in the Understanding, as well as of Determining in the Will, and of Motions in the Body; all which seems to be but Trains of Motion in the Animal Spirits, which once set a going continue on in the same steps they have been used to, which by often treading are worn into a smooth path, and the Motion in it becomes easy and as it were Natural. As far as we can comprehend Thinking, thus *Ideas* seem to be produced in our Minds; or if they are not, this may serve to explain their following one another in an habitual train, when once they are put into that tract, as well as it does to explain such Motions of the Body. A Musician used to any Tune will find that let it but once begin in his Head, the *Ideas* of the several Notes of it will follow one another orderly in his Understanding without any care or attention, as regularly as his Fingers move orderly over the Keys of the Organ to play out the Tune he has begun, though his unattentive Thoughts be elsewhere a wandering. Whether the natural cause of these *Ideas*, as well as of that regular Dancing of his Fingers be the Motion of his Animal Spirits, I will not determine, how probable soever by this Instance it appears to be so: But this may help us a little to conceive of Intellectual Habits, and of the tying together of *Ideas*.

That there are such Associations of them made by Custom in the Minds of most Men, I think no Body will question who has well consider'd himself or others; and to this, perhaps, might be justly attributed most of the Sympathies and Antipathies observable in Men, which work as strongly, and produce as regular Effects as if they were Natural, and are therefore called so, though they at first had no other Original but the accidental Connexion of two *Ideas*, which either the strength of the first Impression, or future Indulgence so united, that they always afterwards kept company together in that Man's Mind, as if they were but one *Idea*. I say most of the Antipathies, I do not say all, for some of them are truly Natural, depend upon our original Constitution, and are born with us; but a great part of those which are counted Natural, would have been known to be from unheeded, though, perhaps, early Impressions, or wanton Phancies at first, which would have been acknowledged the Original of them if they had been warily observed. A grown Person surfeiting with Honey, no sooner hears the Name of it, but his Phancy immediately carries Sickness and Qualms to his Stomach, and he cannot bear the very *Idea* of it; other *Ideas* of Dislike and Sickness, and Vomiting presently accompany it, and he is disturb'd, but he knows from whence to date this Weakness, and can tell how he got this Indisposition: Had this happen'd to him, by an over dose of Honey, when a Child, all the same Effects would have followed, but the Cause would have been mistaken, and the Antipathy counted Natural.

I mention this not out of any great necessity there is in this present Argument, to distinguish nicely between Natural and Acquired Antipathies, but I take notice of it for another purpose, (*viz.*) that those who have Children, or the charge of their Education, would think it worth their while diligently to watch, and carefully to prevent the undue Connexion of *Ideas* in the Minds of young People. This is the time most susceptible of lasting Impressions, and though those relating to the Health of the Body, are by discreet People minded and fenced against, yet I am apt to doubt, that those which relate more peculiarly to the Mind, and terminate in the Understanding, or Passions, have been much less heeded than the thing deserves; nay, those relating purely to the Understanding have, as I suspect, been by most Men wholly over-look'd.

This wrong Connexion in our Minds of *Ideas* in themselves, loose and independent one of another, has such an influence, and is of so great force to set us awry in our Actions, as well Moral as Natural, Passions, Reasonings, and Notions themselves, that, perhaps, there is not any one thing that deserves more to be looked after.

The *Ideas* of *Goblines* and *Sprights* have really no more to do with Darkness than Light; yet let but a foolish Maid inculcate these often on the Mind of a Child, and raise them there together, possibly he shall never be able to separate them again so long as he lives, but Darkness shall ever afterwards bring with it those frightful *Ideas*, and they shall be so joined that he can no more bear the one than the other.

A Man receives a sensible Injury from another, thinks on the Man and that Action over and over, and by ruminating on them strongly, or much in his Mind, so cements those two *Ideas* together, that he makes them almost one; never thinks on the Man, but the Pain and Displeasure he suffered comes into his Mind with it, so that he scarce distinguishes them, but has as much an aversion for the one as the other. Thus Hatreds are often begotten from slight and almost innocent Occasions, and Quarrels propagated and continued in the World.

A Man has suffered Pain or Sickness in any Place, he saw his Friend die in such a Room; though these have in Nature nothing to do one with another, yet when the *Idea* of the Place occurs to his Mind, it brings (the Impression being once made) that of the Pain and Displeasure with it, he confounds them in his Mind, and can as little bear the one as the other.

When this Combination is settled and whilst it lasts, it is not in the power of Reason to help us, and relieve us from the Effects of it. *Ideas* in our Minds, when they are there, will operate according to their Natures and Circumstances; and here we see the cause why Time cures certain Affections, which Reason, though in the right, and allow'd to be so, has not power over, nor is able against them to prevail with those who are apt to hearken to it in other cases. The Death of a Child, that was the daily delight of his Mother's Eyes, and joy of her Soul, rends from her Heart the whole comfort of her Life, and gives her all the torment imaginable; use the Consolations of Reason in this case, and you were as good preach Ease to one on the Rack, and hope to allay, by rational Discourses, the Pain of his Joints tearing asunder. Till time has by disuse separated the sense of that Enjoyment and its loss from the *Idea* of the Child returning to her Memory, all Representations, though never so reasonable, are in vain; and therefore some in whom the union between these *Ideas* is never dissolved, spend their Lives in Mourning, and carry an incurable Sorrow to their Graves.

A Friend of mine knew one perfectly cured of Madness by a very harsh and offensive Operation. The Gentleman, who was thus recovered, with great sense of Gratitude and Acknowledgment, owned the Cure all his Life after, as the greatest Obligation he could have received; but whatever Gratitude and Reason suggested to him, he could never bear the sight of the Operator: That Image brought back with it the *Idea* of that Agony which he suffer'd from his Hands, which was too mighty and intolerable for him to endure.

Many Children imputing the Pain they endured at School to their Books they were corrected for, so joyn those *Ideas* together, that a Book becomes their Aversion, and they are never reconciled to the study and use of them all their Lives after; and thus Reading becomes a torment to them, which otherwise possibly they might have made the great Pleasure of their Lives. There are Rooms convenient enough, that some Men cannot Study in, and fashions of Vessels, which though never so clean and commodious they cannot Drink out of, and that by reason of some accidental *Ideas* which are annex'd to them, and make them offensive; and who is there that hath not observed some Man to flag at the appearance, or in the company of some certain Person not otherwise superior to him, but because having once on some occasion got the Ascendant, the *Idea* of Authority and Distance goes along with that of the Person, and he that has been thus subjected is not able to separate them.

Chapter 37

Of the Connection or Association of Ideas

David Hume

As all simple ideas may be separated by the imagination, and may be united again in what form it pleases, nothing wou'd be more unaccountable than the operations of that faculty, were it not guided by some universal principles, which render it, in some measure, uniform with itself in all times and places. Were ideas entirely loose and unconnected, chance alone would join them; and 'tis impossible the same simple ideas should fall regularly into complex ones (as they commonly do) without some bond of union among them, some associating quality, by which one idea naturally introduces another. This uniting principle among ideas is not to be consider'd as an inseparable connexion; for that has been already excluded from the imagination: Nor yet are we to conclude, that without it the mind cannot join two ideas; for nothing is more free than that faculty: but we are only to regard it as a gentle force, which commonly prevails, and is the cause why, among other things, languages so nearly correspond to each other; nature in a manner pointing out to every one those simple ideas, which are most proper to be united in a complex one. The qualities, from which this association arises, and by which the mind is after this manner convey'd from one idea to another, are three, *viz.* RESEMBLANCE, CONTIGUITY in time or place, and CAUSE and EFFECT.

I believe it will not be very necessary to prove, that these qualities produce an association among ideas, and upon the appearance of one idea naturally introduce another. 'Tis plain, that in the course of our thinking, and in the constant revolution of our ideas, our imagination runs easily from one idea to any other that *resembles* it, and that this quality alone is to the fancy a sufficient bond and association. 'Tis likewise evident, that as the senses, in changing their objects, are necessitated to change them regularly, and take them as they lie *contiguous* to each other, the imagination must by long custom acquire the same method of thinking, and run along the parts of space and time in conceiving its objects. As to the connexion, that is made by the relation of *cause and effect*, we shall have occasion afterwards to examine it to the bottom, and therefore shall not at present insist upon it. 'Tis sufficient to observe, that there is no relation, which produces a stronger connexion in the fancy, and makes one idea more readily recall another, than the relation of cause and effect betwixt their objects.

That we may understand the full extent of these relations, we must consider, that two objects are connected together in the imagination, not only when the one is immediately resembling, contiguous to, or the cause of the other, but also when there is interposed betwixt them a third object, which bears to both of them any of these relations. This may be carried on to a great length; tho' at the same time we may observe, that each remove considerably weakens the relation. Cousins in the fourth degree are connected by *causation*, if I may be allowed to use that term; but not so closely as brothers, much less as child and parent. In general we may observe, that all the relations of blood depend upon cause and effect, and are esteemed near or remote, according to the number of connecting causes interpos'd betwixt the persons.

Of the three relations above-mention'd this of causation is the most extensive. Two objects may be consider'd as plac'd in this relation, as well when one is the cause of any of the actions or motions of the other, as when the former is the cause of the existence of the latter. For as that action or motion is nothing but the object itself, consider'd in a certain light, and as the object continues the same in all its different situations, 'tis easy to imagine how such an influence of objects upon one another may connect them in the imagination.

We may carry this farther, and remark, not only that two objects are connected by the relation of cause and effect, when the one produces a motion or any action in the other, but also when it has a power of producing it. And this we may observe to be the source of all the relations of interest and duty, by which men influence each other in society, and are plac'd in the ties of government and subordination. A master is such-a-one as by his situation, arising either from force or agreement, has a power of directing in certain particulars the actions of another, whom we call servant. A judge is one, who in all disputed cases can fix by his opinion the possession or property of any thing betwixt any members of the society. When a person is possess'd of any power, there is no more required to convert it into action, but the exertion of the will; and *that* in every case is consider'd as possible, and in many as probable; especially in the case of authority, where the obedience of the subject is a pleasure and advantage to the superior.

These are therefore the principles of union or cohesion among our simple ideas, and in the imagination supply the place of that inseparable connexion, by which they are united in our memory. Here is a kind of ATTRACTION, which in the mental world will be found to have as extraordinary effects as in the natural, and to shew itself in as many and as various forms. Its effects are every where conspicuous; but as to its causes, they are mostly unknown, and must be resolv'd into *original* qualities of human nature, which I pretend not to explain. Nothing is more requisite for a true philosopher, than to restrain the intemperate desire of searching into causes, and having establish'd any doctrine upon a sufficient number of experiments, rest contented with that, when he sees a farther examination would lead him into obscure and uncertain speculations. In that case his enquiry wou'd be much better employ'd in examining the effects than the causes of his principle.

Amongst the effects of this union or association of ideas, there are none more remarkable, than those complex ideas, which are the common subjects of our thoughts and reasoning, and generally arise from some principle of union among our simple ideas. These complex ideas may be divided into *Relations, Modes,* and *Substances.* We shall briefly examine each of these in order, and shall subjoin some considerations concerning our *general* and *particular* ideas, before we leave the present subject, which may be consider'd as the elements of this philosophy.

Chapter 38

The Principal Investigations of Psychology Characterised

John Stuart Mill

The subject, then, of Psychology is the uniformities of succession, the laws, whether ultimate or derivative, according to which one mental state succeeds another—is caused by, or at least is caused to follow, another. Of these laws, some are general, others more special. The following are examples of the most general laws.

First, whenever any state of consciousness has once been excited in us, no matter by what cause, an inferior degree of the same state of consciousness, a state of consciousness resembling the former, but inferior in intensity, is capable of being reproduced in us, without the presence of any such cause as excited it at first. Thus, if we have once seen or touched an object, we can afterwards think of the object though it be absent from our sight or from our touch. If we have been joyful or grieved at some event, we can think of or remember our past joy or grief, though no new event of a happy or painful nature has taken place. When a poet has put together a mental picture of an imaginary object, a Castle of Indolence, a Una, or a Hamlet, he can afterwards think of the ideal object he has created without any fresh act of intellectual combination. This law is expressed by saying, in the language of Hume, that every mental *impression* has its *idea*.

Secondly, these ideas, or secondary mental states, are excited by our impressions, or by other ideas, according to certain laws which are called Laws of Association. Of these laws the first is, that similar ideas tend to excite one another. The second is, that when two impressions have been frequently experienced (or even thought of), either simultaneously or in immediate succession, then whenever one of these impressions, or the idea of it, recurs, it tends to excite the idea of the other. The third law is, that greater intensity in either or both of the impressions is equivalent, in rendering them excitable by one another, to a greater frequency of conjunction. These are the laws of ideas, on which I shall not enlarge in this place, but refer the reader to works professedly psychological, in particular to Mr. James Mill's *Analysis of the Phenomena of the Human Mind*, where the principal laws of association, along with many of their applications, are copiously exemplified, and with masterly hand.[1]

These simple or elementary Laws of Mind have been ascertained by the ordinary methods of experimental inquiry; nor could they have been ascertained in any other manner. But a certain number of elementary laws having thus been obtained, it is a fair subject of scientific inquiry how far those laws can be made to go in explaining the actual phenomena. It is obvious that complex laws of thought and feeling not only may, but must be generated from these simple laws. And it is to be remarked that the case is not always one of Composition of Causes: the effect of concurring causes is not always precisely the sum of the effects of those causes when separate, nor even always an effect of the same kind with them. Reverting to the distinction which occupies so prominent a place in the theory of induction, the laws of the phenomena of mind are sometimes analogous to mechanical, but sometimes also to chemical laws. When many impressions or ideas are operating in the mind together, there sometimes takes place a process of a similar kind to chemical combination. When impressions have been so often experienced in conjunction that each of them calls up readily and instantaneously the ideas of the whole group, those ideas sometimes melt and coalesce into one another, and appear not several ideas, but one, in the same manner as, when the seven prismatic colours are presented to the eye in rapid succession the sensation produced is that of white. But as in this last case it is correct to say that the seven colours when they rapidly follow one another *generate* white, but not that they actually *are* white; so it appears to me that the Complex Idea, formed by the blending together of several simpler ones, should, when it really appears simple, (that is, when the separate elements are not consciously distinguishable in it,) be said to *result from*, or *be generated by*, the simple ideas, not to *consist* of them. Our idea of an orange really *consists* of the simple ideas of a certain colour, a certain form, a certain taste and smell, etc., because we can, by interrogating our consciousness, perceive all these elements in the idea. But we cannot perceive, in so apparently simple a feeling as our perception of the shape of an object by the eye, all that multitude of ideas derived from other senses, without which it is well ascertained that no such visual perception would ever have had existence; nor, in our idea of Extension, can we discover those elementary ideas of resistance derived from our muscular frame in which it had been conclusively shown that the idea originates. These, therefore, are cases of mental chemistry, in which it is proper to say that the simple ideas generate, rather than that they compose, the complex ones.

With respect to all the other constituents of the mind, its beliefs, its abstruser conceptions, its sentiments, emotions, and volitions, there are some (among whom are Hartley and the author of the *Analysis*) who think that the whole of these are generated from simple ideas of sensation by a chemistry similar to that which we have just exemplified. These philosophers have made out a great part of their case, but I am not satisfied that they have established the whole of it. They have shown that there is such a thing as mental chemistry; that the heterogeneous nature of a feeling A, considered in relation to B and C, is no conclusive argument against its being generated from B and C. Having proved this, they proceed to show that where A is found B and C were or may have been present; and why, therefore, they ask, should not A have been generated from B and C? But even if this evidence were carried to the highest degree of completeness which it admits of; if it were shown (which hitherto it has not, in all cases, been) that certain groups of associated ideas not only might have been, but actually were present whenever the more recondite mental feeling was experienced, this would amount only to the Method of Agreement, and could not prove causation until confirmed by the more conclusive evidence of the Method of Difference. If the question be whether Belief is a mere case of close association of ideas, it would be necessary to examine experimentally if it be true that any ideas whatever, provided they are associated with the required degree of closeness, give rise to belief. If the inquiry be into the origin of moral feelings, the feeling, for example, of moral reprobation, it is necessary to compare all the varieties of actions or states of mind which are ever morally disapproved, and see whether in all these cases it can be shown, or reasonably surmised, that the action or state of mind had become connected by association, in the disapproving mind, with some particular class of hateful or disgusting ideas; and the method employed is, thus far, that of Agreement. But this is not enough. Supposing this proved, we must try further by the Method of Difference whether this particular kind of hateful or disgusting ideas, when it becomes associated with an action previously indifferent, will render that action a subject of moral disapproval. If this question can be answered in the affirmative, it is shown to be a law of the human mind that an association of that particular description is the generating cause of moral reprobation. That all this is the case has been rendered extremely probable, but the experiments have not been tried with the degree of precision necessary for a complete and absolutely conclusive induction.[2]

It is further to be remembered, that even if all which this theory of mental phenomena contends for could be proved, we should not be the more enabled to resolve the laws of the more complex feelings into those of the simpler ones. The generation of one class of mental phenomena from another, whenever it can be made out, is a highly interesting fact in psychological chemistry; but it no more supersedes the necessity of an experimental study of the generated phenomenon, than a knowledge of the properties of oxygen and sulphur enables us to deduce those of sulphuric acid without specific observation and experiment. Whatever, therefore, may be the final issue of the attempt to account for the origin of our judgments, our desires, or our volitions, from simpler mental phenomena, it is not the less imperative to ascertain the sequences of the complex phenomena themselves by special study in conformity to the canons of Induction. Thus, in respect to Belief, psychologists will always have to inquire what beliefs we have by direct consciousness, and according to what laws one belief produces another; what are the laws in virtue of which one thing is recognised by the mind, either rightly or erroneously, as evidence of another thing. In regard to Desire, they will have to examine what objects we desire naturally, and by what causes we are made to desire things originally indifferent, or even disagreeable to us; and so forth. It may be remarked, that the general laws of association prevail among these more intricate states of mind, in the same manner as among the simpler ones. A desire, an emotion, an idea of the higher order of abstraction, even our judgments and volitions when they have become habitual, are called up by association, according to precisely the same laws as our simple ideas.

Notes

1. When this chapter was written, Professor Bain had not yet published even the first part (*The Senses and the Intellect*) of his profound *Treatise on the Mind*. In this the laws of association have been more comprehensively stated and more largely exemplified than by any previous writer; and the work, having been completed by the publication of *The Emotions and the Will*, may now be referred to as incomparably the most complete analytical exposition of the mental phenomena, on the basis of a legitimate induction, which has yet been produced. More recently still, Mr. Bain has joined with me in appending to a new edition of the *Analysis* notes intended to bring up the analytic science of Mind to its latest improvements.

   Many striking applications of the laws of association to the explanation of complex mental phenomena are also to be found in Mr. Herbert Spencer's *Principles of Psychology*.

2. In the case of the moral sentiments, the place of direct experiment is to a considerable extent supplied by historical experience, and we are able to trace with a tolerable approach to certainty the particular associations by which those sentiments are engendered. This has been attempted, so far as respects the sentiment of justice, in a little work by the present author, entitled *Utilitarianism*.

Chapter 39

The Elementary Law of Association

William James

I shall try to show, in the pages which immediately follow, that there is no other *elementary* causal law of association than the law of neural habit. All the *materials* of our thought are due to the way in which one elementary process of the cerebral hemispheres tends to excite whatever other elementary process it may have excited at some former time. The number of elementary processes at work, however, and the nature of those which at any time are fully effective in rousing the others, determine the character of the total brain-action, and, as a consequence of this, they determine the object thought of at the time. According as this resultant object is one thing or another, we call it a product of association by contiguity or of association by similarity, or contrast, or whatever other sorts we may have recognized as ultimate. Its production, however, is, in each one of these cases, to be explained by a merely quantitative variation in the elementary brain-processes momentarily at work under the law of habit, so that *psychic* contiguity, similarity, etc., are derivatives of a single profounder kind of fact.

My thesis, stated thus briefly, will soon become more clear; and at the same time certain disturbing factors, which co-operate with the law of neural habit, will come to view.

Let us then assume as the *basis* of all our subsequent reasoning this law: *When two elementary brain-processes have been active together or in immediate succession, one of them, on reoccurring, tends to propagate its excitement into the other.*

But, as a matter of fact, every elementary process has found itself at different times excited in conjunction with *many* other processes, and this by unavoidable outward causes. Which of these others it shall awaken now becomes a problem. Shall b or c be aroused next by the present a? We must make a further postulate, based, however, on the fact of *tension* in nerve-tissue, and on the fact of summation of excitements, each incomplete or latent in itself, into an open resultant. The process b, rather than c, will awake, if in addition to the vibrating tract a some other tract d is in a state of subexcitement, and formerly was excited with b alone and not with a. In short, we may say:

> *The amount of activity at any given point in the brain-cortex is the sum of the tendencies of all other points to discharge into it, such tendencies being proportionate (1) to the number of times the excitement of each other point may have accompanied that of the point in question; (2) to the intensity of such excitements; and (3) to the absence of any rival point functionally disconnected with the first point, into which the discharges might be diverted.*

Expressing the fundamental law in this most complicated way leads to the greatest ultimate simplification. Let us, for the present, only treat of spontaneous trains of thought and ideation, such as occur in revery or musing. The case of voluntary thinking toward a certain end shall come up later.

Take, to fix our ideas, the two verses from 'Locksley Hall':

"I, the heir of all *the ages* in the foremost files of time,"

and—

"For I doubt not through *the ages* one increasing purpose runs."

Why is it that when we recite from memory one of these lines, and get as far as *the ages*, that portion of the *other* line which follows, and, so to speak, sprouts out of *the ages*, does not also sprout out of our memory, and confuse the sense of our words? Simply because the word that follows *the ages* has its brain-process awakened not simply by the brain-process of *the ages* alone, but by it *plus* the brain-processes of all the words preceding *the ages*. The word *ages* at its moment of strongest activity would, *per se*, indifferently discharge into either 'in' or 'one.' So would the previous words (whose tension is momentarily much less strong than that of *ages*) each of them indifferently discharge into either of a large number of other words with which they have been at different times combined. But when the processes of '*I, the heir of all the ages*,' simultaneously vibrate in the brain, the last one of them in a maximal, the others in a fading phase of excitement; then the strongest line of discharge will be that which they *all alike* tend to take. '*In*' and not '*one*' or any other word will be the next to awaken, for its brain-process has previously vibrated in unison not only with that of *ages*, but with that of all those other words whose activity is dying away.

But if some one of these preceding words—'heir,' for example—had an intensely strong association with some brain-tracts entirely disjoined in experience from the poem of 'Locksley Hall '—if the reciter, for instance, were tremulously awaiting the opening of a will which might make him a millionaire—it is probable that the path of discharge through the words of the poem would be suddenly interrupted at the word 'heir.' His *emotional interest in that word* would be such that its *own special associations would prevail* over the combined ones of the other words. He would, as we say, be abruptly reminded of his personal situation, and the poem would lapse altogether from his thoughts.

The writer of these pages has every year to learn the names of a large number of students who sit in alphabetical order in a lecture-room. He finally learns to call them by name, as they sit in their accustomed places. On meeting one in the street, however, early in the year, the face hardly ever recalls the name, but it may recall the place of its owner in the lecture-room, his neighbors' faces, and consequently his general alphabetical position; and then, usually as the common associate of all these combined data, the student's name surges up in his mind.

A father wishes to show to some guests the progress of his rather dull child in Kindergarten instruction. Holding the knife upright on the table, he says, "What do you call that, my boy?" "I calls it a *knife*, I does," is the sturdy reply, from which the child cannot be induced to swerve by any alteration in the form of question, until the father recollecting that in the Kindergarten a pencil was used, and not a knife, draws a long one from his pocket, holds it in the same way, and then gets the wished-for answer, "I calls it *vertical*." All the concomitants of the Kindergarten experience had to recombine their effect before the word 'vertical' could be reawakened.

Impartial Redintegration

The ideal working of the law of compound association, were it unmodified by any extraneous influence, would be such as to keep the mind in a perpetual treadmill of

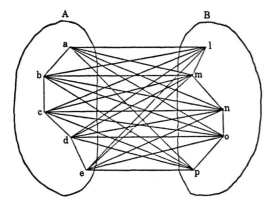

Figure 39.1

concrete reminiscences from which no detail could be omitted. Suppose, for example, we begin by thinking of a certain dinner-party. The only thing which all the components of the dinner-party could combine to recall would be the first concrete occurrence which ensued upon it. All the details of this occurrence could in turn only combine to awaken the next following occurrence, and so on. If a, b, c, d, e, for instance, be the elementary nerve-tracts excited by the last act of the dinner-party, call this act A, and l, m, n, o, p be those of walking home through the frosty night, which we may call B, then the thought of A must awaken that of B, because a, b, c, d, e, will each and all discharge into l through the paths by which their original discharge took place. Similarly they will discharge into m, n, o, and p; and these latter tracts will also each reinforce the other's action because, in the experience B, they have already vibrated in unison. The lines in figure 39.1 symbolize the summation of discharges into each of the components of B, and the consequent strength of the combination of influences by which B in its totality is awakened.

Hamilton first used the word 'redintegration' to designate all association. Such processes as we have just described might in an emphatic sense be termed redintegrations, for they would necessarily lead, if unobstructed, to the reinstatement in thought of the *entire* content of large trains of past experience. From this complete redintegration there could be no escape save through the irruption of some new and strong present impression of the senses, or through the excessive tendency of some one of the elementary brain-tracts to discharge independently into an aberrant quarter of the brain. Such was the tendency of the word 'heir' in the verse from 'Locksley Hall,' which was our first example. How such tendencies are constituted we shall have soon to inquire with some care. Unless they are present, the panorama of the past, once opened, must unroll itself with fatal literality to the end, unless some outward sound, sight, or touch divert the current of thought.

Let us call this process *impartial redintegration*. Whether it ever occurs in an absolutely complete form is doubtful. We all immediately recognize, however, that in some minds there is a much greater tendency than in others for the flow of thought to take this form. Those insufferably garrulous old women, those dry and fanciless beings who spare you no detail, however petty, of the facts they are recounting, and upon the thread of whose narrative all the irrelevant items cluster as pertinaciously as the essential ones, the slaves of literal fact, the stumblers over the smallest abrupt step in thought, are figures known to all of us. Comic literature has made her profit out of them. Juliet's nurse is a classical example. George Eliot's village characters and some of Dickens's minor personages supply excellent instances.

Perhaps as successful a rendering as any of this mental type is the character of Miss Bates in Miss Austen's 'Emma.' Hear how she redintegrates:

> 'But where could *you* hear it?' cried Miss Bates. 'Where could you possibly hear it, Mr. Knightley? For it is not five minutes since I received Mrs. Cole's note—no, it cannot be more than five—or at least ten—for I had got my bonnet and spencer on, just ready to come out—I was only gone down to speak to Patty again about the pork—Jane was standing in the passage—were not you, Jane?—for my mother was so afraid that we had not any salting-pan large enough. So I said I would go down and see, and Jane said: "Shall I go down instead? for I think you have a little cold, and Patty has been washing the kitchen." "Oh, my dear," said I—well, and just then came the note. A Miss Hawkins—that's all I know—a Miss Hawkins, of Bath. But, Mr. Knightley, how could you possibly have heard it? for the very moment Mr. Cole told Mrs. Cole of it, she sat down and wrote to me. A Miss Hawkins—'

But in every one of us there are moments when this complete reproduction of all the items of a past experience occurs. What are those moments? They are moments of emotional recall of the past as something which once was, but is gone forever—moments, the interest of which consists in the feeling that our self was once other than it now is. When this is the case, any detail, however minute, which will make the past picture more complete, will also have its effect in swelling that total contrast between *now* and *then* which forms the central interest of our contemplation.

Ordinary or Mixed Association

This case helps us to understand why it is that the ordinary spontaneous flow of our ideas does not follow the law of impartial redintegration. *In no revival of a past experience are all the items of our thought equally operative in determining what the next thought shall be. Always some ingredient is prepotent over the rest.* Its special suggestions or associations in this case will often be different from those which it has in common with the whole group of items; and its tendency to awaken these outlying associates will deflect the path of our revery. Just as in the original sensible experience our attention focalized itself upon a few of the impressions of the scene before us, so here in the reproduction of those impressions an equal partiality is shown, and some items are emphasized above the rest. What these items shall be is, in most cases of spontaneous revery, hard to determine beforehand. In subjective terms we say that *the prepotent items are those which appeal most to our* INTEREST.

Expressed in brain-terms, the law of interest will be: *some one brain-process is always prepotent above its concomitants in arousing action elsewhere.*

> 'Two processes,' says Mr. Hodgson,[1] 'are constantly going on in redintegration. The one a process of corrosion, melting, decay; the other a process of renewing, arising, becoming.... No object of representation remains long before consciousness in the same state, but fades, decays, and becomes indistinct. Those parts of the object, however, which possess an interest resist this tendency to gradual decay of the whole object.... This inequality in the object—some parts, the uninteresting, submitting to decay; others, the interesting parts, resisting it—when it has continued for a certain time, ends in becoming a new object.'

Only where the interest is diffused equally over all the parts (as in the emotional memory just referred to, where, as all *past*, they all interest us alike) is this law departed from. It will be least obeyed by those minds which have the smallest variety and intensity of interests—those who, by the general flatness and poverty of their aesthetic nature, are kept forever rotating among the literal sequences of their local and personal history.

Most of us, however, are better organized than this, and our musings pursue an erratic course, swerving continually into some new direction traced by the shifting play of interest as it ever falls on some partial item in each complex representation that is evoked. Thus it so often comes about that we find ourselves thinking at two nearly adjacent moments of things separated by the whole diameter of space and time. Not till we carefully recall each step of our cogitation do we see how naturally we came by Hodgson's law to pass from one to the other. Thus, for instance, after looking at my clock just now (1879), I found myself thinking of a recent resolution in the Senate about our legal-tender notes. The clock called up the image of the man who had repaired its gong. He suggested the jeweller's shop where I had last seen him; that shop, some shirt-studs which I had bought there; they, the value of gold and its recent decline; the latter, the equal value of greenbacks, and this, naturally, the question of how long they were to last, and of the Bayard proposition. Each of these images offered various points of interest. Those which formed the turning-points of my thought are easily assigned. The gong was momentarily the most interesting part of the clock, because, from having begun with a beautiful tone, it had become discordant and aroused disappointment. But for this the clock might have suggested the friend who gave it to me, or any one of a thousand circumstances connected with clocks. The jeweller's shop suggested the studs, because they alone of all its contents were tinged with the egoistic interest of possession. This interest in the studs, their value, made me single out the material as its chief source, etc., to the end. Every reader who will arrest himself at any moment and say, "How came I to be thinking of just this?" will be sure to trace a train of representations linked together by lines of contiguity and points of interest inextricably combined. This is the ordinary process of the association of ideas as it spontaneously goes on in average minds. *We may call it* ORDINARY, *or* MIXED, ASSOCIATION.

Another example of it is given by Hobbes in a passage which has been quoted so often as to be classical:

> In a discourse of our present civil war, what could seem more impertinent than to ask (as one did) what was the value of a Roman penny? Yet the coherence to me was manifest enough. For the thought of the war introduced the thought of the delivering up the King to his enemies; the thought of that brought in the thought of the delivering up of Christ; and that again the thought of the thirty pence, which was the price of that treason: and thence easily followed that malicious question; and all this in a moment of time; for thought is quick.[2]

Can we determine, now, when a certain portion of the going thought has, by dint of its interest, become so prepotent as to make its own exclusive associates the dominant features of the coming thought—can we, I say, determine *which* of its own associates shall be evoked? For they are many. As Hodgson says:

> The interesting parts of the decaying object are free to combine again with any objects or parts of objects with which at any time they have been combined before. All the former combinations of these parts may come back into consciousness; one must; but which will?

Mr. Hodgson replies:

> There can be but one answer: that which has been most *habitually* combined with
> them before. This new object begins at once to form itself in consciousness, and to
> group its parts round the part still remaining from the former object; part after part
> comes out and arranges itself in its old position; but scarcely has the process
> begun, when the original law of interest begins to operate on this new formation,
> seizes on the interesting parts and impresses them on the attention to the exclu-
> sion of the rest, and the whole process is repeated again with endless variety. I
> venture to propose this as a complete and true account of the whole process of
> redintegration.

In restricting the discharge from the interesting item into that channel which is
simply most *habitual* in the sense of most frequent, Hodgson's account is assuredly
imperfect. An image by no means always revives its most frequent associate, although
frequency is certainly one of the most potent determinants of revival. If I abruptly utter
the word *swallow*, the reader, if by habit an ornithologist, will think of a bird; if a
physiologist or a medical specialist in throat diseases, he will think of deglutition. If I
say *date*, he will, if a fruit-merchant or an Arabian traveller, think of the produce of the
palm; if an habitual student of history, figures with A.D. or B.C. before them will rise in
his mind. If I say *bed, bath, morning*, his own daily toilet will be invincibly suggested by
the combined names of three of its habitual associates. But frequent lines of transition
are often set at naught. The sight of C. Göring's 'System der kritischen Philosophie' has
most frequently awakened in me thoughts of the opinions therein propounded. The
idea of suicide has never been connected with the volumes. But a moment since, as my
eye fell upon them, suicide was the thought that flashed into my mind. Why? Because
but yesterday I received a letter from Leipzig informing me that this philosopher's
recent death by drowning was an act of self-destruction. Thoughts tend, then, to
awaken their most recent as well as their most habitual associates. This is a matter of
notorious experience, too notorious, in fact, to need illustration. If we have seen our
friend this morning, the mention of his name now recalls the circumstances of that
interview, rather than any more remote details concerning him. If Shakespeare's plays
are mentioned, and we were last night reading 'Richard II,' vestiges of that play rather
than of 'Hamlet' or 'Othello' float through our mind. Excitement of peculiar tracts, or
peculiar modes of general excitement in the brain, leave a sort of tenderness or exalted
sensibility behind them which takes days to die away. As long as it lasts, those tracts or
those modes are liable to have their activities awakened by causes which at other times
might leave them in repose. Hence, *recency* in experience is a prime factor in determining revival in thought.

Vividness in an original experience may also have the same effect as habit or recency
in bringing about likelihood of revival. If we have once witnessed an execution, any
subsequent conversation or reading about capital punishment will almost certainly
suggest images of that particular scene. Thus it is that events lived through only once,
and in youth, may come in after-years, by reason of their exciting quality or emotional
intensity, to serve as types or instances used by our mind to illustrate any and every
occurring topic whose interest is most remotely pertinent to theirs. If a man in his
boyhood once talked with Napoleon, any mention of great men or historical events,
battles or thrones, or the whirligig of fortune, or islands in the ocean, will be apt to draw
to his lips the incidents of that one memorable interview. If the word *tooth* now suddenly appears on the page before the reader's eye, there are fifty chances out of a

hundred that, if he gives it time to awaken any image, it will be an image of some operation of dentistry in which he has been the sufferer. Daily he has touched his teeth and masticated with them; this very morning he brushed them, chewed his breakfast and picked them; but the rarer and remoter associations arise more promptly because they were so much more intense.

A fourth factor in tracing the course of reproduction is *congruity in emotional tone* between the reproduced idea and our mood. The same objects do not recall the same associates when we are cheerful as when we are melancholy. Nothing, in fact, is more striking than our utter inability to keep up trains of joyous imagery when we are depressed in spirits. Storm, darkness, war, images of disease, poverty, and perishing afflict unremittingly the imaginations of melancholiacs. And those of sanguine temperament, when their spirits are high, find it impossible to give any permanence to evil forebodings or to gloomy thoughts. In an instant the train of association dances off to flowers and sunshine, and images of spring and hope. The records of Arctic or African travel perused in one mood awaken no thoughts but those of horror at the malignity of Nature; read at another time they suggest only enthusiastic reflections on the indomitable power and pluck of man. Few novels so overflow with joyous animal spirits as 'The Three Guardsmen' of Dumas. Yet it may awaken in the mind of a reader depressed with sea-sickness (as the writer can personally testify) a most dismal and woeful consciousness of the cruelty and carnage of which heroes like Athos, Porthos, and Aramis make themselves guilty.

Habit, recency, vividness, and emotional congruity are, then, all reasons why one representation rather than another should be awakened by the interesting portion of a departing thought. We may say with truth that *in the majority of cases the coming representation will have been either habitual, recent, or vivid, and will be congruous.* If all these qualities unite in any one absent associate, we may predict almost infallibly that that associate of the going thought will form an important ingredient in the coming thought. In spite of the fact, however, that the succession of representations is thus redeemed from perfect indeterminism and limited to a few classes whose characteristic quality is fixed by the nature of our past experience, it must still be confessed that an immense number of terms in the linked chain of our representations fall outside of all assignable rule. Take the instance of the clock. Why did the jeweller's shop suggest the shirt-studs rather than a chain which I had bought there more recently, which had cost more, and whose sentimental associations were much more interesting? Both chain and studs had excited brain-tracts simultaneously with the shop. The only reason why the nerve-stream from the shop-tract switched off into the stud-tract rather than into the chain-tract must be that the stud-tract happened at that moment to lie more open, either because of some accidental alteration in its nutrition or because the incipient sub-conscious tensions of the brain as a whole had so distributed their equilibrium that it was more unstable here than in the chain-tract. Any reader's introspection will easily furnish similar instances. It thus remains true that to a certain extent, even in those forms of ordinary mixed association which lie nearest to impartial redintegration, *which* associate of the interesting item shall emerge must be called largely a matter of accident—accident, that is, for our intelligence. No doubt it is determined by cerebral causes, but they are too subtle and shifting for our analysis.

Notes

1. *Time and Space*, p. 266. Compare Coleridge: "The true practical general law of association is this: that whatever makes certain parts of a total impression more vivid or distinct than the rest will determine the

mind to recall these, in preference to others equally linked together by the common condition of contemporaeity or of *contiguity*. But the will itself, by confining and intensifying the attention, may arbitrarily give vividness or distinctness to any object whatsoever." (*Biographia Litteraria*, Chap. V.)

2. *Leviathan*, pt. I. chap. III., [chap. 35 in this volume].

Chapter 40

The Appeal of Parallel Distributed Processing

James L. McClelland, David E. Rumelhart,
and Geoffrey E. Hinton

What makes people smarter than machines? They certainly are not quicker or more precise. Yet people are far better at perceiving objects in natural scenes and noting their relations, at understanding language and retrieving contextually appropriate information from memory, at making plans and carrying out contextually appropriate actions, and at a wide range of other natural cognitive tasks. People are also far better at learning to do these things more accurately and fluently through processing experience.

What is the basis for these differences? One answer, perhaps the classic one we might expect from artificial intelligence, is "software." If we only had the right computer program, the argument goes, we might be able to capture the fluidity and adaptability of human information processing.

Certainly this answer is partially correct. There have been great breakthroughs in our understanding of cognition as a result of the development of expressive high-level computer languages and powerful algorithms. No doubt there will be more such breakthroughs in the future. However, we do not think that software is the whole story.

In our view, people are smarter than today's computers because the brain employs a basic computational architecture that is more suited to deal with a central aspect of the natural information processing tasks that people are so good at. We will show through examples that these tasks generally require the simultaneous consideration of many pieces of information or constraints. Each constraint may be imperfectly specified and ambiguous, yet each can play a potentially decisive role in determining the outcome of processing. After examining these points, we will introduce a computational framework for modeling cognitive processes that seems well suited to exploiting these constraints and that seems closer than other frameworks to the style of computation as it might be done by the brain. We will review several early examples of models developed in this framework, and we will show that the mechanisms these models employ can give rise to powerful emergent properties that begin to suggest attractive alternatives to traditional accounts of various aspects of cognition. We will also show that models of this class provide a basis for understanding how learning can occur spontaneously, as a by-product of processing activity.

Multiple Simultaneous Constraints

The mutual influence of syntax and semantics   Multiple constraints operate ... strongly in language processing.... Rumelhart (1977) has documented many of these multiple constraints. Rather than catalog them here, we will use a few examples from language to illustrate the fact that the constraints tend to be reciprocal: The example shows that they do not run only from syntax to semantics—they also run the other way.

It is clear, of course, that syntax constrains the assignment of meaning. Without the syntactic rules of English to guide us, we cannot correctly understand who has done what to whom in the following sentence:

> The boy the man chased kissed the girl.

But consider these examples (Rumelhart 1977; Schank 1973):

> I saw the grand canyon flying to New York.
> I saw the sheep grazing in the field.

Our knowledge of syntactic rules alone does not tell us what grammatical role is played by the prepositional phrases in these two cases. In the first, "flying to New York" is taken as describing the context in which the speaker saw the Grand Canyon—while he was flying to New York. In the second, "grazing in the field" could syntactically describe an analogous situation, in which the speaker is grazing in the field, but this possibility does not typically become available on first reading. Instead we assign "grazing in the field" as a modifier of the sheep (roughly, "who were grazing in the field"). The syntactic structure of each of these sentences, then, is determined in part by the semantic relations that the constituents of the sentence might plausibly bear to one another. Thus, the influences appear to run both ways, from the syntax to the semantics and from the semantics to the syntax.

In these examples, we see how syntactic considerations influence semantic ones and how semantic ones influence syntactic ones. We cannot say that one kind of constraint is primary.

Mutual constraints operate, not only between syntactic and semantic processing, but also within each of these domains as well. Here we consider an example from syntactic processing, namely, the assignment of words to syntactic categories. Consider the sentences:

> I like the joke.
> I like the drive.
> I like to joke.
> I like to drive.

In this case it looks as though the words *the* and *to* serve to determine whether the following word will be read as a noun or a verb. This, of course, is a very strong constraint in English and can serve to force a verb interpretation of a word that is not ordinarily used this way:

> I like to mud.

On the other hand, if the information specifying whether the function word preceding the final word is *to* or *the* is ambiguous, then the typical reading of the word that follows it will determine which way the function word is heard. This was shown in an experiment by Isenberg, Walker, Ryder, and Schweikert (1980). They presented sounds halfway between *to* (actually /t^/) and *the* (actually /d^/) and found that words like *joke*, which we tend to think of first as nouns, made subjects hear the marginal stimuli as *the*, while words like *drive*, which we tend to think of first as verbs, made subjects hear the marginal stimuli as *to*. Generally, then, it would appear that each word can help constrain the syntactic role, and even the identity, of every other word.

Simultaneous mutual constraints in word recognition   Just as the syntactic role of one word can influence the role assigned to another in analyzing sentences, so the identity of one letter can influence the identity assigned to another in reading. A famous example of this, from Selfridge, is shown in figure 40.1. Along with this is a second example

Figure 40.1
Some ambiguous displays. The first one is from Selfridge 1955. The second line shows that three ambiguous characters can each constrain the identity of the others. The third, fourth, and fifth lines show that these characters are indeed ambiguous in that they assume other identities in other contexts. (The ink-blot technique of making letters ambiguous is due to Lindsay and Norman, 1972).

in which none of the letters, considered separately, can be identified unambiguously, but in which the possibilities that the visual information leaves open for each so constrain the possible identities of the others that we are capable of identifying all of them.

At first glance, the situation here must seem paradoxical: The identity of each letter is constrained by the identities of each of the others. But since in general we cannot know the identities of any of the letters until we have established the identities of the others, how can we get the process started?

The resolution of the paradox, of course, is simple. One of the different possible letters in each position fits together with the others. It appears then that our perceptual system is capable of exploring all these possibilities without committing itself to one until all of the constraints are taken into account.

Understanding through the interplay of multiple sources of knowledge   It is clear that we know a good deal about a large number of different standard situations. Several theorists have suggested that we store this knowledge in terms of structures called variously: *scripts* (Schank 1976), *frames* (Minsky 1975), or *schemata* (Norman and Bobrow 1976; Rumelhart 1975). Such knowledge structures are assumed to be the basis of comprehension. A great deal of progress has been made within the context of this view.

However, it is important to bear in mind that most everyday situations cannot be rigidly assigned to just a single script. They generally involve an interplay between a number of different sources of information. Consider, for example, a child's birthday party at a restaurant. We know things about birthday parties, and we know things about restaurants, but we would not want to assume that we have explicit knowledge (at least, not in advance of our first restaurant birthday party) about the conjunction of the two. Yet we can imagine what such a party might be like. The fact that the party was being held in a restaurant would modify certain aspects of our expectations for birthday parties (we would not expect a game of Pin-the-Tail-on-the-Donkey, for example), while the fact that the event was a birthday party would inform our expectations for what would be ordered and who would pay the bill.

Representations like scripts, frames, and schemata are useful structures for encoding knowledge, although we believe they only approximate the underlying structure of knowledge representation that emerges from the class of models we consider elsewhere. Our main point here is that any theory that tries to account for human knowledge using script-like knowledge structures will have to allow them to interact with each other to capture the generative capacity of human understanding in novel situations. Achieving such interactions has been one of the greatest difficulties associated with implementing models that really think generatively using script- or frame-like representations.

Parallel Distributed Processing

In the examples we have considered, a number of different pieces of information must be kept in mind at once. Each plays a part, constraining others and being constrained by them. What kinds of mechanisms seem well suited to these task demands? Intuitively, these tasks seem to require mechanisms in which each aspect of the information in the situation can act on other aspects, simultaneously influencing other aspects and being influenced by them. To articulate these intuitions, we and others have turned to a class of models we call *Parallel Distributed Processing* (PDP) models. These models assume that information processing takes place through the interactions of a large number of simple processing elements called units, each sending excitatory and inhibitory signals to other units. In some cases, the units stand for possible hypotheses about such things as the letters in a particular display or the syntactic roles of the words in a particular sentence. In these cases, the activations stand roughly for the strengths associated with the different possible hypotheses, and the interconnections among the units stand for the constraints the system knows to exist between the hypotheses. In other cases, the units stand for possible goals and actions, such as the goal of typing a particular letter, or the action of moving the left index finger, and the connections relate goals to subgoals, subgoals to actions, and actions to muscle movements. In still other cases, units stand not for particular hypotheses or goals, but for aspects of these things. Thus a hypothesis about the identity of a word, for example, is itself distributed in the activations of a large number of units.

PDP Models: Cognitive Science or Neuroscience?

One reason for the appeal of PDP models is their obvious "physiological" flavor: They seem so much more closely tied to the physiology of the brain than are other kinds of information-processing models. The brain consists of a large number of highly interconnected elements which apparently send very simple excitatory and inhibitory messages to each other and update their excitations on the basis of these simple messages. The properties of the units in many of the PDP models we will be exploring were inspired by basic properties of the neural hardware.

Though the appeal of PDP models is definitely enhanced by their physiological plausibility and neural inspiration, these are not the primary bases for their appeal to us. We are, after all, cognitive scientists, and PDP models appeal to us for psychological and computational reasons. They hold out the hope of offering computationally sufficient and psychologically accurate mechanistic accounts of the phenomena of human cognition which have eluded successful explication in conventional computational formalisms; and they have radically altered the way we think about the time-course of processing, the nature of representation, and the mechanisms of learning.

Examples of PDP Models

In what follows, we review a number of recent applications of PDP models to problems in perception, memory, and language. In many cases, as we shall see, parallel distributed processing mechanisms are used to provide natural accounts of the exploitation of multiple, simultaneous, and often mutual constraints. We will also see that these same mechanisms exhibit emergent properties which lead to novel interpretations of phenomena which have traditionally been interpreted in other ways.

Perception

Perceptual completion of familiar patterns   Perception, of course, is influenced by familiarity. It is a well-known fact that we often misperceive unfamiliar objects as more familiar ones and that we can get by with less time or with lower-quality information in perceiving familiar items than we need for perceiving unfamiliar items. Not only does familiarity help us determine what the higher-level structures are when the lower-level information is ambiguous; it also allows us to fill in missing lower-level information within familiar higher-order patterns. The well-known *phonemic restoration effect* is a case in point. In this phenomenon, perceivers hear sounds that have been cut out of words as if they had actually been present. For example, Warren (1970) presented *legi # lature* to subjects, with a click in the location marked by the #. Not only did subjects correctly identify the word legislature; they also heard the missing /s/ just as though it had been presented. They had great difficulty localizing the click, which they tended to hear as a disembodied sound. Similar phenomena have been observed in visual perception of words since the work of Pillsbury (1897).

Two of us have proposed a model describing the role of familiarity in perception based on excitatory and inhibitory interactions among units standing for various hypotheses about the input at different levels of abstraction (McClelland and Rumelhart 1981, Rumelhart and McClelland 1982). The model has been applied in detail to the role of familiarity in the perception of letters in visually presented words, and has proved to provide a very close account of the results of a large number of experiments.

The model assumes that there are units that act as detectors for the visual features which distinguish letters, with one set of units assigned to detect the features in each of the different letter-positions in the word. For four-letter words, then, there are four such sets of detectors. There are also four sets of detectors for the letters themselves and a set of detectors for the words.

In the model, each unit has an activation value, corresponding roughly to the strength of the hypothesis that what that unit stands for is present in the perceptual input. The model honors the following important relations which hold between these "hypotheses" or activations: First, to the extent that two hypotheses are mutually consistent, they should support each other. Thus, units that are mutually consistent, in the way that the letter *T* in the first position is consistent with the word *TAKE*, tend to excite each other. Second, to the extent that two hypotheses are mutually inconsistent, they should weaken each other. Actually, we can distinguish two kinds of inconsistency: The first kind might be called between-level inconsistency. For example, the hypothesis that a word begins with a *T* is inconsistent with the hypothesis that the word is *MOVE*. The second might be called mutual exclusion. For example, the hypothesis that a word begins with *T* excludes the hypothesis that it begins with *R* since a word can only begin with one letter. Both kinds of inconsistencies operate in the word perception model to reduce the activations of units. Thus, the letter units in each

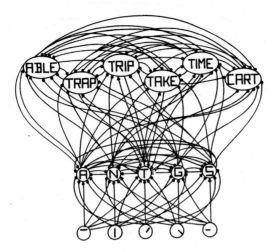

Figure 40.2.
The unit for the letter *T* in the first position of a four-letter array and some of its neighbors. Note that the feature and letter units stand only for the first position; in a complete picture of the units needed from processing four-letter displays, there would be four full sets of feature detectors and four full sets of letter detectors. (From "An Interactive Activation Model of Context Effects in Letter Perception: Part I. An Account of Basic Findings" by J. L. McClelland and D. E. Rumelhart, 1981, *Psychological Review, 88,* p. 380. Copyright 1981 by the American Psychological Association. Reprinted by permission.).

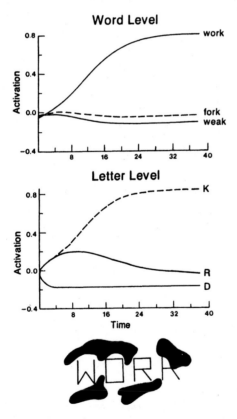

Figure 40.3
A possible display that might be presented to the interactive activation model of word recognition, and the resulting activations of selected letter and word units. The letter units are for the letters indicated in the fourth position of a four-letter display.

position compete with all other letter units in the same position, and the word units compete with each other. This type of inhibitory interaction is often called *competitive inhibition*. In addition, there are inhibitory interactions between incompatible units on different levels. This type of inhibitory interaction is simply called *between-level inhibition*.

The set of excitatory and inhibitory interactions between units can be diagrammed by drawing excitatory and inhibitory links between them. The whole picture is too complex to draw, so we illustrate only with a fragment: Some of the interactions between some of the units in this model are illustrated in figure 40.2.

Let us consider what happens in a system like this when a familiar stimulus is presented under degraded conditions. For example, consider the display shown in figure 40.3. This display consists of the letters *W, O,* and *R,* completely visible, and enough of a fourth letter to rule out all letters other than *R* and *K.* Before onset of the display, the activations of the units are set at or below 0. When the display is presented, detectors for the features present in each position become active (i.e., their activations grow above 0). At this point, they begin to excite and inhibit the corresponding detectors for letters. In the first three positions, *W, O,* and *R* are unambiguously activated, so we will focus our attention on the fourth position where *R* and *K* are both equally consistent with the active features. Here, the activations of the detectors for *R* and *K* start out growing together, as the feature detectors below them become activated. As these detectors become active, they and the active letter detectors for *W, O,* and *R* in the other positions start to activate detectors for words which have these letters in them and to inhibit detectors for words which do not have these letters. A number of words are partially consistent with the active letters, and receive some net excitation from the letter level, but only the word *WORK* matches one of the active letters in all four positions. As a result, *WORK* becomes more active than any other word and inhibits the other words, thereby successfully dominating the pattern of activation among the word units. As it grows in strength, it sends feedback to the letter level, reinforcing the activations of the *W, O, R,* and *K* in the corresponding positions. In the fourth position, this feedback gives *K* the upper hand over *R,* and eventually the stronger activation of the *K* detector allows it to dominate the pattern of activation, suppressing the *R* detector completely.

This example illustrates how PDP models can allow knowledge about what letters go together to form words to work together with natural constraints on the task (i.e.. that there should only be one letter in one place at one time), to produce perceptual completion in a simple and direct way.

Completion of novel patterns   However, the perceptual intelligence of human perceivers far exceeds the ability to recognize familiar patterns and fill in missing portions. We also show facilitation in the perception of letters in unfamiliar letter strings which are word-like but not themselves actually familiar.

One way of accounting for such performances is to imagine that the perceiver possesses, in addition to detectors for familiar words, sets of detectors for regular subword units such as familiar letter clusters, or that they use abstract rules, specifying which classes of letters can go with which others in different contexts. It turns out, however, that the model we have already described needs no such additional structure to produce perceptual facilitation for word-like letter strings; to this extent it acts as if it "knows" the orthographic structure of English. We illustrate this feature of the model with the example shown in figure 40.4, where the nonword *YEAD* is shown in degraded form so that the second letter is incompletely visible. Given the information

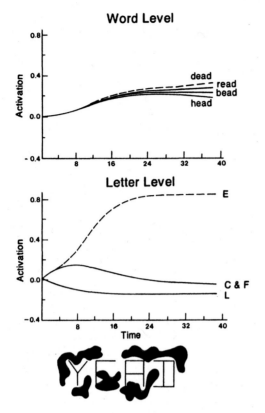

Figure 40.4
An example of a nonword display that might be presented to the interactive activation model of word recognition and the response of selected units at the letter and word levels. The letter units illustrated are detectors for letters in the second input position.

about this letter, considered alone, either *E* or *F* would be possible in the second position. Yet our model will tend to complete this letter as an *E*.

The reason for this behavior is that, when *YEAD* is shown, a number of words are partially activated. There is no word consistent with *Y, E* or *F, A*, and *D*, but there are words which match *YEA_* (*YEAR*, for example) and others which match *_EAD* (*BEAD*, *DEAD*, *HEAD*, and *READ*, for example). These and other near misses are partially activated as a result of the pattern of activation at the letter level. While they compete with each other, none of these words gets strongly enough activated to completely suppress all the others. Instead, these units act as a group to reinforce particularly the letters *E* and *A*. There are no close partial matches which include the letter *F* in the second position, so this letter receives no feedback support. As a result, *E* comes to dominate, and eventually suppress, the *F* in the second position.

The fact that the word perception model exhibits perceptual facilitation to pronounceable nonwords as well as words illustrates once again how behavior in accordance with general principles or rules can emerge from the interactions of simple processing elements. Of course, the behavior of the word perception model does not implement exactly any of the systems of orthographic rules that have been proposed by linguists (Chomsky and Halle 1968, Venesky 1970) or psychologists (Spoehr and Smith 1975). In this regard, it only approximates such rule-based descriptions of perceptual processing. However, rule systems such as Chomsky and Halle's or Venesky's appear to be only approximately honored in human performance as well (Smith and Baker 1976). Indeed, some of the discrepancies between human performance data and rule systems occur in exactly the ways that we would predict from the word perception model (Rumelhart and McClelland 1982). This illustrates the possibility that PDP models may provide more accurate accounts of the details of human performance than models based on a set of rules representing human competence—at least in some domains.

Retrieving Information From Memory

Content addressability   One very prominent feature of human memory is that it is content addressable. It seems fairly clear that we can access information in memory based on nearly any attribute of the representation we are trying to retrieve.

Of course, some cues are much better than others. An attribute which is shared by a very large number of things we know about is not a very effective retrieval cue, since it does not accurately pick out a particular memory representation. But, several such cues, in conjunction, can do the job. Thus, if we ask a friend who goes out with several women, "Who was that woman I saw you with?", he may not know which one we mean—but if we specify something else about her—say the color of her hair, what she was wearing (insofar as he remembers this at all), where we saw him with her—he will likely be able to hit upon the right one.

It is, of course, possible to implement some kind of content addressability of memory on a standard computer in a variety of different ways. One way is to search sequentially, examining each memory in the system to find the memory or the set of memories which has the particular content specified in the cue. An alternative, somewhat more efficient, scheme involves some form of indexing—keeping a list, for every content a memory might have, of which memories have that content.

Such an indexing scheme can be made to work with error-free probes, but it will break down if there is an error in the specification of the retrieval cue. There are possible ways of recovering from such errors, but they lead to the kind of combinatorial explosions which plague this kind of computer implementation.

But suppose that we imagine that each memory is represented by a unit which has mutually excitatory interactions with units standing for each of its properties. Then, whenever any property of the memory became active, the memory would tend to be activated, and whenever the memory was activated, all of its contents would tend to become activated. Such a scheme would automatically produce content addressability for us. Though it would not be immune to errors, it would not be devastated by an error in the probe if the remaining properties specified the correct memory.

As described thus far, whenever a property that is a part of a number of different memories is activated, it will tend to activate all of the memories it is in. To keep these other activities from swamping the "correct" memory unit, we simply need to add initial inhibitory connections among the memory units. An additional desirable feature would be mutually inhibitory interactions among mutually incompatible property units. For example, a person cannot both be single and married at the same time, so the units for different marital states would be mutually inhibitory.

McClelland (1981) developed a simulation model that illustrates how a system with these properties would act as a content addressable memory. The model is obviously oversimplified, but it illustrates many of the characteristics of the more complex models that will be considered in later chapters.

The Jets and The Sharks

Name	Gang	Age	Edu	Mar	Occupation
Art	Jets	40's	J.H.	Sing.	Pusher
Al	Jets	30's	J.H.	Mar.	Burglar
Sam	Jets	20's	COL.	Sing.	Bookie
Clyde	Jets	40's	J.H.	Sing.	Bookie
Mike	Jets	30's	J.H.	Sing.	Bookie
Jim	Jets	20's	J.H.	Div.	Burglar
Greg	Jets	20's	H.S.	Mar.	Pusher
John	Jets	20's	J.H.	Mar.	Burglar
Doug	Jets	30's	H.S.	Sing.	Bookie
Lance	Jets	20's	J.H.	Mar.	Burglar
George	Jets	20's	J.H.	Div.	Burglar
Pete	Jets	20's	H.S.	Sing.	Bookie
Fred	Jets	20's	H.S.	Sing.	Pusher
Gene	Jets	20's	COL.	Sing.	Pusher
Ralph	Jets	30's	J.H.	Sing.	Pusher
Phil	Sharks	30's	COL.	Mar.	Pusher
Ike	Sharks	30's	J.H.	Sing.	Bookie
Nick	Sharks	30's	H.S.	Sing.	Pusher
Don	Sharks	30's	COL.	Mar.	Burglar
Ned	Sharks	30's	COL.	Mar.	Bookie
Karl	Sharks	40's	H.S.	Mar.	Bookie
Ken	Sharks	20's	H.S.	Sing.	Burglar
Earl	Sharks	40's	H.S.	Mar.	Burglar
Rick	Sharks	30's	H.S.	Div.	Burglar
Ol	Sharks	30's	COL.	Mar.	Pusher
Neal	Sharks	30's	H.S.	Sing.	Bookie
Dave	Sharks	30's	H.S.	Div.	Pusher

Figure 40.5
Characteristics of a number of individuals belonging to two gangs, the Jets and the Sharks. (From "Retrieving General and Specific Knowledge From Stored Knowledge of Specifics" by J. L. McClelland, 1981, *Proceedings of the Third Annual Conference of the Cognitive Science Society*, Berkeley, CA. Copyright 1981 by J. L. McClelland. Reprinted by permission.)

Consider the information represented in figure 40.5, which lists a number of people we might meet if we went to live in an unsavory neighborhood, and some of their hypothetical characteristics. A subset of the units needed to represent this information is shown in figure 40.6. In this network, there is an "instance unit" for each of the characters described in figure 40.5, and that unit is linked by mutually excitatory connections to all of the units for the fellow's properties. Note that we have included property units for the names of the characters, as well as units for their other properties.

Now, suppose we wish to retrieve the properties of a particular individual, say Lance. And suppose that we know Lance's name. Then we can probe the network by activating Lance's name unit, and we can see what pattern of activation arises as a result. Assuming that we know of no one else named Lance, we can expect the Lance name unit to be hooked up only to the instance unit for Lance. This will in turn activate the property units for Lance, thereby creating the pattern of activation corresponding to Lance. In effect, we have retrieved a representation of Lance. More will happen than just what we have described so far, but for the moment let us stop here.

Of course, sometimes we may wish to retrieve a name, given other information. In this case, we might start with some of Lance's properties, effectively asking the system, say "Who do you know who is a Shark and in his 20s?" by activating the Shark and 20s units. In this case it turns out that there is a single individual, Ken, who fits the descrip-

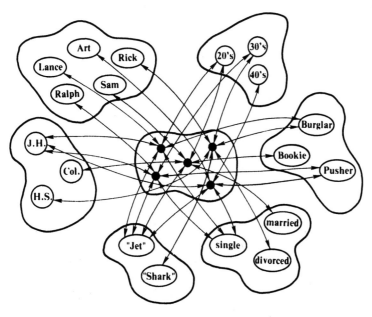

Figure 40.6
Some of the units and interconnections needed to represent the individuals shown in figure 40.5. The units connected with double-headed arrows are mutually excitatory. All the units within the same cloud are mutually inhibitory. (From "Retrieving General and Specific Knowledge From Stored Knowledge of Specifics" by J. L. McClelland, 1981, *Proceedings of the Third Annual Conference of the Cognitive Science Society*, Berkeley, CA. Copyright 1981 by J. L. McClelland. Reprinted by permission.)

tion. So, when we activate these two properties, we will activate the instance unit for Ken, and this in turn will activate his name unit, and fill in his other properties as well.

Graceful degradation   A few of the desirable properties of this kind of model are visible from considering what happens as we vary the set of features we use to probe the memory in an attempt to retrieve a particular individual's name. Any set of features which is sufficient to uniquely characterize a particular item will activate the instance node for that item more strongly than any other instance node. A probe which contains misleading features will most strongly activate the node that it matches best. This will clearly be a poorer cue than one which contains no misleading information—but it will still be sufficient to activate the "right answer" more strongly than any other, as long as the introduction of misleading information does not make the probe closer to some other item. In general, though the degree of activation of a particular instance node and of the corresponding name nodes varies in this model as a function of the exact content of the probe, errors in the probe will not be fatal unless they make the probe point to the wrong memory. This kind of model's handling of incomplete or partial probes also requires no special error-recovery scheme to work—it is a natural by-product of the nature of the retrieval mechanism that it is capable of graceful degradation.

Default assignment   It probably will have occurred to the reader that in many of the situations we have been examining, there will be other activations occurring which may influence the pattern of activation which is retrieved. So, in the case where we retrieved the properties of Lance, those properties, once they become active, can begin to activate the units for other individuals with those same properties. The memory unit for Lance will be in competition with these units and will tend to keep their activation down, but to the extent that they do become active, they will tend to activate their own properties and therefore fill them in. In this way, the model can fill in properties of individuals based on what it knows about other, similar instances.

To illustrate how this might work we have simulated the case in which we do not know that Lance is a Burglar as opposed to a Bookie or a Pusher. It turns out that there are a group of individuals in the set who are very similar to Lance in many respects. When Lance's properties become activated, these other units become partially activated, and they start activating their properties. Since they all share the same "occupation," they work together to fill in that property for Lance. Of course, there is no reason why this should necessarily be the right answer, but generally speaking, the more similar two things are in respects that we know about, the more likely they are to be similar in respects that we do not, and the model implements this heuristic.

Spontaneous generalization   The model we have been describing has another valuable property as well—it tends to retrieve what is common to those memories which match a retrieval cue which is too general to capture any one memory. Thus, for example, we could probe the system by activating the unit corresponding to membership in the Jets. This unit will partially activate all the instances of the Jets, thereby causing each to send activations to its properties. In this way the model can retrieve the typical values that the members of the Jets have on each dimension—even though there is no one Jet that has these typical values. In the example, 9 of 15 Jets are single, 9 of 15 are in their 20s, and 9 of 15 have only a junior high school education; when we probe by activating the Jet unit, all three of these properties dominate. The Jets are evenly divided between the three occupations, so each of these units becomes partially activated. Each has a different name, so that each name unit is very weakly activated, nearly cancelling each other out.

In the example just given of spontaneous generalization, it would not be unreasonable to suppose that someone might have explicitly stored a generalization about the members of a gang. The account just given would be an alternative to "explicit storage" of the generalization. It has two advantages, though, over such an account. First, it does not require any special generalization formation mechanism. Second, it can provide us with generalizations on unanticipated lines, on demand. Thus, if we want to know, for example, what people in their 20s with a junior high school education are like, we can probe the model by activating these two units. Since all such people are Jets and Burglars, these two units are strongly activated by the model in this case; two of them are divorced and two are married, so both of these units are partially activated.[1]

The sort of model we are considering, then, is considerably more than a content addressable memory. In addition, it performs default assignment, and it can spontaneously retrieve a general concept of the individuals that match any specifiable probe. These properties must be explicitly implemented as complicated computational extensions of other models of knowledge retrieval, but in PDP models they are natural by-products of the retrieval process itself.

Representation and Learning in PDP Models

In the Jets and Sharks model, we can speak of the model's *active representation* at a particular time, and associate this with the pattern of activation over the units in the system. We can also ask: What is the stored knowledge that gives rise to that pattern of activation? In considering this question, we see immediately an important difference between PDP models and other models of cognitive processes. In most models, knowledge is stored as a static copy of a pattern. Retrieval amounts to finding the pattern in long-term memory and copying it into a buffer or working memory. There is no real difference between the stored representation in long-term memory and the active representation in working memory. In PDP models, though, this is not the case. In these models, the patterns themselves are not stored. Rather, what is stored is the *connection strengths* between units that allow these patterns to be re-created. In the Jets and Sharks model, there is an instance unit assigned to each individual, but that unit does not contain a copy of the representation of that individual. Instead, it is simply the case that the connections between it and the other units in the system are such that activation of the unit will cause the pattern for the individual to be reinstated on the property units.

This difference between PDP models and conventional models has enormous implications, both for processing and for learning. We have already seen some of the implications for processing. The representation of the knowledge is set up in such a way that the knowledge necessarily influences the course of processing. Using knowledge in processing is no longer a matter of finding the relevant information in memory and bringing it to bear; it is part and parcel of the processing itself.

For learning, the implications are equally profound. For if the knowledge is the strengths of the connections, learning must be a matter of finding the right connection strengths so that the right patterns of activation will be produced under the right circumstances. This is an extremely important property of this class of models, for it opens up the possibility that an information processing mechanism could learn, as a result of tuning its connections, to capture the interdependencies between activations that it is exposed to in the course of processing.

In recent years, there has been quite a lot of interest in learning in cognitive science. Computational approaches to learning fall predominantly into what might be called the "explicit rule formulation" tradition, as represented by the work of Winston (1975), the suggestions of Chomsky, and the ACT* model of J. R. Anderson (1983). All of this work shares the assumption that the goal of learning is to formulate explicit rules (propositions, productions, etc.) which capture powerful generalizations in a succinct way. Fairly powerful mechanisms, usually with considerable innate knowledge about a domain, and/or some starting set of primitive propositional representations, then formulate hypothetical general rules, e.g., by comparing particular cases and formulating explicit generalizations.

The approach that we take in developing PDP models is completely different. First, we do not assume that the goal of learning is the formulation of explicit rules. Rather, we assume it is the acquisition of connection strengths which allow a network of simple units to act *as though* it knew the rules. Second, we do not attribute powerful computational capabilities to the learning mechanism. Rather, we assume very simple connection strength modulation mechanisms which adjust the strength of connections between units based on information locally available at the connection.

Local vs. distributed representation   Before we turn to an explicit consideration of this issue, we raise a basic question about representation. Once we have achieved the insight that the knowledge is stored in the strengths of the interconnections between units, a question arises. Is there any reason to assign one unit to each pattern that we wish to learn? Another possibility—one that we explore extensively in this book—is the possibility that the knowledge about any individual pattern is not stored in the connections of a special unit reserved for that pattern, but is distributed over the connections among a large number of processing units. On this view, the Jets and Sharks model represents a special case in which separate units are reserved for each instance.

Models in which connection information is explicitly thought of as distributed have been proposed by a number of investigators. The units in these collections may themselves correspond to conceptual primitives, or they may have no particular meaning as individuals. In either case, the focus shifts to patterns of activation over these units and to mechanisms whose explicit purpose is to learn the right connection strengths to allow the right patterns of activation to become activated under the right circumstances.

In the rest of this section, we will give a simple example of a PDP model in which the knowledge is distributed. We will first explain how the model would work, given pre-existing connections, and we will then describe how it could come to acquire the right connection strengths through a very simple learning mechanism. A number of models which have taken this distributed approach have been discussed in Hinton and J. A. Anderson's (1981) *Parallel Models of Associative Memory*. We will consider a simple version of a common type of distributed model, a *pattern associator*.

Pattern associators are models in which a pattern of activation over one set of units can cause a pattern of activation over another set of units without any intervening units to stand for either pattern as a whole. Pattern associators would, for example, be capable of associating a pattern of activation on one set of units corresponding to the appearance of an object with a pattern on another set corresponding to the aroma of the object, so that, when an object is presented visually, causing its visual pattern to become active, the model produces the pattern corresponding to its aroma.

How a pattern associator works   For purposes of illustration, we present a very simple pattern associator in figure 40.7. In this model, there are four units in each of two pools. The first pool, the A units, will be the pool in which patterns corresponding to the sight of various objects might be represented. The second pool, the B units, will be the pool in which the pattern corresponding to the aroma will be represented. We can pretend that alternative patterns of activation on the A units are produced upon viewing a rose or a grilled steak, and alternative patterns on the B units are produced upon sniffing the same objects. Figure 40.8 shows two pairs of patterns, as well as sets of interconnections necessary to allow the A member of each pair to reproduce the B member.

The details of the behavior of the individual units vary among different versions of pattern associators. For present purposes, we'll assume that the units can take on positive or negative activation values, with 0 representing a kind of neutral intermediate value. The strengths of the interconnections between the units can be positive or negative real numbers.

The effect of an A unit on a B unit is determined by multiplying the activation of the A unit times the strength of its synaptic connection with the B unit. For example, if the connection from a particular A unit to a particular B unit has a positive sign, when the A unit is excited (activation greater than 0), it will excite the B unit. For this example, we'll simply assume that the activation of each unit is set to the sum of the excitatory and inhibitory effects operating on it. This is one of the simplest possible cases.

Suppose, now, that we have created on the A units the pattern corresponding to the first visual pattern shown in Figure 40.8, the rose. How should we arrange the strengths of the interconnections between the A units and the B units to reproduce the pattern

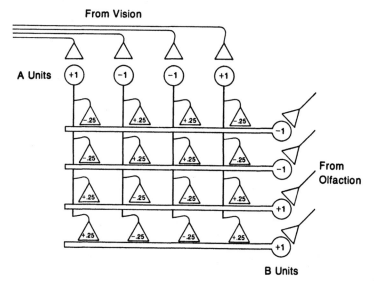

Figure 40.7
A simple pattern associator. The example assumes that patterns of activation in the A units can be produced by the visual system and patterns in the B units can be produced by the olfactory system. The synaptic connections allow the outputs of the A units to influence the activations of the B units. The synaptic weights linking the A units to the B units were selected so as to allow the pattern of activation shown on the A units to reproduce the pattern of activation shown on the B units without the need for any olfactory input.

+1	−1	−1	+1			−1	+1	−1	+1	
−.25	+.25	+.25	−.25	−1		+.25	−.25	+.25	−.25	−1
−.25	+.25	+.25	−.25	−1		−.25	+.25	−.25	+.25	+1
+.25	−.25	−.25	+.25	+1		−.25	+.25	−.25	+.25	+1
+.25	−.25	−.25	+.25	+1		+.25	−.25	+.25	−.25	−1

Figure 40.8
Two simple associators represented as matrices. The weights in the first two matrices allow the A pattern shown above the matrix to produce the B pattern shown to the right of it. Note that the weights in the first matrix are the same as those shown in the diagram in figure 40.7.

corresponding to the aroma of a rose? We simply need to arrange for each A unit to tend to excite each B unit which has a positive activation in the aroma pattern and to inhibit each B unit which has a negative activation in the aroma pattern. It turns out that this goal is achieved by setting the strength of the connection between a given A unit and a given B unit to a value proportional to the product of the activation of the two units. In figure 40.7, the weights on the connections were chosen to allow the A pattern illustrated there to produce the illustrated B pattern according to this principle. The actual strengths of the connections were set to $\pm.25$, rather than ± 1, so that the A pattern will produce the right magnitude, as well as the right sign, for the activations of the units in the B pattern. The same connections are reproduced in matrix form in figure 40.8A.

Pattern associators like the one in figure 40.7 have a number of nice properties. One is that they do not require a perfect copy of the input to produce the correct output, though its strength will be weaker in this case. For example, suppose that the associator shown in figure 40.7 were presented with an A pattern of $(1, -1, 0, 1)$. This is the A pattern shown in the figure, with the activation of one of its elements set to 0. The B pattern produced in response will have the activations of all of the B units in the right direction; however, they will be somewhat weaker than they would be, had the complete A pattern been shown. Similar effects are produced if an element of the pattern is distorted—or if the model is damaged, either by removing whole units, or random sets of connections, etc. Thus, their pattern retrieval performance of the model degrades gracefully both under degraded input and under damage.

How a pattern associator learns   So far, we have seen how we as model builders can construct the right set of weights to allow one pattern to cause another. The interesting thing, though, is that we do not need to build these interconnection strengths in by hand. Instead, the pattern associator can teach itself the right set of interconnections through experience processing the patterns in conjunction with each other.

A number of different rules for adjusting connection strengths have been proposed. One of the first—and definitely the best known—is due to D. O. Hebb (1949). Hebb's actual proposal was not sufficiently quantitative to build into an explicit model. However, a number of different variants can trace their ancestry back to Hebb. Perhaps the simplest version is:

> When unit A and unit B are simultaneously excited, increase the strength of the connection between them.

A natural extension of this rule to cover the positive and negative activation values allowed in our example is:

> Adjust the strength of the connection between units A and B in proportion to the product of their simultaneous activation.

In this formulation, if the product is positive, the change makes the connection more excitatory, and if the product is negative, the change makes the connection more inhibitory. For simplicity of reference, we will call this the *Hebb rule*, although it is not exactly Hebb's original formulation.

With this simple learning rule, we could train a "blank copy" of the pattern associator shown in figure 40.7 to produce the B pattern for rose when the A pattern is shown, simply by presenting the A and B patterns together and modulating the connection strengths according to the Hebb rule. The size of the change made on every trial would, of course, be a parameter. We generally assume that the changes made on each instance are rather small, and that connection strengths build up gradually. The values shown in figure 40.8A, then, would be acquired as a result of a number of experiences with the A and B pattern pair.

It is very important to note that the information needed to use the Hebb rule to determine the value each connection should have is *locally available* at the connection. All a given connection needs to consider is the activation of the units on both sides of it. Thus, it would be possible to actually implement such a connection modulation scheme locally, in each connection, without requiring any programmer to reach into each connection and set it to just the right value.

It turns out that the Hebb rule as stated here has some serious limitations, and, to our knowledge, no theorists continue to use it in this simple form. More sophisticated connection modulation schemes have been proposed by other workers; most important among these are the delta rule, the competitive learning rule, and the rules for learning in stochastic parallel models. All of these learning rules have the property that they adjust the strengths of connections between units on the basis of information that can be assumed to be locally available to the unit. Learning, then, in all of these cases, amounts to a very simple process that can be implemented locally at each connection without the need for any overall supervision. Thus, models which incorporate these learning rules train themselves to have the right interconnections in the course of processing the members of an ensemble of patterns.

Learning multiple patterns in the same set of interconnections   Up to now, we have considered how we might teach our pattern associator to associate the visual pattern for one object with a pattern for the aroma of the same object. Obviously, different patterns of interconnections between the A and B units are appropriate for causing the visual pattern for a different object to give rise to the pattern for its aroma. The same principles apply, however, and if we presented our pattern associator with the A and B patterns for steak, it would learn the right set of interconnections for that case instead (these are shown in figure 40.8B). In fact, it turns out that we can actually teach the same pattern associator a number of different associations. The matrix representing the set of interconnections that would be learned if we taught the same pattern associator both the rose association and the steak association is shown in figure 40.9. The reader can verify this by adding the two matrices for the individual patterns together. The reader can also verify that this set of connections will allow the rose A pattern to produce the rose B pattern, and the steak A pattern to produce the steak B pattern: when either input pattern is presented, the correct corresponding output is produced.

The examples used here have the property that the two different visual patterns are completely uncorrelated with each other. This being the case, the rose pattern produces no effect when the interconnections for the steak have been established, and the steak pattern produces no effect when the interconnections for the rose association are in

$$\begin{bmatrix} - & + & + & - \\ - & + & + & - \\ + & - & - & + \\ + & - & - & + \end{bmatrix} + \begin{bmatrix} + & - & + & - \\ - & + & - & + \\ - & + & - & + \\ + & - & + & - \end{bmatrix} = \begin{bmatrix} & & ++ & -- \\ -- & ++ & & \\ & & -- & ++ \\ ++ & -- & & \end{bmatrix}$$

Figure 40.9
The weights in the third matrix allow either A pattern shown in figure 40.8 to recreate the corresponding B pattern. Each weight in this case is equal to the sum of the weight for the A pattern and the weight for the B pattern, as illustrated.

effect. For this reason, it is possible to add together the pattern of interconnections for the rose association and the pattern for the steak association, and still be able to associate the sight of the steak with the smell of a steak and the sight of a rose with the smell of a rose. The two sets of interconnections do not interact at all.

One of the limitations of the Hebbian learning rule is that it can learn the connection strengths appropriate to an entire ensemble of patterns only when all the patterns are completely uncorrelated. This restriction does not, however, apply to pattern associators which use more sophisticated learning schemes.

Attractive properties of pattern associator models   Pattern associator models have the property that uncorrelated patterns do not interact with each other, but more similar ones do. Thus, to the extent that a new pattern of activation on the A units is similar to one of the old ones, it will tend to have similar effects. Furthermore, if we assume that learning the interconnections occurs in small increments, similar patterns will essentially reinforce the strengths of the links they share in common with other patterns. Thus, if we present the same pair of patterns over and over, but each time we add a little random noise to each element of each member of the pair, the system will automatically learn to associate the central tendency of the two patterns and will learn to ignore the noise. What will be stored will be an average of the similar patterns with the slight variations removed. On the other hand, when we present the system with completely uncorrelated patterns, they will not interact with each other in this way. Thus, the same pool of units can extract the central tendency of each of a number of pairs of unrelated patterns.

Extracting the structure of an ensemble of patterns   The fact that similar patterns tend to produce similar effects allows distributed models to exhibit a kind of spontaneous generalization, extending behavior appropriate for one pattern to other similar patterns. This property is shared by other PDP models, such as the word perception model and the Jets and Sharks model described above; the main difference here is in the existence of simple, local, learning mechanisms that can allow the acquisition of the connection strengths needed to produce these generalizations through experience with members of the ensemble of patterns. Distributed models have another interesting property as well: If there are regularities in the correspondences between pairs of patterns, the model will naturally extract these regularities. This property allows distributed models to acquire patterns of interconnections that lead them to behave in ways we ordinarily take as evidence for the use of linguistic rules.

Here, we describe [such a] model very briefly. The model is a mechanism that learns how to construct the past tenses of words from their root forms through repeated presentations of examples of root forms paired with the corresponding past-tense form. The model consists of two pools of units. In one pool, patterns of activation representing the phonological structure of the root form of the verb can be represented, and, in the other, patterns representing the phonological structure of the past tense can be represented. The goal of the model is simply to learn the right connection strengths between the root units and the past-tense units, so that whenever the root form of a verb is presented the model will construct the corresponding past-tense form. The model is trained by presenting the root form of the verb as a pattern of activation over the root units, and then using a simple, local, learning rule to adjust the connection strengths so that this root form will tend to produce the correct pattern of activation over the past-tense units. The model is tested by simply presenting the root form as a pattern of activation over the root units and examining the pattern of activation produced over the past-tense units.

The model is trained initially with a small number of verbs children learn early in the acquisition process. At this point in learning, it can only produce appropriate outputs for inputs that it has explicitly been shown. But as it learns more and more verbs, it exhibits two interesting behaviors. First, it produces the standard *ed* past tense when tested with pseudo-verbs or verbs it has never seen. Second, it "overregularizes" the past tense of irregular words it previously completed correctly. Often, the model will blend the irregular past tense of the word with the regular *ed* ending, and produce errors like *CAMED* as the past of *COME*. These phenomena mirror those observed in the early phases of acquisition of control over past tenses in young children.

The generativity of the child's responses—the creation of regular past tenses of new verbs and the overregularization of the irregular verbs—has been taken as strong evidence that the child has induced the rule which states that the regular correspondence for the past tense in English is to add a final *ed* (Berko 1958). On the evidence of its performance, then, the model can be said to have acquired the rule. However, no special rule-induction mechanism is used, and no special language-acquisition device is required. The model learns to behave in accordance with the rule, not by explicitly noting that most words take *ed* in the past tense in English and storing this rule away explicitly, but simply by building up a set of connections in a pattern associator through a long series of simple learning experiences. The same mechanisms of parallel distributed processing and connection modification which are used in a number of domains serve, in this case, to produce implicit knowledge tantamount to a linguistic rule. The model also provides a fairly detailed account of a number of the specific aspects of the error patterns children make in learning the rule. In this sense, it provides a richer and more detailed description of the acquisition process than any that falls out naturally from the assumption that the child is building up a repertoire of explicit but inaccessible rules.

There is a lot more to be said about distributed models of learning, about their strengths and their weaknesses, than we have space for in this preliminary consideration. For now we hope mainly to have suggested that they provide dramatically different accounts of learning and acquisition than are offered by traditional models of these processes. We saw earlier that performance in accordance with rules can emerge from the interactions of simple, interconnected units. Now we can see how the aquisition of performance that conforms to linguistic rules can emerge from a simple, local, connection strength modulation process.

Acknowledgments

This research was supported by Contract N00014-79-C-0323, NR 667-437 with the Personnel and Training Research Programs of the Office of Naval Research, by grants from the System Development Foundation, and by a NIMH Career Development Award (MH00385) to the first author.

Note

1. In this and all other cases, there is a tendency for the pattern of activation to be influenced by partially activated, near neighbors, which do not quite match the probe. Thus, in this case, there is a Jet Al, who is a Married Burglar. The unit for Al gets slightly activated, giving Married a slight edge over Divorced in the simulation.

References

Anderson, J. R. 1983. *The architecture of cognition.* Cambridge, MA: Harvard University Press.

Berko, J. 1958. The child's learning of English morphology. *Word, 14,* 150–177.

Chomsky, N., and Halle, M. 1968. *The sound pattern of English.* New York: Harper & Row.

Hebb, D. O. 1949. *The organization of behavior.* New York: Wiley.

Hinton, G. E., and Anderson, J. A., eds. 1981. *Parallel models of associative memory.* Hillsdale, NJ: Erlbaum.

Isenberg, D., Walker E. C. T, Ryder, J. M., and Schweikert J. 1980, November. *A top-down effect on the identification of function words.* Paper presented at the Acoustical Society of America, Los Angeles.

Lindsay, P. H., and Norman, D. A. 1972. *Human information processing: An introduction to psychology.* New York: Academic Press.

McClelland, J. L. 1981. Retrieving general and specific information from stored knowledge of specifics. *Proceedings of the Third Annual Meeting of the Cognitive Science Society,* 170–172.

McClelland, J. L., and Rumelhart, D. E. 1981. An interactive activation model of context effects in letter perception: Part 1. An account of basic findings. *Psychological Review, 88,* 375–407.

Minsky, M. 1975. A framework for representing knowledge. In P. H. Winston (ed.), *The psychology of computer vision* (pp. 211–277). New York: McGraw-Hill.

Norman, D. A., and Bobrow, D. G. 1976. On the role of active memory processes in perception and cognition. In C. N. Cofer, ed., *The structure of human memory* (pp. 114–132). Freeman: San Francisco.

Pillsbury, W. B. 1897. A study in apperception. *American Journal of Psychology, 8,* 315–393.

Rumelhart, D. E. 1975. Notes on a schema for stories. In D. G. Bobrow and A. Collins eds., *Representation and understanding* (pp. 211–236). New York: Academic Press.

Rumelhart, D. E. 1977. Toward an interactive model of reading. In S. Dornic, ed., *Attention & Performance VI.* Hillsdale, NJ: Erlbaum.

Rumelhart, D. E., and McClelland, J. L. 1982. An interactive activation model of context effects in letter perception: Part 2. The contextual enhancement effect and some tests and extensions of the model. *Psychological Review, 89,* 60–94.

Schank, R. C. 1973. Identification of conceptualizations underlying natural language. In R. C. Schank, and K. M. Colby, eds., *Computer models of thought and language* (pp. 187–247). San Francisco: Freeman.

Schank, R. C. 1976. The role of memory in language processing. In C. N. Cofer, ed., *The structure of human memory* (pp. 162–189). Freeman: San Francisco.

Selfridge, O. G., and Neisser, U. 1960. Pattern recognition by machine. *Scientific American, 203,* 60–68.

Smith, P. T., and Baker, R. G. 1976. The influence of English spelling patterns on pronounciation. *Journal of Verbal Learning and Verbal Behavior, 15,* 267–286.

Spoehr, K., and Smith, E. 1975. The role of orthographic and phonotactic rules in perceiving letter patterns. *Journal of Experimental Psychology: Human Perception and Performance, 1,* 21–34.

Venesky, R. L. 1970. *The structure of English orthography.* The Hague: Mouton.

Warren, R. M. 1970. Perceptual restoration of missing speech sounds. *Science, 167,* 393–395.

Winston, P. H. 1975. Learning structural descriptions from examples. In P. H. Winston, ed., *The psychology of computer vision* (pp. 157–209). New York: McGraw-Hill.

Chapter 41

Connectionism and Cognitive Architecture: A Critical Analysis

Jerry A. Fodor and Zenon W. Pylyshyn

1 Introduction

Connectionist or *PDP* models are catching on. There are conferences and new books nearly every day, and the popular science press hails this new wave of theorizing as a breakthrough in understanding the mind (a typical example is the article in the May issue of *Science 86*, called "How we think: A new theory"). There are also, inevitably, descriptions of the emergence of Connectionism as a Kuhnian "paradigm shift". (See Schneider, 1987, for an example of this and for further evidence of the tendency to view Connectionism as the "new wave" of Cognitive Science.)

The fan club includes the most unlikely collection of people. Connectionism gives solace both to philosophers who think that relying on the pseudoscientific intentional or semantic notions of folk psychology (like goals and beliefs) mislead psychologists into taking the computational approach (e.g., P. M. Churchland, 1981; P. S. Churchland, 1986; Dennett, 1986); and to those with nearly the opposite perspective, who think that computational psychology is bankrupt because it doesn't address issues of intentionality or meaning (e.g., Dreyfus & Dreyfus, in press). On the computer science side, Connectionism appeals to theorists who think that serial machines are too weak and must be replaced by radically new parallel machines (Fahlman & Hinton, 1986), while on the biological side it appeals to those who believe that cognition can only be understood if we study it as neuroscience (e.g., Arbib, 1975; Sejnowski, 1981). It is also attractive to psychologists who think that much of the mind (including the part involved in using imagery) is not discrete (e.g., Kosslyn & Hatfield, 1984), or who think that cognitive science has not paid enough attention to stochastic mechanisms or to "holistic" mechanisms (e.g., Lakoff, 1986), and so on and on. It also appeals to many young cognitive scientists who view the approach as not only anti-establishment (and therefore desirable) but also rigorous and mathematical (see, however, note 2). Almost everyone who is discontent with contemporary cognitive psychology and current "information processing" models of the mind has rushed to embrace "the Connectionist alternative".

When taken as a way of modeling *cognitive architecture*, Connectionism really does represent an approach that is quite different from that of the Classical cognitive science that it seeks to replace. Classical models of the mind were derived from the structure of Turing and Von Neumann machines. They are not, of course, committed to the details of these machines as exemplified in Turing's original formulation or in typical commercial computers; only to the basic idea that the kind of computing that is relevant to understanding cognition involves operations on symbols (see Fodor, 1976, 1987; Newell, 1980, 1982; Pylyshyn, 1980, 1984a, b). In contrast, Connectionists propose to design systems that can exhibit intelligent behavior without storing, retrieving, or otherwise operating on structured symbolic expressions. The style of processing carried out in such models is thus strikingly unlike what goes on when conventional machines are computing some function.

Connectionist systems are networks consisting of very large numbers of simple but highly interconnected "units". Certain assumptions are generally made both about the units and the connections: Each unit is assumed to receive real-valued activity (either excitatory or inhibitory or both) along its input lines. Typically the units do little more than sum this activity and change their state as a function (usually a threshold function) of this sum. Each connection is allowed to modulate the activity it transmits as a function of an intrinsic (but modifiable) property called its "weight". Hence the activity on an input line is typically some non-linear function of the state of activity of its sources. The behavior of the network as a whole is a function of the initial state of activation of the units and of the weights on its connections, which serve as its only form of memory.

Numerous elaborations of this basic Connectionist architecture are possible. For example, Connectionist models often have stochastic mechanisms for determining the level of activity or the state of a unit. Moreover, units may be connected to outside environments. In this case the units are sometimes assumed to respond to a narrow range of combinations of parameter values and are said to have a certain "receptive field" in parameter-space. These are called "value units" (Ballard, 1986). In some versions of Connectionist architecture, environmental properties are encoded by the pattern of states of entire populations of units. Such "coarse coding" techniques are among the ways of achieving what Connectionists call "distributed representation".[1] The term 'Connectionist model' (like 'Turing Machine' or 'Van Neumann machine') is thus applied to a family of mechanisms that differ in details but share a galaxy of architectural commitments. We shall return to the characterization of these commitments below.

Connectionist networks have been analysed extensively—in some cases using advanced mathematical techniques.[2] They have also been simulated on computers and shown to exhibit interesting aggregate properties. For example, they can be "wired" to recognize patterns, to exhibit rule-like behavioral regularities, and to realize virtually any mapping from patterns of (input) parameters to patterns of (output) parameters—though in most cases multiparameter, multi-valued mappings require very large numbers of units. Of even greater interest is the fact that such networks can be made to learn; this is achieved by modifying the weights on the connections as a function of certain kinds of feedback (the exact way in which this is done constitutes a preoccupation of Connectionist research and has lead to the development of such important techniques as "back propagation").

In short, the study of Connectionist machines has led to a number of striking and unanticipated findings; it's surprising how much computing can be done with a uniform network of simple interconnected elements. Moreover, these models have an appearance of neural plausibility that Classical architectures are sometimes said to lack. Perhaps, then, a new Cognitive Science based on Connectionist networks should replace the old Cognitive Science based on Classical computers. Surely this is a proposal that ought to be taken seriously: if it is warranted, it implies a major redirection of research.

Unfortunately, however, discussions of the relative merits of the two architectures have thus far been marked by a variety of confusions and irrelevances. It's our view that when you clear away these misconceptions what's left is a real disagreement about the nature of mental processes and mental representations. But it seems to us that it is a matter that was substantially put to rest about thirty years ago; and the arguments that then appeared to militate decisively in favor of the Classical view appear to us to do so still.

In the present paper we will proceed as follows. First, we discuss some methodologi-cal questions about levels of explanation that have become enmeshed in the substantive controversy over Connectionism. Second, we try to say what it is that makes Connec-tionist and Classical theories of mental structure incompatible. Third, we review and extend some of the traditional arguments for the Classical architecture. Though these arguments have been somewhat recast, very little that we'll have to say here is entirely new. But we hope to make it clear how various aspects of the Classical doctrine cohere and why rejecting the Classical picture of reasoning leads Connectionists to say the very implausible things they do about logic and semantics.

1.1 Levels of Explanation

There are two major traditions in modern theorizing about the mind, one that we'll call 'Representationalist' and one that we'll call 'Eliminativist'. Representationalists hold that postulating representational (or 'intentional' or 'semantic') states is essential to a theory of cognition; according to Representationalists, there are states of the mind which function to encode states of the world. Eliminativists, by contrast, think that psycholog-ical theories can dispense with such semantic notions as representation. According to Eliminativists the appropriate vocabulary for psychological theorizing is neurological or, perhaps behavioral, or perhaps syntactic; in any event, not a vocabulary that charac-terizes mental states in terms of what they represent. (For a neurological version of eliminativism, see P. S. Churchland, 1986; for a behavioral version, see Watson, 1930; for a syntactic version, see Stich, 1983.)

Connectionists are on the Representationalist side of this issue. As Rumelhart and McClelland (1986a, p. 121) say, PDPs "are explicitly concerned with the problem of internal representation". Correspondingly, the specification of what the states of a network *represent* is an essential part of a Connectionist model. Consider, for example, the well-known Connectionist account of the bistability of the Necker cube (Feldman & Ballard, 1982). "Simple units representing the visual features of the two alternatives are arranged in competing coalitions, with inhibitory ... links between rival features and positive links within each coalition.... The result is a network that has two dominant stable states". Notice that, in this as in all other such Connectionist models, the commit-ment to mental representation is explicit: the label of a node is taken to express the representational content of the state that the device is in when the node is excited, and there are nodes corresponding to monadic and to relational properties of the reversible cube when it is seen in one way or the other.

There are, to be sure, times when Connectionists appear to vacillate between Repre-sentationalism and the claim that the "cognitive level" is dispensable in favor of a more precise and biologically-motivated level of theory. In particular, there is a lot of talk in the Connectionist literature about processes that are "sub-symbolic"—and therefore presumably *not* representational. But this is misleading: Connectionist modeling is con-sistently Representationalist in practice, and Representationalism is generally endorsed by the very theorists who also like the idea of cognition 'emerging from the sub-symbolic'. Thus, Rumelhart and McClelland (1986a, p. 121) insist that PDP models are "... strongly committed to the study of representation and process". Similarly, though Smolensky (1988, p. 2) takes Connectionism to articulate regularities at the "sub-sym-bolic level" of analysis, it turns out that sub-symbolic states do have a semantics, though it's not the semantics of representations at the "conceptual level". According to Smolensky, the semantical distinction between symbolic and sub-symbolic theories is just that "entities that are typically represented in the symbolic paradigm by [single] symbols are typically represented in the sub-symbolic paradigm by a large number of sub-symbols".[3] Both the conceptual and the sub-symbolic levels thus postulate representational states, but sub-symbolic theories slice them thinner.

We are stressing the Representationalist character of Connectionist theorizing because much Connectionist methodological writing has been preoccupied with the question 'What level of explanation is appropriate for theories of cognitive architecture?' (see. for example, the exchange between Broadbent, 1985, and Rumelhart & McClelland, 1985). And, as we're about to see, what one says about the levels question depends a lot on what stand one takes about whether there are representational states.

It seems certain that the world has causal structure at very many different levels of analysis, with the individuals recognized at the lowest levels being, in general, very small and the individuals recognized at the highest levels being, in general, very large. Thus there is a scientific story to be told about quarks; and a scientific story to be told about atoms; and a scientific story to be told about molecules ... ditto rocks and stones and rivers ... ditto galaxies. And the story that scientists tell about the causal structure that the world has at any one of these levels may be quite different from the story that they tell about its causal structure at the next level up or down. The methodological implication for psychology is this: If you want to have an argument about *cognitive* architecture, you have to specify the level of analysis that's supposed to be at issue.

If you're *not* a Representationalist, this is quite tricky since it is then not obvious what makes a phenomenon cognitive. But specifying the level of analysis relevant for theories of cognitive architecture is no problem for either Classicists or Connectionists. Since Classicists and Connectionists are both Representationalists, for them any level at which states of the system are taken to encode properties of the world counts as a *cognitive* level; and no other levels do. (Representations of "the world" include of course, representations of symbols; for example, the concept WORD is a construct at the cognitive level because it represents something, namely words.) Correspondingly, it's the architecture of representational states and processes that discussions of *cognitive architecture* are about. Put differently, the architecture of the cognitive system consists of the set of basic operations, resources, functions, principles, etc. (generally the sorts of properties that would be described in a "user's manual" for that architecture if it were available on a computer), whose domain and range are the *representational states* of the organism.[4]

It follows, that, if you want to make good the Connectionist theory *as a theory of cognitive architecture*, you have to show that the processes which operate on *the representational states* of an organism are those which are specified by a Connectionist architecture. It is, for example, *no use at all*, from the cognitive psychologist's point of view, to show that the *non*representational (e.g., neurological, or molecular, or quantum mechanical) states of an organism constitute a Connectionist network, because that would *leave open* the question whether the mind is such a network *at the psychological level*. It is, in particular, perfectly possible that nonrepresentational neurological states are interconnected in the ways described by Connectionist models *but that the representational states themselves are not*. This is because, just as it is possible to implement a *Connectionist* cognitive architecture in a network of causally interacting nonrepresentational elements, so too it is perfectly possible to implement a *Classical* cognitive architecture in such a network.[5] In fact, the question whether Connectionist networks should be treated as models at some level of implementation is moot.

It is important to be clear about this matter of levels on pain of simply trivializing the issues about cognitive architecture. Consider, for example, the following remark of Rumelhart's: "It has seemed to me for some years now that there must be a unified account in which the so-called rule-governed and [the] exceptional cases were dealt with by a unified underlying process—a process which produces rule-like and rule-exception behavior through the application of a single process ... [In this process] ... both the rule-like and non-rule-like behavior is a product of the interaction of a very large number of 'sub-symbolic' processes." (Rumelhart, 1984, p. 60). It's clear from the context that Rumelhart takes this idea to be very tendentious; one of the Connectionist claims that Classical theories are required to deny.

But in fact it's not. For, *of course* there are 'sub-symbolic' interactions that implement both rule like and rule violating behavior; for example, quantum mechanical processes do. *That's* not what Classical theorists deny; indeed, it's not denied by anybody who is even vaguely a materialist. Nor does a Classical theorist deny that rule-following and rule-violating behaviors are both implemented by the very same neurological machinery. For a Classical theorist, neurons implement *all* cognitive processes in precisely the same way: viz., by supporting the basic operations that are required for symbol-processing.

What *would* be an interesting and tendentious claim is that there's no distinction between rule-following and rule-violating mentation *at the cognitive or representational or symbolic level*; specifically, that it is not the case that the etiology of rule-following behavior is mediated by the representation of explicit rules.[6] We will argue that it too is *not* what divides Classical from Connectionist architecture; Classical models *permit* a principled distinction between the etiologies of mental processes that are explicitly rule-governed and mental processes that aren't; but they don't demand one.

In short, the issue between Classical and Connectionist architecture is not about the explicitness of rules; as we'll presently see, Classical architecture is not, per se, committed to the idea that explicit rules mediate the etiology of behavior. And it is not about the reality of representational states; Classicists and Connectionists are all Representational Realists. And it is not about nonrepresentational architecture; a Connectionist neural network can perfectly well implement a Classical architecture at the cognitive level.

So, then, what *is* the disagreement between Classical and Connectionist architecture about?

2 The Nature of the Dispute

Classicists and Connectionists all assign semantic content to *something*. Roughly, Connectionists assign semantic content to 'nodes' (that is, to units or aggregates of units; see note 1)—i.e., to the sorts of things that are typically labeled in Connectionist diagrams; whereas Classicists assign semantic content to *expressions*—i.e., to the sorts of things that get written on the tapes of Turing machines and stored at addresses in Von Neumann machines.[7] But Classical theories disagree with Connectionist theories about what primitive relations hold among these content-bearing entities. Connectionist theories acknowledge *only causal connectedness* as a primitive relation among nodes: when you know how activation and inhibition flow among them, you know everything there is to know about how the nodes in a network are related. By contrast, Classical theories acknowledge not only causal relations among the semantically evaluable objects that they posit, but also a range of structural relations, of which constituency is paradigmatic.

This difference has far reaching consequences for the ways that the two kinds of theories treat a variety of cognitive phenomena, some of which we will presently examine at length. But, underlying the disagreements about details are two architectural differences between the theories:

(1) *Combinatorial syntax and semantics for mental representations.* Classical theories —but not Connectionist theories—postulate a 'language of thought' (see, for example, Fodor, 1975); they take mental representations to have *a combinatorial syntax and semantics*, in which (a) there is a distinction between structurally atomic and structurally molecular representations; (b) structurally molecular representations have syntactic constituents that are themselves either structurally molecular or structurally atomic; and (c) the semantic content of a (molecular) representation is a function of the semantic contents of its syntactic parts, together with its constituent structure. For purposes of convenience, we'll sometime abbreviate (a)–(c) by speaking of Classical theories as committed to "complex" mental representations or to "symbol structures".[8]

(2) *Structure sensitivity of processes.* In Classical models, the principles by which mental states are transformed, or by which an input selects the corresponding output, are defined over structural properties of mental representations. Because Classical mental *representations* have combinatorial structure, it is possible for Classical mental *operations* to apply to them by reference to their form. The result is that a paradigmatic Classical mental process operates upon any mental representation that satisfies a given structural description, and transforms it into a mental representation that satisfies another structural description. (So, for example, in a model of inference one might recognize an operation that applies to any representation of the form $P\&Q$ and transforms it into a representation of the form P.) Notice that since formal properties can be defined at a variety of levels of abstraction, such an operation can apply equally to representations that differ widely in their structural complexity. The operation that applies to representations of the form $P\&Q$ to produce P is satisfied by, for example, an expression like "(AvBvC) & (DvEvF)", from which it derives the expression "(AvBvC)".

We take (1) and (2) as the claims that define Classical models, and we take these claims quite literally; they constrain the physical realizations of symbol structures. In particular, the symbol structures in a Classical model are assumed to correspond to real physical structures in the brain and the *combinatorial structure* of a representation is supposed to have a counterpart in structural relations among physical properties of the brain. For example, the relation 'part of', which holds between a relatively simple symbol and a more complex one, is assumed to correspond to some physical relation among brain states.[9] This is why Newell (1980) speaks of computational systems such as brains and Classical computers as *"physical symbol systems"*.

This bears emphasis because the Classical theory is committed not only to there being a system of physically instantiated symbols, but also to the claim that the physical properties onto which the structure of the symbols is mapped *are the very properties that cause the system to behave as it does.* In other words the physical counterparts of the symbols, and their structural properties, *cause* the system's behavior. A system which has symbolic expressions, but whose operation does not depend upon the structure of these expressions, does not qualify as a Classical machine since it fails to satisfy condition (2). In this respect, a Classical model is very different from one in which behavior is caused by mechanisms, such as energy minimization, that are not responsive to the physical encoding of the structure of representations.

From now on, when we speak of 'Classical' models, we will have in mind *any* model that has complex mental representations, as characterized in (1) and structure-sensitive mental processes, as characterized in (2). Our account of Classical architecture is therefore neutral with respect to such issues as whether or not there is a separate executive. For example, Classical machines can have an "object-oriented" architecture, like that of the computer language *Smalltalk*, or a "message passing" architecture, like that of Hewett's (1977) *Actors*—so long as the objects or the messages have a combinatorial structure which is causally implicated in the processing. Classical architecture is also neutral on the question whether the operations on the symbols are constrained to occur one at a time or whether many operations can occur at the same time.

Here, then, is the plan for what follows. In the rest of this section, we will sketch the Connectionist proposal for a computational architecture that does away with complex mental representations and structure sensitive operations. (Although our purpose here is merely expository, it turns out that describing exactly what Connectionists are committed to requires substantial reconstruction of their remarks and practices. Since there is a great variety of points of view within the Connectionist community, we are prepared to find that some Connectionists in good standing may not fully endorse the program when it is laid out in what we take to be its bare essentials.) Following this general expository (or reconstructive) discussion, Section 3 provides a series of arguments favoring the Classical story. Then the remainder of the paper considers some of the reasons why Connectionism appears attractive to many people and offers further general comments on the relation between the Classical and the Connectionist enterprise.

2.1 Complex Mental Representations

To begin with, consider a case of the most trivial sort; two machines, one Classical in spirit and one Connectionist.[10] Here is how the Connectionist machine might reason. There is a network of labelled nodes as in figure 41.1. Paths between the nodes indicate the routes along which activation can spread (that is, they indicate the consequences that exciting one of the nodes has for determining the level of excitation of others). Drawing an inference from A&B to A thus corresponds to an excitation of node 2 being caused by an excitation of node 1 (alternatively, if the system is in a state in which node 1 is excited, it eventually settles into a state in which node 2 is excited; see note 7).

Now consider a Classical machine. This machine has a tape on which it writes expressions. Among the expressions that can appear on this tape are: 'A', 'B', 'A&B', 'C', 'D', 'C&D', 'A&C&D' ... etc. The machine's causal constitution is as follows: whenever a token of the form P&Q appears on the tape, the machine writes a token of the form P. An inference from A&B to A thus corresponds to a tokening of type 'A&B' on the tape causing a tokening of type 'A'.

So then, what does the architectural difference between the machines consist in? In the Classical machine, the objects to which the content A&B is ascribed (viz., tokens of the expression 'A&B') literally contain, as proper parts, objects to which the content A is ascribed (viz., tokens of the expression 'A'.) Moreover, the semantics (e.g., the satisfaction conditions) of the expression 'A&B' is determined in a uniform way by the semantics of its constituents.[11] By contrast, in the Connectionist machine none of this is true; the object to which the content A&B is ascribed (viz., node 1) is causally connected to the object to which the content A is ascribed (viz., node 2); but there is no structural

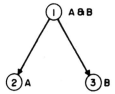

Figure 41.1
A possible Connectionist network for drawing inferences from A & B to A or to B

(e.g., no part/whole) relation that holds between them. In short, it is characteristic of Classical systems, but not of Connectionist systems, to exploit arrays of symbols some of which are atomic (e.g., expressions like 'A') but indefinitely many of which have other symbols as syntactic and semantic parts (e.g., expressions like 'A&B').

It is easy to overlook this difference between Classical and Connectionist architectures when reading the Connectionist polemical literature or examining a Connectionist model. There are at least four ways in which one might be lead to do so: (1) by failing to understand the difference between what arrays of symbols do in Classical machines and what node labels do in Connectionist machines; (2) by confusing the question whether the nodes in Connectionist networks have *constituent* structure with the question whether they are *neurologically distributed*; (3) by failing to distinguish between a representation having semantic and syntactic constituents and a concept being encoded in terms of microfeatures, and (4) by assuming that since representations of Connectionist networks have a graph structure, it follows that the nodes in the networks have a corresponding constituent structure. We shall now need rather a long digression to clear up these misunderstandings.

2.1.1 The role of labels in Connectionist theories   In the course of setting out a Connectionist model, intentional content will be assigned to machine states, and the expressions of some language or other will, of course, be used to express this assignment; for example, nodes may be labelled to indicate their representational content. Such labels often have a combinatorial syntax and semantics; in this respect, they can look a lot like Classical mental representations. The point to emphasize, however, is that it doesn't follow (and it isn't true) that the nodes to which these labels are assigned have a combinatorial syntax and semantics. 'A&B', for example, can be tokened on the tape of the Classical machine *and can also appear as a label in a Connectionist machine* as it does in figure 41.1. And, of course, the expression 'A&B' is syntactically and semantically complex: it has a token of 'A' as one of its syntactic constituents, and the semantics of the expression 'A&B' is a function of the semantics of the expression 'A'. But it isn't part of the intended reading of the diagram that node 1 itself has constituents; the node— unlike its label—has no semantically interpreted parts.

It is, in short, important to understand the difference between Connectionist labels and the symbols over which Classical computations are defined. The difference is this: Strictly speaking, the labels play *no role at all* in determining the operation of a Connectionist machine; in particular, the operation of the machine is unaffected by the syntactic and semantic relations that hold among the expressions that are used as labels. To put this another way, the node labels in a Connectionist machine are not part of the causal structure of the machine. Thus, the machine depicted in figure 41.1 will continue to make the same state transitions regardless of what labels we assign to the nodes. Whereas, by contrast, the state transitions of Classical machines are causally determined *by the structure—including the constituent structure—of the symbol arrays that the machines transform*: change the symbols and the system behaves quite differently. (In fact, since the behavior of a Classical machine is sensitive to the syntax of the representations it computes on, even interchanging *synonymous*—semantically equivalent—representations affects the course of computation). So, although the Connectionist's labels and the Classicist's data structures both constitute languages, only the latter language constitutes a medium of computation.[12]

2.1.2 Connectionist networks and graph structures   The *second* reason that the lack of syntactic and semantic structure in Connectionist representations has largely been ignored may be that Connectionist networks look like general graphs; and it is, of course, perfectly possible to use graphs to describe the internal structure of a complex symbol. That's precisely what linguists do when they use 'trees' to exhibit the constituent structure of sentences. Correspondingly, one could imagine a graph notation that expresses the internal structure of mental representations by using arcs and labelled nodes. So, for example, you might express the syntax of the mental representation that corresponds to the thought that John loves the girl like this:

John → loves → the girl

Under the intended interpretation, this would be the structural description of a mental representation whose content is that John loves the girl, and whose constituents are: a mental representation that refers to *John*, a mental representation that refers to *the girl*, and a mental representation that expresses the two-place relation represented by '→loves→'.

But although graphs can sustain an interpretation as specifying the logical syntax of a complex mental representation, this interpretation is inappropriate for graphs of Connectionist networks. Connectionist graphs are not structural descriptions of mental representations; they're specifications of causal relations. All that a Connectionist can mean by a graph of the form X → Y is: *states of node X causally affect states of node Y*. In particular, the graph can't mean *X is a constituent of Y* or *X is grammatically related to Y* etc., since these sorts of relations are, in general, not defined for the kinds of mental representations that Connectionists recognize.

Another way to put this is that the links in Connectionist diagrams are not generalized pointers that can be made to take on different functional significance *by an independent interpreter*, but are confined to meaning something like "sends activation to". The intended interpretation of the links as causal Connections is intrinsic to the theory. If you ignore this point, you are likely to take Connectionism to offer a much richer notion of mental representation than it actually does.

2.1.3 Distributed representations   The *third* mistake that can lead to a failure to notice that the mental representations in Connectionist models lack combinatorial syntactic and semantic structure is the fact that many Connectionists view representations as being *neurologically distributed*; and, presumably, whatever is distributed must have parts. It doesn't follow, however, that whatever is distributed must have *constituents*; being neurologically distributed is very different from having semantic or syntactic constituent structure.

You have constituent structure when (and only when) the parts of semantically evaluable entities are themselves semantically evaluable. Constituency relations thus hold among objects all of which are at the representational level; they are, in that sense, *within* level relations.[13] By contrast, neural distributedness—the sort of relation that is assumed to hold between 'nodes' and the 'units' by which they are realized—is a *between* level relation: The nodes, but not the units, count as representations. To claim that a node is neurally distributed is presumably to claim that its states of activation correspond to patterns of neural activity—to aggregates of neural 'units'—rather than to activations of single neurons. The important point is that nodes that are distributed in this sense can perfectly well be syntactically and semantically atomic: Complex spatially-distributed implementation in no way implies constituent structure.

There is, however, a different sense in which the representational states in a network might be distributed, and this sort of distribution also raises questions relevant to the constituency issue.

2.1.4 Representations as 'distributed' over microfeatures   Many Connectionists hold that the mental representations that correspond to commonsense concepts (CHAIR, JOHN, CUP, etc.) are 'distributed' over galaxies of lower level units which themselves have representational content. To use common Connectionist terminology (see Smolensky, 1988), the higher or "conceptual level" units correspond to vectors in a "sub-conceptual" space of microfeatures. The model here is something like the relation between a defined expression and its defining feature analysis: thus, the concept BACHELOR might be thought to correspond to a vector in a space of features that includes ADULT, HUMAN, MALE, and MARRIED; i.e., as an assignment of the value + to the first two features and − to the last. Notice that distribution over microfeatures (unlike distribution over neural units) is a relation among representations, hence a relation at the cognitive level.

Since microfeatures are frequently assumed to be derived automatically (i.e., via learning procedures) from the statistical properties of samples of stimuli, we can think of them as expressing the sorts of properties that are revealed by multivariate analysis of sets of stimuli (e.g., by multidimensional scaling of similarity judgments). In particular, they need not correspond to English words; they can be finer-grained than, or otherwise atypical of, the terms for which a non-specialist needs to have a word. Other than that, however, they are perfectly ordinary semantic features, much like those that lexicographers have traditionally used to represent the meanings of words.

On the most frequent Connectionist accounts, theories articulated in terms of microfeature vectors are supposed to show how concepts are *actually* encoded, hence the feature vectors are intended to *replace* "less precise" specifications of macrolevel concepts. For example, where a Classical theorist might recognize a psychological state of entertaining the concept CUP, a Connectionist may acknowledge only a *roughly analogous* state of tokening the corresponding feature vector. (One reason that the analogy is only rough is that which feature vector 'corresponds' to a given concept may be viewed as heavily context dependent.) The generalizations that 'concept level' theories frame are thus taken to be only approximately true, the exact truth being stateable only in the vocabulary of the microfeatures. Smolensky, for example (p. 11), is explicit in endorsing this picture: "Precise, formal descriptions of the intuitive processor are generally tractable not at the conceptual level, but only at the subconceptual level."[14] This treatment of the relation between commonsense concepts and microfeatures is exactly analogous to the standard Connectionist treatment of rules; in both cases, macrolevel theory is said to provide a vocabulary adequate for formulating generalizations that roughly approximate the facts about behavioral regularities. But the contructs of the macrotheory do *not* correspond to the causal mechanisms that generate these regularities. If you want a theory of these mechanisms, you need to replace talk about rules and concepts with talk about nodes, connections, microfeatures, vectors and the like.[15]

Now, it is among the major misfortunes of the Connectionist literature that the issue about whether commonsense concepts should be represented by sets of microfeatures has gotten thoroughly mixed up with the issue about combinatorial structure in mental representations. The crux of the mixup is the fact that sets of microfeatures can overlap, so that, for example, if a microfeature corresponding to '+ has-a-handle' is part of the array of nodes over which the commonsense concept CUP is distributed, then you might think of the theory as representing '+ has-a-handle' as a *constituent* of the concept CUP; from which you might conclude that Connectionists have a notion of constituency after all, contrary to the claim that Connectionism is not a language-of-thought architecture (see Smolensky, 1988).

A moment's consideration will make it clear, however, that even on the assumption that concepts are distributed over microfeatures, '+ has-a-handle' is not a constituent of CUP in anything like the sense that 'Mary' (the word) is a constituent of (the sentence) 'John loves Mary'. In the former case, "constituency" is being (mis)used to refer to a semantic relation between predicates; roughly, the idea is that macrolevel predicates like CUP are defined by sets of microfeatures like 'has-a-handle', so that it's some sort of semantic truth that CUP applies to a subset of what 'has-a-handle' applies to. Notice that while the extensions of these predicates are in a set/subset relation, the predicates themselves are not in any sort of part-to-whole relation. The expression 'has-a-handle' isn't *part of* the expression CUP any more than the English phrase 'is an unmarried man' is part of the English phrase 'is a bachelor'.

Real constituency does have to do with parts and wholes; the symbol 'Mary' is literally a part of the symbol 'John loves Mary'. It is because their symbols enter into real-constituency relations that natural languages have both atomic symbols and complex ones. By contrast, the definition relation can hold in a language where *all* the symbols are syntactically atomic; e.g., a language which contains both 'cup' and 'has-a-handle' as atomic predicates. This point is worth stressing. The question whether a representational system has real-constituency is independent of the question of microfeature analysis; it arises both for systems in which you have CUP as semantically primitive, and for systems in which the semantic primitives are things like '+ has-a-handle' and CUP and the like are defined in terms of these primitives. It really is very important not to confuse the semantic distinction between primitive expressions and defined expressions with the syntactic distinction between atomic symbols and complex symbols.

So far as we know, there are no worked out attempts in the Connectionist literature to deal with the syntactic and semantical issues raised by relations of real-constituency. There is, however, a proposal that comes up from time to time: viz., that what are traditionally treated as complex symbols should actually be viewed as just sets of units, with the role relations that traditionally get coded by constituent structure represented by units belonging to these sets. So, for example, the mental representation corresponding to the belief that John loves Mary might be the feature vector { +*John-subject*; +*loves*; +*Mary-object*}. Here 'John-subject', 'Mary-object' and the like are the labels of units; that is, they are atomic (i.e., micro-) features, whose status is analogous to 'has-a-handle'. In particular, they have no internal syntactic analysis, and there is no structural relation (except the orthographic one) between the feature 'Mary-object' that occurs in the set {John-subject; loves; Mary-object} and the feature 'Mary-subject' that occurs in the set {Mary-subject; loves; John-object}. (See, for example, the discussion in Hinton, 1987 of "role-specific descriptors that represent the conjunction of an identity and a role [by the use of which] we can implement part-whole hierarchies using set intersection as the composition rule." See also, McClelland, Rumelhart and Hinton, 1986, p. 82–85, where what appears to be the same treatment is proposed in somewhat different terms.)

Since, as we remarked, these sorts of ideas aren't elaborated in the Connectionist literature, detailed discussion is probably not warranted here. But it's worth a word to make clear what sort of trouble you would get into if you were to take them seriously.

As we understand it, the proposal really has two parts: On the one hand, it's suggested that although Connectionist representations cannot exhibit real-constituency, nevertheless the Classical distinction between complex symbols and their constituents can be replaced by the distinction between feature sets and their subsets; and, on the other hand, it's suggested that role relations can be captured by features. We'll consider these ideas in turn.

(1) Instead of having complex symbols like "John loves Mary" in the representational system, you have feature sets like { +John-subject; +loves; +Mary-object}. Since this set has { +John-subject}, { +loves; +Mary-object} and so forth as sub-sets, it may be supposed that the force of the constituency relation has been captured by employing the subset relation.

However, it's clear that this idea won't work since not all subsets of features correspond to genuine constituents. For example, among the subsets of { +John-subject; +loves; +Mary-object} are the sets { +John-subject; +Mary-object}) and the set { +John-subject; +loves} which do not, of course, correspond to constituents of the complex symbol "John loves Mary".

(2) Instead of defining roles in terms of relations among constituents, as one does in Classical architecture, introduce them as microfeatures.

Consider a system in which the mental representation that is entertained when one believes that John loves Mary is the feature set { +John-subject; +loves; +Mary-object}. What representation corresponds to the belief that John loves Mary and Bill hates Sally? Suppose, pursuant to the present proposal, that it's the set { +John-subject; +loves; +Mary-object; +Bill-subject; +hates; +Sally-object}. We now have the problem of distinguishing that belief from the belief that John loves Sally and Bill hates Mary; and from the belief that John hates Mary and Bill loves Sally; and from the belief that John hates Mary and Sally and Bill loves Mary; etc., since these other beliefs will all correspond to precisely the same set of features. The problem is, of course, that nothing in the representation of Mary as +Mary-object specifies whether it's the loving or the hating that she is the object of; similarly, mutatis mutandis, for the representation of John as +John-subject.

What has gone wrong isn't disastrous (yet). All that's required is to enrich the system of representations by recognizing features that correspond not to (for example) just being a subject, but rather to being the subject of a loving of Mary (the property that John has when John loves Mary) and being the subject of a hating of Sally (the property that Bill has when Bill hates Sally). So, the representation of John that's entertained when one believes that John loves Mary and Bill hates Sally might be something like +John-subject-hates-Mary-object.

The disadvantage of this proposal is that it requires rather a lot of microfeatures.[16] How many? Well, a number of the order of magnitude of the *sentences* of a natural language (whereas one might have hoped to get by with a vocabulary of basic expressions that is not vastly larger than the *lexicon* of a natural language; after all, natural languages do). We leave it to the reader to estimate the number of microfeatures you would need, assuming that there is a distinct belief corresponding to every grammatical sentence of English of up to, say, fifteen words of length, and assuming that there is an average of, say, five roles associated with each belief. (Hint: George Miller once estimated that the number of well-formed 20-word sentences of English is of the order of magnitude of the number of seconds in the history of the universe.)

The alternative to this grotesque explosion of atomic symbols would be to have *a combinatorial syntax and semantics for the features*. But, of course, this is just to give up the game since the syntactic and semantic relations that hold among the parts of the complex feature +((John subject) loves (Mary object)) are the very same ones that Classically hold among the constituents of the complex symbol "John loves Mary"; these include the role relations which Connectionists had proposed to reconstruct using just sets of atomic features. It is, of course, no accident that the Connectionist proposal for dealing with role relations runs into these sorts of problems. Subject, object and the rest are Classically defined *with respect to the geometry of constituent structure trees*. And Connectionist representations don't have constituents.

The idea that we should capture role relations by allowing features like *John-subject* thus turns out to be bankrupt; and there doesn't seem to be any other way to get the force of structured symbols in a Connectionist architecture. Or, if there is, nobody has given any indication of how to do it. This becomes clear once the crucial issue about structure in mental representations is disentangled from the relatively secondary (and orthogonal) issue about whether the representation of commonsense concepts is 'distributed' (i.e., from questions like whether it's CUP or 'has-a-handle' or both that is semantically primitive in the language of thought).

It's worth adding that these problems about expressing the role relations are actually just a symptom of a more pervasive difficulty: A consequence of restricting the vehicles of mental representation to sets of atomic symbols is a notation that fails quite generally to express the way that concepts group into propositions. To see this, let's continue to suppose that we have a network in which the nodes represent concepts rather than propositions (so that what corresponds to the thought that John loves Mary is a distribution of activation over the set of nodes {JOHN; LOVES; MARY} rather than the activation of a single node labelled JOHN LOVES MARY). Notice that it cannot plausibly be assumed that all the nodes that happen to be active at a given time will correspond to concepts that are constituents of the *same* proposition; least of all if the architecture is "massively parallel" so that many things are allowed to go on—many concepts are allowed to be entertained—simultaneously in a given mind. Imagine, then, the following situation: at time t, a man is looking at the sky (so the nodes corresponding to SKY and BLUE are active) and thinking that John loves Fido (so the nodes corresponding to JOHN, LOVES, and FIDO are active), and the node FIDO is connected to the node DOG (which is in turn connected to the node ANIMAL) in such fashion that DOG and ANIMAL are active too, We can, if you like, throw it in that the man has got an itch, so ITCH is also on.

According to the current theory of mental representation, this man's mind at t is specified by the vector $\{+JOHN, +LOVES, +FIDO, +DOG, +SKY, +BLUE, +ITCH, +ANIMAL\}$. And the question is: *which subvectors of this vector correspond to thoughts that the man is thinking?* Specifically, what is it about the man's representational state that determines that the simultaneous activation of the nodes, {JOHN, LOVES, FIDO} constitutes his thinking that John loves Fido, but the simultaneous activation of FIDO, ANIMAL and BLUE does *not* constitute his thinking that Fido is a blue animal? It seems that we made it too easy for ourselves when we identified the thought that John loves Mary with the vector $\{+JOHN, +LOVES, +MARY\}$; at best that works only on the assumption that JOHN, LOVES and MARY are the only nodes active when someone has that thought. And that's an assumption to which no theory of mental representation is entitled.

It's important to see that this problem arises precisely because the theory is trying to use sets of atomic representations to do a job that you really need complex representations for. Thus, the question we're wanting to answer is: Given the total set of nodes active at a time, what distinguishes the subvectors that correspond to propositions from the subvectors that don't? This question has a straightforward answer if, contrary to the present proposal, complex representations are assumed: When representations express concepts that belong to the same proposition, they are not merely simultaneously active, but also *in construction with each other*. By contrast, representations that express concepts that don't belong to the same proposition may be simultaneously active; but, they are ipso facto *not* in construction with each other.

In short, you need two degrees of freedom to specify the thoughts that an intentional system is entertaining at a time: one parameter (active vs inactive) picks out the nodes that express concepts that the system has in mind; the other (in construction vs not) determines how the concepts that the system has in mind are distributed in the propositions that it entertains. For symbols to be "in construction" in this sense is just for them to be constituents of a complex symbol. Representations that are in construction form parts of a geometrical whole, *where the geometrical relations are themselves semantically significant*. Thus the representation that corresponds to the thought that John loves Fido is not a *set* of concepts but something like a *tree* of concepts, and it's the geometrical relations in this tree that mark (for example) the difference between the thought that John loves Fido and the thought that Fido loves John.

We've occasionally heard it suggested that you could solve the present problem consonant with the restriction against complex representations if you allow networks like this:

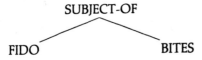

The intended interpretation is that the thought that Fido bites corresponds to the simultaneous activation of these nodes; that is, to the vector { +FIDO, +SUBJECT OF, +BITES}—with similar though longer vectors for more complex role relations.

But, on second thought, this proposal merely begs the question that it set out to solve. For, if there's a problem about what justifies assigning the proposition *John loves Fido* as the content of the set {JOHN, LOVES, FIDO}, there is surely the same problem about what justifies assigning the proposition *Fido is the subject of bites* to the set {FIDO, SUBJECT-OF, BITES}. If this is not immediately clear, consider the case where the simultaneously active nodes are {FIDO, SUBJECT-OF, BITES, JOHN}. Is the propositional content that Fido bites or that John does?[17]

Strikingly enough, the point that we've been making in the past several paragraphs is very close to one that Kant made against the Associationists of his day. In "Transcendental Deduction (B)" of The First Critique, Kant remarks that:

> ... if I investigate ... the relation of the given modes of knowledge in any judgement, and distinguish it, as belonging to the understanding, from the relation according to laws of the reproductive imagination [e.g., according to the principles of association], which has only subjective validity, I find that a judgement is nothing but the manner in which given modes of knowledge are brought to the objective unity of apperception. This is what is intended by the copula "is". It is employed to distinguish the objective unity of given representations from the subjective.... Only in this way does there arise from the relation a *judgement*, that is a relation which is *objectively valid*, and so can be adequately distinguished from a relation of the same representations that would have only subjective validity—as when they are connected according to laws of association. In the latter case, all that I could say would be 'If I support a body, I feel an impression of weight'; I could not say, 'It, the body, is heavy'. Thus to say 'The body is heavy' is not merely to state that the two representations have always been conjoined in my perception, ... what we are asserting is that they are combined *in the object* ... (CPR, p. 159; emphasis Kant's)

A modern paraphrase might be: A theory of mental representation must distinguish the case when two concepts (e.g., THIS BODY, HEAVY) are merely *simultaneously entertained* from the case where, to put it roughly, the property that one of the concepts expresses is predicated of the thing that the other concept denotes (as in the thought: THIS BODY IS HEAVY). The relevant distinction is that while both concepts are "active" in both cases, in the latter case but *not* in the former the active concepts are in construction. Kant thinks that "this is what is intended by the copula 'is'". But of course there are other notational devices that can serve to specify that concepts are in construction; notably the bracketing structure of constituency trees.

There are, to reiterate, two questions that you need to answer to specify the content of a mental state: "Which concepts are 'active'" and "Which of the active concepts are in construction with which others?" Identifying mental states with sets of active nodes provides resources to answer the first of these questions but not the second. That's why the version of network theory that acknowledges sets of atomic representations but no complex representations fails, in indefinitely many cases, to distinguish mental states that are in fact distinct.

But we are *not* claiming that you can't reconcile a Connectionist architecture with an adequate theory of mental representation (specifically with a combinatorial syntax and semantics for mental representations). On the contrary, of course you can: All that's required is that you use your network to implement a Turing machine, and specify a combinatorial structure for its computational language. What it appears that you can't do, however, is have both a combinatorial representational system and a Connectionist architecture *at the cognitive level.*

So much, then, for our long digression. We have now reviewed one of the major respects in which Connectionist and Classical theories differ; viz., their accounts of mental *representations.* We turn to the second major difference, which concerns their accounts of mental *processes.*

2.2 Structure Sensitive Operations

Classicists and Connectionists both offer accounts of mental processes, but their theories differ sharply. In particular, the Classical theory relies heavily on the notion of the logico/syntactic form of mental representations to define the ranges and domains of mental operations. This notion is, however, unavailable to orthodox Connectionists since it presupposes that there are nonatomic mental representations.

The Classical treatment of mental processes rests on two ideas, each of which corresponds to an aspect of the Classical theory of computation. Together they explain why the Classical view postulates at least three distinct levels of organization in computational systems: not just a physical level and a semantic (or "knowledge") level, but a syntactic level as well.

The first idea is that it is possible to construct languages in which certain features of the syntactic structures of formulas correspond systematically to certain of their semantic features. Intuitively, the idea is that in such languages the syntax of a formula encodes its meaning; most especially, those aspects of its meaning that determine its role in inference. All the artificial languages that are used for logic have this property and English has it more or less. Classicists believe that it is a crucial property of the Language of Thought.

A simple example of how a language can use syntactic structure to encode inferential roles and relations among meanings may help to illustrate this point. Thus, consider the relation between the following two sentences:

(1) John went to the store and Mary went to the store.
(2) Mary went to the store.

On the one hand, from the semantic point of view, (1) entails (2) (so, of course, inferences from (1) to (2) are truth preserving). On the other hand, from the syntactic point of view, (2) is a constituent of (1). These two facts can be brought into phase by exploiting the principle that sentences with the *syntactic structure* '(S1 and S2)$_S$' entail their sentential constituents. Notice that this principle connects the syntax of these sentences with their inferential roles. Notice too that the trick relies on facts about the grammar of English; it wouldn't work in a language where the formula that expresses the conjunctive content *John went to the store and Mary went to the store* is *syntactically* atomic.[18]

Here is another example. We can reconstruct such truth preserving inferences as *if Rover bites then something bites* on the assumption that (a) the sentence 'Rover bites' is of the syntactic type **Fa**, (b) the sentence 'something bites' is of the syntactic type ∃x (**Fx**) and (c) every formula of the first type entails a corresponding formula of the second type (where the notion 'corresponding formula' is cashed syntactically; roughly the two formulas must differ only in that the one has an existentially bound variable at the syntactic position that is occupied by a constant in the other.) Once again the point to notice is the blending of syntactical and semantical notions: The rule of existential generalization applies to formulas in virtue of their syntactic form. But the salient property that's preserved under applications of the rule is semantical: What's claimed for the transformation that the rule performs is that it is *truth* preserving.[19]

There are, as it turns out, examples that are quite a lot more complicated than these. The whole of the branch of logic known as proof theory is devoted to exploring them.[20] It would not be unreasonable to describe Classical Cognitive Science as an extended attempt to apply the methods of proof theory to the modeling of thought (and similarly, of whatever other mental processes are plausibly viewed as involving inferences; preeminently learning and perception). Classical theory construction rests on the hope that syntactic analogues can be constructed for nondemonstrative inferences (or informal, commonsense reasoning) in something like the way that proof theory has provided syntactic analogues for validity.

The second main idea underlying the Classical treatment of mental processes is that it is possible to devise machines whose function is the transformation of symbols, and whose operations are sensitive to the syntactical structure of the symbols that they operate upon. This is the Classical conception of a computer: it's what the various architectures that derive from Turing and Von Neumann machines all have in common.

Perhaps it's obvious how the two 'main ideas' fit together. If, in principle, syntactic relations can be made to parallel semantic relations, and if, in principle, you can have a mechanism whose operations on formulas are sensitive to their syntax, then it may be possible to construct a *syntactically* driven machine whose state transitions satisfy *semantical* criteria of coherence. Such a machine would be just what's required for a mechanical model of the semantical coherence of thought; correspondingly, the idea that the brain *is* such a machine is the foundational hypothesis of Classical cognitive science.

So much for the Classical story about mental processes. The Connectionist story must, of course, be quite different: Since Connectionists eschew postulating mental representations with combinatorial syntactic/semantic structure, they are precluded from postulating mental processes that operate on mental representations in a way that is sensitive to their structure. The sorts of operations that Connectionist models do have are of two sorts, depending on whether the process under examination is learning or reasoning.

2.2.1 Learning   If a Connectionist model is intended to learn, there will be processes that determine the weights of the connections among its units as a function of the character of its training. Typically in a Connectionist machine (such as a 'Boltzman Machine') the weights among connections are adjusted until the system's behavior comes to model the statistical properties of its inputs. In the limit, the stochastic relations among machine states recapitulates the stochastic relations among the environmental events that they represent.

This should bring to mind the old Associationist principle that the strength of association between 'Ideas' is a function of the frequency with which they are paired 'in experience' and the Learning Theoretic principle that the strength of a stimulus-response connection is a function of the frequency with which the response is rewarded in the presence of the stimulus. But though Connectionists, like other Associationists, are committed to learning processes that model statistical properties of inputs and outputs, the simple mechanisms based on co-occurrence statistics that were the hallmarks of old-fashioned Associationism have been augmented in Connectionist models by a number of technical devices. (Hence the 'new' in 'New Connectionism'.) For example, some of the earlier limitations of associative mechanisms are overcome by allowing the network to contain 'hidden' units (or aggregates) that are not directly connected to the environment and whose purpose is, in effect, to detect statistical patterns in the activity of the 'visible' units including, perhaps, patterns that are more abstract or more 'global' than the ones that could be detected by old-fashioned perceptrons.[21]

In short, sophisticated versions of the associative principles for weight-setting are on offer in the Connectionist literature. The point of present concern, however, is what all versions of these principles have in common with one another and with older kinds of Associationism: viz., these processes are all *frequency*-sensitive. To return to the example discussed above: if a Connectionist learning machine converges on a state where it is prepared to infer A from A&B (i.e., to a state in which when the 'A&B' node is excited it tends to settle into a state in which the 'A' node is excited) the convergence will typically be caused by statistical properties of the machine's training experience: e.g., by correlation between firing of the 'A&B' node and firing of the 'A' node, or by correlations of the firing of both with some feedback signal. Like traditional Associationism, Connectionism treats learning as basically a sort of statistical modeling.

2.2.2 Reasoning   Association operates to alter the structure of a network *diachronically* as a function of its training. Connectionist models also contain a variety of types of 'relaxation' processes which determine the *synchronic* behavior of a network; specifically, they determine what output the device provides for a given pattern of inputs. In this respect, one can think of a Connectionist model as a species of analog machine constructed to realize a certain function. The inputs to the function are (i) a specification of the connectedness of the machine (of which nodes are connected to which); (ii) a specification of the weights along the connections; (iii) a specification of the values of a variety of idiosyncratic parameters of the nodes (e.g., intrinsic thresholds; time since last firing, etc.) (iv) a specification of a pattern of excitation over the input nodes. The output of the function is a specification of a pattern of excitation over the output nodes; intuitively, the machine chooses the output pattern that is most highly associated to its input.

Much of the mathematical sophistication of Connectionist theorizing has been devoted to devising analog solutions to this problem of finding a 'most highly associated' output corresponding to an arbitrary input; but, once again, the details needn't concern us. What is important, for our purposes, is another property that Connectionist theories share with other forms of Associationism. In traditional Associationism, the probability that one Idea will elicit another is sensitive to the strength of the association between them (including 'mediating' associations, if any). And the strength of this association is in turn sensitive to the extent to which the Ideas have previously been correlated. Associative strength was not, however, presumed to be sensitive to features of the content or the structure of representations per se. Similarly, in Connectionist models, the selection of an output corresponding to a given input is a function of properties of the paths that connect them (including the weights, the states of intermediate units, etc.). And the weights, in turn, are a function of the statistical properties of events in the environment (or of relations between patterns of events in the environment and implicit 'predictions' made by the network, etc.). But the syntactic/semantic structure of the representation of an input is *not* presumed to be a factor in determining the selection of a corresponding output since, as we have seen, syntactic/semantic structure is not defined for the sorts of representations that Connectionist models acknowledge.

To summarize: Classical and Connectionist theories disagree about the nature of mental representation; for the former, but not for the latter, mental representations characteristically exhibit a combinatorial constituent structure and a combinatorial semantics. Classical and Connectionist theories also disagree about the nature of mental processes; for the former, but not for the latter, mental processes are characteristically sensitive to the combinatorial structure of the representations on which they operate.

We take it that these two issues define the present dispute about the nature of cognitive architecture. We now propose to argue that the Connectionists are on the wrong side of both.

3 The Need for Symbol Systems: Productivity, Systematicity, Compositionality and Inferential Coherence

Classical psychological theories appeal to the constituent structure of mental representations to explain three closely related features of cognition: its productivity, its compositionality and its inferential coherence. The traditional argument has been that these features of cognition are, on the one hand, pervasive and, on the other hand, explicable only on the assumption that mental representations have internal structure. This argument—familiar in more or less explicit versions for the last thirty years or so—is still intact, so far as we can tell. It appears to offer something close to a demonstration that an empirically adequate cognitive theory must recognize not just causal relations among representational states but also relations of syntactic and semantic constituency; hence that the mind cannot be, in its general structure, a Connectionist network.

3.1 Productivity of Thought

There is a classical productivity argument for the existence of combinatorial structure in any rich representational system (including natural languages and the language of thought). The representational capacities of such a system are, by assumption, unbounded under appropriate idealization; in particular, there are indefinitely many propositions which the system can encode.[22] However, this unbounded expressive power must presumably be achieved by finite means. The way to do this is to treat the system of representations as consisting of expressions belonging to a generated set. More precisely, the correspondence between a representation and the proposition it expresses is, in arbitrarily many cases, built up recursively out of correspondences between parts of the expression and parts of the proposition. But, of course, this strategy can operate only when an unbounded number of the expressions are non-atomic. So linguistic (and mental) representations must constitute *symbol systems* (in the sense of note 8). So the mind cannot be a PDP.

Very often, when people reject this sort of reasoning, it is because they doubt that human cognitive capacities are correctly viewed as productive. In the long run there can be no a priori arguments for (or against) idealizing to productive capacities; whether you accept the idealization depends on whether you believe that the inference from finite performance to finite capacity is justified, or whether you think that finite performance is typically a result of the interaction of an unbounded competence with resource constraints. Classicists have traditionally offered a mixture of methodological and empirical considerations in favor of the latter view.

From a methodological perspective, the least that can be said for assuming productivity is that it precludes solutions that rest on inappropriate tricks (such as storing all the pairs that define a function); tricks that would be unreasonable in practical terms even for solving finite tasks that place sufficiently large demands on memory. The idealization to unbounded productive capacity forces the theorist to separate the finite specification of a method for solving a computational problem from such factors as the resources that the system (or person) brings to bear on the problem at any given moment.

The empirical arguments for productivity have been made most frequently in connection with linguistic competence. They are familiar from the work of Chomsky (1968) who has claimed (convincingly, in our view) that the knowledge underlying linguistic competence is generative—i.e., that it allows us *in principle* to generate (/understand) an unbounded number of sentences. It goes without saying that no one does, or could, *in fact* utter or understand tokens of more than a finite number of sentence types; this is a trivial consequence of the fact that nobody can utter or understand more than a finite number of sentence tokens. But there are a number of considerations which suggest that, despite de facto constraints on performance, ones knowledge of ones language supports an unbounded productive capacity in much the same way that ones knowledge of addition supports an unbounded number of sums. Among these considerations are, for example, the fact that a speaker/hearer's performance can often be improved by relaxing time constraints, increasing motivation, or supplying pencil and paper. It seems very natural to treat such manipulations as affecting the transient state of the speaker's memory and attention rather than what he knows about—or how he represents—his language. But this treatment is available only on the assumption that the character of the subject's performance is determined by interactions between the available knowledge base and the available computational resources.

Classical theories are able to accommodate these sorts of considerations because they assume architectures in which there is a functional distinction between memory and program. In a system such as a Turing machine, where the length of the tape is not fixed in advance, changes in the amount of available memory *can be affected without changing the computational structure of the machine*; viz., by making more tape available. By contrast, in a finite state automaton or a Connectionist machine, adding to the memory (e.g., by adding units to a network) alters the connectivity relations among nodes and thus does affect the machine's computational structure. Connectionist cognitive architectures cannot, by their very nature, support an expandable memory, so they cannot support productive cognitive capacities. The long and short is that if productivity arguments are sound, then they show that the architecture of the mind can't be Connectionist. Connectionists have, by and large, acknowledged this; so they are forced to reject productivity arguments.

The test of a good scientific idealization is simply and solely whether it produces successful science in the long term. It seems to us that the productivity idealization has more than earned its keep, especially in linguistics and in theories of reasoning. Connectionists, however, have not been persuaded. For example, Rumelhart and McClelland (1986a, p. 119) say that they "... do not agree that [productive] capabilities are of the essence of human computation. As anyone who has ever attempted to process sentences like 'The man the boy the girl hit kissed moved' can attest, our ability to process even moderate degrees of center-embedded structure is grossly impaired relative to an ATN [Augmented Transition Network] parser.... What is needed, then, is not a mechanism for flawless and effortless processing of embedded constructions ... The challenge is to explain how those processes that others have chosen to explain in terms of recursive mechanisms can be better explained by the kinds of processes natural for PDP networks."

These remarks suggest that Rumelhart and McClelland think that the fact that center-embedding sentences are hard is somehow an *embarrassment* for theories that view linguistic capacities as productive. But of course it's not since, according to such theories, performance is an effect of interactions between a productive competence and restricted resources. There are, in fact, quite plausible Classical accounts of why center-embeddings ought to impose especially heavy demands on resources, and there is a reasonable amount of experimental support for these models (see, for example, Wanner & Maratsos, 1978).

In any event, it should be obvious that the difficulty of parsing center-embeddings can't be a consequence of their recursiveness per se since there are many recursive structures that are strikingly easy to understand. Consider: 'this is the dog that chased the cat that ate the rat that lived in the house that Jack built.' The Classicist's case for productive capacities in parsing rests on the transparency of sentences like these.[23] In short, the fact that center-embedded sentences are hard perhaps shows that there are some recursive structures that we can't parse. But what Rumelhart and McClelland need if they are to deny the productivity of linguistic capacities is the much stronger claim that there are no recursive structures that we can parse; and this stronger claim would appear to be simply false.

Rumelhart and McClelland's discussion of recursion (pp. 119–120) nevertheless repays close attention. They are apparently prepared to concede that PDPs can model recursive capacities only indirectly—viz., by implementing Classical architectures like ATNs; so that *if* human cognition exhibited recursive capacities, that would suffice to show that minds have Classical rather than Connectionist architecture at the psychological level. "We have not dwelt on PDP implementations of Turing machines and recursive processing engines *because we do not agree with those who would argue that such capacities are of the essence of human computation*" (p. 119, our emphasis). Their argument that recursive capacities *aren't* "of the essence of human computation" is, however, just the unconvincing stuff about center-embedding quoted above.

So the Rumelhart and McClelland view is apparently that if you take it to be independently obvious that some cognitive capacities are productive, then you should take the existence of such capacities to argue for Classical cognitive architecture and hence for treating Connectionism as at best an implementation theory. We think that this is quite a plausible understanding of the bearing that the issues about productivity and recursion have on the issues about cognitive architecture....

In the meantime, however, we propose to view the status of productivity arguments for Classical architectures as moot; we're about to present a different sort of argument for the claim that mental representations need an articulated internal structure. It is closely related to the productivity argument, but it doesn't require the idealization to unbounded competence. Its assumptions should thus be acceptable even to theorists who—like Connectionists—hold that the finitistic character of cognitive capacities is intrinsic to their architecture.

3.2 Systematicity of Cognitive Representation

The form of the argument is this: Whether or not cognitive capacities are really *productive*, it seems indubitable that they are what we shall call 'systematic'. And we'll see that the systematicity of cognition provides as good a reason for postulating combinatorial structure in mental representation as the productivity of cognition does: You get, in effect, the same conclusion, but from a weaker premise.

The easiest way to understand what the systematicity of cognitive capacities amounts to is to focus on the systematicity of language comprehension and production. In fact, the systematicity argument for combinatorial structure in *thought* exactly recapitulates the traditional Structuralist argument for constituent structure in sentences. But we pause to remark upon a point that we'll re-emphasize later; linguistic capacity is a paradigm of systematic cognition, but it's wildly unlikely that it's the only example. On the contrary, there's every reason to believe that systematicity is a thoroughly pervasive feature of human and infrahuman mentation.

What we mean when we say that linguistic capacities are *systematic* is that the ability to produce/understand some sentences is *intrinsically* connected to the ability to produce/understand certain others. You can see the force of this if you compare learning languages the way we really do learn them with learning a language by memorizing an enormous phrase book. The point isn't that phrase books are finite and can therefore exhaustively specify only *non*-productive languages; that's true, but we've agreed not to rely on productivity arguments for our present purposes. Our point is rather that you can learn *any part of a phrase book without learning the rest*. Hence, on the phrase book model, it would be perfectly possible to learn that uttering the form of words 'Granny's cat is on Uncle Arthur's mat' is the way to say (in English) that Granny's cat is on Uncle Arthur's mat, and yet have no idea at all how to say that it's raining (or, for that matter, how to say that Uncle Arthur's cat is on Granny's mat). Perhaps it's self-evident that the phrase book story must be wrong about language acquisition because a speaker's knowledge of his native language is never like that. You don't, for example, find native speakers who know how to say in English that John loves the girl but don't know how to say in English that the girl loves John.

Notice, in passing, that systematicity is a property of the mastery of the syntax of a language, not of its lexicon. The phrase book model really does fit what it's like to learn the *vocabulary* of English since when you learn English vocabulary you acquire a lot of basically *independent* capacities. So you might perfectly well learn that using the expression 'cat' is the way to refer to cats and yet have no idea that using the expression 'deciduous conifer' is the way to refer to deciduous conifers. Systematicity, like productivity, is the sort of property of cognitive capacities that you're likely to miss if you concentrate on the psychology of learning and searching lists.

There is, as we remarked, a straightforward (and quite traditional) argument from the systematicity of language capacity to the conclusion that sentences must have syntactic and semantic structure: If you assume that sentences are constructed out of words and phrases, and that many different sequences of words can be phrases of the same type, the very fact that one formula is a sentence of the language will often imply that other formulas must be too: in effect, systematicity follows from the postulation of constituent structure.

Suppose, for example, that it's a fact about English that formulas with the constituent analysis 'NP Vt NP' are well formed; and suppose that 'John' and 'the girl' are NPs and 'loves' is a Vt. It follows from these assumptions that 'John loves the girl,' 'John loves John,' 'the girl loves the girl,' and 'the girl loves John' must all be sentences. It follows too that anybody who has mastered the grammar of English must have linguistic capacities that are systematic in respect of these sentences; he *can't but* assume that all of them are sentences if he assumes that any of them are. Compare the situation on the view that the sentences of English are all atomic. There is then no structural analogy between 'John loves the girl' and 'the girl loves John' and hence no reason why understanding one sentence should imply understanding the other; no more than understanding 'rabbit' implies understanding 'tree'.[24]

On the view that the sentences are atomic, the systematicity of linguistic capacities is a mystery; on the view that they have constituent structure, the systematicity of linguistic capacities is what you would predict. So we should prefer the latter view to the former.

Notice that you can make this argument for constituent structure in sentences without idealizing to astronomical computational capacities. There are productivity arguments for constituent structure, but they're concerned with our ability—in principle—to understand sentences that are arbitrarily long. Systematicity, by contrast, appeals to premises that are much nearer home; such considerations as the ones mentioned above, that no speaker understands the form of words 'John loves the girl' except as he also understands the form of words 'the girl loves John'. The assumption that linguistic capacities are productive "in principle" is one that a Connectionist might refuse to grant. But that they are systematic *in fact* no one can plausibly deny.

We can now, finally, come to the point: the argument from the systematicity of linguistic capacities to constituent structure in sentences is quite clear. But *thought is systematic too*, so there is a precisely parallel argument from the systematicity of thought to syntactic and semantic structure in mental representations.

What does it mean to say that thought is systematic? Well, just as you don't find people who can understand the sentence 'John loves the girl' but not the sentence 'the girl loves John,' so too you don't find people who can *think the thought* that John loves the girl but can't think the thought that the girl loves John. Indeed, in the case of verbal organisms the systematicity of thought *follows from* the systematicity of language if you assume—as most psychologists do—that understanding a sentence involves entertaining the thought that it expresses; on that assumption, nobody *could* understand both the sentences about John and the girl unless he were able to think both the thoughts about John and the girl.

But now if the ability to think that John loves the girl is intrinsically connected to the ability to think that the girl loves John, that fact will somehow have to be explained. For a Representationalist (which, as we have seen, Connectionists are), the explanation is obvious: Entertaining thoughts requires being in representational states (i.e., it requires tokening mental representations). And, just as the systematicity of language shows that there must be structural relations between the sentence 'John loves the girl' and the sentence 'the girl loves John,' so the systematicity of thought shows that there must be structural relations between the mental representation that corresponds to the thought that John loves the girl and the mental representation that corresponds to the thought that the girl loves John;[25] namely, the two mental representations, like the two sentences, *must be made of the same parts*. But if this explanation is right (and there don't seem to be any others on offer), then mental representations have internal structure and there is a language of thought. So the architecture of the mind is not a Connectionist network.[26]

To summarize the discussion so far: Productivity arguments infer the internal structure of mental representations from the presumed fact that nobody has a *finite* intellectual competence. By contrast, systematicity arguments infer the internal structure of mental representations from the patent fact that nobody has a *punctate* intellectual competence. Just as you don't find linguistic capacities that consist of the ability to understand sixty-seven unrelated sentences, so too you don't find cognitive capacities that consist of the ability to think seventy-four unrelated thoughts. Our claim is that this isn't, in either case, an accident: A linguistic theory that allowed for the possibility of punctate languages would have gone not just wrong, but *very profoundly* wrong. And similarly for a cognitive theory that allowed for the possibility of punctate minds.

But perhaps not being punctate is a property only of the minds of language users; perhaps the representational capacities of infraverbal organisms do have just the kind of gaps that Connectionist models permit? A Connectionist might then claim that he can do everything "up to language" on the assumption that mental representations lack combinatorial syntactic and semantic structure. Everything up to language may not be everything, but it's a lot. (On the other hand, a lot may be a lot, but it isn't everything. Infraverbal cognitive architecture mustn't be so represented as to make the eventual acquisition of language in phylogeny and in ontogeny require a miracle.)

It is not, however, plausible that only the minds of verbal organisms are systematic. Think what it would mean for this to be the case. It would have to be quite usual to find, for example, animals capable of representing the state of affairs aRb, but incapable of representing the state of affairs bRa. Such animals would be, as it were, aRb sighted but bRa blind since, presumably, the representational capacities of its mind affect not just what an organism can think, but also what it can perceive. In consequence, such animals would be able to learn to respond selectively to aRb situations but quite *un*able to learn to respond selectively to bRa situations. (So that, though you could teach the creature to choose the picture with the square larger than the triangle, you couldn't for the life of you teach it to choose the picture with the triangle larger than the square.)

It is, to be sure. an empirical question whether the cognitive capacities of infraverbal organisms are often structured that way, but we're prepared to bet that they are not. Ethological cases are the exceptions that prove the rule. There *are* examples where salient environmental configurations act as 'gestalten'; and in such cases it's reasonable to doubt that the mental representation of the stimulus is complex. But the point is precisely that these cases are *exceptional*; they're exactly the ones where you expect that there will be some special story to tell about the ecological significance of the stimulus: that it's the shape of a predator, or the song of a conspecific ... etc. Conversely, when there is no such story to tell you expect structurally similar stimuli to elicit correspondingly similar cognitive capacities. That, surely, is the least that a respectable principle of stimulus generalization has got to require.

That infraverbal cognition is pretty generally systematic seems, in short, to be about as secure as any empirical premise in this area can be. And, as we've just seen, it's a premise from which the inadequacy of Connectionist models as cognitive theories follows quite straightforwardly; as straightforwardly, in any event, as it would from the assumption that such capacities are generally productive.

3.3 Compositionality of Representations

Compositionality is closely related to systematicity; perhaps they're best viewed as aspects of a single phenomenon. We will therefore follow much the same course here as in the preceding discussion: first we introduce the concept by recalling the standard arguments for the compositionality of natural languages. We then suggest that parallel arguments secure the compositionality of mental representations. Since compositionality requires combinatorial syntactic and semantic structure, the compositionality of thought is evidence that the mind is not a Connectionist network.

We said that the systematicity of linguistic competence consists in the fact that "the ability to produce/understand some of the sentences is intrinsically connected to the ability to produce/understand certain of the others". We now add that which sentences are systematically related is not arbitrary from a semantic point of view. For example, being able to understand 'John loves the girl' goes along with being able to understand 'the girl loves John', and there are correspondingly close semantic relations between these sentences: in order for the first to be true, John must bear to the girl the very same relation that the truth of the second requires the girl to bear to John. By contrast, there is no intrinsic connection between understanding either of the John/girl sentences and understanding semantically unrelated formulas like 'quarks are made of gluons' or 'the cat is on the mat' or '2 + 2 = 4'; it looks as though semantical relatedness and systematicity keep quite close company.

You might suppose that this covariance is covered by the same explanation that accounts for systematicity per se; roughly, that sentences that are systematically related are composed from the same syntactic constituents. But, in fact, you need a further assumption, which we'll call the 'principle of compositionality': insofar as a language is systematic, a lexical item must make approximately the same semantic contribution to each expression in which it occurs. It is, for example, only insofar as 'the', 'girl', 'loves' and 'John' make the same semantic contribution to 'John loves the girl' that they make to 'the girl loves John' that understanding the one sentence implies understanding the other. Similarity of constituent structure accounts for the semantic relatedness between systematically related sentences only to the extent that the semantical properties of the shared constituents are context-independent.

Here it's idioms that prove the rule: being able to understand 'the', 'man', 'kicked' and 'bucket' isn't much help with understanding 'the man kicked the bucket', since 'kicked' and 'bucket' don't bear their standard meanings in this context. And, just as you'd expect, 'the man kicked the bucket' is *not* systematic even with respect to syntactically closely related sentences like 'the man kicked over the bucket' (for that matter, it's not systematic with respect to the 'the man kicked the bucket' read literally).

It's uncertain exactly how compositional natural languages actually are (just as it's uncertain exactly how systematic they are). We suspect that the amount of context induced variation of lexical meaning is often overestimated because other sorts of context sensitivity are misconstrued as violations of compositionality. For example, the difference between 'feed the chicken' and 'chicken to eat' must involve an *animal/food* ambiguity in 'chicken' rather than a violation of compositionality since if the context 'feed the ...' could *induce* (rather than select) the meaning *animal*, you would expect 'feed the veal', 'feed the pork' and the like.[27] Similarly, the difference between 'good book', 'good rest' and 'good fight' is probably not meaning shift but syncategorematicity. 'Good NP' means something like *NP that answers to the relevant interest in NPs*: a good book is one that answers to our interest in books (viz., it's good to read); a good rest is one that answers to our interest in rests (viz., it leaves one refreshed); a good fight is one that answers to our interest in fights (viz., it's fun to watch or to be in, or it clears the air); and so on. It's because the meaning of 'good' is syncategorematic and has a variable in it for relevant interests, that you can know that a good flurg is a flurg that answers to the relevant interest in flurgs without knowing what flurgs are or what the relevant interest in flurgs is (see Ziff, 1960).

In any event, the main argument stands: systematicity depends on compositionality, so to the extent that a natural language is systematic it must be compositional too. This illustrates another respect in which systematicity arguments can do the work for which productivity arguments have previously been employed. The traditional argument for compositionality is that it is required to explain how a finitely representable language can contain infinitely many nonsynonymous expressions.

Considerations about systematicity offer one argument for compositionality; considerations about entailment offer another. Consider predicates like '... is a brown cow'. This expression bears a straightforward semantical relation to the predicates '... is a cow' and '... is brown'; viz., that the first predicate is true of a thing if and only if both of the others are. That is, '... is a brown cow' severally entails '... is brown' and '... is a cow' and is entailed by their conjunction. Moreover—and this is important—this semantical pattern is not peculiar to the cases cited. On the contrary, it holds for a very large range of predicates (see '... is a red square,' '... is a funny old German soldier,' '... is a child prodigy;' and so forth).

How are we to account for these sorts of regularities? The answer seems clear enough; '... is a brown cow' entails '... is brown' because (a) the second expression is a constituent of the first; (b) the syntactical form '(adjective noun)$_N$' has (in many cases) the semantic force of a conjunction, and (c) 'brown' retains its semantical value under simplification of conjunction. Notice that you need (c) to rule out the possibility that 'brown' means *brown* when it modifies a noun but (as it might be) *dead* when it's a predicate adjective; in which case '... is a brown cow' wouldn't entail '... is brown' after all. Notice too that (c) is just an application of the principle of composition.

So, here's the argument so far: you need to assume some degree of compositionality of English sentences to account for the fact that systematically related sentences are always semantically related; and to account for certain regular parallelisms between the syntactical structure of sentences and their entailments. So, beyond any serious doubt, the sentences of English must be compositional to some serious extent. But the principle of compositionality governs the semantic relations between words *and the expressions of which they are constituents.* So compositionality implies that (some) expressions *have* constituents. So compositionality argues for (specifically, presupposes) syntactic/ semantic structure in sentences.

Now what about the compositionality of mental representations? There is, as you'd expect, a bridging argument based on the usual psycholinguistic premise that one uses language to express ones thoughts: Sentences are used to express thoughts; so if the ability to use some sentences is connected with the ability to use certain other, semantically related sentences, then the ability to think some thoughts must be correspondingly connected with the ability to think certain other, semantically related thoughts. But you can only think the thoughts that your mental representations can express. So, if the ability to think certain thoughts is interconnected, then the corresponding representational capacities must be interconnected too; specifically, the ability to be in some representational states must imply the ability to be in certain other, semantically related representational states.

But then the question arises: *how could* the mind be so arranged that the ability to be in one representational state is connected with the ability to be in others that are semantically nearby? What account of mental representation would have this consequence? The answer is just what you'd expect from the discussion of the linguistic material. Mental representations must have internal structure, just the way that sentences do. In particular, it must be that the mental representation that corresponds to the thought that John loves the girl contains, as its parts, the same constituents as the mental representation that corresponds to the thought that the girl loves John. That would explain why these thoughts are *systematically* related; *and, to the extent that the semantic value of these parts is context-independent, that would explain why these systematically related thoughts are also semantically related.* So, by this chain of argument, evidence for the compositionality of sentences is evidence for the compositionality of the representational states of speaker/hearers.

Finally, what about the compositionality of infraverbal thought? The argument isn't much different from the one that we've just run through. We assume that animal thought is largely systematic: the organism that can perceive (hence learn) that $a\mathbf{R}b$ can generally perceive (/learn) that $b\mathbf{R}a$. But, systematically related thoughts (just like systematically related sentences) are generally semantically related too. It's no surprise that being able to learn that the triangle is above the square implies being able to learn that the square is above the triangle; whereas it would be *very* surprising if being able to learn the square/triangle facts implied being able to learn that quarks are made of gluons or that Washington was the first President of America.

So, then, what explains the correlation between systematic relations and semantic relations in infraverbal thought? Clearly, Connectionist models don't address this question; the fact that a network contains a node labelled X has, so far as the constraints imposed by Connectionist architecture are concerned, *no implications at all* for the labels of the other nodes in the network; in particular, it doesn't imply that there will be nodes that represent thoughts that are semantically close to X. This is just the semantical side of the fact that network architectures permit arbitrarily punctate mental lives.

But if, on the other hand, we make the usual Classicist assumptions (viz., that systematically related thoughts share constituents and that the semantic values of these shared constituents are context independent) the correlation between systematicity and semantic relatedness follows immediately. For a Classicist, this correlation is an 'architectural' property of minds; it couldn't but hold if mental representations have the general properties that Classical models suppose them to.

What have Connectionists to say about these matters? There is some textual evidence that they are tempted to deny the facts of compositionality wholesale. For example, Smolensky (1988) claims that: "Surely ... we would get quite a different representation of 'coffee' if we examined the difference between 'can with coffee' and 'can without coffee' or 'tree with coffee' and 'tree without coffee'; or 'man with coffee' and 'man without coffee' ... context insensitivity is not something we expect to be reflected in Connectionist representations...".

It's certainly true that compositionality is not generally a feature of Connectionist representations. Connectionists can't acknowledge the facts of compositionality because they are committed to mental representations that don't have combinatorial structure. But to give up on compositionality is to take 'kick the bucket' as a model for the relation between syntax and semantics; and the consequence is, as we've seen, that you make the systematicity of language (and of thought) a mystery. On the other hand, to say that 'kick the bucket' is aberrant, and that the right model for the syntax/semantics relation is (e.g.) 'brown cow', is to start down a trail which leads, pretty inevitably, to acknowledging combinatorial structure in mental representation, hence to the rejection of Connectionist networks as cognitive models.

We don't think there's any way out of the need to acknowledge the compositionality of natural languages and of mental representations. However, it's been suggested (see Smolensky, op cit.) that while the principle of compositionality is false (because content isn't context invariant) there is nevertheless a "family resemblance" between the various meanings that a symbol has in the various contexts in which it occurs. Since such proposals generally aren't elaborated, it's unclear how they're supposed to handle the salient facts about systematicity and inference. But surely there are going to be serious problems. Consider, for example, such inferences as

(i)   Turtles are slower than rabbits.

(ii)   Rabbits are slower than Ferraris.

. . . .

(iii)   Turtles are slower than Ferraris.

The soundness of this inference appears to depend upon (a) the fact that the same relation (viz., *slower than*) holds between turtles and rabbits on the one hand, and rabbits and Ferraris on the other; and (b) the fact that that relation is transitive. If, however, it's assumed (contrary to the principle of compositionality) that 'slower than' means something different in premises (i) and (ii) (and presumably in (iii) as well)—so that, strictly speaking, the relation that holds between turtles and rabbits is *not* the same one that holds between rabbits and Ferraris—then it's hard to see why the inference should be valid.

Talk about the relations being 'similar' only papers over the difficulty since the problem is then to provide a notion of similarity that will guaranty that if (i) and (ii) are true, so too is (iii). And, so far at least, no such notion of similarity has been forthcoming. Notice that it won't do to require just that the relations all be similar in respect of their *transitivity*, i.e., that they all be transitive. On that account, the argument from 'turtles are slower than rabbits' and 'rabbits are furrier than Ferraris' to 'turtles are slower than Ferraris' would be valid since 'furrier than' is transitive too.

Until these sorts of issues are attended to, the proposal to replace the compositional principle of context invariance with a notion of "approximate equivalence … across contexts" (Smolensky, 1988) doesn't seem to be much more than hand waving.

3.4   *The Systematicity of Inference*

In Section 2 we saw that, according to Classical theories, the syntax of mental representations mediates between their semantic properties and their causal role in mental processes. Take a simple case: It's a 'logical' principle that conjunctions entail their constituents (so the argument from $P\&Q$ to P and to Q is valid). Correspondingly, it's a psychological law that thoughts that $P\&Q$ tend to cause thoughts that P and thoughts that Q, all else being equal. Classical theory exploits the constituent structure of mental representations to account for both these facts, the first by assuming that the combinatorial semantics of mental representations is sensitive to their syntax and the second by assuming that mental processes apply to mental representations in virtue of their constituent structure.

A consequence of these assumptions is that Classical theories are committed to the following striking prediction: inferences that are of similar logical type ought, pretty generally,[28] to elicit correspondingly similar cognitive capacities. You shouldn't, for example, find a kind of mental life in which you get inferences from $P\&Q\&R$ to P but you don't get inferences from $P\&Q$ to P. This is because, according to the Classical

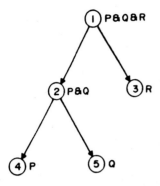

Figure 41.2
A possible Connectionist network which draws inferences from P & Q & R to P and also draws inferences from P & Q to P.

account, this logically homogeneous class of inferences is carried out by a correspondingly homogeneous class of psychological mechanisms: The premises of both inferences are expressed by mental representations that satisfy the same syntactic analysis (viz., $S_1 \& S_2 \& S_3 \& \ldots S_n$); and the process of drawing the inference corresponds, in both cases, to the same formal operation of detaching the constituent that expresses the conclusion.

The idea that organisms should exhibit similar cognitive capacities in respect of logically similar inferences is so natural that it may seem unavoidable. But, on the contrary: there's nothing in principle to preclude a kind of cognitive model in which inferences that are quite similar from the logician's point of view are nevertheless computed by quite different mechanisms; or in which some inferences of a given logical type are computed and other inferences of the same logical type are not. Consider, in particular, the Connectionist account. A Connectionist can certainly model a mental life in which, if you can reason from $P\&Q\&R$ to P, then you can also reason from $P\&Q$ to P. For example, the network in (Figure 41.2) would do.

But notice that *a Connectionist can equally model a mental life in which you get one of these inferences and not the other.* In the present case, since there is no structural relation between the $P\&Q\&R$ node and the $P\&Q$ node (remember, all nodes are atomic; don't be misled by the node *labels*) there's no reason why a mind that contains the first should also contain the second, or vice versa. Analogously, there's no reason why you shouldn't get minds that simplify the premise *John loves Mary and Bill hates Mary* but no others; or minds that simplify premises with 1, 3, or 5 conjuncts, but don't simplify premises with 2, 4, or 6 conjuncts; or, for that matter, minds that simplify only premises that were acquired on Tuesdays ... etc.

In fact, the Connectionist architecture is *utterly indifferent* among these possibilities. That's because it recognizes no notion of syntax according to which thoughts that are alike in inferential role (e.g., thoughts that are all subject to simplification of conjunction) are expressed by mental representations of correspondingly similar syntactic form (e.g., by mental representations that are all syntactically conjunctive). So, the Connectionist architecture tolerates gaps in cognitive capacities; it has no mechanism to enforce the requirement that logically homogeneous inferences should be executed by correspondingly homogeneous computational processes.

But, we claim, you don't find cognitive capacities that have these sorts of gaps. You don't, for example, get minds that are prepared to infer *John went to the store* from *John and Mary and Susan and Sally went to the store* and from *John and Mary went to the store* but not from *John and Mary and Susan went to the store.* Given a notion of logical syntax—the very notion that the Classical theory of mentation requires to get its account of mental processes off the ground—it is a *truism* that you don't get such minds. Lacking a notion of logical syntax, it is a *mystery* that you don't.

3.5 Summary

It is perhaps obvious by now that all the arguments that we've been reviewing—the argument from systematicity, the argument from compositionality, and the argument from influential coherence—are really much the same: If you hold the kind of theory that acknowledges structured representations, it must perforce acknowledge representations with *similar* or *identical* structures. In the linguistic cases, constituent analysis implies a taxonomy of sentences by their syntactic form, and in the inferential cases, it implies a taxonomy of arguments by their logical form. So, if your theory also acknowledges mental processes that are structure sensitive, then it will predict that similarly structured representations will generally play similar roles in thought. A theory that says that the sentence 'John loves the girl' is made out of the same parts as the sentence 'the girl loves John', and made by applications of the same rules of composition, will have to go out of its way to explain a linguistic competence which embraces one sentence but not the other. And similarly, if a theory says that the mental representation that corresponds to the thought that *P&Q&R* has the same (conjunctive) syntax as the mental representation that corresponds to the thought that *P&Q* and that mental processes of drawing inferences subsume mental representations in virtue of their syntax, it will have to go out of its way to explain inferential capacities which embrace the one thought but not the other. Such a competence would be, at best, an embarrassment for the theory, and at worst a refutation.

By contrast, since the Connectionist architecture recognizes no combinatorial structure in mental representations, gaps in cognitive competence should proliferate arbitrarily. It's not just that you'd expect to get them from time to time; it's that, on the 'no-structure' story, *gaps are the unmarked case.* It's the *systematic* competence that the theory is required to treat as an embarrassment. But, as a matter of fact, inferential competences are *blatantly* systematic. So there must be something deeply wrong with Connectionist architecture.

What's deeply wrong with Connectionist architecture is this: Because it acknowledges neither syntactic nor semantic structure in mental representations, it perforce treats them not as a generated set but as a list. But lists, qua lists, have no structure; any collection of items is a possible list. And, correspondingly, on Connectionist principles, any collection of (causally connected) representational states is a possible mind. So, as far as Connectionist architecture is concerned, there is nothing to prevent minds that are arbitrarily unsystematic. But that result is *preposterous.* Cognitive capacities come in structurally related clusters; their systematicity is pervasive. All the evidence suggests that *punctate minds can't happen.* This argument seemed conclusive against the Connectionism of Hebb, Osgood and Hull twenty or thirty years ago. So far as we can tell, nothing of any importance has happened to change the situation in the meantime.[29]

A final comment to round off this part of the discussion. It's possible to imagine a Connectionist being prepared to admit that while systematicity doesn't *follow from*—and hence is not explained by—Connectionist architecture, it is nonetheless *compatible* with that architecture. It is, after all, perfectly possible to follow a policy of building networks that have *a*R*b* nodes only if they have *b*R*a* nodes ... etc. There is therefore nothing to stop a Connectionist from stipulating—as an independent postulate of his theory of mind—that all biologically instantiated networks are, de facto, systematic.

But this misses a crucial point: It's not enough just to stipulate systematicity; one is also required to specify a mechanism that is able to enforce the stipulation. To put it another way, it's not enough for a Connectionist to agree that all minds are systematic; he must also explain *how nature contrives to produce only systematic minds*. Presumably there would have to be some sort of mechanism, over and above the ones that Connectionism per se posits, the functioning of which insures the systematicity of biologically instantiated networks; a mechanism such that, in virtue of its operation, every network that has an *a*R*b* node also has a *b*R*a* node ... and so forth. There are, however, no proposals for such a mechanism. Or, rather, there is just one: The only mechanism that is known to be able to produce pervasive systematicity is Classical architecture. And, as we have seen, Classical architecture is not compatible with Connectionism since it requires internally structured representations.

Notes

1. The difference between Connectionist networks in which the state of a single unit encodes properties of the world (i.e., the so-called 'localist' networks) and ones in which the pattern of states of an entire population of units does the encoding (the so-called 'distributed' representation networks) is considered to be important by many people working on Connectionist models. Although Connectionists debate the relative merits of localist (or 'compact') versus distributed representations (e.g., Feldman, 1986), the distinction will usually be of little consequence for our purposes, for reasons that we give later. For simplicity, when we wish to refer indifferently to either single unit codes or aggregate distributed codes, we shall refer to the 'nodes' in a network. When the distinction is relevant to our discussion, however, we shall explicitly mark the difference by referring either to units or to aggregate of units.

2. One of the attractions of Connectionism for many people is that it does employ some heavy mathematical machinery, as can be seen from a glance at many of the chapters of the two volume collection by Rumelhart, McClelland and the PDP Research Group (1986). But in contrast to many other mathematically sophisticated areas of cognitive science, such as automata theory or parts of Artificial Intelligence (particularly the study of search, or of reasoning and knowledge representation), the mathematics has not been used to map out the limits of what the proposed class of mechanisms can do. Like a great deal of Artificial Intelligence research, the Connectionist approach remains almost entirely experimental; mechanisms that look interesting are proposed and explored by implementing them on computers and subjecting them to empirical trials to see what they will do. As a consequence, although there is a great deal of mathematical work within the tradition, one has very little idea what various Connectionist networks and mechanisms are good for in general.

3. Smolensky seems to think that the idea of postulating a level of representations with a semantics of subconceptual features is unique to network theories. This is an extraordinary view considering the extent to which *Classical* theorists have been concerned with feature analyses in every area of psychology from phonetics to visual perception to lexicography. In fact the question whether there are 'sub-conceptual' features is *neutral* with respect to the question whether cognitive architecture is Classical or Connectionist.

4. Sometimes, however, even Representationalists fail to appreciate that it is *representation* that distinguishes cognitive from noncognitive levels. Thus, for example, although Smolensky (1988) is clearly a Representationalist, his official answer to the question "What distinguishes those dynamical systems that are cognitive from those that are not?" makes the mistake of appealing to complexity rather than intentionality: "A river ... fails to be a cognitive dynamical system only because it cannot satisfy a *large* range of goals under a *large* range of conditions." But, of course, that depends on how you individuate goals and conditions; the river that wants to get to the sea wants first to get half way to the sea, and then to get half way more, ..., and so on; quite a lot of goals all told. The real point, of course, is that states that represent goals play a role in the etiology of the behaviors of people but not in the etiology of the 'behavior' of rivers.

5. That Classical architectures can be implemented in networks is not disputed by Connectionists; see for example Rumelhart and McClelland (1986a, p. 118): "... one can make an arbitrary computational machine out of linear threshold units, including, for example, a machine that can carry out all the

operations necessary for implementing a Turing machine; the one limitation is that real biological systems cannot be Turing machines because they have finite hardware.".

6. There is a different idea, frequently encountered in the Connectionist literature, that this one is easily confused with: viz., that the distinction between regularities and exceptions is merely stochastic (what makes 'went' an irregular past tense is just that the *more frequent* construction is the one exhibited by 'walked'). It seems obvious that if this claim is correct it can be readily assimilated to Classical architecture.

7. This way of putting it will do for present purposes. But a subtler reading of Connectionist theories might take it to be total machine *states* that have content, e.g., the state of *having such and such a node excited*. Postulating connections among labelled nodes would then be equivalent to postulating causal relations among the corresponding content bearing machine states: To say that the excitation of the node labelled 'dog' is caused by the excitation of nodes labelled [d], [o], [g] is to say that the machine's representing its input as consisting of the phonetic sequence [dog] causes it to represent its input as consisting of the word 'dog'. And so forth. Most of the time the distinction between these two ways of talking does not matter for our purposes, so we shall adopt one or the other as convenient.

8. Sometimes the difference between simply postulating representational states and postulating representations with a combinatorial syntax and semantics is marked by distinguishing theories that postulate *symbols* from theories that postulate *symbol systems*. The latter theories, but not the former, are committed to a "language of thought". For this usage, see Kosslyn and Hatfield (1984) who take the refusal to postulate symbol systems to be the characteristic respect in which Connectionist architectures differ from Classical architectures. We agree with this diagnosis.

9. Perhaps the notion that relations among physical properties of the brain instantiate (or encode) the *combinatorial structure* of an expression bears some elaboration. One way to understand what is involved is to consider the conditions that must hold on a mapping (which we refer to as the 'physical instantiation mapping') from expressions to brain states if the causal relations among brain states are to depend on the combinatorial structure of the encoded expressions. In defining this mapping it is not enough merely to specify a physical encoding for each symbol; in order for the *structures* of expressions to have causal roles, structural relations must be encoded by physical properties of brain states (or by sets of functionally equivalent physical properties of brain states).

Because, in general, Classical models assume that the expressions that get physically instantiated in brains have a generative syntax, the definition of an appropriate physical instantiation mapping has to be built up in terms of (a) the definition of a primitive mapping from atomic symbols to relatively elementary physical states, and (b) a specification of how the sturcutre of complex expressions maps onto the structure of relatively complex or composite physical states. Such a structure-preserving mapping is typically given recursively, making use of the combinatorial syntax by which complex expressions are built up out of simpler ones. For example, the physical instantiation mapping **F** for complex expressions would be defined by recursion, given the definition of **F** for *atomic* symbols and given the *structure* of the complex expression, the latter being specified in terms of the 'structure building' rules which constitute the generative syntax for complex expressions. Take, for example, the expression '(A&B)&C'. A suitable definition for a mapping in this case might contain the statement that for any expressions P and Q, $F[P\&Q] = B(F[P], F[Q])$, where the function B specifies the physical relation that holds between physical states $F[P]$ and $F[Q]$. Here property B serves to physically encode, (or 'instantiate') the relation that holds between the expressions P and Q, on the one hand, and the expressions $P\&Q$ on the other.

In using this rule for the example above P and Q would have the values 'A&B' and 'C' respectively, so that the mapping rule would have to be applied twice to pick the relevant physical structures. In defining the mapping recursively in this way we ensure that the relation between the expressions 'A' and 'B', and the composite expression 'A&B', is encoded in terms of a physical relation between constituent states that is identical (or functionally equivalent) to the physical relation used to encode the relation between expressions 'A&B' and 'C', and their composite expression '(A&B)&C'. This type of mapping is well known because of its use in Tarski's definition of an interpretation of a language in a model. The idea of a mapping from symbolic expressions to a structure of physical states is discussed in Pylyshyn (1984a, pp. 54–69), where it is referred to as an 'instantiation function' and in Stabler (1985), where it is called a 'realization mapping'.

10. This illustration has not any particular Connectionist model in mind, though the caricature presented is, in fact, a simplified version of the Ballard (1987) Connectionist theorem proving system (which actually uses a more restricted proof procedure based on the *unification* of Horn clauses). To simplify the exposition, we assume a 'localist' approach, in which each semantically interpreted node corresponds to a single Connectionist unit; but nothing relevant to this discussion is changed if these nodes actually consist of patterns over a cluster of units.

11. This makes the "compositionality" of data structures a defining property of Classical architecture. But, of course, it leaves open the question of the degree to which *natural* languages (like English) are also compositional.

12. Labels aren't part of the *causal structure* of a Connectionist machine, but they may play an essential role in its *causal history* insofar as designers wire their machines to respect the semantical relations that the labels express. For example, in Ballard's (1987) Connectionist model of theorem proving, there is a mechanical procedure for wiring a network which will carry out proofs by unification. This procedure is a function from a set of node labels to a wired-up machine. There is thus an interesting and revealing respect in which node labels are relevant to the operations that get performed when the function is executed. But, of course, the machine on which the labels have the effect is not the machine whose states they are labels of; and the effect of the labels occurs at the time that the theorem-proving machine is constructed, not at the time its reasoning process is carried out. *This* sort of case of labels 'having effects' is thus quite different from the way that symbol tokens (e.g., tokened data structures) can affect the causal processes of a Classical machine.

13. Any relation specified as holding among representational states is, by definition, within the 'cognitive level'. It goes without saying that relations that are 'within-level' by this criterion can count as 'between-level' when we use criteria of finer grain. There is, for example, nothing to prevent hierarchies of levels of representational states.

14. Smolensky (1988, p. 14) remarks that "unlike symbolic tokens, these vectors lie in a topological space, in which some are close together and others are far apart." However, this seems to radically conflate claims about the Connectionist model and claims about its implementation (a conflation that is not unusual in the Connectionist literature). If the space at issue is *physical*, then Smolensky is committed to extremely strong claims about adjacency relations in the brain; claims which there is, in fact, no reason at all to believe. But if, as seems more plausible, the space at issue is *semantical* then what Smolensky says isn't true. Practically any cognitive theory will imply distance measures between mental representations. In Classical theories, for example, the distance between two representations is plausibly related to the number of computational steps it takes to derive one representation from the other. In Connectionist theories, it is plausibly related to the number of intervening nodes (or to the degree of overlap between vectors, depending on the version of Connectionism one has in mind). The interesting claim is not that an architecture offers *a* distance measure but that it offers the *right* distance measure—one that is empirically certifiable.

15. The primary use that Connectionists make of microfeatures is in their accounts of generalization and abstraction (see, for example, Hinton, McClelland, & Rumelhart, 1986). Roughly, you get generalization by using overlap of microfeatures to define a similarity space, and you get abstraction by making the vectors that correspond to *types* be subvectors of the ones that correspond to their *tokens*. Similar proposals have quite a long history in traditional Empiricist analysis; and have been roundly criticized over the centuries. (For a discussion of abstractionism see Geach, 1957; that similarity is a primitive relation—hence not reducible to partial identity of feature sets—was, of course, a main tenet of Gestalt psychology, as well as more recent approaches based on "prototypes"). The treatment of microfeatures in the Connectionist literature would appear to be very close to early proposals by Katz and Fodor (1963) and Katz and Postal (1964), where both the idea of a feature analysis of concepts and the idea that relations of semantical containment among concepts should be identified with set-theoretic relations among feature arrays are explicitly endorsed.

16. Another disadvantage is that, strictly speaking it doesn't work; although it allows us to distinguish the belief that John loves Mary and Bill hates Sally from the belief that John loves Sally and Bill hates Mary, we don't yet have a way to distinguish believing that (John loves Mary because Bill hates Sally) from believing that (Bill hates Sally because John loves Mary). Presumably nobody would want to have microfeatures corresponding to these.

17. It's especially important at this point not to make the mistake of confusing diagrams of Connectionist networks with constituent structure diagrams (see section 2.1.2). Connecting SUBJECT-OF with FIDO and BITES does not mean that when all three are active FIDO is the subject of BITES. A network diagram is not a specification of the internal structure of a complex mental representation. Rather, it's a specification of a pattern of causal dependencies among the states of activation of nodes. Connectivity in a network determines which sets of simultaneously active nodes are possible; but it has no *semantical* significance.

The difference between the paths between nodes that network diagrams exhibit and the paths between nodes that constituent structure diagrams exhibit is precisely that the latter but not the former specify parameters of mental representations. (In particular, they specify part/whole relations among the constituents of complex symbols). Whereas network theories define semantic interpretations over sets of (causally interconnected) representations of concepts, theories that acknowledge complex symbols define semantic interpretations over sets of representations of concepts *together with specifications of the constituency relations that hold among these representations.*

18. And it doesn't work uniformly for English conjunction. Compare: *John and Mary are friends* → *John are friends; or *The flag is red, white and blue* → *The flag is blue*. Such cases show either that English is not the language of thought, or that, if it is, the relation between syntax and semantics is a good deal subtler for the language of thought than it is for the standard logical languages.

19. It needn't, however, be strict truth-preservation that makes the syntactic approach relevant to cognition. Other semantic properties might be preserved under syntactic transformation in the course of mental processing—e.g., warrant, plausibility, heuristic value, or simply *semantic non-arbitrariness.* The point of Classical modeling isn't to characterize human thought as supremely logical; rather, it's to show how a family of types of semantically coherent (or knowledge-dependent) reasoning are mechanically possible. Valid inference is the paradigm only in that it is the best understood member of this family; the one for which syntactical analogues for semantical relations have been most systematically elaborated.

20. It is not uncommon for Connectionists to make disparaging remarks about about the relevance of logic to psychology, even thought they accept the idea that inference is involved in reasoning. Sometimes the suggestion seems to be that it's all right if Connectionism can't reconstruct the theory of inference that formal deductive logic provides since it has something even better on offer. For example, in their report to the U.S. National Science Foundation, McClelland, Feldman, Adelson, Bower & McDermott (1986) state that "... connectionist models realize an evidential logic *in contrast to* the symbolic logic of conventional computing (p. 6; our emphasis)" and that "evidential logics are becoming increasingly important in cognitive science and have a natural map to connectionist modeling." (p. 7). It is, however, hard to understand the implied contrast since, on the one hand, evidential logic must surely be a fairly conservative extension of "the symbolic logic of conventional computing" (i.e., most of the theorems of the latter have to come out true in the former) and, on the other, there is not the slightest reason to doubt that an evidential logic would 'run' on a Classical machine. Prima facie, the problem about evidential logic isn't that we've got one that we don't know how to implement; it's that we haven't got one.

21. Compare the "little s's" and "little r's" of neo-Hullean "mediational" Associationists like Charles Osgood.

22. This way of putting the productivity argument is most closely identified with Chomsky (e.g., Chomsky, 1965; 1968). However, one does not have to rest the argument upon a basic assumption of infinite generative capacity. Infinite generative capacity can be viewed, instead, as a consequence or a corollary of theories formulated so as to capture the greatest number of generalizations with the fewest independent principles. This more neutral approach is, in fact, very much in the spirit of what we shall propose below. We are putting it in the present form for expository and historical reasons.

23. McClelland and Kawamoto (1986) discuss this sort of recursion briefly. Their suggestion seems to be that parsing such sentences doesn't really require recovering their recursive structure: "... the job of the parser [with respect to right-recursive sentences] is to spit out phrases in a way that captures their *local* context. Such a representation may prove sufficient to allow us to reconstruct the correct bindings of noun phrases to verbs and prepositional phrases to *nearby* nouns and verbs" (p. 324; emphasis ours). It is, however, by no means the case that all of the semantically relevant grammatical relations in readily intelligible embedded sentences are local in surface structure. Consider: '*Where* did the man who owns the cat that chased the rat that frightened the girl say that he was going to move to (X)?' or '*What* did the girl that the children loved to listen to promise your friends that she would read (X) to them?' Notice that, in such examples, a binding element (italicized) can be arbitrarily displaced from the position whose interpretation it controls (marked 'X') without making the sentence particularly difficult to understand. Notice too that the 'semantics' doesn't determine the binding relations in either example.

24. See Pinker (1984, Chapter 4) for evidence that children never go through a stage in which they distinguish between the internal structures of NPs depending on whether they are in subject or object position; i.e., the dialects that children speak are always systematic with respect to the syntactic structures that can appear in these positions.

25. It may be worth emphasizing that the structural complexity of a mental representation is not the same thing as, and does *not* follow from, the structural complexity of its propositional content (i.e., of what we're calling "the thought that one has"). Thus, Connectionists and Classicists can agree to agree that *the thought that P&Q* is complex (and has the thought that *P* among its parts) while agreeing to diagree about whether mental representations have internal syntactic structure.

26. These considerations throw further light on a proposal we discussed in Section 2. Suppose that the mental representation corresponding to the thought that John loves the girl is the feature vector

{ + *John-subject;* + *loves;* + *the-girl-object*} where '*John-subject*' and '*the-girl-object*' are atomic features; as such, they bear no more structural relation to '*John-object*' and '*the-girl-subject*' than they do to one another or to, say, '*has-a-handle*'. Since this theory recognizes no structural relation between '*John-subject* and '*John-object*', it offers no reason why a representational system that provides the means to express one of these concepts should also provide the means to express the other. This treatment of role relations thus makes a mystery of the (presumed) fact that anybody who can entertain the thought that John loves the girl can also entertain the thought that the girl loves John (and, mutatis mutandis, that any natural language that can express the proposition that John loves the girl can also express the proposition that the girl loves John). This consequence of the proposal that role relations be handled by "role specific descriptors that represent the conjunction of an identity and a role" (Hinton, 1987) offers a particularly clear example of how failure to postulate internal structure in representations leads to failure to capture the systematicity of representational systems.

27. We are indebted to Steve Pinker for this point.

28. The hedge is meant to exclude cases where inferences of the same logical type nevertheless differ in complexity in virtue of, for example, the length of their premises. The inference from $(AvBvCvDvE)$ and $(-B\&-C\&-D\&-E)$ to A is of the same logical type as the inference from AvB and $-B$ to A. But it wouldn't be very surprising, or very interesting, if there were minds that could handle the second inference but not the first.

29. Historical footnote: Connectionists are Associationists, but not every Associationist holds that mental representations must be unstructured. Hume didn't, for example. Hume thought that mental representations are rather like pictures, and pictures typically have a compositional semantics: the parts of a picture of a horse are generally pictures of horse parts.

On the other hand, allowing a compositional semantics for mental representations doesn't do an Associationist much good so long as he is true to this spirit of his Associationism. The virtue of having mental representations with structure is that it allows for structure sensitive operations to be defined over them; specifically, it allows for the sort of operations that eventuate in productivity and systematicity. Association is not, however, such an operation; all *it* can do is build an internal model of redundancies in experience by altering the probabilities of transitions among mental states. So far as the problems of productivity and systematicity are concerned, an Associationist who acknowledges structured representations is in the position of having the can but not the opener.

Hume, in fact, cheated: he allowed himself not just Association but also "Imagination", which he takes to be an 'active' faculty that can produce new concepts out of old parts by a process of analysis and recombination. (The idea of a unicorn is pieced together out of the idea of a horse and the idea of a horn, for example.) Qua associationist Hume had, of course, no right to active mental faculties. But allowing imagination in gave Hume precisely what modern Connectionists don't have: an answer to the question how mental processes can be productive. The moral is that if you've got structured representations, the temptation to postulate structure sensitive operations and an executive to apply them is practically irresistible.

References

Arbib, M. (1975). Artificial intelligence and brain theory: Unities and diversities. *Biomedical Engineering, 3,* 238–274.

Ballard, D. H. (1986). Cortical connections and parallel processing: Structure and function. *The Behavioral and Brain Sciences, 9,* 67–120.

Ballard, D. H. (1987). Parallel Logical Inference and Energy Minimization. Report TR142, Computer Science Department, University of Rochester.

Broadbent, D. (1985). A question of levels: Comments on McClelland and Rumelhart. *Journal of Experimental Psychology: General, 114,* 189–192.

Chomsky, N. (1965). *Aspects of the theory of syntax.* Cambridge, MA: MIT Press.

Chomsky, N. (1968). *Language and mind.* New York: Harcourt, Brace and World.

Churchland, P. M. (1981). Eliminative materialism and the propositional attitudes. *Journal of Philosophy, 78,* 67–90.

Churchland, P. S. (1986). *Neurophilosophy,* Cambridge, MA: MIT Press.

Dennett, D. (1986). The logical geography of computational approaches: A view from the east pole. In Brand, M. & Harnish, M. (Eds.), *The representation of knowledge.* Tuscon, AZ: The University of Arizona Press.

Dreyfus, H., & Dreyfus, S. (in press). Making a mind vs modelling the brain: A. I. back at a branch point. *Daedalus.*

Fahlman, S. E., & Hinton, G. E. (1987). Connectionist architectures for artificial intelligence. *Computer, 20,* 100–109.

Feldman, J. A. (1986). Neural representation of conceptual knowledge. Report TR189. Department of Computer Science, University of Rochester.

Feldman, J. A., & Ballard, D. H. (1982). Connectionist models and their properties. *Cognitive Science, 6,* 205–254.

Fodor, J. (1975). *The language of thought,* Harvester Press, Sussex. (Harvard University Press paperback).

Fodor, J. D. (1977). *Semantics: Theories of meaning in generative grammar.* New York: Thomas Y. Crowell.

Fodor, J. (1987). *Psychosemantics.* Cambridge, MA: MIT Press.

Geach, P. (1957). *Mental acts.* London: Routledge and Kegan Paul.

Hewett, C. (1977). Viewing control structures as patterns of passing messages. *The Artificial Intelligence Journal, 8,* 232–364.

Hinton, G. (1987). Representing part-whole hierarchies in connectionist networks. Unpublished manuscript.

Hinton, G. E., McClelland, J. L., & Rumelhart, D. E. (1986). Distributed representations. In Rumelhart, D. E., McClelland, J. L. and the PDP Research Group, *Parallel distributed processing: Explorations in the microstructure of cognition. Volume I: Foundations.* Cambridge, MA: MIT Press/Bradford Books.

Kant, I. (1929). *The critique of pure reason.* New York: St. Martins Press.

Katz, J. J., & Fodor, J. A. (1963). The structure of a semantic theory, *Language, 39,* 170–210.

Katz, J., & Postal, P. (1964). *An integrated theory of linguistic descriptions.* Cambridge, MA: MIT Press.

Kosslyn, S. M., & Hatfield, G. (1984). Representation without symbol systems. *Social Research, 51,* 1019–1054.

Lakoff, G. (1986). Connectionism and cognitive linguistics. Seminar delivered at Princeton University, December 8, 1986.

McClelland, J. L., Feldman, J., Adelson, B., Bower, G., & McDermott, D. (1986). *Connectionist models and cognitive science: Goals, directions and implications.* Report to the National Science Foundation, June, 1986.

McClelland, J. L., & Kawamoto, A. H. (1986). Mechanisms of sentence processing: Assigning roles to constituents. In McClelland, Rumelhart and the PDP Research Group (Eds.), *Parallel distributed processing: volume 2.* Cambridge, MA: MIT Press/Bradford Books.

McClelland, J. L., Rumelhart, D. E., & Hinton, G. E. (1986). The appeal of parallel distributed processing. In Rumelhart, McClelland and the PDP Research Group. (Eds.), *Parallel distributed processing: volume 1.* Cambridge, MA: MIT Press/Bradford Books.

Newell, A. (1980). Physical symbol systems. *Cognitive Science, 4,* 135–183.

Newell, A. (1982). The knowledge level. *Artifical Intelligence, 18,* 87–127.

Pinker, S. (1984). *Language, learnability and language development.* Cambridge: Harvard University Press.

Pylyshyn, Z. W. (1980). Cognition and computation: Issues in the foundations of cognitive science. *Behavioral and Brain Sciences, 3 : 1,* 154–169.

Pylyshyn, Z. W. (1984a). *Computation and cognition: Toward a foundation for cognitive science.* Cambridge, MA: MIT Press/Bradford Books.

Pylyshyn, Z. W. (1984b). Why computation requires symbols. *Proceedings of the Sixth Annual Conference of the Cognitive Science Society, Boulder, Colorado, August, 1984.* Hillsdale, NJ: Erlbaum.

Rumelhart, D. E. (1984). The emergence of cognitive phenomena from sub-symbolic processes. In *Proceedings of the Sixth Annual Conference of the Cognitive Science Society, Boulder, Colorado, August, 1984.* Hillsdale, NJ: Erlbaum.

Rumelhart, D. E., & McClelland, J. L. (1985). Levels indeed! A response to Broadbent. *Journal of Experimental Psychology: General, 114,* 193–197.

Rumelhart, D. E., & McClelland, J. L. (1986a). PDP Models and general issues in cognitive science. In Rumelhart, McClelland and the PDP Research Group (Eds.), *Parallel distributed processing, volume 1.* Cambridge, MA: MIT Press/Bradford Books.

Rumelhart, D. E., & McClelland, J. L. (1986b). On learning the past tenses of English verbs. In Rumelhart, McClelland and the PDP Research Group (Eds.), *Parallel distributed processing, volume 1.* Cambridge, MA: MIT Press/Bradford Books.

Schneider, W. (1987). Connectionism: Is it a paradigm shift for psychology? *Behavior Research Methods, Instruments, & Computers, 19,* 73–83.

Sejnowski, T. J. (1981). Skeleton filters in the brain. In Hinton, G. E., & Anderson, A. J. (Eds.), *Parallel models of associative memory.* Hillsdale, NJ: Erlbaum.

Smolensky, P. (1988). On the proper treatment of connectionism. *The Behavioral and Brain Sciences, 11,* 1–74.

Stabler, E. (1985). How are grammars represented? *Behavioral and Brain Sciences, 6,* 391–420.

Stich, S. (1983). *From folk psychology to cognitive science.* Cambridge, MA: MIT Press/Bradford Books.

Wanner, E., & Maratsos, M. (1978). An ATN approach to comprehension. In Halle, M., Bresnan, J., & Miller, G. A. (Eds.), *Linguistic theory and psychological reality*. Cambridge, MA: MIT Press.

Watson, J. (1930). *Behaviorism*, Chicago: University of Chicago Press.

Ziff, P. (1960). *Semantic analysis*. Ithaca, NY: Cornell University Press.

Chapter 42

The Constituent Structure of Connectionist Mental States: A Reply to Fodor and Pylyshyn

Paul Smolensky

The primary purpose of this article is to reply to the central point of Fodor and Pylyshyn's critique of connectionism. The direct reply to their critique comprises section 2 of this paper. In short, I argue that Fodor and Pylyshyn are simply mistaken in their claim that connectionist mental states lack the necessary constituent structure, and that the basis of this mistake is a failure to appreciate the significance of distributed representations in connectionist models. Section 3 is a broader response to the bottom line of their critique, which is that connectionists should re-orient their work towards *implementation* of the classical symbolic cognitive architecture. I argue instead that connectionist research should develop *new formalizations* of the fundamental computational notions that have been given one particular formal shape in the traditional symbolic paradigm.

My response to Fodor and Pylyshyn's critique presumes a certain meta-theoretical context that is laid out in section 1. In this first section I argue that any discussion of the choice of some framework for cognitive modeling (e.g., the connectionist framework) must admit that such a choice embodies a response to a fundamental cognitive paradox, and that this response shapes the entire scientific enterprise surrounding research within that framework. Fodor and Pylyshyn are implicitly advocating one class of response to the paradox over another, and I wish to analyze their critique in this light.

1 The Paradox and Several Responses

In this section, I want to consider the question of what factors go into the decision about what cognitive modeling formalism to adopt, given the choice between the symbolic formalism and the connectionist formalism. I want to argue that the crucial move in deciding this question is to take a stance on the issue that I will refer to as "the Paradox of Cognition," or more simply, "the Paradox."

The Paradox is simple enough to identify. On the one hand, cognition is *hard*: characterized by the rules of logic, by the rules of language. On the other hand, cognition is *soft*: if you write down the rules, it seems that realizing those rules in automatic formal systems (which AI programs are) gives systems that are just not sufficiently fluid, not robust enough in performance, to constitute what we want to call true intelligence. That, quite simply, is the Paradox. In attempting to characterize the laws of cognition, we are pulled in two different directions: when we focus on the rules governing high-level cognitive competence, we are pulled towards structured, symbolic representations and processes; when we focus on the variance and complex detail of real intelligent performance, we are pulled towards statistical, numerical descriptions. The Paradox could be called, somewhat more precisely, The Structure/Statistics Dilemma.[1] The stance one adopts towards the Paradox strongly influences the role that can be played by symbolic and connectionist modeling formalisms. At least five noteworthy stances have been taken on the Paradox, and I will now quickly review them. I will consider each in its purest form; these extreme stances can be viewed as caricatures of the more subtle positions actually taken by cognitive scientists.

The first stance one should always consider when confronted with a paradox is *denial*. In fact, that is probably the most popular choice. The denial option comes in two forms. The first is to *deny the soft*. A more reputable name for this might be *rationalism*. In this response to the Paradox one insists that the essence of intelligence is logic and following rules—everything else is inessential. This can be identified as the motivation behind the notion of ideal competence in linguistics (Chomsky 1965), where soft behavior and performance variability are regarded as mere noise. The fact that there is tremendous regularity in this noise is to be ignored—at least in the purest version of this stance.

The other denial stance is obviously to *deny the hard*. According to this view, rule following is really characteristic of *novice*, not expert, behavior; the essence of real intelligence is its *evasion* of rule-following (Dreyfus and Dreyfus 1986). Indeed, some of the strongest advocates of this position are connectionists who claim "there are no rules" in cognition.

If one rejects the denial options, one can go for the opposite extreme, which I will call *the split brain*.[2] On this view, the head contains both a soft machine and hard machine, and they sit right next to each other. This response to the Paradox is embodied in talk about systems that have "connectionist modules" and "rule-based modules" and some sort of communication between them. There is the right, connectionist brain doing soft, squishy processing, and the left, von Neumann brain doing the hard rule-based processing. Rather than "the split brain," this scene of a house divided—right and left working side-by-side despite their profound differences—might better be called by its French name: *cohabitation*.

Advocates of this response presumably feel they are giving both sides of the Paradox equal weight. But does this response really grapple with the full force of the Paradox? In the split brain, there is a *hard line* that surrounds and isolates the softness, and there is no soft line that demarks the hardness. The softness is neatly tucked away in an overall architecture characterized by a hard distinction between hard and soft processing. The full force of the Paradox insists that the soft and hard aspects of cognition are so intimately intertwined that such a hard distinction is not viable. Not to mention the serious problem of getting the two kinds of systems to intimately cooperate when they speak such different languages.

The third approach to the Paradox is *the fuzzy approach* (Gupta, Ragade, and Yager 1979). Here the basic idea is take a hard machine and coat its parts with softness. One takes a rule-based system for doing medical diagnosis and attaches a number to every rule that says how certain the inference is (Shortliffe 1976; Zadeh 1975, 1983); or one takes a set, and for every member in the set attaches a number which says how much of member of the set it is (Zadeh 1965). In this response to the Paradox, softness is defined to be degrees of hardness. One takes the ontology of the problem that comes out of the hard approach, and one affixes numbers to all the elements of this ontology rather than reconceptualizing the ontology in a new way that intrinsically reflects the softness in the system.

On such ontological grounds, the fourth approach is starting to get rather more sophisticated. On this view, the cognitive machine is at bottom a hard machine; fundamentally, everything works on rules—but the machine is so complex that it *appears soft* when you look at it on a higher level. *Softness emerges from hardness*. This response to the Paradox is implicit in a comment such as, "O.k., maybe my expert system *is* brittle, but that is because it is just a toy system with only 10,000 rules ... if I had the resources, I would build the *real* system with 10^{10} rules, and it would just be as intelligent as the human expert." In other words, if there are enough hard rules sloshing around in the system, fluid behavior will be an emergent property.

In terms of levels of description, here is the picture. There is a level of description at which the cognitive system is hard: the lower level. And there is a level of description at which it is soft: the higher level. That is the sense in which this approach is getting more sophisticated: it uses *levels of analysis* to reconcile the hard and soft sides of the Paradox.

The question here is whether this approach will ever work. The effort to liberate systems built of large numbers of hard rules from the brittleness that is intrinsic to such rules has been underway for some time now. Whether the partial successes constitute a basis for optimism or pessimism is clearly a difficult judgment call.

The fifth and final approach I want to consider is the one that I have argued (Smolensky 1988a) forms the basis of the proper treatment of connectionism. On this view, which I have called the *subsymbolic* approach, the cognitive system is fundamentally a soft machine that is so complex that it sometimes appears hard when viewed at higher levels. As in the previous approach, the Paradox is addressed through two levels of analysis—but now it is the lower level that is soft and the upper level that is hard: now *hardness emerges from softness.*

Having reviewed these five responses to the Paradox, we can now see why the decision of whether to adopt a symbolic computational formalism or a connectionist one is rooted in a stance on the Paradox. The issue is whether to assume a formalism that *gives for free* the characteristics of the hard side of the Paradox, or one that gives for free the characteristics of the soft side. If you decide not to go for combining both formalisms (*cohabitation*), but to take one as fundamental, then whichever way you go, you have got to either *ignore* the other side, or *build it* in the formalism you have chosen.

So what are the possible motivations for taking the soft side as the fundamental substrate on which to build the hard—whatever hard aspects of cognition need to be built? Here are some reasons for giving the soft side priority in that sense.

- A fundamentally soft approach is appealing if you view *perception*, rather than *logical inference*, as the underpinning of intelligence. In the subsymbolic approach, the fundamental basis of cognition is viewed as categorization and other perceptual processes of that sort.
- In overall cognitive performance, hardness seems more the exception than the rule. That cuts both ways, of course. The denial option is always open to say it is only the 3% that is not soft that really characterizes intelligence, and that is what we should worry about.
- An evolutionary argument says that the hard side of the cognitive paradox evolved later, on top of the soft side, and that your theoretical ontogeny should recapitulate phylogeny.
- Compared to the symbolic rule-based approaches, it is much easier to see how the kind of soft systems that connectionist models represent could be implemented in the nervous system.
- If you are going to base your whole solution to the Paradox on the emergence of one kind of computation from the other, then it becomes crucially important to be able to analyze the higher level properties of the lower level system. That the mathematics governing connectionist networks can be analyzed for emergent properties seems a considerably better bet than extremely complex rule-based

systems being analyzable for their emergent properties. The enterprise of analyzing the emergent properties of connectionist systems is rather closely related to traditional kinds of analysis of dynamical systems in physics; it has already shown signs that it may ultimately be as successful.

• Finally, the hard side has had priority for several decades now with disappointing results. It is time to give the soft side a few decades to produce disappointing results of its own.

The choice of adopting a fundamentally soft approach and building a hard level on top of that has serious costs—as pointed out in some detail by Kirsh (1987). The power of symbols and symbolic computation is not given to you for free; you have to construct them out of soft stuff, and this is really very difficult. At this point, we do not know how to pull it off. As Kirsh points out, if you do not have symbols in the usual sense, it is not clear that you can cope with a number of problems. Fodor and Pylyshyn's critique is basically a statement of the same general sort: that the price one has to pay for going connectionist is the failure to account for certain regularities of the hard side, regularities that the symbolic formalism gives you essentially for free.

If the force of such critiques is taken to be that connectionism does not *yet* come close enough to providing the capabilities of symbolic computation to do justice to the hard side of the Paradox, then I personally think that they are quite correct. Adopting the subsymbolic stance on the Paradox amounts to taking out an enormous loan—a loan that has barely begun to be paid off.

If, on the other hand, the force of such critiques is taken to be that connectionism can *never* come close enough to providing the capabilities of symbolic computation without merely implementing the symbolic approach, then, as I will argue in the remainder of this article, I believe such critiques must be rejected.

Where are the benefits of going with the subsymbolic approach to the Paradox? Why is this large loan worth taking out? In my view, the principal justification is that if we succeed in building symbols and symbol manipulation out of "connectoplasm" then we will have an explanation of *where symbols and symbol manipulation come from*—and that is worth the risk and the effort; very much so. With any luck we will even have an explanation how the *brain* builds symbolic computation. But even if we do not get that directly, it will be the first theory of how to get symbols out of anything that remotely resembles the brain—and that certainly will be helpful (indeed, I would argue, crucial) in figuring out how the brain actually does it.

Another potential payback is a way of explaining *why* those aspects of cognition that exhibit hardness should exhibit hardness: why the area of hardness falls where it does; why it is limited as it is; why the symbolic approach succeeds where it succeeds and fails where it fails.

Finally, of course, if the subsymbolic approach succeeds, we will have a truly unified solution to the Paradox: no denial of one half of the problem, and no profoundly split brain.

We can already see contributions leading towards these ultimate results. The connectionist approach is producing new concepts and techniques for capturing the regularities in cognitive performance both at the lower level where the connectionist framework naturally applies and at the higher level where the symbolic accounts are important. (For recent surveys, see McClelland, Rumelhart, and the PDP Research Group 1986; Rumelhart, McClelland, and the PDP Research Group 1986; Smolensky, forthcoming). The theoretical repertoire of cognitive and computer science is being enriched by new conceptions of how computation can be done.

As far as where we actually stand on achieving the ultimate goals, in my opinion, what we have are interesting techniques and promising suggestions. Our current position in the intellectual history of connectionist computation, in my view, can be expressed by this analogy:

$$\frac{\text{current understanding of connectionist computation}}{\text{current understanding of symbolic computation}} : : \frac{\text{Aristotle}}{\text{Turing}}$$

We are somewhere approximating Aristotle's position in the intellectual development of this new computational approach. If there are any connectionist enthusiasts who think that we can really model cognition from such a position, they are, I fear, sadly mistaken. And if we cannot get from Aristotle to (at least) Turing in our understanding of subsymbolic computation, we are not going to get much closer to real cognition than we are now.

One final comment before proceeding to Fodor and Pylyshyn's critique. The account given here relating the choice of a connectionist framework to the hard/soft paradox sheds some light on the question, often asked by observers of the sociology of connectionism: " Why does the connectionist fan club include such a strange assortment of people?" At least in the polite reading of this question, "strange assortment" refers to a philosophically quite heterogenous group of cognitive scientists whose views have little more in common than a rejection of the mainstream symbolic paradigm. My answer to this question is that the priority of the hard has made a lot of people very unhappy for a long time. The failure of mainstream formal accounts of cognitive processes to do justice to the soft side of the Paradox has made people from a lot of different perspectives feel alienated from the endeavor. By assigning to the soft the position of priority, by making it the basis of the formalism, connectionism has given a lot of people who have not had a formal leg to stand on a formal leg to stand on. And they *should* be happy about that.

At this point, "connectionism" refers more to a formalism than a theory. So it is not appropriate to paraphrase the question of the previous paragraph as "What kind of theory would have as its adherents such a disparate group of people?" It is not really a question of a *theory* at all—it is really a question of what kind of *formalism* allows people with different theories to say what they need to say.

Having made my case that understanding the choice of a connectionist formalism involves considering alternative stances towards the Paradox of Cognition, I now proceed to consider Fodor and Pylyshyn's critique in this light.

2 Fodor and Pylyshyn on the Constituent Structure of Mental States

Here is a quick summary of the central argument of Fodor and Pylyshyn (1988).

(1) Thoughts have composite structure.

By this they mean things like: the thought that *John loves the girl* is not atomic; it is a composite mental state built out of thoughts about *John, loves,* and *the girl.*

(2) Mental processes are sensitive to this composite structure.

For example, from any thought of the form $p \ \& \ q$—regardless of what p and q are—we can deduce p.

Fodor and Pylyshyn elevate (1) and (2) to the status of defining the Classical View of Cognition, and they want to say that this is what is being challenged by the connectionists. I will later argue that they are wrong, but now we continue with their argument.

Having identified claims (1) and (2) as definitive of the Classical View, Fodor and Pylyshyn go on to argue that there are compelling arguments for these claims. [They admit up front that these arguments are a rerun updated for the 80's, a colorized version of a film that was shown in black and white some time ago—with the word "behaviorism" replaced throughout by "connectionism."] Mental states have, according to these arguments, the properties of productivity, systematicity, compositionality, and inferential coherence. Without going into all these arguments, let me simply state that for present purposes I am willing to accept that they are convincing enough to justify the conclusion that (1) and (2) must be taken quite seriously. Whatever the inclinations of other connectionists, these and related arguments convince me that denying the hard is a mistake. They do not convince me that I should deny the soft—nor, presumably, are they intended to.

Now for Fodor and Pylyshyn's analysis of connectionism. They assert that in (standard) connectionism, *all representations are atomic*; mental states have no composite structure, violating (1). Furthermore, they assert, (standard) *connectionist processing is association* which is sensitive only to *statistics*, not to *structure*—in violation of (2). Therefore, they conclude, (standard) connectionism is maximally non-Classical; it violates both the defining principles. Therefore connectionism is defeated by the compelling arguments in favor of the Classical View.

What makes Fodor and Pylyshyn say that connectionist representations are atomic? The second figure of their paper says it all—it is rendered here as figure 42.1. This network is supposed to illustrate the standard connectionist account of the inference from *A* & *B* to *A* and to *B*. It is true that Ballard and Hayes wrote a paper (Ballard and Hayes 1984) about using connectionist networks to do resolution theorem proving in which networks like this appear. However, it is a serious mistake to view this as the paradigmatic connectionist account for anything like human inferences of this sort. This kind of *ultra-local* connectionist representation, in which entire propositions are represented by individual nodes, is far from typical of connectionist models, and certainly not to be taken as *definitive* of the connectionist approach.

My central counter-argument to Fodor and Pylyshyn starts with the claim that any critique of the connectionist approach must consider the consequences of using *distributed representations*, in which the representations of high level conceptual entities such as propositions are distributed over many nodes, and the same nodes simultaneously participate in the representation of many entities. Their response, in Section 2.1.3, is as follows. The distributed/local representation issue concerns (they assume) whether each of the nodes in figure 42.1 refers to something complicated and lower level (the distributed case) or not (the local case). But, they claim, this issue is irrelevant, because it pertains to a *between level* issue, and the compositionality of mental states is a *within level* issue.

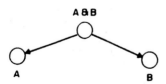

Figure 42.1
Fodor and Pylyshyn's network

My response is that they are correct that compositionality is a within level issue, and correct that the distributed/local distinction is a between level issue. Their argument presumes that because of this difference, one issue cannot influence the other. But this is a fallacy. It assumes that the between-level relation in distributed representations cannot have any consequences on the *within level* structure of the relationships between the representations of *A & B* and the representation of *A*. And that is simply false. There are implications of distributed representations for compositionality, which I am going to bring out in the rest of this section through an extended example. In particular it will turn out that figure 42.1 is no more relevant to a distributed connectionist account of inference than it is to a symbolic account. In the hyper-local case, figure 42.1 is relevant and their critique stands; in the distributed case, figure 42.1 is a bogus characterization of the connectionist account and their critique completely misses its target. It will further turn out that a valid analysis of the actual distributed case, based on suggestions of Pylyshyn himself, leads to quite the opposite conclusion: connectionist models using distributed representations describe mental states with a relevant kind of (within level) constituent structure.

Before developing this counter-argument, let me summarize the bottom line of the Fodor and Pylyshyn paper. Since they believe *standard* connectionism to be fatally flawed, they advocate that connectionists pursue instead a *nonstandard connectionism*. Connectionists should embrace principles (1) & (2); they should accept the classical view and should design their nets to be implementations of classical architectures. The logic implicit here is that connectionist models that respect (1) and (2) must necessarily be implementations of a classical architecture; this is their second major fallacy, which I will return to in section 3. Fodor and Pylyshyn claim that connectionism should be used to implement classical architectures, and that having done this, connectionism will provide not a new cognitive architecture but an implementation for the old cognitive architecture—that what connectionism can provide therefore is not a new paradigm for cognitive science but rather some new information about "implementation science" or possibly, neuroscience.

If connectionists were to follow the implementation strategy that Fodor and Pylyshyn advocate, I do believe these consequences concerning cognitive architecture *would* indeed follow. But I do not believe that it follows from accepting (1) and (2) that connectionist networks must be implementations. In section 3, I argue that connectionists can consistently accept (1) and (2) while rejecting the implementationalist approach Fodor and Pylyshyn advocate.

For now, the goal is to show that connectionist models using *distributed* representations ascribe to mental states the kind of compositional structure demanded by (1), contrary to Fodor and Pylyshyn's conclusion based on the network of figure 42.1 embodying a hyper-local representation.

My argument consists primarily in carrying out an analysis that was suggested by Zenon Pylyshyn himself at the 1984 Cognitive Science Meeting in Boulder. A sort of debate about connectionism was held between Geoffrey Hinton and David Rumelhart on the one hand, and Zenon Pylyshyn and Kurt Van Lehn on the other. While pursuing the nature of connectionist representations, Pylyshyn asked Rumelhart: "Look, can you guys represent a cup of coffee in these networks?" Rumelhart's reply was "Sure" so Pylyshyn continued: "And can you represent a cup without coffee in it?" Waiting for the trap to close, Rumelhart said "Yes" at which point Pylyshyn pounced: "Ah-hah, well, the difference between the two is just the representation of *coffee* and you have just built a representation of *cup with coffee* by combining a representation of *cup* with a representation of *coffee*."

Units	Microfeatures
●	upright container
●	hot liquid
○	glass contacting wood
●	porcelain curved surface
●	burnt odor
●	brown liquid contacting porcelain
●	porcelain curved surface
○	oblong silver object
●	finger-sized handle
●	brown liquid with curved sides and bottom

Figure 42.2
Representation of *cup* with *coffee*

So, let's carry out exactly the construction suggested by Pylyshyn, and see what conclusion it leads us to. We will take a *distributed* representation of *cup with coffee* and substract from it a distributed representation of *cup without coffee* and we will call what is left "the connectionist representation of *coffee*."

To generate these distributed representations I will use a set of "microfeatures" (Hinton, McClelland, and Rumelhart 1986) that are not very micro—but that is always what happens when you try to create examples that can be intuitively understood in a nontechnical exposition. These microfeatures are shown in figure 42.2.

Figure 42.2 shows a distributed representation of *cup with coffee*: a pattern of activity in which those units that are active (black) are those that correspond to microfeatures present in the description of a cup containing coffee. Obviously, this is a crude, nearly sensory-level representation. but again that helps make the example more intuitive—it is not essential.

Given the representation of *cup with coffee* displayed in figure 42.2, Pylyshyn suggests we subtract the representation of *cup without coffee*. The representation of *cup without coffee* is shown in figure 42.3, and figure 42.4 shows the result of subtracting it from the representation of *cup with coffee*.

So what does this procedure produce as "the connectionist representation of *coffee*"? Reading off from figure 42.4, we have a burnt odor and hot brown liquid with curved sides and bottom surfaces contacting porcelain. This is indeed a representation of *coffee*, but in a very particular context: the context provided by *cup*.

What does this mean for Pylyshyn's conclusion that "the connectionist representation of *cup with coffee* is just the representation of *cup without coffee* combined with the representation of *coffee*"? What is involved in combining the representations of figures 42.3 and 42.4 back together to form that of figure 42.2? We assemble the representation of *cup with coffee* from a representation of a *cup*, and a representation of *coffee*, but it is a rather strange combination. It has also got representation of the *interaction* of the cup with coffee—like *brown liquid contacting porcelain*. Thus the composite representation is built from coffee *extracted* from the situation *cup with coffee*, together with *cup* extracted from the situation *cup with coffee*, together with their interaction.

So the compositional structure is there, but it is there in an *approximate* sense. It is *not* equivalent to taking a context-independent representation of *coffee* and a context-

Units	Microfeatures
●	upright container
○	hot liquid
○	glass contacting wood
●	porcelain curved surface
○	burnt odor
○	brown liquid contacting porcelain
●	porcelain curved surface
○	oblong silver object
●	finger-sized handle
○	brown liquid with curved sides and bottom

Figure 42.3
Representation of *cup without coffee*

Units	Microfeatures
○	upright container
●	hot liquid
○	glass contacting wood
○	porcelain curved surface
●	burnt odor
●	brown liquid contacting porcelain
○	porcelain curved surface
○	oblong silver object
○	finger-sized handle
●	brown liquid with curved sides and bottom

Figure 42.4
Representation of *coffee*

independent representation of *cup*—and certainly not equivalent to taking a context-independent representation of the relationship *in* or *with*—and sticking them all together in a symbolic structure, concatenating them together to form the kinds of syntactic compositional structures that Fodor and Pylyshyn think connectionist nets should implement.

To draw this point out further, let's consider the representation of *coffee* once the cup has been subtracted off. This, suggests Pylyshyn, is the connectionist representation of *coffee*. But as we have already observed, this is really a representation of *coffee* in the particular context of being inside a cup. According to Pylyshyn's formula, to get the connectionist representation of *coffee* it should have been in principle possible to take the connectionist representation of *can with coffee* and subtract from it the connectionist representation of *can without coffee*. What would happen if we actually did this? We would get a representation of ground brown burnt smelling granules stacked in a cylindrical shape, together with granules contacting tin. This is the connectionist representation of *coffee* we get by starting with *can with coffee* instead of *cup with coffee*. Or we could start with the representation of *tree with coffee* and subtract off *tree without coffee*. We would get a connectionist representation for *coffee* which would be a representation of brown beans in a funny shape hanging suspended in mid air. Or again we could start with *man with coffee* and get still another connectionist representation of *coffee*: one quite similar to the entire representation of *cup with coffee* from which we extracted our first representation of *coffee*.

The point is that the representation of *coffee* that we get out of the construction starting with *cup with coffee* leads to a different representation of *coffee* than we get out of other constructions that have equivalent status a priori. That means if you want to talk about the connectionist representation of *coffee* in this distributed scheme, you have to talk about a *family of distributed activity patterns*. What knits together all these particular representations of *coffee* is nothing other than a *family resemblance*.

The first moral I want to draw out of this *coffee* story is this: unlike the hyper-local case of figure 42.1, with distributed representations, complex representations *are* composed of representations of constituents. The constituency relation here is a *within level* relation, as Fodor and Pylyshyn require: the pattern or *vector* representing *cup with coffee* is composed of a *vector* that can be identified as a distributed representation of *cup without coffee* together with a *vector* that can be identified as a particular distributed representation of *coffee*. In characterizing the constituent vectors of the vector representing the composite, we are *not* concerned with the fact that the vector representing *cup with coffee* is a vector comprised of the activity of individual microfeature units. The *between level* relation between the vector and its individual numerical elements is *not* the constituency relation, and so section 2.1.4 of Fodor and Pylyshyn (this volume) is irrelevant—there they address a mistake that is not being made.

The second moral is that the constituency relation among distributed representations is one that is important for the analysis of connectionist models, and for explaining their behavior, but it is *not* a part of the causal mechanism within the model. In order to process the vector representing *cup with coffee*, the network does not have to decompose it into constituents. For processing, it is the *between level* relation, not the within level relation, that matters. The processing of the vector representing *cup with coffee* is determined by the individual numerical activities that make up the vector: it is over these lower-level activities that the processes are defined. Thus the fact that there is considerable arbitrariness in the way the constituents of *cup with coffee* are defined introduces no ambiguities in the way the network processes that representation—the ambiguities exist only for us who analyze the model and try to explain its behavior.

Any particular definition of constituency that gives us explanatory leverage is a valid definition of constituency; lack of uniqueness is not a problem.

This leads directly to the third moral, that the decomposition of composite states into their constituents is not precise and uniquely defined. The notion of constituency is important but attempts to formalize it are likely to crucially involve *approximation*. As discussed at some length in Smolensky (1988a), this is the typical case: notions from symbolic computation provide important tools for constructing higher-level accounts of the behavior of connectionist models using distributed representation—but these notions provide approximate, not precise, accounts.

Which leads to the fourth moral, that while connectionist networks using distributed representations *do* describe mental states with the type of constituency required by (1), they do *not* provide a literal implementation of a syntactic language of thought. The context dependency of the constituents, the interactions that must be accomodated when they are combined, the inability to uniquely, precisely identify constituents, the need to take seriously the notion that the representation of *coffee* is a collection of vectors knit together by family resemblance—all these entail that the relation between connectionist constituency and syntactic constituency is *not* one of literal implementation. In particular, it would be absurd to claim that even if the connectionist story is correct then that would have no implications for the cognitive architecture, that it would merely fill in lower level details without important implications for the higher level account.

These conclusions all address (1) without explicitly addressing (2). Addressing (2) properly is far beyond the scope of this paper. To a considerable extent, it is beyond the scope of current connectionism. Let me simply point out that the Structure/Statistics Dilemma has an attractive possible solution that the connectionist approach is perfectly situated to pursue: *the mind is a statistics-sensitive engine operating on structure-sensitive numerical representations*. The previous arguments have shown that distributed representations do possess constituency relations, and that, properly analyzed, these representations can be seen to encode structure. Extending this to grapple with the full complexity of the kinds of rich structures implicated in complex cognitive processes is a research problem that has been attacked with some success but which remains to be definitively concluded (see Smolensky 1987 and section 3). Once we have complex structured information represented in distributed numerical patterns, statistics-sensitive processes can proceed to analyze the statistical regularities in a fully structure-sensitive way. Whether such processes can cope with the full force of the Structure/Statistics Dilemma is apt to remain an open question for some time yet.

The conclusion, then, is that distributed models *can* satisfy both (1) and (2). Whether (1) and (2) can be satisfied to the point of providing an account adequate to cover the *full demands of cognitive modeling* is of course an open empirical question—just as it is for the symbolic approach to satisfying (1) and (2). Just the same, distributed connectionist models do *not* amount to an implementation of the symbolic instantiations of (1) and (2) that Fodor and Pylyshyn are committed to.

Before summing up, I would like to return to figure 42.1. In what sense can figure 42.1 be said to describe the relation between the distributed representation of *A&B* and the distributed representations of *A* and *B*? It was the intent of the *coffee* example to show that the distributed representations of the constituents are, in an approximate but explanation-relevant sense, part of the representation of the composite. Thus, in the distributed case, the relation between the node of figure 42.1 labelled *A & B* and the others is a sort of whole/part relation. An inference mechanism that takes as input the vector representing *A & B* and produces as output the vector representing *A* is a mechanism that extracts a part from a whole. And in this sense it is no different from a symbolic inference mechanism that takes the syntactic structure **A & B** and extracts from it the syntactic constituent **A**. The connectionist mechanisms for doing this are of course quite different than the symbolic mechanisms, and the approximate nature of the whole/part relation gives the connectionist computation different overall characteristics: we do not have simply a new implementation of the old computation.

It is clear that, just as figure 42.1 offers a crude summary of the symbolic process of passing from **A & B** to **A**, a summary that uses the labels to encode hidden internal structures within the nodes, *exactly the same is true of the distributed connectionist case*. In the distributed case, just as in the symbolic case, the links in figure 42.1 are crude summaries of complex processes and not simple-minded causal channels that pass activity from the top node to the lower nodes. Such a causal story applies only to the hyper-local connectionist case, which here serves as the proverbial straw man.

Let me be clear: there is no distributed connectionist model, as far as I know, of the kind of formal inference Fodor and Pylyshyn have in mind here. Such formal inference is located at the far extreme of the hard side of the Paradox, and is not at this point a cognitive process (or abstraction thereof) that the connectionist formalism can be said to have built upon its soft substrate. But at root the Fodor and Pylyshyn critique revolves around the constituent structure of mental states—formal inference is just one setting in which to see the importance of that constituent structure. So the preceeding discussion of the constituent structure of distributed representations does address the heart of their critique, even if a well-developed connectionist account of formal inference remains unavailable.

So, let's summarize the overall picture at this point. We have got principles (1) and (2), and we have got a symbolic instantiation of these in a language of thought using syntactic constituency. According to Fodor and Pylyshyn, what connectionists should do is take that symbolic language of thought as a higher level description and then produce a connectionist implementation in a literal sense. The syntactic operations of the symbolic language of thought then provide an exact formal higher level account.

By contrast, I argue that the distributed view of connectionist compositionality allows us to instantiate the same basic principles of (1) and (2) *without* going through a symbolic language of thought. By going straight to distributed connectionist models we get *new instantiations of compositionality principles*.

I happen to believe that the symbolic descriptions *do* provide useful approximate higher level accounts of how these connectionist models compute—but in no sense do these distributed connectionist models provide a literal implementation of a symbolic language of thought. The approximations require a willingness to accept context sensitive symbols and interactional components present in compositional structures, and the other funny business that came out in the *coffee* example. If you are willing to live with all those degrees of approximation then you can usefully view these symbolic level descriptions as approximate higher level accounts of the processing in a connectionist network.

The overall conclusion, then, is that *the classical and connectionist approaches differ not in whether they accept principles (1) and (2), but in how they formally instantiate them*. To confront the real classical/connectionist dispute, one has to be willing to descend to the level of the particular formal instantiations they give to these nonformal principles. To fail to descend to this level of detail is to miss the issue. In the classical approach, principles (1) and (2) are formalized using syntactic structures for thoughts and symbol manipulation for mental processes. In the connectionist view (1) or (2) are formalized using distributed vectorial representations for mental states, and the corresponding notion of compositionality, together with association-based mental processes that derive their structure sensitivity from the structure sensitivity of the vectorial representations engaging in those processes.

In terms of research methodology, this means that the agenda for connectionism should not be to develop a connectionist implementation of the symbolic language of thought but rather to develop formal analyses of vectorial representations of complex structures and operations on those structures that are sufficiently structure-sensitive to do the required work.

In summary: distributed representations provide a description of mental states with semantically interpretable constituents, but there is no precise formal account of the construction of composites from context-independent semantically interpretable constituents. On this account, there *is* a language of thought—but only approximately; the language of thought does not provide a basis for an exact formal account of mental structure or processes—it cannot provide a precise formal account of the cognitive architecture.[3]

3 Connectionism and Implementation

In section 2 I argued that connectionist research should be directed toward structure-sensitive representations and processes but not toward the implementation of a symbolic language of thought. In this section I want to consider this middle ground between implementing symbolic computation and ignoring structure. Many critics of connectionism do not seem to understand that this middle ground exists. (For further discussion of this point, and a map that explicitly locates this middle ground, see Smolensky 1988b.)

A rather specific conclusion of section 2 was that connectionists need to develop the analysis of distributed (vectorial) representations of composite structures and the kinds of processes that operate on them with the necessary structure sensitivity. More generally, my characterization of the goal of connectionist modeling is to develop formal models of cognitive processes that are based on the mathematics of dynamical systems continuously evolving in time: complex systems of numerical variables governed by differential equations. These formal accounts live in the category of continuous mathematics rather than relying on the discrete mathematics that underlies the traditional symbolic formalism. This characterization of the goal of connectionism is far from universal: it is quite inconsistent with the definitive characterization of Feldman and Ballard (1982), for example. In Smolensky (1988a) I argue at some length that my characterization, called *PTC*, constitutes a Proper Treatment of Connectionism.

A central component of PTC is the relation hypothesized between connectionist models based on continuous mathematics and classical models based on discrete, symbolic computation. That relationship, which entered briefly in the Fodor and Pylyshyn argument of section 2, might be called the *cognitive correspondence principle*: When connectionist computational systems are analyzed at higher levels, elements of symbolic computation appear as emergent properties.

Figure 42.5 illustrates the cognitive correspondence principle. At the top we have nonformal notions: the central hypotheses that the principles of cognition consist in principles of memory, of inference, of compositionality and constituent structure, etc. In the Fodor and Pylyshyn argument, the relevant nonformal principles were their compositionality principles (1) and (2).

The nonformal principles at the top of figure 42.5 have certain formalizations in the discrete category, which are shown one level down on the right branch. For example,

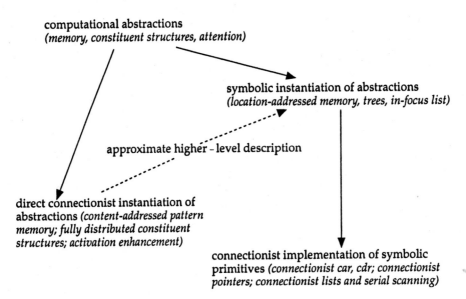

Figure 42.5
PTC vs. implementationalism (reprinted with permission of *The Behavioral and Brain Sciences*)

memory is formalized as standard location-addressed memory or some appropriately more sophisticated related notion. Inference gets formalized in the discrete category as logical inference, a particular form of symbol manipulation. And so on.

The PTC agenda consists in taking these kinds of cognitive principles and finding new ways to instantiate them in formal principles based on the mathematics of dynamical systems; these are shown in figure 42.5 at the lowest level on the left branch. The concept of memory retrieval is reformalized in terms of the continuous evolution of a dynamical system towards a point attractor whose position in the state space is the memory; you naturally get content-addressed memory instead of location-addressed memory. (Memory storage becomes modification of the dynamics of the system so that its attractors are located where the memories are supposed to be; thus the principles of memory storage are even more unlike their symbolic counterparts than those of memory retrieval.) When reformalizing inference principles, the continuous formalism leads naturally to principles of statistical inference rather than logical inference. And so on.

The cognitive correspondence principle states that the general relationship between the connectionist formal principles and the symbolic formal principles—given that they are both instantiations of common nonformal notions—is that if you take a higher level analysis of what is going on in the connectionist systems you find that it matches, to some kind of approximation, what is going on in the symbolic formalism. This relation is indicated in figure 42.5 by the dotted arrow.

This is to be contrasted with an implementational view of connectionism which Fodor and Pylyshyn advocate. As portrayed in figure 42.5, the implementational methodology is to proceed from the top to the bottom not directly, via the left branch, but indirectly, via the right branch; connectionists should take the symbolic instantiations of the nonformal principles and should find ways of implementing *them* in connectionist networks.

The PTC methodology is contrasted not just with the implementational approach, but also with the eliminitivist one. In terms of these methodological considerations, eliminitivism has a strong and a weak form. The weak form advocates taking the left branch of figure 42.5 but ignoring altogether the symbolic formalizations, on the belief that the symbolic notions will confuse rather than enlighten us in our attempts to understand connectionist computation. The strong eliminitivist position states that even viewing the nonformal principles at the top of figure 42.5 as a starting point for thinking about cognition is a mistake; e.g., that it is better to pursue a blind bottom-up strategy in which low-level connectionist principles are taken from neuroscience and we see where they lead us without being prejudiced by archaic prescientific notions such as those at the top of figure 42.5.

In rejecting both the implementationalist and eliminitivist positions, PTC views connectionist accounts as reducing and explaining symbolic accounts. Connectionist accounts serve to refine symbolic accounts, to reduce the degree of approximation required, to enrich the computational notions from the symbolic and discrete world, to fill them out with notions of continuous computation. Primarily that is done by descending to a lower level of analysis, by focussing on the microstructure implicit in these kinds of symbolic operations.

I call this the cognitive correspondence principle because I believe it has a role to play in the developing microtheory of cognition that is analogous to the role that the quantum correspondence principle played in the development of microtheory in physics. The case from physics embodies the structure of figure 42.5 quite directly. There are certain physical principles that arch over both the classical and quantum formalisms: the notions of space and time and associated invariance principles, the principles of energy and momentum conservation, force laws, and so on. These principles at the top of figure 42.5 are instantiated in particular ways in the classical formalism, corresponding to the point one level down on the right branch. To go to a lower level of physical analysis requires the development of a new formalism. In this quantum formalism, the fundamental principles are reinstantiated: they occupy the bottom of the left branch. The classical formalism can be looked at as a higher level description of the same principles operating at the lower quantum level: the dotted line of figure 42.5. Of course, quantum mechanics does not *implement* classical mechanics: the accounts are intimately related, but classical mechanics provides an approximate, not an exact, higher-level account.[4] In a deep sense, the quantum and classical theories are quite incompatible: according to the ontology of quantum mechanics, the ontology of classical mechanics is quite impossible to realize in this world. But there is no denying that the classical ontology and the accompanying principles are theoretically essential, for at least two reasons: (a) to provide explanations (in a literal sense, approximate ones) of an enormous range of classical phenomena for which direct explanation from quantum principles is hopelessly infeasible, and (b), historically, to provide the guidance necessary to discover the quantum principles in the first place. To try to develop lower level principles without looking at the higher level principles for guidance, given the insights we have gained from those principles, would seem, to put it mildly, inadvisable. It is basically this pragmatic consideration that motivates the cognitive correspondence principle and the PTC position it leads to.

In the PTC methodology, it is essential to be able to analyze the higher level properties of connectionist computation in order to relate them to properties of symbolic computation, e.g., to see whether they have the necessary computational power. I now want to summarize what I take to be the state of the art in the mathematical analysis of computation in connectionist systems, and how it relates to Fodor and Pylyshyn's critique. This summary is presented in figure 42.6.

Figure 42.6 shows the pieces of a connectionist model and elements of their analysis. The connectionist model basically has four parts. There is the task that the model is

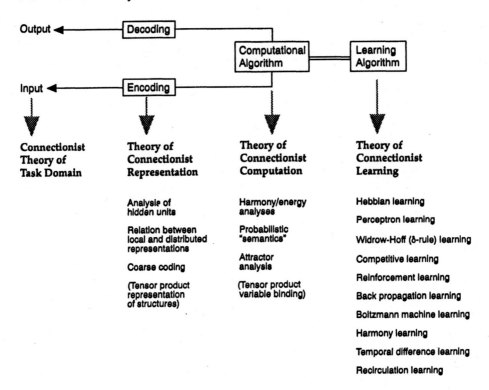

Figure 42.6
Theory of Connectionist models

supposed to perform—for example, to take some set of inputs into a set of outputs described in the terms characteristic of the problem domain. Then there is an actual connectionist network which will perform that mapping from input to output; but between the original task and the model we need methods for encoding and decoding. The encoding must take the problem domain characterization of an input and code it into a form that the network can process, namely, activities of certain input processors. Similarly, the activity of the output processors has to be decoded into some problem domain statement which can be construed as the output of the network. The input-to-output mapping inside the network is the computational algorithm embodied in the network and, more often than not, in addition, there is a learning algorithm which modifies the parameters in the computational algorithm in order to get it to converge on the correct input/output behavior of the correct computation.

In terms of analyzing these four elements of connectionist modeling, things get progressively worse as we move from right to left. In the area of connectionist learning, there are lots of analyses: algorithms for tweaking lower-level connection strengths which will produce reasonable higher level convergence towards the correct input/output mapping. The figure shows as many as would fit conveniently and there are many more.[5]

So, if you think that the problem with connectionism is that a particular learning algorithm has some characteristic you do not like, then chances are there is another learning algorithm that will make you happy. Relative to the rest, the learning theory is in good shape, even though when it comes to theorems about what functions can be learned by a given algorithm, there is very little.

With respect to analyzing the higher-level properties of the algorithms for computing outputs from inputs, there is considerably less theory. The technique of analyzing convergence using a function that measures the "energy" or "harmony" of network states (Ackley, Hinton, and Sejnowski 1985; Cohen and Grossberg 1983; Geman and Geman 1984; Hinton and Sejnowski 1983; Hopfield 1982; Smolensky 1983, 1986a) get us somewhere, as do a few other techniques[6] but it seems rather clear that the state of analysis of connectionist computation is considerably less developed than that of connectionist learning.

After this things get *very* thin. What about the theory behind encoding and decoding, the theory of how to take the kinds of inputs and outputs that have to be represented for cognitive processes and turn them into actual patterns of activity? By and large, it is a black art: there is not much in the way of analysis. People have been getting their hands dirty exploring the representations in hidden units (e.g., Hinton 1986, Rosenberg 1987), but so far I see little reason to believe our understanding of these representations will go further than understanding an occasional node or a few statistical properties. There are a few other simple analyses[7] but they do not take us very far.

At the far left of figure 42.6 is the theory of the task environment that comes out of a connectionist perspective. This is essentially nonexistent. To many, I believe, that is really the ultimate goal: the theory of the domain in connectionist terms.

As figure 42.6 makes clear, there is a very important weak leg here: the connectionist theory of representation. In particular, until recently we have not had any systematic ideas about how to represent complex structures. In fact, it was Fodor and Pylyshyn who really got me thinking about this, and ultimately convinced me. The result was the tensor product technique for generating fully distributed representations of complex structures (Smolensky 1987). For this reason the tensor product representation is dedicated to Fodor and Pylyshyn. This representational scheme is a formalization and generalization of representational techniques that have been used piecemeal in connectionist models. As others have discussed in this volume, the tensor product technique provides a systematic and disciplined procedure for representing complex, structured objects. One can prove that the tensor product representation has a number of nice computational properties from the standpoint of connectionist processing. In this sense, it is appropriate to view the tensor product representation as occupying the lower level corner of figure 42.5: it provides a formalization that is natural for connectionist computation of the nonformal notion of constituent structure, and is a likely candidate to play a role in connectionist cognitive science analogous to that played by constituent structure trees in symbolic cognitive science.

The tensor product representation rests on the use of the tensor product operation to perform in the vectorial world the analog of binding together a variable and its value. Figure 42.6 shows where tensor product variable binding and tensor product representations of structures fit into the overall problem of analyzing connectionist cognitive models.

I hope this last section has made more plausible my working hypothesis that between the connectionist view that Fodor and Pylyshyn attack—denying the importance of structured representations and structure-sensitive processes—and the connectionist methodology they advocate—implementation of the classical symbolic cognitive architecture—there is a promising middle ground on which productive and exciting research can be pursued.

Acknowledgments

This work has been supported by NSF grants IRI-8609599 and ECE-8617947 to the author, and by a grant to the author from the Sloan Foundation's computational neuroscience program.

Notes

1. For related discussions, see, e.g., Gerken and Bever 1986, Greeno 1987.
2. For some somewhat spooky empirical results directly bearing on this issue, see Bever, Carrithers, and Townsend 1987.
3. An important open question is whether the kind of story I have given on *cup of coffee* using these hokey microfeatures will carry over to the kind of distributed representations that real connectionist networks create for themselves in their hidden units—if you make the analysis appropriately sophisticated. The resolution of this issue depends on the (as yet inscrutable) nature of these representations for realistic problems. The nature of the problem is important, for it is perfectly likely that connectionist networks will develop compositional representations in their hidden units only when this is advantageous for the problem they are trying to solve. As Fodor and Pylyshyn, and the entire Classical paradigm, argue, such compositional representations are in fact immensely useful for a broad spectrum of cognitive problems. But until such problems—which tend to be considerably more sophisticated than those usually given to connectionist networks—have been explored in some detail with connectionist models, we will not really know if hidden units will develop compositional representations (in the approximate sense discussed in this paper) when they "should."
4. Many cases analogous to "implementation" *are* found in physics. Newton's laws provide an "implementation" of Kepler's laws; Maxwell's theory "implements" Coulomb's law; the quantum principles of the hydrogen atom "implement" Balmer's formula.
5. Here are a smattering of references to these learning rules; rather than giving historically primary references I have cited recent easily accessible expositions that include the original citations. (In fact I have chosen papers in Rumelhart, McClelland, and the PDP Group 1986, when possible.) For an exposition of Hebbian, perceptron, and Widrow-Hoff or delta-rule learning, see Rumelhart, Hinton, and McClelland 1986 and Stone 1986. For competitive learning see Grossberg 1987, and Rumelhart and Zipser 1986. For reinforcement learning, see Barto, Sutton and Anderson 1983, and Sutton 1987. For back propagation learning see Rumelhart, Hinton and Williams 1986. For Boltzmann machine learning, see Hinton and Sejnowski 1986. For harmony learning, see Smolensky 1986a. Temporal difference learning is reported in Sutton 1987. A simple recirculation learning algorithm is discussed in Smolensky 1987; the idea has been under exploration by Hinton and McClelland for several years, and their first paper should appear in 1988.
6. On giving the computation in connectionist networks semantics based on statistical inference, see Shastri and Feldman 1985; Smolensky 1986a; Golden 1988.
7. For some simple explorations of the relation between local and distributed representations, see Smolensky 1986b. For some observations about the power of the distributed representational technique called "coarse coding," see Hinton, McClelland, and Rumelhart 1986.

References

Ackley, D. H., Hinton, G. E., and Sejnowski, T. J. (1985). A learning algorithm for Boltzmann machines. *Cognitive Science*, 9, 147–169.

Ballard, D. and Hayes, P. J. (1984). Parallel logical inference. *Proceedings of the Sixth Annual Conference of the Cognitive Science Society*. Rochester, NY, June.

Barto, A. G., Sutton, R. S., Anderson. C. W. (1983). Neuronlike elements that can solve difficult learning control problems. *IEEE Transactions on Systems, Man, and Cybernetics* SMC-13, 834–846.

Bever, T. G., Carrithers, C., and Townsend. D. J. (1987). A tale of two brains: The sinistral quasimodularity of language. *Proceedings of the Ninth Annual Conference of the Cognitive Science Society*. 764–773. Seattle, WA, July.

Chomsky, N. (1965). *Aspects of the Theory of Syntax*. Cambridge, MA: MIT Press.

Cohen, M. A. and Grossberg, S. (1983). Absolute stability of global pattern formation and parallel memory storage by competitive neural networks. *IEEE Transactions on Systems, Man, & Cybernetics* SMC-13, 815–826.

Dreyfus, S. E., and Dreyfus, H. L. (1986). *Mind over machine: The power of human intuition and expertise in the era of the computer*. New York: Free Press.

Fodor, J. A. and Pylyshyn. Z. W. (1988). Connectionism and cognitive architecture: A critical analysis. *Cognition, 28*, 2–71.

Feldman, J. A. and Ballard, D. H. (1982). Connectionist models and their properties. *Cognitive Science 6*, 205–254.

Geman, S. and Geman, D. (1984). Stochastic relaxation, Gibbs distributions, and the Bayesian restoration of images. *IEEE Transactions on Pattern Analysis and Machine Intelligence, 6*, 721–741.

Gerken, L. and Bever, T. G. (1986). Linguistic intuitions are the result of interactions between perceptual processes and linguistic universals. *Cognitive Science 10*, 457–476.

Golden, R. (1988). A unified framework for connectionist systems. *Biological Cybernetics*.

Greeno, J. G. (1987). The cognition connection. *The New York Times*, Jan. 4, p. 28.

Grossberg, S. (1987). Competitive learning: From interactive activation to adaptive resonance. *Cognitive Science 11*, 23–63.

Gupta, M., Ragade, R., and Yager, R. (eds.) (1979). *Advances in Fuzzy Set Theory and Applications*. Amsterdam: North-Holland.

Hinton, G. E. (1987). Learning distributed representations of concepts. *Proceedings of the Eighth Annual Meeting of the Cognitive Science Society*. Hillsdale, NJ: Erlbaum 1–12.

Hinton, G. E., McClelland, J. L. and Rumelhart, D. E. (1986). Distributed representations. In J. L. McClelland, D. E. Rumelhart, & the PDP Research Group, *Parallel Distributed Processing: Explorations in the Microstructure of Cognition. Volume 2: Psychological and Biological Models*. Cambridge. MA: MIT Press/ Bradford Books.

Hinton, G. E. and Sejnowski, T. J. (1983a). Analyzing cooperative computation. *Proceedings of the Fifth Annual Conference of the Cognitive Science Society*. Rochester, NY.

Hopfield, J. J. (1982). Neural networks and physical systems with emergent collective computational abilities. *Proceedings of the National Academy of Sciences, USA 79*, 2554–2558.

Kirsh, D. (1988). Paying the price for cognition. *The Southern Journal of Philosophy 26* (supplement).

McClelland, J. L., Rumelhart, D. E., and the PDP Research Group (1986). *Parallel Distributed Processing: Explorations in the Microstructure of Cognition. Volume 2: Psychological and Biological Models*. Cambridge, MA: MIT Press/Bradford Books.

Rosenberg, C. R. (1987). Revealing the structure of NETtalk's internal representations. *Proceedings of the Ninth Annual Meeting of the Cognitive Science Society*, 537–554. Seattle, WA, July.

Rumelhart, D. E., Hinton. G. E. and Williams, R. J. (1986). Learning internal representations by error propogation. In D. E. Rumelhart, J. L. McClelland, & the PDP Research Group, *Parallel Distributed Processing: Explorations in the Microstructure of Cognition. Volume 1: Foundations*. Cambridge, MA: MIT Press/Bradford Books.

Rumelhart, D. E., Hinton. G. E., and McClelland, J. L. (1986). A general framework for parallel distributed processing. In D. E. Rumelhart, J. L. McClelland & the PDP Research Group, *Parallel Distributed Processing: Explorations in the Microstructure of Cognition. Volume 1: Foundations*. Cambridge, MA: MIT Press/Bradford Books.

Rumelhart, D. E., McClelland, J. L. and the PDP Research Group (1986). *Parallel Distributed Processing: Explorations in the Microstructure of Cognition. Volume 1: Foundations*. Cambridge, MA: MIT Press/ Bradford Books.

Rumelhart, D. E. and Zipser, D. (1986). Feature discovery by competitive learning. In D. E. Rumelhart, J. L. McClelland & the PDP Research Group, *Parallel Distributed Processing: Explorations in the Microstructure of Cognition. Volume 1: Foundations*. Cambridge, MA: MIT Press/Bradford Books.

Shastri, L. and Feldman, J. A. (1985). Evidential reasoning in semantic networks: A formal theory. *Proceedings of the International Joint Conference on Artificial Intelligence*. Los Angeles, CA.

Shortliffe, E. H. (1976). *Computer-based Medical Consultations: MYCIN*. New York: American Elsevier.

Smolensky, P. (1983). Schema selection and stochastic inference in modular environments. *Proceedings of the National Conference on Artificial Intelligence*. Washington. D.C.

Smolensky, P. (1986a). Information processing in dynamical systems: Foundations of harmony theory. In D. E. Rumelhart, J. L. McClelland & the PDP Research Group, *Parallel Distributed Processing: Explorations in the Microstructure of Cognition. Volume 1: Foundations*. Cambridge, MA: MIT Press/Bradford Books.

Smolensky, P. (1986b). Neural and conceptual interpretations of parallel distributed processing models. In J. L. McClelland, D. E. Rumelhart, & the PDP Research Group, *Parallel Distributed Processing: Explorations in the Microstructure of Cognition. Volume 2: Psychological and Biological Models*. Cambridge, MA: MIT Press/Bradford Books.

Smolensky, P. (1987). On variable binding and the representation of symbolic structures in connectionist systems. Technical Report CU-CS-355-87, Department of Computer Science, University of Colorado at Boulder, February. (Revised version to appear in *Artificial Intelligence*).

Smolensky, P. (1988a). On the proper treatment of connectionism. *The Behavioral and Brain Sciences*. 11(1).

Smolensky, P. (1988b). Putting together connectionism—again. *The Behavioral and Brain Sciences*. 11(1).

Smolensky, P. (forthcoming). *Lectures on connectionist cognitive modeling*. Hillsdale, NJ: Erlbaum.

Stone, G. O. (1986). An analysis of the delta rule and learning statistical associations. In D. E. Rumelhart, J. L. McClelland, & the PDP Research Group, *Parallel Distributed Processing: Explorations in the Microstructure of Cognition. Volume 1: Foundations.* Cambridge, MA: MIT Press/Bradford Books.

Sutton, R. S. (1987). Learning to predict by the methods of temporal differences. Technical Report 87-509.1, GTE Laboratories, Waltham, MA.

Zadeh, L. A. (1965). Fuzzy sets. *Information and Control, 8*, 338–353.

Zadeh, L. A. (1975). Fuzzy logic and approximate reasoning. *Synthese 30*, 407–428.

Zadeh, L. A. (1983). Role of fuzzy logic in the management of uncertainty in expert systems. *Fuzzy Sets and Systems 11*, 199–227.

Chapter 43

One AI or Many?

Seymour Papert

I do not come to the discussion of connectionism as a neutral observer. In fact, the standard version of its history assigns me a role in a romantic story whose fairytale resonances surely contribute at least a little to connectionism's aura of excitement.

Once upon a time two daughter sciences were born to the new science of cybernetics. One sister was natural, with features inherited from the study of the brain, from the way nature does things. The other was artificial, related from the beginning to the use of computers. Each of the sister sciences tried to build models of intelligence, but from very different materials. The natural sister built models (called neural networks) out of mathematically purified neurones. The artificial sister built her models out of computer programs.

In their first bloom of youth the two were equally successful and equally pursued by suitors from other fields of knowledge. They got on very well together. Their relationship changed in the early sixties when a new monarch appeared, one with the largest coffers ever seen in the kingdom of the sciences: Lord DARPA, the Defense Department's Advanced Research Projects Agency. The artificial sister grew jealous and was determined to keep for herself the access to Lord DARPA's research funds. The natural sister would have to be slain.

The bloody work was attempted by two staunch followers of the artificial sister, Marvin Minsky and Seymour Papert, cast in the role of the huntsman sent to slay Snow White and bring back her heart as proof of the deed. Their weapon was not the dagger but the mightier pen, from which came a book—*Perceptrons*[1]—purporting to prove that neural nets could never fill their promise of building models of mind: *only computer programs could do this.* Victory seemed assured for the artificial sister. And indeed, for the next decade all the rewards of the kingdom came to her progeny, of which the family of expert systems did best in fame and fortune.

But Snow White was not dead. What Minsky and Papert had shown the world as proof was not the heart of the princess; it was the heart of a pig. To be more literal: their book was read as proving that the neural net approach to building models of mind was dead. But a closer look reveals that they really demonstrated something much less than this. The book did indeed point out very serious limitations of a certain class of nets (nowadays known as one-layer perceptrons) but was misleading in its suggestion that this class of nets was the heart of connectionism. *Parallel Distributed Processing,* allowing that the suggestion could have been an honest mistake, lapses into a fairy-tale tone in talking about how things were back in "Minsky and Papert's day." In that far-off time and place, the technical discoveries were still to be made that would open the vision—model connectionism's sustaining myth—of much more powerful neural nets than could then be imagined.

Connectionist writings present the story as having a happy ending. The natural sister was quietly nurtured in the laboratories of a few ardent researchers who kept the faith, even when the world at large let itself be convinced that the enterprise was futile. Who (or what) should be cast in the role of Prince Charming is a problem I shall take up later: Who are the parties to the present-day connectionist love affair? Who woke connectionism? And why now? And what next? But for the moment suffice it to note that the princess has emerged from relative rags and obscurity to win the admiration of all except a few of her sister's disgruntled hangers-on.

The story seems to call for a plea of guilty or innocent: Did Minsky and I try to kill connectionism, and how do we feel now about its resurrection? Something more complex than a plea is needed. Yes, there was *some* hostility in the energy behind the research reported in *Perceptrons*, and there is *some* degree of annoyance at the way the new movement has developed; part of our drive came, as we quite plainly acknowledged in our book, from the fact that funding and research energy were being dissipated on what still appear to me (since the story of new, powerful network mechanisms is seriously exaggerated) to be misleading attempts to use connectionist methods in practical applications. But most of the motivation for *Perceptrons* came from more fundamental concerns, many of which cut cleanly across the division between networkers and programmers.

One of these concerns had to do with finding an appropriate balance between romanticism and rigor in the pursuit of artificial intelligence. Many serious endeavors would never get off the ground if pioneers were limited to discussing in public only what they could demonstrate rigorously. Think, for example, of the development of flying machines. The excitement generated when the Wright brothers made their first flight had a large element of the romantic. And rightly so: it is hard to work up respect for those critics who complained that a short hop on a beach did not prove the feasibility of useful air transportation. When final success cannot be taken as a criterion for judging initial steps, the problem of developing a sensible critical methodology is an essential and often delicate part of any very out-of-the-ordinary endeavor. In the case of artificial intelligence, the problem of critical judgment of partial results is compounded by the fact that a little intelligence is not easily recognized as intelligence. Indeed, in English we have a special word for it: although a short flight is still counted as a flight, a little intelligence is counted as stupidity, and in AI's early stages (where it still is), this is all that can be expected. How, then, does one decide whether the latest "stupidity" of a machine should be counted as a step toward intelligence? The methodology Minsky and I used in *Perceptrons* is best explained through an example.

Parallel Distributed Processing reports an experiment in which a simulated machine (I'll call it Exor) learned to tell whether two inputs, each of which must be either a one or a zero, are different.[2] Exor's learning process consumed 2,232 repetitions of a training cycle; in each repetition the machine was presented with one of the four possible combinations of inputs (one-one, zero-zero, zero-one, one-zero) and a feedback signal to indicate whether it had given the right response ("no" for the first two and "yes" for the others). Smart or stupid? Should one be more impressed by the fact that the thing "learned" at all, or by the fact that it learned so slowly and laboriously?

There was a time, in the early days of cybernetics, when a machine doing anything at all that resembled learning would have been impressive. Today something more is needed to give significance, and in this case the something more is closely related to our allegory. Exor is a neural net, and the task it learned to perform happens, for all its simplicity, to be one of those things a one-layer net cannot do. Knowing this turns the dilemma of judging Exor into an encapsulation of the larger dilemma of judging connectionism. If you want to believe, Exor allows you to proclaim, "Snow White lives." If you don't, Exor's retarded pace of learning allows you to whisper, "But barely." *Perceptrons* set out on a very different tack: instead of asking whether nets are good, we asked what they are *good for.* The focus of enquiry shifted from generalities about kinds of machines to specifics about kinds of tasks. From this point of view, Exor raises such questions as: Which tasks would be learned faster and which would be learned even more slowly by this machine? Can we make a theory of tasks that will explain why 2,232 repetitions were needed in this particular act of learning? The shift in perspective is sharp: interest has moved from making a judgment of the machine to using the performance of the machine on particular tasks as a way to learn more about the nature of the tasks. This shift is reflected in the subtitle of our book—*Perceptrons: An Introduction to Computational Geometry.* We approached our study of neural networks by looking carefully at the kinds of tasks for which their use was being advocated at the time. Since most of these were in the area of visual pattern recognition, our methodology led us into building theories about such patterns. To our surprise, we found ourselves working a new problem area for geometric research, concerned with understanding why some recognition tasks could easily be performed by a given recognition mechanism, while other computations were extremely costly as measured by the number of repetitions needed for a task or the amount of machinery required. For example, a small single-layer perceptron can easily distinguish triangles from squares, but a very large network is needed to learn whether what is put in front of it is a single connected objects or is made up of several parts.

Our surprise at finding ourselves working in geometry was a pleasant one. It reinforced our sense that we were opening a new field, not closing an old one. But although the shift from judging perceptrons abstractly to judging the tasks they perform might seem like plain common sense, it took us a long time to make it. So long, in fact, that we are now only mildly surprised to observe the resistance today's connectionists show to recognizing the nature of our work—and the nature of the problem area into which their own investigations must eventually lead.

The conceit of using the story of Snow White as a metaphor has allowed me to talk about the connectionist counterrevolution without saying exactly what connectionism is or what it is revolting against. A little more technical detail is needed to situate connectionism in the larger field of sciences of mind.

The actual task of recognizing the sameness of the two binary inputs would be a trivial one for a programmer. The first of several remarkable features possessed by Exor is that no one programmed it; it was "trained" to do its task by a strictly behaviorist process of external association of stimuli with reinforcements. It could have been trained by someone who rigorously followed Watson's strictures against thinking about the innards of a system. But if this was its only merit as a model of mental process, the large number of repetitions would negate its interest: machines specifically designed to simulate conditioned reflexes have done so with a psychologically more plausible number of repetitions.

Exor's claim of universality is a stronger feature. Exor is small and limited in power, but it sustains the vision of larger machines that are built on the same principles and that will learn whatever is learnable with no innate disposition to acquire particular behaviors. The prospect of such performance becomes a vindication of something more than neural nets. It promises a vindication of behaviorism against Jean Piaget, Noam Chomsky, and all those students of mind who criticized the universalism inherent in behaviorism's tabula rasa. Behaviorism has been beaten down in another version of the

Snow White story, but the response of academic psychology to connectionism may turn out to be a classic example of the return of the repressed.

Connectionism does more than bring back old-fashioned behaviorism. It brings it back in a form that offers a reconciliation with biological thinking about the brain. The structure of the machine reflects, albeit in an abstract way, a certain model of how brains might conceivably be built out of neurons. Although the actual Exor experiments are, of course, performed by computer programs, these programs are meant to represent what would happen if one connected together networks of units that are held to be neuronlike in the following sense. Each unit in the network receives signals from the others or from sensor units connected to the outside world; at any given time, each unit has a certain level of activation that depends on the weighted sum of the states of activation of the units sending signals to it, and the signals sent out along the unit's "axon" reflect its state of activation. Learning takes place by a process that adjusts the weights (strengths of connections) between the units; when the weights are different, activation patterns produced by a given input will be different, and finally, the output (response) to an input (stimulus) will change. This feature gives machines in Exor's family a biological flavor that appeals strongly to the spirit of our times and yet takes very little away from the behaviorist simplicity: although one has to refer to the neuronlike structure in order to build the machine, one thinks only in terms of stimulus, response, and a feedback signal to operate it.

This presentation of connectionism as behaviorism in computer's clothing helps place *Perceptrons* in perspective: the questions it discusses are a modern form of an old debate originally couched as a humanistic and philosophical discussion of associations and taken up again more recently as a discussion of behaviorism. Such debates often turn around assertions of the form, "*Starting with nothing but* (associations, stimulus and response, or whatever), *you can never get to* (general ideas, language, or whatever)." Discussion of this form has been more or less compelling but seldom anywhere near conclusive to standards of rigor that seemed normal to people trained, as Minsky and I both were, as mathematicians. And indeed, how could the discussion even be formulated with any semblance of rigor in the absence of a tight theory of human thought? And how could one move seriously toward such a tight theory without knowing whether general ideas or whatever can be derived from associations or whatever?

In its narrowest sense, the intention of *Perceptrons* was to avoid for the study of "machine thinking" some of the chicken-and-egg difficulties that have plagued thinking about human thinking. The strategy was to study a class of computational machines that were sufficiently powerful to capture a significant slice of contemporary achievement in AI, yet sufficiently simple to make possible, with the limited analytic tools at our disposal, a rigorous mathematical analysis of their capacities. We chose the class of machines for which the book was named (in honor of Frank Rosenblatt): perceptrons are defined in the book to be a special and especially simple kind of neural net in the same family as Exor. Perceptrons are too simple to be interesting in their own right as models of mental process. But the most promising step toward developing tools powerful enough to analyze more complex systems, including the human mind, seemed to be achieving a thorough understanding of a single case as simple as a perceptron. Many readers, perhaps all except mathematicians, would be shocked to know how simple a machine can be and still elude full understanding of its capabilities. I find it quite awesome to think about how hard it was to confirm or reject our intuitions about the capacities of perceptrons.

Minsky and I both knew perceptrons extremely well. We had worked on them for many years before our joint project of understanding their limits was conceived; indeed, we originally met at a conference where we both coincidentally presented papers with an unlikely degree of overlap in content about what perceptronlike machines could do. With this background we should have been in an exceptional position to formulate strong conjectures about perceptrons. Yet when we challenged ourselves to prove our intuitions it sometimes took years of struggle to pin one down—to prove it true or to discover that it was seriously flawed.

I was left with a deep respect for the extraordinary difficulty of being sure of what a computational system can or cannot do. I wonder at people who seem so secure in their intuitive convictions, or their less-than-rigorous rhetorical arguments, about computers, neural nets, or human minds. One area in which intuition seems particularly in need of rigorous analysis is in dealing with the romantically attractive notion of holistic process.

In the history of psychology, behaviorism and holism (or gestaltism) have been considered polar opposites. Behaviorism fragments the mind into a myriad of separate atoms of a much smaller size than common sense would allow. Holism and gestaltism insist that psychological atoms are bigger than common sense thinks. So it is quite remarkable that connectionism has facets that appeal to each of these schools of thought.

The title of the current bible of connectionism, *Parallel Distributed Processing*, juxtaposes two qualities that are taken in the connectionist movement as prime characteristics certainly of all natural, and probably of effective artificial, embodiments of intelligence. *Parallel* refers to the quality of having many processes go on at the same time: as people walk and talk at the same time, they very likely carry out large numbers of concurrent, mostly unconscious, mental processes. *Distributed* refers to the quality of not being localized: in traditional computers, items of information are stored in particular places, cleanly separated from one another; in neural nets, information is spread out (in principle, a new piece of learning might involve changes everywhere). Much of the sense that deep process is at work in the functioning of nets is related to the suggestion that what ordinary discourse and traditional cognitive theory misleadingly describe as atomistic items of information are holistically represented and yet appropriately evocable.

Parallel plus distributed *feels* right. But work with perceptrons made us acutely aware of ways in which the two qualities are in tension rather than sweet harmony. It is not hard to switch perceptions so as to make the juxtaposition feel intuitively problematic. In ordinary life, customs of separating activities into rooms and offices are founded on experience with the untidy consequences of having everything happening everywhere at the same time. But connectionism is built on the theory—what Sherry Turkle calls a sustaining myth—that a deeper understanding would reveal the naiveté of such everyday analogies. Just as modern physics teaches us not to project our sense of macroscopic events onto the subatomic world, so too deeper understanding of networks will teach us that our metaphors of macroscopic organization may be equally misleading.

Indeed, one can find analogies in physical science that go very strongly against uninformed intuitions about interference—how processes disturb one another. The vibrations of all radio and television waves pass through the same space at the same time, and yet tuning circuits can separate them. Even more incomprehensible, if not frankly shocking to common sense, is the hologram, which records a three-dimensional picture in a fully distributed way: if part of the holographic record is destroyed, no particular part of the picture is lost; there is only a uniform degradation of quality.

These examples plainly say that there is precedent in the physical world for distributed superposition. Enough in the universe is holistic so that the concept of distributed neural net cannot be rejected on general intuitive principles. But not everything is holistic, and commonsense (or even philosophical) opinion is of little use in spotting what is. Specific investigation, sometimes of a subtle and very technical mathematical nature, is needed to find out whether holistic representation is possible in any specific situation and whether (where it can be done) there is an exorbitant price to pay. The Exor machine illustrates, in a simple case, the concept of the cost of holism.

The task that Exor learned can be seen as a superposition of two learnings in the same network: learning to say yes to one-zero and learning to say yes to zero-one. An important fact is that each of these tasks, taken separately, is much easier to learn than the combined task. And this is not an occasional phenomenon: Exor is a very mild case of incurred cost of distribution. One of the research results of *Perceptrons*, and one that required some mathematical labor, shows that in certain situations the degree of difficulty of superposed tasks can exceed the difficulty of each separate task by arbitrary, large factors.

The romantic stance is to make a new network that isn't quite a perceptron and to assume it innocent until proven guilty of the danger of superposition costs. On the whole, connectionist literature does so even when reporting experiments in which the new networks show empirical signs of such costs as those that Exor incurs in its mild way. The rigorous stance assumes the possibility of guilt until innocence can be established: the theorems proved about perceptrons are seen as showing what kind of phenomena need to be precluded before one can make assertions confidently.

I said at the beginning that I would offer some thoughts about Prince Charming. Who woke connectionism? Why this surge of interest and activity? Why now? And I will use my speculations on these themes to comment on the important question, What next?

A purely technical account of Snow White's awakening goes like this: In the olden days of Minsky and Papert, neural networking models were hopelessly limited by the puniness of the computers available at the time and by the lack of ideas about how to make any but the simplest networks learn. Now things have changed. Powerful, massively parallel computers can implement very large nets, and new learning algorithms can make them learn. No romantic Prince Charming is needed for the story.

I don't believe it. The influential recent demonstrations of new networks all run on small computers and could have been done in 1970 with ease. Exor is a "toy problem" run for study and demonstration, but the examples discussed in the literature are still very small. Indeed, Minsky and I, in a more technical discussion of this history (added as a new chapter to a reissue of *Perceptrons*), suggest that the entire structure of recent connectionist theories might be built on quicksand: it is all based on toy-sized problems with no theoretical analysis to show that performance will be maintained when the models are scaled up to realistic size. The connectionist authors fail to read our work as a warning that networks, like "brute force" programs based on search procedures, scale very badly.

A more sociological explanation is needed. Massively parallel supercomputers do play an important role in the connectionist revival. But I see it as a cultural rather than a technical role, another example of a sustaining myth. Connectionism does not use the new computers as physical machines; it derives strength from the "computer in the mind," from its public's largely nontechnical awareness of supercomputers.

I see connectionism's relationship to biology in similar terms. Although its models use biological metaphors, they do not depend on technical findings in biology any more than they do on modem supercomputers. But here too there is a powerful, resonant phenomenon. Biology is increasingly the locus of the greatest excitement. And neurosciences are invading the territory of academic psychology just as psychopharmacology is invading the territory of clinical psychology.

I also see a more subtle, but not less relevant, cultural resonance. This is a generalized turn away from the hard-edged rationalism of the time connectionism last went into eclipse and a resurgent attraction to more holistic ways of thinking. The actual theoretical discussion in the connectionist literature may not be connected in any strict sense to such trends in intellectual fashion. But here again, the concepts of sustaining myth and cultural resonance are pertinent: this time, perhaps, in a two-way process of mutual support.

Voilà Prince Charming: a composite of cultural trends. Reductionist undertones in my discussion do not undermine my good wishes for a happy union with Snow White. The new sense of excitement that is already replacing a certain ho-hum tiredness in cognitive science will ensure the fertility of the union. But the impact of connectionism will come less from the ideas it engenders than from heightened awareness of the problems it avoids.

Notes

1. Marvin Minsky and Seymour Papert, *Perceptrons: An Introduction to Computational Geometry* (Cambridge: MIT Press, 1969).
2. XOR, pronounced as if written *exor*, is a computerist abbreviation for "exclusive or" (i.e., "this or that but not both"). This makes it the perfect name for our simulated machine.

Part V
Innate Ideas

Introduction

The problem of innate ideas is among the most celebrated in the history of philosophy. We begin with a famous passage from Plato in which Socrates demonstrates to Meno that even an uneducated boy has innate knowledge of geometry. Of course, there is a long-standing dispute as to whether Socrates coaxes the knowledge from the boy or essentially supplies the correct answer by skillful use of leading questions. In any case, Plato's thesis is that all of our knowledge is innate, and experience is the occasion for the recollection of that knowledge.

René Descartes supports an alternative version of the innateness thesis. Descartes does not hold that innate ideas are already there waiting to be recalled but argues that we have an innate capacity for generating ideas. So, for example, we are not born with knowledge of geometry, but our innate reasoning ability (the power of thinking) provides our knowledge of geometry.

John Locke attacks the doctrine of innate ideas, providing arguments against both the Platonic and Cartesian positions. Against Descartes, for example, Locke notes that if our ideas are generated by the power of reason, and if reason is to mean deductive reason, then at least the initial stock of ideas will have to come from experience, for no deductive inference mechanism can deduce ideas from nothing. Locke goes on to articulate an empiricist proposal that eschews innate ideas.

Jean Piaget thinks there is a middle ground between the positions of Locke and Descartes. Piaget rejects the contention that ideas are innate, but he also rejects the contention that ideas come from unmediated perception. He holds that our minds have cognitive structures that organize experience but rejects the notion that these structures are the product of an innate biological endowment. Very roughly, it is Piaget's view that a child is born with a certain amount of general native intelligence and can use this to bootstrap his or her way through various stages of conceptual development. Arguing against Chomsky's views on language, Piaget suggests that to posit an innate language organ is "inexplicable" from the perspective of evolutionary biology and that language acquisition can be accounted for on the basis of general intelligence alone.

Jerry Fodor argues for a theory of concept learning that, if correct, would undermine Piaget's bootstrapping model. Fodor argues that in order to learn a predicate in a natural language like English, one must already have a corresponding concept in the language of thought. We cannot learn a natural language (or a new conceptual framework) unless we already have an innate language of thought that is just as rich as that natural language (or conceptual framework).

Noam Chomsky responds to Piaget's remarks on the plausibility of an innate language organ. To the claim of biological inexplicability, Chomsky argues that the development of a language organ is no more problematic than the development of the mammalian eye or the cerebral cortex. On the question of whether general intelligence would suffice for language acquisition, Chomsky describes a rule of English syntax and argues that it is not the rule that a general learning mechanism would select. He concludes that beings that can learn English do not rely solely on general learning mechanisms.

Hilary Putnam argues against Chomsky, suggesting that general intelligence is enough to account for acquisition of the rule Chomsky has in mind if the learner has semantic knowledge—that is, if the learner understands that the string is being used to communicate something about an object and knows which part of the string is being used to speak of the object. Putnam also takes issue with Chomsky on the question of the plausibility of a language organ, suggesting that the development of the mammalian eye appears to be much more gradual than Chomsky claims. Putnam agrees with Piaget that a language organ would be anomalous from the perspective of evolutionary theory. We conclude the exchange with replies to Putnam from both Chomsky and Fodor.

Further Reading

Chomsky, Noam. 1966. *Cartesian Linguistics.* New York: Harper & Row.

Leibniz, G. W. 1981. *New Essays on Human Understanding.* Trans. and ed. by P. Remnant and J. Bennett. Cambridge: Cambridge University Press. (See Book I, "Of Innate Notions.")

Piatelli-Palmerini, M., ed. 1980. *The Debate Between Noam Chomsky and Jean Piaget.* Cambridge, MA: Harvard University Press.

Stich, S., ed. 1975. *Innate Ideas.* Berkeley: University California Press.

Chapter 44

From *The Meno*

Plato

Meno.   And how will you enquire, Socrates, into that which you do not know? What will you put forth as the subject of enquiry? And if you find what you want, how will you ever know that this is the thing which you did not know?

Socrates.   I know, Meno, what you mean; but just see what a tiresome dispute you are introducing. You argue that a man cannot enquire either about that which he knows, or about that which he does not know; for if he knows, he has no need to enquire; and if not, he cannot; for he does not know the very subject about which he is to enquire.

Men.   Well, Socrates, and is not the argument sound?

Soc.   I think not.

Men.   Why not?

Soc.   I will tell you why: I have heard from certain wise men and women who spoke of things divine that—

Men.   What did they say?

Soc.   They spoke of a glorious truth, as I conceive.

Men.   What was it? and who were they?

Soc.   Some of them were priests and priestesses, who had studied how they might be able to give a reason of their profession: there have been poets also, who spoke of these things by inspiration, like Pindar, and many others who were inspired. And they say—mark, now, and see whether their words are true—they say that the soul of man is immortal, and at one time has an end, which is termed dying, and at another time is born again, but is never destroyed. And the moral is, that a man ought to live always in perfect holiness. '*For in the ninth year Persephone sends the souls of those from whom she has received the penalty of ancient crime back again from beneath into the light of the sun above, and these are they who become noble kings and mighty men and great in wisdom and are called saintly heroes in after ages.*' The soul, then, as being immortal, and having been born again many times, and having seen all things that exist, whether in this world or in the world below, has knowledge of them all; and it is no wonder that she should be able to call to remembrance all that she ever knew about virtue, and about everything; for as all nature is akin, and the soul has learned all things, there is no difficulty in her eliciting or as men say learning, out of a single recollection all the rest, if a man is strenuous and does not faint; for all enquiry and all learning is but recollection. And therefore we ought not to listen to this sophistical argument about the impossibility of enquiry: for it will make us idle and is sweet only to the sluggard; but the other saying will make us active and inquisitive. In that confiding, I will gladly enquire with you into the nature of virtue.

Men.   Yes, Socrates; but what do you mean by saying that we do not learn, and that what we call learnings is only a process of recollection? Can you teach me how this is?

Soc.   I told you, Meno, just now that you were a rogue, and now you ask whether I can teach you, when I am saying that there is no teaching, but only recollection; and thus you imagine that you will involve me in a contradiction.

Men.   Indeed, Socrates, I protest that I had no such intention. I only asked the question from habit; but if you can prove to me that what you say is true, I wish that you would.

Soc.   It will be no easy matter, but I will try to please you to the utmost of my power. Suppose that you call one of your numerous attendants, that I may demonstrate on him.

Men.   Certainly. Come hither, boy.

Soc.   He is Greek, and speaks Greek, does he not?

Men.   Yes, indeed; he was born in the house.

Soc.   Attend now to the questions which I ask him, and observe whether he learns of me or only remembers.

Men.   I will.

Soc.   Tell me, boy, do you know that a figure like this is a square?

Boy.   I do.

Soc.   And you know that a square figure has these four lines equal?

Boy.   Certainly.

Soc.   And these lines which I have drawn through the middle of the square are also equal?

Figure 44.1

Boy.   Yes.

Soc.   A square may be of any size?

Boy.   Certainly.

Soc.   And if one side of the figure be of two feet, and the other side be of two feet, how much will the whole be? Let me explain: if in one direction the space was of two feet, and in the other direction of one foot, the whole would be of two feet taken once?

Boy.   Yes.

Soc.   But since this side is also of two feet, there are twice two feet?

Boy.   There are.

Soc.   Then the square is of twice two feet?

Boy.   Yes.

Soc.   And how many are twice two feet? count and tell me.

Boy.   Four, Socrates.

Soc.   And might there not be another square twice as large as this, and having like this the lines equal?

Boy.   Yes.

Soc.   And of how many feet will that be?

Boy.   Of eight feet.

Soc.   And now try and tell me the length of the line which forms the side of that double square: this is two feet—what will that be?

Boy.   Clearly, Socrates, it will be double.

Soc.   Do you observe, Meno, that I am not teaching the boy anything, but only asking him questions; and now he fancies that he knows how long a line is necessary in order to produce a figure of eight square feet; does he not?

Men.   Yes.

Soc.   And does he really know?

Men.   Certainly not.

Soc.   He only guesses that because the square is double, the line is double.

Men.   True.

Soc.   Observe him while he recalls the steps in regular order. (*To the Boy.*) Tell me, boy, do you assert that a double space comes from a double line? Remember that I am not speaking of an oblong, but of a figure equal every way, and twice the size of this—that is to say of eight feet; and I want to know whether you still say that a double square comes from a double line?

Boy.   Yes.

Soc.   But does not this line become doubled if we add another such line here?

Boy.   Certainly.

Soc.   And four such lines will make a space containing eight feet?

Boy.   Yes.

Soc.   Let us describe such a figure: Would you not say that this is the figure of eight feet?

Boy.   Yes.

Soc.   And are there not these four divisions in the figure, each of which is equal to the figure of four feet?

Boy.   True.

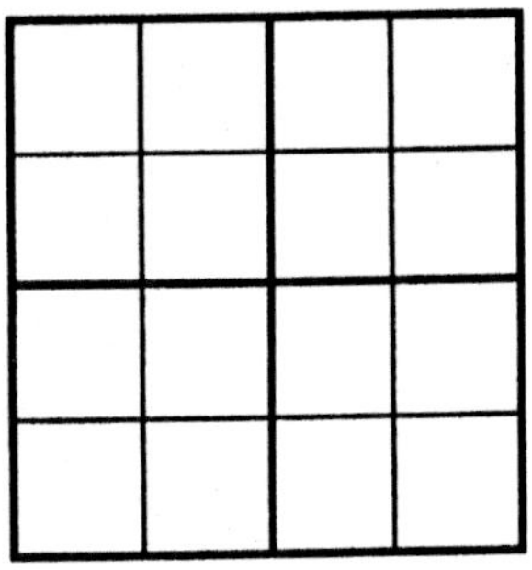

Figure 44.2

Soc.   And is not that four times four?

Boy.   Certainly.

Soc.   And four times is not double?

Boy.   No, indeed.

Soc.   But how much?

Boy.   Four times as much.

Soc.   Therefore the double line, boy, has given a space, not twice, but four times as much.

Boy.   True.

Soc.   Four times four are sixteen—are they not?

Boy.   Yes.

Soc.   What line would give you a space of eight feet, as this gives one of sixteen feet;—do you see?

Boy.   Yes.

Soc.   And the space of four feet is made from this half line?

Boy.   Yes.

Soc.   Good; and is not a space of eight feet twice the size of this, and half the size of the other?

Boy.   Certainly.

Soc.   Such a space, then, will be made out of a line greater than this one, and less than that one?

Boy.   Yes; I think so.

Soc.   Very good; I like to hear you say what you think. And now tell me, is not this a line of two feet and that of four?

Boy.   Yes.

Soc.   Then the line which forms the side of eight feet ought to be more than this line of two feet, and less than the other of four feet?

Boy.   It ought.

Soc.   Try and see if you can tell me how much it will be.

Boy.   Three feet.

Soc.   Then if we add a half to this line of two, that will be the line of three. Here are two and there is one; and on the other side, here are two also and there is one: and that makes the figure of which you speak?

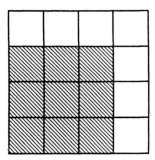

Figure 44.3

Boy.   Yes.

Soc.   But if there are three feet this way and three feet that way, the whole space will be three times three feet?

Boy.   That is evident.

Soc.   And how much are three times three feet?

Boy.   Nine.

Soc.   And how much is the double of four?

Boy.   Eight.

Soc.   Then the figure of eight is not made out of a line of three?

Boy.   No.

Soc.   But from what line?—tell me exactly; and if you would rather not reckon, try and show me the line.

Boy.   Indeed, Socrates, I do not know.

Soc.   Do you see, Meno, what advances he has made in his power of recollection? He did not know at first, and he does not know now, what is the side of a figure of eight feet: but then he thought that he knew, and answered confidently as if he knew, and had no difficulty; now he has a difficulty, and neither knows nor fancies that he knows.

Men.   True.

Soc.   Is he not better off in knowing his ignorance?

Men.   I think that he is.

Soc. If we have made him doubt, and given him the 'torpedo's shock,' have we done him any harm?

Men. I think not.

Soc. We have certainly, as would seem, assisted him in some degree to the discovery of the truth; and now he will wish to remedy his ignorance, but then he would have been ready to tell all the world again and again that the double space should have a double side.

Men. True.

Soc. But do you suppose that he would ever have enquired into or learned what he fancied that he knew, though he was really ignorant of it, until he had fallen into perplexity under the idea that he did not know, and had desired to know?

Men. I think not, Socrates.

Soc. Then he was the better for the torpedo's touch?

Men. I think so.

Soc. Mark now the farther development. I shall only ask him, and not teach him, and he shall share the enquiry with me: and do you watch and see if you find me telling or explaining anything to him, instead of eliciting his opinion. Tell me, boy, is not this a square of four feet which I have drawn?

Boy. Yes.

Soc. And now I add another square equal to the former one?

Boy. Yes.

Soc. And a third, which is equal to either of them?

Boy. Yes.

Soc. Suppose that we fill up the vacant corner?

Boy. Very good.

Soc. Here, then, there are four equal spaces?

Boy. Yes.

Soc. And how many times larger is this space than this other?

Boy. Four times.

Soc. But it ought to have been twice only, as you will remember.

Boy. True.

Soc. And does not this line, reaching from corner to corner, bisect each of these spaces?

Boy. Yes.

Soc. And are there not here four equal lines which contain this space?

Boy. There are.

Soc. Look and see how much this space is.

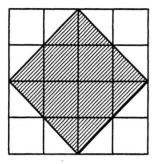

Figure 44.4

Boy.   I do not understand.

Soc.   Has not each interior line cut off half of the four spaces?

Boy.   Yes.

Soc.   And how many spaces are there in this section?

Boy.   Four.

Soc.   And how many in this?

Boy.   Two.

Soc.   And four is how many times two?

Boy.   Twice.

Soc.   And this space is of how many feet?

Boy.   Of eight feet.

Soc.   And from what line do you get this figure?

Boy.   From this.

Soc.   That is, from the line which extends from corner to corner of the figure of four feet?

Boy.   Yes.

Soc.   And that is the line which the learned call the diagonal. And if this is the proper name, then you, Meno's slave, are prepared to affirm that the double space is the square of the diagonal?

Boy.   Certainly, Socrates.

Soc.   What do you say of him, Meno? Were not all these answers given out of his own head?

Men.   Yes, they were all his own.

Soc.   And yet, as we were just now saying, he did not know?

Men.   True.

Soc.   But still he had in him those notions of his—had he not?

Men.   Yes.

Soc.   Then he who does not know may still have true notions of that which he does not know?

Men.   He has.

Soc.   And at present these notions have just been stirred up in him, as in a dream; but if he were frequently asked the same questions, in different forms, he would know as well as any one at last?

Men.   I dare say.

Soc.   Without any one teaching him he will recover his knowledge for himself, if he is only asked questions?

Men.   Yes.

Soc.   And this spontaneous recovery of knowledge in him is recollection?

Men.   True.

Soc.   And this knowledge which he now has must he not either have acquired or always possessed?

Men.   Yes.

Soc.   But if he always possessed this knowledge he would always have known; or if he has acquired the knowledge he could not have acquired it in this life, unless he has been taught geometry; for he may be made to do the same with all geometry and every other branch of knowledge. Now, has any one ever taught him all this? You must know about him, if, as you say, he was born and bred in your house.

Men.   And I am certain that no one ever did teach him.

Soc.   And yet he has the knowledge?

Men.   The fact, Socrates, is undeniable.

Soc.   But if he did not acquire the knowledge in this life, then he must have had and learned it at some other time?

Men.   Clearly he must.

Soc.   Which must have been the time when he was not a man?

Men.   Yes.

Soc.   And if there have been always true thoughts in him, both at the time when he was and was not a man, which only need to be awakened into knowledge by putting questions to him, his soul must have always possessed this knowledge, for he always either was or was not a man?

Men.   Obviously.

Chapter 45

From "Comments on a Certain Broadsheet"

René Descartes

In article *twelve* the author's disagreement with me seems to be merely verbal. When he says that the mind has no need of ideas, or notions, or axioms which are innate, while admitting that the mind has the power of thinking (presumably natural or innate), he is plainly saying the same thing as I, though verbally denying it. I have never written or taken the view that the mind requires innate ideas which are something distinct from its own faculty of thinking. I did, however, observe that there were certain thoughts within me which neither came to me from external objects nor were determined by my will, but which came solely from the power of thinking within me; so I applied the term 'innate' to the ideas or notions which are the forms of these thoughts in order to distinguish them from others, which I called 'adventitious' or 'made up'. This is the same sense as that in which we say that generosity is 'innate' in certain families, or that certain diseases such as gout or stones are innate in others: it is not so much that the babies of such families suffer from these diseases in their mother's womb, but simply that they are born with a certain 'faculty' or tendency to contract them.

In article *thirteen* he draws an extraordinary conclusion from the preceding article. Because the mind has no need of innate ideas, its power of thinking being sufficient, he says, 'all common notions which are engraved in the mind have their origin in observation of things or in verbal instruction'—as if the power of thinking could achieve nothing on its own, could never perceive or think anything except what it receives through observation of things or through verbal instruction, i.e., from the senses. But this is so far from being true that, on the contrary, if we bear well in mind the scope of our senses and what it is exactly that reaches our faculty of thinking by way of them, we must admit that in no case are the ideas of things presented to us by the senses just as we form them in our thinking. So much so that there is nothing in our ideas which is not innate to the mind or the faculty of thinking, with the sole exception of those circumstances which relate to experience, such as the fact that we judge that this or that idea which we now have immediately before our mind refers to a certain thing situated outside us. We make such a judgement not because these things transmit the ideas to our mind through the sense organs, but because they transmit something which, at exactly that moment, gives the mind occasion to form these ideas by means of the faculty innate to it. Nothing reaches our mind from external objects through the sense organs except certain corporeal motions, as our author himself asserts in article nineteen, in accordance with my own principles. But neither the motions themselves nor the figures arising from them are conceived by us exactly as they occur in the sense organs, as I have explained at length in my *Optics*. Hence it follows that the very ideas of the motions themselves and of the figures are innate in us. The ideas of pain, colours, sounds and the like must be all the more innate if, on the occasion of certain corporeal motions, our mind is to be capable of representing them to itself, for there is no similarity between these ideas and the corporeal motions. Is it possible to imagine anything more absurd than that all the common notions within our mind arise from such motions and cannot exist without them? I would like our author to tell me what the corporeal motion is that is capable of forming some common notion to the effect that 'things which are equal to a third thing are equal to each other', or any other he cares to take. For all such motions are particular, whereas the common notions are universal and bear no affinity with, or relation to, the motions.

... It is surely obvious to everyone that, strictly speaking, sight in itself presents nothing but pictures, and hearing nothing but utterances and sounds. So everything over and above these utterances and pictures which we think of as being signified by them is represented to us by means of ideas which come to us from no other source than our own faculty of thinking. Consequently these ideas, along with that faculty, are innate in us, i.e., they always exist within us potentially, for to exist in some faculty is not to exist actually, but merely potentially, since the term 'faculty' denotes nothing but a potentiality. But no one can assert that we can know nothing of God other than his name or the corporeal image which artists give him, unless he is prepared openly to admit that he is an atheist and indeed totally lacking in intellect.

... Later on, in enumerating the forms of perception, he lists only sense-perception, memory, and imagination. We may gather from this that he does not admit any pure understanding, i.e., understanding which is not concerned with any corporeal images, and hence that his view is that we have no knowledge of God, or of the human mind, or of other incorporeal things. The only explanation for this that I can think of is that what thoughts he has on these matters are so confused that he is never aware of having a pure thought, a thought which is quite distinct from any corporeal image.

... By 'innate ideas' I have never meant anything other than what the author himself explicitly asserts to be true, viz. that 'there is present in us a natural power which enables us to know God'. But I have never written or even thought that such ideas are actual, or that they are some sort of 'forms' which are distinct from our faculty of thinking. Indeed, there is no one more opposed than I to the useless lumber of scholastic entities; so much so that I could hardly keep from laughing when I saw the enormous battalion of arguments which the gentleman had painstakingly mustered—quite without malice, no doubt—to prove that 'babies have no actual conception of God while they are in their mother's womb'—as if he were thereby mounting a devastating assault upon me.

Chapter 46

No Innate Principles in the Mind

John Locke

It is an established opinion amongst some men, that there are in the understanding certain *innate principles*; some primary notions, κοιναὶ ἔννοιαι, characters, as it were stamped upon the mind of man; which the soul receives in its very first being, and brings into the world with it. It would be sufficient to convince unprejudiced readers of the falseness of this supposition, if I should only show (as I hope I shall in the following parts of this Discourse) how men, barely by the use of their natural faculties, may attain to all the knowledge they have, without the help of any innate impressions; and may arrive at certainty, without any such original notions or principles. For I imagine any one will easily grant that it would be impertinent to suppose the ideas of colours innate in a creature to whom God hath given sight, and a power to receive them by the eyes from external objects: and no less unreasonable would it be to attribute several truths to the impressions of nature, and innate characters, when we may observe in ourselves faculties fit to attain as easy and certain knowledge of them as if they were originally imprinted on the mind.

But because a man is not permitted without censure to follow his own thoughts in the search of truth, when they lead him ever so little out of the common road, I shall set down the reasons that made me doubt of the truth of that opinion, as an excuse for my mistake, if I be in one; which I leave to be considered by those who, with me, dispose themselves to embrace truth wherever they find it.

There is nothing more commonly taken for granted than that there are certain *principles*, both *speculative* and *practical*, (for they speak of both), universally agreed upon by all mankind: which therefore, they argue, must needs be the constant impressions which the souls of men receive in their first beings, and which they bring into the world with them, as necessarily and really as they do any of their inherent faculties.

This argument, drawn from universal consent, has this misfortune in it, that if it were true in matter of fact, that there were certain truths wherein all mankind agreed, it would not prove them innate, if there can be any other way shown how men may come to that universal agreement, in the things they do consent in, which I presume may be done.

But, which is worse, this argument of universal consent, which is made use of to prove innate principles, seems to me a demonstration that there are none such: because there are none to which all mankind give an universal assent. I shall begin with the speculative, and instance in those magnified principles of demonstration, 'Whatsoever is, is,' and 'It is impossible for the same thing to be and not to be'; which, of all others, I think have the most allowed title to innate. These have so settled a reputation of maxims universally received, that it will no doubt be thought strange if any one should seem to question it. But yet I take liberty to say, that these propositions are so far from having an universal assent, that there are a great part of mankind to whom they are not so much as known.

For, first, it is evident, that all children and idiots have not the least apprehension or thought of them. And the want of that is enough to destroy that universal assent which must needs be the necessary concomitant of all innate truths: it seeming to me near a contradiction to say, that there are truths imprinted on the soul, which it perceives or understands not: imprinting, if it signify anything, being nothing else but the making certain truths to be perceived. For to imprint anything on the mind without the mind's perceiving it, seems to me hardly intelligible. If therefore children and idiots have souls, have minds, with those impressions upon them, *they* must unavoidably perceive them, and necessarily know and assent to these truths; which since they do not, it is evident that there are no such impressions. For if they are not notions naturally imprinted, how can they be innate? and if they are notions imprinted, how can they be unknown? To say a notion is imprinted on the mind, and yet at the same time to say, that the mind is ignorant of it, and never yet took notice of it, is to make this impression nothing. No proposition can be said to be in the mind which it never yet knew, which it was never yet conscious of. For if any one may, then, by the same reason, all propositions that are true, and the mind is capable ever of assenting to, may be said to be in the mind, and to be imprinted: since, if any one can be said to be in the mind, which it never yet knew, it must be only because it is capable of knowing it; and so the mind is of all truths it ever shall know. Nay, thus truths may be imprinted on the mind which it never did, nor ever shall know; for a man may live long, and die at last in ignorance of many truths which his mind was capable of knowing, and that with certainty. So that if the capacity of knowing be the natural impression contended for, all the truths a man ever comes to know will, by this account, be every one of them innate; and this great point will amount to no more, but only to a very improper way of speaking; which, whilst it pretends to assert the contrary, says nothing different from those who deny innate principles. For nobody, I think, ever denied that the mind was capable of knowing several truths. The capacity, they say, is innate; the knowledge acquired. But then to what end such contest for certain innate maxims? If truths can be imprinted on the understanding without being perceived, I can see no difference there can be between any truths the mind is *capable* of knowing in respect of their original: they must all be innate or all adventitious: in vain shall a man go about to distinguish them. He therefore that talks of innate notions in the understanding, cannot (if he intend thereby any distinct sort of truths) mean such truths to be in the understanding as it never perceived, and is yet wholly ignorant of. For if these words 'to be in the understanding' have any propriety, they signify to be understood. So that to be in the understanding, and not to be understood; to be in the mind and never to be perceived, is all one as to say anything is and is not in the mind or understanding. If therefore these two propositions, 'Whatsoever is, is,' and 'It is impossible for the same thing to be and not to be,' are by nature imprinted, children cannot be ignorant of them: infants, and all that have souls, must necessarily have them in their understandings, know the truth of them, and assent to it.

To avoid this, it is usually answered, that all men know and assent to them, *when they come to the use of reason*; and this is enough to prove them innate. I answer:

Doubtful expressions, that have scarce any signification, go for clear reasons to those who, being prepossessed, take not the pains to examine even what they themselves say. For, to apply this answer with any tolerable sense to our present purpose, it must signify one of these two things: either that as soon as men come to the use of reason these supposed native inscriptions come to be known and observed by them; or else, that the use and exercise of men's reason, assists them in the discovery of these principles, and certainly makes them known to them.

If they mean, that by the use of reason men may discover these principles, and that this sufficient to prove them innate; their way of arguing will stand thus, viz. that whatever truths reason can certainly discover to us, and make us firmly assent to, those are all naturally imprinted on the mind; since that universal assent, which is made the mark of them, amounts to no more but this,—that by the use of reason we are capable to come to a certain knowledge of and assent to them; and, by this means, there will be no difference between the maxims of the mathematicians, and theorems they deduce from them: all must be equally allowed innate; they being all discoveries made by the use of reason, and truths that a rational creature may certainly come to know, if he apply his thoughts rightly that way.

But how can these men think the use of reason necessary to discover principles that are supposed innate, when reason (if we may believe them) is nothing else but the faculty of deducing unknown truths from principles or propositions that are already known? That certainly can never be thought innate which we have need of reason to discover; unless, as I have said, we will have all the certain truths that reason ever teaches us, to be innate. We may as well think the use of reason necessary to make our eyes discover visible objects, as that there should be need of reason, or the exercise thereof, to make the understanding see what is originally engraven on it, and cannot be in the understanding before it be perceived by it. So that to make reason discover those truths thus imprinted, is to say, that the use of reason discovers to a man what he knew before: and if men have those innate impressed truths originally, and before the use of reason and yet are always ignorant of them till they come to the use of reason, it is in effect to say, that men know and know them not at the same time.

It will here perhaps be said that mathematical demonstrations, and other truths that are not innate, are not assented to as soon as proposed, wherein they are distinguished from these maxims and other innate truths. I shall have occasion to speak of assent upon the first proposing, more particularly by and by. I shall here only, and that very readily, allow, that these maxims and mathematical demonstrations are in this different: that the one have need of reason, using of proofs, to make them out and to gain our assent; but the other, as soon as understood, are, without any the least reasoning, embraced and assented to. But I withal beg leave to observe, that it lays open the weakness of this subterfuge, which requires the use of reason for the discovery of these general truths: since it must be confessed that in their discovery there is no use made of reasoning at all. And I think those who give this answer will not be forward to affirm that the knowledge of this maxim, 'That it is impossible for the same thing to be and not to be,' is a deduction of our reason. For this would be to destroy that bounty of nature they seem so fond of, whilst they make the knowledge of those principles to depend on the labour of our thoughts. For all reasoning is search, and casting about, and requires pains and application. And how can it with any tolerable sense be supposed, that what was imprinted by nature, as the foundation and guide of our reason, should need the use of reason to discover it?

Those who will take the pains to reflect with a little attention on the operations of the understanding, will find that this ready assent of the mind to some truths, depends not, either on native inscription, or the use of reason, but on a faculty of the mind quite distinct from both of them, as we shall see hereafter. Reason, therefore, having nothing to do in procuring our assent to these maxims, if by saying, that 'men know and assent to them, when they come to the use of reason,' be meant, that the use of reason assists us in the knowledge of these maxims, it is utterly false; and were it true, would prove them not to be innate.

If by knowing and assenting to them 'when we come to the use of reason,' be meant, that this is the time when they come to be taken notice of by the mind; and that as soon as children come to the use of reason, they come also to know and assent to these maxims; this also is false and frivolous. First, it is false; because it is evident these maxims are not in the mind so early as the use of reason; and therefore the coming to the use of reason is falsely assigned as the time of their discovery. How many instances of the use of reason may we observe in children, a long time before they have any knowledge of this maxim, 'That it is impossible for the same thing to be and not to be?' And a great part of illiterate people and savages pass many years, even of their rational age, without ever thinking on this and the like general propositions. I grant, men come not to the knowledge of these general and more abstract truths, which are thought innate, till they come to the use of reason; and I add, nor then neither. Which is so, because, till after they come to the use of reason, those general abstract ideas are not framed in the mind, about which those general maxims are, which are mistaken for innate principles, but are indeed discoveries made and verities introduced and brought into the mind by the same way, and discovered by the same steps, as several other propositions, which nobody was ever so extravagant as to suppose innate. This I hope to make plain in the sequel of this Discourse. I allow therefore, a necessity that men should come to the use of reason before they get the knowledge of those general truths; but deny that men's coming to the use of reason is the time of their discovery.

In the mean time it is observable, that this saying, that men know and assent to these maxims 'when they come to the use of reason,' amounts in reality of fact to no more but this,—that they are never known nor taken notice of before the use of reason, but may possibly be assented to some time after, during a man's life; but when is uncertain. And so may all other knowable truths, as well as these; which therefore have no advantage nor distinction from others by this note of being known when we come to the use of reason; nor are thereby proved to be innate, but quite the contrary.

But, secondly, were it true that the precise time of their being known and assented to were, when men come to the use of reason; neither would that prove them innate. This way of arguing is as frivolous as the supposition itself is false. For, by what kind of logic will it appear that any notion is originally by nature imprinted in the mind in its first constitution, because it comes first to be observed and assented to when a faculty of the mind, which has quite a distinct province, begins to exert itself? And therefore the coming to the use of speech, if it were supposed the time that these maxims are first assented to, (which it may be with as much truth as the time when men come to the use of reason,) would be as good a proof that they were innate, as to say they are innate because men assent to them when they come to the use of reason. I agree then with these men of innate principles, that there is no knowledge of these general and self-evident maxims in the mind, till it comes to be exercise of reason: but I deny that the coming to the use of reason is the precise time when they are first taken notice of; and if that were the precise time, I deny that it would prove them innate. All that can with any truth be meant by this proposition, that men 'assent to them when they come to the use of reason,' is no more but this,—that the making of general abstract ideas, and the understanding of general names, being a concomitant of the rational faculty, and growing up with it, children commonly get not those general ideas, nor learn the names that stand for them, till, having for a good while exercised their reason about familiar and more particular ideas, they are, by their ordinary discourse and actions with others, acknowledged to be capable of rational conversation. If assenting to these maxims, when men come to the use of reason, can be true in any other sense, I desire it may be shown; or at least, how in this, or any other sense, it proves them innate.

The senses at first let in *particular* ideas, and furnish the yet empty cabinet, and the mind by degrees growing familiar with some of them, they are lodged in the memory and names got to them. Afterwards, the mind proceeding further, abstracts them, and by degrees learns the use of general names. In this manner the mind comes to be furnished with ideas and language, the *materials* about which to exercise its discursive faculty. And the use of reason becomes daily more visible as these materials that give it employment increase. But though the having of general ideas and the use of general words and reason usually grow together, yet I see not how this any way proves them innate. The knowledge of some truths, I confess, is very early in the mind; but in a way that shows them not to be innate. For, if we will observe, we shall find it still to be about ideas, not innate, but acquired; it being about those first which are imprinted by external things, with which infants have earliest to do, which make the most frequent impressions on their senses. In ideas thus got, the mind discovers that some agree and others differ, probably as soon as it has any use of memory; as soon as it is able to retain and perceive distinct ideas. But whether it be then or no, this is certain, it does so long before it has the use of words; or comes to that which we commonly call 'the use of reason.' For a child knows as certainly before it can speak the difference between the ideas of sweet and bitter (i.e., that sweet is not bitter), as it knows afterwards (when it comes to speak) that wormwood and sugarplums are not the same thing.

A child knows not that three and four are equal to seven, till he comes to be able to count seven, and has got the name and idea of equality; and then, upon explaining those words, he presently assents to, or rather perceives the truth of that proposition. But neither does he then readily assent because it is an innate truth, nor was his assent wanting till then because he wanted the use of reason; but the truth of it appears to him as soon as he has settled in his mind the clear and distinct ideas that these names stand for. And then he knows the truth of that proposition upon the same grounds and by the same means, that he knew before that a rod and a cherry are not the same thing; and upon the same grounds also that he may come to know afterwards 'That it is impossible for the same thing to be and not to be,' as shall be more fully shown hereafter. So that the later it is before any one comes to have those general ideas about which those maxims are; or to know the signification of those general terms that stand for them; or to put together in his mind the ideas they stand for; the later also will it be before he comes to assent to those maxims;—whose terms, with the ideas they stand for, being no more innate than those of a cat or a weasel, he must stay till time and observation have acquainted him with them; and then he will be in a capacity to know the truth of these maxims, upon the first occasion that shall make him put together those ideas in his mind, and observe whether they agree or disagree, according as is expressed in those propositions. And therefore it is that a man knows that eighteen and nineteen are equal to thirty-seven, by the same self-evidence that he knows one and two to be equal to three: yet a child knows this not so soon as the other; not for want of the use of reason, but because the ideas the words eighteen, nineteen, and thirty-seven stand for, are not so soon got, as those which are signified by one, two, and three.

This evasion therefore of general assent when men come to the use of reason, failing as it does, and leaving no difference between those supposed innate and other truths that are afterwards acquired and learnt, men have endeavoured to secure an universal assent to those they call maxims, by saying, they are generally assented to as soon as proposed, and the terms they are proposed in understood: seeing all men, even children, as soon as they hear and understand the terms, assent to these propositions, they think it is sufficient to prove them innate. For, since men never fail after they have once understood the words, to acknowledge them for undoubted truths, they would infer, that certainly these propositions were first lodged in the understanding, which, without any teaching, the mind, at the very first proposal immediately closes with and assents to, and after that never doubts again.

In answer to this, I demand whether ready assent given to a proposition, upon first hearing and understanding the terms, be a certain mark of an innate principle? If it be not, such a general assent is in vain urged as a proof of them: if it be said that it is a mark of innate, they must then allow all such propositions to be innate which are generally assented to as soon as heard, whereby they will find themselves plentifully stored with innate principles. For upon the same ground, viz. of assent at first hearing and under-standing the terms, that men would have those maxims pass for innate, they must also admit several propositions about numbers to be innate; and thus, that one and two are equal to three, that two and two are equal to four, and a multitude of other the like propositions in numbers, that everybody assents to at first hearing and understanding the terms, must have a place amongst these innate axioms. Nor is this the prerogative of numbers alone, and propositions made about several of them; but even natural philoso-phy, and all the other sciences, afford propositions which are sure to meet with assent as soon as they are understood. That 'two bodies cannot be in the same place' is a truth that nobody any more sticks at than at these maxims, that 'it is impossible for the same thing to be and not to be,' that 'white is not black,' that 'a square is not a circle,' that 'bitterness is not sweetness.' These and a million of such other propositions, as many at least as we have distinct ideas of, every man in his wits, at first hearing, and knowing what the names stand for, must necessarily assent to. If these men will be true to their own rule, and have assent at first hearing and understanding the terms to be a mark of innate, they must allow not only as many innate propositions as men have distinct ideas, but as many as men can make propositions wherein different ideas are denied one of another. Since every proposition wherein one different idea is denied of another, will as certainly find assent at first hearing and understanding the terms as this general one, 'It is impossible for the same thing to be and not to be,' or that which is the foundation of it and is the easier understood of the two, 'The same is not different'; by which account they will have legions of innate propositions of this one sort, without mention-ing any other. But, since no proposition can be innate unless the *ideas* about which it is be innate, this will be to suppose all our ideas of colours, sounds, tastes, figure, etc., innate, then which there cannot be anything more opposite to reason and experience. Universal and ready assent upon hearing and understanding the terms is, I grant, a mark of self-evidence; but self-evidence, depending not on innate impressions, but on some-thing else, (as we shall show hereafter,) belongs to several propositions which nobody was yet so extravagant as to pretend to be innate.

Nor let it be said, that those more particular self-evident propositions, which are assented to at first hearing, as that 'one and two are equal to three,' that 'green is not red,' etc., are received as the consequences of those more universal propositions which are looked on as innate principles; since any one, who will but take the pains to observe what passes in the understanding, will certainly find that these, and the like less general propositions, are certainly known, and firmly assented to by those who are utterly ignorant of those more general maxims; and so, being earlier in the mind than those (as they are called) first principles, cannot owe to them the assent wherewith they are received at first hearing.

If it be said, that these propositions, viz. 'two and two are equal to four,' 'red is not blue,' etc., are not general maxims, nor of any great use, I answer, that makes nothing to the argument of universal assent upon hearing and understanding. For, if that be the certain mark of innate, whatever proposition can be found that receives general assent as soon as heard and understood, that must be admitted for an innate proposition, as well as this maxim, 'That it is impossible for the same thing to be and not to be,' they being upon this ground equal. And as to the difference of being more general, that makes this maxim more remote from being innate; those general and abstract ideas being more strangers to our first apprehensions than those of more particular self-evident propositions; and therefore it is longer before they are admitted and assented to by the growing understanding. And as to the usefulness of these magnified maxims, that perhaps will not be found so great as is generally conceived, when it comes in its due place to be more fully considered.

But we have not yet done with 'assenting to propositions at first hearing and understanding their terms.' It is fit we first take notice that this, instead of being a mark that they are innate, is a proof of the contrary; since it supposes that several, who understand and know other things, are ignorant of these principles till they are proposed to them; and that one may be unacquainted with these truths till he hears them from others. For, if they were innate, what need they be proposed in order to gaining assent, when, by being in the understanding, by a natural and original impression, (if there were any such,) they could not but be known before? Or doth the proposing them print them clearer in the mind than nature did? If so, then the consequence will be, that a man knows them better after he has been thus taught them than he did before. Whence it will follow that these principles may be made more evident to us by others' teaching than nature has made them by impression: which will ill agree with the opinion of innate principles, and give but little authority to them; but, on the contrary, makes them unfit to be the foundations of all our other knowledge; as they are prentended to be. This cannot be denied, that men grow first acquainted with many of these self-evident truths upon their being proposed: but it is clear that whosoever does so, finds in himself that he then begins to know a proposition, which he knew not before, and which from thenceforth he never questions; not because it was innate, but because the consideration of the nature of the things contained in those words would not suffer him to think otherwise, how, or whensoever he is brought to reflect on them. [And if whatever is assented to at first hearing and understanding the terms must pass for an innate principle, every well-grounded observation, drawn from particulars into a general rule, must be innate. When yet it is certain that not all, but only sagacious heads, light at first on these observations, and reduce them into general propositions: not innate, but collected from a preceding acquaintance and reflection on particular instances. These, when observing men have made them, unobserving men, when they are proposed to them, cannot refuse their assent to.]

If it be said, the understanding hath an *implicit* knowledge of these principles, but not an *explicit*, before this first hearing (as they must who will say 'that they are in the understanding before they are known,') it will be hard to conceive what is meant by a principle imprinted on the understanding implicitly, unless it be this,—that the mind is capable of understanding and assenting firmly to such propositions. And thus all mathematical demonstrations, as well as first principles, must be received as native impressions on the mind; which I fear they will scarce allow them to be, who find it harder to demonstrate a proposition than assent to it when demonstrated. And few mathematicians will be forward to believe, that all the diagrams they have drawn were but copies of those innate characters which nature had engraven upon their minds.

There is, I fear, this further weakness in the foregoing argument, which would persuade us that therefore those maxims are to be thought innate, which men admit at first hearing; because they assent to propositions which they are not taught, nor do receive from the force of any argument or demonstration, but a bare explication or understanding of the terms. Under which there seems to me to lie this fallacy, that men are supposed not to be taught nor to learn anything *de novo*; when, in truth, they are taught, and do learn something they were ignorant of before. For, first, it is evident that they have learned the terms, and their signification; neither of which was born with them. But this is not all the acquired knowledge in the case: the ideas themselves, about which the proposition is, are not born with them, no more than their names, but got afterwards. So that in all propositions that are assented to at first hearing, the terms of the proposition, their standing for such ideas, and the ideas themselves that they stand for, being neither of them innate, I would fain know what there is remaining in such propositions that is innate. For I would gladly have any one name that proposition whose terms or ideas were either of them innate. We *by degrees* get ideas and names, and *learn* their appropriated connexion one with another; and then to propositions made in such terms, whose signification we have learnt, and wherein the agreement or disagreement we can perceive in our ideas when put together is expressed, we at first hearing assent; though to other propositions, in themselves as certain and evident, but which are concerning ideas not so soon or so easily got, we are at the same time no way capable of assenting. For, though a child quickly assents to this proposition, 'That an apple is not fire,' when by familiar acquaintance he has got the ideas of those two different things distinctly imprinted on his mind, and has learnt that the names apple and fire stand for them; yet it will be some years after, perhaps, before the same child will assent to this proposition, 'That it is impossible for the same thing to be and not to be'; because that, though perhaps the words are as easy to be learnt, yet the signification of them being more large, comprehensive, and abstract than of the names annexed to those sensible things the child hath to do with, it is longer before he learns their precise meaning, and it requires more time plainly to form in his mind those general ideas they stand for. Till that be done, you will in vain endeavour to make any child assent to a proposition made up of such general terms; but as soon as ever he has got those ideas, and learned their names, he forwardly closes with the one as well as the other of the forementioned propositions: and with both for the same reason; viz. because he finds the ideas he has in his mind to agree or disagree, according as the words standing for them are affirmed or denied one of another in the proposition. But if propositions be brought to him in words which stand for ideas he has not yet in his mind, to such propositions, however evidently true or false in themselves, he affords neither assent nor dissent, but is ignorant. For words being but empty sounds, any further than they are signs of our ideas, we cannot but assent to them as they correspond to those ideas we have, but no further than that. But the showing by what steps and ways knowledge comes into our minds; and the grounds of several degrees of assent, being the business of the following Discourse, it may suffice to have only touched on it here, as one reason that made me doubt of those innate principles.

To conclude this argument of universal consent, I agree with these defenders of innate principles,—that if they are innate, they must needs have universal assent. For that a truth should be innate and yet not assented to, is to me as unintelligible as for a man to know a truth and be ignorant of it at the same time. But then, by these men's own confession, they cannot be innate; since they are not assented to by those who understand not the terms; nor by a great part of those who do understand them, but have yet never heard nor thought of those propositions; which, I think, is at least one half of mankind. But were the number far less, it would be enough to destroy universal assent, and thereby show these propositions not to be innate, if children alone were ignorant of them.

But that I may not be accused to argue from the thoughts of infants, which are unknown to us, and to conclude from what passes in their understandings before they express it; I say next, that these two general propositions are not the truths that first possess the minds of children, nor are antecedent to all acquired and adventitious notions: which, if they were innate, they must needs be. Whether we can determine it or no, it matters not, there is certainly a time when children begin to think, and their words and actions do assure us that they do so. When therefore they are capable of thought, of knowledge, of assent, can it rationally be supposed they can be ignorant of those notions that nature has imprinted, were there any such? Can it be imagined, with any appearance of reason, that they perceive the impressions from things without, and be at the same time ignorant of those characters which nature itself has taken care to stamp within? Can they receive and assent to adventitious notions, and be ignorant of those which are supposed woven into the very principles of their being, and imprinted there in indelible characters, to be the foundation and guide of all their acquired knowledge and future reasonings? This would be to make nature take pains to no purpose; or at least to write very ill; since its characters could not be read by those eyes which saw other things very well: and those are very ill supposed the clearest parts of truth, and the foundations of all our knowledge, which are not first known, and without which the undoubted knowledge of several other things may be had. The child certainly knows, that the nurse that feeds it is neither the cat it plays with, nor the blackmoor it is afraid of: that the wormseed or mustard it refuses, is not the apple or sugar it cries for: this it is certainly and undoubtedly assured of: but will any one say, it is by viture of this principle, 'That it is impossible for the same thing to be and not to be,' that it so firmly assents to these and other parts of its knowledge? Or that the child has any notion or apprehension of that proposition at an age, wherein yet, it is plain, it knows a great many other truths? He that will say, children join in these general abstract speculations with their sucking bottles and their rattles, may perhaps, with justice, be thought to have more passion and zeal for his opinion, but less sincerity and truth, than one of that age.

Though therefore there be several general propositions that meet with constant and ready assent, as soon as proposed to men grown up, who have attained the use of more general and abstract ideas, and names standing for them; yet they not being to be found in those of tender years, who nevertheless know other things, they cannot pretend to universal assent of intelligent persons, and so by no means can be supposed innate;—it being impossible that any truth which is innate (if there were any such) should be unknown, at least to any one who knows anything else. Since, if they are innate truths, they must be innate thoughts: there being nothing a truth in the mind that it has never thought on. Whereby it is evident, if they be any innate truths, they must necessarily be the first of any thought on; the first that appear.

That the general maxims we are discoursing of are not known to children, idiots, and a great part of mankind, we have already sufficiently proved: whereby it is evident they have not an universal assent, nor are general impressions. But there is this further argument in it against their being innate: that these characters, if they were native and original impressions, should appear fairest and clearest in those persons in whom yet we find no footsteps of them; and it is, in my opinion, a strong presumption that they are not innate, since they are least known to those in whom, if they were innate, they must needs exert themselves with most force and vigour. For children, idiots, savages, and illiterate people, being of all others the least corrupted by custom, or borrowed opinions; learning and education having not cast their native thoughts into new moulds; nor by superinducing foreign and studied doctrines, confounded those fair characters nature had written there; one might reasonably imagine that in *their* minds these innate notions should lie open fairly to every one's view, as it is certain the thoughts of children do. It might very well be expected that these principles should be perfectly known to naturals; which being stamped immediately on the soul, (as these men suppose,) can have no dependence on the constitution or organs of the body, the only confessed difference between them and others. One would think, according to these men's principles, that all these native beams of light (were there any such) should, in those who have no reserves, no arts of concealment, shine out in their full lustre, and leave us in no more doubt of their being there, than we are of their love of pleasure and abhorrence of pain. But alas, amongst children, idiots, savages, and the grossly illiterate, what general maxims are to be found? what universal principles of knowledge? Their notions are few and narrow, borrowed only from those objects they have had most to do with, and which have made upon their senses the frequentest and strongest impressions. A child knows his nurse and his cradle, and by degrees the playthings of a little more advanced age; and a young savage has, perhaps, his head filled with love and hunting, according to the fashion of this tribe. But he that from a child untaught, or a wild inhabitant of the woods, will expect these abstract maxims and reputed principles of science, will, I fear, find himself mistaken. Such kind of general propositions are seldom mentioned in the huts of Indians: much less are they to be found in the thoughts of children, or any impressions of them on the minds of naturals. They are the language and business of the schools and academies of learned nations, accustomed to that sort of conversation or learning, where disputes are frequent; these maxims being suited to artifical argumentation and useful for conviction, but not much conducing to the discovery of truth or advancement of knowledge. But of their small use for the improvement of knowledge I shall have occasion to speak more at large.

I know not how absurd this may seem to the masters of demonstration. And probably it will hardly go down with anybody at first hearing. I must therefore beg a little truce with prejudice, and the forbearance of censure, till I have been heard out in the sequel of this Discourse, being very willing to submit to better judgments. And since I impartially search after truth, I shall not be sorry to be convinced, that I have been too fond of my own notions; which I confess we are all apt to be, when application and study have warmed our heads with them.

Upon the whole matter, I cannot see any ground to think these two speculative Maxims innate: since they are not universally assented to; and the assent they so generally find is no other than what several propositions, not allowed to be innate, equally partake in with them: and since the assent that is given them is produced another way, and comes not from natural inscription, as I doubt not but to make appear in the following Discourse. And if *these* 'first principles' of knowledge and science are found not to be innate, no *other* speculative maxims can (I suppose), with better right pretend to be so.

Chapter 47

The Psychogenesis of Knowledge and Its Epistemological Significance

Jean Piaget

Fifty years of experience have taught us that knowledge does not result from a mere recording of observations without a structuring activity on the part of the subject. Nor do any a priori or innate cognitive structures exist in man; the functioning of intelligence alone is hereditary and creates structures only through an organization of successive actions performed on objects. Consequently, an epistemology conforming to the data of psychogenesis could be neither empiricist nor preformationist, but could consist only of a constructivism, with a continual elaboration of new operations and structures. The central problem, then, is to understand how such operations come about, and why, even though they result from nonpredetermined constructions, they eventually become logically necessary.

Empiricism

The critique of empiricism is not tantamount to negating the role of experimentation, but the "empirical" study of the genesis of knowledge shows from the onset the insufficiency of an "empiricist" interpretation of experience. In fact, no knowledge is based on perceptions alone, for these are always directed and accompanied by schemes of action. Knowledge, therefore, proceeds from action, and all action that is repeated or generalized through application to new objects engenders by this very fact a "scheme," that is, a kind of practical concept. The fundamental relationship that constitutes all knowledge is not, therefore, a mere "association" between objects, for this notion neglects the active role of the subject, but rather the "assimilation" of objects to the schemes of that subject. This process, moreover, prolongs the various forms of biological "assimilations," of which cognitive association is a particular case as a functional process of integration. Conversely, when objects are assimilated to schemes of action, there is a necessary "adaptation" to the particularities of these objects (compare the phenotypic "adaptations" in biology), and this adaptation results from external data, hence from experience. It is thus this exogenous mechanism that converges with what is valid in the empiricist thesis, but (and this reservation is essential) adaptation does not exist in a "pure" or isolated state, since it is always the adaptation of an assimilatory scheme; therefore this assimilation remains the driving force of cognitive action.

These mechanisms, which are visible from birth, are completely general and are found in the various levels of scientific thought. The role of assimilation is recognized in the fact that an "observable" or a "fact" is always interpreted from the moment of its observation, for this observation always and from the beginning requires the utilization of logico-mathematical frameworks such as the setting up of a relationship or a correspondence, proximities or separations, positive or negative quantifications leading to the concept of measure—in short, a whole conceptualization on the part of the subject that excludes the existence of pure "facts" as completely external to the activities of this subject, all the more as the subject must make the phenomena vary in order to assimilate them.

As for the learning processes invoked by the behaviorist empiricists on behalf of their theses, Inhelder, Sinclair, and Bovet have shown that these processes do not explain cognitive development but are subject to its laws, for a stimulus acts as such only at a certain level of "competence" (another biological notion akin to assimilation). Briefly, the action of a stimulus presupposes the presence of a scheme, which is the true source of the response (which reverses the SR schema or makes it symmetrical [$S \leftrightarrows R$]). Besides, Pribram has demonstrated a selection of inputs existing even at the neurological level.

Preformation

Is it necessary, then, to turn in the direction of the preformation of knowledge? I will return later to the problem of innateness and will limit myself for the moment to the discussion of the hypothesis of determination. If one considers the facts of psychogenesis, one notes first the existence of stages that seem to bear witness to a continual construction. In the first place, in the sensorimotor period preceding language one sees the establishment of a logic of actions (relations of order, interlocking of schemes, intersections, establishment of relationships, and so on), rich in discoveries and even in inventions (recognition of permanent objects, organization of space, of causality). From the ages of 2 to 7, there is a conceptualization of actions, and therefore representations, with discovery of functions between covariations of phenomena, identities, and so forth, but without yet any concept of reversible operations or of conservation. These last two concepts are formed at the level of concrete operations (ages 7 to 10), with the advent of logically structured "groupings," but they are still bound to the manipulation of objects. Finally, around the age of 11 to 12, a hypothetico-deductive propositional logic is formed, with a combinatorial lattice, "sums of parts," algebraic four-groups, and so on.

However, these beautiful successive and sequential constructions (where each one is necessary to the following one) could be interpreted as the progressive actualization (related to factors such as neurological maturity) of a set of preformations, similar to the way in which genetic programming regulates organic "epigenesis" even though the latter continues to interact with the environment and its objects. The problem is therefore to choose between two hypotheses: authentic constructions with stepwise disclosures to new possibilities, or successive actualization of a set of possibilities *existing from* the beginning. First, let us note that the problem is similar in the history of science: are the clearly distinct periods in the history of mathematics the result of the successive creations of mathematicians, or are they only the achievement through progressive thematizations of the set of all possibilities corresponding to a universe of Platonic ideas? Now, the set of all possibilities is an antinomic notion like the set of all sets, because the set is itself only a possibility. In addition, today's research shows that, beyond the transfinite number "kappa zero" (which is the limit of predicativity), some openings into new possibilities are still taking place, but are in fact unpredictable since they cannot be founded on a combinatorial lattice. Thus, either mathematics is a part of nature, and then it stems from human constructions, creative of new concepts; or mathematics originates in a Platonic and suprasensible universe, and in this case, one would have to show through what psychological means we acquire knowledge of it, something about which there has never been any indication.

This brings us back to the child, since within the space of a few years he spontaneously reconstructs operations and basic structures of a logico-mathematical nature, without which he would understand nothing of what he will be taught in school. Thus, after a lengthy preoperative period during which he still lacks these cognitive instruments, he reinvents for himself, around his seventh year, the concepts of reversibility, transitivity, recursion, reciprocity of relations, class inclusion, conservation of numerical sets, measurements, organization of spatial references (coordinates), morphisms, some connectives, and so on—in other words, all the foundations of logic and mathematics. If mathematics were preformed, this would mean that a baby at birth would already possess virtually everything that Galois, Cantor, Hilbert, Bourbaki, or MacLane have since been able to realize. And since the child is himself a consequence, one would have to go back as far as protozoa and viruses to locate the seat of "the set of all possibilities."

In a word, the theories of preformation of knowledge appear, for me, as devoid of concrete truth as empiricist interpretations, for the origin of logico-mathematical structures in their infinity cannot be localized either in objects or in the subject. Therefore, only constructivism is acceptable, but its weighty task is to explain both the mechanisms of the formation of new concepts and the characteristics these concepts acquire in the process of becoming logically necessary.

Reflective Abstraction

If logico-mathematical structures are not preformed, one must, in contrast, go far back to discover their roots, that is, the elementary functioning permitting their elaboration; and as early as the sensorimotor stages, that is to say, much before language, one finds such points of departure (though without any absolute beginning, since one must then go back as far as the organism itself; see the section on the biological roots of knowledge). What are the mechanisms, then, that provide the constructions from one stage to the other? The first such mechanism I will call "reflective abstraction."

It is, in fact, possible to distinguish three different kinds of abstraction. (1) Let us call "empirical abstraction" the kind that bears on physical objects external to the subject. (2) Logico-mathematical abstraction, in contrast, will be called "reflective"* because it proceeds from the subject's actions and operations. This is even true in a double sense; thus we have two interdependent but distinct processes: that of a projection onto a higher plane of what is taken from the lower level, hence a "reflecting," and that of a "reflection" as a reorganization on the new plane—this reorganization first utilizing, only instrumentally, the operations taken from the preceding level but aiming eventually (even if this remains partially unconscious) at coordinating them into a new totality. (3) We will speak finally of "reflected abstraction" or "reflected thought" as the thematization of that which remained operational or instrumental in (2); phase (3) thus constitutes the natural outcome of (2) but presupposes in addition a set of explicit comparisons at a level above the "reflections" at work in the instrumental utilizations and the constructions in process of (2). It is essential, therefore, to distinguish the phases of reflective abstractions, which occur in any construction at the time of the solution of new problems, from reflected abstraction, which adds a system of explicit correspondences among the operations thus thematized.

Reflective and reflected abstractions, then, are sources of structural novelties for the following reasons: In the first place, the "reflecting" on a higher plane of an element taken from a lower level (for example, the interiorization of an action into a conceptualized representation) constitutes an establishment of correspondences, which is itself already a new concept, and this then opens the way to other possible correspondences, which represents a new"opening." The element transferred onto the new level is then constituted from those that were already there or those that are going to be added, which is now the work of the "reflection" and no longer of the "reflecting" (although initially elicited by the latter). New combinations thus result which can lead to the construction of new operations operating "on" the preceding ones, which is the usual course of mathematical progress (an example in the child: a set of additions creating multiplication).[1] As a rule, all reflecting on a new plane leads to and necessitates a *reorganization*, and it is this reconstruction, productive of new concepts, that we call "reflection"; yet well before its general thematization, reflection comes into action through a set of still instrumental assimilations and coordinations without any conceptual awareness of structures as such (this is to be found all through the history of mathematics). Finally reflected abstraction or retrospective thematization become possible, and although they are found only on preconstructed elements, they naturally constitute a new construction in that their transversal correspondences render simultaneous that which was until now elaborated by successive longitudinal linkings (compare, in scientific thought, the thematization of "structures" by Bourbaki).

Constructive Generalization

Abstraction and generalization are obviously interdependent, each founded on the other. It results from this that only inductive generalization, proceeding from "some" to "all" by simple extension, will correspond to empirical abstraction, whereas constructive and "completive" generalizations in particular will correspond to reflective and reflected abstractions.

The first problem to be solved, then, is that of the construction of successive steps that have been established in the preceding paragraphs. Now, each one of them results from a new assimilation or operation aimed at correcting an insufficiency in the previous level and actualizing a possibility that is opened by the new assimilation. A good example is the passage of action to representation due to the formation of the semiotic function. Sensorimotor assimilation consists only of assimilating objects to schemes of action, whereas representative assimilation assimilates objects to each other, hence the construction of conceptual schemes. Now, this new form of assimilation already was virtual in sensorimotor form since it bore on multiple but successive objects; it was then sufficient to complete these successive assimilations by a simultaneous act of setting into transversal correspondence before passing to the next level. But such an action implies the evocation of objects not presently perceived, and this evocation requires the formation of a specific instrument, which is the semiotic function (deferred imitations, symbolic play, mental image which is an interiorized imitation, sign language, and so on, in addition to vocal and learned language). Now, sensorimotor signifiers already exist in the form of cues or signals, but they constitute only one aspect or a part of the signified objects; on the contrary, the semiotic function commences when signifiers are differentiated from what is thereby signified and when signifiers can correspond to a multiplicity of things signified. It is clear, then, that between the conceptual assimilation of objects between themselves and semiotization, there is a mutual dependence and that both proceed from a completive generalization of sensorimotor assimilation. This generalization embeds a reflective abstraction bearing on elements directly borrowed from sensorimotor assimilation.

Likewise, it would be easy to show that the new concepts inherent in the levels of initially concrete, then hypothetico-deductive operations proceed from completive generalizations as well. It is thus that concrete operations owe their new abilities to the acquisition of reversibility, which has already been prepared by preoperative reversibility; but the reversibility, in addition, requires a systematic adjustment of affirmations and negations, that is to say, an autoregulation which, by the way, is always working within the constructive generalizations (I will return to the subject of autoregulation in the section on necessity and equilibration). As for the hypothetico-deductive operations, these are made possible by the transition from the structures of "groupings" devoid of a combinatorial lattice (the elements of which are disjoint), to the structures of the "set of components" embedding a combinatorial lattice and full generalization of partitions.[2]

These last advances are due to a particularly important form of constructive generalizations, which consist of raising an operation to its own square or a higher power: thus, combinations are classifications of classifications, permutations are seriations of seriations, the sets of components are partitions of partitions, and so on.

Finally, let us call attention to a simpler but equally important form which consists of generalizations by synthesis of analogous structures, such as the coordination of two systems of references, internal and external to a spatial or cinematic process (the 11- to 12-year-old level).

The Biological Roots of Knowledge

What we have seen so far speaks in favor of a systematic constructivism. It is nonetheless true that its sources are to be sought at the level of the organism, since a succession of constructions could not admit of an absolute beginning. But before offering a solution, we should first ask ourselves what a preformationist solution would mean biologically; in other words, what *a priorism* would look like after having been rephrased in terms of innateness.

A famous author has demonstrated this quite clearly: it is Konrad Lorenz, who considers himself a Kantian who maintains a belief in a hereditary origin of the great structures of reason as a precondition to any acquisition drawn from experience. But as a biologist, Lorenz is well aware that, except for "general" heredity common to all living beings or major groups, specific heredity varies from one species to another: that of man, for instance, remains special to our own particular species. As a consequence, Lorenz, while believing as a precondition that our major categories of thought are basically inborn, cannot, for that very reason, assert their generality: hence his very enlightening formula according to which the *a prioris* of reason consist simply of "innate working hypotheses." In other words, Lorenz, while retaining the point of departure of the *a priori* (which precedes the constructions of the subject), sets aside necessity which is more important, whereas we are doing exactly the opposite, that is, insisting on necessity (see the next section), but placing it at the end of constructions, without any prerequisite hereditary programming.

Lorenz's position is therefore revealing: if reason is innate, either it is general and one must have it go back as far as the protozoa, or it is specific (species-specific or genus-specific, for instance) and one must explain (even if it is deprived of its essential character of necessity) through which mutations and under the influence of which natural selections it developed. Now, as research stands at present, current explanations would be reduced for this particular problem to a pure and simple verbalism; in fact, they would consist of making reason the product of a random mutation, hence of mere chance.

But what innatists surprisingly seem to forget is that there exists a mechanism which is as general as heredity and which even, in a sense, controls it: this mechanism is autoregulation, which plays a role at every level, as early as the genome, and a more and more important role as one gets closer to higher levels and to behavior. Autoregulation, whose roots are obviously organic, is thus common to biological and mental processes, and its actions have, in addition, the great advantage of being directly controllable. It is therefore in this direction, and not in mere heredity, that one has to seek the biological explanation of cognitive constructions, notwithstanding the fact that by the interplay of regulations of regulations, autoregulation is eminently constructivist (and dialectic) by its very nature.[3]

It is understandable, therefore, that while fully sympathizing with the transformational aspects of Chomsky's doctrine, I cannot accept the hypothesis of his "innate fixed nucleus." There are two reasons for this. The first one is that this mutation particular to the human species would be biologically inexplicable; it is already very difficult to see why the randomness of mutations renders a human being able to "learn" an articulate language, and if in addition one had to attribute to it the innateness of a rational linguistic structure, then this structure would itself be subject to a random origin and would make of reason a collection of mere "working hypotheses," in the sense of Lorenz. My second reason is that the "innate fixed nucleus" would retain all its properties of a "fixed nucleus" if it were not innate but constituted the "necessary" result of the constructions of sensorimotor intelligence, which is prior to language and results from those joint organic and behavioral autoregulations that determine this epigenesis. It is indeed this explanation of a noninnate fixed nucleus, produced by sensorimotor intelligence, that has been finally admitted by authors such as Brown, Lenneberg, and McNeill. This is enough to indicate that the hypothesis of innateness is not mandatory in order to secure the coherence of Chomsky's beautiful system.

Necessity and Equilibration

We still have to look for the reason why the constructions required by the formation of reason become progressively necessary when each one begins by various trials that are partly episodic and that contain, until rather late, an important component of irrational thought (non-conservations, errors of reversibility, insufficient control over negations, and so on). The hypothesis naturally will be that this increasing necessity arises from autoregulation and has a counterpart with the increasing, parallel equilibration of cognitive structures. Necessity then proceeds from their "interlocking."

Three forms of equilibration can be distinguished in this respect. The most simple, and therefore the most precocious, is that of assimilation and accommodation. Already at the sensorimotor level, it is obvious that in order to apply a scheme of actions to new objects, this scheme must be differentiated according to the properties of these objects; therefore one obtains an equilibrium aimed at both preserving the scheme and taking into account the properties of the object. If however, these properties turn out to be unexpected and interesting, the formation of a subscheme or even of a new scheme has to prove feasible. Such new schemes will then necessitate an equilibration of their own. But these functional mechanisms are found at all levels. Even in science, the assimilation between linear and angular speeds involves two joint operations: common space-time relationships are assimilated while one accommodates for these nonetheless distinct solutions; similarly, the incorporation of open systems to general thermodynamic systems requires differentiating accommodation as well as assimilations.

A second form of equilibrium imposes itself between the subsystems, whether it is a question of subschemes in a scheme of action, subclasses in a general class, or subsystems of the totality of operations that a subject has at his disposal, as for example, the equilibration between spatial numbers and measurement during calculations in which both can intervene. Now, since subsystems normally evolve at different speeds, there can be conflicts between them. Their equilibration presupposes in this case a distinction between their common parts and their different properties, and consequently a compensatory adjustment between partial affirmations and negations as well as between direct or inverted operations, or even the utilization of reciprocities. One can see, then, how equilibration leads to logical necessity: the progressive coherence, sought and finally attained by the subject, first comes from a mere causal regulation of actions of which the results are revealed, after the fact, to be compatible or contradictory; this progressive coherence then achieves a comprehension of linkings or implications that have become deductible and thereby necessary.

The third form of equilibration relies upon the previous one but distinguishes itself by the construction of a new global system: it is the form of equilibration required by the very process of differentiation of new systems, which requires then a compensatory step of integration into a new totality. Apparently, there is here a simple balance of opposing forces, the differentiation threatening the unity of the whole and the integration jeopardizing the necessary distinctions. In fact, the originality of the cognitive equilibrium (and, by the way, further down in the hierarchy, also of organic systems) is to ensure, against expectations, the enrichment of the whole as a function of the importance of these differentiations and to ensure their multiplication (and not only their consistency) as a function of intrinsic (or having become such) variations of the totality of its own characteristics. Here again one clearly sees the relationship between equilibration and progressive logical necessity, that is, the necessity of the *terminus ad quem* resulting from the final integration or "interlocking" of the systems.

In summary, cognitive equilibration is consequently "accretive" (*majorante*); that is to say, the disequilibria do not lead back to the previous form of equilibrium, but to a better form, characterized by the increase of mutual dependencies or necessary implications.

As for experimental knowledge, its equilibration admits, in addition to the previous laws, of a progressive transfer (*passage*) from the exogenous to the endogenous, in the sense that perturbations (falsifications of expectations) are first nullified or neutralized, then progressively integrated (with displacement of equilibrium), and finally incorporated into the system as deducible intrinsic variations reconstructing the exogenous by way of the endogenous. The biological equivalent of this process (compare "from noise to order" in von Foerster)[4] is to be sought in the "phenocopy," as I have endeavored to interpret and to generalize this notion in a recent paper.[5]

Psychogenesis and History of Science

As Holton said, one can recognize certain convergences between psychogenesis and the historical development of cognitive structures;[6] this is what I will attempt to define in an upcoming work with the physicist Rolando Garcia.

In some cases, before seventeenth-century science, one can even observe a stage-by-stage parallelism. For instance, in regard to the relationship between force and movement, one can distinguish four periods: (1) the Aristotelian theory of the two motors with, as a consequence, the model of *antiperistasis*; (2) an overall explanation in which force, movement, and impetus remain undifferentiated; (3) the theory of impetus (or *élan*), conceived by Buridan as a necessary intermediary between force and movement; and (4) a final and pre-Newtonian period in which impetus tends to conflate with acceleration. Now, one notes a succession of four very similar stages in the child. The first one is that one in which the two motors remain rather systematic as residues of animism, but with a large number of spontaneous examples of *antiperistasis* (and this often occurs in very unexpected situations, and not only for the movement of projectiles). During a second stage, an overall notion comparable to "action" intervenes and can be symbolized by *mve*, in which *m* represents the weight, *v* the speed, and *e* the distance covered. During a third period (ages 7 to 10), the "impetus" in the sense of Buridan's middle term spontaneously appears, but with, in addition, the power of "passing through" motionless intermediaries by passing through their "interior" when a movement is transmitted through their mediation. Finally, in a fourth phase, (around the age of 11 to 12), the first inklings of the notion of acceleration appear.

For larger periods of history, obviously one does not find any stage-by-stage parallelism, but one can search for common mechanisms. For instance, the history of Western geometry bears witness to a process of structuration whose steps are those of a centration on an emphasis by Euclid on simply intrafigural relationships, then a construction of interfigural relationships with Cartesian coordinate systems, and then finally a progressive algebrization by Klein. Now one finds, on a small scale, a similar process in children, who naturally begin with the "intrafigural," but who discover around their seventh year that in order to determinate a point on a plane, one measurement is not sufficient, but two are necessary, and they must be orthogonally arranged. After this "interfigural" stage (which is necessary also for the construction of horizontal lines) follows that which we can call the "transfigural" stage, in which the properties to be discovered cannot be read on a single diagram, but necessitate a deduction or a calculation (for example, mechanical curves, relative motions, and so on).

Now, these analogies with the history of science assuredly speak in favor of my constructivism. *Antiperistasis* was not transmitted hereditarily from Aristotle to the little Genevans, but Aristotle began by being a child; for childhood precedes adulthood in all men, including cavemen. As for what the scientist keeps from his younger years, it is not a collection of innate ideas, since there are tentative procedures in both cases, but a constructive ability; and one of us went so far as to say that a physicist of genius is a man who has retained the creativity inherent to childhood instead of losing it in school.

Notes

1. Considering the number of these additions and not only their result.
2. Let us recall that completive generalization is a constructive process essential in mathematics: for example, the transition from passages of groupoids to semigroups, then from there to monoids, then to groups, to rings, and to bodies.
3. It is true that autoregulation is in part innate, but more in terms of functioning than in terms of structures.
4. H. von Foerster, "On Self-organizing Systems and Their Environments," in *Self-organizing Systems*, ed. M. Yovitz and S. E. Cameron (Elmsford, N.Y.: Pergamon Press, 1960).
5. J. Piaget, *Adaptation vitale et psychologie de l'intelligence: Sélection organique et phénocopie* (Paris: Hermann, 1974).
6. G. Holton, *Thematic Origins of Scientific Thought* (Cambridge, Mass.: Harvard University Press, 1973), p. 102.

Chapter 48

How There Could Be a Private Language and What It Must Be Like

Jerry A. Fodor

The first objection I want to consider is an allegation of infinite regress. It can be dealt with quickly (but for a more extensive discussion, see the exchange between Harman, 1969, and Chomsky, 1969).

Someone might say: 'According to you, one cannot learn a language unless one already knows a language. But now consider *that* language, the metalanguage in which representations of the extensions of object language predicates are formulated. Surely, learning *it* must involve prior knowledge of a meta-metalanguage in which its truth definitions are couched. And so on ad infinitum. Which is unsatisfactory'. There is, I think, a short and decisive answer. My view is that you can't learn a language unless you already *know* one. It isn't that you can't learn a language unless you've already *learned* one. The latter claim leads to infinite regress, but the former doesn't; not, at least by the route currently being explored. What the objection has in fact shown is that *either* my views are false *or* at least one of the languages one knows isn't learned. I don't find this dilemma embarrassing because the second option seems to me to be entirely plausible: the language of thought is known (e.g., is the medium for the computations underlying cognitive processes) but not learned. That is, it is innate. (Compare Atherton and Schwartz, 1974, which commits explicitly the bad argument just scouted.)

There is, however, another way of couching the infinite regress argument that is more subtle: 'You say that understanding a predicate involves representing the extension of that predicate in some language you already understand. But now consider understanding the predicates of the metalanguage. Doesn't that presuppose a representation of *its* truth conditions in some meta-metalanguage previously understood? And, once again, so on ad infinitum?' This argument differs from the first one in that the regress is run on 'understand' rather than on 'learn', and that difference counts. For, while I am not committed to the claim that the language of thought is *learned*, I am committed to the claim that it is, in a certain sense, understood: e.g., that it is available for use as the vehicle of cognitive processes. Nevertheless, this objection, like the other one, commits the fallacy of *ignoratio elenchi*: The position attacked is not the one defended.

What I said was that learning what a predicate means involved representing the extension of that predicate; not that understanding the predicate does. A sufficient condition for the latter might be just that one's use of the predicate is always in fact conformable to the truth rule. To see what's at issue here, consider the case of real computers.

Real computers characteristically use at least two different languages: an input/output language in which they communicate with their environment and a machine language in which they talk to themselves (i.e., in which they run their computations). 'Compilers' mediate between the two languages in effect by specifying biconditionals whose left-hand side is a formula in the input/output code and whose right-hand side is a formula in the machine code. Such biconditionals are, to all intents and purposes, representations of truth conditions for formulae in the input/output language, and the ability of the machine to use that language depends on the availability of those definitions. (All this is highly idealized, but it's close enough for present purposes.)[1] My point is that, though the machine must have a compiler if it is to use the input/output language, it doesn't *also* need a compiler for the machine language. What avoids an infinite regression of compilers is the fact that the machine is *built* to use the machine language. Roughly, the machine language differs from the input/output language in that its formulae correspond directly to computationally relevant physical states and operations of the machine: The physics of the machine thus guarantees that the sequences of states and operations it runs through in the course of its computations respect the semantic constraints on formulae in its internal language. What takes the place of a truth definition for the machine language is simply the engineering principles which guarantee this correspondence.

I shall presently return to this point in some detail. For the moment, suffice it to suggest that there are two ways in which it can come about that a device (including, presumably, a person) understands a predicate. In one case, the device has and employs a representation of the extension of the predicate, where the representation is itself given in some language that the device understands. In the second case, the device is so constructed that its use of the predicate (e.g., in computations) comport with the conditions that such a representation would specify. I want to say that the first is true of predicates in the natural languages people learn and the second of predicates in the internal language in which they think.

'But look', you might reply, 'you admit that there is at least one language whose predicates we understand without the internal representation of truth conditions. You admit that, for that language, the answer to: "How do we use its predicates correctly?" is that we just do; that we are just built that way. This saves you from infinite regress, but it suggests that even the regress from the natural language to the inner language is otiose. You argue that we learn "is a chair" only if we learn that it falls under the truth rule ⌜*y is a chair*⌝ *is true iff x is G* and then you say that the question of learning a truth rule for *G* doesn't arise. Why not stop a step sooner and save yourself trouble? Why not say that the question of how we learn "is a chair" doesn't arise either? Explanation has to stop somewhere'.

The answer is that explanation has to stop somewhere but it doesn't have to—and it better not—stop *here*. The question of how we learn 'is a chair' *does* arise precisely because English *is* learned. The question of how *G* is learned does not arise precisely because, by hypothesis, the language in which *G* is a formula is innate. Once again, thinking about computers is likely to be illuminating.

The critical property of the machine language of computers is that its formulae can be paired directly with the computationally relevant physical states of the machine in such fashion that the operations the machine performs respect the semantic constraints on formulae in the machine code. Token machine states are, in this sense, interpretable as tokens of the formulae. Such a correspondence can *also* be effected between physical states of the machine and formulae of the input/output code, but only by first compiling these formulae: i.e., only by first translating them into the machine language. This expresses the sense in which machines *are* 'built to use' their machine language and are *not* 'built to use' their input/output codes. It also suggests an empirical theory: When you find a device using a language it was not built to use (e.g., a language that it has *learned*), assume that the way it does it is by translating the formulae of that language into formulae which correspond directly to its computationally relevant physical states.

This would apply, in particular, to the formulae of the natural languages that speaker/hearers learn, and the correlative assumption would be that the truth rules for predicates in the natural language function as part of the translation procedure.

Admittedly this is just a *theory* about what happens when someone understands a sentence in a language he has learned. But at least it *is* a theory, and one which makes understanding a sentence analogous to computational processes whose character we roughly comprehend. On this view, what happens when a person understands a sentence must be a translation process basically analogous to what happens when a machine 'understands' (viz., compiles) a sentence in its programming language. I shall try to show that there are broadly empirical grounds for taking this sort of model seriously. My present point, however, is just that it is at least *imaginable* that there should be devices which need truth definitions for the languages they speak but not for the language that they compute in. If *we* are such devices, then there is point to asserting that learning English involves learning that ⌜y is a chair⌝ is true iff x is G, even though one denies that learning that requires learning that ⌜y is G⌝, is true iff x is Ψ for any Ψ other than G or 'is a chair'.

I don't, in short, think that the view of language learning so far sketched leads to infinite regress. It does lead to a one-stage regress; viz., from the natural language to the internal code—and that one stage is empirically rather than conceptually motivated. That is, we can imagine an organism which is born speaking and born speaking whatever language its nervous system uses for computing. For such an organism, the question of how it learns its language would, *ex hypothesi*, not arise; and the view that its use of the language is controlled by an internal representation of the truth conditions upon the predicates of that language might well be otiose. All we would need to suppose is that the organism is so constructed that its use of the expressions in the language conforms to the conditions that a truth definition for the language would articulate. But we are not such organisms and, so far as I know, for us no alternative to the view that we learn rules which govern the semantic properties of the expressions in our language is tenable.

To begin with, it may be felt that I have been less than fair to the view that natural language *is* the language of thought. It will be recalled that the main objection to this view was simply that it cannot be true for those computational processes involved in the acquisition of natural language itself. But, though it might be admitted that the *initial* computations involved in first language learning cannot themselves be run in the language being learned, it could nevertheless still be claimed that, a foothold in the language having once been gained, the child then proceeds by extrapolating his bootstraps: The fragment of the language first internalized is itself somehow essentially employed to learn the part that's left. This process eventually leads to the construction of a representational system more elaborate than the one the child started with, and this richer system mediates the having of thoughts the child could not otherwise have entertained.

Surely something that *looks* like this does sometimes happen. In the extreme case, one asks a dictionary about some word one doesn't understand, and the dictionary tells one, in one's own language, what the word means. That, at least, *must* count as using one part of one's language to learn another part. And if the adult can do it by the relatively explicit procedure of consulting a dictionary, why shouldn't the child do it by the relatively implicit procedure of consulting the corpus that adults produce? In particular, why shouldn't he use his observations of how some term applies to confirm hypotheses about the extension of that term? And why should not these hypotheses be couched in a fragment of the very language that the child is learning; i.e., in that part of the language which has been mastered to date?

This begins to seem a dilemma. On the one hand, it sometimes *does* help, in learning a language, to use the language that one is trying to learn. But, on the other hand, the line of argument that I have been pursuing appears to show that it *couldn't* help. For I have been saying that one can't learn P unless one learns something like $\ulcorner P_y \urcorner$ is true iff Gx', and that one can't learn *that* unless one is able to use G. But suppose G is a predicate (not of the internal language but) in the same language that contains P. Then G must itself have been learned and, *ex hypothesi*, learning G must have involved learning (for some predicate or other) that G applies iff *it* applies. The point is that this new predicate must either be a part of the internal language or 'traceable back' to a predicate in the internal language by iterations of the present argument. In neither case however does any predicate which belongs to the same language as P play an essential role in mediating the learning of P.

What makes the trouble is of course that the biconditional is *transitive*. Hence, if I can express the extension of G in terms of, say, H, and I can express the extension of P in terms of G, then I can express the extension of P in terms just of H (namely, $\ulcorner y$ is $P \urcorner$) is true iff Hx. So, introducing G doesn't seem to have gained us any leverage. There doesn't seem to be any way in which the part of a natural language one knows could play an essential role in mediating the learning of the part of the language that one doesn't know. Paradox.

In fact, two closely related paradoxes. We want to make room for the possibility that there is *some* sense in which you can use one part of a language to learn other parts, and we want to make room for the possibility that there is *some* sense in which having a language might permit the thinking of thoughts one could not otherwise entertain. But the views we have so far been propounding seem not to admit of either possibility: Nothing can be expressed in a natural language that can't be expressed in the language of thought. For if something could, we couldn't learn the natural language formula that expresses it.[2]

Fortunately, both paradoxes are spurious and for essentially the same reasons. To begin with the learning case, what the argument thus far shows is this. Suppose F is a (proper) fragment of English such that a child has mastered F and only F at time t. Suppose that F' is the rest of English. Then the child can use the vocabulary and syntax of F to express the truth conditions for the predicates of F' only insofar as the semantic properties of F' terms is already expressible in F. What the child cannot do, in short, is use the fragment of the language that he knows to increase the expressive power of the concepts at his disposal. But he may be able to use it for *other* purposes, and doing so may, in brute empirical fact, be essential to the mastery of F'. The most obvious possibility is to use F for mnemonic purposes.

It is a commonplace in psychology that mnemonic devices may be essential to a memory-restricted system in coping with learning tasks. If, as it seems reasonable to suppose, relatively simple natural language expressions are often coextensive only with quite elaborate formulae in the internal code, it becomes easy to see how learning one part of a natural language could be an essential precondition for learning the rest: The first-learned bits might serve to abbreviate complicated internal formulae, thus allowing the child to reduce the demands on computing memory implicit in projecting, confirming, and storing hypotheses about the truth conditions on the later-learned items. This sort of thing is familiar from teaching the vocabulary of formal systems. Complex concepts are typically not introduced directly in terms of primitives, but rather by a series of interlinking definitions. The point of this practice is to set bounds on the complexity of the formulae that have to be coped with at any given stage in the learning process.[3]

Essentially similar considerations suggest how it might after all be the case that there are thoughts that only someone who speaks a language can think. True, for every predicate in the natural language it must be possible to express a coextensive predicate in the internal code. It does not follow that for every natural language predicate *that can be entertained* there is an *entertainable* predicate of the internal code. It is no news that single items in the vocabulary of a natural language may encode concepts of extreme sophistication and complexity. If terms of the natural language can become incorporated into the computational system by something like a process of abbreviatory definition, then it is quite conceivable that learning a natural language may increase the complexity of the thoughts that we can think. To believe this, it is only necessary to assume that the complexity of thinkable thoughts is determined (*inter alia*) by some mechanism whose capacities are sensitive to the form in which the thoughts are couched. As we remarked above, memory mechanisms are quite plausibly supposed to have this property.

So, I am not committed to asserting that an articulate organism has *no* cognitive advantage over an inarticulate one. Nor, for that matter, is there any need to deny the Whorfian point that the kinds of concepts one has may be profoundly determined by the character of the natural language that one speaks. Just as it is necessary to distinguish the concepts that can be expressed in the internal code from the concepts that can be entertained by a memory-restricted system that computes with the code, so, too, it is necessary to distinguish the concepts that *can* be entertained (*salve* the memory) from the ones that actually get employed. This latter class is obviously sensitive to the particular experiences of the code user, and there is no principled reason why the experiences involved in learning a natural language should not have a specially deep effect in determining how the resources of the inner language are exploited.[4]

What, then, *is* being denied? Roughly, that one can learn a language whose expressive power is greater than that of a language that one already knows. Less roughly, that one can learn a language whose predicates express extensions not expressible by those of a previously available representational system. Still less roughly, that one can learn a language whose predicates express extensions not expressible by predicates of the representational system *whose employment mediates the learning.*

Now, while this is all compatible with there being a computational advantage associated with knowing a natural language, it is *in*compatible with this advantage being, as it were, principled. If what I have been saying is true, than all such computational advantages—all the facilitatory effects of language upon thought—will have to be explained away by reference to 'performance' parameters like memory, fixation of attention, etc. Another way to put this is: If an angel is a device with infinite memory and omnipresent attention—a device for which the performance/competence distinction is vacuous—then, on my view, there's no point in angels learning Latin; the conceptual system available to them by virtue of having done so can be no more powerful than the one they started out with.

It should now be clear why the fact that we can use part of a natural language to learn another part (e.g., by appealing to a monolingual dictionary) is no argument against the view that no one can learn a language more powerful than some language he already knows. One cannot use the definition D to understand the word W unless (a) 'W

means D' is true and (b) one understands D. But if (a) is satisfied, D and W must be at least coextensive, and so if (b) is true, someone who learns W by learning that it means D must already understand at least one formula coextensive with W, viz., the one that D is couched in. In short, learning a word can be learning what a dictionary definition says about it *only for someone who understands the definition.* So appeals to dictionaries do not, after all, show that you can use your mastery of a part of a natural language to learn expressions you could not otherwise have mastered. All they show is what we already know: Once one is able to express an extension, one is in a position to learn that W expresses that extension.

Notes

1. Someone might point out that, if the compiler formulae are biconditional, they could be read as specifying truth conditions for formulae in the *machine language* with the input/output code providing the metalinguistic vehicles of representation. In fact, however, the appearance of symmetry is spurious even if the two languages are entirely intertranslatable. For while the machine uses the machine code formulae without appealing to the compiler, it has no access to formulae in the input/output language except via the translations that the compiler effects. There is thus a useful sense in which, so far as the machine is concerned, machine language formulae express the meanings of formulae in the input/output code but not vice versa.

2. I know of only one place in the psychological literature where this issue has been raised. Bryant (1974) remarks: "the main trouble with the hypothesis that children begin to take in and use relations to help them solve problems because they learn the appropriate comparative terms like 'larger' is that it leaves unanswered the very awkward question of how they learned the meaning of these words in the first place." (p. 27) This argument generalizes, with a vengeance, to *any* proposal that the learning of a word is essential to mediate the learning of the concept that the word expresses.

3. I am assuming—as many psychologists do—that cognitive processes exploit at least two kinds of storage: a 'permanent memory' which permits relatively slow access to essentially unlimited amounts of information and a 'computing memory' which permits relatively fast access to at most a quite small number of items. Presumably, in the case of the latter system, the ability to display a certain body of information may depend critically on the form in which the information is coded. For extensive discussions see Neisser (1967). Suffice it to remark here that one way in which parts of a natural language might mediate further language learning is by providing the format for such encoding.

4. It should nevertheless be stressed that there is a fundamental disagreement between the kinds of views I have been proposing and those that linguistic relativists endorse. For such writers as Whorf, the psychological structure of the neonate is assumed to be diffuse and indeterminate. The fact about development that psychological theories are required to explain is thus the emergence of the adult's relatively orderly ontological commitments from the sensory chaos that is supposed to characterize the preverbal child's experience. This order has, to put it crudely, to come from somewhere, and the inventory of lexical and grammatical categories of whatever language the child learns would appear to be a reasonable candidate if a theorist is committed to the view that cognitive regularities must be reflexes of *environmental* regularities. On this account, the cognitive systems of adults ought to differ about as much as, and in about the ways that, the grammars and lexicons of their languages do and, so far as the theory is concerned, languages may differ without limit.

   On the internal code story, however, all these assumptions are reversed. The child (indeed, the infraverbal organism of whatever species) is supposed to bring to the problem of organizing its experiences a complexly structured and endogenously determined representational system. Similarities of cognitive organization might thus be predicted even over wide ranges of environmental variation. In particular, the theorist is not committed to discovering environmental analogues to such structural biases as the adult ontology exhibits. He is thus prepared to be unsurprised by the prima facie intertranslatability of natural languages, the existence of linguistic universals, and the broad homologies between human and infrahuman psychology. (For further discussion, see Fodor et al., 1974.)

Bibliography

Atherton, M., and Schwartz, R., 1974. "Linguistic Innateness and Its Evidence." *The Journal of Philosophy,* 71: 155–168.
Bryant, P. E., 1974. *Perception and Understanding in Young Children.* New York: Basic Books.

Chomsky, N., 1969. "Linguistics and Philosophy." In S. Hook, ed. *Language and Philosophy*. New York: NYU Press.

Fodor, J., 1975. *The Language of Thought*. Cambridge, MA: Harvard University Press.

Harman, G., 1969. "Linguistic Competence and Empiricism." In S. Hook, ed. *Language and Philosophy*. New York: NYU Press.

Neiser, U., 1967. *Cognitive Psychology*. New York: Appleton.

Chapter 49

On Cognitive Structures and Their Development:
A Reply to Piaget

Noam Chomsky

In his interesting remarks on the psychogenesis of knowledge and its epistemological significance, Jean Piaget formulates three general points of view as to how knowledge is acquired: empiricism, "preformation" ("innatism"), and his own "constructivism." He correctly characterizes my views as, in his terms, a variety of "innatism." Specifically, investigation of human language has led me to believe that a genetically determined language faculty, one component of the human mind, specifies a certain class of "humanly accessible grammars." The child acquires one of the grammars (actually, a system of such grammars, but I will abstract to the simplest, ideal case) on the basis of the limited evidence available to him. Within a given speech-community, children with varying experience acquire comparable grammars, vastly underdetermined by the available evidence. We may think of a grammar, represented somehow in the mind, as a system that specifies the phonetic, syntactic, and semantic properties of an infinite class of potential sentences. The child knows the language so determined by the grammar he has acquired. This grammar is a representation of his "intrinsic competence." In acquiring language, the child also develops "performance systems" for putting this knowledge to use (for example, production and perception strategies). So little is known about the general properties of performance systems that one can only speculate as to the basis for their development. My guess would be that, as in the case of grammars, a fixed, genetically determined system of some sort narrowly constrains the forms that they can assume. I would also speculate that other cognitive structures developed by humans might profitably be analyzed along similar lines.

Against this conception Piaget offers two basic arguments: (1) the mutations, specific to humans, that might have given rise to the postulated innate structures are "biologically inexplicable"; (2) what can be explained on the assumption of fixed innate structures can be explained as well as "the 'necessary' result of constructions of sensorimotor intelligence."

Neither argument seems to me compelling. As for the first, I agree only in part. The evolutionary development is, no doubt, "biologically unexplained." However, I know of no reason to believe the stronger contention that it is "biologically inexplicable." Exactly the same can be said with regard to the physical organs of the body. Their evolutionary development is "biologically unexplained," in exactly the same sense. We can, *post hoc*, offer an account as to how this development might have taken place, but we cannot provide a theory to select the actual line of development, rejecting others that appear to be no less consistent with the principles that have been advanced concerning the evolution of organisms. Although it is quite true that we have no idea how or why random mutations have endowed humans with the specific capacity to learn a human language, it is also true that we have no better idea how or why random mutations have led to the development of the particular structures of the mammalian eye or the cerebral cortex. We do not therefore conclude that the basic nature of these structures in the mature individual is determined through interaction with the environment (though such interaction is no doubt required to set genetically determined processes into motion and of course influences the character of the mature organs). Little is known concerning evolutionary development, but from ignorance, it is impossible to draw any conclusions. In particular, it is rash to conclude either (A) that known physical laws do not suffice in principle to account for the development of particular structures, or (B) that physical laws, known or unknown, do not suffice in principle. Either (A) or (B) would seem to be entailed by the contention that evolutionary development is literally "inexplicable" on biological grounds. But there seems to be no present justification for taking (B) seriously, and (A), though conceivably true, is mere speculation. In any event, the crucial point in the present connection is that cognitive structures and physical organs seem to be comparable, as far as the possibility of "biological explanation" is concerned.

The second argument seems to me a more important one. However, I see no basis for Piaget's conclusion. There are, to my knowledge, no substantive proposals involving "constructions of sensorimotor intelligence" that offer any hope of accounting for the phenomena of language that demand explanation. Nor is there any initial plausibility to the suggestion, as far as I can see. I might add that although some have argued that the assumption of a genetically determined language faculty is "begging the question," this contention is certainly unwarranted. The assumption is no more "question-begging" in the case of mental structures than is the analogous assumption in the case of growth of physical organs. Substantive proposals regarding the character of this language faculty are refutable if false, confirmable if true. Particular hypotheses have repeatedly been challenged and modified in the light of later research, and I have no doubt that this will continue to be the case.

It is a curiosity of our intellectual history that cognitive structures developed by the mind are generally regarded and studied very differently from physical structures developed by the body. There is no reason why a neutral scientist, unencumbered by traditional doctrine, should adopt this view. Rather, he would, or should, approach cognitive structures such as human language more or less as he would investigate an organ such as the eye or heart, seeking to determine: (1) its character in a particular individual; (2) its general properties, invariant across the species apart from gross defect; (3) its place in a system of such structures; (4) the course of its development in the individual; (5) the genetically determined basis for this development; (6) the factors that gave rise to this mental organ in the course of evolution. The expectation that constructions of sensorimotor intelligence determine the character of a mental organ such as language seems to me hardly more plausible than a proposal that the fundamental properties of the eye or the visual cortex or the heart develop on this basis. Furthermore, when we turn to specific properties of this mental organ, we find little justification for any such belief, so far as I can see.

I will not attempt a detailed argument here, but will merely sketch the kind of reasoning that leads me to the conclusions just expressed.

Suppose that we set ourselves the task of studying the cognitive growth of a person in a natural environment. We may begin by attempting to delimit certain cognitive domains, each governed by an integrated system of principles of some sort. It is, surely, a legitimate move to take language to be one such domain, though its exact boundaries and relations to other domains remain to be determined. In just the same way, we might proceed to study the nature and development of some organ of the body. Under this quite legitimate assumption, we observe that a person proceeds from a genetically determined initial state S_0 through a sequence of states $S_1, S_2, \ldots$, finally reaching a "steady state" S_s which then seems to change only marginally (say, by the addition of new vocabulary). The steady state is attained at a relatively fixed age, apparently by puberty or somewhat earlier. Investigating this steady state, we can construct a hypothesis as to the grammar internally represented. We could try to do the same at intermediate stages, thus gaining further insight into the growth of language.

In principle, it is possible to obtain as complete a record as we like of the experience available to the person who has achieved this steady state. We make no such attempt in practice, of course, but we can nevertheless focus on particular aspects of this experience relevant to specific hypotheses as to the nature of S_s and S_0. Assuming a sufficient record E of relevant experience, we can then proceed to construct a second-order hypothesis as to the character of S_0. This hypothesis must meet certain empirical conditions: It cannot be so specific as to rule out attested steady states, across languages; it must suffice to account for the transition from S_0 to S_s, given E, for any (normal) person. We may think of this hypothesis as a hypothesis with regard to a function mapping E into S_s. For any choice of E sufficient to give rise to knowledge of some human language L, this function must assign an appropriate S_s in which the grammar of L is represented. We might refer to this function as "the learning theory for humans in the domain language"—call it LT(H,L). Abstracting away from individual differences, we may take S_0—which specifies LT(H,L)—to be a genetically determined species character. Refinements are possible, as we consider stages of development more carefully.

More generally, for any species O and cognitive domain D that have been tentatively identified and delimited, we may, correspondingly, investigate LT(O,D), the "learning theory" for the organism O in the domain D, a property of the genetically determined initial state. Suppose, for example, that we are investigating the ability of humans to recognize and identify human faces. Assuming "face-recognition" to constitute a legitimate cognitive domain F, we may try to specify LT(H,F), the genetically determined principles that give rise to a steady state (apparently some time after language is neurally fixed, and perhaps represented in homologous regions of the right hemisphere, as some recent work suggests). Similarly, other cognitive domains can be studied in humans and other organisms. We would hardly expect to find interesting properties common to LT(O,D) for arbitrary O,D; that is, we would hardly expect to discover that there exists something that might be called "general learning theory." As far as I know, the prospects for such a theory are no brighter than for a "growth theory," intermediate in level between cellular biology and the study of particular organs, and concerned with the principles that govern the growth of arbitrary organs for arbitrary organisms.

Again, we may refine the investigation, considering intermediate states as well.

Returning to the case of language, to discover the properties of S_0 we will naturally focus attention on properties of later states (in particular, S_s) that are not determined by E, that is, elements of language that are known but for which there appears to be no relevant evidence. Consider a few examples.

The Structure-Dependent Property of Linguistic Rules

Consider the process of formation of simple yes-or-no questions in English. We have such declarative-question pairs as (1):

(1) The man is here—Is the man here?
     The man will leave.—Will the man leave?

Consider the following two hypotheses put forth to account for this infinite class of pairs:

H_1: process the declarative from beginning to end (left to right), word by word, until reaching the first occurrence of the words *is, will,* etc.; transpose this occurrence to the beginning (left), forming the associated interrogative.

H_2: same as H_1, but select the first occurrence of *is, will,* etc., following the first noun phrase of the declarative.

Let us refer to H_1 as a "structure-independent rule" and H_2 as a "structure-dependent rule." Thus, H_1 requires analysis of the declarative into just a sequence of words, whereas H_2 requires an analysis into successive words and also abstract phrases such as "noun phrase." The phrases are "abstract" in that their boundaries and labeling are not in general physically marked in any way; rather, they are mental constructions.

A scientist observing English speakers, given such data as (1), would naturally select hypothesis H_1 over the far more complex hypothesis H_2, which postulates abstract mental processing of a nontrivial sort beyond H_1. Similarly, given such data as (1) it is reasonable to assume that an "unstructured" child would assume that H_1 is valid. In fact, as we know, it is not, and H_2 is (more nearly) correct. Thus consider the data of (2):

(2) The man who is here is tall.——Is the man who is here tall?
     The man who is tall will leave.——Will the man who is tall leave?

These data are predicted by H_2 and refute H_1, which would predict rather the interrogatives (3):

(3) Is the man who here is tall?
     Is the man who tall will leave?

Now the question that arises is this: how does a child know that H_2 is correct (nearly), while H_1 is false? It is surely not the case that he first hits on H_1 (as a neutral scientist would) and then is forced to reject it on the basis of data such as (2). No child is taught the relevant facts. Children make many errors in language learning, but none such as (3), prior to appropriate training or evidence. A person might go through much or all of his life without ever having been exposed to relevant evidence, but he will nevertheless unerringly employ H_2, never H_1, on the first relevant occasion (assuming that he can handle the structures at all). We cannot, it seems, explain the preference for H_2 on grounds of communicative efficiency or the like. Nor do there appear to be relevant analogies of other than the most superficial and uninformative sort in other cognitive domains. If humans were differently designed, they would acquire a grammar that incorporates H_1, and would be none the worse for that. In fact, it would be difficult to know, by mere passive observation of a person's total linguistic performance, whether he was using H_1 or H_2.

Such observations suggest that it is a property of S_0—that is, of LT(H,L)—that rules (or rules of some specific category, identifiable on quite general grounds by some genetically determined mechanism) are structure-dependent. The child need not consider H_1; it is ruled out by properties of his initial mental state, S_0. Although this example is very simple, almost trivial, it illustrates the general problem that arises when we attend to the specific properties of attained cognitive states.

Chapter 50

What Is Innate and Why: Comments on the Debate

Hilary Putnam

I can say in a nutshell what I think about Chomsky and Piaget; neither has good arguments, but there is almost certainly something to what each one says. In this paper I am first going to say why the arguments are not good, and then discuss the more important question of why there is something right to what they say.

I shall begin with Chomsky's arguments. When one reads Chomsky, one is struck by a sense of great intellectual power; one knows one is encountering an extraordinary mind. And this is as much a matter of the spell of his powerful personality as it is of his obvious intellectual virtues: originality; scorn for the faddish and the superficial; willingness to revive (and the ability to revive) positions (such as the "doctrine of innate ideas") that had seemed passé; concern with topics, such as the structure of the human mind, that are of central and perennial importance. Yet I want to claim that his individual arguments are *not good*. I will examine only one example here, but I claim that a similar examination could be carried out on any of the arguments he has offered at this conference, with similar results.

The argument concerns "the process of formation of simple yes-or-no questions in English." In his paper, Chomsky considers "such declarative-question pairs" as:

(1) The man is here.—Is the man here?
    The man will leave.—Will the man leave?

And he considers two hypotheses "put forth to account for this infinite class of pairs" (of course, H_1 has never been "put forth" by anyone, nor would any sane person put it forth):

H_1: process the declarative from beginning to end (left to right), word by word, until reaching the first occurrence of the words *is, will*, etc.; transpose this occurrence to the beginning (left), forming the associated interrogative.

H_2: same as H_1, but select the first occurrence of *is, will*, etc., following the first noun phrase of the declarative.

Chomsky then writes:

Let us refer to H_1 as a "structure-independent rule" and H_2 as a "structure-dependent rule." Thus, H_1 requires analysis of the declarative into just a sequence of words, whereas H_2 requires an analysis into successive words and also abstract phrases such as "noun phrase." The phrases are "abstract" in that their boundaries and labeling are not in general physically marked in any way; rather, they are mental constructions.

A scientist observing English speakers, given such data as (1), would naturally select hypothesis H_1 over the far more complex hypothesis H_2, which postulates abstract mental processing of a nontrivial sort beyond H_1. Similarly, given such data as (1) it is reasonable to assume that an "unstructured" child would assume that H_1 is valid. In fact, as we know, it is not, and H_2 is (more nearly) correct. Thus consider the data of (2):

(2) The man who is here is tall.—Is the man who is here tall?
    The man who is tall will leave.—Will the man who is tall leave?

These data are predicted by H_2 and refute H_1, which would predict rather the interrogatives (3):

(3) Is the man who here is tall?
    Is the man who tall will leave?

Now the question that arises is this: how does a child know that H_2 is correct (nearly), while H_1 is false? It is surely not the case that he first hits on H_1 (as a neutral scientist would) and then is forced to reject it on the basis of data such as (2).

Chomsky's conclusion from all this is the following:

Such observations suggest that it is a property of S_0—that is, of LT(H,L)—that rules (or rules of some specific category, identifiable on quite general grounds by some genetically determined mechanism) are structure-dependent. The child need not consider H_1; it is ruled out by properties of his initial mental state, S_0.

I wish to discuss this example by considering two different questions: (1) can we account for the child's selection of "structure-dependent" hypotheses and concepts in the course of language learning on the basis of general intelligence, without postulating that the preference for H_2 over H_1 is built in, or that a template of a typical human language is built in, as Chomsky wishes us to do; and (2) can we account specifically for the preference of H_2 over H_1 without assuming that such a specific preference is built in? Before discussing these questions, however, I want to consider the vexed question, "What is a grammar?"

The Nature of Grammars

A grammar is some sort of system which—ideally—generates the "grammatical sentences" of a language and none of the ungrammatical ones. And a grammatical sentence is one generated by *the* grammar of the language (or by any adequate one, if one believes as Zellig Harris does that there is no such thing as *the* grammar of a language).[1] This is obviously a circular definition. But how does one break the circularity?

Chomsky suggested long ago (in "Explanatory Models in Linguistics")[2] that a child *hears* people classing sentences as "grammatical" or "ungrammatical"—not, of course, in those words, but by hearing them correct each other or the child—and that he projects a grammar as a simplest extrapolation from such data satisfying some innate constraints.

The trouble with this view is that the factual premise is clearly false. People don't object to all and only *ungrammatical* sentences. If they object at all, it is to *deviant* sentences—but they do not, when they correct each other, clearly say (in a way that a child can understand) whether the deviance was syntactic, semantic, discourse-theoretic, or whatever.

Chomsky asserts that the child is, in effect, supplied with "a list of grammatical sentences" and "a list of ungrammatical sentences" and has to extrapolate from these two lists. But this is surely false. If anything, he is supplied rather with a list of acceptable sentences and a list of sentences that are deviant-for-some-reason-or-other; a grammar of his language will generate (idealizing somewhat) all of the acceptable sentences in the first list, but unfortunately, it will not be the case that it generates none of the deviant sentences in the other list. On the contrary, the grammatical sentences will be a superset of the (finite list of) acceptable sentences, which is *not disjoint from* the (finite list of) deviant sentences.

Moreover, the second list does not have to exist at all. Chomsky has cited evidence that children can learn their first language without being corrected; and I am sure he also believes that they don't need to hear anyone else corrected either. Chomsky might reply to this by scrapping the hypothetical second list (the list of "ungrammatical," or at least, "unacceptable" sentences). He might say that the grammar of an arbitrary language is the simplest projection of any suitable finite set of acceptable sentences satisfying some set of innate constraints. This throws the whole burden of defining what a grammar is on the innate constraints. I want to suggest a different approach: one that says, in quite traditional fashion, that the grammar of a language is a property of the *language*, not a property of the brain of *Homo sapiens*.

Propositional Calculus

Let us start with a simple and well-understood example: the artificial language called "propositional calculus" with its standard interpretation. The grammar of propositional calculus can be stated in many different but equivalent ways. Here is a typical one:

(I)   A propositional variable standing alone is a well-formed formula.

(II)   If A and B are well-formed formulas, so are $\sim A$, $(A \& B)$, $(A \vee B)$ and $(A \supset B)$.[3]

(III)   Nothing is a well-formed formula unless its being so follows from (I) and (II).

The fact that a perfectly grammatical sentence may be deviant for semantic reasons, which is a feature of natural languages, is possessed also by this simple language, since "$p \& \sim p$" (for example) is perfectly grammatical but would not be "uttered" for obvious semantic reasons.

Now consider the "semantics" of propositional calculus as represented by the following inductive definition of *truth* in terms of *primitive truth* (truth for propositional variables, which is left undefined). The fact that primitive truth is left undefined means that this can be thought of as an *interpretation-schema*, which becomes an interpretation when joined to any definition of primitive truth.

Definition:

(i) $\sim A$ is true if and only if A is not true.

(ii) $(A \& B)$ is true if and only if A and B are both true.

(iii) $(A \vee B)$ is true if and only if at least one of A, B is true.

(iv) $(A \supset B)$ is true unless A is true and B is not true.

Notice that the inductive definition of *truth* in propositional calculus parallels (in a sense which could be made precise, but which I will not attempt to make precise here) the inductive definition of *grammatical* in propositional calculus. Now, there are other ways of defining grammatical in propositional calculus with the property that corresponding to them there exist parallel inductive definitions of truth in propositional calculus. But if we limit ourselves to those that are computationally feasible (that is, the corresponding decision program is short, when written in any standard format, and the typical computation is also short), not a great many are known, and they are all extremely similar. In this sense, propositional calculus as an interpreted system possesses an *intrinsic* grammar and semantics.

Let me elaborate on this a little. If Martians exist, very likely they have hit upon propositional calculus, and it may be that when they use propositional calculus their logicians' brains employ different heuristics than our logicians' brains employ. But that does not mean that propositional calculus has a different grammar when used by a Martian and when used by a Terrestrian. The grammar is (any one of) the simplest inductive definition(s) of the set of strings in the alphabet of propositional calculus for which truth is defined—that is, the simplest inductive definition(s) with the property that there exist parallel inductive definitions of truth. Given the semantics of propositional calculus (and no information about the brains of speakers), the class of reasonable grammars is fixed by that semantics, *not* by the structure of the brains that do the processing.

It may seem that I have begged too many questions by introducing the predicate "true"; but it is not essential to my argument. Suppose we do not define "true," but rather "follows from." Any reasonably simple definition of the relation "x follows from y" in propositional calculus will have the property that it presupposes a syntactic analysis of the standard kind. In other words, checking that something is an axiom or a proof, etc., will involve checking that strings and components of strings have the forms (p & q), $\sim$p, (p $\vee$ q), (p $\supset$ q). The grammar (I), (II), (III) not only generates the set of strings over which the relation "follows from" is defined, but it generates it in a way that corresponds to properties of strings referred to in the definition of "follows from."

Coming to natural language: suppose we think of a natural language as a very complicated formalized language whose formalization is unknown. (This seems to be how Chomsky thinks of it.) Suppose we think of the speaker as a computer that, among other things, computes whether certain strings are "true," given certain inputs, or if you don't like "true," as a computer that computes whether certain sequences of strings are "proofs," or computes the "degree of confirmation" of certain strings, and so forth. The fact is that any one of these semantic, or deductive logical, or inductive logical notions will have an *inductive definition* whose clauses parallel or at least presuppose a syntactic analysis of the language.

To come right out with it: I am suggesting (1) that the declarative grammar of a language is the inductive definition of a set of strings which is the set over which semantic, deductive-logical, inductive-logical (and so on) predicates are defined;[4] (2) that it must be in such a form that the inductive definitions of these predicates can easily "parallel" it; (3) that the corresponding decision program must be as computationally feasible as is consistent with (1) and (2). If a language is thought of in this way—as a system of strings with a semantics, with a deductive logic, with an inductive logic, and so on—then it is easy to see how the grammar can be a property of the *language* and not of the speakers' *brains*.

The Nature of Language Learning

Let us consider the linguistic abilities of Washoe (the chimpanzee brought up to use a certain amount of deaf-mute sign language by Alan and Beatrice Gardner). No doubt Chomsky will point out that Washoe lacks many of the syntactic abilities that humans have, and on these grounds he would claim that it is wrong to apply the term "language" to what she has learned. But the application of this term is not what is important. What is important is the following:

1. There is a certain class of words, which I will call *nouns-for-Washoe*, which Washoe associates with (classes of) *things*. For example, Washoe associates the word "grape" (in sign language) with more-or-less stereotypical grapes, "banana" with more-or-less stereotypical bananas, and so forth.

2. There is a *frame*, _____ gives _____ (to) _____, which Washoe has acquired (for example, "Alan gives apple to Trixie").

3. She can project *new* uses of this frame. If you teach her a new word, say "date," she will figure out herself the use she is expected to make of "_____ gives *date* (to) _____."

4. She can use the word "and" to combine sentences. She can figure out the expected use of *p* and *q* from the uses of p and q separately.[5]

Actually Washoe's abilities go far beyond these four capacities; but let us just consider these for now. The only plausible account of what has occurred is that Washoe has "internalized" a rule to the effect that if X is a *noun-for-Washoe*, and A, B, and C are people's names—counting Washoe (of course) as a person—then "A gives X to B" is a sentence, and a rule to the effect that if p, q are sentences so is *p and q*. And these are *structure-dependent rules* which Washoe has learned *without benefit of an innate template for language.*

Nor is this really surprising. Let us introduce a semantic predicate to describe the above tiny fragment of Washoe's "language" (where the "shudder-quotes" are inserted to avoid the accusation of question-begging), say, the predicate "corresponds to the condition that." Here are the "semantic rules" for the fragment in question:

(I)   If X is a *noun-for-Washoe* and B, C are people-names, and X corresponds to things of kind K, and b, c are the people corresponding to B, C, then "B gives X (to) C" corresponds to the condition that b gives something of kind K to c.

(II) If p, q are *sentences-for-Washoe, p and q* corresponds to the condition that the condition corresponding to p and the condition corresponding to q both obtain.

Now, I submit that Washoe is not really interested in learning that certain *uninterpreted* strings of gestures have a certain *uninterpreted* property called "grammaticality." She is interested for practical reasons—reward, approval, and so forth—in learning (I) and (II). But learning (I) and (II) automatically involves learning the grammatical facts that:

(i)   If B, C are people-names and X is a *noun-for-Washoe*, "B gives X (to) C" is a sentence-for-Washoe.

(ii) If p, q are sentences-for-Washoe, so is *p and q.*

For the set of sentences "generated" by the "grammar" (i), (ii) is precisely the set over which the semantic predicate—"corresponds to the condition that_____"—is defined by the inductive definition (I), (II); and the clauses (I), (II) presuppose precisely the syntactic analysis given by (i), (ii). Given that Washoe is trying to learn the *semantics* of Washoe-ese, and the syntax is only a *means* to this end, there are only two possibilities: either her intelligence will be too low to internalize "structure-dependent" rules like (I), (II), and she will fail; or her intelligence will be high enough, and as a corollary we will be able to ascribe to Washoe "implicit knowledge" of the syntactic rules (i), (ii)—not because she "knows" (I), (II) *and in addition* "knows" (i), (ii), but because having the "know-how" that constitutes implicit knowledge of (I), (II) *includes* implicit knowledge of (i), (ii).

But the same thing is true of the child. The child is not trying to learn a bunch of *syntactic* rules as a kind of crazy end-in-itself. He is learning, and he wants to learn, *semantic* rules, and these *cannot* be stated without the use of structure-dependent notions. There aren't even plausible candidates for structure-independent semantic rules. So *of course* (given that his intelligence is high enough to learn language), *of course* the child "internalizes" structure-dependent rules. And given that he must be building up an "inner representation" of abstract structural notions such as *sentence, noun, verb phrase,* and so on in learning to understand the language, the mere fact that H_2 uses such notions and H_1 does not, does *not* make H_2 so much less plausible than H_1.

Chomsky has, so to speak, "pulled a fast one" on us. He presents us with a picture of the child as being like an insanely scientistic linguist. Both are looking at language as a stream of uninterpreted noises; both are interested in an occult property of "grammaticality." From this (crazy) point of view, it is not surprising that H_1 seems infinitely "simpler" than H_2. So—Chomsky springs his carefully prepared trap—"Why doesn't the child try the simpler-but-false hypothesis H_1 *before* the correct hypothesis H_2?"

But this isn't what children (or sane linguists) are like at all. The child is in the process of trying to understand English. He has already tumbled (if Washoe can, so can he!) to the fact that he needs to internalize structure-dependent notions to do this. So the mere fact that H_2 *uses* such notions doesn't at all make it implausible or excessively complex. The point is that the *learning of grammar is dependent on the learning of semantics.* And there aren't even any candidates for structure-independent semantic rules (if there are, they get knocked out pretty early, even by a chimpanzee's brain).

H_1 Considered More Closely

So far I have argued that H_2 is not nearly as weird from the point of view of the intelligent brain unaided by an innate template of language as Chomsky wants to make it seem. But I haven't argued against H_1. So still the question remains, why doesn't the child try H_1?

Let us try applying to this problem the conception of grammar we just sketched (grammar as, so to speak, semantics minus the semantic predicates). H_1 will only be "tried" by the child if the child "tries" some *semantic* hypotheses that correspond to H_1. The child wants to *understand* questions, not just to "flag" them as questions. But it is plausible to assume (and Chomsky himself would assume) that understanding questions involves recovering the underlying declarative. This means that the question-transformation must have an *inverse* the child can perform. H_1 is indeed simple, but *its inverse is horribly complicated.* Moreover, *its inverse uses the full resources of the grammar;* all the notions, such as "noun phrase," that H_1 does not employ have to be employed in recovering the declarative from the output of our application of H_1. So it is no mystery that the child (or its brain) never "tries" such an unworkable semantic theory, and hence never "tries" H_1.

Incidentally, H_1 itself employs "abstract" notions, since it contains the phrase-structure concept "declarative," and applying it, if it were a rule of English, would therefore involve working with notions such as "noun phrase," since these have to be used to recognize declaratives. And some languages do have question-transformations that are as "structure-independent" as H_1 is; for example, in Hebrew one can form a question from a declarative by just prefixing *na im*. But this prefixing operation *does* have a simple inverse, namely, deleting *na im*.

I would like now to discuss Chomsky's more abstract remarks at the beginning of his paper. Let me begin with what he says about intelligence.

Chomsky on General Intelligence

So far I have assumed that there is such a thing as general intelligence; that is, that whatever else our innate cognitive repertoire may include, it *must* include *multipurpose* learning strategies, heuristics, and so forth. But Chomsky appears to deny this assumption explicitly. I quote:

> More generally, for any species O and cognitive domain D that have been tentatively identified and delimited, we may, correspondingly, investigate LT(O,D), the "learning theory" for the organism O in the domain D, a property of the genetically determined initial state. Suppose, for example, that we are investigating the ability of humans to recognize and identify human faces. Assuming "face-recognition" to constitute a legitimate cognitive domain F, we may try to specify LT(H,F), the genetically determined principles that give rise to a steady state (apparently some time after language is neurally fixed, and perhaps represented in homologous regions of the right hemisphere, as some recent work suggests). Similarly, other cognitive domains can be studied in humans and other organisms. We would hardly expect to find interesting properties common to LT(O,D) for arbitrary O,D; that is, we would hardly expect to discover that there exists something that might be called "general learning theory." As far as I know, the prospects for such a theory are no brighter than for a "growth theory," intermediate in level between cellular biology and the study of particular organs, and concerned with the principles that govern the growth of arbitrary organs for arbitrary organisms.

The key notion in this argument is the notion of a "domain." How wide is a domain? Is all of mathematics one domain? If so, what about empirical science? Or are physics, chemistry, and so on, all *different* domains?

If Chomsky admits that a domain can be as wide as empirical science (that there can be a "learning theory for empirical science"), then he has granted that something exists that may fittingly be called "general intelligence." (Chomsky might retort that only exceptionally intelligent individuals can discover new truths in empirical science, whereas everyone learns his native language. But this is an extraordinarily elitist argument: the abilities of exceptionally intelligent men must be *continuous* with those of ordinary men, after all, and the relevant mechanisms must be present at some level of functioning in all human brains.) Even if only physics, or just all of solid-state physics, or just all of the solid-state physics of crystals is one domain, the same point holds: heuristics and strategies capable of enabling us to learn new facts in these areas must be extraordinarily multipurpose (and we have presently no idea what they are). Once it is granted that such multipurpose learning strategies exist, the claim that they *cannot* account for language learning becomes highly dubious, as I argued long ago.[6] (Consider Washoe!)

On the other hand, if domains become so small that each domain can use only learning strategies that are highly specific in purpose (such as "recognizing faces," "learning a grammar"), then it becomes really a miracle that evolution endowed us with all these skills, most of which (for example, higher mathematics, nuclear physics) were not used at all until *after* the evolution of the race was complete (some 100,000-odd years ago). And the analogy with organ growth does not then hold at all: the reason there does not have to be a multipurpose learning mechanism is that there are only limited numbers of organs, whereas there are virtually unlimited numbers of "domains."

The Prospects of General Learning Theory

Chomsky feels that the "prospects" of "general learning theory" are bad. I tend to agree. I see no reason to think that the detailed functioning of the human mind will ever be transparent to the human mind.[7] But the existence of general intelligence is one question; the prospect for a revealing *description* of it is another.

Incidentally, if the innateness hypothesis is right, I am also not optimistic about the prospects for a revealing description of the innate template of language. The examples Chomsky has given us of how to go about inferring the structure of the template (such as the argument about H_1 and H_2) are such bad arguments that they cast serious doubt on the feasibility of the whole program, at least at this point in history (especially if there exist *both* general intelligence *and* an innate template).

On the other hand, we may well be able to discover interesting facts and laws about general intelligence without being able to describe it completely, or to model it by, say, a computer program. There may be progress in studying general intelligence without its being the case that we ever succeed in writing down a "general learning theory" in the sense of a mathematical model of multipurpose learning.

Chomsky on Evolution

Chomsky dismisses Piaget's question regarding how such a thing as an innate template for language might have evolved. But he should not dismiss it. One answer he might have given is this: primitive language first appeared as an *invention*, introduced by some extraordinary member of the species and learned by the others as Washoe learns her fragment of language. Given such a beginning of the instrument, genetic changes to enable us to use the instrument better (including the enlargement of the so-called speech center in the left lobe of normal humans) could have occurred, and would be explained, if they did occur, by natural selection. Presumably Chomsky did not give this answer because (1) he wants to deny that there exists such a thing as general intelligence, and to deny that even the simplest grammar could be internalized by general intelligence alone; and (2) he wants to deny that Washoe's performance is continuous with language learning, and to deny that it has any interest for the study of language learning. But this is surely perverse. If the first language user *already* had a complete innate template, then this could only have been a miraculous break in the evolutionary sequence, as Piaget in effect points out.

Chomsky remarks that we don't know the details of the development of the motor organs either, and this is surely true. We do postulate that they developed bit by bit. This poses difficulties, however, since there are no creatures with two thirds of a wing! But there have been impressive successes in this direction (for example, working out the evolution of the eye). We have found creatures with gliding membranes which are, in a sense, "two thirds of a wing." And we have found eyes with only rods (no cones) and eyes with only cones (no rods). Since the first draft of this paper was written, there have been exciting new suggestions in evolutionary theory.[8]

It is one thing to say that we cannot scientifically explain how certain structures were produced (and the theory of natural selection does not even claim that those structures were *probable*), and quite another to say that we now have scientific reason to postulate a large number of "mental organs" as specific as the various domains and subdomains of human knowledge. Such a mental organization would not be scientifically explicable at all; it would mean that God simply decided to produce these structures at a certain point in time because they were the ones we would need a half a million (or whatever) years later. (Although I don't doubt that God is ultimately responsible for what we are, it is bad scientific methodology to invoke Him as a *deus ex machina*. And, in any case, this is such a *messy* miracle to attribute to Him! Why should He pack our heads with a billion different "mental organs," rather than just making us smart?) On the other hand, if our language capacity did develop bit by bit, even with "jumps," a description of the first bit will almost certainly sound like a description of Washoe. But then we will have conceded that *some* internalization of linguistic rules (at least in prototype form) can be accounted for without innateness.

A Better Argument

But this suggests that there *is* an argument for *some* "innateness" that Chomsky might have used. Consider the phenomenon called "echo-location" in the bat. The bat emits supersonic "noises," which are reflected from the prey (or whatever—for example, a single insect), and the bat can "steer" by these sound-reflections as well as if it had sight (that is, it can avoid fine wires, catch the mosquito that is trying to avoid it, and so forth). Now, examination of the bat's brain shows that there has been a tremendous enlargement of the centers connected with hearing (they fill about seven-eighths of the bat's brain), as compared to other mammals (including, presumably, those in its evolutionary past). Clearly, a lot of the bat's echo-locating ability is *now* "innate."

Suppose Chomsky were to grant that Washoe has protospeech, and thereby grant that general intelligence can account for *some* language learning. He could then *use evolution as an argument for (some) "innateness."* In other words, we could argue that, given the enormous value of the language ability (as central to human life as echo-location is to bat life), it is *likely* that genetic changes have occurred to make the instrument better—for example, the development of the "speech center" in the left lobe. (But caution is needed: if the left lobe is damaged early, speech *can* develop in the right lobe.) This argument is the only one I know of that makes it plausible that there is *some* innate structuring of human language that is not simply a corollary to the innate (that is, genetically predetermined) structuring of human cognition in general. But the argument is not very strong: it could be *general intelligence* that has been genetically refined bit by bit and not a hypothetical language template. Indeed, even species-specific and functionally useless aspects of all human languages could be the product of unknown but genetically predetermined aspects of the overall functioning of the human brain and not clues to the character of a language template; so the mere existence of such aspects is no evidence at all for the template hypothesis.

I think there is an answer that Chomsky can make to this objection; but I will defer it until I have discussed Piaget.

Piaget's "Constructivism"

The view I have been putting forward—that everything Chomsky ascribes to an innate template of language, a "mental organ" specifically designed to enable us to *talk*, can, for all we know, be explained by general intelligence—agrees in broad outline with the view of Piaget. However, there seem to me to be serious conceptual difficulties with this view when it is combined with Piaget's specific account of what general intelligence is like.

Piaget supposes that human intelligence develops in stages, each stage depending on biological maturation (that is, the age of the child) and on the successful attainment of the previous stages. At a certain stage, certain concepts characteristically appear, for example, the concept of "conservation." But what is it to have such a concept as conservation?

I submit that the only coherent account presently available for having the concept of conservation is this: to have the concept is to have mastered a bit of *theory*, that is, to have acquired the characteristic uses of such expressions as "same amount," and some key *beliefs*, expressed by sentences involving such expressions, or equivalent symbolism. I don't claim that all concepts are abilities to use symbolism; an animal that *expects* the water to reach the same height when it is poured from a pot back into the glass might be said to have a minimal concept of conservation, but I claim that anything like the *full* concept of conservation involves the ability to use symbolism with the complexity of language in certain ways. (I don't claim that this is a "tautology"; rather that it is the only coherent account presently available for what full-blown concepts *are*. And I don't claim to have argued this here, but I have discussed this elsewhere;[9] and, of course, this insight is not mine but Wittgenstein's—indeed, it is the main burden of *Philosophical Investigations*.)

But if a maturational schedule *involving the development of concepts* is innate, and *concepts are essentially connected with language*,[10] then Piaget's hypothesis would seem to imply Chomsky's; "constructivism" would entail "nativism."

Of course, Piaget does not commit so crude an error. He does not suppose that the maturational *schedule* is given (that is, innate); what he takes as given is "reflective abstraction"—it is this that "precedes language" and that is supposed to take us from one "step" to the next.

But "reflection" and "abstraction" have *no literal meaning* apart from *language*! If "reflective abstraction" is not literally meant, it is either a metaphor for empiricist "generalization," which is insufficient to account for language learning and use, or a metaphor for we-know-not-what.

It seems to me that Piaget should take the view that "reflective abstraction" is something *like* the use of language in the making of hypothetico-deductive inferences, as Chomsky and Fodor urge, and hence conclude that something *like* the use of language is "innate." This position would have brought him into convergence with Chomsky, instead of into an unnecessary sectarian squabble. Moreover, his own suggestion in 1958 that formal logic is the best model for human reasoning[11] is very consonant with such a position.

Fodor's "Tautology"

In the discussion Fodor said some things that were a little careless. I want to rectify some of these errors, not for the sake of being "picky," but because the discussion becomes hopelessly confused at the critical point if we let them stand.

First a quibble: Fodor and Chomsky are simply wrong when they say that it is a "tautology" that we can't learn anything, unless some innate "prejudices" are "built in". It is not *logically* impossible that our heads should be as empty as the Tin Woodman's and we should still talk, love, and so on; it would just be an extreme example of a *causal anomaly* if it ever happened that a creature with no internal structure did these things. I don't doubt for one moment that our dispositions *do* have a causal explanation, and of course the functional organization of our brains is where one might look for a causal explanation (although I myself think that we won't be able to describe this in very much detail in the foreseeable future).[12] But this still is not a tautology.

Second, it is true that we can't learn how to learn unless we have some prior learning-dispositions: we have to have some dispositions to learn that are not themselves learned, on pain of infinite regress (however, the impossibility of an infinite regress in the real world is hardly a tautology!); but that does not mean that it is *logically necessary* (a "tautology") that the unlearned dispositions be innate. We might (*logically possibly*) acquire a new *unlearned* disposition every five minutes for no cause at all, for example, or for some cause that does not count as a form of "learning." There just aren't any significant tautologies in this area.

The reason this is not *just* a quibble is this: once we pare down Fodor's and Chomsky's big "tautology" to something like this: *as a matter of fact* (not logic!), *no learning without some laws of learning*, we see that no one, least of all the empiricists, has ever denied it. Chomsky's and Fodor's claim that there is a big, mysterious tautology that no one appreciated until Nelson Goodman and that everyone they dislike fails to appreciate is mere rhetoric.

Fodor's Argument for the Innateness of All Concepts

My aim in the remainder of this paper is to develop a modest a priori argument for the Fodor-Chomsky view that something *like* a language-processing capacity must be innate. But if Fodor's argument in *The Language of Thought* were acceptable, *my* work would be all done. So I must first explain why I reject Fodor's argument.

Fodor's argument has two parts. First, he contends that the only model we have presently available for the brain is the all-purpose digital computer. He contends, moreover, that such a computer, if it "learns" at all, must have an innate "program" for making generalizations in its built-in computer language. (Here he goes too fast—this is precisely what I think we need an *argument* for.) Second, he concludes that every predicate that a brain could learn to use must have a *translation* into the computer language of that brain. So no "new" concepts can be acquired: all concepts are innate!

I want to examine this second part of the argument, which is fallacious even if the first part is granted. Fodor's reasoning is as follows: Learning the meaning of a predicate is inferring what the semantic properties of that predicate are, that is, concluding (inductively) to some such generalization as:

(A)   For every x, P is true of x if and only if Q (x).

But if (A) is in brain language, so is Q. (P need not be; P is mentioned, not used in (A). But Q is *used*, not mentioned.) And if (A) is correct, Q is coextensive with P, and is so by virtue of what P *means* (otherwise (A) is not a correct semantic characterization of the meaning of P). So Q is *synonymous* with P; P is not a *new* concept, because there is a predicate (namely, Q) in "brain language" that is synonymous with it. But P is an *arbitrary* predicate the brain can learn to understand—so no new concepts can be learned!

What is wrong with this argument is clear. The assumption is as strong as what Fodor wishes to prove. So all we have to do is show how it could be false, even given Fodor's general outlook, and nothing is left but a simple case of begging the question.

First a point of terminology: Every computer does have a built-in "computer language," but *not* a language that contains quantifiers (that is, the words "all" and "some," or synonyms thereof). Let me explain.

A digital computer is a device that stores its own program and that consults its own program in the course of a computation. It is not at all necessary that the brain be a digital computer in *this* sense. The brain does not, after all, have to be reprogrammed as an all-purpose digital computer does. (One might reply that learning is "reprogramming"; but Fodor is talking about the program *for* learning, not about what is learned, and this program might be stored as the brain's *structure*, not as a code.) Waiving this objection: the program that a digital computer stores consists of "instructions" such as "add the two numbers in address 12" and "go back to step 6"—none of which use the word "all." So generalization (A) *cannot ever be stated* in "machine language," even if the computer's program is a program for making inductive inferences in some formalized language (for example, if the program is that of the hypothetico-deductive machine mentioned earlier). Moreover, machine language does not contain (nor can one introduce into it by definition) such notions as "tree," "cow," "jumps," "spontaneous," "pert," and so on—it only contains such notions as "add," "subtract," "0," "1," "put result in address 17," "go back to instruction so-and-so," and "print out contents of address blah-blah."

Let us suppose, however (what needs to be proved) that our brain is a hypothetico-deductive machine, and that it carries out inference in a formalized language ILL (for Inductive Logic Language) according to some program for eliminative induction. And let us suppose that Fodor is not really talking about the brain's *machine language* when he postulates his "language of thought," but about ILL. Even if so strong an assumption is conceded, his argument still does not work.

To see why it does not work, let us recall that when the speaker has finally mastered the predicate P, on Fodor's model, he is supposed to have acquired a new "subroutine." Even if this subroutine is described initially in ILL or in some special "programming language," or both, it has to have a translation into machine language that the brain's "compiler" can work out, or the brain won't "execute" this subroutine. Let S be the description of the subroutine in question *in machine language*; then even if we grant that the brain learns P by making an induction, it need not be an induction with the conclusion (A). It would suffice that the brain instead conclude:

(B)   I will be doing OK with P if subroutine S is employed.

And *this* can be stated in ILL provided ILL has the concept "doing OK with an item," and ILL contains machine language. But this does *not* require ILL to contain (synonyms for) "face," "cow," "jumps," "spontaneous," "pert," and so on. Fodor's argument has failed.

Fodor suggests that he would claim that the machine language description of how to use, say, "tree" *is* (a form of) the predicate *tree*. But this is simply an extension of use designed to make his thesis an uninteresting "tautology."

Of course, the predicate "doing OK with P" may arouse suspicion. But it should not. The "machine" (the brain) doesn't have to understand this predicate as linguists and philosophers would! The generalization (B) is simply a signal to the machine to add subroutine S to its repertoire of subroutines. (We should keep in mind Dennett's caution that talk of "machine language" is dangerous because we are tempted to confuse *our* abilities with the formalism in question with the machine's abilities.)

Notes

1. Z. S. Harris, *Methods in Structural Linguistics* (Chicago: University of Chicago Press, 1951).
2. N. Chomsky, "Explanatory Models in Linguistics," in *Logic, Methodology and Philosophy of Science*, ed. E. Nagel, P. Suppes, and A. Tarski (Stanford, Calif.: Stanford University Press, 1962).
3. Each formula can be associated with a corresponding statement expressed in ordinary language, namely, "not-A," "A and B," "A or B," "if A, then B."
4. By "declarative grammar" I mean that part of the grammar that generates the declarative sentences of the language. The usual assumption—made also by Chomsky—is that interrogatives, imperatives, and so on are somehow derived from declaratives.
5. What I have given here is a very oversimplified account of Washoe's actual abilities. The interested reader should consult the following works: B. Gardner and R. A. Gardner, "Two-Way Communication with an Infant Chimpanzee," in *Behavior of Non-Human Primates*, ed. A. Schrier and F. Stollnitz (New York and London: Academic Press, 1971), vol. 4, pp. 117–184; B. Gardner and R. A. Gardner, "Teaching Sign Language to the Chimpanzee Washoe" (16-mm sound film), State College of Pennsylvania, Psychological Cinema Register, 1974; B. Gardner and R. A. Gardner, "Comparing the Early Utterances of Child and Chimpanzee," in *Minnesota Symposia on Child Psychology*, ed. A. Pick (Minneapolis, Minn.: University of Minnesota Press, 1974); B. Gardner and R. A. Gardner, "Evidence for Sentence Constituents in the Early Utterances of Child and Chimpanzee," *Journal of Experimental Psychology: General* 104: 244–267, 1975. The last of these references bears directly on Washoe's ability to learn "structure-dependent" rules.
6. See chapter 5 of my *Mind, Language, and Reality* (Cambridge: Cambridge University Press, 1975).
7. I discuss this in my 1976 John Locke Lectures, *Meaning and the Moral Sciences* (London: Routledge and Kegan Paul, 1978).
8. For an account of some of these suggestions, I recommend Stephen Gould's *Ontogeny and Phylogeny* (Cambridge, Mass.: Harvard University Press, 1977).
9. See chapter 1 of my *Mind, Language, and Reality*.
10. It is worth noting in this connection that Piaget's research method (in all but a few experiments) consists of studying *verbal* behavior.
11. J. Piaget and B. Inhelder, *The Growth of Logical Thinking from Childhood to Adolescence* (London: Routledge and Kegan Paul, 1958).
12. This is argued in my John Locke Lectures.

Chapter 51
Discussion of Putnam's Comments
Noam Chomsky

Putnam's discussion of what he calls "the innateness hypothesis" extends an earlier critical analysis of his to which he refers.[1] The earlier criticism, I believe, is based on a series of specific errors and a mistaken conception of the problem at hand. I have discussed all of this in detail elsewhere[2] and will not recapitulate here. Putnam's current "Comments" contain some new arguments, all of them, I believe, erroneous. I will not review them all, but will concentrate on those that are directed specifically to my paper in this volume.

According to Putnam, I advocate the "innateness hypothesis" as he formulates it, and I (and Fodor) attribute to "associationists"—the adversary—the mistake of "denying innate structure (*laws* of learning) altogether." The second of these claims is utterly false. I have repeatedly, consistently, and clearly insisted that all rational approaches to the problems of learning, including "associationism" and many others that I discuss, attribute innate structure to the organism.[3] I am sure that the same is true of Fodor.[4] The question is not whether innate structure is a prerequisite for learning, but rather what it is. Furthermore, the literature is clear and explicit about this point.

For just this reason I have never used the phrase "the innateness hypothesis" in putting forth my views, nor am I committed to any particular version of whatever Putnam has in mind in using this phrase (which, to my knowledge, is his and his alone) as a point of doctrine. As a general principle, I am committed only to the "open-mindedness hypothesis" with regard to the genetically determined initial state for language learning (call it S_0^L), and I am committed to particular explanatory hypotheses about S_0^L to the extent that they seem credible and empirically supported. I have outlined one possible research strategy for determining the nature of S_0^L and sketched a number of properties that it seems reasonable to attribute to S_0^L, pursuing this strategy. Putnam investigates one of these examples, namely, the "structure-dependent" property of syntactic rules, arguing that the point is not well established. He contends that this particular property derives from "general intelligence." If indeed Putnam could characterize "general intelligence" or "multipurpose learning strategies" in some manner, and indicate, however vaguely, how the structure-dependent property of syntactic rules follows from the assumption that innate structure is as characterized, I would be happy to consider the hypothesis that this property should be attributed to "general intelligence" rather than to S_0^L, as I presently suppose to be the case. Nothing will follow, obviously, about the other properties that I argue can plausibly be attributed to S_0^L. Furthermore, if it can be shown that all properties of S_0^L can be attributed to "general intelligence," once this mysterious notion is somehow clarified, I will cheerfully agree that there are no special properties of the language faculty. But Putnam offers not even the vaguest and most imprecise hints as to the nature of the "general intelligence" or "multipurpose learning strategies" that he believes to exist. Therefore, his claim that some particular property of S_0^L can be explained in terms of these notions cannot be assessed.[5] It has the form of an empirical hypothesis, but not the content of one. Furthermore, his specific arguments with regard to the single example he discusses are all based on errors of fact or reasoning. Therefore, I see no reason to qualify the tentative suggestions in my paper with regard to structure dependence.

Putnam considers my two hypotheses H_1 and H_2, advanced to explain the formation of yes-or-no questions in English. He observes that the structure-independent rule H_1 would not be put forth by any "sane person," which is quite true, but merely constitutes part of the problem to be solved. The question is: Why? The answer that I suggest is that the general principles of transformational grammar belong to S_0^L, as part of a schematism that characterizes "possible human languages." It can easily be shown that H_2 can be directly formulated as a transformational rule in accordance with these principles, whereas H_1 cannot. In other words, the property "main verb" or "first occurrence of *is* (etc.) following the first noun phrase" is easily expressed in this particular theory, whereas the property "first occurrence of *is* (etc.)" cannot be expressed without a vast enrichment of theory (technically, it requires quantifiers in structural descriptions of transformations, whereas the former property does not). It follows, then, that a language learner equipped with the principles of transformational grammar as part of S_0^L will formulate H_2 rather than H_1 on the basis of data consistent with both. These principles are not, of course, invented ad hoc for this example; there is independent evidence to support them. Therefore, we have a plausible explanation for the fact that children automatically make the correct "induction" to a hypothesis which on general grounds would be regarded as more complex. Similarly, "sane persons," who also have an intuitive, pretheoretical grasp of the nature of language, will not put forth H_1, despite its great simplicity as compared with H_2. On the other hand, a Martian scientist, not equipped with the principles of transformational grammar as a schematism for human language, would have no hesitation in putting forth H_1. He would not be "insane," but merely "nonhuman"; that is, he lacks S_0^L.

Putnam offers several arguments to the contrary, which I will consider in turn. The first has to do with the data available for language learning. I have argued that we can, under an appropriate idealization, think of the language learner as being supplied with a sample of well-formed sentences and (perhaps) a sample of ill-formed sentences—namely, corrections of the learner's mistakes. No doubt much more information is available, and may be necessary for language learning, although little is known about this matter. Nothing that Putnam says in this connection has the slightest bearing on my (rather innocuous) proposal, as it has actually been formulated. Thus his "false premise" that people object to all and only ungrammatical sentences is one that I have never proposed, and his discussion of deviance is compatible with my views on this subject, as expressed since the mid-1950s. Therefore, I will not comment further on these remarks, which have no relevance to the issue at hand or, as far as I can see, to my expressed views on language learning.

Putnam objects to my conclusion that "the whole burden of defining what a grammar is [falls] on the innate constraints," arguing rather that the grammar of a language is a property of the "language." I find it difficult to make much sense of this part of his discussion, which seems to me quite confused. Before considering his "different approach," consider what he rejects. Is he proposing that only part of the burden of defining what a grammar is falls on the innate constraints? If so, which part? Which part of the burden falls elsewhere, why, and in what manner? No answer is suggested; therefore it is not clear that, and if so how, he is objecting to my conclusion. Note that he could hardly be claiming that none of the burden falls on the innate constraints, that is, that there are no innate constraints on what is a possible grammar, hence a possible human language. Thus even if language is constrained only by Putnam's "general intelligence," it follows that the burden of defining what a language is falls on the innate constraints, and hence the burden of "defining what a grammar is" falls on the innate constraints, if grammar is, as he claims, a property of "language." Thus to begin with, it is quite unclear to what view Putnam believes he is objecting.

In fact, Putnam's counterproposal suggests that he has something different in mind, and that his objection is just misstated. His counterproposal is that "the grammar of a language is a property of the *language*, not a property of the brain of *Homo sapiens*." But this formulation refers to the grammar of a particular language, say English, not to the innate constraints on possible languages and grammars. Apparently, Putnam is confusing the grammars of particular languages (the topic of his counterproposal) with "universal grammar," his notion of "what a grammar is" (the topic of his objection). Let us turn now to his counterproposal, as he formulates it.

The two counterposed views, then, are these: (1) my view, that grammars are represented in the brains of mature speakers, that languages are determined by these grammars, and that speakers of language can communicate to the extent that the languages characterized by the grammars in their brains are alike; (2) Putnam's view, that grammars are not represented in the brains of speakers but are properties of "languages."

It is difficult to compare these views, because Putnam's seems to me barely intelligible and, insofar as it is clear, inconsistent with other positions that he maintains. Let us put aside the fact that such notions as "the English language" are not linguistically definable, but are rather sociopolitical in nature. Consider now Putnam's "different approach." Note first that Putnam agrees, of course, that language is neurally represented (namely, in "the speech center in the left lobe," or the right lobe under early injury; see his "better argument"). It follows, then, that my language is a property of my brain. But Putnam claims that the grammar is a property of this language. Therefore, it is also a property of my brain, contrary to what Putnam asserts. If, as Putnam claims, grammars *are not* properties of brains but *are* properties of languages, then it follows that neither languages nor grammars are "properties of the brain of *Homo sapiens*," which is to say that my knowledge of English (and ability to use English) is not a property of my brain and is not represented in my brain, in the "speech center" or anywhere else. But this is surely not Putnam's view. One might take a different tack and argue that grammar is just an artifact of some sort, but that is not Putnam's approach; he is, it seems, a "realist" as far as grammar is concerned.

One can, perhaps, choose to think of propositional calculus (Putnam's example) as a "mathematical object" with whatever kind of existence we attribute to such "objects," but that has nothing to do with the empirical problem of determining the properties of natural systems such as some human language, as represented (I assume) in the brains of individuals in their mature state, or the problem of determining the properties of S_0^L, whatever these may be. Putnam gives no explanation of his alternative and allegedly "traditional" approach. I doubt that a coherent account is possible as a real alternative to the approach he wants to reject, which takes grammar to be a property of a brain and the "definition" of grammar to belong, in effect, to the theory of S_0^L. I see no need to comment further on Putnam's remarks about propositional calculus, except to note that even these are not free from error.[6]

Putnam proposes that the "declarative grammar of a language is the inductive definition of a set of strings which is the set over which semantic, deductive-logical, inductive-logical (and so on) predicates are defined" and that it must facilitate these definitions, be computationally feasible, etc. Let us grant all of this, for the sake of discussion, putting aside an ample literature that is concerned with the alleged "parallel" between semantic and syntactic properties of natural language.[7] From Putnam's suggestion, nothing follows about grammars being a property of "language" rather than "the speakers' brains," contrary to what Putnam asserts, without argument. The suggestion is entirely compatible with the view that grammars are represented in the brain, and represented in such a way that semantic (etc.) predicates have definitions whose clauses "parallel ... syntactic analysis" (though I think there are adequate grounds to suspect that the latter conclusion is incorrect—an empirical question, which I cannot consider here).

Putnam next turns to Washoe, arguing that she has developed structure-dependent rules. His discussion, however, is vitiated by an equivocation with respect to the notion "structure-dependent." Note that both of my hypotheses, H_1 and H_2, present rules that apply to a sentence, deforming its internal structure in some way (to be precise, the rules apply to the abstract structures underlying sentences, but we may put this refinement aside). Both the structure-independent rule H_1 and the structure-dependent rule H_2 make use of the concepts "sentence," "word," "first," and others; they differ in that H_2 requires in addition an analysis of the sentence into abstract phrases. A rule that does not modify the internal structure of a sentence is neither structure-dependent nor structure-independent. For example, a phrase structure rule, part of a phrase structure grammar in the technical sense of the term, is neither structure-dependent nor structure-independent.

The rule for conjunction that Putnam discusses in his Washoe comments takes two sentences p and q and combines them to form $p \& q$; in the framework of my discussion, it is a phrase structure rule rather than a transformational rule. It is neither structure-dependent nor structure-independent in my sense of these terms, since it does not require an internal analysis of the sentences to which it applies as a sequence of words *or* as a system of phrases. The rule does nothing to the internal structure of the sentences, and thus lies outside the bounds of the present discussion altogether.

Notice that in discussing question formation, I counterposed a structure-dependent and a structure-independent hypothesis, H_2 and H_1, respectively, and raised the question of why one is selected over the other on evidence compatible with both. In discussing conjunction, Putnam does not put forth competing hypotheses. The reason is that neither the notion "structure-dependent" nor the notion "structure-independent" applies in this case. There is no "structure-independent" counterpart to his rule, because it is neither structure-dependent nor structure-independent. Thus even if we were to grant that Washoe has learned her rule, and can form $p \& q$ (in principle) for arbitrary sentences p, q, nothing at all follows with regard to structure dependence or the choice between H_1 and H_2. The other Washoe examples also fall outside the domain of our discussion. They have nothing to do with structure dependence or structure independence; they illustrate substitution of items in a fixed frame. There is, to my knowledge, no evidence that chimpanzees use structure-dependent (or structure-independent) rules, in the sense of my discussion. Clearly, Putnam's account involves no rules of either sort. Therefore, we can put aside the discussion of Washoe, which has no more relevance to the problem under consideration than the discussion of propositional calculus. Both concern a kind of syntax to which the concepts under discussion do not even apply (in the case of propositional calculus, context-free phrase structure grammar; in the case of Washoe, an extremely limited finite-state grammar, perhaps even without any cycles). The same is true of Putnam's Hebrew example, which involves a nontransformational phrase structure rule like the rule introducing an abstract question marker in many treatments of English grammar.

Putnam later argues that my H_1 is itself structure-dependent, again equivocating on the term. I did not patent the terms and Putnam is free to use them as he likes, but in my usage, the rule is plainly not structure-dependent.

It is not clear why Putnam introduced propositional calculus and Washoe into the discussion of structure dependence. Perhaps his argument is that since the child (like Washoe, allegedly) can learn the rule for conjunction, and since this rule is "structure-dependent" (in Putnam's sense, though not mine), then the child will, by some kind of induction, choose the structure-dependent H_2 over the structure-independent H_1. I hesitate to suggest that this is Putnam's implicit argument (there is no explicit argument), since it would be inconsistent with his assertion that both H_1 and H_2 are structure-dependent (in his sense); if this is so, then either could have been posited by "induction," so the original problem remains. Or perhaps Putnam means to suggest that the concept of "structure dependence" in his sense is a notion of "general intelligence" (since Washoe allegedly has it). But that is of no help to his argument, since Washoe also undoubtedly has the notion "before" in time and probably "first," so that these too, by the argument, form part of general intelligence. We are still faced with the problem of why the child selects H_2 over H_1, which "general intelligence" makes available (since it involves only the notions "before" or "first," applying to word sequences). Similarly, if both hypotheses are (as Putnam alleges) "structure-dependent" (in his sense), then we are still left with the original problem: Why is H_2 selected?

Whether or not Putnam has something like this in mind, in case anyone else might be misled into supposing that there is an argument here based on some kind of "induction," let me add a few remarks. Imagine some new concept of "structure dependence" (call it SD*) under which the rule of conjunction and H_2 are structure-dependent (have the property SD*) but not H_1. Suppose further that the child learns the rule of conjunction and others like it which have the property SD*. Can we then account for his choice of H_2, which has the property SD*, over H_1, which does not? Only if we suppose that the predicate SD* is "available" as a projectable predicate for induction. But that is to beg the very question at issue. That is, we can now ask why the child carries out an induction with the predicate SD* instead of another, equally good predicate SI*, which holds of the rule of conjunction and H_1, but not H_2 (for example, consider the property of being a rule that does not deform a sentence in accordance with its internal phrase structure). In short, this pseudo-argument requires that the predicate SD* but not SI* be available for "induction" (learning). The question then arises: why SD* but not SI*? But that is just a variant of our original problem—we have just another variant of the familiar Goodman paradox, except that in this case we cannot even tell which is "grue," SD* or SI*, since neither seems a reasonable choice as a "projectable" predicate.

Putnam next turns to H_1 and H_2 directly, presenting his first real argument that the child "of course" uses structure-dependent rules. He argues that this follows from the fact that the child wants to learn "semantic rules" which cannot be stated without structure-dependent notions. Let us assume, for the sake of argument, that the semantic rules are structure-dependent. Does this explain why the child selects H_2 over H_1? Obviously not. Suppose that in fact English used the structure-independent rule H_1 to form yes-or-no questions. This would pose no problem at all for the formulation of the appropriate semantic rule. The rule for yes-or-no questions merely requires that these be distinguished from declaratives; they can be distinguished by H_1, by H_2, by painting them green, by standing on one's head while saying them, or in any other way, as far as the semantic rule is concerned. The rule asks: Is the corresponding declarative true or false? (Actually, the matter is more complex, but in no way that bears on this discussion.) We will turn in a moment to the matter of finding the "corresponding declarative." But Putnam offers no argument at all to support his claim that H_2 facilitates statement of the relevant semantic rule in a way that H_1 does not. Furthermore, there is no such argument, as the semantics makes clear. I should add that it is very common in discussions of language learning to appeal to "semantics" or "pragmatics" when problems arise. It is often not appreciated just what is at stake. Putnam's argument, which is completely without force, is a clear example of this unfortunate tendency.

Putnam argues that the child must use abstract phrase structure to understand the language, and that therefore H_2 is natural. He fails to add that the child also uses the notions "word" and "first" (presupposed by both H_1 and H_2) to understand the language; thus H_1 is no less "natural," in this regard. We then face again our original question: Why does the child use H_2, which employs analysis into phrases in addition to the notions presupposed in H_1? Putnam's argument is neutral with respect to this question, and therefore goes the way of the preceding ones.

Putnam next claims that (A) *the learning of grammar is dependent on the learning of semantics.* He offers (A) as an apparent paraphrase of his earlier assertion that the grammar must provide for the definition of semantic predicates, but it is certainly no paraphrase of this assertion. Elsewhere, Putnam has been quite clear about the distinction and has indeed advanced a very different and more plausible thesis.[8] Indeed, it is not easy to reconcile (A) with Putnam's earlier observation that the inductive definitions of semantic notions "parallel or at least presuppose a syntactic analysis of the language." If the definitions of the semantic notions presuppose a syntactic analysis (that is, a formal grammar that assigns phrase structure, determines well-formedness, and so on), then how can the learning of this grammar be "dependent on" a (prior?) learning of semantics?[9] But putting this question aside, suppose that (A) is true, in some sense that remains to be explained. Does anything follow concerning H_1 and H_2? Not as far as Putnam has argued or shown. The semantics of yes-or-no questions prefers neither H_1 nor H_2.

Putnam next argues that H_2 is preferable to H_1 because its "inverse" is simple, whereas the inverse of H_1 is "horribly complicated." He does not explain why he believes that this is so. As far as I can see, it is not; the inverses are very similar. In each case, the inverse operation requires that we find the position from which *is* (etc.) has been moved—a position immediately before the predicate. Given H_1, we seek the first such position (and if someone wanted to argue that the inverse of H_1 is in fact simpler, he might note that our search is facilitated by the presence of the word *who* [etc.] in this case). Given H_2, we will seek the "main" position, using the full phrase structure analysis. One can think of various algorithms, none of which, as far as I can see, differentiates between H_1 and H_2. Since Putnam offers no argument, I have to leave it at that.

Note, incidentally, that even if the inverse algorithm must be "structure-dependent," that has no bearing on the choice between H_1 and H_2, that is, on the question of whether it is the first occurrence of *is* (etc.) or the "main" occurrence that is proposed. We cannot argue that because (by assumption) the inverse is structure-dependent, then so is the rule. In fact, even if one were to put forth this illegitimate argument, it would not bear on the essential point. We could then rephrase our original query, asking why it is that the occurrence of *is* after the main noun phrase is moved, rather than the first occurrence after a noun phrase (that is, the leftmost occurrence in "The man who is here is tall").

To allay any lingering confusion about this matter, consider the three relevant question forms:

(I)   Is—the man here?

(II)   Is—the man who is here tall?

(III)   Is—the man who here is tall?

Both Putnam and I are assuming that the language learner is presented with many examples such as (I), and formulates either H_1 or H_2 to account for them. The facts of (II) and (III) show that H_2 was correct. To apply the inverse algorithm in (I), (II), and (III), the child must be able to detect where *is* is missing in the form to the right of—in these expressions. The question has never been studied, but it seems likely that at the stage of language acquisition when children can freely form sentences such as (II) (using H_2), they would have no difficulty in determining where *is* is missing in any of the forms to the right of—in (I), (II), and (III). Indeed, I would not be surprised to learn that they can solve the problem more easily for (III) than for (II). But ability to solve this problem is all that is required for the inverse algorithm to operate. Therefore, Putnam's unargued assertion that the inverse operation for H_1 is "horribly complicated" as compared with the inverse for H_2 seems far from the mark. If in fact it is easier to solve the problem for (III) than for (II), we would have an additional puzzle for the Martian observer, who might have taken this as further support for the obvious hypothesis that H_1 is to be preferred.

These comments exhaust Putnam's arguments concerning structure dependence. As far as I can see, none of them have any force. My conclusions, therefore, remain as stated.

Next, Putnam turns to the question of "general intelligence," beginning with the following assertion:

(IV)   "So far I have assumed that there is such a thing as general intelligence," including "*multipurpose* learning strategies, heuristics, and so forth."

Actually, (IV) is a rather misleading assertion. All that Putnam has so far assumed is that S_0^L, whatever it may be, contains only the general mechanisms for learning. Recall that he gives no hint as to what these are. To invoke an unspecified "general intelligence" or unspecified "multipurpose learning strategies" is no more illuminating than his reference, at one point, to divine intervention. We have no way of knowing what, if anything, Putnam has assumed. The point is worth stressing, since it illustrates a common fallacy in discussions of this sort. The use of words such as "general intelligence" does not constitute an empirical assumption unless these notions are somehow clarified. As matters now stand, very little is asserted by (IV).

Putnam claims that his "multipurpose learning strategies" enable us to learn and create physics. He seems to feel that I should also grant something of the sort, since I insist, naturally, that these achievements are possible. But I am not committed to an empty claim. If Putnam tells us what these "multipurpose learning strategies" are, even in the most vague and informal way, I will be glad to join him in inquiring as to their efficacy in accounting for our learning of physics, etc. In the absence of any proposal, I have nothing to say about the problem. Nor does Putnam, it is crucial to emphasize.

There are, in fact, striking and obvious differences between language learning and the learning (or discovery) of physics. In the first case, a rich and complex system of rules and principles is attained in a uniform way, rapidly, effortlessly, on the basis of limited and rather degenerate evidence. In the second case, we are forced to proceed on the basis of consciously articulated principles subjected to careful verification with the intervention of individual insight and often genius. It is clear enough that the cognitive domains in question are quite different. Humans are designed to learn language, which is nothing other than what their minds construct when placed in appropriate conditions;

they are not designed in anything like the same way to learn physics. Gross observations suffice to suggest that very different principles of "learning" are involved.

As for the proper delimitation of cognitive domains and their nature, I have nothing to add here to earlier discussion, at the Royaumont conference and elsewhere.[10] Where a rich and intricate system of belief and knowledge is rapidly attained in a uniform way on the basis of limited and degenerate evidence, it makes sense to suppose that some "mental organ" with special design is involved, and to try to determine the nature and properties of this "organ" and the cognitive domain related to it, as well as its relations to other systems that form part of the general structure of mind. Progress in delimiting these domains and determining their nature may come through studies analogous to those I have discussed in the case of language, or perhaps in other ways. Putnam asserts that the number of domains is "virtually unlimited" and that the strategies we use "must be extraordinarily multipurpose," although he adds that "we have presently no idea what they are." I know no more about these strategies than Putnam does, or about the delimitation of domains, or about their number or specific character. As far as I can see, we differ here only in that I am disinclined to put forth what appear superficially to be empirical hypotheses where, as we both admit, we have "no idea" as to what the facts may be. I would urge that Putnam too should adopt the "open-mindedness hypothesis" and refrain from putting forth assertions such as (IV) and others that appear in that section of his "Comments."

Putnam argues that if there are such cognitive domains as "learning a grammar," "recognizing faces," and others that are "so small" and have such "highly specific-purpose" learning strategies, then "it becomes really a miracle that evolution endowed us with all these skills," since most of them (for example, mathematics) weren't used until after the evolution of the race was complete. I see no miracle here. Consider the human ability to handle fairly deep properties of the number system. I suppose that this ability is genetically determined for humans, though it is hard to imagine that it contributed to differential reproduction. But we need not suppose that this is a miracle, if true. These skills may well have arisen as a concomitant of structural properties of the brain that developed for other reasons. Suppose that there was selection for bigger brains, more cortical surface, hemispheric specialization for analytic processing, or many other structural properties that can be imagined. The brain that evolved might well have all sorts of special properties that are not individually selected; there would be no miracle in this, but only the normal workings of evolution. We have no idea, at present, how physical laws apply when 10^{10} neurons are placed in an object the size of a basketball, under the special conditions that arose during human evolution. It might be that they apply in such a way to afford the brains that evolved (under selection for size, particular kinds of complexity, etc.) the ability to deal with properties of the number system, continuity, abstract geometrical space, certain parts of natural science, and so on. There are innumerable problems here, but I see no need to appeal to miracles. Nor do the problems that arise seem qualitatively different from familiar problems in accounting for the evolution of physical structures in organisms.

Putnam's further remarks about evolution seem to me mystifying. He feels that I have "dismissed" Piaget's concerns about evolution, but that is quite false. Rather, I remarked that the structures I have been led to postulate for S_0^L, though "biologically unexplained," are not, as Piaget asserts, "biologically inexplicable." Furthermore, I see no specific problem that arises in this connection beyond those that are familiar (if often mysterious) in the case of physical organs. Putnam's further discussion seems to indicate that he agrees. Therefore, I assume that he has somehow misunderstood what I said about this matter.

In my earlier discussion of Putnam's criticisms of the "innateness hypothesis" (see note 2), I noted that his views about evolution seemed to me very curious. Thus in the paper to which he refers,[11] Putnam asserts that "*invoking 'innateness' only postpones the problem of learning; it does not solve it.*" This is a very odd principle, one that would never be put forth in connection with the development of physical organs. If, in fact, the general properties of binocular vision or the fact that we grow arms instead of wings is genetically determined, then it would be senseless to say that "invoking 'innateness' only postpones the problem of the learning of binocular vision or the learning of arms rather than wings." There is no such problem to be "solved." True, a problem remains, but it is not the problem of learning; it is the problem of explaining the origin and development of structures that are innate. I see no reason to take a different approach when we study higher mental faculties. If, indeed, certain properties of language are genetically determined, then "invoking 'innateness'" does not "postpone the problem of learning" with regard to these properties, but rather is the proper move, since there is no "problem of learning" in these respects. Putnam seems to believe otherwise, but I have no idea why.

I will not comment on Putnam's "better argument," except to observe that it does not bear even in a remote way on the questions that I discussed and that seem to me to be the interesting ones, namely, what is the nature of S_0^L, how does it relate to other faculties of mind or to "general intelligence" (whatever it may be), and so on.

Putnam summarizes the view that he has been putting forward as follows: "Everything Chomsky ascribes to an innate template of language, a 'mental organ' specifically designed to enable us to *talk*, can, for all we know, be explained by general intelligence." And he suggests that this conclusion agrees "in broad outline" with Piaget's views. At the level of vagueness at which he discusses the problem, I would not disagree, once his specific arguments are dismissed as fallacious. Thus I agree that "for all we know" some notion of "general intelligence" about which we have "no idea" might explain everything I have ascribed to S_0^L. Similarly, there would be little point in debating the claim that "for all we know" some mysterious force, as to the character of which we have "no idea," might explain everything that physicists try to explain in terms of their complex constructions. Thus, contrary to what Putnam believes, I would not deny his contention. We differ only in that I dismiss it, whereas in contrast he seems to think the contention is important—why, I do not know.

There is much to say about Putnam's discussion of Piaget, but I will not go into the matter here. One point deserves mention, however. Putnam feels that Piaget's approach converges with mine in that the notion of "reflective abstraction" relates to the use of language in inference. At the risk of seeming ungracious, I must demur. My uneasiness with "reflective abstraction" is not that it is placed "apart from language" (as Putnam asserts), but rather that I do not know what the phrase means, to what processes it refers, or what are its principles, any more than I know what Putnam has in mind when he speaks of "general intelligence," "multipurpose learning strategies," and the like. Hence it is impossible for me to take a position on the potential convergence that Putnam perceives.

Putnam argues that Fodor and I misused the term "tautology." He fails to note that the term did not appear in any presented paper, but was introduced in the informal discussion (by whom, I do not recall) and was then used by all participants not in the technical sense of "logical truth" but in the informal sense of "obvious truth." Since one cannot speak with warning-quotes, this may not be explicit in the transcript, but it surely is obvious enough from the context. Since Putnam agrees that the contention at issue is an obvious truth, there is no disagreement here.

Putnam concludes his paper with the claim that Fodor's hypothesis of a "language of thought" makes my hypothesis concerning a "'mental organ' for *speaking* ... totally unnecessary." He offers no hint of an argument in support of this contention. He would be right if the "language of thought" had, in general, the properties of S_0^L. But it is exactly this question that Putnam has failed to address, once errors in argument and incorrect statements of fact are eliminated. I do not state categorically that the thesis is false; only that no argument to support it has been offered by Putnam or anyone else, to my knowledge, whereas there are empirical (though, obviously, nondemonstrative) arguments to the effect that S_0^L has certain properties for which there are no known significant analogues elsewhere. Furthermore, there are real and generally unappreciated difficulties in the thesis that intelligence is "undifferentiated."[12] Perhaps the reason why we can offer no specific analogues elsewhere to the properties postulated for S_0^L is that we just do not know enough about other aspects of cognition, or perhaps postulation of these properties is incorrect. Or perhaps the reason is, as I suspect, that the "mental organ" of language really has special properties, hardly a surprising conclusion, though of course far from a necessary truth.

Perhaps I may conclude with a personal remark. My old friend Hilary Putnam and I have been debating these issues for quite a few years. He begins his discussion here with some kind remarks, for which I am grateful. He even goes so far as to say that if I am unable to provide arguments for what he calls "the innateness hypothesis," then probably no case can be made for it. As noted, I do not feel that he has established any of his points; rather, it seems to me that my arguments stand, as given, with just the qualifications and strictures given. But let me return the compliment. Putnam has remarkable intellectual gifts and an awesome command of many fields of knowledge. Furthermore, more than any other philosopher to my knowledge, he has concerned himself with the problem to which his present comments are addressed, seeking to establish that "general intelligence" or "multipurpose learning strategies" suffice to account for the specific workings of language. I feel that to date, he has not made a case for his contentions, and indeed, has not even succeeded in making clear what these contentions are. Perhaps, then, we may conclude ...

Notes

1. See H. Putnam, *Mind, Language, and Reality* (Cambridge: Cambridge University Press, 1975), chapter 5.
2. See chapters 3 and 6 of my *Language and Mind*, extended edition New York: Harcourt Brace Jovanovich, 1972).
3. For a quite typical example, see chapter 1, section 8 of my *Aspects of the Theory of Syntax* (Cambridge, Mass.: MIT Press, 1965).
4. See J. A. Fodor, T. G. Bever, and M. F. Garrett, *The Psychology of Language* (New York: McGraw-Hill, 1974), pp. 436 ff.
5. We might even argue that his proposal, though nearly vacuous, can indeed be assessed, and rejected. The sole content of his proposal, as it stands, is that the properties of S_0^L are simply "general learning mechanisms," which apply freely in all cognitive domains. But there is evidence that S_0^L contains mechanisms and structures for which it is difficult to find even a vague analogue outside of language, for example, the specific principles of transformational grammar postulated to explain the structure dependence of rules (and much else). Consequently, the belief that the properties of S_0^L are in fact "general learning mechanisms" is quite implausible with regard to its minimal empirical content.
6. For example, when he asserts that "p & ~ p" is "deviant for semantic reasons," and "would not be 'uttered' for obvious semantic reasons." It is not deviant at all, and might well be "uttered" as a line in any proof by *reductio ad absurdum*.
7. See, for example, Otto Jespersen, *The Philosophy of Grammar* (London: Allen & Unwin, 1924); and for some recent discussion, my "Questions of Form and Interpretation," *Linguistic Analysis*, vol. 1, no. 1,1975.
8. See Putnam's *Mind, Languages, and Reality*, volume 2, chapter 4.

9. Perhaps Putnam means that the learning of grammar is "dependent on" the learning of semantics in the sense that semantics provides the goal or motive for the learning of syntax. But if this is what he has in mind, the argument again fails, since as already noted, there is no problem in stating the semantics with the structure-independent rule.

10. See chapter 1 of my *Reflections on Language* (New York: Pantheon, 1975).

11. Putnam, *Mind, Language, and Reality*, chapter 5.

12. See chapters 1 and 4 of my *Reflections on Language* for some discussion.

Chapter 52

Reply to Putnam

Jerry A. Fodor

Not many of Putnam's criticisms seem to me to require extended discussion; and many of those that do have been covered in Chomsky's reply. I shall therefore restrict myself almost exclusively to those of Putnam's remarks that concern things I said at this conference and in my book *Language of Thought*.[1]

Putnam on "Fodor's Tautology"

Professor Putnam thoughtfully reminds me (and Chomsky) that it is "not *logically* impossible that our heads should be as empty as the Tin Woodman's and we should still talk, love, and so on"; it was "a little careless" of me to suggest the contrary. It would have been if I had. In fact, "tautology" is not a term that appears in my formal presentation, nor did I introduce it into the discussion, nor did I suggest (ever or anywhere) that "no one appreciated until Nelson Goodman" that there can be "no learning without some laws of learning." (What I *did* suggest is that the demonstration that there is no induction without an a priori delimitation of the field of *projectible predicates* is owing to Goodman and has profound implications for theories of learning. This remark, which has nothing to do with the existence or otherwise of laws of learning, is one I continue to endorse.) Finally, the sense of "tautology" at issue in the discussion was, of course, *not* "truth of logic," but rather "obvious truth, self-evident truth . . . etc." Putnam denies that his strictures on "tautology" are "just a quibble," but they'll do until a real one comes along.

Putnam on Fodor on the Innateness of All Concepts

Putnam (mis)construes an argument that I gave in *Language of Thought*. I'll work with his version first and then come back to how he got it wrong and why that matters.

> Fodor's reasoning is as follows: Learning the meaning of a predicate is inferring what the semantic properties of that predicate are, that is, concluding (inductively) to some such generalization as
>
> (A) For every x, P is true of x if and only if Q (x).
>
> But if (A) is in brain language, so is Q. (P need not be; P is mentioned, not used in (A). But Q is *used*, not mentioned.) And if (A) is correct, Q is coextensive with P, and is so by virtue of what P *means* (otherwise (A) is not a correct semantic characterization of the meaning of P). So Q is *synonymous* with P; P is not a *new* concept, because there is a predicate (namely, Q) in "brain language" that is synonymous with it. But P is an arbitrary predicate the brain can learn to understand—so no new concepts can be learned!

Putnam has an analysis of what's wrong with this argument: "The assumption is as strong as what Fodor wishes to prove. So all we have to do is show how it could be false . . . and nothing is left but a simple case of begging the question." Now, I suppose that Putnam is being a little careless here, for it is not easy to see how an argument *could* be valid unless its "assumptions" were (at least) as strong as its conclusion. What Putnam must mean to say is that the assumptions are as *tendentious* as the conclusion. But that is surely just false, since the (operative) assumptions are that learning a predicate is learning its meaning, and that language learning is (inter alia) the projection and confirmation of hypotheses. And there is a tradition of making just such assumptions which goes back for literally hundreds of years in philosophy, and which is, to all intents and purposes, simply unquestioned in contemporary cognitive psychology. Indeed, what is puzzling about the argument (if anything is) is exactly that it requires only these fairly banal assumptions to arrive at the wildly paradoxical conclusion that all concepts are innate. (I assume that it's part of the philosopher's job to reveal the paradoxical lurking in the prima facie untendentious—and then to make it go away.)

Now, what can Putnam offer to replace these trouble-making assumptions? Putnam does a very odd thing at this point. Instead of following the doctrine about language learning proposed in such of his papers as "The Meaning of 'Meaning'" (to which doctrine we shall presently return), he suggests that "even if we grant that the brain learns P by making an induction, it need not be an induction with the conclusion (A). It would suffice that the brain instead conclude: (B) I will be doing OK with P if subroutine S is employed." Putnam does not tell us what sort of subroutine S is, and he is thunderously silent on where such subroutines come from, but he remarks (correctly) that S will have to be specifiable in machine language if the machine is to be able to execute it. We may add (as Putnam rather astonishingly does not) that if learning to execute the subroutine S is to be identifiable with learning P, then the machine (brain, etc.) must not only conclude, but conclude *truly*, that it is "doing OK" with P if it uses S. (There is, after all, a distinction between having a predicate and merely believing that you do.) Well, then, what might be the subroutine vis-à-vis P such that, when you have learned to execute *that* subroutine, your belief that you are doing OK with P is *true*? The classic suggestion is, of course, that you must have a procedure for sorting things that do and don't satisfy P by reference to whether they exhibit some property Q. And now if we add that the fact that the possession of Q determines the satisfaction of P is supposed to be a consequence of the meaning of P, what we have is just (A) all over again. In effect, my (A) is a version of Putnam's (B). It is, moreover, the standard version of (B); and Putnam neither suggests how we are to avoid the paradoxes that arise from taking (B) on construal (A), nor proposes a version of (B) that provides an alternative to (A).

Putnam seems to sense this sort of reply in the offing, because he says that I might claim "that the machine language description of how to use, say, 'tree' *is* (a form of) the predicate *tree*. But this is simply an extension of use designed to make his [my] thesis an uninteresting 'tautology.'" It doesn't, however, seem to be an extension of use at all. Putnam has, in effect, endorsed the view that what we learn when we learn "tree" is a set of procedures for using the word. It was, after all, Wittgenstein (and not I) who suggested that the best candidate for meaning is rules-of-use. And Putnam is surely aware of a long philosophical tradition that identifies such rules with (one or another form of) operational *definition* of a term. (This tradition is, by the way, enthusiastically endorsed by the "procedural semanticists" whose work was at issue.)

I think, however, that what Putnam must really have in mind is something quite different from what this argument suggests—something that has very little to do with all this business about "subroutines." I think what he really has in mind is that we should abandon (the classic form of) the proposal that to learn a word is to learn what it means; that is, he wants to distinguish between *learning P* and *learning the meaning of P* and to argue that the latter is *not* necessary for the former (not, at least, if the meaning of P determines logically necessary and sufficient conditions for P's applying). This move, of course, really *is* tendentious, but Putnam argues for it in "The Meaning of 'Meaning'" and, though I think his arguments there do not, in the long run, persuade, I won't try to deal with them here. For present purposes, my point is just that, on *this* account, not any old subroutine S will do vis-à-vis P. We require a very special kind of subroutine associated with "tree" such that something might satisfy the subroutine and fail, for all that, to *be* a tree. Of course, if one can show *that* then one *has* shown that (A) fails; hence that no argument that rests on (A) would prove that the meaning of "tree" is innate.

The trouble is, however, that on this view the meaning of "tree" isn't *learned* either. Indeed, on this view it is quite possible that nobody now knows, or ever will know, the meaning of "tree" (in the traditional sense of, roughly, the essential conditions for being a tree). For, whether something is a tree depends (so the story goes) *not* on its having the properties we learned to associate with "tree" (in particular, it is not determined by the outcome of executing subroutine S) but rather on whether it has those properties that "the progress of science" will (or may) come to tell us that trees must have. And, of course, learning *those* properties (the ones which, as it were, give the *real* meaning of "tree") isn't part of learning "tree."

This is where it becomes important that Putnam has misrepresented the argument I gave in *Language of Thought*. What I did there was *not* to endorse (A) (the principle which, on our present reading, Putnam has brought under attack) but simply to run it as an example of what you would be committed to if you were to hold that to learn a word is to learn its (for example, operational) definition. But, as I pointed out (ad nauseam and with explicit reference to Putnam's views),[2] weaker assumptions than (A) might be made about what is learned when one learns P; and, given the structure of my argument, those weaker assumptions about what is learned will comport with correspondingly weaker conclusions about what is innate. What I endorsed was, in short, an argument scheme: you tell me what you think is learned (when P is learned), and I'll tell you what you must be assuming to be innately available to the learning device. You say: "meanings are learned," and I'll show you that you must assume that meanings are innate; you say: "subroutines are learned," and I'll show you that you must assume that subroutines are innate; in effect, you tell me what sense of "concept" you have in mind when you speak of "concept learning," and I'll show you that you must take concepts *in that sense* to be innate. I don't think there is anything in Putnam's remarks that undermines this strategy; I can't find anything in Putnam's remarks that even bears on it.

Putnam on What Fodor Has Rendered Otiose

Putnam says that "Fodor's hypothesis of a 'language of thought' ... is not ... the same as Chomsky's hypothesis of a 'mental organ' for *speaking*; it even makes the latter hypothesis totally unnecessary." I don't understand *what* Putnam could have in mind here. Perhaps he has confused the question of whether cognitive processes (for example, language learning) presuppose a medium of representation with the question of whether such processes presuppose (unlearned) information couched *in that medium*. As far as I can see, Chomsky's thesis (which, for purposes of discussion, let's take to be that General Linguistic Theory is innate) entails mine on the principle: no (innate) information without (innate) representation. On the other hand, there could be an innate medium of representation without there being innate information about (for example) natural languages (or, I suppose, anything else). I remarked earlier that a tendency not to distinguish between issues about innateness and issues about internal representation is pretty general in Putnam's paper: it may be that this is just a case of it. Alternatively, it may be that Putnam has confused issues about the innateness of *concepts* with issues about the innateness of *beliefs*, the thesis that GLT (General Linguistic Theory) is innate being primarily a claim about the latter while the thesis that LOT (Language of Thought) is innate is primarily a claim about the former. Nor should I wish to suggest that these alternatives are exclusive, since it may be that Putnam is confused about all of them at once.

Putnam on God and Man

Putnam says: "I don't doubt that God is ultimately responsible for what we are ... [but] this is such a *messy* miracle to attribute to Him! Why should He pack our heads with a billion different 'mental organs,' rather than just making us smart?" This is, however, a bad argument even on what appears to be the operative assumption: that God's aesthetic principles are indistinguishable from Putnam's. To see how bad it is, try applying it to any *other* species. Why didn't God make the spider *smart* instead of merely teaching it to eat flies and spin webs? Why endow the robin and the stickleback with a parochial talent for building nests instead of "general intelligence" and a bent for architecture? And what a messy miracle the bee's dance comes to. Clever gods would make clever bees, which could then invent navigation and the telephone in the fullness of time. Sloppy old God! Better consult a philosopher the next time 'round!

The point is, of course, that in all other species cognitive capacities are molded by selection pressures as Darwin taught us to expect. A truly *general* intelligence (a cognitive capacity fit to discover just *any* truths there are) would be a biological anomaly and an evolutionary enigma. Perhaps that is not what Putnam thinks we've got. Since he tells us nothing about what general intelligence is, we have no way of knowing.

The reasonable assumption, in any event, is that human beings have an ethology, just as other species do; that the morphology of our cognitive capacities reflects our specific (in both senses) modes of adaptation. Of course, we are in some respects uniquely badly situated to elucidate its structure (to carry through [what I take to be] the Kantian program). *From in here* it looks as though we're fit to think whatever thoughts there are to think (compare "a billion different mental organs"). It *would*, of course, precisely because we *are* in here. But there is surely good reason to suppose that this is hubris bred of an epistemological illusion. No doubt spiders think that webs exhaust the options.

We know more than spiders do; we can (and should) bear the biological precedents in mind. These precedents suggest that we must seem to angels the way that other species seem to us: organisms whose intelligence is shaped by their history and is therefore fragmentary, task-oriented, and domain-specific. I'll bet that's what the angels say when they are doing anthropology. Assuming that the angels bother.

Notes

1. J. Fodor, The *Language of Thought* (Cambridge, Mass.: Harvard University Press, 1979).
2. Ibid., p. 61.

Index